Politics in
Developing Countries

Politics in Developing Countries

Comparing Experiences with Democracy

Second Edition

edited by

Larry Diamond
Juan J. Linz
Seymour Martin Lipset

LYNNE
RIENNER
PUBLISHERS

BOULDER
LONDON

Cover photograph courtesy of the World Bank

Published in the United States of America in 1995 by
Lynne Rienner Publishers, Inc.
1800 30th Street, Boulder, Colorado 80301

and in the United Kingdom by
Lynne Rienner Publishers, Inc.
3 Henrietta Street, Covent Garden, London WC2E 8LU

Library of Congress Cataloging-in-Publication Data
Politics in developing countries : comparing experiences with
  democracy / edited by Larry Diamond, Juan J. Linz, Seymour Martin
  Lipset.—2nd ed.
    Rev. ed. of Politics in developing countries, which was
selections from the editors' larger work, Democracy in developing
countries.
    Includes bibliographical references and index.
    ISBN 1-55587-541-6 (pbk. : alk. paper)
    1. Developing countries—Politics and government. 2. Comparative
government. 3. Democracy. I. Diamond, Larry Jay. II. Linz, Juan
J. (Juan José), 1926– . III. Lipset, Seymour Martin.
IV. Democracy in developing countries. Selections.
D883.P66 1995
320.3'09172'4—dc20
                                       95-24347
                                         CIP

British Cataloguing in Publication Data
A Cataloguing in Publication record for this book
is available from the British Library.

Printed and bound in the United States of America

    The paper used in this publication meets the requirements
∞ of the American National Standard for Permanence of
    Paper for Printed Library Materials Z39.48-1984.

5 4 3 2 1

Contents

Acknowledgments

This book derives from a twenty-six country study originally published as three volumes under the title *Democracy in Developing Countries*. Like the first edition, it draws together ten particularly important and revealing cases from the three regions we examined: Africa, Asia, and Latin America. And we again sought to produce in one volume a collection of ten cases that would be of maximum possible value to courses in comparative politics. Inevitably, this involved difficult choices. Given the success of the first edition, we sought to deviate as little as possible from the structure of that book, adding only one new case, South Africa.

As with the original multivolume project, this revised edition was made possible by support from the National Endowment for Democracy (NED). NED is a private, nonprofit organization that supports democratic development and, through its new International Forum for Democratic Studies, research and publishing on democracy around the world. We reiterate our gratitude to the NED president, Carl Gershman, and to Marc F. Plattner, co-director of the International Forum. We also appreciate the continued support of the Hoover Institution, with which Diamond and Lipset are affiliated, and of its director, John Raisian. Finally, we would like to thank Marguerite Kramer of the Hoover Institution for her administrative support of this project.

L. D.
J. J. L.
S. M. L.

1

Introduction: What Makes for Democracy?

Larry Diamond, Juan J. Linz, and Seymour Martin Lipset

The ten case studies in this book analyze the political development of a selection of countries from Africa, Asia, Latin America, and the Middle East—or what we term, for lack of a better label, *developing countries.* Although these studies analyze the full sweep of regime evolution and change, we focus on a particular issue in political development that can justifiably be called the preeminent political issue of our times: the struggle for democracy. Beginning from a common theoretical agenda, we seek to explain whether, why, and to what extent democracy has evolved and taken root in the vastly different cultural and historical soils of these countries.

The larger (twenty-six–nation) comparative study from which earlier versions of these case studies were derived was undertaken at a time of tremendous democratic ferment in the developing world.[1] We began our original study in 1985, a decade after the toppling of Western Europe's last three dictatorships (in Portugal, Spain, and Greece), which launched what Samuel Huntington has called the "third wave" of global democratic expansion.[2] Moving from Southern Europe to Latin America, then to East Asia in the mid-1980s and back to Eastern Europe and the former Soviet Union, this wave of democratic transitions finally reached sub-Saharan Africa in the early 1990s. Between 1990 and 1995, roughly twelve African countries initiated multiparty, constitutional regimes, most prominently South Africa. Elsewhere (as in Kenya, Gabon, and Cameroon), some political liberalization occurred, with the legalization of opposition parties and greater scope for dissent, but long-dominant parties rigged themselves back into power. Globally the number of democracies in the world has more than doubled since 1974, and during this period most of the cases in our volume experienced democratic transitions, or at least strong pressures for democratization, as part of this global phenomenon.

The 1980s also witnessed unprecedented growth in international concern for human rights—including, prominently, the rights to choose democratically the government under which one lives and to express and organize

1

around one's political principles and views. As torture, disappearances, and other grave human rights violations became more widespread but were also more systematically exposed and denounced around the world, a renewed and deeper appreciation developed for democratic institutions, which, with all their procedural messiness and sluggishness, nevertheless protect the integrity of the person and the freedoms of conscience and expression. The growth of democratic norms throughout the world was strikingly evidenced in the degree to which authoritarian regimes found it necessary to wrap themselves in the rhetoric and constitutional trappings of democracy or at least to state as their goal the eventual establishment of democracy.

The global advance of democracy in the 1980s and early 1990s was assisted by the demise of its historic ideological rivals. Fascism was destroyed as a vital force in World War II. The appeals of Marxism-Leninism withered with the harsh repressiveness, glaring economic failures, and loss of revolutionary idealism of the existing Communist regimes. More limited, quasi-socialist, or mass-mobilizational models—the Mexican, Yugoslav, and Nasserite models—also lost their aura. Almost universally, military regimes were shorn of any ideological justification and legitimacy beyond a temporary intrusion to correct political and social problems. Democracy became—partly by choice and political learning and partly by default—the only model of government in the world with any broad ideological legitimacy and appeal.

By the early 1990s, however, this ideological hegemony was increasingly under challenge from two forceful and self-confident alternatives. In that large swath of countries from Indonesia to West Africa wherein Islam is a major or the dominant religion, fundamentalist advocates of the Islamic state presented it as the only moral alternative to a "Western" liberal democratic model they denounced as decadent because of its rampant materialism and individualism. Although the radical Islamic regime had demonstrated in Iran and then Sudan its dubious efficacy and blatant disregard for human rights, it nevertheless attracted growing support, particularly among young people disgusted with the corruption, social injustice, economic stagnation, and gross abuses of power of authoritarian regimes in North Africa and the Middle East. The fact that some of these regimes claimed to be democratic only intensified the Islamist view of democracy as corrupt, elitist, and morally bankrupt. Even in Pakistan and, most surprisingly, Turkey, with its distinctive twentieth-century legacy of separation between state and mosque, Islamic parties gained political and ideological ground in the early 1990s.

In East Asia, economically dynamic elites, led by former Singaporean Prime Minister Lee Kuan Yew and Malaysian Prime Minister Mahathir bin Mohamad, rejected the Western emphasis on individual rights as culturally inappropriate and conducive to economic and social decline. However, this defense of a much more constrained, illiberal democracy was challenged by other prominent Asians who found important democratic currents in Asian tradition and culture and who dismissed the denunciations of liberalism as mere self-serving rationalization for authoritarianism.[3]

Even with these regional challenges to democracy's legitimacy, it is a sign of how much the world has changed, both politically and intellectually, that the normative question that stirred such intense debate in the 1960s and 1970s—Why study democracy?—is rarely raised today. Indeed, over the past decade no subject in comparative politics has received more scholarly attention than have the causes, conditions, and challenges of democratic transition and consolidation. Nevertheless, previous historical cycles warn that the 1990s may bring setbacks and even a renewed crisis of confidence in democracy. Recent years have witnessed a significant erosion of democracy in several of our cases (as we indicate below) and throughout much of Latin America.[4]

Outside the West, and the Western Hemisphere, East Asian and other critiques of democracy argue that economic and social rights, and political order, should be considered to be more important than civil and political liberties, and that "enlightened" authoritarian rulers should have the right to use coercive measures, in the name of some higher good, to suppress democratic opposition. For ourselves, neither of these normative suppositions is tenable.

If many undemocratic governments (now and in the past) were committed to serving collective goals rather than the interests of the rulers and were ready to respect human rights (to refrain from torture and indiscriminate violence, to offer due process and fair trials in applying laws that, even if antiliberal, are known in advance, and to maintain humane conditions of imprisonment), we might find these questions more difficult to answer. However, it is highly unlikely that a nondemocratic regime would meet these two requirements; even those that begin with a strong ideological commitment to the collectivity and a professed sensitivity to human rights often become increasingly narrow, autocratic, and repressive.

Even when authoritarian rulers strive to serve collective goals, why should we assume that their conception of the collective good is better than that of any other group in society? Only if we were totally certain that one ideological conception is the expression of historical reason—true and necessary—would we be forced to accept such an authoritarian alternative as better than democracy. To do so, as we know, justifies any sacrifices and ultimately terrible costs in terms of freedom and human lives. Democracy—with its relativism and tolerance (so disturbing to those certain of the truth) and its "faith" in the reasonableness and intelligence of the common people, deciding freely (and with a chance to change their minds every four or five years) and without the use of force—still seems a better option.

Organization of the Study

The contributions to this book are distinctive in that they deal with the entire history of a country's experience with democracy: the establishment, breakdown, re-equilibration, and consolidation of democratic government; periods of democratic persistence, crisis, authoritarianism, and renewal; and all of the ambivalences and oscillations in between. We consider each country's early cultural traditions, analyze (where relevant) the colonial experience, and consider all of its postindependence history, giving special emphasis to post–World War II developments. Whereas most other works focus on limited time spans and particular processes (breakdown, transition, crisis, or consolidation),[5] our authors explain the overall path of a country's political development.

Although it can be enormously fertile, this historical approach is not without methodological problems. In particular, it runs the risk of attributing contemporary political patterns to antecedents far removed in time without clearly demonstrating that those factors (or characteristics resulting from them) are operating at a later time and account for the failure or success of democracy. To overcome this risk, each case study author reviews the country's political history, describing its major experiences with democratic and undemocratic governments—including the structure, nature, and characteristic conflicts and tensions of each regime—and explains the fate of each regime (especially each democratic one): why it persisted, failed, or evolved as it did, and why successive regimes emerged as and when they did. Finally, each author offers a summary theoretical judgment of the most important factors in determining the country's overall degree of success or failure with democratic government and considers its prospects for democracy.

Culturally, the cases in this book encompass much of the enormous variation in the developing world: Brazil, Chile, and Mexico—Christian (largely Catholic) societies of Latin America; India with its mosaic of traditions, including the distinctive Hindu culture; two largely Islamic societies—Turkey (whose secularization has historically been linked with democratization) and Senegal; largely Buddhist Thailand; South Korea with its mixture of Buddhism, Confucianism, and Christianity; multiracial and multiethnic South Africa with its unique historical legacy of apartheid; and a major example—Nigeria—of what Ali Mazrui calls the "triple heritage" of Christianity, Islam, and traditional African religion and culture.

One of the most complex and intractable problems in our world is the tension that exists between the model of ethnically, linguistically, and culturally homogeneous societies that satisfy the ideal of the nation-state and the multiethnic, multilingual societies that face the difficult task of nation building or state building in the absence of the integration and identification we normally associate with the idea of the nation-state. Even in Europe, before the massive and forced transfers (if not destruction) of populations, most states did not satisfy that ideal; outside of Europe, even fewer do. Virtually no African or Asian countries and only a few Latin American countries (in this book, only Chile) seem to satisfy the model. Others, such as Brazil and Mexico, include not only descendants of the conquistadores and European immigrants but also substantial populations (intermixed to varying degrees with the above) of Indians and descendants of black slaves. To the list of relatively homogeneous countries could be added South Korea. Our remaining cases confront us with the problem of democracy in ethnically and culturally divided societies, especially India, Nigeria, and South Africa.

Except for the deliberate exclusion of countries with no prior democratic or semidemocratic experience or no prospect of an opening to freedom, our study encompasses virtually every type of democratic experience in the (non-Communist) developing world. At the beginning of 1995, nine of our ten cases had the formal structure of a constitutional, multiparty democracy; only Nigeria had an explicitly authoritarian (military) regime. However, five of these nine countries (Turkey, Brazil, South Korea, Chile, and, most recently, Thailand) had experienced military rule within the previous ten to fifteen years, and South Africa only completed its transition to democracy in 1994, from the most racially exclusive political system any country has constructed in the modern era. Moreover, at the end of 1994 only three of our nine formally democratic cases were rated by Freedom House as "free"— Chile, South Korea, and South Africa.[6] In the other six cases, problems of corruption, human rights violations, and poor democratic functioning placed them beneath that threshold.

Among the new democracies of the third wave, Chile and South Korea stand out for their progress toward democratic consolidation. However, Chile's democracy remained constrained by some significant authoritarian enclaves of military prerogative entrenched in the 1989 constitution.[7] Similarly, South Korea began its new democracy with significant power still inhering in the military and intelligence apparatus, and the first post-transition president, Roh Tae Woo, was a recently retired general nominated by the ruling party of the military-dominated authoritarian regime.

Most observers also consider Brazil and India to be democratic today, but in recent years both countries have experienced serious strains that might have toppled less resilient democratic systems. Of the remaining four civilian regimes analyzed in this volume, Mexico and Senegal have long been among the classic instances of semidemocracy in the developing world, with multiparty regimes that allow for some significant freedom of expression and partial freedom of organization but without the truly free and fair electoral competition that might displace aging ruling parties from power.

Turkey and Thailand represent ambiguous regime types. Unlike the situations in Mexico and Senegal, there is genuine, relatively open and fair electoral competition, but in each country the military remains a significant political force, constraining the actual authority of elected civilian officials. Our other two African cases represent the opposite poles of promise and frustration in this, Africa's "second liberation." Nigeria had long been regarded as one of the continent's brightest hopes for democracy, with a pluralistic society, a vigorous press, independent associations, and an elite strongly committed (at least rhetorically) to multiparty democracy. All of this went up in flames during four brief years of rapacious corruption, electoral fraud, and political violence (1979–1983). When Nigeria's Second Republic was functioning during the early 1980s, South Africa seemed mired in a war of attrition between the apartheid white minority regime and the liberation forces, led by the banned African National Congress. It took the coming to power of a new, more pragmatic South African president, F. W. de Klerk, to launch the process of negotiation in 1990 by releasing Nelson Mandela from prison and legalizing the ANC. There followed over the subsequent four years one of the most complex, fascinating, and intensively negotiated democratic transitions of the third wave.

Concepts, Definitions, and Classifications

It reflects the political climate of our time that the word *democracy* is used to signify the desirable end state of so many social, economic, and political pursuits or to self-designate and thus presumably legitimate many existing structures. Hence, it is imperative to be as precise as possible about the subject of our study.

In this book, *democracy* signifies a political system, separate and apart from the economic and social systems to which it is joined. Unless the economic and social dimensions are kept conceptually distinct from the political, there is no way to analyze how variation on the political dimension is related to variation on the other dimensions. In addition, we distinguish the concept of political democracy out of a clear and frankly expressed conviction that it is worth valuing—and hence worth studying—as an end in itself.

In this book, then, democracy—or what Robert Dahl terms polyarchy—denotes a system of government that meets three essential conditions:

- Meaningful and extensive competition among individuals and organized groups (especially political parties) for all effective positions of government power through regular, free, and fair elections that exclude the use of force
- A highly inclusive level of political participation in the selection of leaders and policies, such that no major (adult) social group is prevented from exercising the rights of citizenship

- A level of civil and political liberties—freedom of thought and expression, freedom of the press, freedom of assembly and demonstration, freedom to form and join organizations, freedom from terror and unjustified imprisonment—secured through political equality under a rule of law, sufficient to ensure that citizens (acting individually and through various associations) can develop and advocate their views and interests and contest policies and offices vigorously and autonomously.[8]

Also implicit in this definition are the notions that rulers will be held accountable for their actions in the public realm by citizens and their representatives and that multiple channels exist for representation of citizen interests beyond the formal political frameworks of parties, parliaments, and elections.[9]

Although this definition is relatively straightforward, it presents a number of problems in application. For one, countries that broadly satisfy these criteria nevertheless do so to different degrees (and none do so perfectly, which is why Dahl prefers to call them polyarchies). The factors that explain this variation in degrees of popular control and freedom at the democratic end of the spectrum constitute an important intellectual problem, but it is different from the one that concerns us in this book and thus is one we have largely bypassed. We seek to determine why countries do or do not evolve, consolidate, maintain, lose, and reestablish more or less democratic systems of government, and even this limited focus leaves us with conceptual problems.

As we have already suggested, the boundary between democratic and undemocratic (or "less than democratic") is often blurred and imperfect, and beyond it lies a much broader range of variation in political systems. Even if we look only at the political, legal, and constitutional structures, several of our cases appear ambiguous, and this ambiguity is greatly complicated by the constraints on free political activity, organization, and expression, or the major human rights violations, or the substantial remaining political prerogatives of military authorities, or some combination of these that may in practice make the system much less democratic than its formal structure. In all cases, we have tried to pay serious attention to actual practice in assessing and classifying regimes.

All of this underscores the importance of recognizing grades of distinction among less than democratic systems. Whereas isolated violations of civil liberties or modest and occasional vote rigging should not disqualify a country from broad classification as a democracy, we need to categorize separately those countries that allow greater political competition and freedom than would be found in a truly authoritarian regime but less than could justifiably be termed democratic. Hence, we classify as *semidemocratic* those countries in which the effective power of elected officials is so limited or political party competition so restricted, or the freedom and fairness of elections so compromised that electoral outcomes, although competitive, do not produce true popular sovereignty and accountability, or in which civil and political liberties are so uncertain that some political orientations and interests are unable to organize and express themselves peacefully, without fear.

In different ways and to different degrees, Senegal, Mexico, Turkey, and Thailand fit this category of semidemocracy today. Singapore and Malaysia are other classic and long-standing semidemocracies, featuring regular electoral competition between competing parties under civilian, constitutional rule but with entrenched advantages for historically dominant parties and serious constraints on individual liberties and civil society.

Although formally democratic, many of the regimes in the world today (including several contemporary examples in our volume) represent what might be termed *low-quality* democracy. *Low-intensity* democracy, *poor* democracy, and *delegative* democracy are other terms that have been used— primarily in the Latin American context—to describe a system that may have fair, competitive, and open elections; authentic power for elected officials; freedom of expression and of the press (more or less); and at least some independent organizations and media, but that nevertheless lacks accountability, responsiveness, and institutional balance and effectiveness between elections.[10] Such a designation might apply not only to many of the unconsolidated democracies of the third wave, including Argentina and Brazil, but also to longer-functioning systems, such as those in India and Venezuela, that have entered a period of institutional decay and stress.

Even more restrictive is a *hegemonic party system,* in which opposition parties are legal but are denied, through pervasive electoral malpractices and frequent state coercion, any real chance to compete for power. Such a system long prevailed under the domination of the Partido Revolucionario Institucional (PRI) in Mexico, but the political reforms of the 1980s and early 1990s and the unprecedented gains of both right and left opposition parties since the 1988 elections justify a reclassification of the Mexican system as a semidemocracy.

Descending further on our scale of classification, authoritarian regimes permit even less pluralism, typically banning political parties (or all but the ruling party) and most forms of political organization and competition while being more repressive than liberal in their level of civil and political freedom. By paying close attention to actual behavior, one can distinguish a subset of authoritarian regimes that we call *pseudodemocracies* because the existence of formally democratic political institutions, such as multiparty electoral competition, masks (often in part to legitimate) the reality of authoritarian domination. Central America long endured such regimes. Africa now has several, including the regimes in Kenya, Cameroon, and Gabon. Although in some ways this regime type overlaps with the hegemonic regime, it is less institutionalized and is typically more personalized, coercive, and unstable.

Finally are the *totalitarian* regimes, which not only repress all forms of autonomous social and political organization, denying completely even the most elementary political and civil liberties, but also demand the active commitment of citizens to the regime.[11] With the decay, collapse, or at least partial liberalization of most of the world's Communist regimes in the late 1980s and early 1990s, it is debatable whether the totalitarian distinction remains salient. Nevertheless, the totalitarian legacy shapes in distinctive ways the possibilities and conditions for democratization even in post-totalitarian, nondemocratic regimes.

The dependent variable of our study was concerned not only with democracy but also with stability—the persistence and durability of democratic and other regimes over time, particularly through periods of unusually intense conflict, crisis, and strain. A *stable* regime is one whose institutionalization and level and breadth of popular legitimacy make it highly likely to persist, even in the face of crises and challenges. Building these foundations of regime stability is the task of democratic consolidation (which we consider in conclusion). *Partially stable* regimes are neither fully secure nor in imminent danger of collapse. Their institutions have perhaps acquired some measure of depth, flexibility, and value but not enough to ensure them safe passage through severe challenges. *Unstable* regimes are, by definition, highly vulnerable to breakdown or overthrow in periods of acute uncertainty and stress. New regimes, including those that have recently restored democratic government, tend to fall into this category.

Facilitating and Obstructing Factors for Democratic Development

Legitimacy and Performance

All governments rest on some mixture of coercion and consent, but democracies are unique in the degree to which their stability depends upon the consent of a majority of those governed. So intimately is legitimacy tied to democratic stability that it is difficult to know where definition ends and theorizing begins. Almost as a given, theories of democracy stress that democratic stability requires a widespread belief among elites and masses in the legitimacy of the democratic system: that it is the best (or the "least evil") form of government, "that in spite of shortcomings and failures, the existing political institutions are better than any others that might be established," and hence that the democratic regime is morally entitled to demand obedience—to tax and draft, to make laws and enforce them, even, "if necessary, by the use of force."[12]

Democratic legitimacy derives, when it is most stable and secure, from an intrinsic value commitment rooted in the political culture at all levels of society, but it is also shaped (particularly in the early years of a democracy) by the performance of the democratic regime, both economically and politically (through the "maintenance of civil order, personal security, adjudication and arbitration of conflicts, and a minimum of predictability in the making and implementation of decisions").[13] Historically, the more successful a regime has been in providing what people want, the greater and more deeply rooted its legitimacy has tended to be. A long record of successful performance tends to build a large reservoir of legitimacy, enabling the system better to endure crises and challenges.[14] As Valenzuela shows here in the case of Chile, however, such a long accumulation of democratic legitimacy does not confer immunity from breakdown and can be squandered with great speed by a combination of poor leadership, wrong choices, and outmoded political institutions. The democratic breakdowns in Chile and Uruguay during the 1970s, and the institutional decay and instability experienced during the 1980s and early 1990s by such long-standing democracies as India, Venezuela, and Colombia, emphasize that the legitimation and consolidation of democratic institutions are not necessarily permanent achievements but may require continuous adjustment, reform, and renewal to maintain.[15]

Regimes that lack deep legitimacy depend more precariously on current performance and are vulnerable to collapse in periods of economic and social distress.[16] This has been a particular problem for democratic (as well as undemocratic) regimes in the developing world, especially given their tendency to experience an interaction of low legitimacy and low effectiveness. Because of the combination of widespread poverty and the strains imposed by modernization, regimes that begin with low legitimacy also find it difficult to perform effectively, and regimes that lack effectiveness, especially in the area of economic growth, find it difficult to build legitimacy.

However, our own studies and many others caution against drawing too deterministic a linkage between the economic performance of democratic regimes and the probability of their survival. Spain's new democracy experienced a sharp decline of economic growth and an increase in unemployment in the decade following the transition, but it became consolidated nevertheless because of the resolute popular rejection of authoritarian alternatives and the respect for constitutional procedures and freedoms on the part of the ruling and contesting political elites.[17] The same broad distaste for a reversion to authoritarianism made possible the persistence of Latin American democracies through prolonged economic crisis during the 1980s. As Juan Linz and Alfred Stepan have noted, two features of democracies tend to insulate them from the delegitimating consequences of sustained economic downturns: their claims to intrinsic legitimacy based on their democraticness, and the prospect (always at least looming on the horizon) of replacing the incumbent government and its policies constitutionally, through elections.[18] Nevertheless, whereas the political response to such crises in Latin America has so far been to vote out governing parties rather than to embrace extremist ones or reject democratic legitimacy,[19] this situation masks the broad deterioration in democratic institutions and freedoms that occurred during this period.[20] More important, any blithe inference that contemporary democracies are freed from previously presumed performance constraints errs both in its projection of the recent past into the indefinite future and in its ignorance of history. In the short to medium run, perceptions of a democratic regime's socioeconomic efficacy appear "less tightly coupled" to assessments of its political legitimacy than was once assumed, but "in the long run, it erodes the accrued political capital of the regime if it is seen as completely incapable of solving major socioeconomic problems."[21]

Democracies have their peculiar vulnerabilities. One of these is the particularly corrosive effect of corruption on the legitimacy of democratic regimes, even more than on authoritarian ones. This is so in part because under conditions of freedom—with competitive elections, an independent judiciary, an opposition in parliament, and a free press—corruption is likely to be more visible than is the case under authoritarianism. Its scale and its extension to the entire democratic political class—as has repeatedly occurred in Ghana and Nigeria, for example—delegitimize the whole political system rather than disqualify a particular politician or party. Further, the prevalence of political corruption as the primary motive for the pursuit of power (because of the dominance of the state over economic life) reduces the political process to a struggle for power rather than a debate about policies and taints the electoral process while generating cynical and apathetic responses in the electorate (or at least in the bulk of it outside patronage networks). Such widespread corruption also undermines economic development and is one of the major arguments used by the military to justify its overthrow of elected governments, even though its own corruption will likely be as great or greater in time. The February 1991 coup in Thailand was a case in point (as were the unsuccessful coup attempts in the Philippines in 1989 and in Venezuela in 1992).[22]

Although they have not been immune to problems of recession, inflation, and corruption, the more successful democracies in our study have generally experienced relatively steady economic growth, which in turn has benefited their legitimacy. For a time, rapid growth can derive from the bounty of highly marketable natural resources, but as the experiences of Venezuela and Nigeria show, this can be a decidedly mixed blessing. Botswana, too, has benefited from great natural resources (and high levels of foreign aid), but underlying its strong development performance have been sound policies and effective management (which have helped attract foreign aid). State policies have not strangled producers of agricultural exports (in this case, cattle) as they did in much of the rest of tropical Africa.

Table 1.1   Selected Development Indicators

	Chile 1970	Chile 1992	Brazil 1970	Brazil 1992	Mexico 1970	Mexico 1992	Turkey 1970	Turkey 1992
Per Capita GNP, 1966 & 1992[a]	**740**	**2,730**	**280**	**2,770**	**490**	**3,470**	**310**	**1,980**
Real GDP Per Capita in PPP$, 1960 & 1991[b]	3,130	7,060	1,404	5,240	2,870	7,170	1,669	4,840
Per Capita GNP Annual Percentage Growth Rate, 1965–1980, 1980–1991	**0**	**3.7**	**6.3**	**0.4**	**3.6**	**–0.2**	**3.6**	**2.9**
Inflation Rate, 1970–1980, 1980–1992	187.1	20.5	38.6	370.2	18.1	62.4	29.4	46.3
External Debt as Percentage of GNP, 1970 & 1992	**25.8**	**48.9**	**8.2**	**31.2**	**8.7**	**34.1**	**14.7**	**47.8**
Population (in millions), 1966 & 1992	8.7	14	86.5	154	44.9	85.0	31.9	58.5
Population Annual Percentage Growth Rate, 1970–1980, 1980–1992	**1.6**	**1.7**	**2.4**	**2.0**	**2.9**	**2.0**	**2.3**	**2.3**
Projected Population (in millions), 2000 & 2025	15	19	172	224	99	136	68	92
Urban Population as Percentage of Total	**75**	**85**	**56**	**77**	**59**	**74**	**38**	**64**
Life Expectancy at Birth								
Male	59	69	57	64	60	67	55	65
Female	66	76	61	69	64	74	59	70
Infant Mortality Rate (per 1,000 live births)	**78**	**17**	**95**	**57**	**72**	**35**	**147**	**54**
Adult Literacy Rate (in percentages)	89	94	66	82	74	89	52	82
Human Development Index[c]	**0.682**	**0.848**	**0.507**	**0.756**	**0.642**	**0.804**	**0.441**	**0.739**
Percentage of Labor Force in Agriculture, 1965 & 1990–1992	27	19	49	25	49	23	75	47
Percentage of Population in Absolute Poverty, 1980s	**—**	**n.a.**	**—**	**47**	**—**	**30**	**—**	**n.a.**
Income Share of Highest 20 Percent, 1988–1990	—	62.9	—	67.5	—	55.9	—	n.a.
Radios per 100 People, 1990	**—**	**34**	**—**	**38**	**—**	**25**	**—**	**16**

Sources: World Bank, *World Development Report 1983, 1987, 1989, 1994* (New York: Oxford University Press, 1983, 1987, 1989, 1994); United Nations Development Programme (UNDP), *Human Development Report 1994* (New York: Oxford University Press, 1994); World Bank, *World Tables 1987* (Washington, D.C.: World Bank, 1987).

a. GNP per capita is expressed in current U.S. dollars for each year. Comparisons between 1966 and 1992 figures therefore are not controlled for (U.S.) inflation.

b. Estimates real GDP by measuring the relative domestic purchasing power (PPP$) of currencies rather than by using official exchange rates to convert the national currency figures to U.S. dollars. See *Human Development Report 1994*, p. 221, and *World Development Report 1994*, pp. 244–247.

| India | | Thailand | | South Korea | | Nigeria | | Senegal | | South Africa | |
1970	1992	1970	1992	1970	1992	1970	1992	1970	1992	1970	1992
90	**310**	**150**	**1,840**	**130**	**6,790**	**70**	**320**	**2210**	**780**	**550**	**2,670**
617	1,150	985	5,270	690	8,320	1,133	1,360	1,136	1,680	2,984	2,885
1.5	**3.1**	**4.4**	**6.0**	**7.3**	**8.5**	**4.2**	**–0.4**	**–0.5**	**0.1**	**3.2**	**0.1**
8.4	8.5	9.2	4.2	20.1	5.9	15.2	19.4	8.5	5.2	13.0	14.3
14.7	**25.9**	**4.6**	**35.2**	**20.3**	**14.2**	**3.4**	**108.4**	**11.9**	**39.3**	**n.a.**	**n.a.**
498.9	883.6	32.0	58.0	29.5	43.7	60.0	101.9	4.0	7.8	20.8	39.8
2.3	**2.1**	**2.7**	**1.8**	**1.8**	**1.1**	**2.9**	**3.0**	**2.9**	**2.9**	**2.7**	**2.5**
1,016	1,370	65	81	47	53	128	217	10	16	47	69
20	**26**	**13**	**23**	**41**	**74**	**20**	**37**	**33**	**41**	**48**	**50**
50	61	56	67	58	67	40	50	42	48	50	60
49	62	61	72	62	75	43	54	44	50	56	66
137	**79**	**73**	**26**	**51**	**13**	**139**	**84**	**135**	**68**	**79**	**53**
34	50	79	94	88	97	25	52	12	40	—	—
0.254	**0.382**	**0.465**	**0.798**	**0.523**	**0.859**	**0.230**	**0.348**	**0.176**	**0.322**	**0.591**	**0.650**
73	62	82	67	55	17	72	48	83	81	32	13
—	40	—	30	—	5	—	40	—	70[d]	—	n.a.
—	41.3	—	50.7	—	42.2	—	n.a.	—	58.6	—	n.a.
—	8	—	19	—	99	—	17	—	11	—	30

c. The Human Development Index is a composite of three meaures of human development: longevity (life expectancy), knowledge (weighted two-thirds to adult literacy and one-third to mean years of schooling), and standard of living (real GDP per capita adjusted for the cost of living, i.e. in purchasing-power parity). Each of these three measures is expressed in equally weighted scales of 0 to 1, which are averaged in the overal index. In 1970 the highest scorer was Canada at 0.887 and the lowest was Mali at 0.102. In 1992 the highest scorer was again Canada at 0.932 and the lowest was Guinea at 0.191.

d. This figure is for rural areas only (which have a higher poverty rate, often a massively higher one, than urban areas in virtually every country for which the UNDP reports data).

n.a. indicates figures not available. Data are for 1970 and 1992 unless otherwise indicated.

The state has invested prudently in basic infrastructure, and the elite has kept an effective lid on political and administrative corruption. Parastatals have been managed efficiently, and efforts have been made to distribute growth through state investment in education, housing, health, and other social services; unusually effective food distribution programs to relieve the effects of drought; and improved wages in the formal sector.[23] This record of performance contrasts markedly with the bloated, predatory state structures, widespread corruption, and ill-designed, poorly implemented development policies that sucked the economic breath from putative democratic republics in Nigeria and elsewhere in Africa.

Although it is often presumed to have done poorly in delivering material progress, India has actually achieved significant, if incremental, socioeconomic development and would have done much better if its population had not doubled since 1960 to almost 900 million people. As Table 1.1 shows, India has made steady, if unspectacular, economic and social gains since 1970, significantly improving such quality-of-life indicators as literacy, infant mortality, and life expectancy.

The Indian case also demonstrates, however, the long-term costs to economic dynamism and thus, ultimately, to social and political stability of what Das Gupta terms a "large and abysmally wasteful public sector" and a heavily protected and distorted economy. The increasing globalization of economic life, the collapse of India's socialist trading partners, and most of all the growing fiscal and balance-of-payments deficits in India have brought home to the country's elites the fundamental policy lesson of the past decade: that sustainable development in such a context requires stabilization to reduce imbalances and curb inflation, as well as liberalization to sharply reduce state ownership and intervention in the economy while opening it up to international trade and capital movements.

Over the past decade, economic reform has emerged as one of the main performance challenges for new and recent democracies, as well as some long-standing ones such as India's and Venezuela's. Early interpretations of the Chilean experience under the Pinochet dictatorship and of China's explosive economic growth under a marketizing Communist regime argued that authoritarian rule was necessary to impose economic reform over the opposition of various entrenched and favored interest groups, both producers and consumers. However, the cumulative evidence and research in recent years shows overwhelmingly that this conclusion is false. Most authoritarian regimes do not reform their economies because they are too committed to the distribution of rents that derive from state ownership and controls over production, foreign exchange, and trade. To the surprise of many skeptics, a number of democracies (or at least formally democratic systems) have launched economic stabilization and liberalization programs—some of them rather ambitious—without collapsing under the weight of public protest.

Among this growing list of counterexamples are Spain, Argentina, Bolivia, Turkey, Thailand, the Czech Republic, Poland, Hungary, and (particularly with the 1994 inauguration of President Fernando Henrique Cardoso) Brazil. The first stages of reform (especially austerity-inducing stabilization measures) often require strong and insulated political authority, and a measure of surprise, but not beyond what democratic constitutions commonly afford their executive authorities.

Increasingly, it appears that the conditions conducive to successful economic reform are not incompatible with democratic governance. These conditions include political leadership strongly committed to basic structural reform and possessing the political skill necessary to mobilize and craft supporting coalitions; a "relatively strong consensus" among elites on certain fundamental policy principles, thus depoliticizing economic management;[24] political scope (or even incentive) for that leadership to break with the past, as may be afforded when a new party takes power and is "not beholden to the party, faction or group that has previously benefited from state intervention";[25] more generally, the "political capital" to pursue painful policies during an inaugural honeymoon period when political constraints are at their minimum and trust and confidence in government are at their peak;[26] a perception of manifest crisis (as with the hyperinflations in Bolivia in 1985 and Argentina in 1990) that readies the public for radical reform; considerably enhanced state capacity, transforming the civil service at all levels from a patronage resource to a career meritocracy;[27] and a social safety net program that buffers the impact of adjustment on the poor, empowers them in the design of assistance programs, and thereby gives them a stake in the reform process (as well as in the democratic regime).[28] Unfortunately, the historical and political conditions for mobilizing reform coalitions are not necessarily easy to reproduce and may require time, and considerable economic and political learning, to appear.

Economic reform is more likely to be sustainable, and to effect a fundamental economic restructuring over time, if the governments imposing the transitory pain of adjustment are viewed as legitimate by the society, if they consult major social and interest groups and involve them in the design of policies, and if they (along with independent media and policy centers) educate the public about the need for reform.[29] Democracies are advantaged in all of these respects. Further, social safety net programs are more likely to be targeted effectively toward the poor and vulnerable and to incorporate them politically in the process under a democratic (rather than a clientelistic, dominant-party) regime.[30] All things considered, over the long run open information and debate are more likely to yield reform policies that enjoy some public understanding and support, that are better targeted to social needs, and that are less compromised by corruption and the unfair enrichment of political cronies and special interests.

Political Leadership

Although our theoretical orientation gives substantial emphasis to the importance of various structural factors in shaping the prospects for democracy, these are never wholly determinative. As we have just seen, regime performance and viability, not only economically but also politically, are the outcomes in part of the policies and choices political leaders make—acting, to be sure, within the constraints of the structural circumstances they inherit. Even structures and institutions, especially political ones, are shaped by the actions and options of political leaders. The more constraining and unfavorable the structural circumstances, the more skillful, innovative, courageous, and democratically committed political leadership must be for democracy to survive. Even when the obstacles are formidable, democratic breakdowns are not inevitable but are accelerated by poor leadership and bad choices.[31]

In this book, we see repeatedly how inefficacious, weak, and often militant and uncompromising political leadership has contributed to democratic breakdowns in Chile, Brazil, Turkey, South Korea, Thailand, and Nigeria. In some of these cases, it could be argued that structural circumstances were highly unfavorable, but this was often in part a result of the failure of politicians to produce needed economic reforms and institutional innovations. Valenzuela and Özbudun show, for the breakdowns in Chile (1973) and Turkey (1980), how significantly the miscalculations and intransigence of political leaders contributed.

We also see the importance of strong democratic commitments on the part of political leaders—what Linz calls "loyalty" to the democratic system. Democratically loyal leaders reject the use and rhetoric of violence and illegal or unconstitutional means for the pursuit of power, and they refuse to condone or tolerate antidemocratic actions by other participants.[32] The Nigerian case portrays graphically how electoral violence and fraud, thuggery, demagoguery, and widespread political corruption delegitimated and destroyed the Second Republic (1979–1983)—even in the absence of the polarized ethnic conflict that further contributed to the failure of the First Republic (1960–1966). In the case of India, we see the central role of Indira Gandhi's equivocal commitment to democratic values in motivating not only her declaration of emergency rule in 1975 but also her centralization and personalization of political power in the preceding years and after her return to power in 1980. In many developing countries, the erosion or destruction of democratic institutions has come through the actions of elected leaders who proved to be authoritarian in nature and consumed with their own self-aggrandizement: Marcos in the Philippines, Syngman Rhee in South Korea, Nkrumah in Ghana, Obote in Uganda, and Perón in Argentina. This confirms G. Bingham Powell's generalization that democratic breakdown (by executive or military coup) is commonly preceded by "renunciation of the democratic faith by [a country's] elected leaders."[33]

The story, of course, is not all negative. Throughout the developing world, flexible, accommodative, consensual leadership styles have contributed notably to democratic development, as in the early years of institution building under Gandhi and Nehru and a gifted crop of Congress Party leaders in India.

More recently, political leadership has been a notable and oft-neglected factor in the pursuit of democratic consolidation. Of course, it is hard to disentangle the individual from the structural and institutional context that shapes and constrains political options. Nevertheless, with all of its institutional deficiencies and glaring inequalities that Lamounier exposes so sharply in his chapter, it was only by historical accident that Brazil lost—because of an untimely death—a president-elect who was a proven coalition builder and a skilled and committed democrat, to be replaced by a vice president with much more dubious credentials and limited vision and ability. Nor was it inevitable that Brazil's next president (Fernando Collor de Mello) would prove so inept and corrupt that he would be forced to resign in disgrace. Many citizens and friends of Brazil hope the very different course toward economic and political reform Brazil has charted under recently inaugurated President Fernando Henrique Cardoso will again show the scope for effective leadership to broker lasting change.

Elsewhere in Latin America, progress toward democratic consolidation in Chile and Uruguay occurred in no small measure as a result of the pragmatism, political skill, and respect for democratic constitutionalism of the first post-transition presidents, Patricio Aylwin (1990–1994) in Chile and Julio María Sanguinetti (1985–1990; reelected in 1995). Both men handled with great sensitivity, wisdom, and restraint the explosive issue of accountability for past human rights violations by the military while gradually narrowing the scope of military prerogatives and deepening democratic institutions. In our case study of South Korea, we see the way shrewd and forthright political and financial reforms by President Kim Young Sam have helped to cleanse and strengthen the democratic process while diminishing the autonomous power of the military. By contrast, Philippine President Corazon Aquino—despite her honorable intentions and her deserved esteem as a symbol of the people-power revolution—proved to be a timid and lackluster democratic leader, unable to cope effectively with economic disarray, massive social inequality, political crisis and fragmentation, and repeated military coup attempts that nearly toppled her from power.

Accommodating, shrewd, and resourceful political leadership has often been a factor in successful democratic transitions. Our South African case study highlights the intricate pattern of mutual concessions between the ruling National Party (NP) and the ANC leaderships—especially between

President de Klerk and Nelson Mandela—that kept the negotiating process on track through four treacherous years despite deep differences in ideology and political vision, recalcitrant political flanks, doubting constituencies, alarming levels of political violence, and a brutal history of racial domination and distrust. In retrospect, South Africa's peaceful transition has an air of inevitability because, as Friedman notes here, the major parties all understood that in the end, "the society had no option but to negotiate its way out of a stalemate." But it is important to appreciate the indeterminacy of the process at the time and the real possibility of a descent into large-scale sabotage and violence had ANC and NP negotiators failed to craft adequate provisions for power sharing and face saving and had they not, in Friedman's words, "proved adept at bargaining compromises that saved both the transition and the country from crises that threatened irreversible breakdown."

Such flexible and visionary political leadership, which shows keen timing and some real political courage, also figured prominently in the democratic transitions in South Korea and Taiwan. Arguably, South Korea's democratic transition was saved in 1987 (was certainly spared from trauma and bloodshed) by the decision of the ruling party presidential candidate, Roh Tae Woo, to concede to opposition demands (which included direct presidential elections and a host of other democratic reforms). Roh's surprising and dramatic announcement was, in David Steinberg's opinion, "an example of statesmanlike, expedient compromise" in a society in which the incumbents of power had come to see themselves as pure and the opposition as unworthy and where compromise was generally denigrated as "a signal of weakness and lack of resolve."[34]

In Taiwan, Chiang Ching-kuo's leadership was a pivotal factor in the lifting of martial law and the launching of a democratic transition.[35] Following the death of Chiang in January 1988, President Lee Teng-hui, with support from other reform elements in the ruling Kuomintang (KMT) Party, accelerated Taiwan's democratization through a process of sustained political liberalization, constitutional reform, internal party reform, and new elections.[36] To be sure, powerful social structural and international forces were pressing for democratization and constraining the authoritarian option (as was also true in South Korea and South Africa).[37] However, hard-line factions in the party and security establishments were opposed, and a differently inclined political leadership might have succeeded in perpetuating a much more authoritarian political system for some time. Thus, it would be a serious oversight to neglect the distinctive skills, motives, and goals of individual leaders (and the way they fit into broader patterns of strategic interaction among regime factions and between regime and opposition). By contrast, the primary obstacle to the successful completion of a transition under the military regime of General Ibrahim Babangida (1985–1993) in Nigeria proved to be the general himself, along with other top military elites, who were bent on using every ruse to hang on to the rewards and gratifications of power.

Time and again across our cases we find the values, goals, skills, and styles of political leaders and elites making a difference in the fate of democracy. Coulon shows the importance of the personal leadership decisions and skills of Leopold Senghor and Abdou Diouf in opening up Senegal's politics to more democratic pluralism and competition. Valenzuela shows the importance of able, democratically committed, and even visionary political leadership in the founding of democracy in Chile in the early nineteenth century, its adaptation and expansion during periods of turbulent change and growth, and its maintenance during the Great Depression of the 1930s. Demonstrating a different, corollary rule, Levy and Bruhn explain how consistently skilled and effective leadership, with many undemocratic values, long contributed to the stability of Mexico's undemocratic regime.

Political Culture

One important dimension of regime performance is the management of conflict. If political freedom and competition are not to descend into extremism, polarization, and violence, mechanisms are needed to contain conflict within certain behavioral boundaries. One of the most important factors in this regard is a country's political culture; that is, the beliefs and values concerning politics that prevail within both the elite and the mass.

Theorists in the pluralist or liberal tradition identify several values and beliefs as crucial for stable and effective democracy: belief in the legitimacy of democracy; tolerance for opposing parties, beliefs, and preferences; a willingness to compromise with political opponents and, underlying this, pragmatism and flexibility; trust in the political environment, and cooperation, particularly among political competitors; moderation in political positions and partisan identifications; civility of political discourse; and political efficacy and participation, based on principles of political equality but tempered by the presence of a subject role (which gives allegiance to political authority) and a parochial role (which involves the individual in traditional, nonpolitical pursuits).[38] Dahl in particular emphasizes the importance of such a democratic culture among the political elite, especially early on.

Our larger study provides considerable evidence that such presumed features of democratic culture are closely correlated with democratic stability. Those countries that have been the most strongly and stably democratic also appear to have the most democratic political values and beliefs.

Democratic success in developing countries can be traced not only to the growth of democratic values but also to their roots in a country's historical and cultural traditions. Das Gupta points out that from the time of the founding of the Indian National Congress a century ago, "democratic rules of procedure, tolerance of adversaries, and reconciliation of conflicting claims became part of the political education of the participants." But whereas the political culture of bargaining, accommodation, and constitutionalism began with the gradual development of electoral processes under British colonial rule, the process was not confined to the elite level. A major reason for India's democratic development was that elites reached out to mass society to raise political consciousness, develop democratic practices, and mobilize participation—both in electoral politics and in a wide range of voluntary organizations. Political leadership and ideology were crucial in this process, particularly in the person of Mahatma Gandhi, who emphasized the values of liberty, nonviolent and consensual resolution of conflict, and continuous incorporation of excluded groups.[39]

Ambivalence in a country's political culture is also associated with ambivalence in its experience with democracy. Turkey has been torn between a strong consensus on the legitimacy of popular, elective government and the continuing predilection (dating back to Ottoman rule) for organic theories of state, which spawn excessive fear of division, intolerance of political opposition and individual deviation, and a tendency to see politics in absolutist terms. The behavioral manifestations of these values have figured prominently in Turkey's democratic breakdowns and may help to explain the erosion of liberty and the mounting human rights violations by both state authorities and Kurdish separatists in recent years. Nigeria has been torn between a deep and broadly based commitment to political freedom, with popular, accountable government, and a weak inclination toward tolerance and accommodation. Twice this contradiction has led to political chaos, violence, and democratic breakdown. In Nigeria especially, this intolerance has been driven by the high political stakes associated with state control (see below).

Coulon shows the correspondence between the "mixed" political culture of Senegal and the semidemocratic character of the regime. Traditional political cultures in Senegal balanced authoritarian values with "a propensity for debate, political game playing," and constitutional limits on monarchical authority. Liberal, Western cultural influences press further in a democratic direction, but this is undermined by the lack of support for democracy among the neglected and alienated lower classes and the growing interest in authoritarian Islamic doctrines felt by a segment of the elite. Repeated military intervention in Thai politics has derived in part from a military conception of democracy that values "national security, stability, and order" over freedom and participation and dislikes pressure groups and conflict.

In South Africa, a different kind of cultural tension or ambivalence complicates the democratic prospect. Although the electoral process and constitutional protections of political and civil rights enjoy mass legitimacy, the decades of political exclusion, repression, and liberation struggle have bred a culture of intolerance and inflexibility among many individuals and groups that were radicalized by the experience, particularly in the black townships and among the young. These dispositions not only threaten South Africa's capacities for peaceful conflict resolution; they also breed a general cynicism and resistance to state authority that undermine the state's capacity to perform even its most elementary functions, such as the maintenance of order and the provision of services.[40] As Friedman reminds us, effective democracy requires an effective state, and the state cannot be effective unless it commands citizen allegiance, what Gabriel Almond and Sidney Verba called the "subject" role.

It is misleading, however, to infer too much from the contours of a country's political culture at any particular point in time. Perhaps the most important lesson our case studies (and many others) teach us about political culture is that it is plastic and malleable over time. Political culture is not destiny. Just as Latin American countries overcame what was once thought to be their indelibly authoritarian Catholic and Iberian heritage, so Asian countries are not condemned to authoritarian rule by their Confucian or Buddhist cultures, or Middle Eastern countries by the predominance of Islam, or African countries by their ethnic and religious pluralism. All great religious traditions are complex belief systems with multiple (and even conflicting) political implications that are open to different interpretations and reinterpretations over time. Cultural patterns and beliefs do change in response to new institutional incentives, socioeconomic development, and historical experience. Certainly, the experience of brutal dictatorship, repression, and torture has given Latin American elites and mass publics (including not only politicians but liberation theologians and other thinkers and activists on the left) "a renewed appreciation of the virtues of representative government, however flawed."[41] In fact, such political learning—which reshapes the perceptions, tactics, and beliefs of political elites and their followers—has been one of the most important factors facilitating democratic transition and, it is hoped, consolidation during the third wave.[42] In cases as diverse as Chile and South Africa, our authors show here what a crucial foundation of democratic progress it has been.

Social Structure and Socioeconomic Development

One of the most powerful factors that alters political beliefs and values and increases the prospects for stable democracy is socioeconomic development. Since Lipset's 1959 article, which asserted a positive relationship between the level of economic development and a country's chances for stable democracy, dozens of quantitative studies have examined this relationship.[43] Overwhelmingly, the weight of the evidence confirms a strong positive relationship between democracy and socioeconomic development and that this relationship is causal in at least one direction: Higher levels of development generate a significantly higher probability of democracy and of stable democracy. In particular, as countries approach very high levels (or thresholds) of socioeconomic development, democracy becomes highly likely, just as it has historically been rather rare in countries with very low thresholds of development.[44] While per capita national income has been the variable most commonly correlated with democracy, the more important underlying phenomenon appears to be reduction in poverty and improvement in literacy, life expectancy, and so on, as measured by the United Nations Development Programme's (UNDP) Human Development Index (HDI).[45] Improvements in these physical quality-of-life indicators have been particularly dramatic over the past two decades in Chile and South Korea and fairly rapid in Thailand and Mexico as well (see Table 1.1), accounting in part for the growing democratic pressures and possibilities in these countries over the past decade. From this theoretical and empirical perspective, one can see that it is not just the level of socioeconomic development but also its distribution that matters, as the case of Brazil graphically shows (see below).[46]

There are several reasons why socioeconomic development may increase the likelihood of stable democracy. An advanced level of economic development, which produces greater economic security and more widespread education, is assumed to reduce socioeconomic inequality and mitigate feelings of relative deprivation and injustice in the lower class, thus reducing the likelihood of extremist politics.[47] Increased national wealth also tends to enlarge the middle class, which has long been associated in political theory with moderation, tolerance, and democracy.[48] Independent of the impact of changes in class structure, national economic development appears to create a milieu that is more conducive to the emergence of such democratic values as tolerance, trust, and efficacy.[49] Economic development also tends to alter the relationship between state and society, to increase the number and variety of independent organizations that check the state and broaden political participation, and to reduce corruption, nepotism, and state control over jobs and opportunities to accumulate wealth.[50] Finally, economic development thrusts a country into ever greater cultural and economic integration with a world whose most desired markets, capital, goods, technology, and ideas are controlled primarily by democracies. As they have achieved higher levels of economic development, South Korea and Taiwan in particular but also countries such as Turkey, Thailand, Chile, and even South Africa have felt increasing pressure to democratize from Western industrialized democracies—and from their own elites trained in Western (especially U.S.) universities.

Whereas the weight of the evidence supports the Lipset thesis, it does not do so in every respect. The relationships described here are not linear, and at certain stages development may even increase corruption or alter class coalitions in ways more favorable to authoritarian than to democratic rule. In particular, the middle class is by no means always supportive of democracy. In some cases, historically the bourgeoisie has been sympathetic to authoritarian rule and hostile to democracy, and the working class has been a leading force pressing for democratization.[51] Recent studies have emphasized the need to disaggregate the middle class in analyzing its political role. Small-scale entrepreneurs and the professional middle classes, it seems, are more likely to support democratization; the major owners of capital, especially those benefiting from state contracts and largesse, are much more likely to support continued authoritarian rule.

Thus, South Korea's large industrial conglomerates, the *chaebols,* were constrained by the state through the latter's regulatory powers and control of credit, whereas students, professionals, trade unions, and various civil society organizations pressed for democratization. In Taiwan, where the ruling KMT had avoided fostering big capital as had occurred in South Korea, small and medium enterprises, independent of the KMT, joined with labor and the professional middle classes (including intellectuals trained abroad) to pressure for democratization.[52] As Chai-Anan observes, this same distinction between small and large (state-associated) capital has also been apparent in Thailand, with the former spearheading the campaign for genuine democracy.

As countries reach middle stages of development, access to information expands, through radios and newspapers and increasingly to television as well. We see in Table 1.1 that our Latin American cases and South Africa have a ratio of radios to persons (twenty-five to forty radios for every one hundred persons) sufficient to provide access for the majority of households.[53] In these and other industrializing countries, access to television has also been growing (which has become a big factor in Brazilian politics). In addition, literacy and education enable people to discover information for themselves and thus to participate in politics more autonomously.

To be sure, this is only one dimension of development, and high levels of literacy and mass communications have not produced democracy in Singapore, Malaysia, or the many oil-rich states of the Gulf. Moreover, on these as on other measures, India remains fairly underdeveloped, despite considerable progress in recent decades, and yet has maintained a more or less democratic constitutional system. However, beyond the impact of income levels on political beliefs, attitudes, and values, low levels of urbanization, literacy, and communication do make it easier for authoritarian or, as in Senegal, quasi-authoritarian structures to perpetuate themselves and make it more difficult for democratic institutions to consolidate themselves. Clearly, the challenge of building an informed democratic citizenry, capable of scrutinizing government and demanding accountability and responsiveness, is more formidable at these lower levels of development.

Still, it is important to underscore that the relationship between democracy and development is far from perfect. Many other variables can alter the expected impact of the development level on democracy in individual countries. Development enhances the prospects for democracy because—*and to the extent that*—it enhances several crucial intervening variables: democratic values and beliefs, capacities for independent organization and action in civil society (see below), a more equitable class structure (with reduction of absolute poverty), and a less corrupt, interventionist, rent-seeking state. Where, as in the Gulf states, economic growth far outstrips these deeper structural and cultural changes, the level or probability of democracy will be much lower than that expected from the country's level of economic development. But where, as in India, Costa Rica, or Botswana, these intervening variables have emerged through different historical processes—including tradition and the deliberate and effective innovation of political leaders—the level or probability of democracy will be much greater than that which would be predicted merely from the country's per capita GNP. In fact, these three developing democracies and others (such as Mauritius, Jamaica, Trinidad, and Tobago) have survived in large part because they improved the quality of life for their citizens.[54] Thus, economic development is not a prerequisite for democracy: "A premature democracy which survives will do so by (among other things) facilitating the growth of other conditions conducive to democracy, such as universal literacy, or autonomous private organizations."[55]

The accumulation of historical and quantitative evidence cannot, we think, justify the argument, so prevalent in the thinking of the 1960s and 1970s, that poor countries should forget about democracy and concentrate on development; that authoritarian regimes grow more rapidly than democracies; and that democratic political participation must therefore "be held down, at least temporarily, in order to promote economic development" at lower to middle stages of the process.[56] Recent studies have found that democracy either has no independent effect on economic growth or that, on balance, it contributes to growth.[57] The most sophisticated and most recent of these quantitative studies concludes that "regimes do not differ at all in their impact on the growth of per capita income," and thus "democracy can flourish in poor countries if they develop and poor countries can develop under democracy."[58]

Socioeconomic inequality. Democracy and socioeconomic equality are related. In particular, deep, cumulative social inequalities represent a poor foundation for democracy. Historically, this situation has been a contributing factor to the instability of democracy in much of Latin America, including the Dominican Republic, Peru, and most of Central America. By contrast, the historical absence of hacienda agriculture and large landholdings in Costa Rica, and the shortage of agricultural labor that kept rural wages high, bred an egalitarian social culture and what John Booth has termed an "interdependence among classes" that helped significantly to foster the development of democracy.[59]

Perhaps nowhere in the current period does inequality pose a more acute and urgent problem for democracy than in Brazil, where the wealthiest tenth of the population earns the highest percentage of income (51.3 percent) and the poorest fifth earns the second-lowest share (2.1 percent) among the sixty-four countries for which the World Bank currently reports data.[60] Regional inequalities are also severe. The impoverished northeastern region of the country lags behind the more prosperous south by seventeen years in life expectancy, 33 percentage points in adult literacy, and $2,000 (40 percent) in real GDP per capita.[61] Lamounier shows that the marked failure to reduce inequality was an important structural factor that weakened the democratic system and contributed to its breakdown in 1964. As Brazil has become even more urbanized and socially mobilized in the past quarter-century—although income inequality and, by some accounts, even absolute poverty worsened despite the stunning overall rates of economic growth under military rule—"deconcentration" of wealth has become imperative for democratic consolidation. And yet, policies to reduce inequality, such as land reform, carry serious short-term political risks, whereas reducing absolute poverty requires long-term policy commitments that may be politically difficult to sustain. The potential polarizing effects of inequality in Brazil have been evidenced in the growth of urban labor militancy and strife, violent rural land conflicts, and electoral support for populist and radical candidates.

Although comparable income-inequality data are not available for South Africa, its distributive challenge is even more formidable, not only because of the extreme levels of inequality but also because these levels are correlated with race more heavily than is the case in any other country in the world. The disparities in development levels between whites and blacks are four times greater in South Africa than in the United States. In South Africa, blacks have a life expectancy of sixty years and whites of seventy-five years. Blacks have a GDP per capita (in purchasing power parity) of $1,710; for whites the figure is $14,920. In terms of the overall human development index, "If white South Africa were a separate country, it would rank 24 in the world (just after Spain). Black South Africa would rank 123 in the world (just above Congo). Not just two different peoples, these are almost two different worlds."[62] These deep socioeconomic divisions further reinforce the racial polarization of politics and severely challenge the patience and moderation of a majority black population that has had to wait decades for just treatment but that cannot now seek wholesale redistribution of wealth or state spending without driving away the domestic and foreign capital and skills so desperately needed for economic growth. The ruling ANC thus will have to walk a fine line between redistribution and restraint. Its effectiveness in balancing these competing goals will heavily determine whether it can maintain a relatively moderate and accommodating course, preserving democracy while holding on to its constituency.

Population growth.   A socioeconomic problem that is often overlooked in evaluating democratic performance and prospects is that of rapid population growth. Although birthrates tend to decline with higher standards of living and improved socioeconomic opportunities for women (as suggested by the data in Table 1.1), population growth rates nevertheless remain high in most of Asia, Latin America, and especially Africa. Even if countries reduce these annual growth rates toward 2 percent, as Brazil, Mexico, Turkey, Thailand, and India (nearly) managed to do in the 1980s, populations will still *double* in thirty-five years or less. For populations growing annually at rates of 3 percent to 3.5 percent in Nigeria and many other African countries, the doubling time is twenty to twenty-three years. In countries with such rapid growth rates, the age structure is heavily tilted toward children and adolescents, with 40 to 50 percent of the population typically under fifteen years of age.[63] Thus, not only is there a large dependent population to be cared for, schooled, and, ultimately, somehow gainfully employed, but population growth has a hidden momentum that will only be felt fully when these children in turn bear children of their own—even if by that time social, economic, and cultural conditions have been transformed so they do so only at the rate of replacement fertility (i.e., two children per couple).

The political consequences of such rapid population growth follow closely, but not entirely, from the economic ones. To the extent that its population is growing rapidly, a country's economic growth is absorbed each year in providing for its additional people at existing levels of nutrition, schooling, health care, and so on, rather than improving per capita standards. The annual population increments are often large in absolute terms: at current growth rates, more than 3 million additional people each year in Nigeria and Brazil, more than a million a year in Turkey and Thailand, and 18.5 million annually in India. Increasingly, as these countries also become more urbanized, these burgeoning numbers are concentrated in the cities, where violent protest and conflict may be more destabilizing. To the extent that economic growth is rapid enough to provide adequate schooling, training, jobs, and opportunities for these young populations, political stability may not be affected, and population growth rates will decline to the more manageable levels (1 percent or less) found in the advanced industrial countries. But among our cases, only in South Korea has this largely occurred. Birthrates through the remainder of this decade are forecast to fall to 1.3 percent in Chile and Thailand, to 1.4 percent in Brazil, and to 1.7 percent in India. Yet even at that rate, India's population will grow to past a billion by the turn of the century, and the country is projected to add an additional 350 million people in the following quarter-century.[64] In Turkey, Mexico, South

Africa, Nigeria, and Senegal, birth rates will remain near, at, or well above 2 percent annually, generating exploding economic and political demands and expectations these systems will be hard-pressed to meet. The problem is exacerbated by substantial economic inequality because the poor typically have higher birthrates and are less able to provide for their children's future.

If current assumptions are not altered, the resulting stagnation, frustration, and political turmoil may be blamed on economic mismanagement, but rapid population growth should not be overlooked as a contributing factor. National programs to foster family planning and population consciousness must be accelerated—along with efforts to improve health care and education for women and the poor—if population growth rates are to be slowed sufficiently to allow these developing countries a reasonable chance to consolidate and maintain stable democratic government.

In this effort, democracy can be an important asset (contrary to many past assumptions). On average, populations grow more rapidly under authoritarian regimes than under democratic ones.[65] The openness of democracies to public debate and independent organization, and their greater propensity for concern about the status of women—in part because of the ability of women to mobilize politically—give democracies distinct advantages in the effort to reduce fertility rates. This is only one of many ways in which a vigorous civil society serves democracy.

Civil Society

Civil society can be thought of as "the realm of organized social life that is voluntary, self-generating, (largely) self-supporting, autonomous from the state, and bound by a legal order or set of shared rules."[66] It consists of a vast array of organizations, both formal and informal: interest groups, cultural and religious organizations, civic and developmental associations, issue-oriented movements, the mass media, research and educational institutions, and similar organizations. What distinguishes these groups from other collective actors in society is that civil society organizations are concerned with and act in the public realm, relate to the state (without seeking to win control over it), and encompass and respect pluralism and diversity.[67] By contrast, the purpose of groups in *political* society—especially political parties but also electoral alliances, legislative caucuses and coalitions, and the like—is to win and exercise state power.[68]

Conceived in this way, a vigorous and autonomous civil society serves the development of democracy in many ways. The classic function of civil society in political theory, dating back in different respects to such eighteenth- and nineteenth-century thinkers as Ferguson, Hegel, Marx, and de Tocqueville, was to limit state power and to oppose and resist the tyrannical abuse of state power.[69] Since 1974, the "resurrection of civil society" has been a crucial dynamic in undermining the stability of authoritarian regimes and pressuring for democratization.[70] In the Philippines, the Marcos dictatorship was brought down by the coalescence of students, professionals, business owners, workers, priests, teachers, and mothers into the people-power movement that mobilized *half* a million Filipinos to monitor the 1986 elections and then brought them into the streets to take back the election victory Marcos had blatantly tried to steal. In South Korea, massive student and worker demonstrations (emboldened in part by television images from the Philippines) played a key role in pressuring for the institutional concessions that paved the way for democratic transition in late 1987. In Chile, the stunning defeat of the Pinochet dictatorship in the October 1988 plebiscite was achieved against enormous odds only by the heroic organization of a remarkably broad coalition of independent groups that united in the Crusade for Citizen Participation.[71] In Eastern Europe the renaissance of autonomous group activity undermined Communist domination by puncturing the psychology of fear and passivity, revitalizing social morality, regenerating political efficacy, and reporting the shocking truth about the gross abuses of power.[72] Across sub-Saharan Africa (including, very prominently and for many years, South Africa) the pressure for democratic change has come most significantly from the impassioned mobilization and coalescence of students, the churches, professional associations, women's groups, trade unions, human rights organizations, producer groups, intellectuals, journalists, civic associations, and informal networks.[73] Even where this mobilization has fractured and failed to produce democracy, as in Nigeria and Kenya, it has kept the issue of democracy alive and has constrained to some extent the autonomy of the authoritarian state.

After the transition, civil society contributes in diverse and reinforcing ways to deepening, consolidating, and maintaining democracy. First, it continues to provide the means for monitoring and limiting the exercise of state power and for holding officials accountable to the public between elections. Second, a rich associational life supplements the role of political parties in stimulating political participation and increasing citizens' political efficacy and skill. Third, both through the process of participating within organizations and through more deliberate efforts at civic education by organizations and the media, a vigorous civil society can help to inculcate norms of tolerance, trust, moderation, and accommodation that facilitate the peaceful, democratic regulation of cleavage and conflict. Fourth, civil society can enhance the representativeness of democracy by providing additional channels (beyond political parties) for the expression and pursuit of a wide variety of interests, including those of historically marginalized groups, such as women and minorities.

Fifth, as a by-product of successful organizational practice, and in some cases through deliberate programming, civil society organizations identify and train new leaders who at some point may cross over into the political arena and broaden its pool of leadership talent. Sixth, some civic organizations work explicitly to improve democracy: election-monitoring groups such as NAMFREL, the Mexican Civic Alliance, the massive voter education and monitoring efforts in South Africa in 1994; human rights groups, think tanks devoted to democratic reform, and public anticorruption groups such as Poder Ciudadano in Argentina. Civil society also empowers citizens and enhances their oversight of government by the wide dissemination of independent information.

Finally, by enhancing the accountability, responsiveness, inclusiveness, and legitimacy of the political system, civil society also strengthens legitimacy and governability, giving citizens respect for the state and positive engagement with it. Indeed, Robert Putnam and his collaborators have found that traditions and horizontal networks of civic engagement, based on norms of reciprocity, social trust, and cooperation, have significantly accounted for patterns of good governance and economic prosperity in Italy.[74] As they demonstrate, a strong civil society and a strong (i.e., effective) state complement rather than contradict one another.

Our cases demonstrate the significant benefit to democratic development that can be derived from a pluralistic civil society. From its earliest beginnings in the nationalist mobilization against colonial rule a century ago, democracy in India has been invigorated by the presence of a rich array of voluntary associations directed to language reform, legal reform, educational modernization, defense of press freedom, civil liberties, and women's rights. Whereas today strong trade unions and peasant, student, and business associations often align with political parties, they also act autonomously to pursue their own interests, and this political autonomy has increased as new leadership groups within them give greater emphasis to economic issues. Today a vast network of issue-oriented movements also campaigns for social and political reform. Indeed, as formal political institutions have deteriorated in the past two decades, India's associational life has become an increasingly crucial resource for democratic articulation and accountability.

As a strong and autonomous associational life may buttress or foster democracy, so the absence of a vigorous sector of voluntary associations and interest groups or the control of such organizations by a corporatist state can reinforce authoritarian rule and obstruct the development of democracy. Perhaps the classic demonstration of this phenomenon in our study is found in Mexico, where, as Levy and Bruhn indicate, the early encapsulation of mass organizations (especially those of peasants and workers) by a hegemonic ruling party has been a key pillar of stability for the authoritarian regime, and the struggle of labor and other popular movements to break free of corporatist controls is now a key feature of the struggle for democracy. In Turkey, Thailand, South Korea, and other Asian countries, state corporatist controls—and the historical dominance of a powerful, highly centralized state bureaucracy—stunted the development of autonomous associational life and mass media and (particularly in Thailand and Korea) facilitated the ascendance of the military as the leading political force. For decades in these countries, weak institutions in civil and political society were both cause and effect of bureaucratic-authoritarian domination in what seemed a vicious cycle. However, as has occurred in Mexico, economic development has been undermining this pattern of state-society relations and giving rise in each country to a civil society of historically unprecedented pluralism, vigor, autonomy, and resourcefulness.

Yet whether the component elements of civil society will benefit democracy depends on the degree to which they are truly civil and democratic in their spirit and internal structure—pragmatic and willing to compromise, tolerant, and pluralistic. South Africa shows that a civil society with mixed features in these regards can have ambiguous implications for democracy. As Friedman explains, both the white professional and business communities and the black liberation struggle gave rise to an extraordinarily active and pluralistic civil society, which now constitutes the principal force for containing state power. But civil society "is largely an insider phenomenon, [and] even within the insider world, the voice of authentically independent private associations is muted." Many of the black-led organizations in the "struggle," particularly the civic associations based in the townships, manifest dubious representativeness and monopolistic tendencies, claiming a "mandate" to represent a monolithic black community.[75] South Africa's democratic development will be advanced if these popular organizations learn to respect state authority and associational pluralism within the black community; institutionalize democratic rules and procedures; become more autonomous from the ruling ANC; and represent more specific policy agendas.[76]

Although vigor, skepticism, and independence enhance civil society's contribution to democracy, they can also go too far. Interest groups cannot take the place of political parties in a democracy, however much they may supplement their participatory and representational functions. Only parties and their representatives in parliament and government can aggregate multiple societal preferences into clear policy alternatives, negotiate compromises, and enact them into law; only parties can govern in a democracy.

Not only political society but the state as well must be viewed as legitimate by civil society. The state must have sufficient autonomy, legitimacy, capacity, and support to mediate among various interests, balance their claims, and govern on behalf of broader societal interests. However, in the aftermaths of Communist oppression in Eastern Europe and the former Soviet Union and of authoritarian predation, especially in Africa, the dominant political mood is one of cynicism, indiscipline, defiance, and resistance to state authority (and typically toward parties as well). Missing is the crucial link between state strength and societal vigor, the social and cultural capital that is such an important foundation for effective democratic governance: norms of generalized reciprocity—not particularistic, hierarchical bonds of clientage—and networks of civic engagement that foster self-reinforcing patterns of social trust and cooperation. These core elements of what Putnam has called "the civic community" must be developed if democracy is to become effective and secure. If new patterns of civic engagement are gradually to take hold, not only must formal institutions change but organizational entrepreneurs must strive to build a new social context in which "associations proliferate, memberships overlap, and participation spills into multiple arenas of community life."[77]

State and Society

If democracy is to be stable, it must find a balance between a number of competing values: between conflict and consensus, participation and passivity, protest and allegiance, consent and effectiveness, elite conciliation and popular mobilization, and—as we will see shortly—between representativeness and governability.[78] As we have just seen, a balance must also be found between the vigor and dynamism of civil society and the capacity and authority of the state.

As we suggested earlier in our discussion of economic performance, yet another dimension in which balance is needed is the relationship between the state and the economy. Recent studies of the East Asian "miracles" have suggested that rapid economic development can be consistent with different degrees and strategies of state intervention in the economy. Still, all eight "high-performance Asian economies" (including in our study Thailand and South Korea) followed certain basic policy fundamentals: avoiding inflationary financing of budget deficits, maintaining competitive real exchange rates, investing in human capital (especially through basic education), encouraging savings, creating secure bank-based financial systems, limiting price distortions (of labor, capital, and goods), attracting foreign investment and technology, limiting the bias against agriculture, actively promoting manufactured exports, instituting mechanisms (such as land reform, public housing, and farmer assistance) to effect a commitment to shared growth, and establishing an institutional environment generally friendly to business and investment.[79] These policies were facilitated by the insulation of state economic policymakers from excessive political pressures, but as we have already suggested, we do not think authoritarianism is a necessary (or sufficient) condition to achieve such insulation.

An overriding lesson from our cases, as well as from the East Asian experience, is the need to limit direct state ownership and control of the economy. This is important for democracy not only because of the costs to economic development of failing to do so but also because of the perverse political incentives that prevail under statist systems. "The greater the importance of the central state as a source of prestige and advantage, the less likely it is that those in power—or the forces of opposition—will accept rules of the game that institutionalize party conflict and could result in the turnover of those in office."[80] These destructive incentives have been particularly striking in sub-Saharan Africa, where (with a few notable exceptions, such as Botswana and South Africa) state ownership and mediation of socioeconomic resources and rewards have been massive, with relatively few private means of economic accumulation and opportunity. Hence, upward social mobility and the accumulation of personal wealth have depended on getting and maintaining control of, or at least having access to, the state.[81] This situation raises the premium on political power to the point at which no competing party or candidate is willing to abide by the rules of democratic competition or to entertain the prospect of defeat. The result is a zero-sum game—the politics of intolerance, desperation, violence, and fraud.[82]

This desperate character of politics in the swollen African state has heavily motivated the postindependence drive by ruling parties and elites to monopolize power in such countries as Senegal and helps to explain the current unwillingness of the political bosses of Senegal's ruling Socialist Party to allow the opposition parties a fully free and fair chance to compete for power. In Nigeria, where most of the country's wealth is mediated through government contracts, jobs, licenses, development projects, and other state largesse, it has been the single most important factor underlying the failure of all three attempts at democracy. Özbudun notes a similar effect in Turkey, where the ruling party's access to immense state resources, and the clientelistic traditions that gave the political class wide scope in distributing state resources, made being out of power in Turkey very costly, and helped to generate political polarization and democratic instability. Statism also heightens the stakes in the ethnic struggle and makes accommodation between competing groups more difficult.

Another tension between statism and democracy is the former's inducement to pervasive political corruption and rent seeking. By driving the entrepreneurial spirit into the search for unproductive profits, the market distortions that give rise to "rents" retard economic growth. No less serious for democracy, however, are the delegitimating political consequences of corruption: cynicism, alienation, civic withdrawal, and gross violation of the rules of democratic competition in the chase for the corrupt rewards of power. Endemic political corruption has been a major factor undermining support for democratic regimes in the developing world and in paving the way for their overthrow.

The answer to the problem of political corruption is not simply a limited state but rather a professionalized and in some ways strengthened state. Where we find corruption contained (at least so it does not massively distort the incentive structure of politics, business, and society), and where we find states performing relatively effectively—as in the high-performance East Asian economies and (virtually alone among sub-Saharan African states)

Botswana—almost invariably we find more or less meritocratic civil services that are able to attract and retain able, well-educated officials because they pay them well. In such systems, the "rules and procedures governing public sector employment [are] institutionalized and insulated from political interventions." Recruitment and promotion are based on merit and performance, and public employment is accorded high status.[83]

Political Institutions

For several reasons, political institutionalization in general, and of the party system in particular, is strongly related to the persistence and stability of democracy.[84]

First, because institutions structure behavior into stable, predictable, and recurrent patterns, institutionalized systems are less volatile and more enduring, and so are institutionalized democracies. Acting within well-established and normatively shared institutional settings, individuals and groups confine themselves to legal and constitutional methods that eschew the use or threat of force. The outcomes of electoral and other conflicts remain uncertain, but that uncertainty is bounded by rules that protect basic interests, and it is eased by the knowledge that these institutionalized interactions will continue indefinitely, generating a long-term view that induces moderation, bargaining, accommodation, and trust among competing actors.[85]

Second, regardless of how they perform economically, democracies that have more coherent and effective political institutions will be more likely to perform well politically in maintaining not only political order but also a rule of law, thus ensuring civil liberties, checking the abuse of power, and providing meaningful representation, competition, choice, and accountability. Third, over the long run well-institutionalized democracies are also more likely to produce workable, sustainable, and effective economic and social policies because they have more effective and stable structures for representing interests and they are more likely to produce working congressional majorities or coalitions that can adopt and sustain policies. Moreover, a strong party system facilitates governability and effective macroeconomic management even in the face of prolonged economic crisis.[86] Finally, and owing in large measure to the first three factors, democracies that have capable, coherent democratic institutions are better able to limit military involvement in politics and assert civilian control over the military.

Parties and party systems.   The challenge of democratic institutionalization is more formidable today in at least one sense: Political parties, once the linchpin of democratic institution building, now find it much more difficult to establish strong organizations and coherent programs. Parties will never again dominate the arena of mass-membership political actors the way they did in the late nineteenth and early twentieth centuries, when one or two major issues, such as class and the role of the church, organized politics. Today, issues and interests are more diverse, and class identities and organizations are weaker and more permeable. In addition, technological changes have tended to personalize politics, diffuse information, widen interests, and reduce the need for direct face-to-face participation. Thus, political preferences and voting patterns are much more fluid, and "parties that want to aggregate large numbers of votes to govern a country are forced to present a much more diffuse and general appeal."[87]

Nevertheless, political parties remain "the most important mediating institutions between the citizenry and the state," indispensable not only for forming governments but also for constituting effective opposition.[88] Only political parties can fashion diverse identities, interests, and preferences into laws, appropriations, policies, and coalitions. Without effective parties that command at least somewhat stable bases of support, democracies cannot have effective governance.

Political scientists have long debated the ideal number of parties for a stable democracy. Lipset considers the two-party system the most likely to produce moderation, accommodation, and aggregation of diverse interests because it compels each party to fashion broad political appeals, in contrast to the strident and ideological appeals small parties tend to make in a multiparty system to consolidate and mobilize their limited bases.[89] However, the two-party system requires crosscutting cleavages; if the two-party cleavage coincides with other accumulated cleavages (such as ethnicity and religion), it might further polarize conflict sufficiently to produce democratic breakdown and civil strife.[90] Sartori and Linz draw the distinction instead between moderate (with fewer than five relevant parties) and extreme, polarized multiparty systems, with the latter significantly increasing the probability of democratic breakdown.[91] Yet G. Bingham Powell argues, from empirical examination of twenty-nine democracies over time, that a "representational" party system, in which numerous parties exhibit strong linkages to distinct social groups, may contribute to democratic stability by facilitating the involvement of potentially disaffected groups in legitimate politics—provided extremist parties are unable to gain significant support.[92]

Recent analyses of experiences with economic reform confirm the value of a more aggregative party system. Fragmented party systems give rise to bidding wars, trade union militancy, ideological polarization, and weak and unstable coalition governments held together mainly by "extensive, and costly, sidepayments," thus producing "perverse incentives that are detrimental not only to macroeconomic stability but to democratic governance as well."[93] By contrast, aggregative party systems, in which one or two broadly based and centrist parties can consistently obtain electoral majorities or near majorities, are better positioned to resist "class or narrow sectoral interests," maintain policy continuity across administrations, and diminish the influence of political extremes.[94]

Our twenty-six–nation study generally supports the proposition that a system of two or a few parties, with broad social and ideological bases, may be conducive to stable democracy. Of the five most stable democratic systems in our study, two (Venezuela and Costa Rica) have had two-party systems composed of broad, multiclass parties in societies that lack deep social cleavages; two (India and Botswana) have had one-party–dominant systems in which the ruling parties incorporate and aggregate a wide range of ethnic and social interests; and one (Papua New Guinea) has had a moderate multiparty system in which two parties have predominated. In addition, the more stable emerging democracies, such as South Korea and Taiwan, have also been developing two-party-dominant systems, whereas the increasing instability in Venezuela and India in recent years has been associated with the decay of the predominant parties and growing fragmentation of the party system. Historically, fragmentation into a large number of parties that come and go—as has occurred in Thailand and Brazil, among other countries— has been associated with democratic instability and breakdown, not only because such party systems tend toward Sartori's "polarized pluralism" but also because parties in such systems are poorly institutionalized.

A critical consideration for democracy is not merely the number of political parties but also their overall institutional strength, as indicated by Samuel Huntington's criteria of coherence, complexity, autonomy, and adaptability.[95] Among the twenty-six cases in our larger study, we find that when at least one and eventually two or more parties were able to develop some substantive coherence regarding policy and program preferences, some organizational coherence and discipline, some complexity and depth of internal structure, some autonomy from dominance by individual leaders or state or societal interests, and some capacity to adapt to changing conditions—incorporating new generations and newly emergent groups—democracy has usually developed considerable durability and vitality. The early and deep institutionalization of the Congress Party became an important foundation for democratic consolidation in India, just as the personalization of party power and the decay of party organization under Indira Gandhi has reflected and heightened the overall deterioration of democratic institutions since the mid-1960s. For many decades the strength of Chilean parties likewise contributed to stable democracy, with breakdown resulting not from their institutional deterioration but from the polarization of relations among them. In Brazil, the "deinstitutionalization" of the party system that began in the mid-1950s, fragmenting or dividing each of the major parties and thus undercutting their capacity to respond to and harness changing economic and social forces, heavily contributed, as Lamounier shows, to the democratic breakdown in 1964.

Thailand shows vividly the linkage between extreme party fractionalization and the institutional weakness of parties and the party system. With around fifty parties winning representation in parliament in just seven elections from 1975 through 1992, elites have been unable to build strong bases of popular support; to articulate, aggregate, and mobilize political interests; to incorporate emerging interests into the political process; and to cooperate with one another in achieving policy innovations. As a result, the military and bureaucracy have been able to claim many of these functions, making it more difficult for independent democratic forces to establish themselves. The weakness and fragmentation of Thailand's party system was a leading factor in the failure of past democratic attempts (notably the 1974–1976 regime), and, with eleven parties having won legislative seats in the September 1992 elections, it remains an obstacle to the evolution and consolidation of a fully democratic system today.

Party system institutionalization is not only reflected in the internal coherence and the organizational depth and resourcefulness of political parties. An important dimension of institutionalization, and a necessary condition for the persistence of institutions through time, is adaptability.[96] A major weakness in the literature on consociational democracy and elite settlements is its failure to recognize the way in which these institutional foundations of democratic stability can erode and unravel because of failure to adapt to social change and to incorporate new groups.[97] Unfortunately, adaptability and incorporation are fostered by features of internal organization, such as decentralization and openness, that may undermine coherence. The ability of central party leaders to choose closed lists of legislative candidates in proportional representation (PR) electoral systems promotes party coherence and control, but it may undermine the ability of parties to incorporate and appeal to new social forces. Switching to open lists or party "primary elections" to elect party slates would promote adaptability, incorporation, and responsiveness but would undermine party coherence (especially in presidential systems, which are otherwise prone to extremely weak party discipline).

The architects of institutional designs and reforms therefore need to chart careful courses, reconciling in various ways two conflicting needs: the need for political parties to be accessible, accountable, and responsive to their constituencies while also preserving (or generating) mechanisms to foster party discipline and coherence.

Electoral systems. Electoral laws are a principal instrument for trying to shape the contours of the party system. The "effective number of parties" represented in parliament is significantly lower in plurality (single-member–district) electoral systems than in PR ones.[98] This fact constitutes strong grounds for many to prefer majoritarian electoral systems in general and the plurality method in particular. The "efficiency" of democracy—"the ability of elections to serve as a means for voters to identify and choose among the competing government options available"—is best served with a majoritarian electoral system, which can provide clear, coherent governing alternatives (ideally between two parties) that are known to the electorate in advance and also a ready, governing majority.[99] Majoritarian (again especially plurality) systems are also seen to enhance governability by avoiding the need to cobble multiple parties and interests together into shaky coalitions and to enhance accountability by making members of parliament answerable to specific, clearly defined constituencies. However, the more majoritarian the electoral system, the greater the distortion (disproportionality) between votes and seats and the less representative the outcome in giving parliamentary place and voice to all interests and views.

There is no perfect way to reconcile or maximize both efficiency and representativeness, and although both systems have their passionate defenders, we are inclined to conclude, with Ken Gladdish, that the choice of electoral system should depend upon the particular historical patterns of cleavage and conflict in each country and also upon which threats to democracy are judged to be more severe: the possible exclusion, alienation, apathy, and illegitimacy of majoritarian outcomes or the possible paralysis, fragmentation, and polarization of proportional ones.[100]

Of course, the choice is not either-or. In seeking to balance representativeness with governability, many countries have implemented moderate systems of PR that, by modifying the pure proportionality of election results, tend to produce a more manageable number of parties in parliament. As a general rule, the greater the district magnitude (i.e., the greater the number of representatives elected from a single district—up to the point where, as in Israel, the entire country constitutes a single district), the more ideological and sectoral interests shape the voting choice, and the greater the effective number of parties. (Direct accountability to voters also declines with district magnitude.) To try to reduce party fragmentation, political engineers may not only reduce district magnitude (down to the single member), they may also modify proportionality by establishing a minimum percentage of the vote (the "threshold") parties must obtain to win representation in parliament. A common minimum is the 5-percent threshold Germany established (in an innovative, two-tier electoral system that is completely proportional but that elects half of the legislators individually, from single-member districts, and half from party lists). Recent work has shown that the "effective threshold"—the combination of district magnitude and the electoral threshold—is the electoral system variable that has the greatest influence on the effective number of parties in parliament and that its effect on the degree of proportionality of election outcomes is even stronger.[101]

Electoral system design can do much to shape party systems and patterns of political mobilization and cleavage. However, it does not do so completely or necessarily immediately. Seeking to prevent a recurrence of the classic conditions of polarized pluralism that brought down Turkey's democracy in 1980, the Turkish military adopted an unusually high threshold—10 percent—and also banned Marxist-Leninist, religious, and separatist parties (the first two restrictions were lifted in 1987). Yet this has not produced the much hoped for, stable two- or three-party system. Parties that are essentially centrist have dominated since the return to democracy in 1983, but with the growth of corruption, inequality, and various other socioeconomic and political stresses, party support has again become more fragmented. Electoral support for a more radical alternative—the anti-Western, pro-Islamic Welfare Party—has grown to the point where it garnered more than 17 percent of the vote in the October 1991 elections (after failing to exceed the threshold in 1987) and then scored extremely well in local elections. Politics in Turkey is once again becoming more polarized, and violence and terrorism are growing.

The Turkish experience shows the limits as well as the possibilities of electoral engineering. Electoral rules and institutional designs are important, but they cannot completely negate or override other pressures and tendencies. Party systems cannot effectively be enacted by law. The one explicit effort to do that—the Nigerian military's decree and creation of a two-party system—contributed to the instability and failure of that prolonged transition (1986–1993). Although the two parties did span the political and ethnic horizon more broadly than had previous ones, and although the party system had previously been evolving in this direction, the artificial two-party system interrupted more organic processes of party consolidation that had been evolving over many years and generated political tensions within the two parties that were easily manipulated by scheming military autocrats. These tensions figured significantly in the implosion of the putative Third Republic.

Of our ten cases, Brazil and South Africa are the two in which the electoral system is the most problematic and could have the greatest impact on the future of democracy. The electoral system in Brazil, which dates back to 1932, "stands out among similar systems worldwide in promoting the proliferation of parties found in extreme PR systems, but without the system incentives to party discipline that PR typically generates."[102] To be represented in the Federal Chamber of Deputies (the lower house), a party need only win a single seat from a state list, and voters are not required to endorse a complete, "closed" list of candidates but "rather [are to] select a *single* candidate from the bewildering numbers on the various statewide party lists."[103] The result is one of the most paralyzingly fractionalized and undisciplined party systems in the world. A more workable party system requires raising the electoral threshold and switching to closed or partially closed lists. Lamounier has proposed (inter alia) a 5-percent threshold for entry into the chamber and consideration of another crucial feature of the German model, the mixed (two-tier) system of PR-list and single-member districts (within a system that is proportional in its overall allocation of seats).[104]

Interest in the German model is also growing in South Africa, where the election of the national parliament (and the regional ones) by pure PR from large regional districts has left no means for specific territorial communities to be represented and to hold their representatives accountable. There appears to be a consensus, however, for maintaining a low electoral threshold that will continue to enable sharply defined interests, such as the white right and more militant blacks, to have a place in the parliament rather than be tempted to challenge the entire system from outside it.

Electoral rules are the most powerful tool available for reorganizing politics relatively rapidly. Precisely for that reason, the bias should be for stability: "Healthy partisan competition requires that the electoral system . . . be broadly supported and not be changed too frequently, [particularly not] for narrow partisan purposes."[105] Change should be approached cautiously and, if needed, should as much as possible take the form of modest and specific reforms (such as raising the electoral threshold or introducing a German-style, two-tier system of representation).[106] The best time by far to develop the right electoral rules is at the dawn of a new democracy rather than when a profound political crisis, as in Italy, requires a sweeping political overhaul.[107]

Constitutional structure.   Although presidential government is associated with the world's longest and most successful democratic experience, that in the United States, its record in the developing world exhibits several characteristic problems. For one, a presidential system tends to concentrate power in the executive branch and to facilitate claims to plebiscitarian legitimacy. This may make the president too strong, thereby facilitating abuse of power. It may even pave the way for executive coups against democracy, as happened repeatedly in Africa after independence or as President Jorge Serrano attempted in Guatemala in May 1993. The latter often occurs, however, because a president feels his or her position is too weak. Second, presidentialism can give rise to a paralyzing deadlock between the executive and the legislature, and competing claims to democratic legitimacy. This problem of dual legitimacy is particularly severe when different parties (or coalitions) control the presidency and the legislature or where—as in Brazil—legislative representation is fragmented among many parties. The problem of presidential weakness is often exacerbated by constitutional provisions that explicitly limit the power of the office (and that often bar reelection) precisely out of fear of its abuse. Either of these scenarios—concentration of power or division and deadlock (or even a constant struggle between these two tendencies)—is particularly dangerous for nascent or fragile democracies, in which the separation of powers and checks and balances between branches of government are not well established.

The third problem with presidentialism is tied to and exacerbated by its majoritarian nature, which tends to make politics a zero-sum game in which power sharing is difficult and legislative coalitions are much more difficult to form and maintain. This is all the more reason presidentialism fits poorly with PR electoral systems that give rise to multiple parties. Fourth, presidentialism, with its fixed terms, rigidifies outcomes, possibly sticking a nation—even for several years—with a government that has utterly lost public confidence and support. Temporal rigidity makes it much more difficult for a presidential system to handle succession crises as well.[108]

The advantages of a parliamentary system lie in its greater flexibility. An executive who has lost popular support can be turned out of office before his or her term has ended. Coalitions can be formed to reach across significant political divisions, and these can be reformed in light of shifting political issues and fortunes, making for more than a zero-sum game. Because they are associated with a greater number of parties, parliamentary systems are somewhat less conducive to the polarization of politics between two or three major political parties, each identified with major class or ethnic cleavage groups. (However, combined with PR, parliamentary systems are more prone to polarized pluralism.) Moreover, presidential coalitions typically have little incentive to cohere (and often real incentives to fragment) following the election, whereas in a parliamentary multiparty system the parties have to assume responsibility to support a government that would otherwise fall.

The theoretical case for these advantages lies largely with the experience of parliamentary democracy in Western Europe and the disastrous experience with presidentialism in some Latin American countries, especially Chile. Valenzuela demonstrates the lack of fit between a highly polarized and competitive multiparty system—which, because it could not generate electoral majorities, necessitated bargaining and coalition-making—and a presidential system of centralized authority, zero-sum outcomes, and fixed terms. The contradictions "came to a tragic head in the Allende years," culminating in 1973 in a breakdown of democracy that could have been avoided. In the late 1980s, the debilitating rigidities of presidentialism became manifest in Brazil and Peru, where presidents whose programs had failed catastrophically and whose political support had evaporated were forced to limp through their remaining terms with virtually no capacity to respond effectively to the deepening economic and political crises.

Legislatures and courts.   In most developing countries that have operated presidential systems, particularly in Latin America but also the Philippines and parts of Africa, an additional problem has been the exalted status of the presidency in relation to weak and heavily manipulated legislative and judicial branches. In Latin America, the executive's responsibility for writing implementational legislation and his or her control over a vast, patronage-rich state bureaucracy "is supplemented by far-reaching decree powers that are rarely checked by Congress or courts, even if they are of questionable constitutionality."[109] In the post-transition period in Latin America this has given rise to what Guillermo O'Donnell has termed "delegative democracy," in which elections delegate sweeping and largely unaccountable authority to whomever wins the presidential election, and parties and independent interest groups are weak and fragmented.[110] To be effective, presidential systems require some independence on the part of the legislature to scrutinize the executive branch, check its excesses, and impose what O'Donnell calls "horizontal accountability." If they are to perform and balance these roles effectively, legislatures must not only be based upon a relatively consolidated party system, but they must also have autonomous capacities to gather and process information, as through a congressional research service and a professionally staffed committee structure. They must also be held accountable, through politically autonomous mechanisms, for detecting and punishing corruption. All of this seems a distant prospect, however, unless legislatures become composed of stronger, more disciplined and purposeful political parties.

We also stress the importance to democracy of a strong and independent judiciary. A powerful judiciary can be the bulwark of a democratic constitution, defending both its integrity (and hence political freedom and due process) and its preeminence as the source of democratic legitimacy. More generally, the judiciary is the ultimate guarantor of the rule of law and thus of the accountability of rulers to the ruled, which is a basic premise of democracy. During the authoritarian emergency in India, "a beleaguered and partially 'captured' Supreme Court still struck down a constitutional amendment, enacted by parliament, that would have destroyed an 'essential feature' of the constitution."[111]

Unfortunately, judicial systems in much of the developing world are feeble and ineffective, crippled by endemic corruption, intimidation, politicization, and lack of resources and training. This results in chronic human rights problems, even in formally democratic systems. The problem is intensified in countries such as Colombia, where huge volumes of drug money overwhelm institutional integrity and capacity. Part of the answer lies in reforms (such as those recently adopted in Costa Rica, Colombia, and Ecuador) to professionalize, depoliticize, insulate, and decentralize the judicial system. In addition, judges, prosecutors, and investigators need more training and resources, higher pay to deter temptation, and more effective and honest police to protect them from criminal retribution and to attack organized crime more aggressively.

Stronger and more autonomous institutions—including government auditing agencies and means to monitor the personal assets of public officials—are also needed specifically to combat corruption. The judicial system can hardly remain chaste when the rest of the political system is saturated with corruption, as Diamond explains for the case of Nigeria. The impetus for reform can only come from outside the political system, however, from a civil society that organizes vigorously to reclaim and reform democracy.

Ethnic and Regional Conflict

For several reasons, ethnicity (loosely defined)—meaning any highly inclusive, distinctive group identity based on culture and common origin, including language, religion, nationality, race, and caste—represents the most difficult type of cleavage for a democracy to manage.[112] Because ethnicity taps cultural and symbolic issues—basic notions of identity and the self, of individual and group worth and entitlement—the conflicts it generates are intrinsically less amenable to compromise than those revolving around issues of material or functional conflict. When the struggle is over the distribution of material costs and benefits, the latter are divisible in a variety of ways. At bottom, ethnic conflicts revolve around exclusive conceptions of legitimacy and symbols of worth. Thus they yield competing demands that tend to be indivisible and therefore zero-sum. As Donald Horowitz has asked, "How does a policymaker divide up the 'glorification' of the national language?"[113]

In deeply divided societies, ethnicity—in contrast to other political cleavages, such as those of class or functional interest—appears permanent and all-encompassing, predetermining who will be included and excluded from power and resources. Democratic elections take on the character of a census and produce a zero-sum game: One ethnic group or coalition or party wins by its sheer demographic weight, and others, in losing, see themselves as becoming excluded not only from the government but also from the larger political community.[114] This fear of permanent exclusion is not unreasonable. The comparative historical record is replete with cases in which a particular ethnic group or narrow coalition—often a distinct minority of the total population—entrenched itself in power indefinitely once it won state control.[115]

At the extreme, different nationality groups may not identify with the state at all. This poses a particular problem for democracy because agreement on the legitimate boundaries and nature of the state—and on who its citizens are—is a prerequisite for the establishment of viable democratic institutions.[116]

For all of these reasons, many scholars have expressed profound skepticism about the possibility for stable democracy in societies in which multiple ethnic identities become politicized. Examining the wave of African and Asian democratic implosions during the 1950s and 1960s, Alvin Rabushka and Kenneth Shepsle concluded that "democracy . . . is simply not viable in an environment of intense ethnic preferences." In what they termed *plural societies* (essentially, deeply divided ones), in which ethnic differences are mobilized to high salience through cohesive political organization, multiethnic coalitions inevitably break down, brokerage institutions disappear, all distributive (not to mention cultural) issues are reflected through the prism of ethnicity, and ethnic moderation becomes untenable.[117] A number of comparative and statistical analyses have seemed to confirm this pessimism.[118]

One means by which democracies manage, soften, complicate, and contain conflict is through the presence or even the generation of crosscutting cleavages. When people who are divided on one line of cleavage, such as religion, interact and find common ground with one another around a different line of cleavage, such as class, they experience psychological "crosspressures" that tend to moderate their political views and induce them generally toward greater tolerance and accommodation.[119] But such crosscutting cleavage tends to be scarce or weakly felt in the deeply divided societies of Africa and Asia. This is so not only because these societies manifest little class and functional complexity that could crosscut ethnicity. It also has to do with two other features of ethnicity. First, in deeply divided societies, ethnic allegiances are all-encompassing, seeping into "organizations, activities, and roles to which they are formally unrelated."[120] Second, in many deeply divided societies, other objective lines of cleavage cumulate with ethnicity rather than crosscut it, so some ethnic groups are distinctly richer, better educated, and more advanced in industry and commerce than others or are represented disproportionately in the military and bureaucracy.

One of the most vexing aspects of ethnicity for democracy is the extent to which politicians mobilize it shamelessly for their own immediate political advantage. In Nigeria, political mobilization of ethnic consciousness and fear heavily drove the political dynamics that led to the breakdown of the First Republic and the onset of the civil war, and it has been a recurrent feature of electoral politics ever since. In India, the recent intensification and politicization of religious conflict between Hindus and Muslims, which erupted into deadly rioting (claiming more than 1,000 lives) in December 1992, is not the product of "ancient hatreds" but of present-day militant politicians and intellectuals who seek to ride to power by relocating the basis of Indian identity from secular, pluralistic culture to Hindu religious identity and sacred traditions that are sharply distinguished from alien traditions.[121]

Yet as the Nigerian case shows, democracy—with its processes of bargaining, coalition building, and political learning—offers better prospects than authoritarianism for peacefully managing ethnic conflict.[122] If ethnic conflict stems more from the rational pursuit of political opportunities and incentives than from visceral and immutable passions, it can presumably also be contained by restructuring institutions to generate incentives for accommodation and mutual security.

Managing ethnic conflict.   Our own country studies and many others attest
to the complexity and diversity of ethnic conflict situations and thus to the
inappropriateness of any one, specific formula for conflict management.
Nevertheless, there are some broad lessons to be learned and some specific
institutional arrangements worth noting.

The most general lesson involves the paramount need to avoid the
indefinite and complete exclusion from power of particular groups (whether
majority or minority). Majoritarian electoral systems are thus particularly
dangerous in divided societies. Rather, different ethnic groups should be
induced to pool votes or form coalitions. All significant groups must be
given a share of political power—some stake in the system at some level. No
minority should be allowed to establish a permanent political hegemony at
the center.

Most of all, no one should be denied equal citizenship in the state
because of nationality or ethnicity. "In a multi-national, multi-cultural setting, the chances to consolidate democracy are increased by state policies
which grant inclusive and equal citizenship, and which give all citizens a
common 'roof' of state-mandated, and enforced, constitutional rights."[123]
These include the rights of ethnic minorities to use their own culture, religion, and language, as well as to participate in economic and political life
fully, free from discrimination. Encroachments on these rights have contributed to the sense of exclusion and the secessionist sentiment and violence among the Kurds in Turkey, and they now cloud democratic prospects
in many of the former Communist states of Eastern Europe and the former
Soviet Union. Yet secessionist leaders themselves often have little respect
for democracy. In return for constitutionally protected group and individual
rights, minority leaders must recognize their obligation to affirm the legitimacy and territorial integrity of the state.[124]

One of the stronger generalizations that emerged from our larger study
is the danger for democracy of excessive centralization of state power.
Where major ethnic or regional cleavages exist that are territorially based,
the relationship is by now self-evident and axiomatic: The absence of provisions for devolution and decentralization of power, especially in the context of ethnoregional disparities, feeds ethnic insecurity, violent conflict,
and even secessionist pressures.[125]

Secessionist pressures carry a dual threat. Unless they are resolved by
political means, through institutions such as autonomy, federalism, or—in
the extreme—separate statehood, they can lead to the imposition of authority by force and the deterioration or breakdown of democratic rule.
Alternatively, a democratic center can be criticized for its ineptitude in creating, or its weakness in handling, the secessionist crisis, thus opening the
way for military intervention. These dangers have threatened or damaged
democratic regimes in Peru, Sri Lanka, India, the Philippines, and Sudan,
and they figured prominently in the failure of Nigeria's first democratic

attempt in the 1960s. Although India has benefited from the multiple, complex character of religious, linguistic, and regional identities—fragmented and crosscut by caste and class formations—its more recent failure to provide a sense of effective political inclusion and equality to diverse ethnic communities (especially Sikhs and Muslims and especially at the state level), or at least to find some stable formula for accommodating and managing diversity, has been a major source of instability. Das Gupta's conclusion from the Indian experience is confirmed by our wider evidence: "When ethnic leaders are allowed to share power, they generally act according to the rules of the regime," but when the state responds to ethnic mobilization with exclusion, repression, or manipulation of conflict for the short-term gain of the ruling party, violence festers.

In deeply divided societies, meaningful devolution of power—typically through federalism—is an indispensable instrument for managing and reducing conflict. In India, federalism has functioned, even during lengthy periods of one-party dominance, to give opposition parties a stake in the system, to expand political access to new groups, to give regional and ethnic minorities some autonomous control over resources and local affairs, and to compartmentalize conflicts at the state level so as to minimize their pressure on the center. In Nigeria, federalism has functioned in similar ways during the two most recent democratic experiments, facilitating a more complex politics less prone to polarization. These important conflict-reducing functions have led the ANC constitutional negotiators in South Africa to agree to significant devolution of power to independently elected regional (and eventually municipal) governments—a variant of federalism (although the permanent constitutional provisions remain to be negotiated)—despite the ANC's historical commitment to unitary government.

Decentralization.   Decentralization is important to democracy not only to manage ethnic and regional cleavage. Local government that is accountable to local electorates is an important element of the democratic process. In Mexico, centralization and strong presidentialism have been important pillars of one-party hegemony and have become major targets of groups seeking democratic reform. Throughout Latin America, centralization of government power has entrenched the political exclusion of the poor and shielded long-standing authoritarian enclaves from grassroots mobilization to dismantle coercive, violently abusive, and clientelistic practices.[126] In Turkey, state centralization—as reflected in the absence of any tradition of autonomous municipalities and in the dependence of municipal and provincial administrations on the central government—has not only obstructed peaceful resolution of the Kurdish insurgency, it has also increased the stakes for all parties in winning the central government, resulting in the tendency toward violence and intolerance in the electoral struggle. In Thailand, a highly centralized state bureaucracy manifests cynicism and suspicion of democratic politics. In Senegal, the unresponsiveness to popular concerns and the distance of a highly centralized state from popular reach have not only fueled a sometimes violent resistance movement in the geographically isolated and culturally distant Casamance region but have also undermined the legitimacy of the semidemocratic regime throughout the country. By contrast, the substantial power of local elected councils over community development and services can be a source of democratic vitality, as it has been in Botswana, where opposition party control of some local councils has somewhat mitigated the effect of continuing one-party dominance at the center and thus enhanced commitment to the system.

The devolution and democratization of power at the local level serve democratic consolidation by removing barriers to participation, enhancing the responsiveness and accountability of government, testing innovations in governance, diminishing the winner-take-all character of politics, and giving opposition or minority political parties and social forces a chance to have a share of power, to learn the complexities of governing, and to establish political credibility and responsibility by developing experience first at lower levels of power.[127] In the past few years, Latin American countries have implemented a number of reforms to decentralize government and democratize power at the local level. Colombia, Venezuela, Chile, Nicaragua, Panama, and Paraguay instituted direct elections for mayors and other municipal officials; Colombia and Venezuela also instituted elections for state governors.

Although the capacity for institutional reform is an important condition for democratic persistence, one should not assume that the opportunity is always open. Particularly in deeply divided societies, the window of opportunity to establish accommodative institutions may be only a brief historical moment in time that is either seized or lost—a stalemate in civil war, a regime or leadership transition, the inauguration of a new democracy. At that moment, new policies and constitutional rules must be enacted to generate mutual security and encourage interethnic accommodation, or the room for political maneuver may be drastically narrowed, "and a dynamic of societal conflict will intensify until democratic consolidation becomes increasingly difficult, and eventually impossible."[128]

The Military

In most of the countries in our larger study, democracy has been threatened or overturned by military establishments that regard themselves "as the privileged definers and guardians of the national interest."[129] Typically, however, military role expansion is induced by the corruption, stagnation, and malfunctioning of democratic institutions to the point at which the military is increasingly called upon to maintain order and comes to see itself as the country's only salvation. In virtually every instance among our ten cases of democratic breakdown by military coup, these interventions have come in the wake of manifest political and economic crises and low levels of regime legitimacy: Brazil in 1964; Chile in 1973; Turkey in 1960 and 1980 (and the "half-coup" in 1971); South Korea in 1961; Thailand in 1976 and 1991; and Nigeria in 1966, 1983, and 1993. The military's size, autonomy, professional doctrine, and role conception may determine its threshold for intervention but do not constitute an independent cause of democratic breakdown. Thus, the single most important requirement for keeping the military at bay is to make democracy work, to develop its institutional capacities so it accrues broad and unquestioned legitimacy.

This is not to say that factors external to the political process do not shape the military's disposition to intervene. External Communist threats, or perceptions of Communist support for indigenous insurgencies, heightened the military's readiness to intervene and rule on behalf of "national security" not only in much of Latin America but also in Thailand and especially South Korea. However, repeated interventions in politics over decades have shaped the mentality of many officers and the formal role conception and organization of the armed forces in ways that continue to impinge upon and constrain the quality and extent of democracy. Once military role expansion occurs, it tends to advance, or at least endure, placing numerous areas of public policy under unaccountable military control.[130]

In Pakistan, Turkey, Thailand, and much of Latin America, new or recent democratic regimes have managed to coexist with powerful militaries by making a strategic decision not to challenge seriously their institutional power and prerogatives. Even in the more democratic Southern Cone countries (Chile, Argentina, and Uruguay), the intimidating power of the military has prevented the pursuit of legal accountability for past human rights violations and constitutes an important obstacle to democratic consolidation. Indeed, in Chile—where General Pinochet has embedded military autonomy into the constitution—it may constitute the main obstacle.

New and insecure democracies must therefore find ways to strengthen (or to begin to develop) civilian control over the military while constraining the military increasingly strictly to the core national security functions appropriate for it to perform in a democracy: defense of external boundaries and sea lanes; combatting of armed threats to the civilian, constitutional order from terrorism, insurgency, and the drug trade; readiness for emergency disaster relief; and participation in international peacekeeping.[131] This requires reducing military influence over nonmilitary issues within the state and eliminating military ownership of or control over nonmilitary institutions. Ultimately, it also means that even on issues directly related to the military and to national security—such as strategy, deployment, and expenditures—military decisionmaking must be subjected to civilian scrutiny and control, thus, it is hoped, enabling a reduction in the size and budget of the armed forces. Finally, control of the military requires that the right of the

military to regulate or intervene in politics and civil society (even informally) be eliminated.

Democratic consolidation demands an active strategy of civilian
empowerment, through which civilian scholars and policy specialists
acquire credible expertise in military and intelligence affairs, legislatures
develop the capacity to monitor military and intelligence systems routinely
and responsibly, and democratic state leaders implement "a well conceived,
politically led strategy toward the military [that] narrows their involvement
in state regulation of conflict, builds effective procedures for civilian control, seeks to increase military professional capacities, and lessens the
risks—for the polity and for the military—of further military intervention."[132] Given the power of the military in these societies, reduction of military prerogatives must be a gradual process that relies on bargaining,
engagement, dialogue, and consensus building rather than blunt confrontation.

The risks of military resistance or rebellion against reform measures
will be minimized if civilian leaders seek to reduce the perceived costs to the
military by always according it a position of high status, honor, and income
and by refraining from using it as a power resource or from interfering in the
process of routine promotions and discipline. Unfortunately, as Brazil,
Chile, and other Latin American countries have found, it may also be necessary to offer amnesty for human rights violations, but this should not deter
society from a thorough effort "to exorcise the ghosts of a dark past" through
the systematic discovery and reporting of the truth by an independent and
impartial government commission, as in Chile and Argentina.[133]

International Factors

In an influential theoretical movement that dominated academic thinking in
the 1970s, dependency theorists maintained that political exclusion and
repression of popular mobilization were inevitable concomitants of peripheral status in the global division of labor and the dependent character of capitalist economic development.[134] The authors of the case studies in this book
reject that assumption and attribute the course of political development and
regime change primarily to internal structures and action. Nevertheless, they
do recognize the ways national political regimes and regime change have
been shaped by a variety of international factors, including colonial rule,
intervention, cultural diffusion, and demonstration effects from abroad.

Any accounting of the colonial legacy has to include not only the
authoritarian and statist character of the colonial state, which heavily influenced political norms and models in the postcolonial states, but also the liberal and democratic values conveyed by the British colonizers (and, to a
much lesser extent, by the French), which gave India, Sri Lanka, Jamaica,
and other British colonies some significant preindependence experience in

self-governance and scope for democratic, pluralist expression and organization.[135] The fact that this experience was much shorter in Africa helps to explain why the democratic legacy in countries such as Nigeria and Ghana was weaker.[136] At the same time, the longer and more liberal participatory French colonial presence in Senegal helps to explain why its postindependence experience was less repressive than those elsewhere in Francophone Africa.

In the postcolonial period and for Turkey and Thailand, which were never colonized, cultural diffusion of democratic norms and models has remained an important stimulant of democratic progress, particularly with the internationalization of the mass media and the rapid increase in the number of foreign students in the United States and other Western democracies. Demonstration effects (or what Schmitter has called "contagion") may also exert a powerful external influence, although these tend to be most potent regionally "among countries that [are] geographically proximate and culturally similar."[137] Since the mid-1970s, demonstration effects—and the phenomenon Samuel Huntington has termed "snowballing"—have contributed to democratic transitions throughout Latin America, the sudden collapse of Communist regimes throughout Eastern Europe in 1989, and the wave of African regime openings in the early 1990s.

The diffusion, demonstration, snowballing, and contagion effects underlying the wavelike expansion of democracy involve more than earlier transitions providing models for later ones. As other (particularly geographically or ideologically proximate) authoritarian regimes fall, the psychological and political context in the remaining regimes alters. Oppositions become inspired and emboldened. Ruling elites lose confidence. As democracy gains greater regional and international momentum, more external resources flow to democratic movements and less to the authoritarian regimes. Powerful international actors become more willing to exert pressure against the remaining authoritarian regimes, which become more isolated. That these effects are preeminently regional in scope is indicated not only by the close temporal clustering of regime changes within regions but also by the regional clustering of regimes scarcely touched by these trends: most of all the Middle East (where a nondemocratic, Islamic fundamentalist model is diffusing) and also East and Southeast Asia, where Communist, authoritarian, and semiauthoritarian regimes (along with some democratic ones) persist. If China undergoes significant political liberalization at some point in the coming years, it would likely generate potent demonstration effects in Asia's nondemocratic regimes.

Historically, the industrialized democracies have been ambivalent about fostering democracy abroad and have often seen it in their interest to support authoritarian regimes, as well as to sanction, subvert, and overthrow popularly elected ones that appeared unfriendly to their geopolitical interests.[138] This policy orientation began to change in the late 1970s under U.S.

President Jimmy Carter, and democratic pressure and assistance from the Western democracies accelerated notably during the 1980s and early 1990s.

Under certain conditions—weak or eroding internal legitimacy, ruling elite divisions, significant democratic mobilization from political and civil society—international diplomatic and economic pressures can contribute to democratization or political liberalization. When carefully applied, diplomatic pressures have worked to narrow the domestic support of authoritarian regimes and to aggravate the divisions within them. Carter administration human rights pressure on Uruguay and especially Argentina, including cutoffs of military and economic aid and other sanctions, had this kind of effect while bringing significant improvements in those human rights situations.[139] President Carter's human rights policies and diplomatic initiatives also supported democratic transition in Peru, "prevented an authoritarian relapse" in Ecuador in 1978, and in that same year deterred vote fraud in the Dominican Republic's presidential election.[140]

Pressure from the Reagan administration, the U.S. Congress, and international public opinion, interacting with rising domestic mobilization and a loss of business confidence, led Philippine dictator Ferdinand Marcos to call the 1986 presidential "snap election" that independent election observers judged he lost to Corazon Aquino. In the tense days following the February 7 vote, a deliberate U.S. policy to "accelerate the transition" helped to frustrate Marcos's effort to retain power through massive electoral fraud.[141] During the Reagan years, U.S. diplomatic and economic pressure, and its symbolic support for human rights and peaceful democratic change, ultimately contributed to democratic transitions in Chile and South Korea as well, while preventing planned military coups in El Salvador, Honduras, and Bolivia in the early 1980s and in Peru in January 1989.[142] "In each case, however, international support for democracy *reinforced* domestic groups and sectors of the military opposed to military intervention."[143]

Regional pressure can also make a difference. At its historic June 1991 Santiago meeting, the Organization of American States (OAS) adopted a resolution mandating steps to promote and defend democracy following its rupture anywhere in the region. Two years later, when Guatemalan President Jorge Serrano attempted to seize absolute power in an *autogolpe,* the OAS member states stood united in warning "that Guatemala would face political isolation and economic sanctions if constitutional rule remained disrupted."[144] Again, however, OAS and international pressure worked as rapidly as it did only because of the massive mobilization of Guatemalan civil society.[145]

Several other dimensions of international engagement affected democratic prospects during the 1980s and the early 1990s. Economic sanctions and the general international isolation of the apartheid regime played a role in inducing South Africa's business establishment and, ultimately, the ruling National Party elites in South Africa to opt for a negotiated transition to democracy. The movements (to varying degrees) by the major Western donors toward conditioning aid on human rights, democracy, and good governance pressed a number of African regimes to legalize opposition parties and hold competitive, internationally monitored elections that in several countries (such as Benin, Zambia, Madagascar, and Malawi) led to the defeat of the ruling party. Elsewhere, as in Kenya, donor pressure forced political liberalization and reform, but factionalism among democratic forces squandered the opportunity for full democratization.[146]

Conditionality can be especially potent when it is embedded in standing provisions of a bilateral relationship or multilateral charter. The requirement of the European Community (now the European Union, or EU) that its member states manifest "truly democratic practices and respect for fundamental rights and freedoms" provided an important incentive for democratic consolidation in Spain, Portugal, and Greece.[147] That same incentive now operates in Turkey and the new democracies of Central and Eastern Europe, all of which seek admission to the EU. Similar conditionality attaches to membership in the Council of Europe, which several East European democracies have recently obtained, and to lending from the European Bank for Reconstruction and Development. Increasingly, would-be autocrats have to ponder the heavy price their country would pay in loss of aid, capital, trade, investment, and symbolic status if they were to roll back democracy. And formally democratic regimes like Turkey's must weigh the impact of their policies on ethnic minorities and other human rights issues against these valued goals.

External political assistance to democratic movements and regimes can also advance the democratic prospect. Following the model of the German party foundations, which gave important assistance to democratic parties and the democratization process in Spain and Portugal during the 1970s (and to other countries before and thereafter), the United States established the National Endowment for Democracy in the early 1980s. Similar nongovernmental organizations to promote democracy and human rights, with public funding, have been established in Canada and Great Britain, and official aid organizations—such as the Swedish International Development Authority and the U.S. Agency for International Development—are also heavily involved in assisting the development of democratic organizations in civil society as well as effective legislative, judicial, and local government institutions. These international assistance efforts have helped significantly to lay the groundwork in civil society for successful democratic transitions, and to support free and fair elections—especially founding elections in countries such as the Philippines, South Korea, Chile, Nicaragua, Bulgaria, Zambia, and South Africa—through the provision of technical assistance, support for independent organizations, and international observer teams.

Currently, dozens of governmental, quasi-governmental, and nongovernmental actors provide thousands of grants and projects to strengthen the political, cultural, and societal foundations of democracy in post-transition settings.[148]

Economic assistance can also give an important boost to the consolidation of new and vulnerable democracies, particularly those having to implement extremely painful stabilization and structural adjustment measures. In these contexts, economic assistance can help significantly by writing off portions of a country's external debt, providing cash for a currency stabilization fund, and helping to underwrite a social safety net (such as unemployment compensation) for those displaced by economic reform measures. In the early 1990s, Poland benefited significantly from the first two types of assistance.

Beyond assistance, diplomacy, and sanctions, there is also the blunter instrument of force or even conquest. Several of the world's now established democracies were imposed by foreign powers following defeat in war or colonization.[149] But the democratic successes of Allied occupation after World War II in Germany, Austria, and Japan are not likely to be replicable, and certainly no democrat would wish for war as a means of implanting democracy. U.S. military action did help to save the Aquino presidency from a coup attempt and to topple the Noriega dictatorship in Panama in 1989, and international (mainly U.S.) forces restored Haiti's democratically elected president, Jean-Bertrand Aristide, to power in 1994. But at most, such interventions can provide an opportunity for democracy, the outcome of which will be largely determined by domestic actors and structures.

Overall, the importance of the international and regional contexts for democratization and democratic consolidation, or at least their positive effect, appears to have increased significantly over the past two decades. This increase is not merely a result of the discrete actions, policies, and assistance programs of established democracies and multilateral institutions (as well as nongovernmental actors) but also of the cumulative effect of all of these efforts in generating a global normative climate inhospitable to authoritarian rule. This climate and its underlying policies have been heightened by the end of the Cold War, with its powerful competing geostrategic rationales, and by the growing conviction that the expansion of democracy serves international peace and security. However, whether the collective emphasis on democracy and democracy promotion will endure with the rise of new strategic threats, real or perceived, remains to be seen.

Consolidating Democracy

In this chapter we have surveyed the principal structural and institutional factors that facilitate and obstruct the development of democracy. But in the end, democracy does not arrive or persist by some political or sociological "hidden hand." Structural factors make democracy more or less likely but neither inevitable nor impossible. Democracy is more likely—in particular, more likely to survive—where poverty and inequality are limited and levels of education and income are generally high; where cultural norms value democracy, tolerance, bargaining, and accommodation, and efficacious citizens join together in a wide range of civil society organizations; where ethnic pluralism is limited, or different ethnic and nationality groups form coalitions and feel secure with one another; where military prerogatives and roles are limited, and a country's valued regional and international ties depend on its being or becoming democratic. But no country that has become democratic has done so under purely favorable structural conditions. Democracy cannot commence without democrats—political leaders and players who, for whatever motives, commit themselves to advancing their interests and waging their conflicts according to written (and unwritten) rules that institutionalize uncertainty.

The literature on democratic transitions has identified political leadership, regime factionalism, elite settlement, political pacts, contingent choice, strategic interaction, and similar behavioral phenomena as the key variables that drive democratic transitions.[150] Yet social structures and historical legacies circumscribe and confine the choices available to various political actors at a particular time. As Terry Lynn Karl has argued, "Structural and institutional constraints determine the range of options available to decision makers and may even predispose them to choose a specific option."[151]

This same interplay between structure and choice, history and contingency, institutions and action shapes the effort to consolidate democracy. Consolidation is the process by which democracy becomes so broadly and profoundly legitimate and so habitually practiced and observed that it is very unlikely to break down. As Linz and Stepan have argued, consolidation is signaled by three interrelated changes:

> Behaviorally . . . no significant national social, economic, political or institutional actor in the country spends significant resources attempting to achieve their objectives by creating a non-democratic regime or by seceding from the state.
>
> Attitudinally . . . a strong majority of public opinions holds the belief that democratic procedures and institutions are the most appropriate way to govern collective life in a society such as theirs, and . . . support for anti-system alternatives is quite small [and] isolated. . . .
>
> Constitutionally . . . governmental and non-governmental forces alike become habituated to the resolution of conflict within the specific laws, procedures and institutions sanctioned by the new democratic process.[152]

To be sure, democratic consolidation is heavily facilitated by favorable structural, cultural, and historical factors. A long prior historical tradition of democracy and party politics, as in Chile and Uruguay, adds significantly to the legitimacy of a restored democracy. So does a recent historical experience with authoritarian rule that is widely discredited, as in Argentina and many of the former Communist countries, or a process of social and economic change—as in Spain, South Korea, and Taiwan—that alters the class structure of society, its political values, and its relationship to the industrialized democracies. Constitutional and electoral system designs that intelligently channel the underlying patterns of cleavage and tension can bound the uncertainty of democratic competition sufficiently to encourage all democratic actors to habituate themselves to the rules much more quickly and unconditionally.

However, democratic consolidation is essentially a process of "crafting," an exercise of conscious leadership and strategy—like state building, a work of art.[153] One of the first and most important elements of this crafting comes at the very beginning, with the design of a new constitution and electoral system, or later—and with greater risk and difficulty—in the struggle to redesign flawed institutions imposed by the authoritarian regime or resurrected from the past. Precisely because the constitution sets the parameters and structures the incentives for the democratic game, it is crucially important to adopt a constitution—through means that produce broad popular consent and legitimacy—as soon as possible in the life of a new democracy. It is no less important to configure institutions so as to foster accommodation and mutual security, discourage polarization and exclusion, protect ethnic minorities, and in general give all major social, economic, and political actors a stake in the system. If democratic forces do not act early and wisely to set the right institutional parameters, the "constitutional moment" may pass, and the quest for consolidation may be gravely handicapped from the start.[154]

After the transition, elected leaders of government and their interlocutors among the parties face several other characteristic challenges of statecraft: to gradually narrow military prerogatives and roles and establish civilian control; to stabilize and restructure the economy to facilitate sustainable economic growth over the long run; to overcome ethnic insecurity and even violent insurgency; to control high rates of crime, violence, and lawlessness.

Many of these challenges require not just state reform but also state *building*. Economic reform means not only getting the state out of owning, running, and over-regulating a vast array of enterprises but also empowering it to perform effectively the enabling and regulating functions any modern market economy needs: maintaining a stable currency; controlling monopolies; protecting the environment; encouraging capital formation; providing education, infrastructure, and other public goods; and raising equitably and efficiently the revenue to pay for these public goods and services. In most new democracies, this requires modernizing the state bureaucracy and paying it sufficiently well to attract trained and committed talent, as well as to deter corruption.

State building is crucial in a second sense as well. A democratic order presumes, first, order; unless fragile new democracies such as Russia and South Africa can impose the authority of the state—with its monopoly on the use of legitimate force—over heavily armed private mafias, gangs, and militias, democracy is not possible. Democrats must therefore walk a fine line between protecting the individual from the state and mobilizing the state to protect the individual from predatory and anarchic forces in society. This balance can only be struck with the construction of a modern police force and legal system that gradually institutionalize a true rule of law.

To consolidate democracy, elected leaders must therefore tackle multiple tasks. They must build institutions, reform institutions, and in some cases dismantle institutions (such as a military intelligence apparatus that spies on domestic civilian life). They must manage the economy and deal with some of the major problems their society confronts, even if progress on the latter is selective and incremental. Procedurally, they must govern with sufficient accountability and faithfulness to law and constitution to enhance the legitimacy of the constitutional system (compensating for the inevitable shortcomings in their substantive performance). Although short-term economic performance is important, the experience of third-wave democracies suggests it may be less important than establishing the proper institutional frameworks for economic growth and governmental effectiveness in the long run.

Effectiveness at these governmental and state-building tasks demands effective engagement by political and civil society. Political parties remain essential for meeting several of the governance challenges of consolidation: forming a government that has sufficient legislative support to act decisively on the key policy challenges; structuring relations between government and opposition not only to define policy alternatives and heighten accountability but also to pursue broader consensus on the most urgent policy challenges; and mobilizing a sufficient base of popular support, among both party loyalists and allied groups in society, to enable the government to carry out difficult reforms and innovations.

Yet in the contemporary world, political parties alone cannot mobilize sufficient support, participation, or accountability. Civil society organizations and the mass media thus have crucial roles to play in stimulating participation and cultivating the habits and norms of democratic citizenship, as well as in educating mass publics and mobilizing them behind political, economic, and social reforms. This is not to minimize the myriad conflicts over values and interests that will also be played out in the clash of parties and interest groups, but there, too, civil society can help to consolidate democracy by giving voice and power to previously marginalized or voiceless groups. No less critical is the role civil society must play—and *only* civil society can play—in scrutinizing the state and political arenas and securing accountability. Democratic consolidation is not possible—and once achieved, later risks unraveling—when citizens perceive their elected officials to be a class apart, serving their own interests at the expense of society.

As boundaries erode and ties proliferate, international actors of all kinds have real scope to help develop the formal institutions and practices of democracy, to help educate new democracies about the range and implications of institutional choices, to help empower civil society actors and techniques, to help facilitate economic reform and cushion its pain, and to deter antisystem forces from resisting reform by threatening or overthrowing democracy. Of course, these international influences are secondary and not decisive. But to democratic leaders faced with multiple forbidding obstacles to consolidation, timely, generous, discreet, and carefully structured support must appear welcome and may even help to tip the balance. For heavily indebted middle-income countries, it may at least buy democratic leaders more room for maneuver to enact reforms and thus speed the process of consolidation. In some of the impoverished countries of Asia and Africa, debt relief and development assistance—heavily conditioned on democracy and reform—along with help in building democratic institutions, may make possible an otherwise impossible challenge of developing democracy.

Another, more subtle international variable may also bear on the prospects for democratic consolidation and survival. As Samuel Huntington in particular has noted, the expansion of democracy during the third wave has coincided with the international dominance of the United States and other Western democracies.[155] Democratic transitions during this period have been driven by powerful indigenous political conflicts and aspirations, but they have also drawn inspiration from the successful examples of democracy in the West. Ironically, as democracy has expanded at the periphery over the past twenty years, it has weakened at the core. Italy and Japan are undergoing wrenching political transformations as they seek to purge entrenched patterns of political corruption and reorganize their party and electoral systems.[156] Western Germany is still struggling to incorporate its eastern *Länder* and to overcome the "wall in the mind."[157] And in the United States, electoral participation, civic engagement, and trust in government have steadily declined for decades, as government appears unable to respond effectively to deep structural problems in the society and the economy.[158]

It is a dangerous fallacy to view consolidation as a one-time, irreversible process. Democracies come and go. Over time, they may become legitimated, institutionalized, and consolidated. But as their institutions decay and democratic beliefs and practices erode, they may also become deconsolidated. Arguably, this is what has happened to Venezuela and India as they struggle to re-equilibrate. Decay has not by any calculus progressed as far in Italy or Japan, not to mention the United States. But even established democracies have demagogues who blame the failings of society on democracy itself. One should not assume that in the face of severe societal crisis and prolonged governmental inefficacy and corruption, these demagogues could not gain a wider following.

In contrast to all other regime types, democracies depend for their survival almost exclusively on a widely shared belief in their legitimacy. This belief is passed on from one generation to the next, but it must be renewed in each generation—not only through faith and ritual but also through practice and performance. What enables performance to continue to be effective, and institutions to work and command legitimacy, is not just stability but periodic adaptation and reform as well. Reform is the challenge presently facing the world's established democracies, and their success in meeting that challenge will affect not only the quality of their own political systems but, most likely, the prospects for democracy worldwide.

Notes

1. For all twenty-six case studies, see Larry Diamond, Juan J. Linz, and Seymour Martin Lipset, eds., *Democracy in Developing Countries,* vols. 2, *Africa;* 3, *Asia;* and 4, *Latin America* (Boulder, Colo.: Lynne Rienner Publishers, 1988 and 1989).

2. Samuel P. Huntington, *The Third Wave: Democratization in the Late Twentieth Century* (Norman: University of Oklahoma Press, 1991). Philippe Schmitter identifies the post-1974 democratic expansion as a fourth wave, with previous waves beginning in 1848 and after World Wars I and II. Philippe C. Schmitter, "The International Context of Contemporary Democratization," *Stanford Journal of International Affairs* 2, no. 1 (Fall–Winter 1993): 1–29.

3. On this debate see the interview with Lee Kuan Yew, *Foreign Affairs* 73, no. 2 (March–April 1994): 109–126; Kim Dae Jung, "Is Culture Destiny: The Myth of Asia's Anti-Democratic Values," *Foreign Affairs* 73, no. 6 (November–December 1994): 189–194; and Francis Fukuyama, "Confucianism and Democracy," *Journal of Democracy* 6, no. 3 (April 1995): 20–33.

4. On the problems and constraints of democratic functioning in Latin America, see Guillermo O'Donnell, "Delegative Democracy," *Journal of Democracy* 5, no. 1 (January 1994): 55–69; and Larry Diamond, "Democracy in Latin America: Degrees, Illusions, and Directions for Consolidation," in Tom Farer, ed., *Beyond Sovereignty: Collectively Defending Democracy in the Americas* (Baltimore: Johns Hopkins University Press, 1995).

5. This neglect is overcome to some extent in Arend Lijphart's creative and enterprising study, *Democracies: Patterns of Majoritarian and Consensus Government in Twenty-One Countries* (New Haven, Conn.: Yale University Press, 1984). However, Lijphart's focus is mainly on political structure, and the comparison is limited to the continuous and stable democracies of the advanced industrial countries.

6. *Freedom Review,* January–February 1995; and Freedom House, *Freedom in the World, 1994–1995* (New York: Freedom House, 1995). Each year since 1973, Freedom House has rated every country in the world on twin seven-point scales that measure political rights (of contestation, opposition, and participation) and civil liberties (of expression, information, organization, due process, and so on). On each scale, a rating of one signifies the most free and seven the least free. Countries whose average score on the two scales is 2.5 or lower are considered "free," whereas those that range from 3 to 5.5 are termed "partly free" and those from 5.5 to 7.0 "not free."

7. On this point, see as well Manuel Antonio Garretón, "Redemocratization in Chile," *Journal of Democracy* 6, no. 1 (January 1995): 146–158.

8. Robert A. Dahl, *Polyarchy: Participation and Opposition* (New Haven, Conn.: Yale University Press, 1971), pp. 3–20; Joseph Schumpeter, *Capitalism, Socialism and Democracy* (New York: Harper and Row, 1942); Seymour Martin Lipset, *Political Man,* expanded and updated ed. (Baltimore: Johns Hopkins University Press, 1981), p. 27; Juan Linz, *The*

Breakdown of Democratic Regimes: Crisis, Breakdown, and Reequilibration (Baltimore: Johns Hopkins University Press, 1978), p. 5. Also, Joseph E. Ryan, "Survey Methodology," *Freedom Review* 26, no. 1 (January–February 1995): 10–12 (or in the 1993–1994 or 1994–1995 *Freedom in the World*). See in particular the Freedom House checklists of political rights and civil liberties.

    9. Philippe C. Schmitter and Terry Lynn Karl, "What Democracy Is . . . and Is Not," *Journal of Democracy* 2, no. 3 (Summer 1991): 75–88.

    10. O'Donnell, "Delegative Democracy"; see also Francisco C. Weffort, "'New Democracies': Which Democracies?" Woodrow Wilson Center for International Scholars, Washington, D.C., January 1992. For a definitive analysis of the vast array of terms denoting such "diminished subtypes" of democracy, see David Collier and Steven Levitsky, "Democracy 'with Adjectives': Finding Conceptual Order in Recent Comparative Research," paper presented to the Annual Meeting of the American Political Science Association, New York, September 1–4, 1994.

    11. The distinction between authoritarian and totalitarian regimes has a long intellectual history. See Juan J. Linz, "Totalitarian and Authoritarian Regimes," in Fred I. Greenstein and Nelson W. Polsby, eds., *Handbook of Political Science* (Reading, Mass.: Addison-Wesley, 1975), vol. 3, pp. 175–411.

    12. Linz, *Breakdown of Democratic Regimes*, pp. 16–17. See also Lipset, *Political Man*, p. 64; and Dahl, *Polyarchy*, pp. 129–131.

    13. Linz, *Breakdown of Democratic Regimes*, p. 20.

    14. Lipset, *Political Man*, pp. 67–71.

    15. Larry Diamond, "Conclusion: Causes and Effects," in Larry Diamond, ed., *Political Culture and Democracy in Developing Countries* (Boulder, Colo.: Lynne Rienner Publishers, 1993), pp. 425–432.

    16. Lipset, *Political Man*, pp. 64–70; Dahl, *Polyarchy*, pp. 129–150; and Linz, *Breakdown of Democratic Regimes*, pp. 16–23.

    17. Juan Linz and Alfred Stepan, "Political Crafting of Democratic Consolidation or Destruction: European and South American Comparisons," in Robert A. Pastor, ed., *Democracy in the Americas: Stopping the Pendulum* (New York: Holmes and Meier, 1989), pp. 41-47.

    18. Juan J. Linz and Alfred Stepan, *Problems of Democratic Transition and Consolidation: Southern Europe, South America, and Post-Communist Europe* (Baltimore: Johns Hopkins University Press, forthcoming), Chapter 5.

    19. Karen L. Remmer, "The Political Impact of Economic Crisis in Latin America in the 1980s," *American Political Science Review* 85, no. 3 (September 1991): 777–800.

    20. Diamond, "Democracy in Latin America."

    21. Linz and Stepan, "Political Crafting of Democratic Consolidation or Destruction," p. 43.

    22. On the role of corruption in the 1991 coup in Thailand, see Catharin Dalpino, "Thailand's Search for Accountability," *Journal of Democracy* 2, no. 4 (Fall 1991): 61–72. The relationship between corruption and democracy is also examined historically, comparatively, and prescriptively in the articles by Michael Johnston, Larry Diamond, and Robert Klitgaard in that issue. These four articles also appear in Larry Diamond and Marc F. Plattner, eds., *The Global Resurgence of Democracy* (Baltimore: Johns Hopkins University Press, 1993), pp. 193–244.

    23. John D. Holm, "Botswana: A Paternalistic Democracy," in Diamond, Linz, and Lipset, *Democracy in Developing Countries: Africa*, pp. 196–199.

    24. Karen L. Remmer, "The Political Economy of Elections in Latin America, 1980–91," *American Political Science Review* 87, no. 2 (June 1993): 402.

    25. Barbara Geddes, "Challenging the Conventional Wisdom," *Journal of Democracy* 5, no. 4 (special issue on Economic Reform and Democracy) (October 1994): 115.

    26. Remmer, "The Political Economy of Elections in Latin America, 1980–91"; Adam Przeworski, *Democracy and the Market: Political and Economic Reforms in Eastern Europe and Latin America* (Cambridge: Cambridge University Press, 1991), pp. 164–165.

    27. Moisés Naím, "Latin America: The Second Stage of Reform," *Journal of Democracy* 5, no. 4 (October 1994): 32–48.

    28. Carol Graham, *Safety Nets, Politics, and the Poor: Transitions to Market Economies* (Washington, D.C.: Brookings Institution, 1994). In at least some developing countries, such

programs can supplement existing welfare and poverty alleviation efforts. In the transition from socialism, however, as in Eastern Europe and the former Soviet Union, a key element of the reform challenge is to construct from scratch an entirely new system for welfare delivery and income maintenance. Przeworski, *Democracy and the Market*, p. 161.

29. These issues and extensive evidence for the compatibility of democracy and economic reform are found in a number of the contributions to the *Journal of Democracy* 5, no. 4 (October 1994), and to the larger volume containing that special issue: Larry Diamond and Marc F. Plattner, eds., *Economic Reform and Democracy* (Baltimore: Johns Hopkins University Press, 1995). See also Larry Diamond, "Democracy and Economic Reform: Tensions, Compatibilities, and Strategies for Reconciliation," in Edward Lazear, ed., *Economic Transition in Eastern Europe and Russia: Realities of Reform* (Stanford, Calif.: Hoover Institution Press, 1995), pp. 107–158.

30. Graham, *Safety Nets, Politics, and the Poor.*

31. Juan J. Linz and Alfred Stepan, eds., *The Breakdown of Democratic Regimes*, 4 vols. (Baltimore: Johns Hopkins University Press, 1978).

32. Linz, *Breakdown of Democratic Regimes*, pp. 27–38. For extensive evidence of the role of violence and terror, and party reactions to them, in the breakdown or persistence of democracies, see G. Bingham Powell Jr., *Contemporary Democracies: Participation, Stability, and Violence* (Cambridge, Mass.: Harvard University Press, 1982), pp. 155–170.

33. Ibid., Powell, p. 174.

34. Sung-joo Han, "South Korea: Politics in Transition," in Diamond, Linz, and Lipset, *Democracy in Developing Countries: Asia*, p. 285.

35. For an early influential analysis emphasizing the crucial importance of Chiang's leadership vision and skill, see Ramon H. Myers, "Political Theory and Recent Political Developments in the Republic of China," *Asian Survey* 27, no. 9 (September 1987): 1007, 1019–1021.

36. On President Lee's leadership role, see Ramon H. Myers, "Building the First Chinese Democracy: The Crises and Leadership of President Lee Teng-hui," in Jason C. Hu, ed., *Quiet Revolutions on Taiwan, Republic of China* (Taipei: Kwang Hwa Publishing Co., 1994), pp. 43–72.

37. For an analysis of the full range of economic, social, and international (as well as political and institutional) factors giving rise to the democratic transition in Taiwan, see Hung-mao Tien, *The Great Transition: Political and Social Change in the Republic of China* (Stanford, Calif.: Hoover Institution Press, 1989); Tun-jen Cheng and Stephan Haggard, eds., *Political Change in Taiwan* (Boulder, Colo.: Lynne Rienner Publishers, 1992); and Yun-han Chu, *Crafting Democracy in Taiwan* (Taipei: Institute for National Policy Research, 1992).

38. Gabriel A. Almond and Sidney Verba, *The Civic Culture* (Princeton, N.J.: Princeton University Press, 1963); Sidney Verba, "Conclusion: Comparative Political Culture," in Lucian W. Pye and Sidney Verba, eds., *Political Culture and Political Development* (Princeton, N.J.: Princeton University Press, 1965), pp. 512–560; Dahl, *Polyarchy*, pp. 129–162; Lipset, *Political Man;* Seymour Martin Lipset, *The First New Nation* (New York: W. W. Norton, 1979), part 3; Robert D. Putnam, with Roberto Leonardi and Raffaella Y. Nanetti, *Making Democracy Work: Civic Traditions in Modern Italy* (Princeton, N.J.: Princeton University Press, 1993); and Larry Diamond, "Introduction: Political Culture and Democracy," in Diamond, *Political Culture and Democracy in Developing Countries*, pp. 10–15.

39. Richard Sisson, "Culture and Democratization in India," in Diamond, *Political Culture and Democracy in Developing Countries*, pp. 37–66.

40. These patterns are not unique to South Africa but have commonly emerged in response to the depredations of authoritarian rule throughout Africa. See Naomi Chazan, "Between Liberalism and Statism: African Political Cultures and Democracy," in Diamond, *Political Culture and Democracy in Developing Countries*, pp. 67–105.

41. Paul E. Sigmund, "Christian Democracy, Liberation Theology, and Political Culture in Latin America," in Diamond, *Political Culture and Democracy in Developing Countries*, p. 343. See also Robert Barros, "The Left and Democracy: Recent Debates in Latin America," *Telos* 68 (1986): 49–70; Linz and Stepan, "Political Crafting of Democratic Consolidation or Destruction," p. 47; and Larry Diamond and Juan J. Linz, "Introduction: Politics, Society, and Democracy in Latin America," in Diamond, Linz, and Lipset, *Democracy in Developing Countries: Latin America*, p. 12.

42. Nancy Bermeo, "Democracy and the Lessons of Dictatorship," *Comparative Politics* 24 (April 1992): 273–291.

43. Seymour Martin Lipset, "Some Social Requisites of Democracy," *American Political Science Review* (March 1959): 69–105, republished as "Economic Development and Democracy," in Lipset, *Political Man,* Chapter 2. For a review of this literature, see Larry Diamond, "Economic Development and Democracy Reconsidered," *American Behavioral Scientist* 35, no. 4–5 (March–June 1992): 450–499, also published in Gary Marks and Larry Diamond, eds., *Reexamining Democracy: Essays in Honor of Seymour Martin Lipset* (Newbury Park, Calif.: Sage Publications, 1992), pp. 93–139.

44. Dahl, *Polyarchy,* pp. 67–68; Samuel P. Huntington, "Will More Countries Become Democratic?" *Political Science Quarterly* 99, no. 2 (Summer 1984): 201.

45. United Nations Development Programme, *Human Development Report 1994* (New York: Oxford University Press, 1994), pp. 90–101.

46. Diamond, "Economic Development and Democracy Reconsidered," pp. 465–468.

47. Lipset, *Political Man,* p. 45.

48. Ibid., p. 51; Dahl, *Polyarchy,* p. 81.

49. Alex Inkeles and Larry Diamond, "Personal Qualities as a Reflection of Level of National Development," in Frank Andrews and Alexander Szalai, eds., *Comparative Studies on the Quality of Life* (London: Sage Publications, 1980), pp. 73–109.

50. Lipset, *Political Man,* pp. 51–52.

51. Dietrich Rueschemeyer, Evelyne Huber Stephens, and John D. Stephens, *Capitalist Development and Democracy* (Chicago: University of Chicago Press, 1992).

52. Tun-jen Cheng, "Democratizing the Quasi-Leninist Regime in Taiwan," *World Politics* 41 (1989): 471–499.

53. The fifty-five (predominantly African and Asian) countries the UNDP ranks as having "low human development" have an average of 9 radios, 2.4 televisions, 2.1 daily newspapers, and 0.7 telephones per 100 people, compared to the seventeen developing countries with high human development, which average 47 radios, 17.7 televisions, 27.8 daily newspapers, and 18.7 telephones per 100 people. UNDP, *Human Development Report 1994,* Table 2, pp. 132–133.

54. The ten developing countries with populations above one million that maintained democracy, or at least a constitutional near-democracy, continuously from 1965 (India, Sri Lanka, Costa Rica, Colombia, Venezuela, Jamaica, Trinidad and Tobago, Botswana, Mauritius, and Papua New Guinea) reduced their infant mortality by a median annual rate of 3.25 percent from 1965 to the late 1980s, compared with a median annual reduction of 2.3 percent among ten of the most prominent continuous dictatorships in this period. Diamond, "Economic Development and Democracy Reconsidered," p. 487. Between 1960 and 1992, Botswana realized the greatest absolute increase in its score on the Human Development Index of any of the 114 countries for which the UNDP presents time series data (except for Malaysia, with which it was tied). UNDP, *Human Development Report 1994,* p. 96.

55. Lipset, *Political Man,* p. 29.

56. Samuel P. Huntington and Joan M. Nelson, *No Easy Choice: Political Participation in Developing Countries* (Cambridge, Mass.: Harvard University Press, 1976), p. 23.

57. For a review of several decades of literature examining this issue, see Adam Przeworski and Fernando Limongi, "Political Regimes and Economic Growth," *Journal of Economic Perspectives* 7, no. 3 (1993): 51–69.

58. Adam Przeworski and Fernando Limongi, "Democracy and Development," paper presented to the Nobel Symposium "Democracy's Victory and Crisis," Uppsala University, Sweden, August 27–30, 1994, p. 14.

59. John Booth, "Costa Rica: The Roots of Democratic Stability," in Diamond, Linz, and Lipset, *Democracy in Developing Countries: Latin America,* pp. 389–391.

60. World Bank, *World Development Report* 1994 (New York: Oxford University Press, 1994), Table 30, pp. 220–221. The top fifth of Brazil's income earners also take the highest share in the world (67.5 percent). See Table 1.1 for comparisons with other cases in this volume. The Brazilian data are from 1989.

61. United Nations Development Programme, *Human Development Report 1994,* p. 99.

62. Ibid., p. 98.

63. Michael P. Todaro, *Economic Development in the Third World,* 2d ed. (New York: Longman, 1981), p. 165.

64. World Bank, *World Development Report 1994,* Table 25, p. 210.

65. See Przeworski and Limongi, "Democracy and Development," pp. 9, 10, and 18 (Table 5). For their entire sample of regimes across several decades, democracies averaged population growth rates of 1.48 percent and dictatorships of 2.51 percent. This is not some artifact of the association between democracy and higher levels of development. Dictatorships exhibited higher (often substantially higher) average rates of population growth in every one of ten levels of per capita GDP.

66. Larry Diamond, "Rethinking Civil Society: Toward Democratic Consolidation," *Journal of Democracy* 5, no. 3 (July 1994): 5. Many of the themes in this section are elaborated in that article.

67. Ibid., pp. 6–7.

68. On the distinction between civil society and political society, see Alfred Stepan, *Rethinking Military Politics* (Princeton: Princeton University Press, 1988), Chapter 1; and Linz and Stepan, *Problems of Democratic Transition and Consolidation.*

69. See, for example, John Keane, ed., *Civil Society and the State: New European Perspectives* (London: Verso, 1988); Bronislaw Geremek, "Civil Society Then and Now," *Journal of Democracy* 3, no. 2 (April 1992): 3–12; Samuel P. Huntington, "Will More Countries Become Democratic?" *Political Science Quarterly* 99, no. 2 (Summer 1984): 204; Lipset, *Political Man,* p. 52.

70. O'Donnell and Schmitter, *Transitions from Authoritarian Rule: Tentative Conclusions About Uncertain Democracies,* Chapter 5.

71. For a first-person account, see Monica Jimenez de Barros, "Mobilizing for Democracy in Chile: The Crusade for Participation and Beyond," in Larry Diamond, ed., *The Democratic Revolution: Struggles for Freedom and Pluralism in the Developing World* (New York: Freedom House, 1992), pp. 73-88.

72. Christine Sadowski, "Autonomous Groups as Agents of Democratic Change in Communist and Post-Communist Eastern Europe," in Diamond, *Political Culture and Democracy in Developing Countries,* pp. 163–195.

73. John W. Harbeson, Donald Rothchild, and Naomi Chazan, eds., *Civil Society and the State in Africa* (Boulder, Colo.: Lynne Rienner Publishers, 1994); Peter Lewis, "Political Transition and the Dilemma of Civil Society in Africa," *Journal of International Affairs* 27, no. 1 (Summer 1992): 31–54; Naomi Chazan, "Africa's Democratic Challenge: Strengthening Civil Society and the State," *World Policy Journal* 9 (Spring 1992): 279–308; Chazan, "Between Liberalism and Statism," pp. 67–105; and Michael Bratton and Nicolas van de Walle, "Toward Governance in Africa: Popular Demands and State Response," in Goran Hyden and Michael Bratton, eds., *Governance and Politics in Africa* (Boulder, Colo.: Lynne Rienner Publishers, 1992), pp. 27–56.

74. Putnam, *Making Democracy Work,* Chapters 4–6. Putnam and his fellow researchers found that a significant correlate of successful (democratic) government was the dense presence of "horizontally ordered groups," even sports clubs, choral societies, and cultural associations that might seem to fall outside our definition of civil society. However, in empowering citizens "to engage in collective deliberation about public choices" (p. 115), such groups turn out to manifest a concern with collective welfare—the civic good—that marks them as elements of civil society.

75. On this point, see also Steven Friedman, "An Unlikely Utopia: State and Civil Society in South Africa," *Politikon* 19, no. 1 (December 1991): 5–19.

76. Kehla Shubane and Pumla Madiba, "The Struggle Continues?: Civic Associations in the Transition," Research Report No. 25 (1992), Centre for Policy Studies, Johannesburg, South Africa; see also Diamond, "Civil Society and Democratic Consolidation," pp. 66–67.

77. Putnam, *Making Democracy Work,* p. 183.

78. See, for example, Larry Diamond, "Three Paradoxes of Democracy," *Journal of Democracy* 1, no. 3 (Summer 1990): 48–60, and "Democracy as Paradox," in Ehud Sprinzak and Larry Diamond, eds., *Israeli Democracy Under Stress* (Boulder, Colo.: Lynne Rienner Publishers, 1993), pp. 21–43.

79. World Bank, *The East Asian Miracle: Economic Growth and Public Policy* (New York: Oxford University Press, 1993), pp. 8–25, 347–360, and passim.

80. Seymour Martin Lipset, "The Social Requisites of Democracy Revisited," *American Sociological Review* 59, no. 1 (February 1994): 4.

81. Richard L. Sklar, "The Nature of Class Domination in Africa," *Journal of Modern African Studies* 17, no. 4 (December 1979): 531-552.

82. Larry Diamond, "Class Formation in the Swollen African State," *Journal of Modern African Studies* 25, no. 4 (December 1987): 567–596.

83. World Bank, *The East Asian Miracle,* pp. 352–353.

84. Samuel P. Huntington, *Political Order in Changing Societies* (New Haven: Yale University Press, 1968); Jonathan Hartlyn and Arturo Valenzuela, "Democracy in Latin America Since 1930," in Leslie Bethell, ed., *The Cambridge History of Latin America, Vol. VI: Latin America Since 1930: Economy, Society, and Politics* (Cambridge: Cambridge University Press, 1994); see also Diamond, "Democracy in Latin America."

85. O'Donnell, "Delegative Democracy;" see also Adam Przeworski, "Some Problems in the Study of the Transition to Democracy," in Guillermo O'Donnell, Philippe C. Schmitter, and Laurence Whitehead, eds., *Transitions from Authoritarian Rule: Comparative Perspectives* (Baltimore: Johns Hopkins University Press, 1986), pp. 56–61.

86. Stephan Haggard and Robert R. Kaufman, "The Political Economy of Inflation and Stabilization in Middle Income Countries," in Haggard and Kaufman, eds., *The Politics of Economic Adjustment* (Princeton: Princeton University Press, 1992) pp. 270–313, and in the same volume "Economic Adjustment and the Prospects for Democracy," pp. 342–358; and Michael Coppedge, "Institutions and Democratic Governance in Latin America," revised version (August 1993) of paper prepared for the conference on Rethinking Development Theories in Latin America, Institute of Latin American Studies, University of North Carolina–Chapel Hill, March 11–13, 1993, p. 16.

87. Juan J. Linz, "Change and Continuity in the Nature of Contemporary Democracies," in Marks and Diamond, *Reexamining Democracy,* pp. 184–186.

88. Lipset, "The Social Requisites of Democracy Revisited," p. 14.

89. Lipset, *First New Nation,* pp. 307–308.

90. Ibid., pp. 308–310; Linz, *Breakdown of Democratic Regimes,* p. 24.

91. Giovanni Sartori, *Parties and Party Systems: A Framework for Analysis* (Cambridge: Cambridge University Press, 1976), pp. 131–140; Linz, *Breakdown of Democratic Regimes,* pp. 25–27. From this perspective, to be relevant a party must be potentially useful in the formation of a coalition government or must have "power of intimidation" politically. Polarized pluralism encompasses not only extreme multipartyism but such other factors as antisystem parties, irresponsible oppositions, outbidding between parties, and ideological polarization.

92. Powell, *Contemporary Democracies,* pp. 154–157, 206, 222–223.

93. Haggard and Kaufman, "The Political Economy of Inflation and Stabilization," p. 279, and "Economic Adjustment and the Prospects for Democracy," p. 343.

94. Haggard and Kaufman, "The Political Economy of Inflation and Stabilization," pp. 279–280.

95. Huntington, *Political Order in Changing Societies,* pp. 12–24.

96. Ibid.

97. John Peeler, "Elite Settlements and Democratic Consolidation: Colombia, Costa Rica, and Venezuela," in John Higley and Richard Gunther, eds., *Elites and Democratic Consolidation in Latin America and Southern Europe* (Cambridge: Cambridge University Press, 1992), pp. 81–112; Diamond, "Introduction: Political Culture and Democracy," and "Conclusion: Causes and Effects," in Diamond, *Political Culture and Democracy in Developing Countries,* pp. 5–6, 427–428.

98. The "effective number of parties" is a technical expression for measuring the degree of fragmentation in parliament (or in the popular vote for parliament). Although it is a continuous scale, intuitively it might be thought of as roughly the number of parties "significant" enough to shape the formation of government and the dynamics of the political system. Electoral system design and choice have attracted a vast literature that is well beyond the scope of this chapter to canvass. Some key works include Maurice Duverger, *Political Parties: Their Organization and Activity in the Modern State* (New York: Wiley, 1963); Douglas Rae, *The Political Consequences of Electoral Laws* (New Haven: Yale University Press, 1967); Lijphart, *Democracies;* Bernard Grofman and Arend Lijphart, eds., *Electoral Laws and Their Consequences* (New York: Agathon Press, 1986); Rein Taagepera and Matthew S. Shugart,

Seats and Votes: The Effects and Determinants of Electoral Systems (New Haven: Yale University Press, 1989); Matthew S. Shugart and John M. Carey *Presidents and Assemblies: Constitutional Design and Electoral Dynamics* (Cambridge: Cambridge University Press, 1992); Donald Horowitz, *A Democratic South Africa: Constitutional Engineering in a Divided Society* (Berkeley: University of California Press, 1991); and Arend Lijphart, *Electoral Systems and Party Systems: A Study of Twenty-Seven Democracies, 1945–1990* (Oxford: Oxford University Press, 1994), which provides clear evidence (Table 5.1 and passim) of the greater tendency of PR toward multipartyism.

99. Shugart and Carey, *Presidents and Assemblies,* p. 7.

100. Ken Gladdish, "Choosing an Electoral System: The Primacy of the Particular," *Journal of Democracy* 4, no. 1 (January 1993): 53–65. On the trade-off between governability and representativeness, see also Diamond, "Three Paradoxes of Democracy." For a debate on the merits of PR compared with plurality systems, see the chapters by Arend Lijphart, Guy Lardeyret, and Quentin Quade in Larry Diamond and Marc F. Plattner, *The Global Resurgence of Democracy* (Baltimore: Johns Hopkins University Press, 1993), pp. 146–177.

101. Lijphart, *Electoral Systems and Party Systems.*

102. Bolivar Lamounier, "Brazil at an Impasse," *Journal of Democracy* 5, no. 3 (July 1984): 79.

103. Ibid., p. 80. As Lamounier notes, the current system "combines the worst of all worlds: It ends up being as individualistic as the Ango-Saxon single-member district system, but without the latter's requirement that representatives be accountable to geographic constituencies." Ibid.

104. Ibid., p. 86.

105. Lijphart, *Electoral Systems and Party Systems,* p. 151.

106. Ibid., Chapter 7.

107. Gianfranco Pasquino, "Italy: The Twilight of the Parties," *Journal of Democracy* 5, no. 1 (January 1994): 18–29, and "The Birth of the 'Second Republic,'" *Journal of Democracy* 5, no. 3 (July 1994): 107–113.

108. The seminal critique of presidentialism is Juan J. Linz, "Presidential or Parliamentary Democracy: Does It Make a Difference?" in Juan J. Linz and Arturo Valenzuela, eds., *The Failure of Presidential Democracy* (Baltimore: Johns Hopkins University Press, 1994). An earlier and abbreviated version, "The Perils of Presidentialism," appeared in the *Journal of Democracy* 1, no. 1 (Winter 1990): 51–70. For a debate on this essay, see the critiques by Donald Horowitz and Seymour Martin Lipset and the reply by Linz in the *Journal of Democracy* 1, no. 3, pp. 73–91, republished (along with Linz's *Journal* essay) in Diamond and Plattner, *The Global Resurgence of Democracy,* pp. 108–145. Further evidence and debate appears in *The Failure of Presidential Democracy.* The unstable marriage between presidentialism and PR in Latin America is demonstrated by Scott Mainwaring, "Presidentialism in Latin America," *Latin American Research Review* 25, no. 1 (1990): 157–179, and "Presidentialism, Multipartyism, and Democracy," *Comparative Political Studies* 26, no. 2 (July 1993): 196–228; see also Arturo Valenzuela, "Latin America: Presidentialism in Crisis," *Journal of Democracy* 4, no. 4 (October 1993): 3–16. The case for presidentialism, a critique of parliamentarism, and consideration of hybrid forms are considered in Shugart and Carey, *Presidents and Assemblies.*

109. Coppedge, "Institutions and Democratic Governance in Latin America," p. 7.

110. O'Donnell, "Delegative Democracy."

111. Richard L. Sklar, "Developmental Democracy," *Comparative Studies in Society and History* 29, no. 4 (October 1987): 694.

112. This section draws from Larry Diamond and Marc F. Plattner, "Introduction," in Diamond and Plattner, eds., *Nationalism, Ethnic Conflict, and Democracy* (Baltimore: Johns Hopkins University Press, 1994), pp. xviii–xxix.

113. Donald Horowitz, *Ethnic Groups in Conflict* (Berkeley: University of California Press, 1985), p. 224. The notions of group entitlement and legitimacy and their linkage to individual feelings of worth, on the one hand, and to intergroup conflict, on the other, are explored extensively in this seminal work.

114. Donald L. Horowitz, "Ethnic Conflict Management for Policymakers," in Joseph V. Montville, ed., *Conflict and Peacemaking in Multiethnic Societies* (Lexington, Mass.: Lexington Books, 1990), pp. 115–116.

115. Donald L. Horowitz, "Democracy in Divided Societies," in Diamond and Plattner, *Nationalism, Ethnic, Conflict, and Democracy,* pp. 35–55.

116. Robert A. Dahl, *Democracy and Its Critics* (New Haven: Yale University Press, 1989), p. 207; see also Linz and Stepan, *Problems of Democratic Transition and Consolidation,* Chapter 2; and Juan J. Linz, "State Building and Nation Building," *European Review* 1, no. 4 (1993): 355–369. There is no simple democratic way of settling the disjunction between nation and state, as Linz emphasized (p. 366), quoting the famous dictum of Ivor Jennings, "The people cannot decide until somebody decides who are the people." Although he generally rejected the notion of socioeconomic preconditions for democracy, Dankwart A. Rustow similarly posited "national unity" as a background condition for democracy. See his "Transitions to Democracy: Towards a Dynamic Model," *Comparative Politics* 2, no. 3 (April 1970): 337–363.

117. Alvin Rabushka and Kenneth Shepsle, *Politics in Plural Societies: A Theory of Democratic Instability* (Columbus, Ohio: Charles E. Merrill), pp. 62–92. Quote is from page 86.

118. Dahl, *Polyarchy,* pp. 108–111; Rupert Emerson, "The Prospects for Democracy," in Michael F. Lofchie, ed., *The State of the Nations* (Berkeley: University of California Press, 1971), pp. 248–249; Michael T. Hannan and Glenn P. Carrol, "Dynamics of Formal Political Structure: An Event-History Analysis," *American Sociological Review* 46 (January 1981): 19–35; Powell, *Contemporary Democracies,* pp. 40–53, 157.

119. Lipset, *Political Man,* pp. 70–79.

120. Horowitz, *Ethnic Groups in Conflict,* pp. 7–8.

121. Ashutosh Varshney, "Contested Meanings: India's National Identity, Hindu Nationalism, and the Politics of Anxiety," *Daedalus* 122, no. 3 (Summer 1993): 227–261.

122. The worst incidents of ethnic and religious conflict in Nigeria, including the civil war, have occurred under military, not civilian constitutional, rule.

123. Linz and Stepan, *Problems of Democratic Transition and Consolidation,* Chapter 2.

124. Janusz Bugajski, "The Fate of Minorities in Eastern Europe," in Diamond and Plattner, *Nationalism, Ethnic Conflict, and Democracy,* pp. 102–116. Needless to say, the way in which, and the degree to which, minority groups' rights are explicitly recognized and protected varies somewhat in appropriateness across countries.

125. Even where groups are not territorially concentrated, governments can grant them certain provisions for autonomous self-government of their cultural and religious affairs, such as special courts (in Islam, Shari'a courts) in which parties can mutually agree to have civil and family matters adjudicated.

126. Jonathan Fox, "Latin America's Emerging Local Politics," *Journal of Democracy* 5, no. 2 (April 1994): 105–116.

127. Ibid. See also Lipset, *Political Man.*

128. Linz and Stepan, *Problems of Democratic Transition and Consolidation,* Chapter 2; see also Horowitz, "Democracy in Divided Societies," pp. 53–54.

129. Carlos H. Waisman, "Argentina: Autarkic Industrialization and Illegitimacy," in Diamond, Linz, and Lipset, *Democracy in Developing Countries: Latin America,* pp. 59–110.

130. Stepan, *Rethinking Military Politics.*

131. Louis Goodman, presentation to the Asia Foundation Conference Democratization in Asia: Meeting the Challenges of the 1990s, Chiang Mai, Thailand, December 7–12, 1992.

132. Stepan, *Rethinking Military Politics,* pp. 138–139.

133. Jamal Benomar, "Justice After Transitions," *Journal of Democracy* 5, no. 2 (April 1994): 14. The above strategy for reducing the autonomous power of the military is elaborated in Diamond, "Democracy in Latin America."

134. See the review in Peter Evans, *Dependent Development: The Alliance of Multinational State and Local Capital in Brazil* (Princeton, N.J.: Princeton University Press, 1979), pp. 25–54.

135. For an analysis of the impact of colonial rule on subsequent political development in Africa, see L. H. Gann and Peter Duignan, *Burden of Empire: An Appraisal of Western Colonialism in Africa South of the Sahara* (Stanford, Calif.: Hoover Institution Press, 1967), pp. 253–272; Robert Jackson and Carl Rosberg, "Popular Legitimacy in African Multi-Ethnic States," *Journal of Modern African Studies* 22, no. 2 (June 1984): 177–198; Michael Crowder, "Whose Dream Was It Anyway? Twenty-Five Years of African Independence," *African Affairs* 86, no. 342 (January 1987): 11–18; Diamond, "Introduction: Roots of Failure, Seeds of Hope,"

in Diamond, Linz, and Lipset, *Democracy in Developing Countries: Africa,* pp. 6–10; and Crawford Young, *The African Colonial State in Comparative Perspective* (New Haven: Yale University Press, 1994). Several statistical analyses have found that a British colonial legacy has a positive effect on democracy, at least through the 1970s. See especially Kenneth A. Bollen and Robert Jackman, "Economic and Noneconomic Determinants of Political Democracy in the 1960s," *Research in Political Sociology* 1 (Greenwich: JAI Press, 1985): 27–48; and Seymour Martin Lipset, Kyoung-ryung Seong, and John Charles Torres, "A Comparative Analysis of the Social Requisites of Democracy," *International Social Science Journal* 45 (May 1993): 155–175.

136. Chazan, "Between Liberalism and Statism."

137. Huntington, *The Third Wave,* p. 102; see also Schmitter, "The International Context of Contemporary Democratization," pp. 18–19.

138. For an analysis of political development doctrines in U.S. foreign policy between 1947 and 1968, and the frequent conflict between the goals of fighting the expansion of communism and promoting democracy abroad, see Robert Packenham, *Liberal America and the Third World: Political Development Ideas in Foreign Aid and Social Science* (Princeton, N.J.: Princeton University Press, 1973). More recent tensions between democracy promotion and anticommunism during the Reagan years are explored in Thomas Carothers, *In the Name of Democracy: U.S. Policy Toward Latin America in the Reagan Years* (Berkeley: University of California Press, 1991). U.S. policies to promote democracy over the course of the twentieth century are analyzed in Tony Smith, *America's Mission: The United States and the Worldwide Struggle for Democracy in the Twentieth Century* (Princeton, N.J.: Princeton University Press, 1994). U.S. effforts to promote, or "export," democracy to Latin America are historically and critically assessed from a number of country and thematic perspectives in Abraham Lowenthal, ed., *Exporting Democracy: The United States and Latin America* (Baltimore: Johns Hopkins University Press, 1991), 2 volumes.

139. Kathryn Sikkink, "The Effectiveness of U.S. Human Rights Policy: Argentina, Guatemala, and Uruguay," paper presented to the World Congress of the International Political Science Association, Buenos Aires, July 21–25, 1991. Uruguay's first post-transition democratic president, Julio Sanguinetti, declared shortly after taking office in 1984, "The vigorous policies of the Carter Administration were the most important outside influence on Uruguay's democratization process." Quoted in Huntington, *The Third Wave,* p. 96.

140. Ibid., pp. 96–97.

141. George P. Shultz, *Turmoil and Triumph: My Years as Secretary of State* (New York: Charles Scribner's Sons, 1993), pp. 608-642.

142. Huntington, *The Third Wave,* p. 95. On the U.S. efforts to induce and support democratic transition in Chile, see Carothers, *In the Name of Democracy,* pp. 150–163; on South Korea, see Shultz, *Turmoil and Triumph,* pp. 976–980.

143. J. Samuel Fitch, "Democracy, Human Rights and the Armed Forces," in Jonathan Hartlyn, Lars Schoultz, and Augusto Varas, eds., *The United States and Latin America in the 1990s: Beyond the Cold War* (Chapel Hill: University of North Carolina Press, 1993), p. 203 (emphasis in the original).

144. Francisco Villagrán de León, "Thwarting the Guatemalan Coup," *Journal of Democracy* 4, no. 4 (October 1993): 124.

145. However, Sikkink concludes that U.S. human rights pressure over the years has not been particularly effective in Guatemala, and she cautions that even superpower pressure for democratization may be ineffective unless it is applied in a comprehensive and forceful manner, clearly conveyed through multiple channels and utilizing a wide range of policy instruments, and unless a moderate faction exists within the authoritarian regime that is prepared to be receptive to such pressure. Sikkink, "U.S. Human Rights Policy," pp. 32–38.

146. Larry Diamond, "Promoting Democracy in Africa," in John W. Harbeson and Donald Rothchild, eds., *Africa in World Politics,* 2d ed. (Boulder, Colo.: Westview Press, 1995); Joel Barkan, "Kenya: Lessons from a Flawed Election," *Journal of Democracy* 4, no. 3 (July 1993): 85-99.

147. Laurence Whitehead, "International Aspects of Democratization," in O'Donnell, Schmitter, and Whitehead, *Transitions from Authoritarian Rule,* p. 21; also Huntington, *The Third Wave,* pp. 87–89; and Schmitter, "The International Context of Contemporary Democratization," pp. 24–26. "More than any other international commitment, full EC mem-

bership has served to stabilize both political and economic expectations," in Schmitter's view, for three reasons: EC membership's permanent nature, the comprehensive and "complex inter-dependence" it generates, and the "lengthy, public, multilateral," and consensual nature of EC deliberations, which makes it much less likely that other criteria could overrride the stated democratic ones in certifying a country for membership (p. 26).

148. Larry Diamond, "Promoting Democracy," *Foreign Policy,* no. 87 (Summer 1992): 25–46, and "Promoting Democracy in the 1990s" in Axel Hadenius, *Democracy's Victory and Crisis: Nobel Symposium 1994* (Cambridge: Cambridge University Press, forthcoming); Thomas Carothers, "The NED [National Endowment for Democracy] at 10," *Foreign Policy,* no. 95 (Summer 1994): 123–138; and Joel D. Barkan, "Can Established Democracies Nurture Democracy Abroad? Lessons from Africa," in Hadenius, *Democracy's Victory and Crisis.*

149. Dahl, *Polyarchy,* p. 197.

150. See, for example, Rustow, "Transitions to Democracy"; O'Donnell, Schmitter, and Whitehead, *Transitions from Authoritarian Rule;* Adam Przeworski, "Democracy as a Contingent Outcome of Conflicts," in Jon Elster and Rune Slagstad, eds., *Constitutionalism and Democracy* (Cambridge: Cambridge University Press, 1988) pp. 59–80; Michael G. Burton and John Higley, "Elite Settlements," *American Sociological Review* 52 (1987): 295–307; John Higley and Michael G. Burton, "The Elite Variable in Democratic Transitions and Breakdowns," *American Sociological Review* 54 (1989): 17–32; Terry Lynn Karl, "Dilemmas of Democratization in Latin America," *Comparative Politics* 23, no. 1 (October 1990): 1–21, republished in Dankwart A. Rustow and Kenneth Paul Erickson, *Comparative Political Dynamics: Global Research Perspectives* (New York: HarperCollins, 1991), pp. 163–191; Giuseppe Di Palma, *To Craft Democracy: An Essay on Democratic Transitions* (Berkeley: University of California Press, 1990); and Gary Marks, "Rational Sources of Chaos in Democratic Transitions," in Marks and Diamond, *Reexamining Democracy,* pp. 47–69.

151. Karl, "Dilemmas of Democratization in Latin America" (1991 publication), p. 171.

152. Linz and Stepan, *Problems of Democratic Transition and Consolidation,* Chapter 1.

153. On the latter, see Linz, "State Building and Nation Building," especially pp. 360–362.

154. On the need to "constitutionalize" revolution and regime change early and wisely, see Bruce Ackerman, *The Future of the Liberal Revolution* (New Haven: Yale University Press, 1992), Chapter 4.

155. Huntington, *The Third Wave,* pp. 284–287.

156. Pasquino, "Italy: The Twilight of the Parties," and "The Birth of the Second Republic"; and Frank McNeil, "Japan's New Politics," *Journal of Democracy* 5, no. 1 (January 1994): 5–17, and "The Rock of Sisyphus or Road to Reform," *Journal of Democracy* 5, no. 3 (July 1994): 101–106.

157. Hans-Dieter Klingemann and Richard I. Hofferbert, "Germany: A New 'Wall in the Mind'?" *Journal of Democracy* 5, no. 1 (January 1994): 30–44.

158. On the decline of civic engagement in U.S. politics, government, and civil society, see Robert D. Putnam, "Bowling Alone: America's Declining Social Capital," *Journal of Democracy* 6, no. 1 (January 1995): 65–78.

2

Chile:
Origins and Consolidation of
a Latin American Democracy

Arturo Valenzuela

With the inauguration of President Eduardo Frei Ruiz-Tagle on March 11, 1994, the Chilean people witnessed the installation of the second democratic administration since the sixteen-year-long dictatorship of Augusto Pinochet. Frei's predecessor, Patricio Aylwin Azocar, who gained the presidency when the general lost a plebiscite on his continued rule, successfully steered the country back to civilian rule, reestablishing the democratic traditions that had set Chile apart from most of its neighbors on the South American continent.

Before the 1973 breakdown of democracy, which led to the longest and most brutal authoritarian interlude in the nation's history, Chile would have been classified, following the criteria used by the editors of this book, as a high success, a stable and uninterrupted case of democratic rule. For most of the preceding one hundred years, Chilean politics had been characterized by a high level of party competition and popular participation, open and fair elections, and strong respect for democratic freedoms. Indeed, Bollen, in one of the most comprehensive cross-national efforts to rank countries on a scale of political democracy, placed Chile in the top 15 percent in 1965, a score higher than that of the United States, France, Italy, or West Germany. For 1960, Chile's score was higher than that of Britain.[1]

However, synchronic studies such as Bollen's fail to account for the fact that Chile's democratic tradition was not a recent phenomenon but goes back several generations. In the nineteenth century, Chile developed democratic institutions and procedures, setting the country apart from many of its European counterparts, as well as its Latin American neighbors. As Epstein has noted, in Europe "political power was not often effectively transferred from hereditary rulers to representative assemblies no matter how narrow their electorates until late in the nineteenth century."[2] By contrast, Chile had, by the turn of the century, experienced several decades in which political

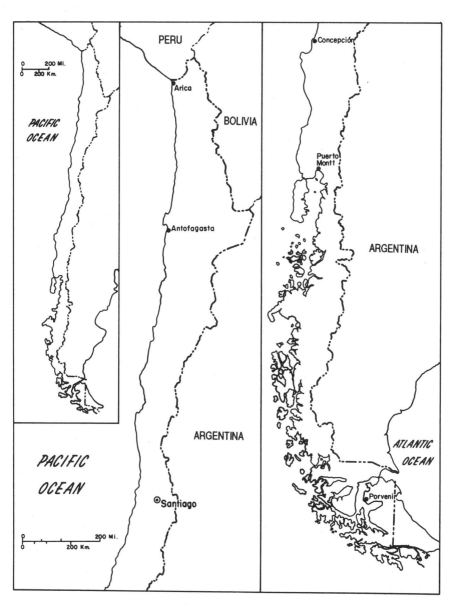

CHILE

authority was vested in elected presidents, and Congress wielded substantial influence over the formulation of public policy.[3] Indeed, from 1830 until 1973, all Chilean presidents were followed in office by their duly elected successors. Deviations to this pattern occurred only in 1891, in the aftermath of a brief civil war, and in the turbulent period between 1924 and 1932, when four chief executives felt pressured to resign in an atmosphere of political and social unrest and military involvement in politics. In 143 years, Chile experienced only thirteen months of unconstitutional rule under some form of junta, and only four months under a junta dominated exclusively by the military. And, though the executive was preeminent in the decades after independence, Congress gradually increased its prerogatives, becoming an important arena for national debate and one of the most powerful legislatures in the world.

Dahl has noted that the development of democracy entails not only establishing institutions for public contestation and leadership renewal, but also popular sovereignty.[4] In nineteenth-century Chile, citizenship was sharply restricted, first to men who owned property and later to those who were literate. Thus, Chile was only a partial democracy, according to the definition used here, until well into the twentieth century, when women's suffrage was established, the literacy requirement abolished, and eighteen-year-olds given the right to vote.[5] It must be stressed, however, that Chile did not deviate substantially from other nascent democracies in extending citizenship. In 1846, only 2 percent of the Chilean population voted, but this figure was comparable to that in Britain in 1830, Luxembourg in 1848, the Netherlands in 1851, and Italy in 1871. In 1876, two years after it had abolished the property requirement, Chile had 106,000 registered voters, compared to 84,000 in Norway for a comparable adult male population. Secret voting was established in Chile shortly after its adoption in Britain, Sweden, and Germany, and before its adoption in Belgium, Denmark, France, Prussia, and Norway.[6]

Reflecting the profound social changes brought about by urbanization, incipient industrialization, and a booming export economy, Chile's middle- and then working-class groups were incorporated into the democratic political game by the second decade of the twentieth century. With the rise of an organized left, Chilean politics became sharply polarized between vastly different conceptions of what the country's future should be. This division, articulated by powerful and institutionalized parties functioning within the framework of Chile's presidential system, placed increasing strains on democracy. In the 1970s, these strains contributed to the breakdown of democracy soon after the first leftist candidate in Chilean history had been elected to the nation's highest office.

The years of military rule had a profound effect on the life of the nation. Chile, one of the most politicized and participatory countries in the world, became one of the most depoliticized. Political parties were banned or dismantled, their leaders killed, exiled, or persecuted. Representative institutions including the national congress and local governments were closed down, with all authority devolving on a four-person military junta dominated increasingly by army commander Pinochet.

The junta sought to change the underlying physiognomy of national politics convinced that the leaders, parties, and ideologies of the past could be rendered obsolete by a combination of harsh discipline and revolutionary economic and social policies. Blaming Chile's woes not only on the Marxist regime of Salvador Allende but also on Chile's statist and protectionist policies forged over several administrations, the junta slashed state subsidies and government spending, dramatically lowering tariff barriers to encourage export-led economic growth.

Although the social costs were extremely high, by the mid-1980s Chile's military rulers succeeded in setting the country on a course of dynamic development. Pinochet failed, however, to eliminate the parties and politicians he held responsible for the nation's shortcomings. They were far more rooted in society than the military leaders had believed; they gradually rebuilt their ties to militants and followers and stunned Pinochet by defeating him decisively in his own prearranged plebiscite on September 11, 1988.

To accomplish this historic event, however, party leaders were forced to moderate their ideological disputes and forge a new consensus aimed at making democracy work. The hard lessons of the hyper-polarization of the 1960s and the repressive years of military rule contributed to the development of a strong and cohesive multiparty coalition that formed the base of support for the government of Patricio Aylwin, inaugurated on March 11, 1990.

This chapter begins with a historical overview of the major trends in Chilean politics. It is not intended to cover all periods in equal depth; rather, it gives disproportionate attention to those historical developments that are especially important in formulating analytical arguments about the development and breakdown of Chilean democracy. Following this is a theoretical assessment of the applicability to the Chilean case of several leading hypotheses generated by social scientists to account for the emergence of democratic politics. The third part analyzes the breakdown of democracy, highlighting those variables that best explain the complex process resulting in the 1973 military coup. The fourth gives an overview of military rule in Chile, explaining how authoritarian politics was first institutionalized and why the transition back to democracy was so slow and painful. It ends with a brief evolution of the first civilian administration after the end of military rule and an assessment of the future course of Chilean democracy.

Historical Overview

Origins and Consolidation of Chilean Democracy, 1830s–1960s

As in the rest of Latin America, attempts in Chile to inaugurate republican institutions, based on democratic principles inspired by the framers of the U.S. Constitution, met with resounding failure.[7] For a quarter-century after Chile's declaration of independence from Spain in 1810, the new nation alternated between dictatorship and anarchy. The war of independence was a prolonged and bloody civil "war to the death," as much as a war to end colonial rule, as many Chileans supported the royalist cause. The final defeat of Spanish forces left the territory's administrative and governing institutions in shambles, and local elites bitterly divided by regional, family, ideological, and personal disputes. Gone were the complex, far-flung patrimonial bureaucracy and the mediating power of the Crown, which for centuries had imposed a traditional style of political authority over a distant colony. In 1830, the clear military victory of one coalition of forces permitted the inauguration of a concerted effort to institute political order and encourage economic progress. However, despite the able leadership of Cabinet Minister Diego Portales and military President Joaquín Prieto, and the establishment of a new constitution in 1833, coup attempts and conspiracies continued to plague Chile; Portales himself was assassinated in 1837 by troops he had thought loyal.

Portales's death was widely, though probably erroneously, blamed on interference in Chilean affairs by General Andrés Santa Cruz, the ruler of the Peru-Bolivia Confederation and a powerful rival for hegemony in Pacific commerce. The Bolivian dictator, after gaining control over Peru, had made no secret of his ambition to extend his empire southward. In response, Portales engineered, in 1836, a declaration of war, an unpopular move widely condemned in political circles. Ironically, Portales's death helped galvanize support for the war among disparate Chilean political factions; incensed at foreign intervention, several groups agreed to back an expeditionary force to Peru.

The war effort and the resounding victory achieved by the Chilean military had a profound impact. Individuals of all stations enthusiastically welcomed home the returning expeditionary force. The victory ball at the presidential palace was attended by rival families who had not spoken to each other in years, helping to heal long-standing wounds and forge a sense of common purpose. In the wake of triumph, authorities decreed a broad amnesty and the restitution of military ranks and pensions for those defeated in the civil war of 1830. As historian Encina notes, defeat of the Chilean forces would have magnified political divisions and seriously imperiled the already tenuous governmental stability. Military success gave the Prieto government and Chile's fledgling institutions a new lease on life.[8]

The 1837–1838 war had another, equally important consequence for Chile's political development. It created a national hero, the first Chilean leader to rise unambiguously above factional disputes. General Manuel Bulnes, the embodiment of national unity, was easily able to succeed Prieto in the presidential elections of 1840, a transition facilitated by Prieto's willingness to leave office in favor of his nephew. In his two terms, Bulnes took two important steps to implement the principles set forth in the nation's republican constitution, principles that were nothing less than revolutionary at the time.[9]

In the first place, Bulnes refused to rule autocratically, giving substantial authority to a designated cabinet carefully balanced to represent some of the most important factions of the loose governing coalition. And though executive power was paramount, Bulnes permitted growing autonomy of the courts and the legislature. In time, Congress became increasingly more assertive, delaying approval of budget laws in exchange for modifications in cabinet policy. The cabinet's response to growing congressional activism was not to silence the institution but to capture it by manipulating the electoral process. Ironically, while this practice was condemned by opponents as a perversion of suffrage, it contributed to reinforcing the legitimacy of the legislature as a full-fledged branch of government. Eventually, as presidents changed ministers or as political coalitions shifted, even legislatures originally elected through fraud became centers for the expression of opposition sentiments, reinforcing presidential accountability to legislative majorities.

In the second place, Bulnes firmly exchanged his role as commander-in-chief of the armed forces for that of civilian president. Under his guidance, the professional military was sharply cut back, its personnel thinned out, and many of its assets sold. Instead, and to the dismay of his former military colleagues, Bulnes poured resources into the National Guard, a force of citizen soldiers closely tied to the government patronage network, who served as a ready pool of voters for government-sponsored candidates. In his last presidential address to the nation, Bulnes proudly described the reduction of the regular army and the expansion of the militia as the most convincing evidence of his administration's fidelity to republican institutions.[10]

The transition to a new president, however, was not easy. Many of the country's elites rejected the candidacy of Manuel Montt, a civil servant and cabinet minister of middle-class extraction, to succeed Bulnes. His candidacy was also rejected by elements in the professional army, who believed Bulnes would support a revolt to prevent Montt's accession to power and thus ensure the continuity of leadership from his native area of Concepción. When a revolt was attempted, however, Bulnes personally led the National Guard to defeat the rebel forces.

With the mid-nineteenth-century development of a new class of government functionaries and political leaders who espoused the liberal creed, the state gained substantial autonomy from the traditional landed elite, the pillar of social and economic power. State autonomy was reinforced by the government's success in promoting economic progress, particularly the booming export trade in wheat and minerals, which encouraged economic elites to give the authorities substantial leeway in policy formulation and implementation. Just as important, however, the export-import trade gave the authorities a ready and expanding source of income from customs duties, without their having to make the politically risky decision to tax property or income. Ironically, had the Chilean economy been more balanced and less dependent on foreign trade, the state would have been much more vulnerable to the immediate and direct pressures of economic elites. In Chile, economic "dependency" contributed to strengthening, not weakening, the state.[11] From 1830 to 1860, customs revenues, which represented 60 percent of all revenues, increased sevenfold, enabling the Chilean state to undertake extensive public-works projects, including constructing Latin America's second railroad, and to invest large sums of money in education, which officials believed to be the key to prosperity and national greatness.

In time, however, the state, rapidly extending its administrative jurisdiction and public-works projects throughout the national territory and actively promoting domestic programs in education and civil registries, clashed sharply with landowners, the church, and regional interests. Discontent in the ranks of the conservative landed elite was such that it led to the formation of the country's first real party, the Conservative Party, in direct opposition to Montt's administration. The Conservatives were committed to preserving the traditional order, and defending the values and interests of the church. At the same time, and also in opposition to the state, a group of ideological liberals, influenced by the Revolution of 1848 in France, pressed to accelerate secularization and decentralization and to expand suffrage and democratization. The secular-religious issue, with state elites taking a middle ground, would become the most salient political cleavage in nineteenth-century Chile, and the basis for crystalizing partisan alignments.

By 1859, discontent with the government from various quarters was such that a disparate coalition, composed of aristocratic Conservatives, regional groups, and the newly formed Radical Party representing the anticlerical and mining interests, challenged the government by force. In particular, the dissidents objected to the widespread state intervention in the 1858 congressional election, in which the government obtained a large majority in the Chamber of Deputies. Once again, however, state officials, with strong support from provincial interests and urban groups, were able to make use of the National Guard to put down the revolt. In the process, they put to rest the lingering center-periphery cleavages that had challenged central authority from the days of independence. The new president, following earlier precedents, granted a national amnesty and incorporated many dissidents into policymaking positions. Even the Radical Party obtained congressional representation in the next election.

The monopoly that the government had obtained over the country's most effective fighting forces made it difficult for Conservatives and other opposition elements to contemplate victory through armed challenge. Because of official intervention in the electoral process, moreover, opponents were unable to wrest control of the state from incumbents. Ironically, Conservatives soon realized that they had no choice but to push for expanded suffrage if they were to succeed in capturing the state. Even more oddly, in opposing the government they structured alliances of convenience in Congress with their nemeses, the staunchly ideological liberals, who were worried about electoral intervention and the authorities' refusal to press for increased democratization. This strategic adoption of a "liberal" creed by conservative forces in a traditional society explains one of the most extraordinary paradoxes of Chilean history: the legislative alliance of ultramontane Catholics and radical liberals, both seeking for different reasons the fulfillment of democratic ideals.

Clearly, the Conservatives did not become democrats because of an ideological conversion, though many with close ties to England had come to believe that parliamentary government was a requirement for any civilized nation-state. But they correctly perceived that representative institutions were in their best interest, and the only real alternative once military solutions to domestic conflicts no longer seemed viable. Conservatives were forced to make the liberal creed their own precisely because they had lost ground to a new political class, which had gained strength by dominating the state. In turn, the pragmatic "liberals" (known as the Montt-Varistas) were not acting irrationally when they resisted attempts to expand suffrage and bar official manipulation of the electoral process. They fully realized that in an overwhelmingly rural society, with traditional landlord-peasant relationships, the Conservatives would beat them at the polls and challenge their monopoly of power.[12]

Under the leadership of Conservative José Manuel Irarrazaval, who became a champion of electoral reform, the right sought to advance its interests through the democratic electoral process, rather than through military conspiracies or direct ties with elements of the central bureaucracy, as was the case in many other countries at the time. As a result, the church, hostile to electoral democracy in much of Latin Europe, also came to accept the legitimacy of suffrage in generating public officials. From a position of strength in Congress, the Conservatives, together with Radicals and ideological liberals and over the objections of the executive, successfully pressed for a series of reforms that restricted presidential power. The president was limited to a single five-year term, and his veto power was restricted. The adoption of the Electoral Reform Act in 1874 tripled the electorate from 50,000 to 150,000 voters over the 1872 total.[13]

Nevertheless, official intervention in the electoral process did not end with electoral reform, and the stakes in controlling the state continued to increase. With its victory in the War of the Pacific (1879–1883), Chile gained vast new territory and rich nitrate deposits. Customs duties climbed to over 70 percent of government income, eliminating the need for property taxes and swelling state coffers. President José Manuel Balmaceda (1886–1891) refused to give in to congressional demands that ministers serve with congressional approval. He also balked at proposals that local governments be given substantial autonomy from the central administration, and that local notables be given control of the electoral process. When his cabinet was censured, Balmaceda sought to govern without congressional approval, adopting the national budget by decree. Finally, a civil war broke out between Congress, backed by the navy, and the president, backed by the army; Balmaceda was defeated in August 1891 and committed suicide.

With the country in disarray and the president dead, a junta headed by a navy captain, the vice-president of the Senate, and the president of the Chamber of Deputies assumed control of the government for three months. This marked the first time since 1830 that political power had been exercised in a manner not prescribed by the constitution. But the brief period of unconstitutional rule did not involve imposing an authoritarian regime, nor did the military as an institution involve itself in politics except to take orders from civilian leaders. The cabinet continued to be a civilian cabinet, and Congress remained in session with virtually no interruption.

The victory of the congressional forces ushered in almost four decades of parliamentary government (1891–1927), in which the center of gravity of the political system shifted from the executive to the legislature, from the capital to local areas, and from state officials and their agents to local party leaders and political brokers. Politics became an elaborate log-rolling game centered in Congress, in which national resources were divided for the benefit of local constituents. Democratization, implied by these changes, had important effects on the political system. With the expansion of suffrage and local control of elections, parliamentary parties expanded beyond the confines of congressional corridors and became national networks with grassroots organizations.

Just as significant, however, was the emergence of parties outside the congressional arena (in Duverger's terms) in response to increased democratization and to other dramatic changes taking place in Chilean society.[14] While the Conservatives initially gained from electoral reform and were able to dominate the politics of the Parliamentary Republic, they did not foresee that the country's social structure would change so quickly in a quarter-century, and that electoral reform would soon benefit a new group of parties with far different agendas. The urban population, which accounted for 26 percent of the total in 1875, had soared to 45 percent by 1900. Nitrate production, employing between 10 and 15 percent of the population, spawned a host of ancillary industries and created a new working class, which soon found expression in new political parties when the traditional parties, particularly the modern Radicals, failed to provide the leadership required to address its grievances.

Both the state and private employers were slow to recognize the legitimacy of working-class demands and often brutally repressed the infant labor movement. But the openness of the political system, and the sharp competition among traditional parties searching for alliances to maximize electoral gain, permitted the development of electorally oriented class-based parties. By 1921, the year the Chilean Communist Party was officially founded, it had elected two members to Congress; four years later, it achieved representation in the Senate. Thus, to the secular-religious cleavage of the nineteenth century was added the worker-employer cleavage of the early twentieth century—generative cleavages that would shape the basic physiognomy of Chile's contemporary party system.

The 1920s were years of considerable political upheaval. The invention of synthetic nitrates during World War I led to the collapse of the Chilean nitrate industry, with far-reaching ramifications for the whole economy. The cumbersome and venal Parliamentary Republic fell increasingly into disrepute, criticized by the right for allowing politics to become corrupt and overly democratic; denounced by the center and left for its inability to address national problems. President Arturo Alessandri (1920–1924) violated political norms by becoming an activist president and pressing for change in the face of congressional inaction and opposition. In September 1924, a group of young military officers unsheathed their swords in the congressional galleries, demanding reforms and the defeat of a congressional pay increase. Bowing to the unprecedented pressure, Alessandri resigned his post and left the country in the hands of a military junta—the first time in over 100 years that military men had played a direct role in governing the nation.

Senior officers, however, objected to the reform agenda of their younger colleagues; uncomfortable with the responsibility of governing, they soon began to defer to civilian leaders of the right. This prompted a national movement to have Alessandri return, backed by younger officers who identified with the September *pronunciamiento*. In January 1925, the president resumed his position, marking the end of the first extraconstitutional government since 1891. During Alessandri's term, the 1925 Constitution was adopted with the expectation that it would increase the power of the president. It was the first full reform of the basic document since the Constitution of 1833, but it also embodied many elements of continuity.

Alessandri's elected successor, Emiliano Figueroa, proved unable to stand up to political pressures and the growing influence of Minister of War Colonel Carlos Ibañez, a military officer who had participated in the 1924 movement. In 1927 Figueroa resigned, and Ibañez was elected with broad support from all major parties, who sensed the country's and the military's demand for a "nonpolitical" and forceful chief executive. During his administration, Ibañez sought to alter fundamentally Chilean politics by introducing "efficient and modern" administrative practices, disdaining the role of Congress in cabinet appointments and resorting to emergency and executive measures, such as forced exile, in attempting to crush labor and opposition political parties. It is important to stress, however, that Ibañez's government was not a military dictatorship. While his authority derived in large measure from support in the barracks, army officers did not govern. The vast majority of cabinet officials were civilians, though most were newcomers to politics who criticized the intrigues of the traditional political class.

Ibañez soon discovered that he, too, could run out of political capital. His inability to curb the influence of parties, and his growing isolation, combined with the catastrophic effects of the Great Depression (in which Chilean exports dropped to a fifth of their former value) and mounting street unrest, finally led the demoralized president to submit his resignation in July 1931. After a period of political instability, which included the resignation of yet another president and the ninety-day "Socialist Republic" proclaimed by a civil/military junta that attempted to press for social change, elections were scheduled in 1932. Once again, Arturo Alessandri was elected to a full constitutional term, thereby restoring the continuity of Chile's institutional system. During his second administration, Alessandri was far more cautious than during his first, successfully bringing the country out of the depression with firm austerity measures and reaffirming the value of institutions based on democratic values and procedures at a time when they were under profound attack in Europe.

The 1938 presidential election represented another major turning point in Chilean politics and a vivid confirmation of the extent to which ordinary citizens had become the fundamental source of political authority. In an extremely close election, the center, in a Popular Front alliance with the Marxist left, captured the presidency, and Radical Pedro Aguirre Cerda was elected. Despite the often bitter opposition of the right, the government for a decade expanded social-welfare policies, encouraged the rise of legal unionism, and actively pursued import-substituting industrialization through a new Corporación de Fomento de la Producción (Corporation for the Development of Production). The trend toward urbanization continued: in 1940, 53 percent of the population lived in cities; by 1970, that figure had increased to 76 percent.

By 1948, the new Cold War climate abroad and the increased local electoral successes of the Communist Party were making both Socialists and Radicals increasingly uneasy. Encouraged by Radical leaders, President Gabriel González Videla dissolved the Popular Front, outlawed the Communist Party, and sent many of its members to detention camps. These actions, combined with the wear of incumbency and general dissatisfaction with the opportunistic Radicals, contributed to the election of Carlos Ibañez as president in 1952 on an anti-party platform. But Ibañez, unable to govern without party support, was forced to shift his initial populist programs to a severe austerity plan that contributed to wage and salary declines. He was succeeded in 1958 by conservative businessman Jorge Alessandri, the former president's son, who edged out socialist Salvador Allende by only 2.7 percent of the vote. Alessandri applied more austerity measures, provoking cries for profound reform from a populace tired of spiraling inflation and economic stagnation. In the 1964 presidential elections, fear of the growing strength of the left led Chile's traditional rightist parties to reluctantly support Eduardo Frei, the candidate of the new Christian Democratic Party, which had replaced the Radicals as the largest party in Chile and the most powerful party of the center. With massive financial assistance from the United States, the Frei government attempted to implement far-reaching reforms, but after dissolving their tacit alliance with the right, the Christian Democrats were unable to increase their share of the vote. In 1970, claiming to have been betrayed by Frei's reformist policies, the right refused to support Christian Democratic candidate Radomiro Tomic, making possible the election of leftist candidate Salvador Allende and his Popular Unity coalition, with only 36.2 percent of the vote. The Christian Democratic and Popular Unity governments are treated in more detail in the discussion of the breakdown of Chilean democracy, below.

Characteristics of Chilean Politics at Mid-Century[15]

By the 1930s, with the rise of Marxist parties at a time of electoral expansion, the Chilean party system, in Lipset and Rokkan's terms, had become complete.[16] In addition to the traditional Conservative and Liberal parties that had emerged from church-state cleavages in the early nineteenth century, and the Radical Party that had developed later in that century out of similar divisions, Communist and Socialist parties had now developed in response to a growing class cleavage. The only new party to emerge after the 1930s, the Christian Democratic Party, was an offshoot of the Conservatives, which sought to address social and economic issues from the vantage point of reform Catholicism.

Yet this "complete" system was characterized by sharp social polarizations in which the organized electorate was divided almost equally among the three political tendencies. Although numerous small parties appeared after 1932, the six major parties continued to dominate politics, commanding over 80 percent of the vote by the 1960s. Elections and politics became a national "sport," as parties became so deeply ingrained in the nation's social fabric that Chileans would refer to a Radical or a Communist or a Christian Democratic "subculture." Parties helped to structure people's friendships and social life. Partisan affiliation continued to be reinforced by both class and religion, so that Christian Democratic elites were more likely to go to Catholic schools and universities and come from upper-middle-class backgrounds, while Socialist elites went to public schools and state universities and came from lower-middle-class backgrounds. Communist strength was heavily concentrated in mining communities and industrial areas, Christian Democrats appealed to middle-class and women voters, while the right retained substantial support in rural Chile.

The major parties framed political options not only in municipal and congressional elections but also in private and secondary associations. The penetration of parties into Chilean society was such that even high school student associations, community groups, universities, and professional societies selected leaders on party slates. Political democracy helped democratize social groups and erode historic patterns of authoritarian social relations.

It is crucial to stress that there were no giants in the Chilean political system. No single party or tendency could win a majority and impose its will. This pattern had clear implications for the functioning of Chile's presidential system.

Since majorities were impossible to achieve, Chilean presidents were invariably elected by coalitions or were forced to build governing coalitions with opposing parties in Congress after the election. However, because pre-election coalitions were constituted primarily for electoral reasons, in an atmosphere of considerable political uncertainty, they tended to disintegrate after a few months of the new administration.

Ideological disputes were often at the root of coalition changes, as partisans of one formula would resist the proposals of opponents. But narrow political considerations were also important. Since a president could not succeed himself, leaders of other parties in his coalition often realized they could best improve their fortunes in succeeding municipal and congressional elections by disassociating themselves from the difficulties of incumbency in a society fraught with economic problems. In the final analysis, only by proving their independent electoral strength in nonpresidential elections could parties demonstrate their value to future presidential coalitions.

Since Chilean presidents could not dissolve Congress in case of an impasse or loss of congressional support, they needed to build alternative alliances in order to govern. Parties assured their influence by requiring that candidates nominated for cabinet posts seek their party's permission (*pase*) to serve in office. Presidents, required continually to forge working coalitions, were repeatedly frustrated by the sense of instability and permanent crisis that this bargaining process gave Chilean politics.

An image of Chile's party system as excessively competitive and polarized, however, is incomplete and inaccurate. The collapse of party agreements, the censure of ministers, and the sharp disagreement over major policy issues captured the headlines and inflamed people's passions. But the vast majority of political transactions were characterized by compromise, flexibility, and respect for the institutions and procedures of constitutional democracy. Over the years, working agreements among political rivals led to implementing far-reaching policies, including state-sponsored industrialization; comprehensive national health, welfare, and educational systems; agrarian reform; and copper nationalization. Agreements were also structured around the more mundane aspects of politics. Congressmen and party leaders of different stripes would join in efforts to promote a particular region or to provide special benefits to constituency groups and individuals.[17]

This pattern of give-and-take can be attributed to three mutually reinforcing factors: a pragmatic center; the viability of representative arenas of decisionmaking and neutrality of public institutions; and the imperatives of electoral politics. Compromise would have been difficult without the flexibility provided by center parties, notably the Radical Party, which inherited the role of the nineteenth-century Liberals as the fulcrum of coalition politics. The Radicals supported, at one time or another, the rightist presidencies of the two Alessandris in the 1930s and 1960s and governed with support of the right in the late 1940s. In the late 1930s and through most of the 1940s, however, they allied with the left to form Popular Front governments under a Radical president, and in the 1970s, a substantial portion of the party supported Salvador Allende, though by then the party's strength had been severely eroded.

Accommodation and compromise were also the hallmarks of democratic institutions such as the Chilean Congress, whose lawmaking, budgetary, and investigatory powers provided incentives for party leaders to set aside disagreements in matters of mutual benefit. Indeed, the folkways of the legislative institution, stemming from years of close working relationships in committees and on the floor, contributed to the development of legendary private friendships among leaders who were strong public antagonists. Just as significant, however, were such prestigious institutions as the armed forces, the judiciary, and the comptroller general, respected for their "neutrality" and remoteness from the clamor of everyday politics. These institutions provided an important safety valve from the hyperpoliticization of most of public life. The legitimacy of public institutions was further reinforced by a strong commitment to public service, which extended from the presidential palace to the rural police station. Although electoral fraud and vote-buying by political party machines were common, financial corruption remained very rare in Chilean public life, and the vigilance of the Congress and the courts helped prevent wrongdoing for personal gain by public office-holders.

Finally, the press of continuous elections forced political leaders to turn away from ideological pursuits and attend to the more mundane side of politics, such as personal favors and other particularistic tasks inherent in a representative system. Congressmen and senators had to look after their party brokers in municipalities and neighborhoods, making sure to provide public funds for a local bridge or jobs for constituents. Often political leaders from different parties joined in advancing the common interests of their constituencies, setting aside acrimonious, abstract debates over the role of the state in the economy or Soviet policy in Asia. In Chile, the politics of ideology, rooted in strong social inequalities, was counterbalanced by the clientelistic politics of electoral accountability reinforced by that same inequality. As will be noted below, many of these elements disappeared during the later 1960s and early 1970s, putting the democratic system under great strain and ultimately contributing to its total collapse.

Origins of Chilean Democracy:
A Theoretical Assessment

Because it is one of the few cases in which a democratic government was successfully established in the mid-nineteenth century, and an especially dramatic example of democratic failure, Chile constitutes a valuable paradigmatic case in the effort to construct theoretical propositions explaining the origins, consolidation, and breakdown of democratic regimes. Its theoretical utility is enhanced by the fact that there are no comparable cases of democratic development outside the Western European–North American context, or among primarily Catholic or export-oriented countries. As a deviant case, which has been largely neglected in scholarly literature, Chile can serve as a useful test for the validity of theoretical propositions generated by observing the experience of other countries, primarily European.[18]

The most prominent theses aimed at explaining the development of democracy assume that political practices and institutions can be understood by reference to a series of historical, cultural, or economic determinants. It is the central argument of this chapter that such approaches fall short in accounting for Chilean exceptionality, and that the Chilean case can be best explained by considering political factors as independent variables in their own right. This section will review the "determinants" of democracy embodied in what can be called the colonial-continuity thesis, the political-culture thesis, and the economic-class-structure thesis.[19] It will then turn to an analysis of those political variables that are most helpful in understanding Chile's political evolution, variables that can add to the development of theoretical propositions to be tested in other contexts.

Naturally, any hypotheses derived from the Chilean case or any single case will remain tentative until subjected to systematic comparative analysis drawing on a broader sample of carefully chosen observations. Without comparative evidence it would be difficult to identify those factors that are generalizable and constitute necessary conditions for the development of democratic practices and institutions, and those that are unique to and ultimately incorrect for explaining the single case.

The Colonial-Continuity Thesis

According to the colonial-continuity thesis, democratic practices will flourish in postcolonial regimes if institutions for self-rule, even if limited, were in place for several generations during colonial times, and if the transition from colony to independent state was accomplished without too much violence and destruction of those institutions. Both these conditions figure prominently in accounts of the outcome of the British decolonization experiences of the eighteenth and twentieth centuries.[20] It is clear that this thesis cannot account for the Chilean case. Although Chile was a more isolated colony than the major centers of Spanish rule in the new world, there is no evidence that the colony was able to gain the necessary autonomy to develop institutions of self-rule that would carry it into the postindependence period. Chile was subject to the same patrimonial administration and mercantilistic policies that discouraged expressions of political or economic independence and frowned on participatory institutions as contrary to the fundamental conception of monarchical rule. The colonies were the personal property of the king, subject to his direct control. Moreover, the Chilean wars of independence were profoundly disruptive of the previous political order, plunging the nation into a fratricidal conflict that tore asunder institutions and political practices that had been in place for generations. Although Chileans later established democratic rule, this accomplishment had little to do with the political experiences gained in colonial times.[21]

There is, however, a variant of the continuity thesis that must be addressed because it constitutes the principal explanation found in the historiographical literature dealing with Chilean exceptionality. According to this thesis, Chile deviated from the pattern that held sway in nineteenth-century Latin America not because its colonial institutions were more liberal, but because its postindependence institutions were more conservative. This argument holds that Diego Portales, the cabinet minister who dominated the government of President Prieto during the 1830s, helped to establish firm and authoritarian rule equivalent to that of the Spanish Crown during the colonial era, thus rescuing Chile from misguided liberals enamored with unrealistic federal formulae and excessive freedoms.[22] Chile succeeded not because it broke from the colonial past, this argument holds, but because it reimposed that past. Morse articulates the point:

> Chile was an example perhaps unparalleled of a Spanish American country which managed, after a twelve-year transitional period, to avoid the extremes of tyranny and anarchy with a political system unencumbered by the mechanisms and party rhetoric of exotic liberalism. . . . The structure of the Spanish patrimonial state was recreated with only those minimum concessions to Anglo-French constitutionalism that were necessary for a nineteenth century republic which had just rejected monarchical rule.[23]

It is disingenuous to argue, as most Chileans do, that Portales forged Chile's institutions single-handedly. The minister was in office for only a total of three years, had little to do with drafting the 1833 Constitution, and died in office at a time when his government was under serious challenge.[24] Regardless of Portales's role, it is also profoundly mistaken to argue that Chile's concessions to Anglo-French constitutionalism were minimal. The political system established by the Constitution of 1833 was qualitatively different from the colonial system of the past, bearing far greater resemblance to the institutions and practices followed in the North American colonies, and the compromises struck at the constitutional convention in Philadelphia, than to the institutions set up by the Castilian rulers.

In Weberian terms, Chile's new constitutional formula substituted rational-legal authority for traditional authority; that is, it replaced the authority of a hereditary monarch, whose power was inherent in his person by virtue of divinely ordained practices going back generations, with the authority of an elected president whose power derived from the office as defined by law. Moreover, rather than recreating colonial patterns of political domination, nineteenth-century Chilean politics from the outset expanded the concept of citizenship (a radical notion at the time) and affirmed the legitimacy of elected assemblies to claim political sovereignty equally with the chief executive.

When viewed in this light, the achievements of the forgers of Chilean institutionality are very significant in contrast to those of their North American counterparts, who fashioned their institutions and practices by drawing on generations of experience with self-rule within the political framework of Tudor England.[25]

The Political-Culture Thesis

Perhaps the most influential set of propositions associated with the development of democratic institutions are those that hold that democracy requires a country's citizens, or at the very least its politically active elites, to share the liberal beliefs and values that are the hallmark of the Enlightenment. These include values conducive to accepting the equality of all people and their fundamental worth, values tolerating opposition and the free expression of ideas, and values celebrating the legitimacy of moderation and compromise. In short, they are the values associated with participatory politics as opposed to authoritarian patterns of governance. These political-culture variables have figured prominently in efforts to explain the general failure of democracy in Latin America and in Latin Europe, and the success of democracy in Protestant Europe and the United States. Democracy succeeded in the United States, this argument holds, because the British colonies were populated by settlers already imbued with more egalitarian values stemming from the Enlightenment and the Protestant Reformation. By contrast, the colonizers of Latin America brought aristocratic and feudal values reinforced by a Catholic faith stressing the importance of hierarchy, authority, corporativism, and the immutability of the traditional social order.[26]

But if the absence of democracy in Latin America is explained by the lack of appropriate beliefs, how can we account for the Chilean case? Were Chileans, located in one of the most remote colonies of the empire and dominated by an aristocracy of Basque descent, less tied to royal institutions? Or was the Chilean church more liberal or less influential in the social and political life of the colony? None of the historical evidence supports these contentions. To the contrary, Chile's isolation had made the colony one of the most traditional on the continent. Royalist sentiment was as strong in Chile as anywhere else, and troops who fought with the Spaniards to suppress the insurrection were recruited locally. Similarly, the church was as conservative as in other countries and retained the strong backing of the local aristocracy despite its close ties with the colonial power. Chilean elites were no less Catholic than the political elites of other former colonies.[27]

A variant of the political-culture thesis holds that it is not so much the religious traditions or political practices of the past that condition political beliefs and attitudes, but the authority relations found in secondary spheres of society: the workplace, the family, or the educational system.[28] Of particular importance in a predominantly agricultural society are the social relations of production resulting from the country's land-tenure system. Where land is concentrated in a small number of estates with traditional patron-client authority relations, this thesis argues, political values will be hierarchical and authoritarian. Where land is divided more equally and exploited by family farmers and contract labor, political values will be more egalitarian and democratic, facilitating the development of democratic politics. This is the argument that Booth makes in attempting to account for democratic development in Costa Rica.[29] Dahl echoes this approach when he suggests that the Chilean case can be explained by "considerable equality in distribution of land and instruments of coercion, reinforced by norms favoring social and political equality."[30]

However, Dahl's argument also fails to stand up to historical scrutiny. Chile's system of social relations and stratification was one of the most rigid and traditional on the continent, based on large landed estates and semifeudal relationships of authority between landlord and peasant. Authority relations in the family and in the educational system, still under church tutelage, were also authoritarian and hierarchical.[31] The wars of independence disrupted the country's social structure less than they did elsewhere. As Dominguez notes, "Chile lagged behind the other colonies, although it had experienced economic growth and mobilization. Its society had been transformed the least. The social bonds within it remained strong. Centralization had not been advanced nor had society been pluralized. Traditional elites remained strong, and traditional orientations prevailed."[32] Throughout the nineteenth and well into the twentieth century, the traditional nature of social relations in the countryside remained one of the most striking features of the Chilean social structure. Despite the rise of an urban working class and the democratization of other spheres of social life, rural social relations were not significantly altered until the 1960s, when agrarian reform was finally undertaken as national policy.[33]

There is no reason to assume that the evolution of democratic politics in Chile in the nineteenth century was due to more "favorable" political-culture variables. The failure of cultural explanations to account for the Chilean case raises serious questions about the underlying assumption that there is a direct fit between societal values and political institutions. It is very unlikely that Chile had societal values comparable to those of Norway, Australia, or the United States (though they may not have been too dissimilar to those found in class-conscious Britain), yet the political outcomes were not dissimilar. Several students of democracy have argued that "stable" democracy is the product not only of liberal and participatory values, but of a mixture of participatory and deferential ones. However, in the absence of a clearly defined set of values that relate to democracy, it is difficult to ascertain which mix is appropriate. As a result, there is a real temptation to engage in circular reasoning: If a particular regime was stable or had the requisite democratic characteristics, it was assumed it had ipso facto the appropriate value structure.

Although egalitarian and democratic values were not necessary to structure democratic institutions and procedures, the Chilean case suggests that the exercise of democratic practices over a period of time encourages the development of certain norms of political conduct and reinforces belief in the legitimacy of the rules of the game. As early as the 1850s, Chilean political elites of different ideological persuasions worked together in Congress to advance common objectives, thus developing habits of flexibility and compromise. The Radicals, who were excluded from decisionmaking roles in Argentina until after the 1912 Saenz Peña law, were invited to serve in cabinets fifty years earlier in Chile.

As an industrial working class developed, moreover, Chilean elites, despite serious objections to accepting the principle of collective bargaining at the workplace and brutal repression of the incipient labor movement, accepted the legitimate role of working-class parties in the arena of electoral competition and eventually in the corridors of power. Democratic institutions came to be accepted by most Chileans as the best way to resolve disagreements and set national policy. By the mid-twentieth century, ordinary Chileans took great pride in their civic duties, participating enthusiastically in an electoral process that made Chile distinctive among Third World nations. In sum, Chilean democracy emerged without strongly held democratic values. But the practice of democracy itself instilled norms of give-and-take, tolerance, and respect for fundamental liberties that were widely shared by the population as a whole.[34]

This does not mean that democratic politics in Chile were centrist-oriented and devoid of sharp conflict. In 1891, after thirty years of domestic tranquility, the strongly felt political antagonisms generated by the executive-congressional impasse spilled onto the battlefield, a conflict that nonetheless pales by comparison with the U.S. Civil War, which also took place eighty years after the Declaration of Independence. The deep ideological disagreements of twentieth-century Chile continuously challenged the country's institutions and practices. The Chilean case and those of other highly polarized political systems like Italy, France, and Finland show that consensus on the fundamentals of public policy can be relatively low, while consensus on the rules and procedures for arriving at policy decisions can be high.

It was not moderation that made Chilean democracy function; it was Chilean democracy that helped moderate political passions and manage deep-seated divisions. A democratic political culture is not an abstract set of beliefs or psychological predispositions governing interpersonal relations in the body politic, but practical and ingrained traditions and working relations based on regularized patterns of political interaction in the context of representative institutions. As will be noted below, with the breakdown of democracy, Chile lost not only representative rule, but the institutional fabric that helped define many of the values of democratic human conduct.

The Economic-Class-Structure Thesis

While there is broad variation in studies emphasizing the economic determinants of democracy, they can be divided into two categories: those relating democracy to overall levels of economic development; and those focusing on the contribution to the creation of democratic institutions of particular groups or classes that emerge as a result of economic transformations in society.

The first group draws on the insights of "modernization" theory, arguing that economic development leads to more complex, differentiated, secularized, and educated societies, opening the way for the rise of new groups and institutions that find expression in democratic practices.[35] In addition, economic growth is said to provide channels for upward mobility and for ameliorating the sharp social disparities found in poor societies, disparities that undermine democratic performance. Empirical evidence for these propositions was advanced in a host of cross-national studies conducted in the late 1960s, inspired by Lipset's classic article on the "economic correlates of democracy."[36] The main difficulty with these studies in explaining the Chilean case is that they are ahistorical. Chile in the nineteenth century, like most incipient democracies of the time, was a rural, pre-industrial society with very low levels of personal wealth and literacy, yet it met many of the criteria for democratic performance. In the twentieth century, as several authors have noted, Chile was clearly an outlier, exhibiting many of the characteristics of economic underdevelopment while boasting high scores on democratic performance.[37] As Linz has argued, explanations that draw on levels of economic development do not contribute much to our understanding of the origins and development of democratic politics.[38]

Scholars writing in a Marxist tradition have argued that the most important variable is not overall economic development, but the rise of rural and urban middle classes capable of challenging the monopoly of landed elites and breaking their political power. Based on his reflections on the European case, Therborn attributes the rise of democracy to the emergence of agrarian bourgeois groups, giving particular emphasis to "the strength of these agrarian classes and the degree of their independence from the landowning aristocracy and urban big capital."[39] Moore goes further, presenting a more complex argument. For Moore, as for Therborn, the development of a bourgeoisie was central to the development of democracy. However, whether a country actually followed a democratic path depended on how agriculture was commercialized, whether or not it became "labor repressive" or "market commercial."[40]

As with the political-culture thesis, it is difficult to accept the applicability of the economic-class-structure thesis to the Chilean case. As noted earlier, Chilean agriculture remained "labor repressive" well into the twentieth century, retaining a high concentration of land ownership. And though, as Dominguez notes, Chilean agriculture was geared by the eighteenth century to the export of wheat, wheat production was never commercialized as in North America. As in czarist Russia, it was expanded with only minimal modifications to the traditional manorial system.[41] By the same token, and despite some interpretations of Chilean history that stress the rise of an urban bourgeoisie as the key liberalizing force, Chile did not develop a strong and independent urban-based bourgeoisie before the development of democratic rules and procedures. Although mining interests became powerful and some of the most prominent mine owners were identified with the Radical Party, it is mistaken to identify Chilean mining interests as representatives of a new and differentiated bourgeois class. Other, equally prominent mine owners had close ties to the Conservative Party, and many members of the Chilean elite had both mining and agricultural interests.[42]

However, the most telling argument against the economic-class-structure thesis has already been anticipated in the historical discussion at the beginning of this chapter. The rise of democracy in Chile—including the limitations on presidential authority, the expansion of legislative prerogatives, and the extension of suffrage—took place not over the objections of the conservative landed elites but, as in Britain, at their instigation. If the traditional landowning class, which championed the Roman Catholic church, decided to support suffrage expansion and the development of democratic institutions, then theoretical explanations that hold that democracy emerges only with the destruction of that class are less than adequate. This is a central point, to which we will return.

The Political-Determinants Thesis

An examination of various theses dealing with the historical, cultural, and economic "determinants" of democracy suggests that they are not particularly useful in explaining the Chilean case. What is more, the Chilean case, as one of successful democratic development that does not conform to the principal arguments of those theses, raises serious questions about their overall validity. However, from this evidence alone it would be clearly mistaken to argue that these factors play no substantial role in democratic development. A "liberal" colonial tradition, egalitarian values, economic development, and a variegated social structure are undoubtedly conducive to the implementation and acceptance of institutions of self-governance. Indeed, a perspective such as the one advocated here, the political-determinants thesis, which stresses the importance of discrete political variables and even historical accidents as independent variables, need not eschew the economic and cultural constants nor shy away from developing generalizations that relate socioeconomic to political variables. The point is that these cultural and economic variables are hardly determinants of democratic practices. They may very well be powerful contributory conditions; but they are not necessary or sufficient ones.

A historical review of the development of Chilean political institutions immediately suggests the utility of the "political-crisis" literature developed by political scientists. According to this literature, all countries face severe challenges in developing democratic institutions and, depending on the timing and sequence of those challenges, have greater or lesser success in achieving democratic stability.[43] Although the challenges vary in kind and number, most authors view the crises of national identity (creating a sense of national community over parochial loyalties), authority (establishing viable state structures), and participation (incorporating the citizenry into the political system) as crucial.

In addition, the sequence and timing of the appearance of these problems on the historical scene can seriously affect the political outcome. As Nordlinger puts it, "the probabilities of a political system developing in a nonviolent, non-authoritarian, and eventually democratically viable manner are maximized when a national identity emerges first, followed by the institutionalization of the central government, and then the emergence of mass parties and mass electorate."[44] It can be argued that Chile followed this "optimal" sequence and that the timing was also favorable, particularly with respect to the emergence of the participation crisis, which did not become a critical issue until after central authority structures had been consolidated.[45]

National identity.   It is doubtful that Chileans considered themselves a nation before independence, because there were far fewer mechanisms of social communication and exchange than in North America and a far more ubiquitous set of colonial authority structures.[46] However, the clear-cut military victory in the war against the Peru-Bolivia Confederation, a victory without parallel in Latin America, gave the small, divided nation a powerful new sense of confidence and purpose, creating tangible symbols of patriotism and nationality. These feelings were reinforced with the victory of Chilean forces in the War of the Pacific, which led to the incorporation of large portions of Peruvian and Bolivian territory into national boundaries.

Political authority.   Rustow has noted the importance of distinguishing between establishing and consolidating institutions of democracy. Consolidation involves a lengthy process of "habituation," which is not necessarily unilinear; there can be reversals and even breakdown.[47] In consolidating political authority in Chile, five factors were critically important: leadership; state autonomy; government efficacy; civilian control of the armed forces; and conservative support for democratic rules.

The first important element was leadership. General Bulnes, drawing on his command of the most powerful armed forces in the country and his widespread popularity, could have easily used his position to establish personal rule, following the pattern of notable Latin American *caudillos* such as Paez in Venezuela, Rosas in Argentina, or Santa Ana in Mexico. Instead, like Washington in the United States, he insisted on working within the framework of established political institutions and chose to leave office at the end of his term, making way for his successor. His willingness while in office to underscore the autonomy of the courts, accept the role of Congress in policy, and allow ministerial cabinets to formulate the government's program set a precedent for his successor and future administrations, and helped to establish the legitimacy of democratic institutions.[48]

The second important factor was state autonomy. A crucial legacy of Bulnes's and, later, Montt's respect for constitutionally mandated institutions was the development of politics and government service as a vocation. An impressive group of functionaries and legislators emerged who were committed to strengthening and expanding the secular state. By 1860, more than 2,500 people worked for the state, not including local officials, construction workers, and members of the armed forces. All of Chile's nineteenth-century presidents save one had extensive congressional experience before being elected to office, and five who took office before 1886 began their careers in the Bulnes administration. Between Bulnes and Pinochet, only two of Chile's twenty-two presidents were career military officers, and both of those were freely elected with political-party support in moments of political crisis.[49]

The third element was governmental efficacy. Under the leadership of the first three presidents to serve after 1830, the Chilean economy performed relatively well. This not only brought credit to the new institutions and leaders of the independent nation, but more importantly, it gave the government elites time and autonomy to begin state consolidation. By the time important interests sought to stop the expansion of the secular state, it had garnered significant political, financial, and military strength.[50]

The fourth factor was control of the armed forces by civilian governmental leaders. By deliberately refusing until after the War of the Pacific to create a professional military establishment, while retaining close political control over an effective national militia, Chilean officials were able to establish a monopoly over the control of force and a tradition of civilian supremacy over the military. The military challenges of 1851 and 1859 were defeated, discouraging dissident elites from gathering their own military force to challenge national authority structures.

The fifth factor was conservative support for democratic rules. This factor is directly related to the development of state autonomy and control of the military. Control of the military prevented aggrieved sectors of the elites from resorting to insurrectionary movements in order to prevent state action or to capture the state by force. Thus such elites, including conservative landholders, were forced to turn to democratic procedures already in place, and indeed to seek their expansion, in order to preserve and advance their interests. Far from being a minor footnote in history, this support of the Chilean conservatives for liberal rules was of central importance. It led to the creation of a Conservative Party, committed to representative institutions, which had no exact parallel in Latin America or Latin Europe.

This leads to a basic proposition: that the origins and evolution of democratic institutions and procedures are determined more by the choices made by key elites seeking to maximize their interests within the framework of specific structural and political parameters, than they are by abstract cultural or economic factors. Chilean elites, initially hostile to democracy, came to embrace democratic rules as a conscious choice for political survival, in the process contributing to the strengthening of those institutions over the years.[51] Where political elites have fewer incentives to support democratic institutions, and, in particular, where resorting to force to prevent the distribution of power through the expansion of citizenship is a viable option for those elites, the consolidation of democratic authority structures is seriously jeopardized.

√√ *Participation.*   Perhaps the greatest challenge to the consolidation of stable democracy is the expansion of citizenship rights to non-elite elements, and the incorporation into the political process of new groups and classes. Like

Britain and Norway, but unlike Latin Europe, the consolidation of democratic institutions in Chile benefited from a gradual extension of suffrage, less in response to pressures from below than as a consequence of inter-elite rivalries and strategies to maximize electoral gain. Like Britain, but unlike Latin Europe, Chile found in the elites of the Conservative Party the driving force in the first pivotal extension of suffrage in 1874. This took place a dozen years before the French Third Republic teetered on the brink of collapse with Boulangisme, and twenty-five years before the French right, still resisting republicanism and democracy, became embroiled in the Dreyfus Affair. It also took place forty years before the pope lifted the *non-expedit* that barred Catholics from participating in Italian elections.

The extension of suffrage in Chile clearly benefited the Conservatives who controlled the countryside, but it also benefited middle-class sectors who identified with the growing urban-based Radical Party. Forty-two years before the adoption of the Saenz Peña Law in Argentina, which forced reluctant Conservatives to suddenly expand the electoral system to permit the Radical Party's eruption on the political stage, Chile had initiated the gradual expansion of suffrage, permitting middle-class sectors to become full participants in ministerial and congressional politics.

In a classic case of what Merton calls the unanticipated consequences of purposive social action, the expansion of suffrage in Chile also soon benefited the growing working class.[52] But the entry of the working class into politics in Chile was also gradual, coming both after the consolidation of parliamentary institutions and after middle-class parties had become full actors in the political process. Indeed, in the 1910s, suffrage expansion was actually limited by complex electoral rules and byzantine electoral pacts in which the working-class parties became full participants.

The gradual expansion of suffrage and incorporation of new groups in Chile had some clear implications for the country's democratic development. Had the pressure for full participation coincided with attempts to set up democratic institutions, it is difficult to see how these could have survived. At the same time, however, it is important to stress that in Chile, suffrage expansion and party development occurred prior to the growth of a powerful and centralized state bureaucracy. The growth of the public sector was consequently shaped by organizations whose primary goals were electoral success and accountability. This reinforced the viability of representative institutions. Where strong bureaucracies emerged before strong parties or legislatures, as in Brazil or Argentina, informal or officially sponsored linkage networks without popular representation were much more likely to develop, encouraging corporatist and authoritarian patterns of interest representation.[53]

In sum, the political-determinants thesis suggests that the development of democracy must be understood as a complex process that owes much to fortuitous events and variables, such as leadership, that defy quantification and precise definition. It is a long and difficult course, subject to challenges and reversals as societal conditions and the correlations of political forces change. Its chances of success are better in some contexts than others and may depend on the timing and sequence of fundamental societal challenges.

In the final analysis, however, democracy involves human choice by competing groups and leaders who must determine whether peaceful mechanisms for the resolution of conflict, based on the concept of popular sovereignty, provide them with the best possible guarantees under the circumstances. More often than not, this choice may stem from an inconclusive struggle for power; a situation of stalemate where there are no clear winners. That being so, democracy can be understood as resulting from a set of compromises—second-preference choices—in which the concurrence of non-democrats may be as important as the support of democrats. Once democracy is structured, it provides the key rules of the game, defining the parameters for action and the strategies to be pursued by relevant actors. In time, democratic rules may be accepted as the only proper norms for political conduct, but only if democracy continues to provide guarantees to all politically relevant players, even if it is not the preferred system of all.

The Breakdown of Chilean Democracy

Chilean Politics and the Dialectic of Regime Breakdown

The breakdown of Chilean democracy did not occur overnight. Several developments contributed to the erosion of the country's system of political compromise and accommodation, even before the 1970 election of President Salvador Allende. These included the adoption of a series of reforms aimed at making Chilean politics more "efficient," and the rise of a new and more ideological center, less willing to play the game of political give-and-take.[54]

In 1958, a coalition of the center and left joined in enacting a series of electoral reforms aimed at abolishing what were considered corrupt electoral practices. Among the measures was the abolition of joint lists, a long-established tradition of political pacts that permitted parties of opposing ideological persuasions to structure agreements for mutual electoral benefit. While this reform succeeded in making preelection arrangements less "political," it also eliminated an important tool for cross-party bargaining. More important were reforms aimed at curbing congressional authority, promulgated in the guise of strengthening the executive's ability to deal with Chile's chronic economic troubles. Congressional politics were viewed by chief executives and party elites of various political persuasions as excessively incremental and old-fashioned; the antithesis of modern administrative practices. In the name of modernity, the executive was given control of the budgetary process in 1959, and Congress was restricted in its ability to allocate fiscal resources. Indeed, under the Christian Democratic administration (1964–1970), government technocrats pushed strongly to restrict entirely congressional allocations of funds for small patronage projects, even though these represented an infinitesimal portion of the total budget.

The most serious blow to congressional authority came with the constitutional reforms enacted in 1970, this time through a coalition of the right and center. Among other provisions, the reforms prohibited amendments not germane to a given piece of legislation and sanctioned the use of executive decrees to implement programs approved by the legislature in very broad terms. More significantly, it barred Congress from matters dealing with social security, salary adjustments, and pensions in the private and public sectors—the heart of legislative bargaining in an inflation-ridden society.[55]

These reforms went a long way toward cutting back on many of the traditional sources of patronage and log-rolling, reducing the most important political arena for compromise in Chilean politics. Again, the principal motivation was to strengthen executive efficiency. It is clear, however, that the 1960 reformers were also convinced they would be able to win the 1970 presidential election and did not want to have to deal with a difficult Congress in which the left had a strong presence. Ironically, it was the left that won the presidency, leaving a legislature with reduced powers in the hands of the right and center.

Although these changes were significant, they were symptomatic of other far-reaching changes in Chilean politics, the most notable of which was the rise in the 1960s of a new center party with a markedly different political style. Unlike their predecessor, the pragmatic Radicals, the Chilean Christian Democrats conceived of themselves as a new and vital ideological force in Chilean politics, a middle road between Marxist transformation and preservation of the status quo. The Christian Democrats believed they would be capable of capturing the allegiance of large portions of the electorate from both sides of the political divide, and become a new majority force. In the early 1960s, they began an unprecedented effort at popular mobilization, appealing to women and middle-class voters, as well as factory workers and especially shanty-town dwellers. Their determination to transform the physiognomy of Chilean politics was strengthened by their success in capturing the presidency under the leadership of Eduardo Frei in 1964, in an electoral coalition with the right, and by their impressive victory in the 1965 congressional race, the best showing by a single party in Chile's modern history. Their success presented a serious challenge to the parties of both the right and left. The right was practically obliterated in the 1965 election, while the left redoubled its efforts to maintain its constituents and to appeal with a more militant cry to Chile's most destitute citizens.

Once in office and heartened by their electoral success, the Christian Democrats sought to implement their "revolution in liberty" by disdaining the traditional coalition politics of the past. They were particularly hard on the now-diminished Radicals, refusing any overtures for collaboration. Unlike the Radicals, they were unwilling to tolerate clientelistic and log-rolling politics or to serve as an effective bridge across parties and groups. Although they enacted critical copper "Chileanization" legislation in concert with the right, and agrarian reform in coalition with the left, the Christian Democrats went out of their way to govern as a single party and refused to deal with opponents unless they had to. At the same time, they expended large amounts of state resources and vast amounts of U.S. foreign-aid funds on programs that were clearly designed to enhance their electoral superiority at the expense of both right and left.[56]

The Christian Democrats' rigid posture added to the growing radicalization of elites on the left (particularly the Socialist Party), who feared the electoral challenge of the center party, and to profound resentment among elites on the right, who felt betrayed by the reforms, especially in land redistribution, enacted by their erstwhile coalition partners. Radicalization of the left was also profoundly affected by international events, notably the Cuban Revolution, which set a new standard for the Latin American left to emulate.

Had the Christian Democrats succeeded in becoming a genuine center majority, the increased ideological tension would not have had such serious institutional repercussions. But despite vast organizational efforts and extraordinary levels of foreign aid from the Johnson administration in Washington, which was anxious to promote Chile as a showcase of democracy on a continent fascinated by Cuba, they did not succeed in breaking the tripartite deadlock of Chilean politics.

As a result, even when it became apparent that the Christian Democrats would not be able to win the 1970 presidential election in their own right, they were unable to structure preelection coalitions with either the right or the left. The bulk of the Radical Party joined in supporting Salvador Allende, who stunned most observers by edging out rightist Jorge Alessandri by a plurality of 36.2 percent to 34.9 percent of the vote. Christian Democratic candidate Radomiro Tomic received only 27.8 percent of the vote.

The election of Allende was not the result of growing radicalization or political mobilization. Nor was it due, in Huntington's terms, to the inability of Chile's political institutions to channel societal demands. Allende won even though he received a smaller percentage of the vote than he had received in his loss to Frei in the two-way race of 1964. Electoral analysis suggests that a greater percentage of newly mobilized voters voted for the right than for the left. The election results simply underscored the repercussions of the failure of the right and center to structure a preelection coalition.[57]

Because no candidate received an absolute majority, the election had to be decided in Congress, forcing the creation of a postelection coalition.

Christian Democrats joined legislators of the left in confirming Allende's accession to the highest office in the nation. But the president's minority status, and his lack of majority support in Congress, meant that like other presidents before him, he would have to tailor his program to the realities of coalition politics in order to succeed, even though the very reforms that the right and the Christian Democrats had enacted made such compromises more difficult. But compromise was easier said than done. Important elements in the Unidad Popular (Popular Unity, UP) coalition, including Allende's own Socialist Party, were openly committed to a revolutionary transformation in the socioeconomic order and the institutional framework of Chilean politics. Furthermore, the coalition was unwieldy and fractious, with parties and groups competing as much with one another for spoils and popular support as with the opposition.

At the same time, Allende's election touched off an extraordinary reaction from other sectors of Chilean society, who feared a pro-Moscow, Marxist-Leninist system might be established in Chile, to their detriment. They encouraged sabotage, subversion, and foreign intrigue. On both sides of Chile's divided party system, the commitment to change or preservation of the status quo now exceeded the commitment to the principles and practices of Chile's historic democracy.

Under these circumstances, structuring a center coalition committed to social change within the framework of traditional liberties and democratic guarantees was crucial to the system's survival. However, like the Christian Democrats before them, many leaders of the UP coalition became convinced that bold use of state power could break the political deadlock and swing the balance to the left. This misconception led them to enact a host of ill-conceived redistributive and stimulative economic measures, which aggravated inflation and generated serious economic difficulties. When combined with measures of questionable legality to bring private business under state control, these policies alienated not only Chile's corporate elite, but also small businessmen and much of Chile's middle class.

In an atmosphere of growing suspicion and violence, the lines of communication between leaders and followers of opposing parties eroded, accentuating the polarization of Chilean politics. At several key junctures, and despite pressures from both sides, attempts were made to forge a center consensus and structure the necessary compromises that would have saved the regime. But center groups and moderate politicians on both sides of the political divide abdicated their responsibility in favor of narrower group stakes and short-term interests. The involvement of "neutral" powers, such as the courts and the military, only served to politicize those institutions and pave the way for the military coup, a coup that undermined the very institutions of compromise and accommodation moderate leaders had professed to defend. With the failure of Congress, parties, the courts, and other state institutions to serve as viable arenas to resolve conflict, politics became more and more confrontational; contending groups resorted to mobilizing ever greater numbers of their followers to "prove" their power capabilities. Politics spilled out of the chambers of government onto the streets, exacerbating an atmosphere of fear and confrontation.[58]

The Chilean breakdown was a complex and dialectical process, in which time-tested patterns of accommodation were eroded by the rise of a center unwilling to bridge the gap between extremes, by the decline of institutional arenas of accommodation in the name of technical efficiency, and by the hardening of ideological distance between leaders with radically different conceptions of a good society. It was also the product of gross miscalculations, extremism, narrow group stakes, and the lack of courage in key circumstances. Breakdown was not inevitable. While human action was severely circumscribed by the structural characteristics of Chilean politics and by the course of events, there was still room for choice, for a leadership willing to prevent the final denouement. Nor did most Chileans want a military solution to the country's problems. Surveys taken in the weeks before the coup indicated an overwhelming support for democracy and a peaceful outcome of the political crisis.[59]

Political Structures and Regime Breakdown:
A Critique of Presidentialism

Although it was not inevitable, the breakdown of Chilean democracy raises serious questions about the viability of particular institutional forms of governance in democratic regimes. It is a premise of this chapter that in Chile there was an inadequate fit between the country's highly polarized and competitive party system, which was incapable of generating majorities, and a presidential system of centralized authority.[60]

The starting point for this argument must be a recognition that through much of the twentieth century, presidentialism in Chile was in crisis. By definition, a presidential election is a zero-sum game that freezes the outcome for a fixed period of time. In Chile, the winner invariably represented only a third of the electorate, and yet, as the head of government and head of state, he felt responsible for the national destiny as the embodiment of popular sovereignty. As minority presidents, however, Chilean chief executives received weak legislative support or outright congressional opposition. And since they could not seek reelection, there was little incentive for parties, including the president's, to support him beyond mid-term. The fixed terms for both president and Congress contributed to an atmosphere of ungovernability and a feeling of permanent crisis, alleviated only by the willingness of centrist parties or politicians to provide last-minute reprieves to beleaguered presidents in exchange for ambassadorial appointments or concessions on policy.

Paradoxically, the response to this problem of governance was to seek an increase in presidential power. The resolution of the country's pressing social and economic problems required strong leadership, it was argued, and such leadership should not be thwarted by ideological wrangling and the narrow partisan interest of the parties and the legislature. However, increased presidential power only aggravated the problem by further reducing arenas for accommodation and by making executive-legislative relations more bitter. Indeed, the stronger the power of the presidency as a separate constitutional actor, the greater were the disincentives for structuring presidential support among parties and groups jealous of their autonomy and future electoral prospects.

In Chile, there was an inverse correlation between the power of the presidency and the success of presidential government. The stronger the president, the weaker the presidential system—a perverse logic that came to a tragic head in the Allende years. A parliamentary system of government would have defused the enormous pressures for structuring high-stakes coalitions around a winner-take-all presidential option, which only reinforced political polarization. At the same time, it would have eliminated the stalemate and confrontation in executive-legislative relations. Had Chile had a parliamentary regime in the early 1970s, Allende's government might have fallen, but democracy would have survived. The working majority in Congress that elected Allende to the presidential post would have had to continue for him to have retained his position. This was not out of the question. The Christian Democrats were close to the UP government on many key points of substance, as attested by the near-agreements at several key junctures of the unfolding drama of the UP years. And, had the coalition collapsed, it is quite likely that a Christian Democrat, or perhaps a member of the small leftist Radical Party, would have formed a new government with support from elements on the right.

It is important to stress that parliamentary politics would have had the opposite effect of presidential politics on party distance. It would have contributed to moderating Chilean politics by reinforcing the time-honored traditions of give-and-take honed by generations of politicians. Moderate leaders on both sides of the congressional aisle would have gained strength, encouraging centripetal drives toward coalition and compromise, rather than being outclassed by maximalist leaders who thrived in the public arenas of high-stakes electoral battles. Moreover, legislators of all parties would have thought twice about abandoning hard-fought coalition arrangements if they had faced the prospect of immediate reelection, and the greater accountability of having been part of an agreement to structure executive authority.

Military Rule in Chile

With the collapse of democracy, Chile was abruptly transformed from an open and participatory political system into a repressive and authoritarian one. Few Chileans could have imagined in September 1973 that military intervention would lead to a government so alien to institutions and traditions dating from the nation's founding. Fewer still would have believed that Chile would produce an authoritarian regime capable of outlasting other contemporary military governments on the continent, or that General Pinochet, the obedient commander who assured President Allende of his undivided loyalty, would achieve a degree of personal power rare in the annals of modern dictatorship. How could this transformation have taken place? What happened to Chilean institutions under military rule? How did the transition back to democracy take place?

Soon after the coup, it became clear that Chile's military commanders, with no personal experience of direct involvement in politics, were not about to turn power back to civilian leaders after a brief interregnum. From the outset, they articulated two basic aims.[61] The first was to destroy the parties of the left and their collaborators. The Chilean military did not interpret its intervention as a simple military coup aimed at replacing a government, but as an all-out war to crush an enemy that it believed had infiltrated close to half the population. However, military leaders were convinced that it was not only foreign Marxists who were to blame for Chile's predicament. They thought the left had been able to make inroads because of the inherent weaknesses of liberal democracy, which they saw as encouraging corruption and demagoguery. Thus, their second objective was to engineer a fundamental restructuring of Chilean political institutions and political life, aimed at "cleaning" impurities from the body politic while creating a new political order of committed and patriotic citizens, dedicated to modernizing the country and projecting its grandeur to a hostile world.

The junta had a clear idea of how to pursue its first objective; it simply took the years of training, awesome firepower, and many contingency plans that had been developed to protect the constitutional government, and applied them to the new task of finding and neutralizing the enemy. Military units moved in to "clean up" neighborhoods that were strongholds of the left, as if they were securing enemy territory during wartime.[62] Thousands of party leaders, trade-union officials, and community activists associated with the parties of the left were "neutralized" through arrests, exile, and, in some cases, death. Labor unions were sharply circumscribed, parties were banned or declared in "recess," and internal elections were prohibited or closely monitored in all private organizations including professional associations and nonprofit agencies. Citizens, who during the Allende years and before had been repeatedly enlisted for one cause or another, now turned inward and avoided public affairs entirely, either out of fear of reprisals or outright support for military rule. Politics, which for generations had revolved around parties and interest groups that penetrated all levels of society, was now confined to small groups of individuals and cabals in the inner corridors of power.

The junta, however, had a much hazier conception of how political power should be structured, no experience in governing, and no precise blueprint for its foundational program. In the first months and years, the military governed in an ad hoc and arbitrary fashion, at times racked by internal tension. Gradually, however, the commanders succeeded in establishing a degree of national political authority rare among Latin American military regimes. Ironically, a major reason for this achievement was that, in contrast to other bureaucratic authoritarian regimes in the Southern Cone, the Chilean military successfully invoked Chile's tradition of political stability and concern for legality to reinforce its own political control. By drawing on the ubiquitous power of the Chilean state and utilizing constitutional principles from Chile's presidentialist tradition, while, at the same time, restoring the principle of military obedience to constituted authority, Chile's commanders were able to structure efficient, if not fully legitimate, governing institutions. An important ingredient of this process was elevating General Pinochet to the role of president of the republic, while he retained his posts as commander-in-chief of the army and a voting member of the four-man junta. Further aiding the consolidation of political rule by Pinochet and his colleagues was the successful effort to implement far-reaching socioeconomic transformations of a more revolutionary nature than those attempted by their elected predecessors.[63]

It should be stressed that Pinochet did not resort to populist or charismatic rule, as did Juan Perón in Argentina and Getúlio Vargas of Brazil, nor was power based on developing a corrupt political machine like those of Paraguay's Alfredo Stroessner or the Somoza clan of Nicaragua. In Chile, the consolidation of political power and one-man rule was due to four fundamental factors. First, Pinochet and his advisers were able to draw on the framework of traditional constitutional legality to justify one-man rule. Second, they could rely on the disciplined and hierarchical nature of the armed forces and the growing power of the secret police. Third, they enjoyed the strong and uncritical support of much of the business community and sectors of the middle class. And fourth, they were able to take advantage of continued sharp divisions in the opposition, which continued to fuel widespread fear among influential Chileans that an end to military rule would permit the left to resurge and once again challenge the socioeconomic status quo.

Constitutional Tradition and the Rise of Pinochet

In the immediate aftermath of the coup, the commanders of the army, navy, and air force, and the director general of the Carabineros (Chile's paramilitary police) constituted themselves as a governmental junta, which would exercise executive, legislative, and constitutional authority through unanimous agreement of its members. General Pinochet was selected to be junta president by virtue of his position as leader of the oldest military branch. He argued initially, however, that the junta presidency would rotate on a periodic basis among the commanders. Junta members also agreed to divide up policy areas so that each of the services would handle the affairs of different ministries. Even the appointment of university presidents was parceled out among the services, so that Pinochet named the army general who became president of the University of Chile, while Admiral Merino appointed one of his own colleagues to the top post at the Catholic University.

Pinochet, however, moved swiftly to assert his position as more than *primus inter pares*. Although Air Force General Gustavo Leigh was, in the early days, the most articulate, visible, and hardline member of the junta, Pinochet proved to be more politically skillful and ambitious.[64] But, Pinochet owed his ascendancy to more than his personal qualities. Ministers and other governmental officials automatically turned to the junta leader for direction, as they had always done to Chile's constitutional presidents. Soon, Pinochet was far better informed than the other junta members about government issues and began to make day-to-day decisions, including top government appointments, without consulting his colleagues. The growing junta staff, which he "generously" provided from the ranks of the army, and the increasingly assertive secret police, both reported directly to Pinochet.

At the same time, key conservative civilian and military legal advisers, even some of those who worked for other junta members, became increasingly uncomfortable with the concept of collegial rule, fearing that divided authority would lead to incoherent policies and regime instability. Ironically, they were profoundly influenced by Chilean constitutional law and the traditional practices of a strong presidential system. They could not conceive of a system of authority that did not reproduce the structure of Chile's presidential constitution, with its clear separation of powers between executive, legislative, and judicial branches. Working directly with Pinochet, they gradually proposed to the junta, which was overwhelmed by legislative detail and legal and policy complexities, the adoption of several measures aimed at "rationalizing" military rule in conformity with constitutional doctrine.

The most important of these was Decree Law 527 of June 26, 1974, which directly took the constitutional framework of the 1925 Constitution and applied it to the military government. It specified that the junta would exercise legislative and constitutional powers, while the junta president would have executive power as "Supreme Chief of the Nation."[65] The judiciary, which had shown a strong willingness to support the coup and defer to the armed forces on issues of personal liberties, would remain independent though subject to funding authorizations provided by the junta. Although the other commanders objected to Pinochet's new title, they went along with the measure, persuaded that it was necessary for the efficient administration of a country whose legal corpus was designed for a presidential regime. They were startled and displeased when Pinochet unexpectedly called a ceremony in which he donned the presidential sash.

Although the new statute was designed to institutionalize military authority by providing it with the legitimacy of Chile's presidentialist constitution, it failed to institute a genuine separation of powers. While Pinochet became the nation's chief executive, he continued to serve as one of the four junta members. Since all junta measures required a unanimous vote for adoption, any junta member could block legislation he did not approve of. Because Pinochet could resort to widespread executive authority to implement policy initiatives, the unanimity rule clearly worked in his favor. He could either work with the junta or ignore it; but the junta could not function without his consent. As the chief executive to whom ministers, government officials, and an expanding presidential staff reported, Pinochet had incomparably better information than did his colleagues. The junta soon became a weak legislature overwhelmed by initiatives from a large and complex state, ably administered by political and economic advisers and a growing secret police—all of whom owed exclusive loyalty to the president.

As Pinochet's powers grew, his relationship with the junta became more and more conflictive. General Leigh in particular bitterly opposed Pinochet's ambitions and growing prerogatives, as well as the growing influence over public and economic policy of a group of free-market economists protected by Pinochet. Leigh blocked, in mid-1977, Pinochet's proposal to have junta laws approved by a majority rather than by unanimity. At the end of that year, he also blocked Pinochet's request for junta approval of a referendum endorsing "President Pinochet in his defense of the dignity of Chile" in the face of widespread international criticisms of Chilean human-rights policy. Leigh perceived this as a move on the president's part to gain popular legitimacy for his mandate and to increase further his supremacy over the junta. Pinochet, in the face of junta objections, called the referendum anyway, invoking executive authority.

The tension between Pinochet and Leigh worsened as the two men continued to clash. But the president, making use of his now-considerable powers of persuasion, was able to get the other junta members to side with him against General Leigh. On July 28, 1978, with the support of the other two junta members, he forcibly and illegally removed General Leigh from office, risking an open and armed confrontation with the air force in order to accomplish his ends.[66] With this coup within the coup, Pinochet resolved his principal obstacle to unipersonal control of the Chilean state, control that was formally embodied in a legal foundation that reflected the constitutional practices of the past and gave the general the authority of Chile's traditional presidents without the constraints of a democratic political order.

With the defeat of opposition within the government, Pinochet moved with more confidence to design a new constitutional framework for the country's and his own future. In early 1980, a group of conservative legal advisers sent a constitutional draft to the Council of State for approval and revision. The draft, though based on the 1925 Constitution, called for a further increase in presidential authority, including a provision that reduced the autonomy of legislative bodies, and another that enabled the president to appoint several members of the Senate. The constitution also created a National Security Council, composed primarily of the armed forces commanders, with the authority to rebuke any governmental institution, elected or non-elected, if its actions were deemed to be a threat to the national security. Finally, it outlawed parties and politically banned individuals for supporting doctrines that are based on the notion of "class struggle" or that "violate the integrity of the family."[67]

The Council of State also proposed a number of transitional provisions, calling for a return to democracy and open presidential elections by 1985. Although a Congress would be named before then, Pinochet would be allowed to continue as president until that date. However, Pinochet rejected these proposals. He made it clear to his advisers that he wanted a document that would enable him to stay in office at least until 1997, or through two more eight-year "constitutional" terms. When his advisers hesitated on the grounds that such a formula would be widely rejected even by the political right, Pinochet agreed to a compromise whereby the four armed forces commanders (including himself) would select his successor in late 1988 or early 1989, subject to ratification in a popular plebiscite. But he managed to alter the constitution in one way that would make it easier for him to remain in office: The document specifically exempted him, by name, from the provision barring Chilean presidents from succeeding themselves in office.[68] In a 1980 plebiscite, held without electoral registration and in a climate that gave opponents few opportunities to challenge the government publicly, the new constitution was approved by the voters, establishing Pinochet de jure as the most powerful leader in Chilean history.

Military Obedience to Authority

Ironically, military obedience to governmental authority, a second important factor in Chile's long democratic tradition, also abetted Pinochet's efforts at consolidating dictatorial supremacy. During the UP years, Chile's armed forces had become increasingly politicized, as officers openly called for the resignation of commanders unwilling to move to overthrow the constitutional government. Pinochet himself was forced to shift at the last minute from a position of loyalty to the elected government to support for a coup when he realized that "his" generals were in open revolt. In the immediate aftermath of the coup, military leaders moved quickly to reestablish the lines of authority within the institution and to stress the professional and "nondeliberative" character of the armed forces.

Pinochet proved his shrewdness by retiring those members of his cohort who had led in planning the coup, while at the same time promoting officers who had remained loyal to the institutional chain of command. He thus eliminated potential rivals among officers who had, ironically, forced the military to intervene, while seeking to mold the officer corps into a loyal group of followers completely beholden to Pinochet for their careers. All colonels promoted to the rank of general were required to provide the army commander with a signed letter of resignation, which Pinochet could use at any moment to end a general's career.

But, loyalty was assured with more than the threat of sanctions. Under military rule, officers enjoyed privileges that they had never dreamed of. In addition to increases in pay and fringe benefits, officers could look forward to attractive rewards such as ambassadorships or membership on boards of public and semipublic corporations. Government service provided military men with responsibility and status they had never before enjoyed in the nation's history.[69]

More important for regime stability than the privileges accorded officers was the reestablishment of traditional norms of obedience to authority and hierarchy of rank, practices that had eroded in the turbulent final months of the Allende government. This meant that to a degree unheard of in other military regimes the Chilean authorities were able to establish a sharp separation between the military as institution and the military as government.[70] High-ranking officers were often brought into governmental positions that ranged from cabinet posts, heads of state agencies, and ambassadorships, to university presidencies and local governorships.[71]

However, once in government service, officers no longer took orders from their immediate military superiors but reported instead to their superiors in government, either military or civilian. As government officials, they could discuss policy with their military and civilian counterparts but were barred from discussing these matters with military colleagues serving a strictly military command. Indeed, officers in the military line of duty could be dismissed from the services for discussing politics or policy with fellow officers or with civilians. And for the duration of the Pinochet years, military men were not allowed to remain for long periods of time in governmental duties, continuously being rotated back to military command. Officers who were not deemed to be completely reliable found that their careers were terminated, cutting short a chance for a lucrative and prestigious post and retirement with high pensions. By serving both as president and commander-in-chief of the army with direct responsibility over the institution, and by strictly observing the separation of the military as government from the military as institution, Pinochet avoided the inherent tensions that develop in military regimes between officers occupying government positions and those serving in the institution itself.[72]

Aiding the general's ascendancy and ability to control the armed forces in the early years was the growing power of the secret police. The DINA (Dirección de Inteligencia Nacional or National Bureau of Intelligence), under the direction of Colonel Manuel Contreras, a close friend of the Pinochet family, soon became a law unto itself. It eliminated with efficient brutality the clandestine leadership of leftist parties in Chile and carried out with impunity a series of high-risk political assassinations abroad, aimed at silencing prominent critics of the regime. But DINA's power extended beyond its role in fighting the resistance movement. The secret organization came to be feared in military and governmental circles as DINA agents reported on the personal lives and political proclivities of prominent officers and advisers. It soon developed its own cadres of experts in fields including economic policy, as DINA officers sought to take control of sectors of the Chilean state, particularly the nationalized industries. Pinochet made use of Contreras's services to counter other advisory groups and to strengthen his hand vis-à-vis the junta and the military.[73]

Regime Support in the Business Community

The durability of Chile's military regime cannot be understood without underscoring the latitude the military government enjoyed in pursuing its policies. Although business groups were profoundly affected by the economic policies that transformed Chile from a state-supported, import-substituting industrialization economy to an export-oriented one, the business community was reticent to criticize the regime for fear of undermining its strength. For Chile's business leaders, democracy had meant the electoral triumph of political forces bent on destroying them. No matter how objectionable the Pinochet government was because of its radical free-market policies, it remained a far preferable alternative to the uncertainties of democratic politics. Many people in Chile's middle classes, despite serious reverses, shared these views. This provided the Chilean military government with autonomy not enjoyed by its counterparts in countries such as Argentina and Brazil, allowing it to pursue policies unencumbered by the potentially damaging opposition of business and elite groups.

As such, business had little direct influence in the formulation of public policy. Policies were made by an economic team that had the complete confidence of the president, and substantial latitude to implement policies without consulting affected groups. The use of a group of neutral technocrats with no strong constituency support, but with a clear and sophisticated understanding of economic policy, helped insulate the president from societal pressures and demands, contributing further to his increasing powers.

Opposition to Dictatorship and the Defeat of Pinochet

The coup that ended Chile's long trajectory of democratic politics was applauded by many sectors of society, while condemned by others. Chile's rightist parties welcomed the new authorities and soon agreed to disband, confident that the military would represent their interests. The Christian Democrats, Chile's largest party, reluctantly accepted the coup as the inevitable result of the Popular Unity government's policies. However, Christian Democrats were not prepared to accept the diagnosis of the country's new rulers that democracy was also at fault and that military rule should be maintained for an indefinite period of time. Soon, the Christian Democrats began to join the parties of the left in strong criticism of the regime's human-rights abuses and its redrafting of the nation's institutional structures. By the late 1970s, Christian Democrats were able to begin a dialogue with elements on the left, as both groups attempted to come to terms with their collective responsibility in the failure of Chile's political order.

It was not until 1983, however, that Chile's political parties reasserted themselves, signaling that the regime's efforts to obliterate them from national life had failed.[74] The spontaneous protest movement, begun at the urging of a group of labor leaders, surprised the party leadership as much as it surprised the regime. The government's swift repressive measures against labor, rendered vulnerable by high levels of unemployment, opened the door for the party leadership to gain control over the burgeoning opposition movement. In the moderate opposition, the Christian Democrats sought to create a broad alliance with small groups on the right and left in order to structure a proposal for an alternative government that would press the armed forces to negotiate. On the left, the Communist Party, which had countenanced an armed strategy against the regime, sought to mobilize popular discontent through increasingly militant protests in the expectation that the regime would capitulate.

This division, between those that sought peaceful mobilization in order to engage in negotiations with the authorities and those that sought sharp and even violent confrontations in order to render the country ungovernable, was the key to understanding the paralysis of Chile's opposition after 1983.[75] When the regime's intransigence led important sectors on the right to join with the center and moderate left and sign a National Accord for Transition to Democracy in 1985, calling for free elections and significant modifications in the 1980 Constitution, the fragile alliance failed. Some groups accused the right of trying to halt political mobilization in Pinochet's favor; others accused the left of trying to undermine possible negotiations with the armed forces while alienating middle-class support for the opposition.

At the root of this division was the continued polarization of Chilean politics between a strong Marxist left, which advocated far-reaching socioeconomic reforms, and a rejuvenated right, which refused to have any of the economic gains of authoritarianism threatened. While significant political learning took place in broad quarters of Chilean party life, with Socialists embracing democratic practices as important ends in their own right, and

Christian Democrats vowing not to pursue single-party strategies for their own gain, mistrust remained high as elements on both extremes pressed for radically divergent solutions.

Antidemocrats on both sides made it difficult for centrist forces to pursue concerted policies. Moderate Socialists feared that too many concessions to the regime would lead to a loss of support among the faithful, who might be attracted by the more militant line of the Communist Party or socialist groups affiliated with them. Democratic rightists feared that they would be isolated and outflanked by Pinochet supporters who argued that any compromise with the opposition is nothing but an opening to the Communist Party. The Christian Democrats, in turn, were immobilized by sharp internal divisions over fears that the party might move too close to either the left or the right. The same logic of polarization that made it difficult to maintain a center consensus and finally helped bring Chilean democracy crashing down in 1973 conspired against structuring a broad and coherent opposition movement to force the military from power. Widespread rejection of the Pinochet regime as illegitimate could not translate into an early return to democracy for lack of a clear alternative.[76]

Paradoxically, it was the regime that provided the opposition with a rationale for unity and a means to define the transition process in its favor. Although no opposition leader accepted the legitimacy of the plebiscite formula spelled out in the 1980 Constitution, calling instead for open and fair presidential elections as soon as possible, by 1987 most seemed resigned to accepting the plebiscite as a fact of political life. At first, opposition leaders called on Chileans to register in the electoral roles, while still pressing for open presidential elections. Gradually and reluctantly, they began to call on their followers to register to vote NO in the plebiscite that would ratify the individual chosen by the armed forces chiefs to serve the next eight-year presidential term beginning on March 11, 1989.[77]

The Communist Party and sectors of the socialist left strongly objected to this "participation in the legality of the regime." They were convinced that registering and voting would simply serve to further legitimize the regime, since they felt that the authorities would not permit a negative result and would resort to fraud if necessary to impose their candidate.

Moderate opposition leaders, on the other hand, argued that the plebiscite represented a valuable tool for popular mobilization and an important opportunity to try to defeat the regime at its own game—the only viable alternative for an opposition that had not succeeded in overthrowing the dictatorship through other means. Reluctantly they agreed to go further than asking citizens to vote: They also proceeded to register their political parties according to government regulations, which limited in several ways the autonomy of party organizations and forced them to engage in a national campaign to collect signatures from potential members, many of whom feared committing themselves publicly to a particular party or movement.

Party registration was necessary to entitle opposition groups to name poll watchers to monitor the fairness of the election. The principal groups to register were the Christian Democrats and a loose coalition of left-of-center groups that called itself the Party for Democracy.

By December 1987 it became clear Chileans were prepared to register and vote in large numbers, forcing party leaders to structure a united effort in an attempt to win the NO vote in the plebiscite. A massive television campaign on the part of the authorities and growing evidence of the use of public resources to bolster the official candidate helped further to galvanize opposition groups into action. The Communist Party soon became isolated as its allies on the left decided to join the NO command.

In governmental circles there was considerable speculation that Pinochet might not be the candidate selected by the four commanders-in-chief (including Pinochet as commander of the army). Many leaders on the right felt that the government needed to project its institutions into the future without being tied to the figure of one man. They also feared that Pinochet was too controversial a leader, one around whom the opposition could unite in a simple zero-sum decision. An alternative candidate, preferably a civilian, would contribute to dividing the opposition and depersonalizing the regime. Two of the four commanders shared this view.

In late August 1988, however, Pinochet was named the candidate. He was determined to be selected and used the force of his personality and the weight of his office to obtain the designation. Leaders on the right had not been willing to go too far in proposing an alternative for fear of antagonizing the chief executive. Businessmen who were still heavily indebted to the state were not about to jeopardize key loans by coming out publicly for an alternative. Without strong vocal support from the right for another candidate, the dissenting commanders were not able to press for an alternative, particularly since Pinochet's supporters argued effectively that he was the country's most prominent figure and could win popular support.

Government and military leaders were confident that an improved economy, a massive housing and public-works program, and a saturation television campaign would tip the balance in favor of the regime. In particular, they felt that most Chileans did not want uncertainty and the fear of a return to a Marxist government; that television and other media could effectively remind them of the dangers of not supporting the regime. Furthermore, key government officials and advisers in both the military and civilian sectors repeatedly stressed that their evidence pointed to a strong victory for Pinochet as the only candidate to appear on the ballot. They noted that the disarray and divisions in the opposition would only strengthen the government's position.

The Chilean authorities came under considerable pressure internally and internationally to stage a fair contest, even though the plebiscite formula was widely criticized as undemocratic. Chile's tradition of fair and free elections, combined with the military regime's own desire to assert its legitimacy, contributed to the structuring of virtually fraud-proof voting procedures. The contest was unequal, however, because the government used substantial resources for media efforts on behalf of its "record" and made ample use of the authority of provincial leaders and mayors to give an advantage to the YES campaign. The opposition was able to turn to television only in the last month, after Pinochet had been officially nominated, and then was restricted to fifteen minutes of free air time a day, to be shared in equal amounts with the YES campaign.

To the surprise of most people, particularly in the government, the opposition groups mounted an extraordinarily successful media and door-to-door campaign in the last few weeks before the elections. With limited resources and relying on volunteer workers, they successfully countered the "fear" campaign of the government by stressing a positive and upbeat message. NO came to denote happiness and the future, while the YES campaign remained mired in the past. The drive to produce advertisements, to recruit poll watchers, to set up an effective parallel vote count, and to conduct door-to-door campaigns cemented further the unity of the sixteen parties that formed the NO command. International support, particularly through the U.S. National Endowment for Democracy, channeled through the National Democratic Institute for International Affairs, contributed important resources for the media campaign and for the computer system designed to monitor the electoral count.

The victory of opposition forces by a 12-percent margin was a stunning achievement. Ninety-seven percent of the registered voters (representing 92 percent of the eligible population) went to the polls, and the opposition won in all but two of the country's twelve regions. Pinochet lost among most categories of voters, including women and provincial dwellers.

Two elements were critical in making it possible for the NO vote to win and to derail plans by some elements close to Pinochet to create a climate of violence that they hoped would lead to canceling the plebiscite. First, elements in the military and in the civilian political right expected a fair contest and would not have tolerated any disruption of the process. Pinochet was the most powerful person in the country, but Chile's institutions were not "personalized." Even in the army, institutional loyalties and respect for "legality" were more important factors than allegiance to the ambitions of the commander-in-chief. Second, opposition leaders were successful in persuading voters to stay home, waiting calmly for results on election night, and to celebrate peacefully the next day. The violence that some elements in the regime had expected simply did not materialize. The Communist Party played an important role by insisting that its own militants refrain from organizing street demonstrations.

The election showed clearly how easy it is for an authoritarian regime to engage in collective self-delusion. Countless polls and newspaper accounts suggested that once the voters got over their skepticism about the election's fairness, the NO vote stood a good chance of winning. And yet, Pinochet, his advisers, and his supporters in the military and the business community were absolutely convinced that the government could not lose. All the information transmitted up the chain of command was designed to reinforce the president's wishes, to the point that negative information was filtered out. A generalized contempt for politics and politicians, even those supporting the regime, made it difficult for officials to sense the mood of the country, one that strongly supported a return to Chile's democratic traditions.

Redemocratization and Prospects for the Future

The defeat of General Pinochet in the 1988 plebiscite paved the way, following Pinochet's own constitution, for open presidential and congressional races a year later. In the December 14, 1989, election Christian Democratic Party president Patricio Aylwin, supported by the parties that backed the NO campaign, handily defeated the architect of Pinochet's economic recovery, former Minister of Finance Hernán Büchi, by 55.2 percent of the vote to 29.4 percent, with independent businessman Javier Errázuriz obtaining 15.4 percent. The opposition coalition also won a majority of the contests for seats in both chambers of the legislature.

Despite considerable initial uncertainty, including fears of an authoritarian reversal, the four-year Aylwin administration was extraordinarily successful in setting the country on a solid course of redemocratization and notable economic progress. Although Chile's historical legacy of democratic governance was the principal factor facilitating a smooth transition process, two other developments were crucial in explaining why the country was able to move from authoritarianism to democracy with relative ease and why Chile's democratic future is highly auspicious.

First and foremost, Chile's transition was spearheaded by a coalition of disciplined and coherent political parties with strong societal roots. Not only did the military fail to destroy them, but the struggle against dictatorship forced opposition parties to set aside the bitter disputes of the past, fashioning a strong multiparty commitment to ensure that the first transitional government would work. Party leaders joined the cabinet and worked closely with one another, their congressional representatives, and the new president to design policies that would address the challenges of the nation with prudence and moderation, making the Aylwin government one of the most successful administrations in twentieth-century Chile. By expanding the free-market economic policies begun under the Pinochet regime, the new government was able to attract record levels of foreign investment.

The close ties between coalition parties and labor and popular groups, coupled with the weakness of the Communist Party in the postauthoritarian period, gave the authorities the necessary political space to deepen the free-market economic reforms of the military government without engendering significant social unrest. Thus, the government expanded social spending without incurring deficit spending, making a significant dent in poverty and inequality. By the end of Aylwin's administration, the country had experienced several years of sustained economic progress, making Chile the fastest-growing economy in Latin America. At the same time, Aylwin was able to draw on his considerable popular support and the cohesiveness of his coalition to address the demand for an accounting of human-rights violations by appointing a "truth" commission while averting risky trials of former military officers.

In the second place, Chile's transition was abetted by the fact that it took place within the framework of the constitutional legacy of the military regime. By challenging Pinochet within his own legality, opposition sectors tacitly accepted that legality. After the plebiscite they had hoped to introduce fundamental changes in Pinochet's constitutional order. Opposition from the military and sectors of the right, coupled with the fact that Pinochet had garnered 43 percent of the vote, made it impossible to contemplate a wholesale dismantling of the 1980 Constitution.

The victorious opposition and the Pinochet government did agree to a few key constitutional changes prior to the 1989 election. These included tempering the prohibition against parties of the left, downgrading the veto power of the military-dominated National Security Council, and expanding the size of the Senate to decrease the importance of the designated senators. In turn, by agreeing to these changes, which were ratified in a second plebiscite in July 1989, the democratic forces openly acknowledged the legitimacy of the military constitution while agreeing to additional modifications in the constitution aimed at further insulating the military from civilian accountability. A resolution, albeit partial, of some of the more objectionable elements in the Pinochet Constitution would help to remove volatile constitutional reform issues from the agenda of the new civilian government.

The opposition's acquiescence to a transition following the rules established by the authoritarian regime was also critical in providing the military and its supporters with institutional guarantees that they would not be overwhelmed by representatives of the majority. These rules included the institution of the designated senators, as well as an electoral law clearly drafted to favor parties of the right. Despite its loss of the majority of the popular vote, the right obtained strong representation in the parliament and an effective majority in the Senate, as "institutional senators," appointed by the outgoing regime, sided with the right. The strong rightist presence in the legislature, combined with constitutional provisions enabling Pinochet and the other commanders to stay in their posts until well past the end of the Aylwin government, also insulated the military from possible retribution.

Although leaders of the Aylwin coalition strongly criticized these "authoritarian" enclaves, they provided the right with a significant voice in policy matters, thereby reinforcing its still tentative commitment to civilian rule and strengthening its orientation toward electoral, as opposed to conspiratorial, politics. Thus, the government had to bargain with the right on tax increase and social spending matters, as well as on constitutional reforms reestablishing elected local governments and reducing the presidential term from eight to six years.

Paradoxically, whereas the legacies of the Pinochet Constitution may have facilitated a peaceful transition in a political climate still marked by considerable mistrust, a strong case can be made that over the long haul they may prove counterproductive, undermining the progress of democratic reforms. Designated senators are widely viewed in Chile as illegitimate, and the autonomy of military commanders and institutions is bound to lead to serious conflicts in the future. More significant, however, the exaggerated powers of the presidency as outlined in the military constitution are likely to generate serious institutional and political controversies. In the transition government, congressional leaders, working closely with party leaders in the executive, were willing to accept strong presidential prerogatives to avoid subverting the new government. Hyper-presidentialism, however, created strong resentment among legislative elites of the governing coalition while undermining the critical role the legislature can play as an arena for accommodation and compromise as well as oversight of executive authority.

An exaggerated presidentialism is particularly serious in Chile given the survival of the country's strong multiparty system. Sixteen years of military rule coupled with deliberate policies aimed at creating a moderate two-party system failed to create a system with fewer than five important party organizations, none of which can expect to command a majority of the vote on its own. Indeed, Chileans continued to have high levels of party identification, with over 60 percent of voters saying they identified with particular party organizations.[78] Equally striking is the continued division of the electorate into the proverbial thirds of Chilean politics, with roughly equal thirds each identifying with the right, center, and left.

In this context, it is unlikely that any president will command a majority of the vote or obtain majority support from his or her party in the legislature, thereby requiring multiparty coalitions for governance. Although the Aylwin government succeeded in structuring such a coalition, its unity was based on the common struggle against authoritarianism and the fear of a democratic reversal. As Chilean politics moves from the heroic politics of the transition period to "normal" politics revolving around policy differences and competition for power, the unity of the Aylwin and Frei coalitions is bound to fray.

Indeed, "new" issues in Chilean politics such as divorce and abortion could introduce wedges in the Christian Democratic–Socialist alliance. The fact that Christian Democrats have led the two postauthoritarian coalition governments will also be a source of tension as Socialists argue that in the next contest it will be their turn to gain the presidency. Exaggerated presidentialism is likely to exacerbate conflict by centering too much power in one person, thus risking the transformation of the legislature into an arena of negative opposition. Although competition and conflict are normal in democratic contexts, Chilean political elites should attempt to ensure that the country's institutions are able to channel them without straining the democratic order.

Despite these misgivings there is considerable room for optimism as Chile enters the final years of the twentieth century. The sharp and bitter conflicts of the past have been attenuated by a painful learning experience and the end of the Cold War. The dramatic success of Chile's economic reforms promises to help the country emerge from the ranks of the underdeveloped world within a generation. In overcoming the wrenching crisis of the recent past by turning to their country's historical democratic traditions, Chileans have set the foundation for a promising future as a democratic nation.

Notes

1. Kenneth A. Bollen, "Comparative Measurement of Political Democracy," *American Sociological Review* 45, no. 3 (June 1980): pp. 370–390. See also Robert W. Jackman, "On the Relations of Economic Development to Democratic Performance," *American Journal of Political Science* 17, no. 3 (August 1973): pp. 611–621; and his "Political Democracy and Social Equality: A Comparative Analysis," *American Sociological Review* 39, no. 1 (February 1974): pp. 29–44.

2. Leon Epstein, *Political Parties in Western Democracies* (New York: Praeger, 1967), p. 192. For a discussion of the rise of parliamentary opposition in Western Europe, see the excellent collection in Robert Dahl, ed., *Political Oppositions in Western Democracies* (New Haven, CT: Yale University Press, 1966). See also Dahl's *Polyarchy: Participation and Opposition* (New Haven, Conn.: Yale University Press, 1971).

3. Some countries, including Britain and Norway, developed political contestation with parliamentary responsibility before Chile did. Others, such as Belgium and the Netherlands, began to develop parliamentary influence at around the same time. The Swedish king was able to choose ministers without regard to parliamentary majorities until 1917, though the parliament's views were taken into consideration earlier. Italy was not unified until the 1860s and did not establish a system of parliamentary rule until the 1880s. Republican France dates from 1871, and many observers, noting the importance of the Napoleonic bureaucracy, question the degree of authority wielded by the French parliament. Because of the importance of the monarchies in Europe, Chile comes closer to the United States in the origins and evolution of its political institutions. For historical discussions of these issues, see Dahl, *Political Oppositions;* and Stein Rokkan, *Citizens, Elections, Parties* (Oslo: Universitetsforlaget, 1970).

4. See Dahl, *Polyarchy,* ch. 1. Dahl's definition informs the discussion of democracy in Chapter 1 of this volume.

5. Women were able to vote in national elections for the first time in 1952. The voting age was reduced from twenty-one to eighteen and illiterates were given the right to vote with the constitutional reforms of 1970. The best discussion of Chilean electoral practices can be found in Federico Gil, *The Political System of Chile* (Boston: Houghton Mifflin, 1966). The 1970 reforms are discussed in Guillermo Piedrabuena Richards, *La reforma constitucional* (Santiago: Ediciones Encina, 1970). The intricacies of the electoral system are described in Mario Bernaschina G., *Cartilla electoral* (Santiago: Editorial Jurídica de Chile, 1958). For an overview of electoral participation, see Atilio Borón, "La evolución del régimen electoral y sus efectos en la representación de los intereses populares: El caso de Chile," estudio no. 24 (Santiago: Escuela Latinoamericana de Ciencia Política y Administración Pública, FLACSO, April 1971).

6. Voting data for Europe can be found in Stein Rokkan, *Citizens*. Voting data on Chile are found in J. Samuel Valenzuela, *Democratización vía reforma: La expansión del sufragio en Chile* (Buenos Aires: Ediciones del IDES, 1985). This is the best study of the critical decisions that led to suffrage expansion in Chile in the nineteenth century, underscoring the important role of the Conservatives in that process. As such, it is an important revisionary study in Chilean historiography.

7. This section draws extensively from J. Samuel Valenzuela and Arturo Valenzuela, "Chile and the Breakdown of Democracy," in *Latin American Politics and Development,* ed. Howard J. Wiarda and Harvey F. Kline (Boston: Houghton Mifflin, 1979), pp. 234–249. The author is grateful to J. Samuel Valenzuela for his contribution to this work and to much of the thinking that is reflected in this chapter. See also Arturo Valenzuela, *Political Brokers in Chile: Local Government in a Centralized Polity* (Durham, N.C.: Duke University Press, 1977), ch. 8.

8. Francisco Antonio Encina, *Historia de Chile,* vol. 9 (Santiago: Editorial Nacimiento, 1941–1942), p. 493; cited in Arturo Valenzuela, *Political Brokers,* p. 175.

9. This thesis is at variance with standard interpretations that attribute to Diego Portales a pivotal role in forming the Chilean institutional system. See Arturo Valenzuela, *Political Brokers,* ch. 8; and his "El mito de Portales: La institucionalización del régimen político chileno en el siglo XIX," unpublished manuscript.

10. Chile, *Documentos parlamentarios correspondientes al segundo quinquenio de la administración Bulnes, 1846–1850,* vol. 3 (Santiago: Imprenta del Ferrocarril, 1858), p. 795.

11. Some of the generalizations from the "world-system" and "dependency" literature to the effect that dependent capitalist development leads to weak states does not fully apply to the Chilean case.

12. This section draws heavily on Arturo Valenzuela and J. Samuel Valenzuela, "Los orígenes de la democracia: Reflexiones teóricas sobre el caso de Chile," *Estudios públicos* 12 (Spring 1983): pp. 3–39; and J. S. Valenzuela, *Democratización.*

13. In 1863, the total electorate was about 22,000. By 1878, the electorate had expanded sevenfold. See J. S. Valenzuela, *Democratización,* pp. 118–119.

14. Mauice Duverger, *Political Parties* (New York: John Wiley, 1965), pp. xxiii–xxxvii.

15. This section draws heavily on Arturo Valenzuela, *The Breakdown of Democratic Regimes: Chile* (Baltimore, Md.: Johns Hopkins University Press, 1978), ch. 1.

16. Seymour Martin Lipset and Stein Rokkan, *Party Systems and Voter Alignments* (New York: Free Press, 1967), pp. 50, 56.

17. For a discussion of this, see Arturo Valenzuela, *Political Brokers.*

18. An exception to this generalization is Dahl's *Polyarchy.* Not only has Chile been neglected in the broader literature, Latin America in general has been left out. The volumes of the Committee on Comparative Politics of the Social Science Research Council had only a few studies dealing with Latin America, and Latin America did not figure prominently in the theoretical efforts of the 1960s. In his excellent study of parties in Western democracies, Epstein acknowledges that a few Latin American countries meet his criteria for inclusion but leaves them out "mainly because the whole of Latin America is customarily treated along with developing nations" (emphasis added). See Epstein, *Political Parties,* p. 4. For a discussion of the place of Latin America in the literature on comparative politics, see Arturo Valenzuela, "Political Science and Latin America: A Discipline in Search of Political Reality," in *Changing Perspectives in Latin American Studies,* ed. Christopher Mitchell (Stanford, Calif.: Stanford University Press, 1988).

19. These terms are designed to group in analytically similar categories propositions that

are sometimes advanced in more discrete fashion. They are drawn from previous work of the author on the subject, some of which has been done in collaboration with J. Samuel Valenzuela. I have attempted to address within each category the relevant variables advanced in this book. I do not treat what can be called the national-cohesiveness thesis because it is not as relevant to the Chilean case. Ethnic, regional, and center-periphery cleavages were defused in the early half of the nineteenth century.

20. The importance of gradual evolution without significant upheaval is stressed by Dahl in *Polyarchy,* pp. 40–47. The continuity of institutions from the colonial period is one of the points advanced by Seymour Martin Lipset in his provocative study of the United States, *The First New Nation* (New York: Doubleday, 1967), pp. 106–107. For a discussion of differences in the colonial experience, see Rupert Emerson's classic *From Empire to Nation* (Boston: Beacon Press, 1960).

21. Chile inaugurated a polyarchy through a struggle for independence that led to the collapse of the remnants of the old colonial regime and not, as Dahl holds, through an evolutionary process comparable to that of England or Sweden. In this sense, the Chilean case is closer to that of France than England. See Dahl, *Polyarchy,* p. 42.

22. See Frederick Pike, *Chile and the United States, 1880–1962* (Notre Dame, Ind.: University of Notre Dame Press, 1963), p. 11. The literature on Portales is voluminous. An influential work that argues this thesis is Alberto Edwards Vives, *La fronda aristocrática* (Santiago: Ediciones Ercilla, 1936), pp. 50–51. For a sampling of views see B. Vicuña Mackenna, J. Victorino Lastarria, and R. Sotomayor Valdés, *Portales: Juicio histórico* (Santiago: Editorial del Pacífico, 1973).

23. Richard Morse, "The Heritage of Latin America," in *The Founding of New Societies,* ed. Louis Hartz (New York: Harcourt, Brace and World, 1964), pp. 163–164. See also Hartz's comments on the Chilean case on p. 88 of that work.

24. For an elaboration of this argument see Arturo Valenzuela, *Political Brokers,* ch. 8.

25. See Samuel P. Huntington, *Political Order in Changing Societies* (New Haven, Conn.: Yale University Press, 1968), ch. 2.

26. David Martin argues that "the incidence of pluralism and democracy is related to the incidence of those religious bodies which are themselves inherently pluralistic and democratic. . . . Such bodies . . . are much more prevalent in the Anglo-American situation than elsewhere. . . . In Russia and Latin America democratic and individualistic Protestantism arrived late in the process and could not have an important effect." See his *A General Theory of Secularization* (New York: Harper and Row, 1978), p. 25. For an influential essay dealing with Latin America along these same lines, see Seymour Martin Lipset, "Values, Education and Entrepreneurship," in *Elites in Latin America,* ed. Seymour Martin Lipset and Aldo Solari (New York: Oxford University Press, 1963). See also Howard Wiarda, "Toward a Framework for the Study of Political Change in the Iberic-Latin Tradition: The Corporative Model," *World Politics* 25, no. 2 (January 1973): pp. 206–235. For a classic work that links liberal values stemming from the Protestant tradition with the growth of democracy in the United States, see Louis Hartz, *The Liberal Tradition in America* (New York: Harcourt, Brace and World, 1955).

27. See Jorge I. Dominguez, *Insurrection or Loyalty* (Cambridge, Mass.: Harvard University Press, 1979) for a discussion of some of these points.

28. Harry Eckstein, *Division and Cohesion in a Democracy: A Study of Norway* (Princeton, N.J.: Princeton University Press, 1966).

29. See John A. Booth, "Costa Rica: The Roots of Democratic Stability," in *Democracy in Developing Countries: Vol. 4, Latin America,* eds., Larry Diamond, Juan J. Linz, and Seymour Martin Lipset (Boulder: Lynne Rienner, 1989).

30. Dahl, *Polyarchy,* p. 140.

31. For a description of Chile's hacienda system, see George M. McBride, *Chile: Land and Society* (New York: American Geographical Society, 1936). For the origins, the classic study is Mario Góngora, *Origen de los inquilinos del Valle Central* (Santiago: Editorial Universitaria, 1960). See also Arnold J. Bauer, *Chilean Rural Society from the Spanish Conquest to 1930* (New York: Cambridge University Press, 1975).

32. Dominguez, *Insurrection,* p. 141.

33. See Robert Kaufman, *The Politics of Land Reform in Chile, 1950–1970* (Cambridge, Mass.: Harvard University Press, 1972); and Brian Loveman, *Struggle in the Countryside: Politics and Rural Labor in Chile, 1919–1973* (Bloomington: Indiana University Press, 1976).

34. Chile is a good illustration of Dankwart Rustow's argument that democracies must go through a "habituation" phase before they are consolidated. See his "Transitions to Democracy: Toward a Dynamic Model," *Comparative Politics* 2, no. 3 (April 1970): pp. 337–363.

35. See Daniel Lerner, *The Passing of Traditional Society* (New York: Free Press, 1958). See also S. N. Eisenstadt, "Social Change, Differentiation and Evolution," *American Sociological Review* 29 (June 1964): pp. 375–387.

36. Seymour Martin Lipset, "Some Social Requisites of Democracy: Economic Development and Political Legitimacy," *American Political Science Review* 53, no. 1 (March 1959): pp. 69–105. For collections of articles on "empirical democratic theory," see J. V. Gillespie and B. A. Nesvold, eds., *Macroquantitative Analysis: Conflict, Development and Democratization* (Beverly Hills, Calif.: Sage Publications, 1971); and Charles Cnudde and Deane Neubauer, eds., *Empirical Democratic Theory* (Chicago: Markham, 1969). For an excellent review of this literature, see Leonardo Morlino, "Misure di Democrazia e di Libertá: Discusione di Alcune Analisi Empiriche," *Rivista Italiana di Scienza Política* 5, no. 1 (April 1975): pp. 131–166.

37. See, for example, Phillips Cutright, "National Political Development: Measurement and Analysis," *American Sociological Review* 28, no. 2 (April 1963): pp. 253–264; and Bollen, "Comparative Measurement of Political Democracy."

38. Juan Linz, "Totalitarian and Authoritarian Regimes," in *Handbook of Political Science,* vol. 3, ed. Fred I. Greenstein and Nelson W. Polsby (Reading, Mass.: Addison Wesley, 1975), p. 182. As Dahl notes, the United States in the nineteenth century did not meet the development criteria but met the political criteria. See Dahl, *Polyarchy,* p. 72.

39. Goran Therborn, "The Rule of Capital and the Rise of Democracy," *New Left Review* 103 (May–June 1977): pp. 3–41. Therborn adds that the rarity of bourgeois democracy in capitalist Third World countries is a result of the vulnerability of commodity-oriented economies, which give the "indigenous bourgeoisie little room for maneuver vis-à-vis the exploited classes." In such contexts there is an "intertwining of capitalist with feudal, slave or other pre-capitalist modes of exploitations . . . impeding the development of impersonal rule of capital and free labor market, thereby seriously limiting the growth of both the labor movement and an agrarian petty bourgeoisie." Ibid., pp. 1, 32. Although he is not dealing with the development of democracy per se, Immanuel Wallerstein argues that peripheral states in the world system were much weaker in part because the social structure of export economies did not permit the development of bourgeois sectors. See his *The Modern World System,* 2 vols. (New York: Academic Press, 1974, 1980).

40. Barrington Moore, *Social Origins of Dictatorship and Democracy: Lord and Peasant in the Making of the Modern World* (Boston: Beacon Press, 1966). As he notes, for democracy to emerge, "the political hegemony of the landed upper class had to be broken or transformed. The peasant had to be turned into a farmer producing for the market instead of for his own consumption and that of the overlord. In this process the landed upper class either became an important part of the capitalist and democratic tide, as in England, or, if they came to oppose it, they were swept aside in the convulsions of revolutions (France) or civil war (U.S.). In a word the landed upper classes either helped to make the bourgeois revolution or were destroyed by it." Ibid., pp. 429–430. Moore's analysis, though brilliant in scope, leaves much to be desired in terms of clarity. For a valuable critique, see Theda Skocpol, "A Critical Review of Barrington Moore's Social Origins of Dictatorship and Democracy, " *Politics and Society* 4 (Fall 1973): pp. 1–34. See also Joseph V. Femia, "Barrington Moore and the Preconditions for Democracy," *British Journal of Political Science* 2 (January 1972): pp. 21-6; and Ronald Dore, "Making Sense of History," *Archive Européenes de Sociology* 10 (1969): pp. 295–305.

41. See Dominguez, *Insurrection,* p. 131.

42. Influential works of Chilean historians in this vein include Julio César Jobet, *Ensayo crítico del desarrollo económico-social de Chile* (Santiago: Editorial Latinoamericana, 1965); and Hernán Ramirez Necochea, *Historia del movimiento obrero en Chile, antecedentes siglo XIX* (Santiago: Editorial Austral, 1956). The most fully developed version of this thesis is in Luis Vitale, *Interpretación marxista de la historia de Chile* (Frankfurt: Verlag Jugend und Politik, 1975). Maurice Zeitlin's *The Civil Wars in Chile: 1851 and 1859* (Princeton, N.J.: Princeton University Press, 1984) draws uncritically from the work of Vitale and others.

43. See Leonard Binder et al., *Crises and Sequences in Political Development* (Princeton, N.J.: Princeton University Press, 1971). For a volume of essays applying the framework to par-

ticular cases, see Raymond Grew, ed., *Crises of Political Development in Europe and the United States* (Princeton, N.J.: Princeton University Press, 1978). Influential earlier studies that anticipate the arguments in these books include Dankwart Rustow, *A World of Nations* (Washington, D.C.: Brookings Institution, 1967); Lipset and Rokkan, eds., *Party Systems and Voter Alignments;* and Gabriel Almond, Scott Flanigan, and Roger Mundt, eds., *Crisis, Choice and Change: Historical Studies of Political Development* (Boston: Little, Brown, 1973). Although some of these works focus on political development more generally, and not on the development of democracy as such, their framework is oriented toward democratic regimes rather than other regime types.

44. Eric Nordlinger, "Political Development, Time Sequences and Rates of Change," in *Political Development and Social Change,* 2d ed., ed. Jason L. Finkle and Robert W. Gable (New York: John Wiley, 1971), p. 458. This argument is made in Rustow, *World of Nations,* pp. 120–123.

45. Of the three crises, the most difficult to deal with is that of national identity. Its definition is imprecise, and in the absence of survey-research data it is virtually impossible to find empirical evidence to document its relative strength. Much of this analysis has to be speculative and informed by general historical accounts. Particularly useful in capturing the mood of Chile in the early period is the work of Diego Barros Arana, which is also an eyewitness account. In particular, see his *Un decenio de la historia de Chile,* 2 vols. (Santiago: Imprenta Universitaria, 1906.)

46. See Richard Merritt, "Nation-Building in America: the Colonial Years," in *Nation Building,* ed. Karl W. Deutsch and William J. Foltz (New York: Atherton Press, 1966; and Karl Deutch, *Nationalism and Social Communication: An Inquiry into the Foundations of Nationality,* 2d ed. (Cambridge, Mass.: MIT Press, 1966). Lipset discusses the question of national identity in the United States in his *First New Nation,* ch. 2.

47. See Rustow, "Transitions to Democracy."

48. For a discussion of Washington's impact, see Lipset, *First New Nation,* pp. 18–23.

49. For lists of all Chilean presidents, cabinet officials, and members of Congress from independence until the 1940s, see Luis Valencia Avaria, *Anales de la república,* 2 vols. (Santiago: Imprenta Universitana, 1951). Most presidents had extensive parliamentary experience.

50. On the question of efficacy, see the arguments of Juan J. Linz in *The Breakdown of Democratic Regimes: Crisis, Breakdown and Reequilibration* (Baltimore, Md.: Johns Hopkins University Press, 1978), pp. 20–21.

51. For an elaboration of this argument, see Valenzuela and Valenzuela, "Orígenes de la democracia."

52. R. K. Merton, "The Unanticipated Consequences of Purposive Social Action," *American Sociological Review* 1 (1936): pp. 894–904.

53. This point is made in Arturo Valenzuela and Alexander Wilde, "Presidentialist Politics and the Decline of the Chilean Congress," in *Legislatures in Development: Dynamics of Change in New and Old States,* ed. Joel Smith and Lloyd Musolf (Durham, N.C.: Duke University Press, 1979), p. 194.

54. The material in this section is taken from the author's *Breakdown.* For other books on the Chilean breakdown, see Paul Sigmund, *The Overthrow of Allende and the Politics of Chile* (Pittsburgh, Penn.: Pittsburgh University Press, 1977); Lan Roxborough, Phil O'Brien, and Jackie Roddick, *Chile: The State and Revolution* (New York: Holmes and Meier, 1977); and Manuel A. Garretón and Tomás Moulian, *Análisis coyuntural y proceso político: Lasfases del conflicto en Chile (1970–73)* (San José, Costa Rica: Editorial Universitaria Centro-Americana, 1978). The last-named is drawn from the comprehensive and detailed daily account of the most important events of the Allende administration, published in Manuel Antonio Garretón et al., *Cronología del período 1970–73,* 9 vols. (Santiago: Facultad Latinoamericana de Ciencias Sociales, 1978), an invaluable publication including extensive indices to parties, individuals, and events. In the immediate aftermath of the coup, a host of primarily more polemical works were published. For a review essay of thirty-one books, see Arturo Valenzuela and J. Samuel Valenzuela, "Visions of Chile," *Latin American Research Review* 10 (Fall 1975): pp. 155–176.

55. See Valenzuela and Wilde, "Presidentialism and Decline of Congress," pp. 204–210.

56. The most comprehensive study of U.S. involvement was conducted by the U.S. Select Committee to Study Govermental Operations with respect to Intelligence Activities (Church

Committee) of the 94th Congress, 1st Session. See its *Covert Action in Chile 1963–1973* (Washington, D.C.: Government Printing, 1975).

57. The fact that Allende received fewer votes in 1970 than in 1964 suggests that his victory was not the result of an increase in popular discontent and mobilization fueled by a worsening socioeconomic crisis. An examination of socioeconomic indicators in the late 1960s does not support the argument that the lot of the average Chilean was becoming worse or that political mobilization was exceeding historic levels. Survey data also support the view that a majority of voters would have preferred a center-right to a center-left coalition. Huntington's thesis, in *Political Order,* that political order collapses when political institutions are too weak is not supported by the Chilean case. Chile's parties prior to the election of Allende were very strong (perhaps too dominant), and political mobilization was the product of deliberate strategies on the part of the parties and the government to bring people into the political process, rather than the product of widespread discontent or anomic behavior. In Chile, the election of Allende and the economic and social crisis of the Allende years was more the product of the sharp political crisis than vice-versa. For a full elaboration of this argument, see my *Breakdown,* ch. 3. An article that argues that mobilization in Chile became excessive is Henry Landberger and Tim McDaniel, "Hypermobilization in Chile, 1970–73," *World Politics* 28, no. 4 (July 1976): pp. 502–543.

58. For the concept of neutral powers, see Linz, *Breakdown,* pp. 76–80. For a discussion of the growing confrontation, suggesting that mobilization was more the result of political crisis than its cause, see Valenzuela, *Breakdown,* p. 34.

59. Seventy-two percent of those polled thought Chile was living through extraordinary times, but only 27 percent of the respondents felt the military should be involved in the political process. See Valenzuela, *Breakdown,* p. 65. The Chilean case suggests that even where democratic norms are widespread and deeply rooted in a society, political crisis resulting from institutional struggles and competing claims can seriously erode democratic practices. A democratic political culture is no guarantee for the maintenance of democratic institutions.

60. This argument is elaborated in Arturo Valenzuela, "Orígenes y características del sistema de partidos políticos en Chile: Una proposición para un gobierno parlamentario," *Estudios Públicos* 18 (Fall 1985): pp. 87–154; and my "Party Politics and the Failure of Presidentialism in Chile," in *The Failure of Presidential Democracy,* ed. Juan J. Linz and Arturo Valenzuela (Baltimore: Johns Hopkins University Press, 1994). The author is grateful to Juan Linz for his reflections on this subject. See the suggestive discussion in Linz, *Breakdown,* pp. 71–74; and his "Democracy, Presidential or Parliamentary: Does It Make a Difference?" in Linz and Valenzuela.

61. This section draws on Pamela Constable, and Arturo Valenzuela, *A Nation of Enemies: Chile Under Pinochet* (New York: Norton, 1994).

62. This section is based on interviews, conducted in August 1987, with high-ranking military officers who commanded troops during the coup and were responsible for "cleaning up" or "neutralizing" Santiago neighborhoods.

63. A valuable discussion of the neoconservative economic policies applied by the Chilean military regime is Pilar Vergara, *Auge y caída del neoliberalismo en Chile* (Santiago: FLACSO, 1985).

64. This section is based on extensive interviews with advisers close to the junta and General Pinochet in 1973–1978. See Arturo Valenzuela, "The Military in Power: the Consolidateion of One-Man Rule," in *The Struggle for Democracy in Chile: 1982–1990* ed. Paul Drake and Ivan Jaksic, (Lincoln: University of Nebraska Press, 1991).

65. For the text of Decree Law 527, see Eduardo Soto Kloss, *Ordenamiento constitucional* (Santiago: Editorial Jurídica de Chile, 1980), pp. 145–153.

66. These observations are based on interviews conducted with General Leigh in Santiago, Chile, during November 1985. An excellent published interview is in Florencia Varas, *Gustavo Leigh: El general disidente* (Santiago: Editorial Aconcagua, 1979). Pinochet retired eighteen air force generals before finding one who would accept his action and replace Leigh on the junta. Had Leigh had better intelligence, the conflict might have been much more dramatic.

67. See Chile, *Constitución de la República de Chile 1980* (Santiago: Editorial Jurídica, 1981). See Article 8, p. 13, for that language.

68. See transitional articles 16 and 27 in *Constitución.*

69. For an excellent study that gives a picture of rising military expenditures for personnel, see Jorge Marshall, "Gasto público en Chile 1969–1979," *Colección estudios cieplan* 5 (July 1981): pp. 53–84.

70. As such, the Chilean military regime was of the military but not by the military. I am indebted to the excellent work of Genaro Arriagada for this insight. See his *La política militar de Pinochet* (Santiago: Salesianos, 1985).

71. For an article detailing the service of military men in government positions, see Carlos Huneeus and Jorge Olave, "La Partecipazione dei Militari nei Nuovi: Autoritatismi in una Prospettive Comparata," *Rivista Italiana di Scienza Politica* [Rome] 17, no. 1 (April 1987), pp. 65–78.

72. See Alfred Stepan's now classic elaboration of this problem in *The Military in Politics: Changing Patterns in Brazil* (Princeton, N.J.: Princeton University Press, 1971).

73. Senior officers such as General Oscar Bonilla, perhaps the most powerful general at the time of the coup, were not successful in their attempts to control Contreras. Bonilla died in an accident of suspicious nature. Many civilian advisers came to fear that Contreras could come to threaten Pinochet, though the general succeeded in playing various groups off against each other. Contreras was finally fired and the DINA restructured as relations between the United States and Chile deteriorated following U.S. demands for extradition of Contreras to the United States for his alleged involvement in the assassination of Orlando Letelier, Allende's foreign minister, in the streets of Washington. For studies that deal with the Letelier case and provide insights into the DINA, see John Dinges and Saul Landau, *Assassination on Embassy Row* (New York: Pantheon, 1980); and Taylor Branch and Eugene M. Propper, *Labyrinth* (New York: Viking, 1982).

74. For a discussion of political parties under authoritarianism see Arturo Valenzuela and J. Samuel Valenzuela, "Political Oppositions Under the Chilean Authoritarian Regime," in *Military Rule in Chile: Dictatorship and Oppositions,* ed. J. Samuel Valenzuela and Arturo Valenzuela (Baltimore, Md.: Johns Hopkins University Press, 1986).

75. See Pamela Constable and Arturo Valenzuela, "Is Chile Next?" *Foreign Policy* 63 (Summer 1986): pp. 58–75.

76. See Adam Przeworski's persuasive critique of the notion that the lack of legitimacy is a sufficient condition for the breakdown of a regime in "Some Problems in the Study of the Transition to Democracy," in *Transitions from Authoritarian Rule,* ed. Guillermo O'Donnell, Philippe C. Schmitter, and Laurence Whitehead (Baltimore, Md.: Johns Hopkins University Press, 1986).

77. This section is based on field research conducted by the author in Chile in 1987 and 1988. For a more detailed description of the events leading up to the plebiscite, see Pamela Constable and Arturo Valenzuela, "Plebiscite in Chile: End of the Pinochet Era?" *Current History* 87 (January 1988): pp. 29–33, 41; and Pamela Constable and Arturo Valenzuela, "Chile's Return to Democracy," *Foreign Affairs* (Winter 1989/90): pp. 169–186. See also Arturo Valenzuela, "Government and Politics," in *Chile: A Country Study,* ed. Rex A. Hudson (Washington, D.C.: Federal Research Division, Library of Congress, 1995), pp. 199–273.

78. Valenzuela, "Government and Politics," p. 244.

3

Brazil:
Inequality Against Democracy

Bolívar Lamounier

Political scientists have repeatedly emphasized the advantages of viewing democracy as a political subsystem rather than as a total pattern of society. The study of democratic breakdowns has given them every reason to insist on that view, since it has shown that in many cases dictatorship could have been avoided through institutional change and conscious political effort. Observing processes of "opening" (*abertura*) or "decompression" in authoritarian regimes has certainly reinforced that preference, not least because the importance of prior institution building came clearly to light during some of these processes. Democracy, then, is a political subsystem, not a total pattern of social organization. But how sharply can we draw the line between the development of political institutions and the substantive democratization of society? How should we approach the fact that enormous tensions develop between these concepts—especially when we move from the dilemmas of democratic opening to those of democratic consolidation?

The Brazilian case is certainly worth examining in this connection. Recall that on March 31, 1964, a military coup overthrew President Goulart and inaugurated the longest period of ostensible authoritarian rule in Brazil's history. More than two decades later, on January 15, 1985, the Electoral College instituted by the military to ratify their presidential nominations elected Tancredo Neves—a civilian and a moderate oppositionist since 1964 to the presidency of the republic. The Brazilian authoritarian regime was ending by peaceful means. Seven years later, in 1992, Fernando Collor de Mello, elected president in 1989, was impeached on charges of corruption and replaced by vice president Itamar Franco—again in an orderly way. Obviously, these are not the kinds of changes that take place in countries without a fair degree of institutional development. Protest and popular resistance played an important role in both cases, but there was also an element of flexibility among power holders and a weight of their own among traditional representative institutions.

Can we then say that the Brazilian political system is fully democratic

or fully consolidated? The answer to this question transcends the Brazilian case. It depends on our evaluation of the historical record, but also on our conceptualization of democracy and on our models of consolidation. Our first step here should be an attempt to determine Brazil's position on the scale of democracy employed in this book. Few would have major doubts about Brazil's position; it is clearly not a case of high success or of extreme failure. The optimist would think of Brazil as a "mixed success," noting that we have some democratic tradition, despite many interruptions, and that civilian rule is again in place after twenty years of ostensible military domination. The pessimist will prefer to speak of "partial development," rejecting the view that democracy has been the dominant pattern. Mixed or partial, both will agree that we are a case of unstable democracy, since the democratic system cannot be said to be fully institutionalized in Brazil.

Facing sharp inequality and major social strains, a political system—democratic or authoritarian—can hardly be said to be institutionalized completely. In some cases, democracy succeeds in becoming accepted as a framework for an endless series of substantive changes. Not every contender accepts it as an end in itself, but all or at least the key ones trust that its continuing practice will make substantive outcomes more compatible at some future date. The distinction between state and democratic institutions properly so called is not as simple as it seems when one is still close to the historical process of state building. Brazilian history can be told as a series of steps toward state formation or toward democracy, depending on one's viewpoint. This has an important bearing on the evaluation of democratic development and seems to demand some conceptual refinement.

From Geisel to Tancredo: Opening Through Elections

Gradual and peaceful, the Brazilian *abertura* of the 1970s and early 1980s seems unique by virtue of a third characteristic: It was essentially an opening through elections. It was not a result of sharp mass mobilization and was not precipitated by dramatic or external events, as in Portugal, Greece, and Argentina. In this sense, Brazil must be distinguished even from Spain, if we consider that the death of Franco brought the Spanish political system to an inevitable moment of restructuring. The Brazilian process had no such moment. Here, a gradual accumulation of pressures was channeled through the electoral process. Election results functioned as indicators of the degree to which the authoritarian regime was losing legitimacy and, in turn, helped to aggregate further pressures against it.[1]

Taking the period 1964–1984 as a whole and ignoring for a while certain moments of authoritarian exacerbation, three important democratic formalisms seem to have been at work, channeling the opening process in the direction just described: (1) an element of self-restraint on the part of military institutions; (2) electoral rules and practices kept at an acceptable level of credibility, despite some manipulations; and (3) a clear (and after 1974 virtually unanimous) preference on the part of the opposition to play the electoral game and to avoid violent confrontation. The Brazilian opening has a strong element of deliberate decompression, starting with the Geisel administration (1974–1978). It amounted, from this point of view, to recognition among the regime's power holders that an indefinite monopoly of power, or even "Mexicanization" by means of a hegemonic party, would not be viable. The opposition seems on the whole to have evaluated the situation correctly and to have sought to explore the political spaces that appeared at each moment. The formidable impact of the 1974 elections helped it to organize under the label of the MDB—Brazilian Democratic Movement—while at the same time establishing bridges among a variety of social movements and associations then increasingly (re)politicizing.

It would be naive to gloss over the tensions inherent in these changes, as if the actors were simply following a previously conceived blueprint. The point is rather that both sides, government and opposition, found enough space to redefine their respective roles through several stages, since each perceived what it stood to gain from the continuity of the process. The opposition was capable of extracting important concessions while at the same time organizing itself as a powerful electoral force. The government also benefited in many ways. Most importantly, it saw a gradual reduction in the costs of coercion. Decompression helped it to contain the growing autonomy of the repressive apparatus, which had led to violations of human rights and seriously compromised the country's image abroad. In short, the government could capitalize on the political benefits of an atmosphere of progressive "normalcy," as if exchanging losses of legitimacy arising from discontent with its past for gains based on the increasing credibility of its intentions as to the future. Paradoxically, the erosion of authoritarian legitimacy since 1974 amounted to a revitalization of governmental authority—since such authority was thus invested in the role of conductor of the decompression (later rebaptized normalization and eventually redemocratization).

I have said that the electoral game was the institutional expression of an implicit negotiation between the parliamentary opposition and the liberal sectors of the military—or of the regime as a whole. Three examples will make these arguments more concrete. All three refer to the legitimation, in practice, of a congressional majority that the government would hardly have been capable of putting together if it had not had semidictatorial powers. The first is the so-called Pacote de Abril (April Package) of 1977. Using the "revolutionary" powers of the Institutional Act 5, President Geisel decreed several measures designed to preserve a majority for the Aliança Renovadora Nacional (ARENA, the government party) in the Senate, to make an oppositionist victory for the lower chamber unlikely, and to postpone the return to direct state gubernatorial elections from 1978 to 1982.[2] Despite the incredibly massive and arbitrary nature of this intervention, the opposition chose not to reject the electoral process and went confidently to the polls. In so doing it legitimized the new authoritarian parameters; the actual election results confirmed ARENA's majority, though by a small margin. This meant that the government, with an absolute majority in both houses and controlling all but one of the twenty-three states, kept a complete monopoly of the presidential succession and of the political initiative. On the other hand, because it had such a monopoly, the government agreed to relinquish the supraconstitutional powers of Act 5 in December 1978, and negotiated a fairly comprehensive amnesty law, finally approved the following August.

The second example is the party reform of 1979, which ended the compulsory two-party structure established by the first "revolutionary" government in 1965. Knowing that the continuity of the electoral disputes within the two-party framework would inevitably lead to a major defeat, perhaps forcing the regime to violate its own rules, the Figueiredo government (1979–1984) resorted to its majority in both houses and changed the party legislation, precipitating the return to a multiparty system. The ambiguity of the opening process was again brought to the surface. On one hand, the procedure was formally impeccable, since the government did have the majority, and the reform was demanded even by some sectors of the opposition; on the other, the evident intention was to break up the opposition party, the MDB, in order to keep the agenda under control for a more extended period of time and to set the conditions under which the new party structure would be formed.

The third example is the imposition, in November 1981, of a new set of electoral rules, requiring a straight party vote at all levels (councilman, mayor, state and federal deputy, governor, and senator). This effectively prohibited any kind of alliance among the opposition parties in the 1982 elections. Care was thus taken to avoid a serious defeat for the government, since that election would affect the composition of the Electoral College that would choose the next president, in January 1985. Again, though the straight ticket helped the government's party in the overall count, many thought that it would (and certainly did) help the opposition in some key states. Also, despite its manipulative intent, this new set of rules was approved by a congressional majority that had, just a month before, broken up over two bills deemed essential to the government's interests.[3]

Although my focus in this chapter is mainly political and institutional, I must note as well the economic legitimation of the authoritarian governments up to 1984. With the exception of the first three years (1964–1966), the post-1964 governments gave an enormous impetus to modernization and economic growth. The rapid internationalization of the economy and the heavily regressive effect of government policies on income distribution eventually alienated many sectors initially favorable to the authoritarian experiment. However, during most of the post-1964 period, growth rates were high enough to grant the regime an important claim to legitimacy. Under the Médici administration, which was the most repressive and culturally stagnant, such rates were extremely high (the Brazilian "economic miracle").

Geisel, chosen for the presidency in 1973, started the decompression project exactly when the international environment began to become severely adverse. However, his economic policies were designed not only to sustain high rates of growth but, through an ambitious strategy of import substitution in basic sectors, to reduce Brazil's external dependency significantly. With the help of hindsight, it is not difficult to question some of these measures, which aggravated our external debt intolerably. However, this was not an authoritarian government lost in its internal contradictions and without any semblance of a project. On the contrary: in addition to engaging the opposition in gradual political decompression, Geisel's administration was sometimes praised by representatives of the opposition, who perceived his economic policies as nationalistic and antirecessionist.[4]

The first two years of Figueiredo's administration (1979–1980) can be regarded as a continuation of Geisel's strategy, but 1981 was a clear dividing line. On the economic side, sustaining high rates of growth became clearly impossible, after the second oil and the interest-rate shocks of 1979. Politically, Figueiredo's unwillingness to support a thorough investigation of a terrorist attempt against a May 1 artistic show in Rio de Janeiro struck a heavy blow to the credibility of the *abertura*. The attempt was seemingly planned by the information and security agencies. The lack of a thorough investigation thus brought to the surface with stunning clarity the suspicion that the whole process was subject to a military veto, regardless of electoral results or of public-opinion trends.

The election of 1982 inaugurated a fundamentally different situation. Together, the opposition parties constituted a majority (albeit small) in the lower chamber. Even more important, gaining a large number of local and ten of the twenty-three state governments, including São Paulo and Rio de Janeiro, the opposition now had significant bases of power. The only secure institutional instruments of containment at the disposal of the regime were now the Senate and the Electoral College, both severely questioned in their legitimacy.[5] This strange "diarchy," pitting the military-bureaucratic system against state governments and a lower chamber enjoying stronger popular legitimacy, was bound to affect the presidential succession, and thereby the fate of the regime. A proposed amendment to the constitution, determining that Figueiredo's successor would be chosen by direct election, set the stage for a major popular campaign, led by the opposition parties and supported by the oppositionist state governments. This was the *diretas já* (direct elections now), marked by a series of impressive popular rallies, which not only revealed the further loss of regime legitimacy but also paved the way for a formal dissidence (the Frente Liberal) within the government party, the Partido Democrático Social (PDS). The proposed amendment failed to get the two-thirds majority in the Chamber, but after the vote the situation was close to irreversible. Combined, the Frente Liberal and the largest of the opposition parties, the PMDB, established the Democratic Alliance and led Tancredo Neves to victory in the Electoral College in January 1985. Tancredo died without taking office and was succeeded in the presidency by José Sarney, a PDS dissident who had been nominated for vice president.

It can thus be said that the outcome of the opening process became clear only when the moving horizon that guided it during ten years became completely exhausted. Deep recession and the succession crisis combined to make the implicit negotiation virtually impossible after 1982; or rather, to make it possible only insofar as it was embodied in the already existing institutional rules, without further manipulation. The presidency, as an expression of military tutelage over the political system, was forced to stay neutral in the succession struggle.

This rather peculiar process of decompression was made possible because, in the initial stages, the opposition party was fighting for institutional positions almost totally emptied of real power. Up to 1982, the state governments were chosen indirectly, in effect appointed by the federal government. Congress had completely lost its main functions and prerogatives. The docility of the government party (ARENA) and of the (indirectly elected) "bionic" senators, one-third of the upper house, made it hopelessly weak. Hence, the return to civilian rule did not amount to a clear-cut return to a preexisting order. Congress, political parties, the federation: all of these regained some prestige and strength but did not automatically invest themselves in their traditional roles, first because the traditions themselves were modest, and second because the country had changed immensely under authoritarian rule. To understand the prospects for democracy in Brazil, one must appreciate these historical traditions and legacies.

Institutional History: An Overview

Our interpretation of the Brazilian *abertura* stressed that the electoral process and conventional representative institutions had preserved their potential as vehicles for an orderly and peaceful transition. This element seems to have been missed by some academic theories and pieces of journalistic analysis that depicted a far more petrified authoritarian regime. Linz, one of the few scholars who did pay attention to this problem, correctly observed that the Brazilian authoritarian rulers would have had a hard time if they had seriously decided to search for an alternative and durable legitimacy formula.

Our reconstruction of Brazilian institutional history starts with a view of the nineteenth-century empire as an extremely difficult and slow process of state building. In fact, that process is best seen as a Hobbesian construction, not in the vulgar sense of violent or tyrannical domination, but just the opposite way, meaning that certain legal fictions had to be established lest naked force become imperative—and even then, it might not be available in the requisite amount. Stretching further, the empire will be regarded as a political system that developed in order to build a state, not the other way around.[6]

The concept of representation will help us bring the process of state building into the analysis. In fact, the original or Hobbesian meaning of representation is simply formal authorization: It is the fiction that creates the state as an institution. It is prior to Dahl's legitimate contestation, since it corresponds to establishing the state framework within which contestation may later take place.[7] The democratic components of the concept appear at a more advanced stage. Social conflict and participation demands give rise to the descriptive image of representation; i.e., the notion that representative bodies should be like a sample or miniature, reflecting society's diversity. Increasing conflict and cultural strains may at the same time give rise to a demand for symbolic representation; i.e., institutions or charismatic leaders embodying a collective self-image of the nation. A fourth concept eventually emerges, focusing on the behavior of representatives. It expresses itself in the demand for faithfulness and relevance, for greater coherence in the party system, greater independence for unions and other associations, and the like. It corresponds, in short, to a more watchful state of public opinion. Let us now see what these ideas look like in historical perspective.[8]

The Empire: Hobbesian State Building

The only Portuguese colony in the New World, Brazil's political path after independence was completely different from that followed by her Spanish-speaking neighbors. Independence, obtained in 1822, was already marked by a unique feature: It came without a war against the Portuguese metropolis. A proclamation by the regent prince effected the separation and turned Brazil into an independent monarchy. After some years of instability, the monarchical form of government succeeded in establishing a stable political order and in keeping the integrity of the national territory.

The key factor accounting for stability during most of the nineteenth century was the existence of a cohesive political elite entrusted with the legal control of the country. The political system, considered more broadly, was a coalition of the rural aristocracy with the bureaucratic elite, but at the top these two sectors became strongly integrated. Recruited among landowners, urban merchants, and miners, this political elite was trained in the spirit of Roman law, Portuguese absolutism, and mercantilism.[9] The ideological unity of the elite helped it cope with threats to territorial integrity, despite the centrifugal tendencies inherent in continental size, inadequate means of communication and transportation, the thinness of the economic linkages among provinces and regions, and the absence of a strong sense of national identity. Another important factor, in contrast with the old Spanish colonies, lies in the field of civil-military relations. During the empire, there was no threat to civil hegemony in Brazil. A parliamentary monarchy thus developed. The whole arrangement was elitist, no doubt, but cabinets were elected and governed, liberals and conservatives rotated in office, and representative practices thus developed to some extent.

The "artificial" character of this political system has been frequently pointed out. Constitutional arrangements gave the emperor the so-called moderating power, which placed him above parties and factions, in fact allowing him to make and unmake majorities when he decided to dissolve parliament and call new elections. The two parties hardly differed, it is said, and had no significant roots in society. Elections not only tended to return the same people but were frequently fraudulent. This account is as correct as it is anachronic; it completely misses the fact that here we are not talking about descriptive representation in a highly differentiated society, but rather about Hobbesian authorization in the course of state building. In order to understand this, we must take a broader look at the function of elections and at the way in which they were regulated up to 1930.[10]

The endless series of electoral reforms and the constant accusations of fraud were primarily a result of the absence of any independent judicial organization to manage elections. The whole process, from voter registration (or rather, recognition) to counting ballots and proclaiming results was, in one way or another, subject to the interference of those involved and especially of police authorities subject to the provincial governors. To this extent, the importance of elections was indeed reduced. But local councils did affect the choice of state and national deputies. The government was thus constantly concerned with elections at all levels; in fact, it is said that the main function of the provincial governor, under the empire, was to win elections. From our Hobbesian standpoint, it may be deduced that losing them too frequently would force the central government to resort to its *ultima ratio;* i.e., open intervention.

Not a few observers have gone as far as to say that in Brazil, elections were totally farcical, and that more "authentic" results would have been achieved through a plain recognition of whomever held power in a given region or locality; or, on the other extreme, through complete centralization. The argument seems persuasive simply because it skips the difficult step. If recognition in this sense means granting a legal title to rule (as elections do), at that time it would have been tantamount to unleashing an endless series of small civil wars, since in each case public authority would be bestowed on a specifically named individual or faction, to the exclusion of others. The central government would thus be multiplying the conflicts it was seeking to avoid.

It is equally evident that the imperial government did not possess material capabilities to intervene everywhere and "centralize" power, as the recipe goes. Centralization did occur, but in a different sense. The representative mechanism of the empire operated by means of a highly aristocratic two-party system. Rotation between the two was partly a matter of elections, but it also had a lot to do with imperial inducement. The whole point of this courtly and apparently alien system was actually to control the processes of party formation. Monarchical government meant that, contrary to the United States, we did not have the formative impact of presidential elections. Formation through class conflict was out of the question, given the rudimentary state of the productive structure and the low level of social mobilization. But two other alternatives can still be imagined, and the empire carefully controlled both. One was parties of principle, in Burkean language; i.e., parties based on religious or otherwise doctrinal views. Some initiatives of this kind appeared toward the end of the century and were adequately controlled or repressed. The other, certainly more significant, was a gradual evolution from kinship groups (with their private armies) toward nationally organized parties. Something of this sort happened in Uruguay, for example. Brazil's territorial extension made it far less likely, but, in any case, it was prevented exactly by the flexible rotation allowed at the top of the pyramid and managed by the emperor.

The nineteenth-century constitutional monarchy was clearly not a democratic system. Its equilibrium rested largely on the bureaucracy, but this arrangement worked well only as long as it was attractive to a few key actors. When it ceased to be attractive to landowners and slave owners, and when new interests, most notably the military, became more differentiated, it fell without anyone to defend it and without violence.

The First Republic: Hobbes II

When Marshall Deodoro da Fonseca marched before the troops in Rio de Janeiro, on November 15, 1889, signaling the change of the regime, military discontent with the monarchy had already gone a long way. During most of the nineteenth century, the military had played virtually no role in Brazilian politics. The Paraguayan war (1865–1870), however, led to the development of a strong professional army. Victorious, the military decided to claim a share in power and greater respect from society. This was also the time when Comtean positivism and republican ideas began to penetrate military circles, starting a long tradition of military politicization.[11]

Another major source of opposition to the political system of the empire were the São Paulo coffee growers. One of the links between the bureaucratic elite and the landowners under the empire was the underlying agreement to preserve slavery. But the coffee plantations of São Paulo, which developed rapidly during the last decades of the century, depended on wage labor, and indeed on the free labor of European migrants. Republican ideas thus became clearly linked to economic modernization. But the republic was, at the beginning, just as bad for the coffee growers; first because an inexperienced military exerted decisive influence and made the system potentially very unstable, and second because the unitary monarchy gave way to extreme federative decentralization. The republican Constitution of 1891, closely inspired by the U.S. model, gave a great deal of autonomy to the states, including extensive fiscal rights. The country thus faced a precocious "ungovernability" syndrome. The weakness of the central government affected, very adversely, the interests of the more dynamic sectors of the economy, which were exactly those located in São Paulo. For the *paulista* coffee growers, the fiscal and exchange policies were vital.

These elements do not exhaust the picture but go a long way to explain the changes that took place in the political system of the First Republic, producing a generalized feeling that the "real" Brazil had little to do with its liberal constitution. First, the political leaders of the two major states, São Paulo and Minas Gerais, decided to establish between themselves the backbone of a functioning polity. A key aspect of the pact was that they would alternate controlling the federal executive. From this vantage point, they went on to develop a new "doctrine," called politics of the governors: They would support whichever oligarchy was dominant in each of the other states, in exchange for support for their arrangement at the federal level. The central government thus refrained from passing judgment on the quality of the political practices of each state.[12] This was the new guise of the Hobbesian construction. Needless to say, it went rather far to making liberal "formalities" indeed a farce. The legislative and judicial branches were decisively reduced to a secondary role; Congress became increasingly docile and lost its potential as a locus of party formation; and opposition was curbed in most of the states, so much so that statewide single parties became the rule.

The end of slavery and the extension of voting rights to large numbers of town dwellers and rural workers made it imperative for the federal government to be sure it would gain these votes. The governor's role thus became one of disciplining an extended electoral base, which he did by granting extensive extralegal authority to local bosses, in exchange for electoral support. This is the root of the phenomenon of *coronelismo,* which did so much to demoralize the electoral process in the eyes of the urban middle class up to 1930 and to generalize the notion that electoral institutions were somehow "alien" to Brazilian soil. Another result of this process of state building was to make the relationship between political and private power—the latter based on land ownership—extremely transparent and resilient to change.

In exchange for the votes they garnered, the *coronéis* (backland bosses) received support from the oligarchy in control of the state machinery, thus reproducing further down the scale the arrangement between the states and the federal government. Control of the state machinery thus became rather literally a matter of life and death, since in addition to hiring and firing it could easily arrest or release.

Hobbes III: Getúlio Vargas

It is in many ways astounding that the political system of the First Republic lasted forty-one years. In addition to the modest development of the urban middle strata and to the very incipient advances toward forming an industrial working class, that longevity was facilitated by the hierarchical character of nonurban politics, which was the real center of gravity of the whole construction. The votes of the peasants and other lower strata were controlled by rival factions of *coronéis,* who tended to be unified in a single pyramid because of the single-party structures in the states.

In October 1930, the First Republic was terminated by a revolutionary movement led by Getúlio Vargas, who until then was a rather conventional politician from the southernmost state, Rio Grande do Sul. The Revolution of 1930 cannot be described by a single set of causes. It was a reflection of regional cleavages as well as of urban middle-class and military discontent. It was made possible by the obsolescence of the political pact between the two major states, Minas Gerais and São Paulo. The rapid development of the latter toward modern capitalist agriculture and even toward industrialization gradually unbalanced the initial arrangements. However, São Paulo was hit hardest by the international crisis of 1929; other important states, Minas Gerais included, thus made a bid for greater power and influence.[13]

The main institutional result of the movement headed by Getúlio Vargas was an irreversible increase in central authority: The federative excesses of the First Republic were curtailed; government intervention in the economy was legitimized to a far greater degree; and, last but not least, important changes in representation concepts and practices were quickly introduced. Descriptive and symbolic meanings of representation finally made headway into the legal and political culture.

Descriptive representation is based on the notion that representative bodies ought somehow to look like a sample of society. It is therefore a demand that the Hobbesian process of formal authorization be enriched, in order to bring the diversity of social cleavages into those bodies. Perhaps we should stress the word *enriched,* since, for the 1930s, it is not always possible to speak of an articulate demand on the part of autonomous and identifiable social groups. A great deal of the legislation adopted must be understood as having a preemptive character (as was clearly the case with corporatism in the field of labor organization). In the electoral field, the introduction of a scheme of proportional representation (through the Electoral Code of 1932) was intimately linked to other changes, in an overall design intended to enhance governmental authority. Indeed, the revolution rapidly moved to lower the voting age to eighteen, to extend the right to vote to women, to introduce the secret ballot, and to create an Electoral Court in charge of the whole process, from voter registration to certifying the victor.

These advances beg the question of how efficacious voting rights could be at that moment. But the point is that the First Republic had seriously degraded parliamentary and electoral institutions. To recover them would, of course, have a democratizing impact in the long run; but there was a pressing problem of reorganizing and reasserting authority in the short run. The revolution, after all, had decisively strengthened the federal executive vis-à-vis states and regions; signs of left/right polarization and especially resistance to a quick return to institutional normalcy were quite visible.

The provisional government was thus obliged to meet, and drew a great deal of legitimacy from meeting, the prior demand for "moralization of electoral practices." What most attracted Assis Brasil (the main author of the Electoral Code of 1932) to proportional representation (PR) was the enhancement he thought it would give to government legitimacy and stability, rather than the faithful representation of social diversity. Because it represented the (electoral) minority, PR strengthened its involvement with the state system and its acceptance of the majority. Also, PR was based on larger geographical divisions (actually, the states), thus making the mandate truly independent, in the Burkean sense, instead of the almost imperative mandate that might result from small districts under the direct influence of landowners and local potentates. It should also be noted that Assis Brasil's model prevails even today insofar as the representation of the different states in the federal Chamber is concerned. The latter is based on the over-representation of the smaller and on the under-representation of the very large states (especially São Paulo), thus introducing considerations of federative equilibrium, and not simply of electoral justice, in the composition of the lower chamber. In recent years this has been much criticized, but at that time the logic was clearly the same that underlies Assis Brasil's reference to minority support.

It was also thought that PR on a broad geographical basis would practically force the consolidation of the other elements of the electoral reform, such as the secret ballot and administration of the electoral process by an independent Electoral Court. It is noteworthy that one of the most capable analysts of Brazilian institutional history, Nunes Leal, hardly emphasizes the element of proportionality when he discusses the reform of the early 1930s. The important aspect for him is the advance toward "moralization"; i.e., the Electoral Court. This is also remarkable in that Nunes Leal was deeply skeptical about the development of representative democracy in Brazil without a major change in the agrarian structure. Even so, he wrote, in 1948,

> Despite the excesses and frauds that may have occurred here and there, most testimonies have been favorable to the electoral laws of the early thirties. The gravest accusations against our system of political representation ended simply as a consequence of the fact that those laws withdrew the prerogative of certifying who was elected from the chambers themselves. The *ins* ended up defeated in some states and a numerous opposition, later reinforced by contestation in the presidential election, found its way even to the Federal Chamber.[14]

One irony of modern Brazil is that these initial and decisive advances toward Dahlian democratization were in part instrumental to the new Hobbesian/Getúlian thrust. Moreover, they were in part effected under the auspices of protofascist thinking.[15] The forty-one years of the first republican constitution had given rise to a deep strain in political culture: Liberal forms had come to be regarded as an alien factor, distorting or corrupting the "true" nature of Brazilian society. There arose a demand for "authentic" representation, for an institutional structure truly adapted to Brazilian reality. For some, this meant an improvement, but for others it meant the suppression of electoral, party, and parliamentary institutions. The Constitutional Congress of 1934 included a section of "corporatist" deputies, an experiment that did not take root and would never be repeated. But corporatist views of representation were widely propagated and became in fact the framework within which so-called social rights were extended to the urban working class.[16] Such views were part and parcel of the Getúlian thrust toward an authoritarian (as distinguished from totalitarian) integration of the political order. Under Getúlio Vargas's guidance, protofascist thinking quickly became antifascist; i.e., an edge against the further development of mobilizational fascism. More than that, it became an ideological framework helping him effectively to repress the two extremes, *integralistas* and Communists, starting in 1935 and leading to the formal announcement of the dictatorial Estado Novo (1937–1945).

The two pillars of this move toward a far more centralized state structure must be considered, since they embodied the presence, apparently for the first time in Brazilian history, of a comprehensive experiment in symbolic representation. One was the increasingly charismatic nature of the presidential office, with Getúlio Vargas in the role of founding father. At the time, however, this was a limited and cautious change, compared with the more portentous events that would soon take place in Argentina with Perón.

In Brazil, the charismatic presidency developed without a confrontation with the system's element of limited pluralism (in Linz's sense): A de facto federation continued to exist, with strongly oligarchical features within each state; the church's traditional legitimacy went on receiving a great deal of deference; and the elite (strange as this may sound) did not give up its reverence for legal culture and for the Brazilian legal tradition.

Another pillar in the emergence of Getúlian representation was the reinforcement, and, indeed, a considered invention of certain symbols of national identity. It is surely possible to assert that at this time we witness the emergence of culture policy; that such policy was closely associated with a process of nation (as opposed to state) building; and finally that both would have long-range effects in crystallizing a whole new notion of representation in Brazilian political culture. This cultural construction vigorously asserted that zero-sum conflict could not reasonably emerge in Brazilian society. This view became truly encompassing and persuasive in part because it was espoused by leading intellectuals and artists, but also because it reflected important historical and social traits. It was, first, a celebration of past success in keeping together such a vast territory, this in turn always associated with the notion of unlimited opportunity. Second, it suggested that Brazilian social structure had indeed evolved in the direction of increased equality and mobility, not least in the field of race relations.[17] Third, it was a view of Brazilian politics; it effectively retrieved the experience of the early empire, especially Conciliation, when elite restraint and skill put an end to regional and factional struggles. But in the 1930s, a subtle turn seems to have occurred: Instead of reinforcing its nascent negative image as oligarchical, intra-elite behavior, this cultural construction came to regard political flexibility and realism as an emanation of similar traits in the social system, implying that Brazilian politics at its best would always be flexible. Finally, it was a reassertion, on a grand scale, of the conservative (patriarchal) view of conflict as childish behavior: an image that could only be persuasive in a country that had virtually no experience with principled politics and that felt threatened by its emergence in the guise of communism and mobilizational fascism.

The Failure to Consolidate: 1945–1964

Getúlio Vargas was forced to resign on October 29, 1945. His fall and the subsequent developments had a lot to do with the changed international environment. The defeat of the Axis powers in World War II had discredited the Estado Novo internally and externally, despite the fact that it did not belong to the family of mobilizational fascism. At least at first sight, the democratic "experiment" that followed the fall of the Estado Novo had very favorable conditions to prosper and succeed. The international environment was certainly favorable; the domestic economy was not under unusual strain; the armed forces had developed a high degree of organization and an antipersonalistic outlook as a result of their close attention to the weakness of Italian fascism; and the Getúlian dictatorship had led to the emergence of a vigorous liberal opposition, with outstanding parliamentary leadership: the União Democrática Nacional (UDN). The deepest of all Brazilian evils, in the eyes of Nunes Leal, the sin of *governismo,* seemed to have ended.[18] The transition had once again been peaceful: If the lack of a clear break with the Estado Novo made further democratization more difficult later on, the absence of bloody cleavages could have made it easier.

Why did the democratic system then fail to consolidate itself in the next twenty years? The first difficulty was the important institutional contradiction that had developed after 1930 and as a consequence of the Estado Novo. Authority now seemed to bifurcate in a truly charismatic image of the presidency on one side, and an enormous assertion of the parliamentary institution—not least because of the formation of the UDN in the struggle against Vargas—on the other. This was not an immediate threat, since Vargas withdrew to a silent role after his downfall, but became extremely serious when he came back, riding the tide of a direct presidential election in 1950. The political system was now torn between an executive with strong Caesarist overtones and a parliamentary center of gravity that pulled toward some sort of congressional or party government. Needless to say, Vargas's second presidency was extremely tense, and the contradiction was aggravated instead of diluted by his suicide in August 1954.[19]

Second, this newly assertive and formally powerful Congress was essentially made up of notables. It understandably had not developed a technical substructure to speak of and was not supported by a modern party system. In order to appreciate this difficulty, it is necessary to recall that the scope of government intervention had been enormously enlarged since 1930. The bureaucracy, traditionally large by virtue of the patrimonial origins of the Brazilian state, had again been expanded and modernized after the revolution. The legislature had constitutional powers but lacked everything else it needed to supervise and check this massive amount of policy-making.[20]

Interpretations of the 1964 breakdown have diverged a great deal. Stating his preference for those that stress the "internal sociopolitical situation" rather than "causes exogenous to the polity," Merquior aptly summarizes this literature:

> Government instability, the disintegration of the party system, virtual paralysis of legislative decision-making, equivocal attitudes on the part of President Goulart, not least with regard to his own succession; the threat of an ill-defined agrarian reform; military concern with government-blessed sergeants' mutinies; and mounting radicalism on both the right and the left . . . all of this compounded by soaring inflation and, of course, by the haunting ghost of the Cuban revolution.[21]

The fate of the party system should be specifically noted. I have suggested that from 1945 onward Brazil had for the first time some basic conditions to develop a competitive party structure. Most observers seem to agree that the start was promising, but that the new party system underwent a sharp deinstitutionalization from the second half of the 1950s up to 1964. Some impute this to sheer erosion; i.e., rapid social mobilization in the wake of industrialization and urbanization, decreasing efficacy of traditional control mechanisms of the patron-client type, and so forth. Others place greater emphasis on institutional regulations, especially the electoral system based on PR and the preferential vote (open party lists). The fact, however, is that from Jânio Quadros's presidential resignation (August 1961) to the military takeover (March 1964), the party system was overpowered by the worst of all worlds. It became highly fractionalized and subject to increasing radicalization at the same time that each of the major parties was internally divided; the tide of antiparty populism became truly exponential (the election of Jânio Quadros to the presidency in 1960 being an example); and the party traditionally identified with moderation and equilibrium, the Partido Social Democrático (PSD), became fragmented.[22]

However, we must guard against an overly political interpretation. On a broader canvas, the fragmentation of the party system was itself associated with the overall process of economic and social change. This relationship operated in two ways. On one hand, urbanization and social mobilization eroded traditional attachments and social-control mechanisms. On the other, the lack of substantial advance toward deconcentration (reduction of social inequality) left the parties, individually and as a system, without strong bases of popular support. This was the structural framework within which older ideological and institutional conflicts were acted out, setting the stage for the military takeover. On March 31, 1964, the incumbent president, João Goulart, Getúlio Vargas's political heir, was ousted from office and sent to exile.

Thus, Brazil moved rapidly toward instituting the form of democracy—political contestation and participation—but failed to consolidate democracy by reducing socioeconomic inequality. Unable to channel social conflict toward concrete policies, the party system entered a cycle of deinstitutionalization, rather than of consolidation in the new democratic mold. Had there been substantial advances toward reducing inequality, there might have been major conflict among the parties and along class lines, but not the combination of radicalism and populism that took place in big cities, plus survival or even reassertion of basically clientelistic structures in the less developed areas of the country. The crisis of the party system was thus rather telling and cannot be understood simply in terms of the traditional view of those parties as being premodern, preideological, or otherwise not ripe for serious representative democracy. It was more in the nature of an induced suicide, by means of which the society seems to have expelled an extraneous body: a trend toward stronger political representation in the absence of any substantial deconcentration.

An Overview of the Overview

Brazilian institutional development was, so to speak, preeminently state-centered. It must be understood in terms of the prolonged process of state-building and the cautious strategies on which it was based, since a small central elite and state structure were confronted with the challenge of preserving territorial unity in a country of continental dimensions. Today's heavy bureaucratic machinery; the ponderous legalistic ethos, despite the fact that legal norms are frequently bypassed; the continuing weight of clientelism and of conservative interests based on land ownership, not to speak of the increasingly tutelary role of the military since the Estado Novo—all these can be traced to or partly explained by that fundamental thrust of our state formation. These aspects of state building have also been held responsible for what is felt to be an absence of public authority, or a lack of differentiation of the political system vis-à-vis societal structures. This is often phrased as an absence of political institutions properly so-called. This chapter has argued, to the contrary, that there has been significant institution building, though not necessarily of a formally democratic character. Certain aspects of the post-1964 regime, which are surely relevant for understanding the *abertura,* are clearly related to that prior institutional development.

The literature on the authoritarian experiment rightly stresses that its economic project was one of capitalist modernization and greater integration in the world capitalist system; and further, that this led, from 1967 on, to a strategy of accelerated industrial growth rather than of income redistribution or of reduction of absolute poverty. It is also correctly said that the initial perceptions led policymakers to curb labor unions and "progressive" organizations; and finally, that this overall thrust, combined with the need to repress guerrilla activities, ended up engaging the regime, from 1968 to 1974, in a highly repressive phase, with very high costs in terms of human rights. Yet, two features of the post-1964 regime helped preserve institutional continuity, which in this context meant a chance for a peaceful resumption of democracy. The first was the impersonal concept of government, which materialized in: (1) tighter rules to contain politicization among the military; (2) conservation of the presidency as an elective office, at least through an Electoral College; and (3) keeping the traditional limit on the presidential term and the norm against reelection.[23]

The second feature was the preservation of the representative system. Needless to say, representation here meant formal authorization, in the Hobbesian sense; but it now took place within institutional parameters that not even the military could afford to ignore or distort completely. Interestingly, the pre-1964 party structure was not immediately suppressed.

The decision to terminate the old parties was made only in October 1965, eighteen months after the coup, and was immediately followed by the creation of at least a "provisional" party structure; i.e., the two-party system that was to remain until 1979. The military governments obviously manipulated the conditions under which elections were held in the ensuing twenty years but did not try to do away with the electoral mechanism as such or to replace it by a totally different doctrine of representation.

Theoretical Review

State-building in Brazil left a highly contradictory legacy for contemporary democratic development. As a skillful extension of central regulatory capabilities, it was constantly oriented toward keeping intra-elite conflict at a low level and preventing the eruption of large-scale political violence. But this preemptive pattern of growth undoubtedly made Brazilian society too "backward" from the standpoint of autonomous associational participation. This, in turn, gave the elites and the bureaucracy an excessive latitude to define policy priorities, crystallized unjustifiable income differentials, and left the political system constantly exposed to a dangerous legitimacy gap.

Overall Historical Pattern

Brazil was a part of the Portuguese Empire from 1500 to 1822. During those three centuries, it was in essence a commercial (as opposed to a settlement) colony, featuring mining and large-scale plantations based on slave labor. Even the colonizers were few, since the Portuguese population was pathetically small compared to the vast world empire it tried to build. These are some of the reasons why the colonial system left neither a powerful central authority nor an integrated national community in its wake.

The comparative question with respect to Brazil's colonial past, then, is not so much one of democratic tradition, imported or indigenous.[24] It is rather the relatively smooth transition to a process of political development that we see as consciously oriented toward long-range goals. Political competition and the appropriate institutions began to develop under the empire, at a time when mass political participation was totally absent. From then on, political changes became comparatively nonviolent, allowing enough room for the contending groups to accommodate their differences afterwards. Since the nineteenth century, large-scale violence has been increasingly controlled, and bitter memories have not accumulated, at least not among the political elite.

Robert Dahl's theoretical judgment that democracy is better off when peaceful contestation among elites precedes mass participation may be accepted, but requires some qualifications in the Brazilian case. First, there is a matter of degree, since that process finally led to a state structure that seems excessively strong vis-à-vis civil society: too large and clientelistic to be effectively controlled by the citizenry and constantly reinforced by the constraints of so-called late industrialization. Second, the Dahlian sequence seems to have left serious strains in terms of legitimacy and political culture, as indicated by the alleged excess of conciliation and elitist character of the political system.

State Structure and Strength

Historians who see a strong state in Brazil in the nineteenth century normally stress that the empire kept the country's territorial integrity, though compelled to use force against important separatist movements. Other analyses attempt to trace the bureaucratic organization of the Brazilian government directly back to the Portuguese absolutist state. But these arguments overstate the case, since they overlook the fact that state structures never became entirely distinguished qua public authority. Symbiotic arrangements with private power (e.g., landed wealth) were part and parcel of a gradual extension of regulatory capabilities. The effectiveness of the central authority in keeping public order and eventually in undertaking social changes is, then, recent in Brazilian history. It is difficult to see how it could exist at a time when the national army hardly existed, or even before it developed organizational responses to its own internal divisions.[25]

The organizational "maturity" of the army would appear only after the Revolution of 1930. From the 1930s onward, the armed forces developed an increasingly tutelary conception of their role vis-à-vis civilian institutions and society as a whole. Thus, in 1945 they pressured Getúlio Vargas out of office, on the understanding that the days of the Estado Novo were gone. Friction with elected presidents or with their ministers was evident throughout the 1950s and early 1960s. In 1961, following Jânio Quadros's resignation from the presidency, the military ministers actually vetoed the transfer of power to the elected vice president, João Goulart. This move brought the country to the brink of civil war and was defeated only because the military ministers failed to achieve unitary backing for their position among the regional commanders. In 1964, with substantial popular support, the military overthrew Goulart and took power.

However, this tutelary role should not be taken to mean that the Brazilian military is quintessentially opposed to democratic principles and institutions. The tutelary self-conception clearly belongs to the broader authoritarian ideology that presided over the last phase of state building; i.e., the Getúlian thrust of the 1930s. That ideology includes elements that, paradoxically, help sustain some of the institutional mechanisms of representative democracy. Being, at root, antipopulist and nonmobilizational, it stresses the distinction between private and public roles—hence the limits on the duration of mandates, the electoral calendar, and, more generally, the importance of keeping the legislature, at least as an institution capable of being reactivated—all of these clearly practiced by the post-1964 regime.

Brazil's political development has also benefited from the paucity of direct armed challenges to the state in this century and the effective repression since the 1930s of those few that did occur. Ethnic separatism has been virtually nonexistent in modern Brazil. In this regard, too, state building was brought to a conclusion that certainly favors democracy.

On the other hand, the procedures and justifications used to repress armed challenges, in the 1930s and again after 1964, led to threatening precedents. In both cases, those challenges were treated in terms of "internal war," far more than as unlawful behavior that perhaps could be dealt with by judicial or political means. The legislature, political parties, the judiciary: all of these came out clearly weakened vis-à-vis the executive (which in fact meant the military). With the military directly in power after 1964, this trend became far more serious. First there came the arrests, proscriptions, and similar measures designed to curb opposition and promote societal demobilization. From 1968 to 1974, confronting armed underground movements, the regime adopted widespread censorship and all sorts of cover-up of repressive practices. The cost of this phase in terms of human rights was not as high as that endured by Argentina shortly afterward, but it cannot be underestimated as a negative effect for democratic prospects. As argued in my first section, some of the military seem to have recognized that they had gone too far, when they opted (circa 1973) for a gradual "opening from above."

The description of the Brazilian military as exerting a tutelary role and as having directly established an authoritarian regime that would last for twenty-one years obviously does not square well with the emerging image of a vigorous "civil society." In fact, there have been exaggerations in applying the latter concept to the Brazilian case. It is true, of course, that Brazilian society has become highly differentiated and complex. Combined with resistance to the military regime, this has led to a rapid increase in associational politicization. But a more appropriate reading of this trend would update the picture of a society marked by unusually low participation and predominantly organized along corporatist lines. Corporatist political organization (i.e., based essentially on occupational criteria) traditionally facilitated control by the state (as in the case of labor unions) and the petrification of differential privileges among professions, the gradient of such differences being guaranteed by the state.

After twenty years of military-authoritarian rule (1964–1984), no one will doubt that the Brazilian state is highly centralized vis-à-vis the federation, or that it directly controls a large proportion of the economy. Since the nineteenth century, the predominant concern with state building, and the high degree of cohesion of the political elite contrasting with the dispersion and abysmal poverty of the general populace, meant that the central authorities enjoyed a wide margin of discretion to make choices in economic policy.

Development Performance

Disregarding redistributive issues for a moment, there can be no question that Brazilian governments have been consistently seeking to promote economic growth for a long time, and that their record is fairly impressive. The Brazilian economy is now among the ten or twelve largest in the world, bigger than Australia's. This rank is the result of continuously high rates of growth since the early 1930s, and especially of steady advances toward industrialization. The average growth rate of GDP during this whole period has been about 6 percent a year, with a peak of 10 percent a year from 1968 to 1974. Industrial growth rates have been twice or thrice that of agriculture; in 1968, ten times higher. This growth pattern accounts for the vast scale of the structural changes the country has undergone (see Table 3.1), which Santos finds at least as impressive as that promoted by Meiji restoration in Japan or by the Soviet government in its initial two decades.[26]

Some structural aspects of Brazil's "late-developer" pattern of growth must be underlined if we are to understand its political implications. Far from deconcentrating state power, the growth record mentioned above has greatly reinforced it. Reacting to the constraints brought by World War I and by the crisis of 1929, subsequent governments assumed an increasingly direct role in the economic sphere. Starting with the Volta Redonda steel complex, in 1942, state and mixed enterprises were created to foster industrial infrastructure. Foreign trade was regulated not only through fiscal and exchange policies, but also through government entities specifically designed to supervise the commercialization of coffee, sugar, and other commodities. Four decades later, Hewlett could aptly describe the Brazilian state as "a significant producer of basic industrial goods and infra-structural items, an important agent of protection and subsidy, a powerful regulator of economic activity, and the determiner of the direction of national economic development."[27]

Needless to say, this record of growth underlies the proven ability of the Brazilian political system to avoid the generalization of zero-sum perceptions and expectations. But these successes have not been sufficient to dilute the illegitimacy syndrome that permanently surrounds the political system, if not authorities in general. In fact, the Brazilian state, having relied heavily on economic growth for legitimacy, has been reasonably successful in promoting growth but seems rather far from overcoming its legitimacy deficit. In theory, the state can manipulate the supply of key inputs and thus start altering the many perverse aspects of the growth pattern, but it cannot readily do that in practice, as Hewlett points out, since interfering with the market conditions toward which major enterprises are oriented would often mean reducing the rate of growth—hence, losing legitimacy. Moreover, insufficient domestic savings, technological dependence, and other imbalances have increasingly led the country, since the 1950s, to a strategy of growth-cum-debt and inflationary financing. In the 1970s and early 1980s, as is well known, foreign debt skyrocketed to over $100 billion and inflation rapidly moved to the three-digit altitude. Only after successive failures in the attempt to control inflation by means of heterodox shocks between 1986 and 1990 did policymakers, academic economists, and the business community become convinced that a thorough revision of this state-centered growth model had become imperative.

In conclusion, Brazilian development from the 1930s through the late 1970s can thus be said to have very positive and very negative aspects. High rates of growth (hence variable-sum perceptions among different strata of society) coexist with dramatic imbalances—regionally, against the northeast; sectorally, against small-scale agriculture and rural labor; by class, against the poor in general. But there is no persuasive evidence that those positive or negative aspects are predominantly associated by the mass public with either democratic or authoritarian governments. Memories of high growth flash back on democratic (e.g., Kubitschek, 1955–1960) as well as on extreme authoritarian (e.g., Médici, 1969–1973) administrations.

A significant distinction emerged in the 1970s and early 1980s among the educated, urban middle class. In this segment, there undoubtedly was an increase in the proportion of those thinking that the military-authoritarian regime achieved growth at an unacceptable social cost: income concentration; neglect of welfare investments; denationalization of economy and culture; damage to the environment; corruption. This change was crucially important for the Brazilian political *abertura,* expressing itself in electoral mobilization as well as in the political activation of professional and civic associations of numerous types.

Concerning corruption, very important changes have taken place. Up to 1964, corruption was clearly perceived in a patrimonial rather than in a capitalistic framework. The widespread feeling that politicians are corrupt was then primarily focused on clientelistic (patronage) practices. Undue use of public funds for private enrichment was not unknown, of course, but it was perceived as associated with only a few practices (e.g., dubious credits to landowners and co-optation of union leaders). Under the military governments, the context and, therefore, the whole perception of corruption underwent an enormous change—perhaps we should say that both moved to an exponential scale. Accelerated industrialization, increasing internationalization of the economy, the whole strategy of growth-cum-debt—all of these took place, we must recall, without any effective parliamentary oversight and often under the protection of pervasive press censorship. No wonder, then, that the idea of corruption became associated with financial scandals, alleged "commissions" in foreign dealings, and so on; the number of known cases being sufficient, needless to say, to lend credence to the most extravagant generalizations.

Since the transition, the growth of investigative journalism, the impeachment of President Collor in 1992, and a scandal involving members of the congressional Budget Commission in 1993 have substantially changed this long-standing picture of governmental corruption and public complacency. It is not far-fetched to say that Brazilian political culture has gained an important ethical dimension in recent years, which is bound to have practical and institutional consequences during the remainder of the 1990s. If this assumption proves correct, democracy will come out stronger. In a country historically marked by poverty and inequality, insufficient governability, and a political culture strongly affected by corrupt practices, it comes as no surprise that even as remarkable a record of economic growth as Brazil's should for so long have fallen short of full legitimation as a democratic regime.

Class Structure, Income Distribution, and Social Organization

No matter how one measures them, levels of income inequality and mass poverty in Brazil are among the worst in the world. The main determinants of present income differentials and class structure undoubtedly have their roots in the pattern of land appropriation inherited from the colonial past. Concentration of landed wealth and use of the best land to produce export commodities have always been the major "push" factors behind the enormous supply of cheap labor constantly flocking to the cities.[28] Rapid industrial growth oriented toward a predominantly middle-class market, high rates of population growth, and the insufficiency of investment in basic welfare services have combined to maintain extreme inequalities and indeed to make a mockery of the "trickle-down" theory of indirect redistribution.[29] Needless to say, the full implications of Brazilian-size poverty and inequality for democratic prospects must also take into account that the country has now become highly urbanized and "mobilized" (in Deutsch's sense).

Throughout the empire and the First Republic, both working class and urban middle strata were numerically unimportant. The vast majority of the population lived in rural areas or in very small villages and towns, where society was steeply stratified. Here, there was no middle class worth speaking of. At the bottom were the peasants, a sprinkling of very poor independent farmers, and similar strata in the towns. At that time, a crisis in the coffee business was tantamount to economic recession, but it did not necessarily mean that a large number of laborers lost their jobs. From World War II onward, the picture started changing dramatically. Total population grew from 41 million in 1940 to 146 million in 1990; during this same half century, urban population grew from 13 to 119 million, the population living in the nine largest cities from 6 to 48 million, and voters from 6 to over 80 million. These changes were accompanied by major shifts in the labor force out of agriculture and into industry and services (see Table 3.1).

Table 3.1   Socioeconomic Change in Brazil, 1940–1990

	1940	1950	1960	1970	1980	1990
Population (in millions)	41.2	51.9	70.1	93.1	119.1	145.6
Percent of population in urban areas	31.2	35.1	45.1	55.9	67.6	75.0
Percent of population in metropolitan areas (nine largest cities)	15.2	17.9	21.5	25.5	29.0	33.0
Percentage of the labor force in:						
Agriculture	67.4	60.2	54.5	44.6	30.5	22.8
Industry	12.6	13.3	12.4	18.1	24.9	22.7
Services	19.9	26.4	33.1	37.8	44.6	54.5
Per capita gross national product (GNP) (in U.S. dollars)	391[a]	444	640	960	1,708	2,680

Sources: For population data: *Fundação IBGE* (Censos Demográficos e Tabulações Avançadas de 1980). For GNP: *Conjuntura Econômica* 26, no. 11 (1972), and *Gazeta Mercantil* (1970-1985).
    a. Data for 1947.

Despite the impressive overall rates of economic growth during the "economic miracle" period of the military regime (the late 1960s and early 1970s), there is ample evidence that income differentials and some telling indicators of basic welfare (such as infant mortality) went on worsening. By the early 1970s, several studies were showing that income inequality had increased relative to the early 1960s. Writing in 1976, Graham offered the following summary of the evidence:

(a) income concentration (as measured by the standard Gini index) increased overall, and in all regions, during the sixties; (b) the rates of concentration were more pronounced in the more developed (and most rapidly growing) areas like São Paulo and the south than in the lesser developed regions; (c) real income increased in all areas; (d) average monthly real income per urban worker increased much more rapidly (43 percent) than income per agricultural worker (14 percent), thereby increasing the intersectoral income differentials during the decade; (e) these intersectoral income differentials stood out much more dramatically in the northeast than in São Paulo and the center and south.[30]

Using data from 1960 to 1980, Serra reported continuing income concentration through the 1970s. The lowest 20% of the economically active population had gone from 3.9% of total income in 1960 to 3.4% in 1970, to 2.8%

in 1980; the top 10%, from 39.6% to 46.7%, to 50.9%.[31] This means that the governmental policies practiced throughout this period, at best, did not counteract structural forces making for greater inequality; at worst they aggravated their effect. Slow growth, soaring inflation, and a sharp deterioration of social services throughout the 1980s and early 1990s further worsened this picture. By the end of the 1990s, the top tenth of the population was earning 51.3% of all income, the top fifth more than two-thirds (67.5%), and the bottom fifth 2.1%. These figures represent the single worst income distribution of the sixty-five countries for which the World Bank currently reports data (forty-five of them in the developing and post-communist worlds).[32] Combined with the massive character of absolute poverty that prevails in the northeast and in the outskirts of all major cities, this degree of income concentration is undoubtedly one of the steepest challenges to democratic consolidation.

In terms of class structure, the starting point must be the corporatist order imposed from above in the 1930s.[33] This system can be seen as a highly successful attempt to control, not to say petrify, the process of class formation, by which we mean development of differentiated collective identities and autonomous political organization. The lowest extremity of the class structure, made up of landless peasants and very poor small farmers, was not regulated in a strict sense, since they lacked the occupational differentiation that formed the basis of the whole system; rather, they were excluded from it. The upper extremity, made up of large landowners, provided another parameter—untouchable property rights. But this should not be confounded with total political autonomy, much less with monolithic control of the state: The political sphere (embodied in the military, the bureaucracy, and the political "class") retained considerable decisional discretion.

Between these two extremes, a corporatist gradient was imposed on the rest of society; i.e., on urban wage labor and middle-class independent occupations in general. The privilege of "representing" a given sector was thoroughly subjected to state (legal) control, as well as to effective means to circumscribe each sector's agenda-building and other overt political moves. This pattern applied even to industrial and commercial entrepreneurs, through corporatist pyramids exactly paralleling those of urban labor. As Santos points out, this whole structure remained virtually unchanged through the "democratic experiment" based on the Constitution of 1946. Attempts at self-organization on the part of rural labor, in the early 1960s, were quickly repressed by the post-1964 regime, obviously with full applause and cooperation from the landowners, who saw such attempts as outright subversion.

Ironically enough, serious and lasting "subversion" of the regulated order would occur, first as the result of the scale of the economic changes induced by the military governments; second, as an unintended by-product of some of their "modernizing" reforms; and finally, in that context of large-scale structural change, from the reactivation of "civil society" during the political opening. Development of large-scale industry led entrepreneurs, especially in the heaviest and most dynamic sectors, to organize in new types of associations, pulling themselves out of the traditional corporatist framework. Ousted, as it were, from the administration of social-security funds, labor leaders found themselves with nothing to offer their constituencies; nothing but more authentic leadership. This was the origin of so-called new unionism, which thrived in the most dynamic sectors of the economy and struck a blow against the old corporatist structure. Trying to sidestep political clientelism in their attempt to extend social security to the rural areas, the military governments stimulated the formation of rural labor unions. From 1976 to 1983, unionized rural labor increased from slightly over 3 to more than 8 million, accounting now for more than half of total union membership in the country, even though rural labor accounts for only 30 percent of the economically active population. Needless to say, rural unions did not conform to the passive blueprint that the government probably conceived for them. In less than two decades, they had a national leadership, undertook successful strikes, and indeed placed land reform firmly on their agenda. The politicization of the urban middle strata has not lagged behind. White-collar unions, neighborhood organizations, and associations of numerous types quickly emerged, undoubtedly reflecting the increasing complexity and, in many ways the increasing technical and professional sophistication of Brazilian urban life.

The conclusion, then, is that, in Brazil, medieval economic inequalities exist side-by-side with a dynamic and increasingly sophisticated society. So-called external dependency does not mean that an indigenous bourgeoisie failed to develop. There is, in fact, a modern entrepreneurial class, in industry as well as agriculture. This class has become much more affirmative in the last decade, profiting from the process of political opening. Perceiving that it could not unconditionally count on the military or on elected politicians, it became highly and autonomously organized. This process in fact underwent a remarkable acceleration during the 1980s, first in view of the Constitutional Congress (1987–1988) and also because successive attempts to control inflation by means of heterodox plans (such as the introduction of generalized price controls) politicized the economy to a very great extent.

I have so far emphasized the economic bases and the organizational aspects of class formation. Needless to say, the picture becomes much less politicized when we look at the rank and file and especially at class consciousness. A very large proportion of the urban working class is young, politically inexperienced, indeed made up of recent migrants. Wage strikes can be mobilized without much difficulty, but both unions and political parties must reckon with a great deal of instability, indeed of volatility, when it comes to broader electoral or ideological disputes.

Although the stagnation and inflation of the 1980s worsened this picture, Brazilian development, as I have repeatedly stressed, has been able to create a basically non-zero-sum perception of social conflict. Overall, spatial mobility has been extremely high and has, in fact, meant better life chances for poor migrants. The belief in upward social mobility is probably not as deep today as it was in the 1950s, but access to education and to consumption has increased considerably with increases in total income. Some fashionable descriptions of Brazilian society as being rigidly hierarchical must, then, be taken with a grain of salt. The concentration of property, twenty-one years of authoritarian rule, and huge income inequalities have not meant petrification of status inequality.

On the other hand, socioeconomic inequalities do tend to cumulate to some extent. Although extremely high correlation among education, occupation, income, and, say, "honor," certainly does not exist, the overall structure of inequalities has an evident regional component. The southeast (where São Paulo is located) and the extreme south are "rich" regions, whereas the northeast, with 35 million inhabitants, is one of the major examples of mass poverty in the world. This regional disparity has an important overlap with the country's ethnic differentiation. Blacks and *pardoes* account for well over two-thirds of the northern and northeastern states, while the reverse proportion obtains in the southeast and the south. These definitions are known to be very imprecise in Brazilian population statistics, but the difference is large enough to merit attention.

Nationality and Ethnic Cleavages

Political conflict among language or religious groups is virtually nonexistent in Brazil. On these two dimensions, let alone nationality, the country is comparatively very homogeneous. The picture is much more complex in the field of race relations. Interpretations range from the belief in a genuinely "peaceful" evolution to the notion that underprivileged minorities (especially blacks) lack collective identity and organization as a consequence of white economic and political domination. The extremes do seem to agree that overt ethnic strife is not prevalent. There can be no doubt, however, that poverty and color are significantly correlated.[34] Blacks, and especially black women, are disproportionately locked in low-status and low-income occupations.

But the country does have an overarching national identity. Living generations have virtually no memory of separatist movements or politically relevant subcultures, whether based on language, race, or religion. It can, of course, be said that this high degree of cultural uniformity reflects a process of authoritarian state building under colonial and then imperial government. The fact, however, is that Brazil is not presently confronted with serious ethnic or cultural strife. Given the immense burden that socioeconomic cleavages place on the political agenda, this relative homogeneity is clearly a positive factor for democratic development.

Political Structure

The formal structure of the Brazilian state has varied a great deal since in-dependence (see Table 3.2), but the concentration of power in the national executive has been a constant. Accepted as a hallmark of state building and, more recently, as necessary for the sake of economic development and national security, that concentration was often carried out at the expense of state and local governments, of legislative and judicial powers, and even more clearly of the party system.[35]

The First Republic (1889–1930) tried to adapt the U.S. model, provid-ing for a popularly elected president and granting extensive autonomy to the provinces, now called states, of the old unitary empire. The result was full of perverse effects, as the "politics of the governors" decisively weakened the national legislature and judiciary and seriously compromised elections and party competition. In practice, the republican government became as oligarchical and probably less legitimate than the empire, in the eyes of the relevant strata. This process of political decay eventually led to the Revolution of 1930 (and, in 1937, to Vargas's Estado Novo), which again concentrated federal power, but now within a framework of nonmobiliza-tional, partyless authoritarian rule.

The Revolution of 1930 is undoubtedly the "founding" mark of the modern Brazilian political system, but again with contradictory effects in terms of democratic prospects. In the short run, advances in "stateness" (bureaucratic reach, military complexity, greater regulation of economy) were certainly favorable, since they reduced the scope of private power and made purely praetorian involution thenceforth unlikely. In the long run, however, some of those advances seem to have outlived their function. The corporatist system of labor relations has certainly been detrimental to the political organization of the working class. The conventional PR electoral system then established has clearly not contributed to developing a stable party system. Worse still, the presidential office became overloaded with contradictory expectations. For professional politicians, it became the ulti-mate distributor of patronage, credits, and public investments, and the arbiter among regional interests. For the newly mobilized urban masses, after 1945, it was the focal point of demands for better wages and improve-ments in living conditions. From the viewpoint of the military estab-lishment, it came to be the very embodiment of national security, implying containment of both "oligarchical" and "mob" rule.

These cross-pressures and institutional deficiencies were clearly opera-tive in the 1964 breakdown. The democratic experiment initiated in 1945 was based, in comparison with the earlier periods, on a far stronger repre-sentative system. The national legislature and the main political parties start-ed as fundamental political actors. However, growing social mobilization and persistent inflation made it impossible for the two major parties (UDN and PSD) to retain their initially safe electoral advantage. As a typical "insti-tutional" party, the PSD became increasingly vulnerable to a bipolar (left

Table 3.2 Brazilian Political Structure Since Independence

Regimes	Form of Government	Party System	Civil/Military Relations	Social Mobilization	Demise
EMPIRE (1822–1889)	Unitary state; parliamentary monarchy *cum* "moderating power"	Two parties (Liberal and Conservative) since the 1830s; district voting (very unstable rules)	Civil hegemony through National Guard; weak army	Extremely low	Republican military coup; no resistance
FIRST REPUBLIC (1889–1930)	Directly elected president; highly decentralized federation	One-party systems at state level; multi-member district voting; unstable rules	Increasing tension between military (especially young officers) and politicians	Very low	Revolutionary movement headed by Getúlio Vargas; three weeks fighting
REVOLUTION OF 1930 (1930–1937)	Provisional government headed by Vargas; in 1937, Weimar-inspired constitution with strong corporatist leanings	Numerous, unstable party groupings; growing fascist/communist polarization	Army becoming dominant national institution	Growing significantly in urban areas	Vargas's coup, with military backing, leads to Estado Novo
ESTADO NOVO (1937–1945)	Authoritarian, nonmobilizational regime; Getúlio Vargas dictator	None; all parties and elections suppressed	Army identified with regime through national security ideology	Growing rapidly; population 31% urban in 1940	Senior army officers force Vargas to resign, 1945; controlled redemocratization
DEMOCRATIC REGIME (1946–1964)	Directly elected president; weak federation and powerful national legislature	Multiparty system with 13 parties; increasing polarization at end of period; PR electoral system	Frequent friction between military factions and civilian governments; threats of military intervention	Fairly high, increasing even in rural areas; population 45% urban in 1960	Military coup with substantial popular backing in middle strata ousts President Goulart

MILITARY REGIME (1964–1985)	Republican form; presidency *de facto* monopoly of the military; military nominations ratified by Electoral College up to 1978; federation severely weakened	Compulsory two-party system from 1965 on; partial return to pluralism in 1979, still barring communist parties; PR electoral system	Unmistakable hegemony of military as institution, guaranteeing "technocratic" governments	Very high; population 67% urban in 1980	Very gradual, negotiated transition culminating in election of Tancredo Neves (civilian, oppositionist) through Electoral College
SARNEY ADMINISTRATION (1985–1990)	Direct election of president reestablished as constitutional principle; growing influence of states and legislature; Constitutional Congress, 1987	Multiparty system; no legal restrictions on Marxist parties; moderates (PMDB/ PFL) control both chambers from early 1987 on; PR electoral system	Civilian control formally guaranteed; military influence remains strong	Very high	
COLLOR AND FRANCO ADMINISTRATIONS (1990–1994)	Republican and presidential system confirmed in plebiscite held on April 21, 1993	Nineteen parties represented in Federal Chamber, with a Laakso-Taagepera fragmentation score of 8.5	Military presence in political arena low to insignificant	Very high, but without strong political consequences except with regard to the impeachment process; deep recession weakens labor unions	First president directly elected in twenty-nine years; Collor is impeached on charges of corruption on December 29, 1993; Vice President Itamar Franco confirmed in office after Collor's impeachment; Fernando Henrique Cardoso is elected president on first ballot of the elections held on October 3, 1994

and right) opposition, roughly as suggested by Sartori's "polarized pluralism" model.[36]

The erosion of party and congressional support meant that Goulart (1961–1964) had to carry the full burden of maintaining institutional equilibrium exactly when the Caesarist ghost that so often surrounds Latin American presidentialism came, full-bodied, to the fore. The Caesarist dilemma stems from the need to cope with stringent and clearly defined contradictory situational constraints. Frustrating mass demands in the name of austerity or economic rationality alienates diffuse support and thus deprives the president of the one resource that makes him strong vis-à-vis elected politicians. If, on the contrary, he chooses to court those demands too closely, the specter of a mob-based dictatorship is immediately raised by the propertied classes and, often, by the military organization. The middle course is often unavailable because of the very weakness and inconsistency of the party system. When the difficulties inherent in these situational constraints are compounded by ambiguous personal behavior, as was evidently the case in the Goulart presidency, the breaking point is near.

Leadership

From 1961 to 1964, President Goulart proved unable to escape the Caesarist trap. He in fact made it more inexorable by allowing too much room for doubt as to his intention to abide by the constitutional rules that would govern his succession. Few analysts would dispute that Goulart's equivocal behavior was a crucial precipitating factor in the democratic breakdown.[37] The important question, then, is how does it come about that a country with an important institutional history and a fairly impersonal conception of governing falls prey to that sort of populistic retrogression and thence to breakdown?

Part of the answer may indeed be an oversupply of leaders willing to violate the rules of the game. The pattern was set by Getúlio Vargas, in 1930 and especially with the Estado Novo coup of 1937. Liberal opposition to the *varguista* tradition, after 1945, often displayed the same ambiguous behavior of which Goulart was later accused. Prominent UDN leaders, like Carlos Lacerda, were not only *golpistas* but, in fact, strongly inclined to (and skillful at) impassioned demagogic rhetoric.

Yet, personalistic leadership has not been as successful as implied in the common lore. Getúlio Vargas did not establish a personality cult comparable to that of Perón in Argentina. Former president Juscelino Kubitschek (1955–1960) is remembered as a modernizer and a "nice guy," not as a power-seeking *caudillo*. Jânio Quadros ascended to the presidency in 1960, riding a protest vote that he cleverly mobilized by means of a rancorous, theatrical style. In August 1961, he resigned, claiming that the country was ungovernable (in his terms, of course). His decision was fateful in the ensu-

ing years, but is it not a blessing for our hypothesis that the Brazilian political system has developed antibodies against wild personalism? His successful comeback as the elected mayor of São Paulo in 1985 would seem to
deny our view, but it is noteworthy that Quadros has carefully confined his
Poujade-like, protofascist appeal to the electoral arena, never daring to
establish some sort of paramilitary apparatus.

The leadership problem cannot therefore be considered simply as a lack
of men with the appropriate skills and civic virtues, and not even as an
absence of antibodies against irresponsible demagogues. It is rather the
inherent instability of democracy amid rapid social mobilization and
extreme inequality, trying to escape the Scylla of Caesarist *caudillismo* and
the Charybdis of uninspiring, clientelistic politics. A proper understanding
of the leadership problem must then consider, in addition to the already cited
situational constraints, some underlying cultural elements that contribute to
shaping them.

Political Culture

Brazilian political culture is sometimes said to embody an unchanging
Iberian propensity toward monolithism, and thus to be irreducibly inimical
to democratic development. We argue that, on balance, the effects of political culture may indeed be negative, but hardly for that reason. The views
that do operate in the political system (i.e., those put forward by influential
writers, journalists, and the like) show a pervasive and persistent concern,
indeed an obsession, with the alleged incongruence between elite and mass
culture. Since the early decades of this century, outstanding writers of different persuasions have insisted that powerful cultural strains tend to undermine the idea of a Western-style democracy in Brazil. Alberto Torres was
only one among hundreds who emphasized the discrepancy between the
"legal" Brazil, expressed in political institutions, and the "real" one, embodied in actual social behavior.

Somehow, popular culture came to be seen as the only real thing, while
political institutions became irremediably artificial. What is certainly
disturbing in this dichotomous approach is that, through it, we may be
unconsciously demanding a degree of congruence among different spheres
of society, and especially between "center" and "periphery" that does not in
fact exist anywhere among advanced democracies. The starting point is the
Aristotelian ideal that social institutions (familial, educational, religious)
must buttress and reinforce the overarching principle of legitimacy. But that
ideal is then used to imply that democratic political principles are irrelevant
or illegitimate when they fail to mold each and every subsystem. Even in the
advanced democracies, we find, as in Brazil, that knowledge of and support
for democratic rules of the game are undoubtedly correlated with education
and other indicators of social status. In Brazil, this is hardly surprising, if we

consider that elite political socialization has been closely associated, since the nineteenth century, with the law schools (hence with a reverence for legal culture) as well as with a free press and more recently with a sizable and reasonably cosmopolitan academic community.[38]

The dichotomous view just described derives historically from the state-centered pattern of political development and from the fact that elite contestation preceded, by far, the expansion of participation. In fact, elite culture became political at a time when the bulk of the populace, poor and widely dispersed over a large territory, was totally excluded from the system. In 1900, the illiteracy rate among the population over fifteen was 75 percent. There thus arose an excessive predominance of state over societal development and hence a deep anxiety, among opinion makers, that liberal-democratic development would not be viable under such conditions.

However, this picture has changed in surprising ways during the decompression process of the 1970s and especially since the transition to civilian rule in 1985. The Aristotelian craving for congruence remains, but its contents and ideas to correct incongruence have become more complex. Under the impact of high social mobilization (see Table 3.1), of repoliticization and, of course, of protest against income inequality, there appeared an Augustinian strand, according to which the people are good and the state is evil. Stimulated by religious movements and by abundant leadership coming from the now much larger wage-earning middle sectors, the implied correction is no longer to replace liberal by authoritarian politics, as in the 1920s, but rather to substitute some sort of Rousseauan "participatory" for representative democracy.

The historical sequence of institutional development, combined with persistently wide income differentials and other factors, thus seemed to have produced very negative cultural conditions for representative democracy. These negative effects do not derive from a would-be unitary world view, but rather from a pervasive utopian standard against which democratic development is constantly measured by the leadership of some popular movements and by influential opinion makers. The impact of these trends on parliamentary politics has increased noticeably as the PT (Workers' Party) became stronger in Congress, among the clergy and academics, and especially among grassroots reform movements. The usual pessimistic account of Brazilian political culture must be qualified in many ways. Consideration of some positive developments that took place despite allegedly authoritarian Iberian origins and recent authoritarian experiences may be useful as an antidote. First, since the establishment of the Electoral Court, in 1932, there has been unmistakable progress toward orderliness and fairness in administering the electoral process. On the side of the voters, sheer size (95 million registered voters in 1994) allied to social mobilization has made the assumption of individual autonomy increasingly realistic. Despite abysmal poverty and the prevalence of patron-client relationships in many regions, there can be no doubt that the electoral process now operates with the requisite quantum of aggregate uncertainty.

Second, there is no monolithic domination, not even at the local level. This is in part a consequence of the overall changes in the electoral process and in part of local rivalries even among landowners. The image of monolithism has been frequently maintained by students of Brazilian social structure, but they tend to underestimate the impact of political and electoral competition when it is not linked to ideological or class cleavages.

Third, as I noted earlier, even the authoritarian ideology of the 1920s and 1930s (and hence the idea of military tutelage) has been tempered by antipopulist elements that help sustain some democratic institutions and practices. Hence, the limits on the duration of mandates, the electoral calendar, and, more generally, the importance of keeping the legislature as an institution capable of being reactivated—all these clearly practiced by the post-1964 regime.

Fourth, as noted above, a significant degree of social mobility exists, despite severe income inequality. Here, the cultural process of modernization does seem to have an impact of its own, judging from the increasingly informal character of social relationships. Urban living and mass communications work massively in the direction of an egalitarian culture.

Finally, the development of representative institutions, in a general way, clearly implies that primitive *caudillismo* and unitary blueprints are not deemed desirable or realistic by the political elite. Three features seem to characterize the Brazilian "doctrine" of representation. One is the recognition of diversity among the elite. This should not be understood primarily in ideological terms and even less in terms of cultural or ethnic segmentation. It is rather an acceptance of the fact that politics involves constant division and disagreement, making monolithic rule inconceivable. This recognition is deeply rooted in the country's cultural and legal system because, if for no other reason, it was historically a sine qua non for holding the provinces and local governments together.

The second feature is the electoral process. Countless writers have seen a puzzle, or worse, a mimetic disease, in the Brazilian tendency to import such profoundly "alien" liberal institutions. But the fact is that electoral mechanisms, with many of the classical provisions for fair competition, have strong roots in Brazil. Despite the equally countless instances of violence, fraud, and manipulation that can be cited, it is perfectly legitimate to speak of a Brazilian electoral tradition, and even more to recognize that the recent struggle against authoritarian rule has reinforced it.

The third feature, which has the military institution as its main guardian, is the notion that the government must be an impersonal entity. Hence the military's fundamental dislike for any kind of plebiscitarian *caudillismo* and their (reluctant, no doubt) understanding that elections are the ultimate safeguard against some sort of personalistic appropriation of the state.

Do these three features of Brazilian political culture amount to an unambiguous concept of "democratic" representation? Not quite: one indication that they do not are the powerful cultural strains that constantly delegitimize the representative process. Public debate is full of references to the "elitist" character of such institutions. The image of politicians is incessantly associated with clientelism, co-optation, and conciliation—the last being a reference to the early nineteenth century, but also a way of saying that our pluralism is still oligarchical, without substantive meaning for the average citizen. Indeed, what we can assume, in the Brazilian case, is that substantial institutional development was achieved in the past, but some authoritarian traits of the state-building process and of the social structure are still reflected in the democratic system.

International Factors

The international environment is a positive factor for representative democracy—especially now that the Cold War is over—but it was negative on the economic dimension during the 1980s, especially in view of the tremendous internal impact of the debt crisis. Brazil is a fully Western nation in cultural terms, and a dependent (if you will) part of the world capitalist system. One (oft-neglected) consequence of this is that Brazilian elites, including the military, do not ignore the risks involved in toying with fundamentally different principles of political organization. Brazil's territory acquired its present shape a long time ago. Nature provided most of the solution to Brazil's frontier problem. Diplomatic efforts polished it up early in this century. Participation in foreign wars and military readiness are unknown to the vast majority of Brazilians. Were it otherwise, the weight of the military vis-à-vis civilian institutions would undoubtedly be much greater than it has been. Proper understanding of the negative effects of the economic dimension requires a broad historical perspective. Dependency on export commodities, with its attendant instability, was extremely high until the 1950s at least. Import-substituting industrialization began during World War I but was insufficient to alter that basic link to the external world until roughly the mid-1970s.

An important change took place in the 1950s. Under Juscelino Kubitschek, the Brazilian government gave up its formerly cautious strategy and started emphasizing durable consumer goods as a means to accelerate industrial growth. The automobile industry was the driving force of that new phase. The impact of industrialization on the overall social structure became thenceforth much greater. A rapidly expanding population, large cities, and the demonstration effect of foreign consumption patterns now made for permanent tension, leaving no option but constantly high rates of growth. Major inflationary pressures, the need to increase exports at any price, and, of course, to attract investments and credits now became permanent features of the economic system. Internationalization had come to stay.

This, in a rough sketch, is the background of Brazil's deep involvement in the international debt crisis. Having again accelerated growth in the late 1960s and early 1970s, the military governments, especially under President Geisel (1974–1978), undertook major new steps toward import substitution, this time in basic or "difficult" sectors.[39] The premise of that effort, needless to say, was the easy credit situation of that decade. The oil and interest-rate shocks of the late 1970s and early 1980s thus caught Brazil in an extremely vulnerable position.

Prospects for Democratic Consolidation

Reconceptualizing Democratic Consolidation

Liberalization and participation are described by Dahl as distinct theoretical dimensions of democratization. However, when we think about consolidating democracies recently reinstated as a consequence of authoritarian demise, socioeconomic conditions must be incorporated more effectively into our models. It is a trivial observation that a large amount of genuine political democracy tends to be incompatible with a rigid or unequal society, or even with a low rate of change toward greater mobility and equality. Thus, when we think about consolidation, social and economic conditions cannot remain in the category of purely external correlates or prerequisites. They must be "politicized," i.e., brought into the model, and this for two important reasons. The first is that, like liberalization and participation, those conditions will necessarily appear to political actors as objects of decision, and therefore as so many choices they will be forced to make. Land reform is the obvious example in Third World countries. Whether and how such choices are faced may make the difference between keeping and losing support; the loss may transcend individual leaders and parties and extend to the newly constituted democratic system as a whole. The second reason has to do with the change from procedural to substantive demands in the course of redemocratization. Cast in a different theoretical language, this means that, once achieved, formal democracy becomes an Olsonian collective good. Since it already exists and benefits everyone, the incentive to defend and protect it decreases sharply.[40] In Third World countries, the implications of this fact are obviously more dramatic, since elites have not completely consolidated pluralism among themselves, frequently perceive conflicts as zero-sum, and are vastly more threatened by the substantive demands of the masses.

It thus seems clear that we need, not two, but three dimensions. The graphic representation of democratic consolidation would thus be a cube made up of Dahl's liberalization and participation plus another dimension referring to policy advances toward structural deconcentration, which means greater equality, social mobility, and the like. Taking all three dimensions at once, the dilemmas of democratic consolidation will, I believe, appear in a more realistic light. If our questions about the democratic character of the present Brazilian political system were to deal only with Dahl's two-dimensional scheme, the answer would be unequivocally positive. Looking at the "liberalization" axis, we would find that all legal restrictions on political competition have been lifted and that the franchise is now among the broadest in the world. If difficulties remain, they are somehow produced by hidden vetoes (e.g., expectations concerning military behavior), by the sheer weight of certain resources (e.g., bureaucratic power), and by other, "nonpolitical" determinants (e.g., those determining the concentration of power in the societal environment of the political system).

Probing somewhat further, it seems possible to combine Dahl's liberalization and participation into a single dimension, which would be representation; i.e., strength of the representative system. Where contestation becomes the normal way of doing things among political elites and where such elites are regarded as adequate foci for support or as spokesmen for demands arising from participation, what we have is a strong representative system. We can thus come back to a two-dimensional space, with strength of the representative system on one axis and advances toward social change, or deconcentration, on the other (see Figure 3.1).

The "New Republic" period (1985–1990) and the extreme political isolation in which President Collor (1990–1992) found himself, quite aside from the corruption charges that finally brought him down, have shown that the reinstatement of formal democracy may be a far cry from true consolidation. On the horizontal axis of Figure 3.1, the new civilian government was faced with what might be called the vicious circle of transition. The prior authoritarian suppression of politics and the prolonged struggle for redemocratization dammed up enormous (substantive) expectations, which could not (in fact cannot) be met in the short run. Not meeting them at an adequate rate, the government quickly loses the support it needs in order to undertake more forceful policies, the lack of which reinforces the circle. The "moving horizon" that worked so well during the decompression process at the institutional level (i.e., on the vertical axis) thus seems far more difficult to sustain when it comes to our horizontal axis.

Toward Deconcentration?

The proposition that greater equality helps sustain democracy is certainly correct in the long run, but the concrete steps and policies that will reduce inequality may also undermine support for the democratic system in the short run. This is evident enough when we speak of deconcentrating income and wealth, and especially land ownership. Virtually any policy intended to achieve deconcentration produces visible and immediate losses and thus

Figure 3.1 Representation, Deconcentration, and Democratization

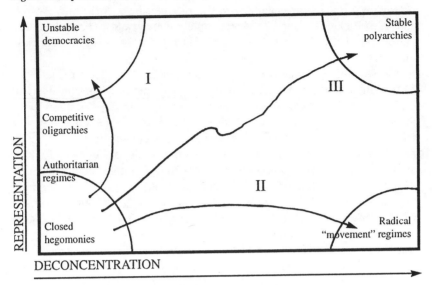

tends to change the basis of political support, often in the direction of unde-mocratic forces. But there is, in addition, the worst face of inequality, so-called absolute poverty. The problem here is that a truly substantial effort would have to be sustained over many years; this presupposes a degree of consistency in political support and implementation that seems unlikely in fragile, underdeveloped democracies. In order to consolidate itself, a func-tioning democratic system should be capable not only of undertaking sub-stantial measures to reduce inequality but, also, of conveying to the deprived majority that such measures are serious efforts undertaken on their behalf; and at the same time, that underdevelopment and the pattern of inequalities traditionally associated with it cannot be overcome on short notice.

The New Republic clearly did not find a consistent answer to these problems and made them worse, as it failed to control soaring inflation. The initial idea was to launch an "emergency program" of assistance (while at the same time designing alternative economic policies and starting a moder-ate, long-range land-reform project). There would be, for example, a milk program directed toward groups known to have a desperate nutritional deficit. The results of this phase could not have been more disastrous. Insufficient production, inadequate implementation networks, and political disputes all combined to paralyze such initiatives. Toward the end of 1985, these difficulties were compounded by the ghosts of hyperinflation and an unprecedented strike wave in the subsequent few months. The "illegitimate" origins of Sarney's presidency (i.e., the fact that he was the conservative side of the ticket, as Tancredo Neves's running mate, and that both had been elected indirectly) began to be recalled. Support for the government rapidly dwindled.

It is therefore probably correct to infer that the so-called Cruzado Plan had political as well as economic objectives. The stabilization plan and monetary reform introduced by President Sarney on February 28, 1986, were decisive in stopping a dangerous erosion of authority. Popular acquiescence to the plan immediately reinforced presidential leadership. But, clearly, such acquiescence was entirely due to the price freeze, the difficulties of which began to appear rather soon. In a country with tremendous income inequalities, the redistribution of money income implicit in the price freeze quickly led to an explosive demand for consumer goods of all kinds. Entrepreneurs responded to the price freeze by reducing supply and enhancing their political organization. To make things worse, a decisive election was scheduled to take place in November (state deputies and governors, and federal deputies and senators, the latter two making up the Constitutional Congress). Sarney's enormous popularity after the economic reforms of February was the one big asset of the governing Democratic Alliance, hence the enormous pressures to go on with the price freeze, despite the evident distortions to which it was giving rise. Confronted with an enlarged demand and a reduced internal supply, the government resorted to massive imports of food products. The result was that reserves fell sharply. By early 1987, readjustment measures had proved insufficient and the country had no alternative but to declare a partial default on foreign-interest payments.

The irony, or tragedy, is that the Cruzado Plan was the closest thing to actual income redistribution in several decades; it was also the one moment in which the government seemed capable of gaining widespread support. But short-run euphoria should not obscure the dark contours of the broader picture. To begin with, bold measures like the Cruzado Plan reflect the institutional weakness of the political system, not its sources of institutional strength. Presidential authority was reinforced by the populist, indeed Caesarist components of the situation, not by the denser substrata of the country's power structure. It is perhaps unnecessary to point out that not every government faces such an opportunity; that the gains were short-lived; and indeed that such a sweeping reform was introduced through a decree-law, and not by means of a prior amalgamation of party and congressional support.

Brazilian Democracy from the 1980s to the 1990s

Sharp social inequality poses a constant challenge to democratic institutions, but the Brazilian case can also be read as a showcase of the relevance of institutional "formalisms" for the growth of democracy. A fair degree of self-restraint among the military during the authoritarian period (1964–1985), the transition from authoritarian rule through a gradual expansion of the electoral arena (and not as a consequence of some abrupt event—for example, the Falklands-Malvinas war in Argentina), and the intense search for institutional reorganization during the late 1980s and early 1990s come readily to mind as illustrations of that assertion. With ten years of hindsight, it seems clear that the depth of the economic crisis and the resilience of democracy have both been greater than what one would have expected in 1985, when the transition to civilian rule was formally completed.

In addition to its protracted (1974–1985) character, Brazilian redemocratization was completed under a very adverse set of circumstances. During the last military administration (that of General Figueiredo, 1978–1985), the overheated Brazilian economy was hit hard by the oil and interest rate shocks and by the Mexican default in 1982, which led to a sudden interruption of the flow of foreign lending to Brazil as well. High-growth-oriented policies underwent a sharp reversal in the period 1981–1984, plunged the country into its worst recession ever, and led to a sharp cut in government social expenditures.

These almost unbearable economic constraints and the protracted nature of the decompression process thus led to a sharp fall of aggregate authority in the political system from 1981 to 1985: on one hand, the military could veto but not really make policy; on the other, the emerging civilian leadership was already liable to erosion of its authority since it controlled key state governments but could not yet make policy at the national level. Highly symbolic events like the *diretas já* (direct elections now!) mobilization of 1984, the campaign to elect opposition candidate Tancredo Neves through the Electoral College in January 1985, and the shock caused by his untimely death without taking office in April of that year misled many analysts into thinking that the new democratic leadership had gained the people's hearts and minds—some even to the extreme view that a compact elite had somehow engineered an *arreglo* (compromise) to keep the levers of power under tight control. My view is, on the contrary, that both military and civilian leaders were sharply weakened by the crisis of the early 1980s, and this mutual debilitation planted the seeds of a crisis that lasted for the next ten years.

In his well-known *Polyarchy,* Robert Dahl included the "centralized control of the economy," regardless of the form of ownership, among the conditions he considered negative for democracy.[41] In Brazil, the implications of state intervention in the economy have gone far beyond the issue of bureaucratic-military power. Unlike the Chilean dictatorship, the Brazilian military did not prepare the transition to a more market-oriented economy. On the contrary, the military greatly expanded the public entrepreneurial sector, leaving the tasks of reforming this sector and finding a solution for the underlying fiscal imbalances to the emerging civilian leadership. To make things worse, neither the policymaking and business communities nor the academic community was convinced of the need for such reforms in the mid-1980s. Although disastrous with regard to social equity and monetary order, the Brazilian state-centered model was highly successful as a growth engine, and this record of past success made its ideological legacy accordingly much heavier than that in either Argentina or Chile, for example.

Throughout the 1980s, as economic and political difficulties grew worse, the phrase "the crisis is more political than economic" became standard jargon but few analysts explained exactly what it meant. My view is that it reflected this very adverse set of circumstances: a sharp fall in the aggregate amount of political authority as a result of the mutual debilitation of both military and civilian leaders; economic structures and ideologies still strongly skewed toward state interventionism, despite domestic and worldwide trends indicating the need to open up the economy and enhance market forces; and the formidable pressure of accumulated substantive demands. Add to this the highly fragmented nature of the Brazilian party system and one can readily understand why Brazilian politicians quickly overloaded the reform agenda and engaged in piecemeal and often cumbersome procedures. Lacking interlocutors capable of aggregating issues for negotiation, the Brazilian political system succumbed to what I have elsewhere dubbed the *hyper-active paralysis syndrome:* a tendency to believe in the miraculous power of institutional reforms while paying no heed to the fact that excessive inter- and intra-party fragmentation made such reforms either politically unviable or too costly.[42]

A full-fledged constitution-making Congress was elected in late 1986. This Congress insisted on working from scratch, accepting no previous draft and not wanting even an internal grand commission to set guidelines. The task of providing the new democracy with a new constitution was thus entrusted to a Congress with no internal coherence. As a sovereign constitution-making body, this Congress theoretically had the power and seemed inclined to shorten the term of office of President Sarney (who had taken office upon the death of Tancredo Neves and had ambiguous democratic credentials at this time because of his prior association with the military regime). The crisis potential imbedded in this situation ended up being diluted, but after the collapse of the Cruzado Plan in late 1986, Sarney never recovered the popularity and authority he briefly enjoyed.

Lacking constructive leadership from the executive, the constitution-making Congress finally adopted a text on October 5, 1988, that was not only wildly detailed but that was also disastrous for governability since it greatly aggravated existing fiscal imbalances, maintained and in some cases expanded state economic interventionism and nationalism, and took no steps to attenuate the unparalleled battery of incentives to party fragmentation implicit in Brazilian electoral and party laws. In fact, it ratified the questionable combination of a presidential system with multipartyism and a highly permissive proportional electoral system; gave a lease on life to old-fashioned nationalist rhetoric and paternalistic welfare provisions; and last but not least, confirmed in a democratic way, with strong support from the labor unions, the corporatist system established by Vargas's dictatorship (1937–1945)—which had been branded as "fascist" throughout the preceding forty years.

Needless to say, the newly revised constitution did little to allay apprehensions about the fragility of Brazilian democracy under the Sarney administration. Perhaps because they were conscious of such difficulties, the constitution makers added two highly controversial clauses, one requiring a plebiscite on presidential versus parliamentary government (as well the possible return to a monarchical system) to be held after five years, and another providing for a full revision of the constitution by unicameral vote and absolute majority (instead of 60 percent separately in the House and Senate). The plebiscite was held in April 1993 and the attempt to revise the constitution was made in October of that year. Both were fiascos because of the inability of the party system to engender consistent support for any change.[43]

Eighty-two million voters went to the polls in November 1989 to elect Sarney's successor—the first direct and totally free presidential election in twenty-nine years. By that time the inflation rate had soared to 50 percent a month, and the proportion of voters willing to rate Sarney's administration as "excellent" or "good" had plummeted to 8 percent in the electorate as a whole and to about half that figure among the highly schooled. The stage was, thus, set for a difficult and, as it turned out, extremely radicalized election. The two largest parties—Partido do Movimento Democrático Brasileiro (PMDB) and Partido da Frente Liberal (PFL)—which made up the governing Democratic Alliance, were discredited to the point of receiving only 4 percent and 1 percent of the vote, respectively, for their presidential candidates. The front-runners were Fernando Collor de Mello of the Partido da Reconstrução Nacional (PRN) and Luís Inácio "Lula" da Silva of the Workers' Party (PT).

Despite his determination to curb inflation and to tackle the intractable problem of public-sector reform, President Collor was bound to fail in view not only of his lack of parliamentary support but also, as it turned out, of the corrupt practices and entourage he tolerated and allowed to grow around the presidential palace. In May 1992, a congressional committee started the dramatic and, for Brazil, unprecedented investigations that led to an overwhelming impeachment vote in late September. Forced to step down, Collor was succeeded by Vice President Itamar Franco, a former senator known for his strongly nationalist and statist views. In other words, Brazil seemed to be exchanging one terrible problem (a president the country came to reject as corrupt) for another: a president who seemed not to assign a high priority to curbing inflation and even less to understanding that in order to achieve this goal tough structural reforms, even constitutional reforms, and a thorough reshuffling of the public sector would be needed. In fact, from his inauguration in September 1992 until March 1993 President Franco did little to prove that such apprehensions were unfounded. By that time he had already fired three finance ministers and submitted economic agents to a continuous flow of contradictory signals. The press devoted substantial space to what it defined as a crisis climate and did not shun speculations about the dangers posed to democratic stability. Proposals to shorten Franco's term of office and to move up the elections scheduled to take place in October 1994 began to proliferate.

The stage was again set for another radicalized election, with Lula (Workers' Party) possibly facing Paulo Maluf (mayor of São Paulo) as his right-wing opponent. Under such conditions, Lula's victory, perhaps even on the first ballot, looked like a foregone conclusion. With Congress highly divided, as usual, and now facing a serious corruption scandal, important legislation tended to be made by decree-law ("provisional measures"). Considerable apprehension thus began to mount among investors, both domestic and foreign, and not without reason since it seemed unlikely that a serious effort at fiscal balance and market-oriented reform could be made under a party strongly influenced by Marxist and religious reform groups of every description.

It was at this juncture that Franco took an audacious step, appointing Fernando Henrique Cardoso as finance minister and making him virtually prime minister of a de facto parliamentary government. A world-renowned sociologist and respected senator, Cardoso had been in charge of the foreign ministry since the beginning of Franco's term. His appointment to the Finance Ministry and the first-rate team of economic advisers he immediately mobilized quickly renewed hopes that a serious effort to control inflation would be made and dissipated apprehensions of a serious political crisis.

Putting together a coalition favorable to the effort toward monetary stabilization (the "Real Plan") undertaken by Cardoso and capable of electing him to the presidency proved easier than most observers would have thought when he was appointed finance minister. In fact, he not only won over Lula but won on the first ballot, with 54 percent of the vote compared to Lula's 27 percent. The expectation that Brazil was headed toward intense left-right polarization, which might harden resistance to economic reform and perhaps even increase the chance of political instability, simply did not materialize. Cardoso's performance as finance minister and the initiation of the stabilization process quickly allayed such fears.

Cardoso's victory over six opponents, including three former state governors and the most important labor leader in Brazil's history, was clearly an enormous political accomplishment. First, it was a very important step toward the consolidation of representative democracy in Brazil—party fragility and the excessively "consociational" character of the underlying institutional system notwithstanding.[44] Second, it was an exceptionally clear mandate for the continuation of the economic policies Cardoso came to personify—monetary stability and market-oriented reforms—provided such policies are combined with a serious effort to ameliorate social conditions over the next few years.

Conclusion

Despite sharp social inequalities and the extremely adverse circumstances under which the transition from military rule was completed, Brazilian democracy survived rather well the polarization of the 1989 presidential elections and the crisis that led to the impeachment of President Fernando Collor de Mello in 1992. In 1994 the country escaped the prospect of a dangerously radicalized right-left election scenario.

Contrary to most predictions, the 1994 campaign was rather mild. As indicated, the election can be said to have been "polarized" only in statistical terms and only because of the provision for a run-off election in the context of a multiparty system. In a two-party system, the outcome would clearly have been a landslide for Cardoso. This conjecture is borne out by the low intensity of the campaign at the grass roots, despite the well-known dedication of the PT faithful. This convergent pattern is clearly more conducive to political stability and government effectiveness than a highly antagonistic one would have been.

Although Cardoso's standing as a public figure has long been formidable, his growth as a presidential candidate was clearly a consequence of his role as initiator of the stabilization plan and, *contrario sensu,* of the voters' perception that Lula and the PT stood against the plan. Indeed, support for Cardoso grew spectacularly in the two weeks following the currency change of July 1, 1994—before an actual improvement in purchasing power could be felt among the lowest-income groups. Thus, his success is best understood as a consequence of a *receptive predisposition*—that is, a preexisting demand for monetary stability: a positive attitude born of the discomfort associated with an unstable monetary environment and of at least a dim understanding that stabilization was the necessary first step toward economic recovery. Among middle- and high-schooled voters, there is substantial evidence that economic attitudes have changed markedly over the past decade, with a greater value placed on monetary stability and public-sector reform. Old "statist" beliefs have grown weaker even among left-of-center voters, who now demand concentration of resources and managerial talent on social policies rather than on steel mills and other large industrial projects, as used to be the case in the heyday of state-centered, import-substituting industrialization.

Another important feature of the 1994 election is that Cardoso and the group of economists who designed the Real Plan repeatedly emphasized that complementary reforms, some requiring constitutional amendments, were needed to ensure fiscal balance and consolidate monetary stability. They also forcefully advocated reducing the entrepreneurial role of the public sector through privatization and "flexibilization"—an awkward term I reproduce here only to be faithful to their campaign terminology—of the existing constitutional monopolies in oil and telecommunications in order to allow for public-private partnerships.

The question, of course, is whether the Cardoso administration will have the necessary backing in Congress and among state governors to undertake such changes. The 1994 gubernatorial elections were very favorable to Cardoso: his Party of Brazilian Social Democracy (PSDB) elected the governors of the three largest states (São Paulo, Minas Gerais, and Rio de Janeiro) and altogether six of the twenty-seven governors. Despite the proverbial fragmentation of the Brazilian party system, which makes it virtually impossible for a president to have a stable majority in Congress, even weaker presidents (even Collor) have been able to win passage of needed legislation. *Contrario sensu,* in 1986 the PMDB-PFL alliance, which backed Sarney, came out with an absolute majority in both the House and the Senate and all of the then twenty-three state governorships—and the result could not have been worse.

The Brazilian "problem" of the 1980s and early 1990s was, therefore, more complex. Party weakness and congressional fragmentation were among the key ingredients of that protracted crisis, but at least two other contributing factors must be taken into account. One was the still dense statist ideological legacy: the state-centered industrialization model continued to be perceived as successful, and, hence, most of Brazilian society was still sending contradictory signals as to which route Congress should take. The other factor was insufficient presidential leadership—in part a result of the protracted nature of the Brazilian transition from military to civilian rule from the mid-1970s to the mid-1980s, which weakened the presidential office as such, and in part a result of the fact that each president, from General Figueiredo to Itamar Franco, for different reasons failed to provide constructive leadership.

It is plausible to assume that this trend will be reversed in the course of Cardoso's term of office, not only by virtue of his intellect but also because society and public opinion have changed significantly since the mid-1980s. A decisive change may thus take place, albeit informally, in the functioning of the political system. Reinforcing this optimistic view is the substantial modernization the private sector has undergone in recent years and the probability that the stabilization plan will greatly constrain future congressional and executive behavior, pushing both branches toward implementing the required complementary public-sector reforms.

If these conjectures prove correct, there is no doubt that the left-wing and nationalist parties—mainly the PT, the PCdoB (Communist Party of Brazil), and the PDT (Democratic Labor Party)—which staunchly opposed constitutional revision in 1993, will face severe limits in their range of influence. Although their combined seat share (23 percent) in the House in the 1994–1998 legislature is more than twice as large as their 10 percent share during the Constitutional Congress of 1987–1988, the present higher figure will probably mean less influence, given that both global and domestic ideological parameters have changed. The difficulties ahead are, therefore, rooted more in the complexity of the issues themselves than in the distribution of congressional and gubernatorial seats among the different parties. The generic concept of "achieving fiscal balance" hides a variety of very difficult political issues—such as accelerating privatization, revising the distribution of revenues and responsibilities among the three levels of government, simplifying the tax system, redesigning the private-public mix in the social security system, and balancing the accounts of the state public banks. As President Cardoso took office at the beginning of 1995, the agenda continued to be overloaded, but few could doubt that the constellation of political and societal resources needed to face that agenda was far greater than at any time since the return of democracy a decade previously.

Notes

This chapter (except for the last section) was initially drafted in 1986. Luís Aureliano Gama Andrade, Wanderley G. Santos, Amaury de Souza, and my colleagues at IDESP all made valuable suggestions to improve the initial version.

1. The Movimento Democrático Brasileiro (opposition) elected sixteen of the twenty-two senators in 1974 (renovating one-third of the Senate), with a strong showing in the more urban and modernized states. An extended discussion of the structure of electoral competition as a factor capable of preventing authoritarian consolidation in Brazil can be found in Bolívar Lamounier, "Authoritarian Brasil Revisited," in *Democratizing Brazil,* ed. Alfred Stepan (Oxford and New York: Oxford University Press, 1988).

2. One of these measures was the introduction of indirect elections for one-third of the senators. These senators were quickly nicknamed "bionic" and were never accepted as legitimate by public opinion. Another measure was the severe curtailing of electoral propaganda through radio and television, generalizing restrictions previously applied only in the municipal election of 1976.

3. One of these bills aimed at increasing contributions to finance the social-security system; the other attempted to extend the *sublegendas* (triple candidacies in each party) to the gubernatorial elections.

4. Cardoso was probably the first scholar to stress that the Brazilian authoritarian regime did not pursue stagnant economic policies; that it was, on the contrary, decidedly modernizing. See Fernando H. Cardoso, "Dependent-Associated Development: Theoretical and Practical Implications," in *Authoritarian Brazil: Origins, Outputs, Future,* ed. Alfred Stepan (New Haven, Conn.: Yale University Press, 1973). On economic policy in the 1970s, see Bolívar Lamounier and Alkimar R. Moura, "Economic Policy and Political Opening in Brazil," in *Latin American Political Economy: Financial Crisis and Political Change,* ed. Jonathan Hartlyn and Samuel A. Morley (Boulder, Colo.: Westview Press, 1986). For a comprehensive

overview of economic and political developments since the 1930s, see Bolívar Lamounier and Edmar Bacha, "Democracy and Economic Reforms in Brazil," in ed. Joan Nelson, *Precarious Balance: Democracy and Economic Reforms in Eastern Europe and Latin America* (San Francisco: ICS Press).

5. In addition to the "bionic" senators, created in 1977, the government majority increased the weight of the smaller states in the Electoral College through Constitutional Amendment 22 of 1982. The traditional but now controversial over-representation that those states enjoy in the federal chamber was thus unacceptably extended to the presidential succession. It is worth noting that the opposition assimilated even this change when it decided to present Tancredo Neves to the Electoral College as a presidential candidate.

6. Bureaucratic continuity has led many historians to accept the naive idea that Brazil inherited a ready-made state from the Portuguese at the time of independence in 1822. The more cautious view that Brazilian state building was "completed" by 1860 or 1870 may be accepted, but even this with important qualifications. See J. G. Merquior, "Patterns of State-Building in Brazil and Argentina," in *States in History,* ed. John A. Hall (London: Blackwell, 1986).

7. On the formation of a central power as a precondition for peaceful competition, see the excellent treatment of the English case in Harvey Mansfield, Jr., "Party Government and the Settlement of 1688," *American Political Science Review* 63, no. 4 (1964): pp. 933–950; on the U.S. case, see Richard Hofstadter, *The Idea of a Party System* (Berkeley and Los Angeles: University of California Press, 1972).

8. My treatment of these questions is evidently inspired by Hannah Pitkin's now-classic work. However, searching for different images of representation in the Brazilian case, we placed them in a historical sequence she may not have intended, at least not as a general rule. See Hannah Pitkin, *The Concept of Representation* (Berkeley and Los Angeles: University of California Press, 1972).

9. See José Murilo de Carvalho, *A Construção da Ordem* (Rio de Janeiro: Editora Campus, 1980).

10. The classic here is Victor Nunes Leal, *Coronelismo, Enxada e Voto: O Município e a Regime Representativo no Brasil* (Rio de Janeiro: Editora Forense, 1948).

11. On the evolution of military institutions, see Edmundo Campos Coelho, *Em Busca da Identidade: O Exército e a Política na Sociedade Brasileira* (Rio de Janeiro: Editora Forense, 1976); José Murilo de Carvalho, "As Forças Armadas na Primeira República: O Poder Desestabilizador"; Belo Horizonte, UFMG, *Cadernos do Deportamento de Ciencia Política* no. 1, March 1974. On the nineteenth-century National Guard, see Fernando Uricoechea, *O Minotauro Imperial* (São Paulo: Difel, 1978).

12. Control of the credentials commission (Comissao de Verificação de Poderes) of the federal chamber was the key to the system, since through it undesirable deputies eventually elected in the states would not be allowed to take up their position. This became popularly known as *degola* (beheading). Souza provides an excellent treatment of this question: "If the sedimentation of the [state] oligarchies was essential to consolidate the federation, it was also the reason for its future weakness. Contrary to the imperial framework, rotation in power among state oligarchies now became impossible." See Maria do Carmo Campello de Souza, "O Processo Político-Partidário na Velha República," in *Brasil em Perspectiva,* ed. Carlos Guilherme Mota (São Paulo: Difel, 1971), p. 203.

13. There is an extensive literature on the Revolution of 1930. Especially useful for our purposes is Campello de Souza, "Processo Politico-Partidário." See also Boris Fausto, ed., *O Brasil Republicano,* 3 vols (São Paulo: Difel, 1978, 1982, and 1983); and Paulo Brandi, *Getulio Vargas—Da Vida para a História* (Rio de Janeiro: Zahar Editores, 1985).

14. Nunes Leal, *Coronelismo,* p. 170-171.

15. Protofascism is used here in the same sense given to it by James Gregor, *The Ideology of Fascism* (New York: Free Press, 1969), ch. 2. He deals with important theoretical precursors, such as Gumplowicz, Pareto, and Mosca, stressing their antiparliamentarianism, their view on the relation between elite and mass, on the function of political myths, and the like.

16. On the corporatist "regulation" of citizenship, see Wanderley Guilherme dos Santos, *Cidadania e Justiça* (Rio de Janeiro: Editora Campus, 1979). Comprehensive accounts of the corporatist features of the labor relations system can be found in P. Schmitter, *Interest Conflict and Political Change in Brazil* (Stanford, Calif.: Stanford University Press, 1971); Amaury de

Souza, *The Nature of Corporatist Representation: Leaders and Members of Organized Labor in Brazil* (Ph.D. Diss., Massachusetts Institute of Technology, 1978); and Youssef Cohen, *The Manipulation of Consent: The State and Working Class in Brazil* (Pittsburgh: University of Pittsburgh Press, 1991).

17. The name of Gilberto Freyre comes readily to mind in connection with race relations and nationality in Brazil. On these themes, see T. Skidmore, *Black into White* (New York: Oxford University Press, 1974). The impact of these developments in Brazilian political culture was of course enormous in the 1930s and as a support to the Estado Novo. The factual importance of these core beliefs has been recognized quite broadly in the ideological spectrum since then. On intellectuals and culture policy in that period, see Simon Schwartzman et al., *Tempos de Capanema* (Rio de Janeiro: Paz e Terra, 1984); Sérgio Miceli, *Intelectuais e Classe Dirigente no Brasil (1920–1945)* (São Paulo: Difel, 1979); Lúcia Lippi de Oliveira, *Estado Novo—Ideologia e Poder* (Rio de Janeiro: Zahar Editores, 1982).

18. On the downfall of the *Estado Novo*, see Maria do Carmo Campello de Souza, *Estado e Partidos no Brasil* (São Paulo: Editora Alfa-Omega, 1976); T. Skidmore, *Politics in Brazil: An Experiment in Democracy* (New York: Oxford University Press, 1968); Peter Flynn, *Brazil: A Political Analysis* (Boulder, Colo.: Westview Press, 1975). On the UDN, see Maria Vitória Benevides, *UDN e Udenismo* (Rio de Janeiro: Paz e Terra, 1981)

19. The literature on Vargas's second government is surprisingly small. In addition to the works of Flynn and Skidmore, already cited, see Maria Celina Soares D'Araujo, *O Segundo Governo Vargas, 1951–1954* (Rio de Janeiro: Zahar Editores, 1982); and Edgard Carone, *A República Liberal II* (São Paulo: Difel, 1985).

20. Useful data on bureaucratic growth under the Estado Novo can be found in Maria do Carmo Campello de Souza, *Estado e Partidos Politicos*. On economic policymaking from the 1930s to the mid-1950s, see John Wirth, *The Politics of Brazilian Development 1930–1954* (Stanford, Calif.: Stanford University Press, 1970); and Luciano Martins, *Pouvoir et développement économique au Brésil* (Paris: Editions Anthropos, 1976).

21. J. G. Merquior, "Patterns of State-Building," p. 284.

22. An overview of these hypotheses and of the relevant literature can be found in Bolívar Lamounier and Rachel Meneguello, *Partidos Políticos e Consolidação Democrática: O Caso Brasileiro* (São Paulo: Editora Brasiliense, 1986), sect 4. Rigorous analysis of the crisis leading to 1964 was pioneered by Wanderley Guilherme dos Santos, *The Calculus of Conflict: Impasse in Brazilian Politics* (Ph.D. Diss., Stanford University, 1974). Important works for the understanding of executive-legislative relations in the 1950s and early 1960s include: Celso Lafer, *The Planning Process and the Political System in Brazil* (Ph.D. Diss., Cornell University, 1970); Maria Vitória Benevides *O Governo Kubitschek* (Rio de Janeiro: Paz e Terra, 1976); and Lúcia Hippolito, *PSD: De Raposas e Reformistas* (Rio de Janeiro: Paz e Terra, 1984).

23. On the ambiguities of military-directed institution building after 1964, see Juan Linz, "The Future of an Authoritarian Situation or the Institutionalization of an Authoritarian Regime: The Case of Brazil," in Stepan, *Authoritarian Brazil;* Bolívar Lamounier, "Authoritarian Brazil revisited"; Wanderley Guilherme dos Santos, *Poder e Política: Crônica do Autoritarismo Brasileiro* (Rio de Janeiro: Forense. 1978). Roett synthesized those ambiguities as follows: "In Brazil, although the latitude given to the civilian political process is severely compromised, it does exist. The commitment to political participation—limited, elitist, and manipulable as it is—is strongly rooted in Brazilian constitutional history. Geisel's efforts at decompression were part of that historical belief that there should be a more open system." See Riordan Roett, "The Political Future of Brazil," in *The Future of Brazil,* ed. William Overholt (Boulder, Colo.: Westview Press, 1978).

24. Before independence and especially before the intensification of mining, in the early eighteenth century, the local chambers (*câmaras municipais*) were almost exclusively made up of landowners and had virtually unlimited authority, concentrating executive, legislative, and judiciary functions. Their members were chosen by means of a crude electoral system set forth in the *ordenações* of the Portuguese Crown. During the nineteenth century, detailed regulations were established to control local and statewide elections. Needless to say, the franchise was limited and voting was not secret. In addition, the empire kept the tradition of not allowing a clear distinction between legislative and executive functions at the local level; an elected local executive would appear only under the republic, and especially after 1930.

25. On bureaucratic continuity, see Raimundo Faoro, *Os Donos Do Poder* (Porto Alegre: Editora Globo, 1958); for a comparative analysis, see Merquior, "Patterns of State-Building"; on the military organization, see Coelho, *Em Busca da Identidade.*

26. See Wanderley Guilherme dos Santos, "A Pós-'Revoluçao' Brasileira," in *Brasil: Sociedade Democrática,* ed. Hélio Jaguaribe (Rio de Janeiro: José Olympio Editora, 1985).

27. Sylvia A. Hewlett, "The State and Brazilian Economic Development," in Overholt, *Future of Brazil,* p. 150.

28. Russet calculated Gini coefficients for inequality in land tenure circa 1960 in forty-seven countries and found Brazil to be the thirty-sixth from low to high concentration. See Bruce M. Russet, "Inequality and Instability: The Relation of Land Tenure to Politics," in *Readings in Modern Political Analysis,* ed. Robert A. Dahl and Deanne E. Neubauer (Englewood Cliffs, N.J.: PrenticeHall, 1968), pp. 150–162. There is no reason to assume that landed property is less concentrated today than in the 1960s. What did happen was that agrarian social relations became thoroughly capitalist. Landed property in Brazil was never "feudal" in a technical sense. Land was essentially used for capitalist purposes; i.e., to produce for a market or to function as a reserve of value in a highly inflationary economy. True, social relations were often paternalistic and exploitative, but this, too, is now undergoing rapid change.

29. The literature on growth and income distribution in this period is, of course, voluminous. A convenient starting point is Ricardo Tolipan and Artur Carlos Tinelli, eds. *A Controvérsia sobre Distribuição de Renda e Desenvolvimento* (Rio de Janeiro: Zahar Editores, 1975); see also Edmar Bacha, *Os Mitos de uma Década* (Rio de Janeiro: Editora Paz e Terra, 1976); and World Bank, *World Development Report 1983* and *World Development Report 1986* (New York: Oxford University Press, 1986).

30. Douglas H. Graham, "The Brazilian Economy: Structural Legacies and Future Prospects," in Overholt, *Future of Brazil,* p 122

31. See José Serra, "Ciclos e Mudanças Estruturais na Economia Brasileira do Pós-Guerra," in *Desenvolvimento Capitalista no Brazil—Ensaios sobre a Crise,* no. 2, eds. L. G. Belluzzo and Renata Coutinho (São Paulo: Editora Brasiliense, 1983), p. 64.

32. World Bank, *World Development Report 1994.*

33. The following account of class structure in relation to the corporatist system draws heavily on dos Santos's important essay, "Pós-'Revoluçao' Brasileira."

34. See dos Santos, "Pós-'Revoluçao' Brasileira," p. 258; see also Carlos A. Hasenbalg, *Discriminação e Desigualdades Raciais no Brasil* (Rio de Janeiro: Ediçoes Graal, 1979).

35. On Brazilian party history, see Lamounier and Meneguello, *Partidos Políticos.*

36. See works cited in note 22, above.

37. Alfred Stepan, "Political Leadership and Regime Breakdown: Brazil," in *The Breakdown of Democracies,* ed. Juan Linz and Alfred Stepan (Baltimore, Md.: Johns Hopkins University Press, 1978).

38. The importance of law schools throughout the nineteenth century and up to 1945 is beyond dispute. Resistance to Vargas's Estado Novo and again to the post-1964 military governments gave them a new lease on life. The Brazilian Lawyers Association was a basic reference point for the opposition during the decompression period.

39. A detailed analysis of Geisel's economic and political strategies can be found in Lamounier and Moura, "Economic Policy and Political Opening"; see also, Lamounier and Bacha, "Democracy and Economic Reforms."

40. Perhaps we can interpret in this light the familiar finding that support for the democratic "rules of the game" is often more a matter of elite ethos than of mass attitudes. On "collective goods" as a tool in political analysis, see Mancur Olson, Jr., *The Logic of Collective Action* (New York: Schocken Books, 1968).

41. Robert A. Dahl, *Polyarchy; Participation and Opposition* (New Haven, Conn.: Yale University Press, 1971) pp. 57–61.

42. Bolívar Lamounier, "Impasse in Brazil," *Journal of Democracy* 5, no. 3 (July 1994): pp. 72–87.

43. For an analysis of the presidential-parliamentary debate, see my chapter "Brazil: Towards Parliamentarism?" in Juan J. Linz and Arturo Valenzuela, eds. *The Failure of Presidential Democracy* (Baltimore: Johns Hopkins University Press, 1994); plebiscite results and a brief analysis of the reasons parliamentarism was defeated can be found in pp. 289–290.

44. On the "consociational" nature of Brazilian institutional arrangements, see my chapter "Institutional Structure and Governability in the 1990s," in Maria D'Alva G. Kinzo, ed. *Brazil: Economic, Social and Political Challenges of the 1990s* (London: British Academic Press, 1992); also Lamounier and Bacha, "Democracy and Economic Reforms."

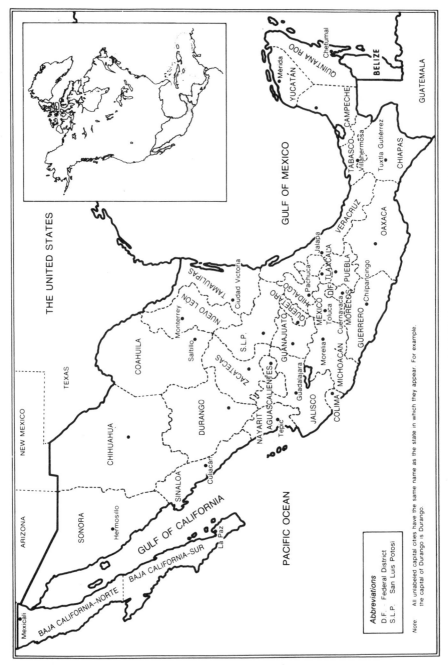

MEXICO

4

Mexico: Sustained Civilian Rule Without Democracy

Daniel C. Levy and Kathleen Bruhn

A lone among the Latin American countries examined in this comparative project series ("Democracy in Developing Countries"), Mexico
has had no significant experience with democratic rule. Despite substantial
increases in the level of competition and the cleanness of elections, Mexican
politics has long disdained the public competition and accountability integral to liberal democracy. Mexico has yet to pass the ultimate test of democratic governance: acceptance of alternation in power. Instead, with the victory of Ernesto Zedillo in the 1994 presidential election, Mexico's
Institutional Revolutionary Party (PRI) became the longest-ruling party still
on the planet.

Nevertheless, Mexico merits inclusion in our comparative study for
three reasons: (1) the nation's overall importance, (2) theoretical insights
distinguishing the bases of democratic and stable civilian rule, and (3)
notable democratizing developments in recent years. The first reason is
obvious; this chapter focuses on the others.[1]

The dominant theme here is that many factors commonly associated
with good prospects for democracy have been present in Mexico without
effecting that result. Moreover, the very achievement of Mexico's major
political success—stable civilian rule—has presented obstacles to democratization. Naturally, observers have long realized that democracy and stability are empirically and analytically separable, but a strong tendency lumps
the two together as one desired outcome. Many of the hypotheses orienting
this comparative project illustrate the tendency. Although distinct measures
are developed for democracy and stability, democratic stability appears as
the key dependent variable.

Among recent attempts to explore difficulties in achieving democracy
and stability together, some have concentrated on the reasons democracies
fall. For other nations discussed in this volume, but not Mexico, one can
analyze democratic periods, democratic breakdown (or consolidation), and
"redemocratization." Another line of inquiry concerns the conditions under

which authoritarian regimes become democratic.[2] But the literature on that process deals overwhelmingly with military regimes—typically very exclusionary and coercive—and to a limited extent with narrow personalistic regimes. Unlike either military authoritarian or personalistic rule, Mexico's authoritarianism has much of the institutionalization, breadth, forms, pacts, and legitimacy often associated with democratic government.

In fact, in Mexico many factors associated with democratic stability have promoted a civilian authoritarian rule that has managed the most impressive political stability in all of Latin America regardless of regime type. No other major Latin American nation has sustained civilian rule throughout the postwar period; Mexico's predates that period. In terms of our measures of stability, no regime in the region matches Mexico's in durability and legitimacy built through periods of change, conflict, and challenge. Despite recent evidence that support and legitimacy have declined substantially (including stronger electoral opposition, increased nonpartisan identification, a more vigorous civil society, and even the emergence of an armed guerrilla movement in the southern state of Chiapas in 1994), Mexico has ranked in the category of stable polities, albeit bordering on partially stable. Unlike Latin American systems that are partially stable because they have not consolidated new democratic regimes, Mexico's main difficulty concerns erosion of consolidated authoritarianism.

Assessments of stability have been clearer than assessments of democracy in Mexico. The latter have been influenced excessively by dominant paradigms in comparative politics in general and in Latin American studies in particular. An irony is that interpretations of Mexican politics changed so much while the system itself remained remarkably stable. In line with burgeoning literature on political development, Mexico was typically depicted in the 1950s and most of the 1960s as incompletely but increasingly democratic. Probably the most cited work emphasized an evolution toward Western democracy in rising interest-group activity, participation, inclusiveness, national identity, legitimacy, and functional specialization along with declining personalism. Mexico fell short on its citizenship base and leadership selection largely because the regime had pursued "suitable social and economic conditions" before democratic goals, but those conditions had made Mexico ready for democracy.[3] Subsequently, however, Mexico was almost consensually depicted as authoritarian, with democratic tendencies not ascendent. Juan Linz's seminal work on authoritarianism was widely employed by Mexicanists, and Mexico was even tied overzealously to bureaucratic authoritarianism. More recently, interpretations of complex blends of authoritarianism and pluralist forces have developed.[4]

From 1945 to 1985, while many Latin American countries suffered military rule, Mexico ranked between third and seventh among twenty nations on the best-known, if controversial, ratings for Latin American democracy.[5] Mexico ranks lower today, however, because most other cases currently fit our basic definition of democracy. Mexico has fallen short on three elements of democracy, although increasing qualification on all three now makes Mexico a borderline case: (1) Mexico has lacked meaningful and extensive competition among organized groups for major government office, although competition is increasing; (2) participation has not reliably extended to leadership selection through fair elections, although elections have been regular; and (3) civil and political liberties have been insufficient to guarantee the integrity of competition and participation, but they have been significant and variable rather than minimal. Mexico falls into the lowest category (failure/absence) in the "Democracy in Developing Countries" six-part "summary scale" of democratic experience because there has been no extended period of democracy. However, democratic space has increased considerably in recent years, and the future is probably more hopeful than ever.

Regarding this study's classification of democratic stability, Mexico has come closest to the "hegemonic party" system. The dominant party has not tolerated genuine challenges (i.e., alternatives) to its rule, it claims almost all subfederal posts, and electoral fraud continues. Still, the party does not regularly take the high vote percentage cited for hegemonic systems: Indeed, in 1994, for the first time, the ruling party acknowledged receiving less than 50 percent of the presidential vote. More broadly, this volume's overall definition of democracy is heavily weighted toward electoral dimensions, long a weak area for Mexico. Even before recent democratization, the Mexican case suggests that hegemonies are not necessarily the least democratic of authoritarian nations.

In terms of the study's overall typology, we would currently classify Mexico as a "semidemocracy" making progress toward democracy. Democracy remains too generous a term until Mexico improves its performance on each of the three defining criteria of democracy just considered, and until the PRI either demonstrates or credibly signals its willingness to accept alternation in power at the national level. Yet too harsh are once valid designations of "authoritarian regime" or "hegemonic party system," even if qualified by noting strong pressures for democracy. In some cases, including the 1994 presidential election and several state elections, outcomes reflect considerable competition and do not significantly diverge from popular preferences. In democracy, such standards would become regular and widespread, and conditions for opposition competition would become more equal. On the stability dimension, Mexico comes near the editors' concept of "partially stable," though still much closer to stable than unstable. So far, the regime has remained able to withstand very trying crises, and it is deeply institutionalized. Still, "stable" now sounds a little strong given recent uncertainties, political change, increased violence (including a local guerrilla rebellion), and the repeated economic shocks of the past decade.

This chapter identifies basic roots of Mexico's complex system of sustained civilian rule without democracy and, more specifically, considers the editors' hypotheses about stable democracy. Finally, it analyzes prospects for democratization and the role the United States might play.

An Undemocratic Past: Review and Analysis

Mexico's political heritage is authoritarian. There is less democratic precedent to analyze than in the other Latin American countries considered in this comparative project; viable democratic rule has been virtually absent. As in the Dominican Republic, so in Mexico, democratic experiments have historically proved ineffective, in contrast to certain authoritarian periods.

Great precolonial civilizations, such as the Aztec, presaged a pattern of relatively strong authoritarian rule. Spain's centuries-long rule was similar in that respect. Some observers see not only precedent but causal roots in these experiences. According to Octavio Paz, the Aztec *tlatoani* introduced impersonal, priestly, institutional rule, and colonialism introduced Arabic-Hispanic reverence for the personal *caudillo:* "I repeat: there is a bridge that reaches from *tlatoani* to viceroy, viceroy to president."[6] And much has been made of the contrast between authoritarian and "liberal" colonizations by Spain and England, respectively.

Independence (1821) brought neither democracy nor stability. Federalist-centralist conflicts were among the most important. The lack of stability crippled hopes for economic growth, which in turn contributed to further instability. Despite examples of autonomous local rule, liberal projects were weak. Liberal rule was extremely short-lived until the Reform (1855–1876), probably the closest Mexico has come to democracy until recent times. It featured a belief that democracy, however restricted, was compatible with stability and growth; a liberal constitution; substantial liberties; some significant elections; and some socioeconomic mobility and educational expansion along with attacks on large landholders, including the church. On the other hand, the Reform was limited in mass inclusiveness and was hostile to Indian communitarianism. Yet democracy often begins with public contestation restricted to certain groups. Mexico's liberal experiment failed because it could not build sufficient strength. French imperial intervention, although eventually beaten back, was debilitating. Mostly, liberal democratic forms were used by antidemocratic forces. Regional *caciques* used decentralized authority to block reform. As it often has in Latin America, Congress represented *cacique* and other oligarchic interests in conflict with a liberal executive.[7] The weakness of liberal experiments with decentralized political authority did not go unnoticed by twentieth-century leaders.

Always fragile, the Reform faded after leader Benito Juárez's death in 1872. A split over the 1876 presidential succession opened the way for a military coup, and Porfirio Díaz became supreme dictator. The regime was repressively authoritarian: Gone were free elections; diminished was freedom of the press. As is common for Latin America, some democratic formalities were preserved, but Díaz's reference to Congress as his herd of tame horses was indicative of the basic realities. Nevertheless, under the *porfiriato* independent Mexico achieved political stability and economic growth for the first time. In its positivist notions of progress through permanent evolution, its support for development through foreign trade and investment, its preference for rational administration by *científicos,* and most of all, its model of economic growth without distribution and political stability without democracy, the *porfiriato* offers broad historical parallels to the contemporary regime.

Among factors that ultimately brought down the *porfiriato* (1910), contemporary optimists about democracy might speculate on both repressiveness and economic growth leading to calls for democracy. However, the main reason for the regime's fall was its unwillingness to allow political mobility among the elite.[8] Representatives of the new national bourgeoisie, such as northerner Francisco Madero, demanded access to power. When Díaz reneged on his pledge not to seek reelection in 1910 and then attempted electoral fraud, Madero called for a popular uprising in support of his claim to have won. Díaz fell within a few months, and Madero became president. Madero's agenda envisioned a relatively limited form of political democracy, basically "a return to '57," the Reform Constitution, and "free suffrage, no reelection." Congress was autonomous from the executive and was the scene of powerful debates among very antagonistic forces. True division of power (federalism) and separation of power (including judicial review) became priorities.

But such democratization proved largely irrelevant for Mexico. Democratic structures did not lead to the destruction of Porfirian forces including *caciques,* governors, bureaucrats, the military, and a partially revitalized church. Madero even appointed former Díaz aides to government positions, whereas he tended to exclude revolutionary groups. In other words, this democratic leader, so popular in 1911, neither destroyed the old order nor constructed a viable new one. Although a good deal of the literature on transitions to democracy stresses the need for pacts among elites, probably the major weakness in Madero's approach was his reluctance to address socioeconomic problems and popular demands (especially for land) and his consequent failure to strengthen democratic forces by adding a mass base. Of course, whether Madero could have successfully done so is unknown. After his assassination by reactionary forces (covertly aided by the United States), other leaders would incorporate the masses—undemocratically.

Revolutionary warfare among various armies broke out again, bringing mass mobilization and, especially, death and destruction. By 1916, a million Mexicans had died and nearly as many had emigrated from a population of just under 14 million in 1910. Compared, for example, with Emiliano

Zapata's peasant army and its demands for land reform, Venustiano Carranza's ultimately victorious constitutionalists were not committed to fundamental socioeconomic change. In subsequent years, some observers would even question whether a real revolution had occurred. Nevertheless, the revolution became a symbol of mass involvement, progressive change, and nationalism, skillfully manipulated by the regime to bolster its legitimacy. By 1940, the revolution was "institutionalized," the fragile stability forged since 1916 safely deepened.

Two crucial factors in building this postrevolutionary stability were pacts among those elites not destroyed by the revolution and the organized integration of mass groups.[9] President Carranza only partly recognized these two necessities, but he accepted provisions that gave the 1917 Constitution strong mass appeal as a legacy of the revolution. These included a minimum wage, an eight-hour workday, workmen's compensation, land reform, and notable nationalist measures. Equally significant, the constitution ambiguously blended democratic aspirations with authoritarian realities, on the one hand stressing popular sovereignty, free elections, guarantees for individual rights, federalism, and separation of powers but on the other hand laying the bases for a potent central government in general and a strong presidency in particular.

Between them Carranza's two powerful successors, Alvaro Obregón and Plutarco Elías Calles, extended the state's ties to and control over mass agrarian and urban labor interests. Yet when their terms ended (1928), the regime's stability was still much in doubt. All three presidents had plotted to rule beyond their constitutional terms; two had been assassinated. Major groups still competed violently, and none was powerful enough to end the nation's political stalemate.

At this point, Mexico experienced three moments of great political leadership, the kind associated in many ways with democratic consolidation. However, the leadership that stabilized Mexico's civilian rule would be undemocratic not only in means, not unusual in democratic consolidations, but also in ends. First, Calles engineered a grand pact among elite power-holders. Convincing them that without compromise they faced defeat, renewed armed conflict, or endless uncertainty, he brought them to support the creation of a civilian institution (the party) that would centralize authority for the regime on the basis of bargains, including elite circulation through peaceful means. Second, Calles's successor, Lázaro Cárdenas, fortified the party by creating and incorporating mass organizations within it. He did so in large part to block Calles's personalistic attempt to perpetuate his rule from behind the scenes. Cárdenas used his personal influence within the mass organizations to counteract Calles's edge among elites—in the process winning their allegiance not only to himself but also to the regime.[10] Critically, however, Cárdenas stressed the leadership of the state rather than the formation of autonomous organizations of masses. His modes were corporatist, and he openly opposed bourgeois democracy.

Finally, the immensely popular Cárdenas peacefully relinquished power to a moderate successor (1940), ending the succession of presidents who had tried to dominate the country beyond their constitutional terms and setting a valuable precedent. By this time the regime was sufficiently institutionalized to pave the way for more than a quarter-century of maximum strength and stability, followed finally by a continuing period of greater turmoil.

Civilian Rule Without Democracy

This section analyzes four topics identified as crucial to democratic development. For each, the analysis explores how basic features evolved, how they serve civilian stability but not democracy, and how recent reforms and popular challenges have altered these traditional bases of support for the system.

State-Society Relations

State relations with mass groups approximate "state corporatism" much more than pluralism.[11] The regime has significant control over organizations that bring the masses into the system. Through unions and other organizations affiliated with the ruling party, the state has had the capacity to influence strike behavior, restrain wage demands, and mobilize support for the system. In most of Mexico, autonomous participation and demand formulation are seriously limited. In fact, much of the Mexican population is unorganized and politically "marginal"; it does not express discontent, or it asks for help from a political mediator without demanding rights. Even formal, organized groups often react to, more than participate meaningfully in, policy formation.[12]

The state's encapsulation of mass organizations had obviously antithetical effects on the chances for democracy. It greatly limited the democratizing option available in Venezuela's *trienio* when the AD (Accíon Democrática) party could organize peasants and workers in opposition to the military rulers. Those groups have already been organized in Mexico into a single undemocratic party controlled by the state. On the other hand—also as in Venezuela—the early incorporation of mass groups (especially labor) promoted stability and civilian rule.[13] It gave the regime a wide base, which helped counterbalance the armed forces and which in some periods was used to boost the regime's autonomy from business. Mainly, however, incorporation protected the state from organized dissent on the left by making the formation of popular alliances extremely difficult. The Mexican regime has repeatedly been able to effect austere economic policies that would bring revolt in other nations. Thus, the regime's undemocratic control of a mass base has sustained civilian rule and stability.

This dominant pattern of state-controlled incorporation was never absolute or unchallenged, however. By the 1990s, moreover, state-society relations had become considerably more complex and problematic for the regime. In part, this resulted from the deterioration of traditional corporatist institutions, particularly key peasant and labor unions, which gradually lost much of their power to mobilize support for the regime. On the one hand, economic development tended to reduce the centrality of unions, as Mexico became an increasingly urban society with a large informal sector and an ever more mobile workforce. By the early 1980s, only about 20 percent of the economically active population was unionized.[14] On the other hand, the regime's insistence on control and union sacrifices tended to delegitimize the unions' leadership. A classic example is the fate of the dominant union within the labor sector, the Confederation of Mexican Workers (CTM), and its ninety-four-year-old leader Fidel Velázquez, a member of the CTM leadership since Cárdenas created it and grafted it onto the PRI. Velázquez and the CTM came to symbolize everything that was wrong with the Mexican labor movement: its capture by leaders with absolute and seemingly perpetual dominance, its flourishing corruption and personalism, and its tendency to sacrifice the interests of union members at the president's behest. Such labor leaders helped make Mexican unions "moderate" but neither autonomous nor democratic.[15] Occasionally, when independent labor movements threatened to become powerful, the regime resorted to severe repression (as in the late 1950s), but it has usually relied on the undemocratic internal structure of organized labor and its ties to the regime.[16]

For a long time, economic growth allowed the regime to use these controls sparingly. Carefully funneled benefits to organized labor helped sustain the relationship. However, the economic crisis of the 1980s compelled unprecedented sacrifices from labor. To control inflation, President de la Madrid initiated the first of several pacts that put a freeze on both wages and some prices—a major reason wages rose slower than inflation during the 1980s. Real minimum wages fell by 40 to 50 percent between 1982 and 1988.[17] Despite some hard bargaining, complaints, and threatened strikes, the labor movement seemed remarkably docile.[18] Not surprisingly, this affected popular support for labor unions: 31 percent of the labor candidates appointed by the CTM lost to opposition candidates in the 1988 election.[19]

Into this context came renewed activity from independent labor movements and dissident factions of official movements (including the Tendencia Democrática of the electrical workers union, as well as factions of the teachers, miners, and telephone workers unions). In addition, relatively autonomous popular-sector organizations became increasingly common and significant as formulators of demands and forums for popular participation. One basic reason has been disenchantment with government, particularly given the consequences of continued economic crisis. A second, more specific catalyst was the earthquakes of 1985; the government appeared impotent in reacting. A third factor has been political organization by activists from leftist currents who saw little hope in electoral opposition, preferring self-organization of the masses to deal with urgent problems. Individuals have formed associations to deal with urban problems such as homelessness, tenant conditions, schooling, and other public services. Although spontaneous association has considerable precedent in Mexico, some see these organizations as the key to "an initial democratization of Mexico's political institutions."[20] Recent behavior can be contrasted to Fagen and Tuohy's well-known depiction of "depoliticized" urban life, where management substitutes for politics and most people believe government should or will handle their political affairs.[21] The new vibrancy in Mexican politics alters traditional state-society patterns associated with stability; indeed, it has resulted both from the state's success in modernizing and diversifying society and from its declining legitimacy.

However, the tendency to use the increasing democratic space has been greatest among more privileged groups, particularly middle-class intellectuals, students, and business. State-business relations have long epitomized another pattern of state-society relations. Reasonable scholarly debate exists over how to characterize this linkage. Some "peak" business associations have been established by the government, mandatory and dependent on government in matters ranging from subsidies to leadership selection. But a good case can be made that domestic business, even including older associations such as the Confederation of Industrial Chambers and the National Chamber of Manufacturing Industry, has long worked with the government because of mutual self-interest and "inducements" more than coercion and "constraints"; has been economically strong and politically able to influence regulatory, trade, and other policies; and has expressed a "sectorial consciousness" involving some "adversary relationship with political elites."[22] In any case, this more pluralist view holds for newer associations, such as the Entrepreneurial Coordinating Council and the Mexican Employers' Confederation, and increasingly for traditional ones. Two developments in particular raised the level of business activism: the economic populism of President Luis Echeverría in the early 1970s and the nationalization of the banking system by President Lopez Portillo in 1982. The bank nationalization impressed many business elites with their own vulnerability to presidential authority and encouraged them to take a more active and critical role in politics, even to the point of supporting the conservative opposition National Action Party (PAN).

Under the administration of Carlos Salinas (1988–1994), the government-business relationship improved considerably. His decision to open up the economy and to seek a free-trade agreement with the United States did not please many of the business sectors that had benefited extensively from state protection and subsidies. Nevertheless, the Mexican government in the 1990s developed close cooperation and communication with those business groups able to take advantage of—and support—the economic opening.

The juxtaposition of business and labor relations with the state illustrates how the balance between freedom and corporatist controls usually depends on social class. Similarly, tolerance has usually extended to middle-class groups. Granted, middle-class dependence on the state goes far beyond what is found in the United States in terms of employment opportunities and professional associations. But intellectuals and other professionals have been much freer than workers to control their affairs and even to criticize the government. Despite the potential corporatist tie of depending heavily on the state for income, Mexico's public universities have substantial autonomy from the government. Furthermore, groups within the public universities have considerable freedom of expression and power to affect institutional policies, as the massive student demonstrations against academic reforms proposed in 1986 illustrate.[23] Private institutions, holding 19 percent of the nation's more than one million enrollments, add significantly to state-society pluralism.[24]

Even these groups have been targets of repression, as in the infamous events of 1968 when the government killed hundreds of protesting university students. The slaughter was a watershed in views about Mexican democratization: It convinced many of the regime's unalterably repressive nature. To be sure, the student protests of 1968 were unprecedented for the widespread questions they so actively raised about the lack of democracy in Mexico. And 1968 serves as a chilling and restraining reminder of the state's potential for violent response to protest, a response much more commonly visited on poorer groups.[25] However, limits on protests have varied; behavior that lies within the "logic" of this authoritarian system is not inevitable behavior, and at times, other Mexican leaders have been more tolerant.

One rule usually demarking zones of permitted and unpermitted freedoms is also central to Mexico's exclusion from the democratic category: Organized dissent that poses a realistic alternative to the regime is forbidden. Violations may bring harsh repression along with co-optation. Even this formidable restriction leaves some room for pluralism, especially at the level of *individual* freedoms.[26] Religion provides an example of both the restrictions and the possibilities. After the revolution finally broke the church's tremendous political-economic power, a *modus vivendi* allowed it considerable autonomy in religious-cultural-educational affairs—beyond what the constitution ostensibly permitted. In turn, the church has not been allowed the opposition voice heard in Brazil, Chile, Nicaragua, and elsewhere in Latin America—although some Mexican church leaders have recently supported opposition party calls for democratization, and some priests support popular struggles. Meanwhile, individuals are free to worship (or not) as they please. Recent improvements in the state-church relationship have included the reestablishment of diplomatic relations with the Vatican and revision of restrictive legislation.

These points about societal freedom—its limits and its growth—are further illustrated by analysis of the media and public debate. Outright repression and censorship exist. Reporters have been intimidated and even killed. More often, self-censorship, encouraged by overlapping elite interests in "macro" orientations such as growth and stability without major redistribution, reinforces "micro" tools such as dependence on government advertising revenue and corrupt stipends for reporters. In return, the government counts on fairly favorable reporting and the ability to restrict or manipulate information about critics of the regime. As a result, citizens often lack the information needed to ensure responsible democracy with accountability. Where the media come closest to escaping such restrictions—in the print media—we tend to see elite pluralism. Most independent publications are not only expensive but also appeal to the educated minority. Electronic media remain much safer in content. Television's conservative banality is crucial. Thus, the most vigorous areas of contestation are the ones that reach the least inclusive audience. Additionally, considerable room exists for rather abstract, if fundamental, critiques of the state but much less for practical critiques including policy alternatives and investigative reporting of top government officials.[27] Where found, such coverage is often limited to what various officials and others have said, avoiding in-depth analysis.

Nevertheless, coverage of true dissent has increased significantly. Repression of the nation's leading independent newspaper in 1976 was followed by a gradual opening, which led to the greatest media freedom contemporary Mexico has known. Opposition parties and independent movements receive increasing coverage by print media (although still far inferior to coverage of the PRI) and even limited access to television. During the 1994 presidential campaign, the government agreed to Mexico's first ever televised debate between the top presidential candidates. The debate may have influenced the order of finish of the two opposition parties, PAN and the Party of the Democratic Revolution (PRD).[28] There has also been a dramatic growth in public opinion polls concerning everything from electoral choices to policy preferences and general attitudes toward government and democracy. All of this has contributed to a new era of democratic challenge.

But the regime has not maintained stability by taking such challenges lying down. Motivated by the strong showing of leftist presidential candidate Cuauhtémoc Cárdenas in 1988, by his electoral alliance with many of the new popular movements, and by the manifest inability of the corporatist unions to mobilize sufficient votes for the PRI, Carlos Salinas moved to mend fences between the state and civil society. No sooner had he been inaugurated than he announced the creation of the National Solidarity Program to "repair the tattered social safety net . . . inherited from the economic crisis and austerity" but also to effect the "rearrangement of state-society relations, and of the coalition supporting the ruling [party]."[29] Solidarity is the umbrella for well over twenty separate programs, most of which concentrate on infrastructural improvement, welfare, and support for productive activities. Like many previous government spending programs, Solidarity was intended to win political support for the regime. However, its design attempted to differentiate it from populism in terms of its fit within a neoliberal market economy, its promotion of local participation and demand formation (including some material contributions to projects from the beneficiaries themselves), and its bypassing of the PRI in favor of direct links between the federal government and local populations.

The effect of Solidarity on state-society relations remains a subject of considerable controversy. Some point to enhanced democratic discussion and grassroots organization with at least some independence from the PRI.[30] Others deny that Solidarity committees have become counterweights to the state or the PRI. Whether official or not, links to the PRI appear relatively common, and participation seems limited to a small percentage of the affected population. Program constraints also limited independent demand-making capacity. Furthermore, Solidarity probably undermined the strength of opposition parties by improving the image of the PRI and by contributing to breaches between the left and its popular movement allies.

Government Centralization

In turning now from state-society relations to the structure of the government, we deal less with elements intrinsic to democracy and more with elements hypothetically associated with democracy. That is, a system with widespread freedoms and pluralism is more democratic than one in which state corporatism rules society, whereas decentralized governments can exist in undemocratic systems and centralized governments can exist in democratic systems.

The editors have hypothesized a strong association between decentralization and democracy. The Mexican case supports this hypothesis, but only indirectly, as it combines centralization with the absence of democracy. Much clearer is that centralization—geographically and in the presidency—has been crucial to civilian stability. As González Casanova's classic analysis showed, Mexico City–based presidentialism with a hegemonic party ended military and legislative conspiracies as well as divisively unstable rule by regional and other *caudillos*. "Respect for the balances of power would have been respect for the conspiracies of a semi-feudal society."[31]

The construction of central authority and national identity is a major problem for new nations. Mexico failed to establish stable central government until the late nineteenth century under Porfirio Díaz. Following the turmoil of the revolution and even into the 1930s, regional and village strongmen ruled outside the grasp of Mexico City. Such decentralized power had nothing to do with democracy but reflected local fiefdoms. Overcoming centrifugal antidemocratic forces is often a prerequisite to democratic consolidation. In Mexico, the centralization of power by key political leaders (Obregón, Calles, and Cárdenas) proved crucial to stability but not democracy.

Mexico formally has a federalist structure with thirty-one states (plus the Federal District), which in turn are divided into over 2,000 supposedly free municipalities. State political structures parallel the national structure except that their legislatures are unicameral. In practice, a range of daily and other activities are handled by states, and the federal government usually intervenes only when conflicts are not locally contained. However, the very infrequency of explicit interventions reflects (as we saw in state-labor relations) ongoing national government control over basic policy. In essence, presidents appoint the official party's gubernatorial candidates and depose troublesome governors. National cabinet ministries have delegates in each state, and stationed military officers represent national authority. States have limited funds and depend on the national government for most of their income. Similarly, municipalities depend on states and the national government for leadership and funds. Most municipalities lack independent income beyond very small appropriations and fees from licenses and fines. Political careers are made in Mexico City, not at the grass roots.

Because centralization limits the power of subnational governments, the regime has accepted some opposition victories. Only since 1989 has this included governorships, always for the PAN. More common have been municipal opposition gains, but the PRI still holds the vast majority of all municipalities.[32] Sometimes, as following the leftist victory in Juchitán, Oaxaca, in 1981, the regime has used violence to oust a municipal opposition. More often, the centralized party-government structure itself makes it hard for the opposition to use municipal victories to consolidate electoral strength and prove its capacity to govern.

Centralization of power in Mexico City has also meant centralization of power in the presidency. Constitutional provisions about the separation of powers within the federal government have had no more impact than provisions about the division of powers between federal and state governments. Mexico achieved stability not by defying authoritarian tendencies toward the enormous concentration of authority in one leader but by limiting the leader's term. Apt are references to Mexico's "king for six years." The president has been central to policymaking, agenda setting, conflict resolution, government appointments, control over the party, and so forth. Cardoso even called the Mexican president perhaps more powerful than any Southern Cone military president.[33]

Such assessments probably underestimate four factors, however. One involves the comparative limits of the Mexican state's control over society; the Mexican president can be no more powerful than his government. Second are the terrible disorders, rivalries, and duplications rampant in the Mexican federal bureaucracy. Third is presidential immunity from criticism has eroded in the past two decades, reflected in increasing attacks on presidents, once unthinkable. Fourth are trends toward more effective separation of power within the national government, and increasingly assertive subnational actors.

The presidency nonetheless has remained very powerful, largely because Congress and the judiciary have been so weak. Congressional debate and opposition continued into the 1920s but died with regime consolidation. Executive initiatives have been approved unanimously or overwhelmingly. The main function of Congress has been to legitimize executive action. Since the 1970s, however, political reform has expanded opposition representation. Particularly after the 1988 election awarded opposition parties nearly half the seats in the Chamber of Deputies plus their first Senate representation, Congress has seen expanded coalition building, revelations about unpopular government actions, and much more vigorous debate.[34] The opening has included the appearance of cabinet officers to answer questions posed by the legislative opposition. Still, Congress's role remains more reactive than proactive; it has yet to develop independent policymaking ability.

The judiciary has played a more important role than the legislature (until recently) but also a limited one. It has been a place for privileged actors to protect their interests even against executive initiatives, particularly in the case of landlords working against land reform. Although it has handled disputes among citizens, it has not limited executive authority by interpreting the constitution or executive actions. No parallel has emerged for the liberalization occurring in the legislature. Except for the special electoral court, which in 1994 demonstrated its new independence by reversing several PRI congressional victories, "judicial reform" has usually meant speeding up the decisionmaking process, not to increasing autonomy from the executive.[35]

Presidential power depends ultimately on a rarity in Latin American politics (and in Mexican history from independence until roughly the 1930s): subordination of the military to civilian government. In the postwar era, only Costa Rica—which abolished its standing army—has enjoyed similar immunity from military interference. Outside Mexico, military subordination is generally associated with the establishment and defense of democracy. Mexico produced no democratic rule. Nonetheless, as in Costa Rica, skilled political leadership was crucial in establishing civilian supremacy.

Presidents Obregón, Calles, and Cárdenas, themselves revolutionary generals (like all presidents until 1946) adeptly timed and executed measures to subordinate the military. These included purges and other forced retirements and transfers (which minimized loyalty to given officers), welcome opportunities for corruption within the service and for business employment outside it, dependence on government salaries and social security, professionalization, cuts in military funding, creation of a viable political party, and incorporation of mass organizations into civilian structures. Since 1946, all presidents have been civilians.

Since the institutionalization of the regime, there have been no coups or serious threats of coups. The military has not been a powerful interest group blocking policies it does not like and forcing others. Its share of government expenditures has been famously low. The military has not been integrated with the civilian right. All of these factors distinguish Mexico from most of Latin America and help us understand the nation's stability.

Some signs of increasing military strength have recently appeared in role, stature, funding, modernization, and appointments of retired generals.[36] Still, a major change in the military's role remains unlikely. The civilian regime would probably have to weaken so much that it would need continual assistance to quell protests over austerity or electoral fraud. To this point, the Mexican military has loyally sustained rather than threatened civilian rule, but its loyalty is not to democracy.

Centralization and presidentialism have recently come under increasing attack. Disaffection runs especially high in the industrial north, although Mexico does not face the separatist threats that undermine stability in some nations. Many Mexicans consider decentralization necessary for increased participation and democratization. Decentralization or limits on presidential power could lower the stakes enough for the ruling party to accept alternation in power, as well as give opposition parties more opportunities to acquire experience in governing. Decentralization in implementation and, more controversially, in decisionmaking is increasingly linked to regime effectiveness and stability as well. President de la Madrid, although duly citing the historical necessity of centralization, called it "a grave limitation": "Centralist mentalities have become obstacles that distort democracy."[37] His administration claimed to have expanded municipal autonomy and increased access to local resources. In its 1988 campaign, the official party made decentralization a major theme, and during Salinas's term, emphasis was placed on local participation, particularly through Solidarity.

Additional limits to centralization and presidential power include the increasing presence of opposition parties and popular movements in particular regions, extensive privatization, and neoliberal trade opening. In the early 1980s, the president headed a vast network of federal agencies and state-owned companies (parastatals) employing 17 percent of the nation's workforce. By 1991, the number of parastatals had fallen from over 1,000 to just 269.[38] Major companies, including telephones, airlines, and banks, passed into private hands. Moreover, with entrance into the General

Agreement on Tariffs and Trade (GATT) and the negotiation of the North American Free Trade Agreement (NAFTA), the Mexican government constrained its ability to use traditional economic instruments like tariffs and import controls. Decisions formerly subject to executive approval could now be made in boardrooms.

But obstacles to decentralization remain enormous. Centralization goes beyond political to economic and social realms. Politically, decentralization means taking away resources and privileges, such as the power of appointment, from entrenched union-party leaders and state administrators, who therefore resist. Moreover, since the ruling party holds together largely on the basis of patron-client networks anchored by presidential power, decentralization or limits on presidentialism could cause the party to split and thus threaten stability. Decentralization or less presidentialism could also endanger national policy coherence, and this engages technocratic resistance. Modernizers have not renounced the idea of an influential state. Slimming down the state also streamlines policymaking, restores presidential control in what had become an overbureaucratized system, and allows top technocrats to distribute subsidies on the basis of evaluated performance.[39] Overall, decentralization involves risks. Even if overcentralization blocks democracy and threatens stability, sudden decentralization might threaten it even more.

The Party and Electoral Systems

Integral to both state corporatism and centralization is the dominance of the Institutional Revolutionary Party. The editors hypothesize that deeply institutionalized competitive parties are conducive to stable democracy. The PRI is deeply institutionalized. It has held power longer than any other currently ruling party in the world and has reached widely into society. Yet this institutionalization has been conducive to a distinctly undemocratic stability. It has helped to encapsulate groups and to preclude alternative institutionalized parties.

From independence until the revolution, parties were mostly political clubs. The elections in which they participated "were not a mechanism of popular voting but a legitimization of military force."[40] Of seventy-one governments (1823–1911), only seventeen were elected by constitutional norms. Even these involved indirect elections, open balloting, and so forth. The elected president almost always came from the incumbent party or group. Nonetheless, all new governments felt obliged to seek popular-constitutional legitimization through elections. Again, democratic ideology is juxtaposed with undemocratic reality.

Even after the revolution, parties continued to be weak, transitory, dependent on a single leader, without mass bases, and multitudinous. Then the new party, continually juggled and deepened from 1929 to 1946 (when it became the PRI), replaced anarchic conflict and made elites play by institutionalized and legal rules. From 1929 to 1933, the number of parties dropped from fifty-one to four.[41] Mass organizations were incorporated. Civilian rulers built a strong institution that could organize and distribute resources, thus helping to subordinate the military. Such developments are often associated with transitions to democracy, but in Mexico competition among elites did not encompass open public contestation, and mass incorporation was corporatist.

Not surprisingly, then, the PRI has not concentrated on the functions expected of democratic parties. Its main mission has been neither to aggregate nor to articulate demands. It has not truly competed for power. Although it has always been "in power," the PRI has not had a major role in policymaking. Instead, it has concentrated on other party functions, directed to the service of the government of which it is really a part (although party and government personnel are formally distinct). These functions include mobilizing support for the regime, suppressing dissent, gathering and manipulating information, distributing welfare and patronage, engaging in political socialization and recruitment, handling particularistic grievances, and providing an ideological rationale for government action. Unlike what one expects of democratic party systems, the PRI's hegemonic rule has sustained socioeconomic inequalities, but the PRI wins its largest vote from the least privileged groups.

In 1988, it appeared that the PRI had stumbled into critical difficulties. Again we see that challenges to political stability suggest increased hopes for democratization. This is a source of both great strength and great weakness for the PRI. On the one hand, fear that alternation in the national government would mean a loss of stability is probably one of the key factors behind the PRI's victory in possibly the cleanest and certainly the most scrutinized election in Mexican history—the 1994 presidential election—despite its candidate's manifest inability to arouse popular enthusiasm. On the other hand, so integral is the PRI to the regime that all of the regime difficulties already cited (e.g., the beleaguered presidency and the need for decentralization) are PRI difficulties as well. In fact, the PRI is crucial to the overall crisis of the "political class" that has so adeptly managed key aspects of Mexico's postrevolutionary affairs.[42] For some time, the party's ability to legitimize the regime had declined. High abstention rates (roughly 50 percent in 1979, 1985, and 1988) went together with a downward trend in the PRI's share of the votes cast (see Table 4.1). The PRI's decline accelerated suddenly in 1988 when even official tallies gave the party only a slim majority in the presidential vote and in congressional seats. For the first time, the PRI faced a strong challenge from the left in the shape of presidential candidate Cuauhtémoc Cárdenas, who won an unprecedented 31 percent of the official presidential vote. Indeed, many continue to believe Cárdenas won the 1988 election but was denied election by massive electoral fraud. His

Table 4.1   Electoral Support and Legislative Representation, 1946–1994

Year	% of Congressional Vote[a]				% of Congressional Seats			
	PRI	PAN	Left[b]	Other	PRI	PAN	Left	Other
1946	73.5	2.2	.5	23.8	94.3	2.7	0	0
1949	93.9	5.6	—	.5	96.6	2.7	—	0
1952	74.3	8.7	15.9[c]	1.5	93.8	3.1	1.2	1.9
1955	89.9	9.2	—	1.0	94.4	3.7	—	1.9
1958	88.2	10.2	—	1.5	94.4	3.7	—	1.2
1961	90.2	7.6	—	1.7	96.6	2.8	—	.5
1964	86.2	11.5	—	2.1	83.3	9.5	—	7.1
1967	83.3	12.3	—	4.2	84.0	9.0	—	7.1
1970	83.2	14.2	—	2.4	83.6	0.4	—	7.0
1973	77.4	16.3	—	6.0	81.8	10.8	—	7.4
1976	84.8	9.0	—	5.8	82.3	8.4	—	9.3
1979	74.0	11.5	5.3[d]	9.1	74.0	10.8	4.5	10.8
1982	69.3	17.5	5.9[e]	7.3	74.5	12.8	4.3	8.3
1985	68.1	16.3	6.3[f]	9.2	72.3	10.3	6.0	11.5
1988	51.1	18.0	29.6[g]	1.3	52.0	20.2	27.8[h]	—
1991	61.5	17.7	8.9[i]	12.0	64.0	17.8	8.2	10.0
1994	50.3	25.8	16.7[j]	7.2[k]	60.0	23.8	14.2	2.0

Sources: Contienda electoral en las elecciones de diputados federales (Mexico, D.F.: Instituto Federal Electoral, 1991); Silvia Gomez Tagle, *Las estadísticas electorales de la reforma política* (Mexico, D.F.: Colegio de Mexico, 1990); *Relación de los 3000 Distritos Federales Electorales* (Mexico, D.F.: Instituto Federal Electoral, 1991); *Elecciones federales 1994: resultados definitivos* (Mexico City: Instituto Federal Electoral, 1994); Mireya Cuellar and Nestor Martinez, "Profundas Inequidades," *La Jornada* 23 (October 1994): p. 1.

a. For comparability, congressional vote is used for all years, including presidential election years (1946, 1952, 1958, etc.). Presidential vote tends to correspond closely to congressional vote (although prior to 1988 most "other" parties co-nominated the PRI's candidate), except for 1976, when the PAN did not run a candidate. Figures reflect percentage of *valid* vote and may not sum to 100% because of rounding and the omission of votes for nonregistered candidates from the "other" category.

b. "Left" refers to the independent left, not the left or center-left parties that functioned as parties allied for all practical purposes to the PRI. Dash marks indicate no legal independent left parties in that year.

c. This represents the congressional vote associated with the candidacy of Miguel Henriquez Guzmán, an independent leftist candidate closely linked to Lázaro Cárdenas.

d. Vote of the Mexican Communist Party (PCM).

e. Vote of the Unified Mexican Socialist Party (PSUM, formed mostly by the ex-PCM) plus the vote of the trotskyist Revolutionary Workers Party (1.3%) and the tiny Social Democratic Party (.2%).

f. Vote of the PSUM (3.4%), Revolutionary Workers Party (1.3%), and Mexican Workers Party (1.6%).

g. Vote of the Cárdenas coalition plus the Revolutionary Workers Party (.6%).

h. Seats won by the Cárdenas coalition. However, all coalition members returned quickly to alliance with the PRI except the Mexican Socialist Party (4.5% of seats), which formed the PRD bench and gave its registry to the new party.

i. Vote of PRD (8.3%) plus the Revolutionary Workers Party (.6%).

j. Vote of the PRD. Although leftist, the new Workers' Party (*Partido del Trabajo*) has strong ties to the government and gets large amounts of funding from unclear sources. Its independence is questionable.

k. This figure represents the total vote of six separate parties, only one of which (the Workers' Party) received enough to keep its legal registry and qualify for proportional representation seats.

performance shattered the PRI's mantle of invincibility. Even as he claimed victory, Carlos Salinas conceded the end of the era of nearly one-party rule.

The PRI's crisis is a culmination of both relatively sudden problems, such as the imposition of austerity, and long-run problems. It has been difficult for a party built to handle a basically rural and uneducated society to adapt its structure and practices to modern Mexico. It has been even harder for a party established without true democratic functions—indeed, to avoid the risks of intra-elite competition—to compete openly for citizen support.[43] Efforts to reform the PRI naturally produce further tensions within the party and so far have shown few results.

In truth, most PRI reforms have aimed less at democratizing *per se* than at reviving legitimacy and combating opposition parties.[44] Probably the most ambitious pre-1980s reform attempt, undertaken by PRI president Carlos Madrazo in the mid-1960s, envisioned primaries and some separation of party from government. It was beaten back by vested PRI interests. In 1986, a new "Democratic Current" was almost immediately denounced by party and labor leaders as disloyal, selfish, and unnecessary. The Current at first carefully emphasized its party credentials and limited its demands to internal party reform. But from the outset it challenged key aspects of presidential power, calling for a broad dialogue within the party over economic and social policy and suggesting that aspirants to the PRI presidential candidacy campaign openly before the public instead of waiting for the president to designate a successor, as in the past.

Nevertheless, de la Madrid followed traditional practice by handpicking the PRI's next candidate for president, Carlos Salinas—of all possible candidates the one whose policy preferences most infuriated the Current. Having failed to change either the PRI's practices or its policies, the Current (including Cárdenas) left the PRI to challenge it from outside. Genuine reform in the PRI may yet occur, and candidate Zedillo pledged to separate the PRI from the government, but reason for skepticism exists. Despite their mutual antipathy, the technocrats that run the government and the politicians that dominate many PRI organizations are bound together. Technocratic annoyance with the inefficiency and corruption of PRI bureaucrats does not change their need for political support and cooperation with PRI politicians to pass their programs in Congress, whereas PRI dissatisfaction with the rewards distributed by technocrats does not diminish their need for rewards and state authority to hang on to their positions. PRI reformers have a notoriously unsuccessful record.

If democracy has been weak within the PRI, it has also been weak in the party system overall. Opposition parties have existed, and some have expressed considerable dissent. But until recently, they have served mostly to legitimize PRI-regime rule by providing a facade of competition. In fact, most opposition parties were largely government-sponsored and cooperated with the PRI.

On the left, independent parties have enjoyed legal registry only since the electoral reform of 1977. However, whether clandestine or participating in elections, left parties have been handicapped by government hostility and by the lack of a trade union or a peasant base (already captured by PRI corporatism) and have generally had little mass appeal.[45] The left also suffered from intense internal conflicts that led to the formation of countless parties, quasi-parties, and currents, although many of these groups were finally unified by 1987 in the Mexican Socialist Party. In 1988, Cuauhtémoc Cárdenas led dissident leftist PRI members into a powerful coalition with this Socialist Party and other left-center parties (although his campaign was perhaps as much "populist" as "leftist"). After the election, the *cardenistas* merged with the Socialist Party to form the PRD. This party failed to consolidate Cárdenas's original electoral base, falling to 8.2 percent of the valid vote in the 1991 federal congressional election. Even the return of Cárdenas as a presidential candidate in 1994 could not lift the party to more than 17 percent of the official vote. Although unrelenting government persecution explains many of the PRD's problems, the party also suffered from debilitating internal divisions, weak local organization, and a tendency toward personalism. Its program remained vague and often contradictory, offering few specific alternatives. In addition, as the economy improved under Salinas, levels of protest began to decline.[46]

Nevertheless, the PRD (and the ghost of its 1988 threat) gave the left a higher political profile in terms of both competition and debate. The percentage of congressional districts in which left parties came in first or second increased between 1985 and 1994 from 5.3 percent (and no first-place finishes) to 30.7 percent of all districts.[47] In several states the left developed a capacity to beat the PRI on at least a municipal level. Moreover, with the ideological convergence of the Salinas PRI and the right, the PRD became virtually the only sustained critic within the party system of the government's economic and social policies. Although the left's confrontational stance and its reluctance to negotiate with the government frustrated some opportunities to advance electoral reform, it served a purpose as a voice of popular inconformity (although not the only one). In this sense, the PRD contributed to the development of multiparty democracy.

Yet as Table 4.1 shows, the main beneficiary of electoral opening since 1988 has not been the left but the better organized, more pragmatic, and more consolidated right—concentrated essentially in one party: PAN, formed in 1939. For most of its history PAN functioned as an institutionalized opposition, not pressing seriously to defeat the PRI. But beginning in the 1980s, a growing portion of the party favored all-out competition in a democratic setting and resorted increasingly to civil disobedience and mobilization to protest electoral fraud. Unlike the PRI, PAN selects candidates rather openly. In recent years, however, ideological and programmatic distinctions between the PRI and the PAN have narrowed, especially in the area of economic reform. The PRI moved steadily to the right during the 1980s.

At the same time, the PAN's attractiveness to sectors of business alienated by the 1982 bank nationalization led to a marked business orientation and some movement away from its roots in Catholic social thought. The PAN and the PRI increasingly preferred cooperation with one another to conflict that might aid the advance of the left. This has been particularly important because since 1988 the PRI has lacked a sufficient majority to pass constitutional amendments unaided. The PAN even supported passage of a 1990 electoral reform that many observers (and some PAN legislators) felt would hurt the PAN. Its more cordial relationship with the PRI led to serious problems within the party, including several public resignations by party leaders and accusations of selling out to the government. Nevertheless, accommodation paid off handsomely. The government accepted electoral wins by the PAN—including governorships of several important states, such as Baja California and Jalisco—when less than six years earlier it had denied PAN *municipal* victories (although in the case of Jalisco, the government may have been relieved that the vote was not even close, so that it could acknowledge the PAN victory without risking a harsh reaction from the local PRI). The PAN also took the opportunity to portray itself as the only "safe" opposition (compared with the "unsafe" left opposition), which contributed to its record electoral performance in 1994.

The PAN does not attract a major portion of labor or the peasantry, as Christian Democratic parties have in nations such as Chile and Venezuela. Its strongest bases have historically been limited to certain regions, particularly the north and urban areas, and to privileged groups. Much of its vote has always been a protest vote. In 1994, the PAN recaptured much of the middle-class protest vote that had gone to Cárdenas in 1988.

The PAN also benefited from recent electoral reforms that made electoral fraud more difficult and improved the competitive position of opposition parties. Prior to 1977, electoral reform had been very limited. Universal suffrage was achieved through reforms in 1954 and 1973, but electoral reforms from 1929 to 1954 greatly inhibited opposition-party formation and representation. The 1977 reforms reversed this trend. They allowed parties to register more easily and granted public funds and free media time. Most dramatically, however, the reforms greatly expanded opposition representation in the Chamber of Deputies. Although 300 seats were still allotted among the plurality winners in each district, first 100 (1977) and then 200 seats (1986) were reserved for distribution according to proportional representation (PR). The 1977 law reserved the seats for minority parties; later versions did not but restricted the majority party to a total of 315 seats (as of 1994; 350 in the 1988 election) and to 300 seats if the majority party receives less than 60 percent of the national vote. The later electoral reforms also provided that each party's share of the PR seats would be proportional to its share of the national vote (but only those parties winning at least 1.5 percent of the vote are eligible for PR seats).

The 1994 package of electoral reforms contains some of the most far-reaching changes yet, replacing party representatives on the board of the Federal Electoral Institute with "citizen councilors" elected by at least two-thirds of the Congress and making it illegal for parties to transport groups to the polls on election day, a long-standing PRI practice. For the first time, the PRI did not have an automatic majority on the governing electoral board, although it retained effective control.[48] Even critics on both the left and the right have generally acknowledged that the electoral system now provides more freedom, information, exposure, and alternative positions.

Why the opening? Mostly, reforms responded to declining legitimacy, opposition threats to boycott the electoral system, or non-electoral threats to the regime. They were intended to stabilize the regime and to make sure dissent would be institutionalized and channeled, not spontaneous.[49] The 1994 reforms, referred to privately as the "Chiapas package," were partly a response to the new guerrilla movement that surfaced in Chiapas on New Year's Day 1994. Among its demands, the "Zapatista Army" included democratization of the regime and clean elections. Through electoral liberalization, the regime has tried to divert dissent into institutional channels, control cries for democratization, divide opposition forces, portray itself as the safe center, and increasingly draw upon electoral legitimacy to compensate for declining revolutionary legitimacy and performance failures. Nevertheless, the regime did not intend full-blown democratization. Thus, at various times "reform" provisions have aimed at ensuring the PRI a legislative majority, even were it to gain fewer than half the votes, and at guaranteeing continued PRI dominance on the electoral body that supervises elections (now reduced to de facto veto power over the selection of those who serve). PRI leaders have blocked measures imposing reform on states.[50] Key factors such as access to media for campaign advertising and federal financial support remain proportional, by law, to each party's previous electoral strength. Perhaps most important, the PRI still has all the backing of the state.

Yet increasing reliance on electoral legitimacy implies certain vulnerabilities. First, by stressing its ability to win elections, the regime has raised the cost of blatant electoral fraud, as have improved opposition organization and heightened international attention (especially in the wake of NAFTA). If opposition parties threaten to defeat the PRI, the regime must weigh more carefully than ever the costs of using its weapon of last resort. Second, for many in Mexico the only truly credible election is an election the PRI loses. This results in part from long experience with PRI "electoral wizards," in part from disbelief that a party regarded with such widespread cynicism could actually win, and in part from self-serving opposition attempts (especially by the PRD) to question the legitimacy of elections it loses. Protests of fraud now mention not only traditional methods such as ballot stuffing but also more sophisticated manipulation of voters and above all—and with justification—"structural fraud," referring to the PRI's massive advantages in resources, organization, media attention, and state connections. So a potential contradiction emerges: The purpose of reform is to legitimate PRI victories by making electoral competition credible, but convincing electoral competition increases the possibility of losing—of democratic alternation in power. So far, the PRI has not credibly faced up to this possibility, preferring to shoulder the tremendous economic costs of winning elections "cleanly," including lavish campaigns, two new national voter registries in five years, an extensive mobilization program, and manipulation of government social programs for electoral purposes, as well as continued traditional fraud on a more limited, targeted, and local scale.

The regime appears inclined at times to bolster the opposition's showing in elections, but not to the point that those oppositions could win—especially at the national level and on the left. The main function of Mexican elections is still not to select parties, leaders, and policies through open choice but instead to ratify the regime's right to rule and to offer the hope of mobility and regularized renewal necessary to maintain that rule.

Increasingly, however, elections have become a purgatory for the PRI—an arduous and exhausting process in which victories are met with protests and only losses win praise. Whereas protest was once confined to PAN states, it now affects even states like Chiapas and Oaxaca, where the PRI won 80 to 90 percent of the official vote as recently as 1988. Hunger strikes, roadblocks, demonstrations, boycotts, occupation of government buildings, and repeated denunciations have become common tactics. The government is increasingly forced to respond to popular concerns in order to maintain its advantages—evidence of democratic influence at work, even in the absence of party alternation. Pressure for free and honest elections is stronger than ever. In no other way can one explain the government's willingness to spend so lavishly to win the 1994 presidential election credibly. The Federal Electoral Institute estimated spending about $730 million on the 1994 electoral registry alone, "equivalent to having built 48,000 new classrooms."[51] In sum, prospects for clean elections are good, although still uncertain, but prospects for elections with equal conditions for competition appear a long way off.

Performance and Support

Until the 1970s at least, Mexico's strong civilian rule brought widely envied economic success and societal support. Like many nations in Latin America, Mexico relied heavily on import substitution. Unlike others, Mexico achieved average annual economic growth of over 6 percent from 1940 to 1970 and held its inflation low (under 5 percent annually) in the latter half of the period. Given the repeated economic crises of recent times, these earlier sustained achievements are especially worth remembering.

Economic growth promoted enormous social change. Only about one-fourth of the labor force remains in agriculture. A large middle class has developed, although it is still dwarfed by the lower class. Mexico has pulled itself to an average position among the larger, relatively developed Latin American nations with its 69.7-year life expectancy at birth, its infant mortality rate of 56 per 1,000 live births, its 87-percent adult literacy, and its dramatic improvements in caloric intake, access to primary schools, and energy consumption.[52] The regime has also used economic growth to promote selective social modernization. Even amid socioeconomic crisis in 1986, the president could point out that 86 million school textbooks were distributed free that year, that one in three Mexicans was in school, and that between 1970 and 1986, the average number of years of schooling for the over-fifteen population had doubled (from three to six).[53]

Of course, even official national figures show not just progress but also underdevelopment. Moreover, these figures obscure regional and class inequality, both tragically high in Mexico. Such outcomes have been consistent with Mexico's striking internal contrasts in the distribution of power and freedom. In fact, government policies have contributed to inequalities. Promotion of capital-intensive industrialization has brought severe problems for rural Mexico and for employment of the less privileged. Hyperurbanization often means urban dwellers also suffer from a lack of piped water and sewage systems and from increasing water, soil, and air pollution. Government social expenditures and services have been very unequally directed, in ways that reward some potentially dangerous groups while repressing and marginalizing others. Social services for unionized workers are a good example. Consistent with Mexico's elite pluralism, a wide network of private organizations, including schools, universities, and hospitals, is available for the privileged.[54] Consequently, economic successes under civilian rule have been compatible with what a World Bank study called one of the world's worst profiles of income distribution.[55] As Table 4.2 shows, the profile did not improve even during decades of growth and selective mobility.

Nevertheless, careful manipulation of the fruits of economic success has long been associated with political strength and high support levels. That manipulation helped sustain a myth of continual progress, which provided legitimacy. In fact, Mexicans have taken pride in their political system and credited it for many of the social and personal material successes they have seen, despite cynicism about politicians and low evaluations of the daily performance of government. Even much of the left has granted legitimacy for the regime's progressive record in some socioeconomic and particularly nationalist matters.[56]

Thus far, hypotheses linking economic growth to the development of democratic government have not been supported in Mexico. Nor does Mexico fit the notion that dependent industrialized development leads at a certain point to instability followed by military rule. Instead, Mexican

Table 4.2   Income Distribution in Mexico, 1950–1992

Income group (deciles)	Percentage of income earned[a]				
	1950	1963	1977	1984[b]	1992
1–2 (lowest 20 percent)	4.7	3.5	3.3	4.8	4.3
3–5	12.7	11.5	13.4	16.0	14.1
6–8	23.7	25.4	28.2	29.7	27.4
9–10 (highest 20 percent)	58.9	59.6	55.1	44.5	54.2

Sources: Daniel C. Levy and Gabriel Székely, *Mexico: Paradoxes of Stability and Change,* 2nd ed. (Boulder, CO: Westview Press, 1987), based on data from ECLA for 1950 and 1963, and Mexico's Secretaría de Programación y Presupuesto for 1977. Figures for 1984 calculated by Diana Alarcón González, based on government figures, in *Changes in the Distribution of Income in Mexico and Trade Liberalization* (Tijuana: El Colegio de la Frontera Norte, 1994). 1992 data from *Encuesta nacional de ingresos y gastos de los hogares* (Mexico, D.F.: Instituto Nacional de Estadística, Geografía, e Informática, 1992), p. 39.

a. Estimates may vary slightly due to calculations by different sources. Similar estimates for 1963 and 1977 appear in Enrique Hernández-Laos and Jorge Córdoba, *La distribución del ingreso en Mexico.* (México, D.F.: Centro de Investigación para la Integración Social, 1982). Slightly less favorable data are reported in Werner Baer, "Growth with Inequality," *Latin American Research Review* 21, no. 2 (1986), p. 198.

b. Alarcón's data may reflect improvement between 1977 and the onset of the economic crisis in 1981/82. However, her estimates for 1989 come quite close to government estimates for 1992, and confirm a deterioration during the crisis of the 1980s.

economic and social modernization has long reinforced stable, undemocratic civilian rule. It is probably the economic reversal of the 1980s that most clearly brought pressures on the regime and contributed to increased electoral opposition. Many see the main roots of the crisis in policies designed for political, not economic, efficiency that built support from business, the middle class, organized labor, and even less privileged groups: protracted import substitution, a variety of credits and subsidies (e.g., for energy, universities, public transportation), low taxes, and bloated public employment. Unable to meet its expenditures, the government borrowed heavily; this, combined with a plunge in revenue as world oil prices fell sharply, caused Mexico to face a foreign debt of over $100 billion, blocked and even negative growth, inflation rates of roughly 100 percent, socially devastating declines in employment and real wages, and rising political protest. In contrast, the sudden crisis of the next decade was widely attributed less to deep-seated structural problems (many of which were addressed in a decade of major economic reforms) and more to specific policy mistakes, especially in fiscal management.

Significant government corruption also tarnished the regime's legitimacy. Perhaps a more modernized society has decreasing tolerance for corruption. In any case, the struggle against corruption has become part of the struggle for democratic accountability. Thus, de la Madrid made what appeared to be the most serious in a line of presidential commitments to curb corruption. Some measures were taken, such as requiring financial statements from top government appointees and punishing a few ex-officials, but by virtually all accounts the cleanup campaign was disappointing. Salinas also began his term with promises to clean up corruption, even daring to arrest the powerful and notoriously corrupt head of the petroleum workers union. However, these efforts appeared less calculated to change political practices than to move against symbols, with whom, in addition, Salinas had personal quarrels.

President Zedillo's arrest of the brother of former president Salinas as intellectual author of the murder of a top PRI official in September 1994 was the most dramatic action to date, breaking a long tradition of immunity for presidents and their families. Yet it remained unclear at this writing whether the arrest would—as announced—usher in a period of broad accountability of public officials or stay an isolated action.

As with the PRI's undemocratic internal structure, corruption has figured in the regime's performance and legitimacy. We have already seen that opportunities for corruption helped bring the military under civilian control. Additionally, corruption has provided some flexibility in an often unresponsive bureaucracy. It has provided an incentive for major and minor actors to seek rewards within the system and to rely on the peaceful turnover of personnel. It has provided glue for many implicit political pacts among elites and has been integral to patron-client and state-society relationships.

But corruption on the Mexican scale is not compatible with significant democratization and the need for accountability. Corruption, therefore, joins the list of factors that may have promoted stability in nondemocratic Mexico yet could undermine stability now.

Theoretical Analysis

We have tried to show how several factors commonly associated with democratic stability have in Mexico long contributed to stable civilian rule that is not democratic. We now turn more fully and explicitly to an examination of this study's hypotheses about democracy. A major problem in so doing is that the hypotheses deal with factors that contribute to democracy, whereas Mexico has not been a democracy. We can repeatedly identify where Mexico has lacked a characteristic associated with democracy, but such counterfactual analysis offers only indirect evidence to sustain the hypothesis.

Political Culture and Legitimacy

Evidence on the impact of political culture on democracy in Mexico remains inconclusive. On the one hand, works on Mexico's "national character" have

often depicted hierarchical, authoritarian, submissive, and other undemocratic inclinations. They suggest that such character traits help promote
Mexico's authoritarian politics; political culture both explains and legit-
imizes the political system. Certainly, Mexicans have been remarkably
accepting of their political system. Whether because of a national trait of
stoicism, or the fear of disorder, or belief in the regime's positive orientations, Mexicans have at a minimum not rebelled even when their aspirations
have been long frustrated, and many have maintained pride in their system.[57] On the other hand, most social scientists have been either skeptical or
hostile to such interpretations. Political culture may reinforce the system or
even result from political learning in an authoritarian institutional framework, but it is "striking how much of Mexican politics can be comprehend-
ed by a model of the rational political actor."[58] Still others argue that the
political culture is basically at odds with the political structure. They find
that Mexicans support participation and dissent and oppose censorship.[59]

If evidence on deep values remains inconclusive, evidence on behavior
is not. Mexico's regime has not been precariously superimposed on a society filled with democratic practices. The society never was so constituted,
and the revolution brought new and strong but mostly undemocratic institutions. State corporatism goes hand in hand with hierarchical, authoritarian
rule inside mass institutions such as unions. And it goes hand in hand with
limited mass participation, encapsulated and restricted to official channels;
patrimonial networks; and petitions rather than aggregated demands.
Allowing for increased grassroots participation, the rule has been to hope
that government acts. Efficacy increases with socioeconomic status, however.[60] Participation by elites is much freer and more influential, but elite institutions (media, intellectual publications, businesses, private schools, and
universities) often operate undemocratically. Pluralism exceeds democracy.

Yet elites do display a behavioral norm hypothesized (in this book and
elsewhere) to be powerfully associated with democracy. This is the disposition to compromise. Postrevolutionary politics provide ample evidence of
flexibility, bargaining, moderation, restraint, and pacts that avoid "fights to
the finish."[61] In Mexico, acceptance of such norms has contributed to regime
consolidation and stability without democracy. First, although elite pacts in
democracies often limit mass participation, Mexico's corporatist mass inclusion is distinctly antidemocratic. Second, the restraint in the elite pacts has
covered the exclusion of open, organized competition for rulership.

However, this long-standing elite propensity to compromise may now
face grave challenges even from within the PRI. The 1994 assassination of
PRI presidential candidate Luis Donaldo Colosio in Tijuana marked the first
murder of a president or heir apparent since the foundation of the governing
party after the murder of president-elect Obregón. The arrest of a "second
gunman" tied to the local PRI confirmed public suspicions of PRI involvement. Investigation of the later murder of a top PRI functionary not only
resulted in the arrest of the president's brother and accusations against

Salinas himself, but also raised concerns about the influence of narco-politics on the Mexican political elite. As norms of complicity break down, norms of compromise may face more severe tests.

For decades, the Mexican case has presented interesting clues about the relationship between political culture and democracy but not information that strongly confirms or disconfirms major project hypotheses.

Historical Sequences

Mexico scores low on the historical dimensions associated with democracy. Mexico lacks sustained, successful democratic precedents or even many experiments with democratic government. If the present regime has precedents, they are chiefly authoritarian. Where it democratizes, it innovates.

Moreover, Mexico has not followed Robert Dahl's favored route of early liberal contestation followed by mass incorporation.[62] Rather, Calles, Cárdenas, and others adeptly incorporated mass organizations into a corporatist system. If elite pacts in nations such as Venezuela limited the masses' ability to obtain socioeconomic benefits, Mexico's pacts excluded them from democracy. Mexico's pacts were aimed at controlling masses mobilized by the revolution and established viable, ingenious alternatives to open elite contestation for power. However, if one were to highlight the persistent marginality of unorganized Mexico and the rise of new groups, or if one were to reserve "inclusiveness" for independent mass participation, Mexico might rank low historically on that dimension. In that case, recent political reforms expanding contestation, coupled with longer-standing and expanding personal freedoms, might give some sense of liberalization preceding inclusiveness.

Class, Ethnic, and Religious Cleavages

Key hypotheses on class structure and cumulative cleavages do not suggest favorable conditions for democracy in Mexico. The distribution of wealth is terribly unequal. Despite massive land reform, large agribusiness and an impoverished, massive peasantry divide the land very unequally in terms of both the size and desirability of plots. Mexican agriculture is not characterized by middle-class farming. Moreover, many cleavages are cumulative. A profile of the most disadvantaged commonly depicts the low-income, Indian peasant living in the rural south.

Indians form the largest ethnic minority, perhaps 10 percent of the population (depending on definition), although ethnic diversity is determined largely by the "European-Indian" mixes among Mestizos. The revolution brought some respect for Indian identity, and pockets of self-governance exist (with some direct democratic selection of leaders and policies). Mostly, however, the Indian population continues to be either marginalized or integrated into a servile underclass, despite some mobility for individuals. In turn, the "rule of law" and the state are often seen as oppressive alien forces by Indian communities. Of interest are increasing signs of ethnically based political demands.[63] Overall, however, Indian distinctiveness hardly translates into pluralist politics.

The regime has been effective in defusing the destabilizing potential of great societal diversity and cumulative cleavages. One way has been to grant autonomy to groups and institutions (e.g., religious) that avoid mainstream politics. This fits Juan Linz's now classic notion of authoritarian regimes.[64]

Second, the regime handles much of its politics in ways that cut across class cleavages—not on basic distributive policies but on symbolic and organizational ones. Symbolically, it has successfully used nationalism even if the concept means somewhat different things to different groups. Organizationally, it has structured itself on "vertical" patron-client relationships. This reinforces hierarchy and other undemocratic societal norms. The "formation of horizontal alliances based on common class interests is impeded," and the relationships serve "to maintain the separation between ideology and its social base."[65]

Third, as noted earlier, the regime has been sophisticated in managing privileged groups differently from other groups. Allowing for important flexibility and other qualifications, state relationships with mass organizations are corporatist, whereas state relationships with elite groups are much more pluralist. But autonomous elite organizations have not usually been run democratically, nor, perhaps more to the point, have they pressured for democratization. Instead, they have normally accepted a stable nondemocracy that has granted them considerable material reward and a substantial if restricted degree of freedom.[66]

State Structure and Strength

Although state strength is a necessary condition for democratic stability, it is not sufficient. Lack of strength may doom a democratic experiment, but in Mexico state strength has meant the stability of an undemocratic system.

Building authority was a historic accomplishment of the postrevolutionary regime. The regime centralized power, maintained order, and preserved civilian rule. It created an adept political class while controlling mass groups and excluding organized challenges to its rule. Nonetheless, the state has not been the nearly omnipotent political force much of the literature on Mexican authoritarianism has depicted. Its power has been limited by business and the middle class, and it has had to work out deals and make compromises with organized labor and even with less privileged groups. We have seen, for example, that the state lacked the capacity to tax sufficiently to pay for the political bargains it struck.

Moreover, the neoliberal shrinking of the state may further weaken it.

One element in the regime's political strength was its early and sustained control over key parts of the economy. Unaccompanied by great bureaucratic professional autonomy from partisan politics, such statism is hypothesized to diminish prospects for democracy. However, it is simply impossible to know whether a causal relationship holds in Mexico, although the idea is in vogue in some business circles.

What is clearer is that statism promoted civilian stability. It provided populist legitimacy; the nationalization of oil (1938) is a notable example. And it gave the regime tremendous political leverage. Even though the Mexican economy has for the most part been privately owned, the state has owned such sectors as oil, mining, electricity, railroads, and, since 1982, banks. It has been heavily involved in regulation, subsidies, public investments, public credits, and so forth. It has established institutions such as the Central Bank (1925), the National Development Bank (1934), and a tremendous network of parastatal agencies. Measures such as the public expenditures share of GDP show an expanded state role as recently as 1982 (from 22 percent in 1970 to 44 percent in 1983).[67] But de la Madrid undertook a reversal, and Salinas accelerated the pace. Citing the counterproductive political effects of statism but concerned chiefly about economic crisis and inefficiencies, these presidents repeatedly cut state expenditures, employment, and subsidies. They sold off many state enterprises and brought Mexico first into the GATT and then into NAFTA. The state remains powerful but is no longer as important a gatekeeper to economic wealth. It is possible that these reforms will create new counterweights to state authority. It is also possible that reform will only spread power differently among elites, with government and business more equal partners, but not open up participation opportunities to ordinary citizens along basically democratic lines.

Political Structure and Leadership

The structural reality of Mexico's undemocratic civilian rule has been overwhelmingly centralized. Mexico's has been a presidential system with only limited roles for the judiciary, the legislature, and state and local government. More liberalism, although still restricted, has been evident regarding the rule of law, freedom of the media, and other liberties. But the party system was long characterized by PRI hegemony and integration with the regime. The PRI has generally been pragmatic. It has been at least somewhat inclusionary and has built a multiclass base. It has kept the vote for extremist parties very small. Yet as with other successes of the centralized party regime, these have served civilian stability without democracy. Earlier interpretations of a political structure purposefully or ineluctably evolving into liberal forms have proved naive. On the other hand, the recent ineffectiveness of centralized forms has raised interesting speculations about future changes in Mexico's political structure.

Like the political structure, political leadership in postrevolutionary Mexico has proven unusually effective, and this effectiveness has been crucial to sustaining civilian rule without democracy. In fact, leadership and structure have been intertwined. Leaders have created and respected structures strong enough to condition behavior but flexible enough to allow for change and continual leadership.

Mexico takes second place to no nation in the skill and will of leadership to build a viable civilian system out of a past characterized mostly by weak political rule. We have highlighted the formative leadership acts of Carranza, Obregón, Calles, and Cárdenas in establishing legitimate, inclusive, centralized, civilian rule. Their acts provide powerful evidence for those political scientists who have championed the resurgence of "politics" and "choice" as major variables in studies of development. For example, Gabriel Almond and Robert Mundt write that a rational prediction from coalition theory would have pointed toward a military coup in the 1930s, but Cárdenas pulled off the "most striking" leadership success discussed in their volume featuring choice in a number of nations.[68] But unlike leaders in the Venezuelan case or in contemporary Argentina, Brazil, and other Latin American nations, Mexico's civilian leaders have not generally acted out of a commitment to democracy. On the contrary, some Mexican leaders have been hostile to democracy as a foreign, unworkable model, whereas others have been indifferent, and still others see democracy as an ideal too risky. Yet another view, however, is that realities have changed to where blocking democratization has become too risky.

Political learning has been crucial to Mexico's civilian success, but most leaders have not set competitive democracy as their goal, and the lessons they have learned have been undemocratic ones. Again, unlike Venezuela, with its *trienio,* not to mention Argentina, Brazil, and (at an extreme) Uruguay, Mexico has not had a modern liberal experiment that made headway before failing. Mexico would have to look back to the Reform for even a mixed record with liberal politics; the Madero interlude at the beginning of the revolution represents more recent failure. Most of the nineteenth century and the first two revolutionary decades suggested to elites the impracticality of decentralized systems and the dangers of excessive competition among elites. The revolution also impressed on them the need for elite pacts to forestall devastating actions by the masses.

In essence, the institutionalization of the system institutionalized these attitudes, converting the PRI into a school par excellence for nondemocratic political managers. They became very good at their jobs, forming a political class that could boast many of the traits of successful professions, including comparative autonomy, status, authority, and power, as well as control over training and rites of entry. Since the 1940s (with due qualifications for the deterioration elaborated previously), Mexico's leaders have shaped politics in ways largely associated with establishing, or even the smooth functioning of, democracy. Yet for each aspect, the shaping has been distinctly undemocratic. The party has incorporated and legitimized but has also encapsulated. Sexennial rule has guaranteed mobility, turnover, renewal, and flexibility but not public choice of leaders. Leaders have denounced disloyalty to the system and violence against the system but have regarded some democratic dissent as disloyal and have used violence against peaceful dissenters. They have contained conflicts and managed crises enviably, but their tools have been predominantly undemocratic. Formative leaders shrewdly forged pacts among conflicting elites, and subsequent leaders have continually bargained, compromised, and disciplined themselves and their followers to accept less than optimal outcomes. Such procedures have excluded democratic opponents, limited mass participation, and often worked against mass material interests. Leaders have also subtly varied their approaches (depending on time, place, policy field, and constituency) in ways that show a greater sensitivity to and understanding of the public than most authoritarian regimes have, but such sophistication is not synonymous with democracy. Thus, we see corporatism mixed with pluralism, repression with co-optation and acquiescence, and continuity with flexibility.

Economic Development

Political leadership also played a major role in establishing Mexico's decades of high growth with low inflation, one of the regime's key sources of legitimacy and stability. Why did sustained growth not produce democracy?

One explanation concerns Mexico's failure to attain the kind of sustained growth hypothesized to promote democracy, growth whose fruits are well distributed. Mexico's have been horribly maldistributed. A middle class grew, but with a debatable commitment to democracy (as in comparative politics generally) and substantial dependence on the state. Moreover, the rise of the middle class has not been part of a generalized equalization of wealth or a broad movement involving coalitions with mass groups. In fact, a second possible explanation for the lack of democratization is that the growth argument is by itself irrelevant to democracy or even that growth may serve the interests of reigning undemocratic regimes. In Mexico, growth contributed to the legitimacy and power of such a regime. It allowed it to manipulate, reward, and claim credit. And in the aftermath of 1988, economic recovery and stabilization went along with the PRI's electoral recovery, at least through 1994.

A third explanation, compatible with the first two, distinguishes growth from economic development. In Mexico, sustained growth brought about considerable economic developmental changes in social structure that eventually promoted pressures for broad democratization and liberalization. Growth per se may also provide some opposition forces with resources needed for democratization. In short, there is much to conventional development theses about an association between growth and social change and between both and the chances for democracy.[69] Still, chances are far from certainties. The record shows that decades of growth produced comparatively limited pressures for democracy in Mexico and more limited results. The strongest calls for democratization came when growth was reversed—although they did not go away with renewed growth.

To sum up, economic growth may increase the chances for democracy eventually but for a long time may shore up almost any regime. After all, the fall of Latin American authoritarian regimes, like Latin American democracies, has been tied to economic failure more than success. In Mexico, growth has been integral to the stability of civilian authoritarian rule.

International Factors

As with so many other variables in this comparative study, international factors hypothesized to be conducive to democratic stability have, in Mexico, contributed to stability without democracy. First, Mexico has not been a significant target of external subversion since the regime consolidated power. But such fortune is much more likely to sustain than to create democracy. Second, the major source of diffusion—given realities of geography, continual back-and-forth migration, trade, investment, and cultural and media might—has long been the United States, a democracy. Third, Mexico received extraordinary foreign assistance from the United States and other democracies, although the emphasis is recent. Whereas the second and third realities are postulated to have democratizing influences even on undemocratic systems, Mexican leadership limited the degree of political dependency and influence that accompany economic dependency on the United States.

For example, Mexico followed a progressive foreign policy, largely in order to protect itself from leftist subversion. The only Latin American nation not to break diplomatic relations with Communist Cuba, Mexico was never targeted the way Bolivia, Venezuela, and others were. Comparatively sympathetic to the Sandinistas and to the guerrillas in El Salvador, Mexico again achieved an at least tacit agreement that leftists outside Mexico would not encourage independent leftists inside.[70]

In the past, such progressivism enhanced legitimacy by demonstrating independence from the United States. Given a historical legacy of U.S. military conquest—costing Mexico about half its national territory—and an ongoing contrast of wealth and culture, it is not surprising that Mexicans would feel alienation as well as respect for their neighbor. Something seen as a U.S. model—and liberal democracy as defined in this book fits here—was not simply seen positively. Even defenders of democracy have stressed the need for democracy "Mexican style," although they also recognize that the regime uses the nationalist card to discredit basic democratic concepts associated with the United States. Moreover, U.S. leverage has given priority to stability, not democratization. So despite the fact that it has depended on the United States for almost two-thirds of its imports and exports, roughly 80 percent of its tourism, and roughly 70 percent of its foreign investment, Mexico has maintained a notable degree of independence from U.S. influence.

Two recent developments may alter this traditional situation: the passage of NAFTA, and the peso/debt crisis that began in December 1994. Both developments have implications for Mexican stability, democracy, and U.S. leverage. On the positive side, preferences for electoral forms (partly due to greater deference to foreign sensibilities) may result from the expanded interchange implied by NAFTA, Mexico's increasing dependence on foreign investment, and vulnerability to conditions attached to the U.S. loans Mexico desperately needed to avoid default on its dollar-denominated debt. This is one factor in the government's willingness to accept opposition electoral victories, to permit foreign election observers for the first time in 1994 (before the peso/debt crisis, but after NAFTA), and to spend money on transparent elections. If NAFTA results in economic growth and development, civil society might also acquire resources and incentives to participate politically.

Mexico's financial crisis of the mid-1990s gave civil society actors ample incentives to participate politically. Few societies could view with equanimity the dramatic declines in living standards implied by wage freezes, a devaluation of 40–50 percent in the value of the peso versus the dollar, higher interest rates (50 percent or more) on many outstanding loans, and increases of 30–50 percent in sales taxes, the price of gas, and basic services like transportation and utilities. The shock of yet another emergency austerity program after Mexicans had come to believe in promises of prosperity under NAFTA made disillusionment worse. Yet it is not clear that these incentives will benefit democratization. The crisis may well exacerbate social conflicts in the short term. At least for the immediate future, it appears unlikely that the economy can create sufficient jobs for those displaced by international competition, who lose their jobs due to a wave of bankruptcies spurred by rising interest rates on private business debt, or who enter the the Mexican job market—approximately one million workers each year. Nor will protest necessarily follow democratic means. The guerrilla movement that surfaced in January 1994 deliberately timed its first strike for the day NAFTA went into effect and has condemned the trade agreement's impact, especially on the peasants of southern Chiapas. Violent or highly confrontational protests in turn may undermine both economic recovery and political stability. In such circumstances, even if democratic transition occurs as a political solution to escalating social conflict, it would be difficult to consolidate a stable democracy.

Prospects and Policy Implications

However much cited variables may have contributed to sustaining civilian stability without democracy, Mexican politics is changing. Of course, it has constantly changed, and one of the strengths of the system and its leadership has been their flexibility. The question here is whether contemporary changes will add up to more than adaptation within a nondemocracy. In an important sense, factors that have reinforced stability have blocked democratization. That does not prove, however, that they will always do so. Nor does it suggest that instability is likely to produce democracy. Major change is a necessary but insufficient condition for democratization.

Positive Prospects for Democratization

Numerous political uncertainties represent some hope for democratization. First, the erosion of undemocratic practices widens the possibility for democratic alternatives and strengthens opposition voices. Second, the regime's realization that traditional bases of stability are endangered stimulates liberalizing moves aimed at protecting stability. Third, some of the uncertainties themselves involve a degree of opening. To be sure, the second and third points involve liberalization rather than transformation toward a democracy, as defined here. Nevertheless, just as Mexico has long enjoyed several aspects of democracy, so it may increase the degree of democracy. Moreover, continued liberalization would, in turn, increase the pressures for such practices as free elections among truly competitive alternative parties.

The following recapitulates some of the major recent political changes that involve uncertainties. Regarding state-society relations, the vitality of civil society and some freedoms (e.g., media freedom) have expanded. Middle-class, business, and even grassroots popular groups have organized more autonomously and become more critical of the regime, and a "third sector" of private, nonprofit organizations or nongovernment organizations (NGOs) is developing.[71] Regarding centralized regime power, the presidency has been tarnished, the legislature is increasingly a forum of debate and dissent, and perceptions are widespread that geographical centralization is excessive and that significant decentralization must somehow be achieved. Regarding the party system, the PRI (like the political class overall) has lost support and its aura of invincibility, whereas an independent left has appeared and the independent right has grown substantially. Although many recent elections have been times of delegitimation more than popular affir-

mation, pressures for honest elections continue to be strong, probably unde-
niably so. Electoral reforms have opened the system significantly and made
it easier to monitor fraud. Regarding the regime's performance, the economic crises of the 1980s and 1990s have eroded the regime's legitimacy,
perhaps permanently. Economic opening, even if ultimately successful in
purely economic terms, might well reduce the regime's tools of control.

Political reform, uncertainty, and regime weakness have contributed to
increased calls for democratization. Such calls are not new, of course. For
years, some observers argued that democratization was necessary for
socioeconomic development and, therefore, for political stability. These
observations did not fare well historically, but they appear valid for the long
run. Perhaps circumstances have changed enough in Mexico that more elites
now recognize their validity. At any rate, previous calls for democratization
were not nearly as widespread and sustained as today's. Nor did they enjoy
the degree of free space for development dissenters now have.

Naturally, proponents of democratization are not united. They do not
hold identical views of what democracy means nor of how to pursue it.
Voices on the right argue in terms partly consistent with major hypotheses
of this project: A highly centralized state with massive power concentrated
in an unchecked presidency, which exercises extensive corporate controls
over society and the economy, is incompatible with democracy. By contrast,
most of the left argues that democratization requires a large and revitalized
state assuming a central role in economic policy and social change, although
others emphasize increased autonomy of societal organizations and internal
democratization within labor unions, neighborhood organizations, and other
institutions. Finally, one may question the sincerity of certain democratic
banners on both the right and the left. For some, such banners are but a tool
in the play for power. For others, democracy is a worthy pursuit but princi-
pally a means toward higher priorities. Thus, some business leaders see
democracy largely as a way to weaken government and achieve growth and
profits, just as others want a revitalized state to suppress labor and grant
concessions to business, and some intellectuals see democracy as a means of
mass mobilization to achieve better socioeconomic distribution.

Another way to see hopeful signs for democratization is to focus on the
many ways in which Mexico ranks high on variables associated with democracies. We have argued that Mexico shows that many of the variables are
compatible with a civilian rule that is effective, stable, and undemocratic.
That thesis has allowed, however, that Mexico's high standing on some of
the variables may have built certain pressures for democratization. The
notion of "zones" of lower and higher probabilities for democracy may be
useful in assessing Mexico's future. Economic growth, industrialization,
urbanization, the growth of a middle class, increased education and other
indices of rising expectations among even the poorer classes, the persistence
of at least formal structures of liberal government, growing if still inconclu-

sive evidence of some political cultural affect for democracy—these and other factors put Mexico in a higher zone of probability for democracy than would have been the case even a decade ago.[72]

Recent research on transitions to democracy also suggests some hopes for democratization in Mexico, although Guillermo O'Donnell rightly labels Mexico "a type by itself" (largely because the regime is so institutionalized). First, authoritarian regimes constantly evolve. Second, transitions usually occur through evolution, not sudden overthrows. Third, democracy usually results from stalemate and dissensus, not from a clear plan based on consensus. Fourth, successful transitions usually begin with elite calculations and initiatives, not independent mass mobilization. When the regime initiates liberalization, it runs risks of losing the initiative amid rising expectations and mobilizations, but it can sometimes control the pace of change, experiment, retreat, and so forth. Fifth, democratization often emerges from situations with seemingly low initial probabilities for it.[73] In sum, the initial lack of a clear or massive movement toward democracy in Mexico does not preclude democratization. And the experimental, evolutionary, regime-led notion of transition could allow further societal liberalizations involving press freedom, criticism (with or without viable organized mass alternatives to the regime), and party and electoral reform. Reform within the PRI, expanded representation for oppositions, and opposition victories in localities and even states have now occurred and can intensify without immediate threat to the regime's rule. Nor after the shock of 1988 does it seem naive to speculate on even the transfer of national government to the opposition or at least on opposition appointments to cabinet positions, although as of 1994, both options appeared to have been postponed again. Indeed, President Zedilló startled observers by naming a PANista to the crucial post of attorney general, responsible for investigating rising violence within the political elite and the involvement of drug traffickers.

The Brazilian case is particularly interesting for speculations on Mexico.[74] Brazilian authoritarian rule was comparatively long and economically successful on its own terms, with massive inequalities. Repression was comparatively limited in the years prior to transition. In fact, constitutional forms persisted almost throughout the dictatorial period, and the limited term of the presidency proved significant. Elections took on increasing importance even as the regime manipulated the rules. Transition was stimulated by long-term factors, but an economic downturn critically undermined support for the regime. Nonetheless, unlike some other cases, democratization was not precipitated by mass mobilizations but by elite accommodations. In short, the Brazilian case illustrates how democratization need not be an all-or-nothing proposition. This fact can make the prospect less threatening for the Mexican regime, which realizes that some political changes are necessary. Indeed, some of the massive efforts made to "buy the vote" (especially through Solidarity), although criticized by the opposition for the advantage it gives to the PRI, indicate a certain electoral responsiveness on the part of the regime.[75]

Negative Prospects for Democratization

But some factors continue to point away from full-blown democratization, if decreasingly so. This is especially evident if we refer to democratization as a transition toward democratic government and not just further liberalization. Obviously, transformation is less common than continuity. Beyond that, Mexican authoritarianism has been uniquely long-lasting and institutionalized. Unlike other authoritarian regimes, Mexico's has always justified itself as permanent (albeit evolving) rather than transitory en route to democracy.

Not all factors commonly associated with democracy are found in Mexico. Mexico lacks significant experience with democratic government (although increasingly liberalized elections and more opportunities for opposition governments may provide important experience). Despite its declining legitimacy, the regime has not been discredited in the dramatic way that sometimes leads to democratic transitions (e.g., in Argentina), unless the economic crisis of the 1990s—often laid at the feet of Salinas and his successor—marks a crucial turning point that leads major sectors of the ruling coalition to prefer democracy as an alternative system of rule. Not all criticism of the Mexican regime concerns its lack of democracy. The political-cultural attachment of the masses to democracy is questionable, and elites have given uncertain evidence of such attachment. Opposition parties, indeed organized oppositions in general, have not yet overcome their marginalization. Corporatist controls have precluded both independent mass-based institutions (unions or parties) and sudden mobilization of the unorganized. The state retains a large role in politics and even in the economy. Poverty remains widespread, wealth painfully concentrated.

Prospects for liberalization are also constrained by the risks of transition.[76] Fear is a central notion in the relevant literature; in Mexico, the fear of transition has dominated the perceived need for or benefits of transition. To be sure, even before the 1988 elections some in the regime, as well as critics, believed the system required major changes. President de la Madrid spoke repeatedly of how changes in demographics, urbanization, education, communications, and class structure have created "a new vigor in society," a greatly expanded "civil society" that requires political changes. As in Colombia, there is a widespread perception that conditions that called for structures of restricted, stable civilian rule have been superseded. But also as in Colombia, powerful political incentives are built into the status quo. Even the "soft-liners" within the Mexican regime have usually focused on modernizing measures (including liberalizing ones) that would not produce a liberal democracy. Wayne Cornelius writes that the regime, and indeed the elites in general, regard two-party or multiparty competition and alternation in power as an alien concept.[77] "Democracy" has meant the PRI as the "party of majorities," with opposition voice allowed. Some even argue that a return to economic normalcy is all that is required for politics to return to normal. And many, whatever their ultimate hopes, believe that times of great economic change, and of some inevitable political change, require steadying reliance on established political structures and practices. To many in the PRI, this was the great danger posed by Cárdenas—that he wanted to "abandon the Noah's Ark . . . built to survive the flood of 1910."[78]

Crucially, fear of transition is not limited to the regime or even the elites overall. As Carlos Monsiváis has emphasized, the regime has succeeded in portraying alternatives to it as disasters, as fascism, communism, or anarchy.[79] Anarchy is particularly frightening to many Mexicans, perhaps because of the nation's history, and many have felt they could little afford democracy, which has been associated with some of Mexico's greatest social disorder.[80] Their system has provided them with relative social peace and political tranquility, economic growth, mobility, selective rather than pervasive repression, a degree of political liberty, and substantial national pride.

In sum, the prospects for business as usual in Mexico are more uncertain than at any time since the consolidation of the postrevolutionary political regime. The emergence of yet another economic crisis brought on by fiscal mismanagement has again led some of the regime's erstwhile business allies to consider alternatives publicly. Mexico now faces a substantial likelihood of, on the one hand, democratic transition, and on the other, authoritarian regression. The contrast reflects the fact that the unravelling of Mexico's undemocratic political system implies risks to stability, to which some may respond in a reactionary fashion, while others seize the opportunity to promote democratic compromise. One should not underestimate the resilience of the Mexican political system, or its capacity to handle even the severe challenges to its legitimacy which it now confronts. Much may depend on whether any opposition force (democratic or antidemocratic) can constitute itself as a credible, viable alternative, but in the past, Mexico's version of sustained civilian authoritarianism derived its longevity from its highly effective methods to prevent precisely this development. The difficult task of democratic reformers will be to relax some of these constraints and allow the growth of democratic alternatives, without provoking further concern about political instability, chaos, or reactionary violence by supporters of an authoritarian peace.

U.S. Policy

If democratization merits increasing attention but remains uncertain, what should the United States do? The conventional scholarly wisdom has been: not much. We concur, although that view has come under increasing attack by U.S. public opinion and many political leaders in both parties.

Not all attempts by one nation to encourage democracy in another are wrong, but several demanding criteria ought to be present. They usually are not. First, a viable alternative to the present regime must exist. Second, that alternative should be more democratic than the present regime. Third, a rather limited role by the foreign nation should have a high probability of making a substantial positive impact.

None of these conditions has characterized the case of Mexico and the United States. Much of this chapter has concerned why no viable alternative to the regime has been organized. Leading opposition parties and groups have not yet proved their governing ability or democratic credentials, although the PAN at least can now claim some experience governing at the state level. Even if a viable and democratic alternative existed—and both the right and the left in Mexico say it now does—U.S. efforts might have either an insignificant or a negative impact. For one thing, the Mexico-U.S. relationship is particularly sensitive, given historical, geographical, economic, and cultural realities. Repeated military interventions and threats contributed to turmoil, not democracy, and left a legacy of mistrust about the democratic giant to the north. In the early 1980s, perceptions that Ambassador John Gavin and U.S. Republican Party leaders supported the PAN probably hurt that opposition party, as the PRI identified it with a still arrogant, interfering neighbor.

Beyond the particular sensitivities of Mexico-U.S. relations lie broader obstacles to government efforts to encourage democracy. Recent literature generally concludes that in peacetime, the overall international role in democratization is secondary.[81] Regardless of whether the United States deserves any credit for the wave of Latin American democratization in the 1980s, its clearest successes have come in protesting grievous human-rights abuses; such abuses have been less characteristic of Mexico than of the military regimes. Mexico's economic opening, now crisis, and heavy dependence on U.S. and other international loan guarantees and investment may well increase U.S. leverage, but questions remain about the usefulness and appropriateness of exercising that leverage to push for immediate democratization. This comparative study of developing democracies reminds us of the variability, complexity, and uncertainty of the conditions that promote democracy. Particular cases present their own dynamics, as we have repeatedly seen for Mexico. Even if we could identify clearly the factors associated with democracy, we would be left with a standard research-policy question: How do we move from the present to the desired future? Rallying cries and simplifications by various U.S. voices and administrations to the contrary, we know little about this.

In reality, U.S. pressures have not concerned democratization, or most other aspects of Mexican domestic politics, as much as Mexican economic and foreign policy. Again, we really do not know what economic and foreign policies, against which the United States has brought pressure, have been identifiably associated with the stability of Mexico's civilian rule.

Regarding foreign policy, for example, the United States has often failed to recognize that Mexico has based its foreign policy not on naive leftist notions or anti-Americanism but on sober judgments about its own security from external threats and from domestic delegitimation. If U.S. pressure "worked"—in the sense of influencing Mexican foreign policy—impacts on Mexico's political stability might have been negative.

A more reasonable course for the U.S. government is to support Mexico's political stability. This can be done in the hope that stability will allow for democratization but mostly in the realization that instability is even less likely to produce democratization and that stability is important on other grounds. If these assumptions are accepted, several oft-cited measures to support stability make sense. Some are not particular to Mexico (such as guaranteeing the safety valve of migration and not discouraging tourism and investment). Moreover, the United States should temper the arrogance that views Mexico's troubles as the simple result of poor policy, not to mention political-cultural backwardness. Instead, the United States should respect the successes of the Mexican political system and the enormous difficulties and dilemmas of meeting present challenges. Efforts to use loan assistance to force compliance with harsh economic policies may have productive results, leading to the very destabilization the loans were intended to prevent.

None of this is to deny the U.S. government a right to express critical opinions about Mexican politics, including its most undemocratic aspects, but advocacy and heavy pressure are different matters. Nor is it to ignore the potential contribution of some nongovernmental actors to strengthen civil society organizations within Mexico. Increased foundation aid to academic institutions and scholarship recipients seems legitimate and hopeful, as do the greatly expanded exchanges of information and resources between nongovernmental organizations in the United States and Mexico, improving the capacity of Mexican organizations to make demands and monitor their own elections. As long as U.S. donors and partners bear in mind the importance of allowing Mexican organizations to define their own goals, such contact can encourage democratization by building institutions with autonomy from the government.

To conclude, the possibilities of external influence on democratization are limited, and there is much to lose by pushing arrogantly or overzealously. U.S. self-interest is clearly linked to Mexican stability, markets, labor, resources, and growth. Mexicans also have much to lose: their unparalleled stability, prospects for economic growth, even their enhanced freedoms and liberalization, prized despite their limited reach. Much remains to criticize and work for politically, but perhaps major improvements remain less likely in the short term than major losses.

Should Mexico continue to liberalize and even democratize without shattering its stability, it will have achieved a truly historic and magnificent political feat. Our understanding of the conditions for Third-World democracy would be profoundly affected. For most of the century, however, Mexican reality has shown how many conditions conducive to sustained civilian rule can have neutral or even negative implications for democracy.

Notes

We thank John Bailey and Gabriel Székely, as well as the series editors, for their comments on earlier drafts of this chapter. Bruhn became co-author for this revised and updated version of the original publication by Levy.

1. Mexico's population, over 80 million, ranks second in Latin America and eleventh in the world; its economic size ranks roughly fifteenth among market economies; and its geography makes its fate vital for the United States. We use democracy in the sense of a desired result, democratization as movement in that direction, and liberalization as movement in terms of at least increased freedoms.

2. On breakdown, see Juan Linz and Alfred Stepan, eds., *The Breakdown of Democratic Regimes* (Baltimore, Md.: Johns Hopkins University Press, 1978). On democratization, see Guillermo O'Donnell, Philippe C. Schmitter, and Laurence Whitehead, eds., *Transitions from Authoritarian Rule: Prospects for Democracy* (Baltimore, Md.: Johns Hopkins University Press, 1986).

3. Robert Scott, *Mexican Government in Transition* (Urbana: University of Illinois Press, 1964), pp. 16, 300–301.

4. See, for example, the citations and analysis in Daniel C. Levy and Gabriel Székely, *Mexico: Paradoxes of Stability and Change,* 2d ed. (Boulder, Colo.: Westview Press, 1987), ch. 4.

5. Kenneth F. Johnson and Philip L. Kelly, "Political Democracy in Latin America," *LASA* Forum 16, no. 4 (1986): pp. 19–22. According to the Statistical Abstract of Latin America (SALA), vol. 30 part I (Los Angeles: UCLA, 1993), Mexico ranked number 5 in Latin America (as of 1985); the 1990 Freedom House Ratings, however, gave Mexico only a 4 on political rights and a 4 on civil rights, with 1 the most free score and 7 the least (SALA, p. 276).

6. Octavio Paz, *The Other Mexico: Critique of the Pyramid,* tr. Lysander Kemp (New York: Grove Press, 1972), pp. 102, 111. Some Indian villages enjoyed self-government in the precolonial and colonial eras.

7. See, for example, Juan Felipe Leal, "El estado y el bloque en el poder en México: 1867–1914," *Latin American Perspectives* 11, no. 2 (1975): p. 38.

8. For an analysis of elite composition and circulation (or lack of it) during the *porfiriato,* see Peter Smith, *Labyrinths of Power* (Princeton: Princeton University Press, 1979).

9. A standard work on the integration is Arnaldo Córdova, *La formación del poder en México,* 8th ed. (Mexico City: Serie Popular Era, 1980). See also John Higley and Richard Gunther, eds., *Elites and Democratic Consolidation in Latin America and Southern Europe* (Cambridge: Cambridge University Press, 1992).

10. Two major accounts are Tzvi Medín, *Ideología y praxis político de Lázaro Cárdenas* (Mexico City: Siglo XXI, 1976); and Wayne A. Cornelius, "Nation Building, Participation, Distribution: Reform Under Cárdenas," in *Crisis, Choice, and Change: Historical Studies of Political Development,* ed. Gabriel A. Almond, Scott C. Flanigan, and Robert J. Mundt (Boston: Little, Brown, 1973), pp. 394, 429, 462.

11. We use the terms as elaborated in Philippe C. Schmitter's widely cited "Still the Century of Corporatism?" in *The New Corporatism,* ed. Frederick Pike and Thomas Stritch (Notre Dame, Ind.: University of Notre Dame Press, 1974), pp. 93–105.

12. On political marginality, see Pablo González Casanova, *Democracy in Mexico,* tr. Danielle Salti (London: Oxford University Press, 1970), pp. 126–134; on reacting, see Susan Kaufman Purcell, *The Mexican Profit-Making Decision: Politics in an Authoritarian Regime* (Berkeley: University of California Press, 1975).

13. On the consequences of early incorporation, see Ruth Berins Collier and David Collier, *Shaping the Political Arena* (Princeton: Princeton University Press, 1991); and Robert R. Kaufman, "Mexico and Latin American Authoritarianism," in ed. José Luis Reyna and Richard S. Wienert, *Authoritarianism in Mexico* (Philadelphia: ISHI, 1977), pp. 220–221. See Evelyn Stevens, *Protest and Response in Mexico* (Cambridge, Mass.: MIT Press, 1974), pp. 276–277, on how activists have been unable to attract mass followings.

14. Pablo González Casanova, *El estado y los partidos políticos en México* (Mexico City: Ediciones Era, 1985), p. 48.

15. See, for example, Jesús Silva Herzog, *La revolución mexicana en crisis* (Mexico City: Ediciones Cuadernos Americanos, 1944), pp. 22–34; and for a similar point on peasants, see Gerrit Huizer, "Peasant Organization in Agrarian Reform in Mexico," in *Masses in Latin America*, ed. Irving Louis Horowitz (New York: Oxford University Press, 1970), pp. 445–502.

16. Raúl Trejo Delarbre, "El movimiento obrero: Situación y perspectivas," in ed. Pablo González Casanova and Enrique Florescano, *México, hoy*, 5th ed. (Mexico City: Siglo XXI, 1981), pp. 128–130.

17. Total wage income fell a cumulative 40 percent between 1983 and 1988, whereas the real minimum wage fell 48.5 percent. See Nora Lustig, *Mexico: The Remaking of an Economy* (Washington, D.C.: Brookings Institution, 1992), pp. 68–69. For other representative estimates, see Sidney Weintraub, *Transforming the Mexican Economy* (Washington, D.C.: National Planning Association, 1930), p. 13; and Ruth Berins Collier, *The Contradictory Alliance* (Berkeley: University of California Press, 1993), p. 128.

18. Kevin Middlebrook makes this point in his article "Dilemmas of Change in Mexican Politics," *World Politics* 41 (October 1988): pp. 120–141.

19. See Juan Reyes del Campillo, "La selección de los candidatos del partido Revolucionario Institucional," in ed. Juan Felipe Leal, Jacqueline Peschard, and Concepción Rivera, *Las elecciones federales de 1988 en México* (Mexico City: Universidad Nacional Autónoma de Mexico, 1988), p. 96.

20. Jorge G. Castañeda, "Mexico at the Brink," *Foreign Affairs* 64 (Winter 1985–1986): p. 293.

21. Richard Fagen and William Tuohy, *Politics in a Mexican Village* (Stanford, Calif.: Stanford University Press, 1969).

22. Dale Story, *Industry, the State, and Public Policy in Mexico* (Austin: University of Texas Press, 1986), pp. 105, 195. See also John J. Bailey, *Governing Mexico: The Statecraft of Crisis Management* (London: MacMillan, 1988), ch. 6; and Sylvia Maxfield and Ricardo Anzaldúa, *Government and Private Sector in Contemporary Mexico* (La Jolla: University of California, San Diego, Center for U.S.-Mexican Studies, 1987).

23. On intellectuals, see Roderic A. Camp, *Intellectuals and the State in Twentieth-Century Mexico* (Austin: University of Texas Press, 1985); on public universities, see Daniel C. Levy, *University and Government in Mexico: Autonomy in an Authoritarian System* (New York: Praeger, 1980).

24. Although this case cannot settle the debate over whether national political democratization requires democratizing society's associational life, it is pertinent that Mexico's mass-based organizations are notoriously undemocratic. For example, both labor and peasant elections are controlled and corrupt. Practice varies among the associations of more privileged classes; many media, intellectual, and student associations are far from open and free. See, for example, Camp, *Intellectuals*, p. 225.

25. See Sergio Zermeño, *México: Una democracia utópica: El movimiento estudiantil del 68* (Mexico City: Siglo XXI, 1978); and Levy, *University*, pp. 28–33, 39–41.

26. In Frank Brandenburg's apt label for the regime, "liberal Machiavellian," "liberal" refers to tolerance more than the Dahl/O'Donnell-Schmitter sense of contestation. Brandenburg, *The Making of Modern Mexico* (Englewood Cliffs, N.J.: Prentice Hall, 1964), pp. 141–165. Disturbing evidence of intolerance has long come from brutal repression of peasant actions and, recently, from reports about human-rights abuses, including torture.

27. Levy and Székely, *Mexico*, ch. 4.

28. The poor performance of PRD candidate Cuauhtémoc Cárdenas knocked him immediately from a solid second place in the polls to third, where he remained. Meanwhile, the feisty performance of the PAN candidate helped give his party its best national showing ever.

29. Wayne Cornelius, Ann Craig, and Jonathan Fox, "Mexico's National Solidarity

Program," in *Transforming State-Society Relations in Mexico,* ed. Wayne Cornelius, Ann Craig, and Jonathan Fox (La Jolla, Calif.: University of California, San Diego, Center for U.S.-Mexican Studies, 1994), p. 3.

30. By official figures, Solidarity led to the formation of 150,000 community-based committees in the first five years of the program, perhaps one-third of which "were fully functional, had real presence in their communities, and were capable of making some demands upon government." Ibid., p. 20.

31. González Casanova, *Democracy,* p. 68.

32. By 1994, the PAN governed three states: Baja California (since 1989), Chihuahua (since 1992), and Guanajuato (through an interim governor named after a strongly disputed 1991 election). Despite the greater independence of state governments and unusually good PRI-PAN relations under Salinas, the PAN could not convert these states into lasting PAN majorities; it lost all three in the 1994 presidential election. For analyses of opposition municipal and state governments, see eds. Victoria Rodríquez and Peter Ward, *Opposition Government in Mexico: Past Experiences and Future Opportunities* (Albuquerque: University of New Mexico Press, 1995). Whereas some observers find local political participation minimal, others see competition within the PRI that includes citizen support for political wings or for candidates proposing popular policies (e.g., improvement of water or electrical systems). Alvaro Arreola Ayala, "Elecciones municipales," in ed. Pablo González Casanova, *Las elecciones en México: Evolución y perspectivas* (Mexico City: Siglo XXI, 1985), pp. 330–336.

33. Fernando Henrique Cardoso, "On the Characterization of Authoritarian Regimes in Latin America," in *The New Authoritarianism in Latin America,* ed. David Collier (Princeton, N.J.: Princeton University Press, 1979), pp. 42–43.

34. Kevin J. Middlebrook, "Political Liberalization in an Authoritarian Regime: The Case of Mexico," in O'Donnell, Schmitter, and Whitehead, *Transitions from Authoritarian Rule: Latin America,* p. 140.

35. Norman Cox, "Changes in the Mexican Political System," in ed. George Philip, *Politics in Mexico* (London: Croom Helm, 1985), p. 20; Scott, *Mexican Government,* pp. 267–271.

36. A prominent recent source is Roderic Camp, *Generals in the Palacio: The Military in Modern Mexico* (New York: Oxford University Press, 1992).

37. Miguel de la Madrid, *Los grandes problemas nationales de hoy* (Mexico City: Editorial Diana, 1982), p. 139.

38. *El nuevo perfil de la economía mexicana* (Mexico City: Secretaria de Hacienda y Crédito Público, 1991), p. 15.

39. See John Bailey, "Centralism and Political Change in Mexico," in Cornelius, Craig, and Fox, *Transforming State-Society Relations in Mexico,* pp. 117, 102; Daniel C. Levy, "Mexico: Towards State Supervision?" in eds. Guy Neave and Frans van Vught, *Government and Higher Education Relationships Across Three Continents* (Oxford: Pergamon, 1994), pp. 241–263.

40. Gustavo Ernesto Emmerich, "Las elecciones en México, 1808–1911: Sufragio electivo, no reelección?" in González Casanova, *Elecciones,* p. 64.

41. Luis Javier Garrido, *El partido de la revolución institucionalizada 1929–45* (Mexico City: Siglo XXI, 1982); González Casanova, *Democracy,* p. 34.

42. This class has been comparatively distinct from the nation's economic elites, despite greatly overlapping interests. Martin C. Needler has compared it to the East European "new class" described by Djilas, except that it has been more legitimate and effective in its ownership of state power. See Needler, *Mexican Politics: The Containment of Conflict* (New York: Praeger, 1982), pp. 131–133. Intertwined with the official party, the political class has lacked career service and merit characteristics, but its strength has been tied to its politicization. Recently, however, the class's coherence has been weakened by a surge of technocrats who rise to high posts based on special educational credentials rather than apprenticeship with the party, elective office, public universities, mass organizations, and so forth. See especially, Miguel Angel Centeno, *Democracy Within Reason* (University Park, Penn.: Pennsylvania State University Press, 1994). Additionally, economic opening and diminishing ratios of state expenditures to GDP could mean diminished resources to reward and sanction (e.g., through subsidies and protectionism).

43. Bailey, *Governing,* ch. 7.

44. Implemented reforms have been limited to measures such as selecting candidates

with local appeal and varying selection methods. PRI candidates for some 1984 municipal posts were selected after open party assemblies or secret votes rather than merely by appointment from above. See Cox, "Changes," p. 28.

45. On leftist weaknesses and platforms, see, for example, Barry Carr, "Mexico: The Perils of Unity and the Challenge of Modernization," in ed. Barry Carr and Steve Ellner, *The Latin American Left* (Boulder, Colo.: Westview Press, 1993).

46. For an analysis of the formation and subsequent struggles of the PRD, see Kathleen Bruhn, *Taking on Goliath: The Emergence of a New Cardenista Party and the Struggle for Democracy in Mexico.* Ph.D. dissertation, Stanford University (Ann Arbor: University Microfilms, 1993).

47. Data from official voting results, from the *Registro Nacional de Electores* (1985) and the *Instituto Federal Electoral* (1991). Calculations by Bruhn. "1985 second-place finishes" adds the vote of the two independent left parties (PMT and PSUM) that merged into the Mexican Socialist Party in 1987 and into the PRD in 1989.

48. The head of the board is a presidential appointee (the secretary of the interior); the PRI kept the power to veto any citizen councilor (since no combination of opposition votes could reach two-thirds); and at least two board members represent the majority party in the House and Senate, respectively.

49. Juan Molinar, *El tiempo de la legitimidad* (Mexico City: Cal y Arena, 1991); Villoro, "Reforma," pp. 355-357; and Middlebrook, "Political Liberalization," pp. 126-128.

50. Some states then chose reform anyway. See Jorge Madrazo, "Reforma política y legislación electoral de las entidades federativas," in González Casanova, *Elecciones,* pp. 293-302.

51. Packet of information for foreign observers, provided by the Instituto Federal Electoral, 1994.

52. Table 1.1 herein; Inter-American Development Bank (IDB), *Economic and Social Progress in Latin America,* 1986 Report (Washington, D.C.: IDB, n.d.), p. 314; *Anuario Estadístio de los Estados Unidos Mexicanos* (Mexico, D.F.: INEGI, 1993), pp. 20, 39, 124; and World Bank, *Social Indicators of Development: 1991–1992* (Baltimore: World Bank, 1992), p. 204.

53. Miguel de la Madrid, "Cuarto informe de gobierno," *Comercio Exterior* 36, no. 9 (1986): p. 760.

54. See, for example, Daniel C. Levy, *Higher Education and the State in Latin America: Private Challenges to Public Dominance* (Chicago: University of Chicago Press, 1986), pp. 114-170.

55. World Bank, *World Development Report,* 1980 (Washington, D.C.: World Bank, 1980), pp. 156–157.

56. Gabriel A. Almond and Sidney Verba, *The Civic Culture* (Boston: Little, Brown, 1963); Ann L. Craig and Wayne A. Cornelius, "Political Culture in Mexico: Continuities and Revisionist Interpretations," in ed. Gabriel A. Almond and Sidney Verba, *The Civic Culture Revisited* (Boston: Little, Brown, 1980), p. 375. See also Fagen and Tuohy, *Politics,* pp. 38–39, 136–137.

57. The three respective explanations of acceptance are emphasized in, for example, Paz, *The Other;* Fagen and Tuohy, *Politics;* and Almond and Verba, *Civic Culture.*

58. Susan Kaufman Purcell and John F. H. Purcell, "State and Society in Mexico: Must a Stable Polity Be Institutionalized?" *World Politics* 32, no. 2 (1980): pp. 204–205. See Craig and Cornelius, "Political," pp. 341, 385–386, fn. 35, on the different positions. A prominent recent example of the causal political-cultural approach, bitterly denounced in Mexico, is Alan Riding, *Distant Neighbors: A Portrait of the Mexicans* (New York: Knopf, 1985).

59. John Booth and Mitchell Seligson, "The Political Culture of Authoritarianism in Mexico: A Reexamination," *Latin American Research Review* 19, no. 1 (1984): pp. 110–113. The authors report uniformly strong democratic values, although less among women, the less educated, and the working class than in the middle class. But their data come from developed urban areas known for dissent from the PRI regime. Also, expressed values do not seem quite so at odds with the system when one acknowledges that it permits some degree of free expression, demonstration, etc.; it does not permit organized alternatives, and the one issue on which the authors report a majority of undemocratic responses was on critics seeking office. Craig and Cornelius, "Political," pp. 348–350, report conflicting data regarding "working-class authoritarianism."

60. Rafael Segovia, *La politicización del niño mexicano,* 2d ed. (Mexico City: El Colegio de México, 1982); Craig and Cornelius, "Political," p. 369. Family socialization and interrelations are often described as intolerant and undemocratic. However, the introduction of more participatory educational practices (e.g., Montessori schools) may have a democratizing influence.

61. In a sense, then, elites have developed a degree of "trust" in their pacts even though interpersonal trust is low. On the generally low degree of trust in Mexican society, see Craig and Cornelius, "Political," p. 372.

62. Robert Dahl, *Polyarchy: Participation and Opposition* (New Haven, Conn.: Yale University Press, 1971).

63. Guillermo Bonfil Batalla, "Los pueblos indígenas: Viejos problemas, nuevas demandas," in González Casanova and Florescano, *México, hoy,* pp. 100–107.

64. Juan J. Linz, "Totalitarian and Authoritarian Regimes," in ed. Fred I. Greenstein and Nelson W. Polsby, *Handbook of Political Science,* vol. 3 (Reading, Mass.: Addison-Wesley, 1975).

65. Respective quotations from Larissa Lomnitz, "Social Structure of Urban Mexico," *Latin America Research Review 16,* no. 2 (1982): p. 69; and Purcell and Purcell, *"State and Society,"* p. 226.

66. Mexico's elite autonomous organizations have not usually served as "training grounds" for democracy. The public university is the best example of a substantially autonomous organization that has trained most of Mexico's (undemocratic) political elite. Relevant skills are the ability to mobilize and manipulate mass groups, bargaining, and leadership.

67. Bailey, *Governing,* Table 6.1.

68. Gabriel A. Almond and Robert J. Mundt, "Crisis, Choice, and Change: Some Tentative Conclusions," in Almond and Mundt, *Crisis,* pp. 635, 637.

69. Perhaps Mexico's unequal socioeconomic development has facilitated autonomous political participation for some privileged groups alongside mobilized participation by mass groups. See Samuel P. Huntington and Joan Nelson, *No Easy Choice* (Cambridge, Mass.: Harvard University Press, 1976). Such a view appears consistent with this chapter's corporatist-pluralist contrasts.

70. Daniel C. Levy, "The Implications of Central American Conflicts for Mexican Politics," in ed. Roderic A. Camp, *Mexico's Political Stability: The Next Five Years* (Boulder, Colo.: Westview Press, 1986), pp. 235–264.

71. Joe Forewaker, *Popular Mobilization in Mexico* (Cambridge: Cambridge University Press, 1993); Daniel C. Levy, "Outside the University: Mexico's Private Research Contexts in Comparative Perspective," in ed. David Lorey, *Cycles and Trends in Mexican University Education* (Los Angeles: UCLA Center for Latin American Studies, forthcoming).

72. Whether "success" by itself would ever undermine an authoritarian regime, particularly a well-institutionalized one, is an interesting question, but perhaps more pertinent is whether success sets the general conditions for democracy to the point that crises (economic disaster, military defeat, scandal) leading to instability, or at least turmoil, may in fact bring democratization.

73. Guillermo O'Donnell, "Introduction to the Latin American Cases," pp. 5, 15; and Luciano Martins, "The 'Liberalization' of Authoritarian Rule in Brazil," p. 72, both in O'Donnell, Schmitter, and Whitehead, *Transitions: Latin America;* and especially O'Donnell and Schmitter, *Transitions from Authoritarian Rule: Tentative Conclusions About Uncertain Democracies* (Baltimore, Md.: Johns Hopkins University Press, 1986), pp. 48–72; also, Alfred Stepan, "Paths Toward Redemocratization: Theoretical and Comparative Considerations," in O'Donnell, Schmitter, and Whitehead, *Transitions from Authoritarian Rule: Comparative Perspectives,* pp. 72–74.

74. See Lamounier's chapter in this volume, and also Martins, "Liberalization," pp. 72–74.

75. Juan Molinar and Jeffrey Weldon, "Electoral Determinants and Consequences of National Solidarity," in eds. Cornelius et al., *Transforming State-Society Relations in Mexico,* p. 141.

76. The theoretical argument is developed in Adam Przeworski, "Some Problems in the Study of the Transition to Democracy," in O'Donnell, Schmitter, and Whitehead, *Transitions,* pp. 47–63; and in O'Donnell and Schmitter, *Transitions,* pp. 7–16, 48–49.

77. Wayne A. Cornelius, "Political Liberalization in an Authoritarian Regime: Mexico, 1976–1985," in Gentleman, *Mexican.*

78. Statement observed by Bruhn at internal PRI conference "Democracy and Modernization," April 29, 1991, Mexico City.

79. Carlos Monsiváis, "La ofensiva ideológica de la derecha," in Casanova and Florescano, *México, hoy,* p. 315. This underscores Przeworski's point ("Some Problems," pp. 50–53) that perceptions of alternatives as well as of the present regime are critical to choices about pushing for transition.

80. It is curious that Mexico's most democratic presidents—Juárez and Madero—are also associated with the outbreak of armed conflicts: Juárez with the Conservatives and the French, and Madero with the Mexican Revolution.

81. Abraham Lowenthal, ed., *Exporting Democracy: The United States and Latin America,* 2 vols. (Baltimore, Md.: Johns Hopkins University Press, 1991).

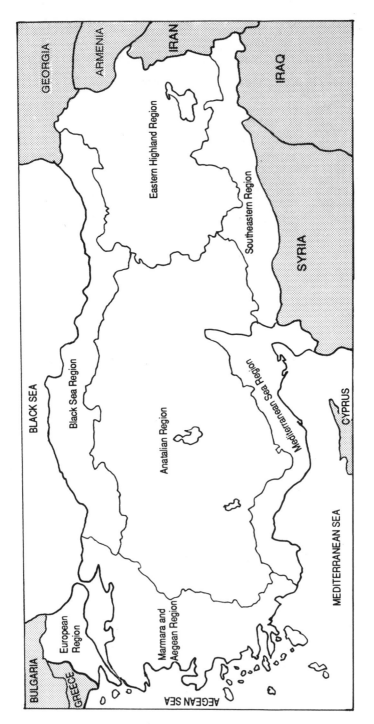

TURKEY

5

Turkey: Crises, Interruptions, and Reequilibrations

Ergun Özbudun

The record of democratic development in Turkey has been somewhat mixed. On the one hand, Turkey has remained committed to a democratic regime for almost fifty years with only relatively brief interruptions. Presently it is the only democratic country in the entire Middle East (with the single exception of the very special case of Israel). By most socioeconomic indicators, Turkey is a middle-rank, developing country, with a per capita income of about $2,800 in 1994. However, Turkey's democratic process has been interrupted thrice in the last quarter of a century, which indicates a rather high degree of political instability. At best then, Turkey can be placed in the category of unstable democracies.

If the record of democratic development in Turkey is mixed, so are the factors that may have a bearing on Turkey's overall degree of success with democratic government. Culturally most Turks, elite and non-elite, seem to be committed to a democratic regime; yet this commitment does not always seem to be based on a set of profoundly felt concomitant democratic values, such as tolerance, compromise, and respect for individuality. The military shares the society's commitment to democracy, yet it also displays certain elitist attitudes and a tendency to see itself as the true guardian of the national interest. The major political parties have been non-ideological and committed to democracy; yet their leaderships have not always shown a propensity for compromise and accommodation even in the face of a grave and imminent threat to the regime; furthermore, they have not been immune to polarizing influences, as was the case in the 1970s. The society is relatively homogeneous and well-integrated; yet ethnic or sectarian conflict can sometimes become violent. The rate of economic growth has on the whole been quite respectable; yet economic inequalities have also increased and are continuing to do so; moreover, there seem to exist serious obstacles to sustained economic growth in the future.

The Development of
Representative and Democratic Government

The Ottoman Empire

Turkey differs from most of the developing countries of today in that it never experienced a colonial past. On the contrary, the Ottoman Empire—which at its zenith at the end of the sixteenth century comprised the entire Middle East (excluding Iran), North Africa, Southeastern Europe (including Hungary), and southern Russia—left a powerful legacy not only in the contemporary politics of its principal heir, the Republic of Turkey, but also upon those of other "successor states" to the empire.[1] A study of the development of democracy in Turkey cannot therefore be attempted without reference to its Ottoman past.

It is generally agreed that the Ottoman state conformed much more closely to a "bureaucratic empire" than to a European-style feudal system.[2] The Ottoman society was divided into two major classes. The *askeri,* literally the "military," included those to whom the sultan had delegated religious or executive power, namely officers of the court and the army, civil servants, and *ulema* (religious functionaries). The *reaya,* on the other hand, comprised all Muslim and non-Muslim subjects who paid taxes but who had no part in the government. "It was a fundamental rule of the empire to exclude its subjects from the privileges of the 'military.'"[3] This accorded well with the fundamental concepts of state and society in the Ottoman Empire, which held that the social order was of divine origin and hence immutable. It was the sultan's duty to maintain this order, assisted by the members of the *askeri* class, by keeping everyone in his appropriate social position. Thus the state was above and independent of the society. Political power did not derive from the society, but was imposed upon it by the will of God (in effect, by conquest) from outside.[4] It was this primacy of politics over society that was to affect the nature of social and political changes in the Ottoman Empire for many centuries.

Two features of the Ottoman system reinforced the rigid dichotomy between the ruler and the ruled. One was the recruitment (*devsirme*) system, which was a periodic levy on the male children of Christian subjects, reducing them to the status of slaves and training them for service to the state. Since these slaves legally became the sultan's property, and he could take their lives and confiscate their wealth without legal process, they were in no position to challenge his authority. Furthermore, their removal from their former social environments prevented the development of locally entrenched, semiautonomous elements in the provinces.

A second feature, which was also instrumental in maintaining a strong central authority over the large territories of the empire, was the Ottoman land tenure system. This system vested in the state the original ownership of all the land, and limited the rights of the fief holders (*sipahi*) to the collection of taxes and the supervision of peasants under their jurisdiction. In return for the land grant, the *sipahi* were expected to recruit, train, and support a local contingent of soldiers; the fiefs were granted by the central government and could be taken away by it. Furthermore, the largest fiefs (*hass*) were perquisites of office. "The Ottoman feudal system seems to have differed from that of Western Europe chiefly in that the principal feudatories held their lands temporarily, in virtue of their offices. Hence the monarchy was exposed to little danger from the rivalry of this class of its tenants-in-chief."[5]

Two other significant social groups were the *ulema* (the class of religious scholars), and the merchants and artisans. Although part of the ruling class, the *ulema* differed from the "military" proper and the administrators in that it consisted of freeborn Muslims. However, the *ulema* did not constitute a hierarchy independent of government, since the most important among its members held appointive posts and hence were completely dependent on the state. As for merchants the Ottoman state, unlike its Western European counterparts, did not pursue mercantilist policies and did not favor the emergence of a powerful merchant class. Another factor that hindered the growth of a politically influential merchant class was the "ethnic division of labor." Non-Muslim minorities took the lead in mercantile activities, especially in international trade. But this group, so important in the development of early mercantile capitalism in Western Europe, was barred from the opportunity of converting such economic power into a significant political role because of the Islamic character of the state.

Thus, with no feudalism comparable to that of Western Europe, no hereditary aristocracy, no independent church hierarchy, no strong and independent merchant class, no powerful guilds, no self-governing cities, and with a ruling institution (i.e., the administration and the army) staffed with slaves, the Ottoman Empire represented a close approximation of an Oriental despotism. In the West, non-governmental intermediary social structures operated relatively independently of government and played a cushioning role between the state and the individual. The church was the foremost of these corporate structures such as the guilds, free cities, and the like. These had no parallels in the Ottoman Empire.

Islamic law does not as a rule recognize corporate entities. For all the theoretical supremacy of the *sharia* (Islamic law), even the religious class does not have a corporate identity. At least in Sunni (orthodox) Islam it forms part of the state bureaucracy, dependent upon the state for its appointments, promotions, and salaries. Similarly, in the Ottoman Empire, neither the cities nor the artisan guilds played any autonomous role comparable to their counterparts in Western Europe.[6] This dichotomy between the ruler and the ruled led to a class consciousness very different from that of the West, "that of *askeri* on the one hand and of their opponents on the other. . . . The saliency of these strata replaced the European saliency of strata connected with the production and distribution of goods and services."[7]

The bureaucratic nature of the Ottoman state and the concentration of political power in the hands of the sultan and his military and civilian bureaucrats explain the absence of representative institutions throughout the history of the empire until the last quarter of the nineteenth century. This contrasts sharply with the feudal tradition in Western Europe, which contained within itself the germs of representative and constitutional government. Western European feudalism implied a legally defined division of powers between a relatively weak central authority and local centers of power. It also implied some idea of representation for the estates, regardless of the frequency with which assemblies of estates were actually called. To this was added the corporate autonomy of the church, the cities, and the guilds. From this medieval social and political pluralism and division of powers, it was a relatively easy step to modern constitutionalism, the rule of law, and modern representative institutions.

The Ottoman state, however, was not entirely devoid of the idea of "consultation" in the conduct of governmental affairs. It was an established custom for the Ottoman government to convene an assembly of leading civilian, military, and religious officials to discuss important matters of policy especially in times of stress. While it clearly had no representative character, this body nevertheless gave support to the notion that important policy decisions should be based on deliberations and consultations in a broader council. Such a consultative assembly was institutionalized in 1838 by Mahmud II, in the form of the "Grand Council of Justice." Mahmud's successor, Abdulmecid I, gave the council the responsibility of discussing and drafting new laws on matters of civil rights and taxation. In practice it "successfully operated as the principal Ottoman legislative organ. . . . All the important *Tanzimat* [Reform] decrees and regulations were prepared by it and over ninety percent of its recommendations were promulgated without change."[8]

In the next few decades, known as the "Reform" period in the Ottoman Empire, the development of representative institutions followed two different routes. One was the increasingly important role of the central legislative council and the effort to broaden its social base without, however, introducing the elective principle. The second was the establishment of local administrative councils based on limited elections. The elective principle in local administration was introduced in the Danube Province in 1864 and then extended in 1867 to the rest of the country. This provided for the election of only the lowest level of local officials (commune headmen) but attached semielected administrative councils to the centrally appointed governors of the each of the three tiers of local administration. A somewhat more representative institution was the "general assembly" created for each province. It was indirectly elected with largely advisory powers.[9]

The First Ottoman Parliament (1876–1878)

The next step was to be the linking of the elective principle adopted at the local level with the practice of non-elective legislative councils at the center. The first Ottoman legislature based on elections came into being with the constitution of December 23, 1876. Interestingly, Midhat Pasha, the leader of the constitutionalist faction, hoped to be able to convene a parliament even before the constitution was officially promulgated. Therefore, a Provisional Electoral Regulation was promulgated on October 28, while the constitution itself was still being debated in the drafting committee, which was composed of high-ranking civil servants.

Despite the limited and indirect nature of the suffrage and certain incidents of interference in the electoral process by provincial governors, it is generally agreed that the first legislative elections in the Ottoman Empire produced a Chamber of Deputies broadly representative (in a sociological sense) of various national and religious communities. While the Muslims, who outnumbered non-Muslims by a considerable ratio in the country, had a majority in the chamber, the Christians and the Jews were proportionally much better represented. The Turks as an ethnic group were a minority of the deputies as a whole, sharing the Muslim seats with Arabs, Albanians, Bosnians, and others. Although a large percentage of the deputies were former government officials, there were also many others representing other professions.[10]

The Chamber of Deputies had two sessions between March 19, 1877, and February 14, 1878, when it was indefinitely prorogued by Sultan Abdulhamid II. Although officially the fiction was maintained that the constitution was still in force, the Chamber of Deputies was not reconvened until the Young Turk revolution of 1908 forced Abdulhamid to do so. It is impossible to analyze here the full political context of the first experiment with constitutional government in the Ottoman Empire or the reasons for its failure. Suffice it to say that the introduction of constitutional and representative government was the work of a very small group of reformist government officials and intellectuals; it was based neither on broad support, nor on organized political parties. Consequently, Abdulhamid's prorogation of the chamber did not lead to any strong public reaction. On the contrary his absolutist rule, emphasizing the Islamic character of the state, seems to have been quite popular with the conservative, anti-Western mood of public opinion.

The fundamental political cleavage in the Ottoman Empire until the nineteenth century can be described as a center-periphery cleavage between the political ins and outs. The ins were "the incumbents of the Ottoman institutions. The outs were people who were excluded from the state."[11] Beginning in the eighteenth century, this cleavage was complicated by another one that resulted from the efforts of Westernization. The adoption

of, first, Western military technology and, then, Western laws and administrative practices was strongly opposed by the old religious and military
elites. This opposition was motivated not only by religious grounds, but also
by the fear that such reforms would undermine their power and status in the
society. In contrast to the older center-periphery cleavage this one was located at the very center. The Westernization movement undertaken by bureaucrats fractured the old intraelite unity, and produced a conflict that remained
for many years one of the principal cleavages in Turkish political life. The
political implications of this culture change, first under the Ottoman reformers and then under the leadership of Kemal Ataturk, will be discussed more
fully below.

The first Ottoman experiment with constitutional government reflects
the emergence of yet another line of cleavage. This one pitted the constitutionalists (called the "Young Ottomans") against the supporters of monar-
chic autocracy. This was also an intraelite conflict, since both the constitutionalists and the autocratic *tanzimat* reformers came from the ranks of the
Westernized, official elite. The Young Ottomans did not represent either the
local notables or urban merchants. However, their advocacy of a parliament
put them in a dilemma, one that was to be faced by many generations of
future modernizers: the modernizers wanted to have a parliament as an alternative (and modern) source of legitimacy. But they soon realized that when
a parliament was convened, it "did not increase the power of modernizing
officials vis-à-vis the Sultan, but that it rather increased the power of notables against state officials."[12] In fact, the Young Ottomans were often bitterly critical of the abuses of local notables, and charged them with repressing
the countryside. The short life of the first Ottoman Parliament provided clear
manifestations of the deep conflict between the central bureaucratic elite
and the local (peripheral) forces.[13] It is also a good example of unanticipated and undesired consequences democratization poses for modernizers in
traditional or developing societies.

The Second Constitutionalist Period (1908–1918)

The electoral process was reinstated in 1908 after thirty years of absolutist
monarchical rule when military-popular uprisings in Macedonia compelled
Abdulhamid II to restore the constitution. This was a victory for the
reformist-constitutionalist wing of the official bureaucratic elite organized
in the underground Society for Union and Progress, which in time transformed itself into a political party. Indeed the second constitutionalist period witnessed, for the first time, the emergence of organized political parties
and party competition. The 1908 elections gave the Society for Union and
Progress a comfortable majority in the Chamber of Deputies. Of the other
two elections held in this period, only that of 1912 was relatively competitive. Because of the administrative pressures exerted by the Unionist gov-

ernment and restrictions on opposition activities, this election came to be known as the "big stick election." The 1914 election was not contested by any opposition party.[14]

The democratic experiment of the second constitutionalist period is generally too easily dismissed as one that quickly degenerated into an internecine struggle poisoned by coups and countercoups, political assassinations and martial law courts, government manipulation of elections and repression of the opposition, becoming finally an outright party dictatorship. While this diagnosis contains a great deal of truth, the same period (especially until the Unionists' coup of 1913) also provided the first extended Turkish experiment with competitive elections, organized political parties, and the parliamentary process. The beginnings of mass politics in Turkey should also be sought in this period. Unlike the earlier military, bureaucratic, intellectual cliques, the Union and Progress, "had too broad a social base and too heterogeneous a class structure to be elitist. . . . The Committee was the first political organization in the Empire to have a mass following and this gave the politics of the day a populist basis."[15] Finally, under the crust of virulent and mutually destructive political struggles of the period, one can discern the beginnings of "issue-oriented politics," which pitted the modernizing, unifying, centralizing, standardizing, nationalist, authoritarian, and statist Union and Progress against three types of opposition: the liberals who favored parliamentary democracy, administrative decentralization, more reliance on private initiative, and a more Ottomanist policy (i.e., a policy aimed at creating an "Ottoman" identity around the common fatherland and dynasty, regardless of religion, language, and ethnicity); religious traditionalists who were opposed to the secularist aspects of the Unionist policies; and the non-Turkish minorities (whether Muslim or non-Muslim) who felt threatened by the nationalist and centralizing drive of the Union and Progress.[16]

The National Liberation Period (1918–1923)

With the defeat of the Ottoman Empire in World War I, the Ottoman government collapsed in fact, if not in theory. While the Istanbul government maintained a shaky existence during the Armistice years (1918–1922) under the control of the Allies' occupation armies, a new governmental structure was developed in Anatolia by the nationalists resisting the occupation.

The era of national liberation is a most interesting period in Turkey's constitutional history, and is full of constitutional innovations. Following the arrest and deportation of many deputies with nationalist sympathies by the Allied occupation forces and the consequent dissolution of the Chamber of Deputies on March 18, 1920, Mustafa Kemal, the leader of the nationalist forces in Anatolia, called for the election of a new assembly "with extraordinary powers" to convene in Ankara. This body, called the "Grand

National Assembly," was fundamentally different from the Ottoman Parliament in that it combined legislative and executive powers in itself. It was a real constituent and revolutionary assembly, not bound by the Ottoman constitution.

The Grand National Assembly enacted a constitution in 1921. This was a short but very important document. For the first time it proclaimed the principle of national sovereignty, calling itself the "only and true representative of the nation." Legislative and executive powers were vested in the Assembly. The ministers were to be chosen by the Assembly individually from among its own members. The Assembly could provide instructions to the ministers and, if deemed necessary, change them.

In the entire Turkish history, the political influence of the legislature reached its peak during the period of national liberation. The theory of legislative supremacy was also followed in practice. The Assembly closely supervised all aspects of administrative activity. Under the most difficult external and internal circumstances, Kemal and his ministers ruled the country in close cooperation with the Assembly and never attempted to ignore it.

In the months following the victorious termination of the War of Independence and the abolition of the sultanate in the fall of 1922, Mustafa Kemal formed a political party based on populist principles, which was named the People's Party (later the Republican People's Party, or RPP). In the 1923 elections it won almost all of the Assembly seats. However, the newly elected Assembly was also far from being an obedient instrument of the leadership. Disagreements on constitutional and other questions soon became manifest. In November 1924, twenty-nine deputies resigned from the People's Party and formed the Progressive Republican Party. The new opposition party was led by some prestigious generals closely associated with Kemal during the War of Independence. In its initial manifesto the party emphasized economic and particularly political liberalism, including a commitment to "respect religious feelings and beliefs." The manifesto stated its opposition to despotism, and stressed individual rights, judicial independence, and administrative decentralization. It promised not to change the constitution without a clear popular mandate. The Progressive Republican Party was strongly supported by the Istanbul press, and started to set up local organizations in big cities and in the eastern provinces.

Behind these publicly claimed policy differences also lay the personal estrangement of the Progressive leaders from Kemal, and their concern about his growing personal power. At a more fundamental level, however, their opposition reflected a more conservative mentality that Frey sees as typical of postindependence crises in developing countries. Behind all the ideas of the Progressive Republican Party, he argues that "there lay the conservative aim of making the new Turkey—if there was ever to be a new Turkey in any basic sense—conform as far as possible to the customs and traditions of the old. Change was to be gradual and evolutionary, not swift and revolutionary in the Kemalist mode."[17]

The Consolidation of the Republic

Justification for crushing the Progressive Republican Party was found in the Seyh Sait rebellion that erupted in eastern Anatolia in February 1925. The rebellion quickly reached serious dimensions. Consequently, the more moderate government of Fethi was replaced by a new one headed by Ismet Inönü, who favored more radical methods to deal with the rebellion. Legislation passed in March gave the government broad powers to ban all kinds of organization, propaganda, agitation, and publications that could lead to reaction and rebellion or undermine public order and security. Martial law was declared, and the Independence Tribunals (revolutionary courts created in 1920 to deal with treasonable activities) were reactivated. The Progressive Republican Party was shut down on June 3, 1925, by a decision of the Council of Ministers, which implicated it in the revolt, although no concrete proof of such connection was established. The suppression of the opposition party and much of the independent press marked the end of the first, semipluralistic phase of the Kemalist regime.

The following period can be characterized as the consolidation phase of the new republican regime. Between 1925 and 1945 the country was ruled by a single-party regime, with the exception of a brief and unsuccessful attempt to introduce an opposition party, the Free Republican Party, in 1930. This was a period of radical secularizing reforms such as the banning of religious orders; the adoption of the Swiss civil code to replace the *sharia;* acceptance of other Western codes in the fields of penal, commercial, and procedural law; the closing of religious schools; the outlawing of the fez; the adoption of a Latin alphabet and the international calendar; the repeal of the constitutional provisions that made Islam the official religion of the state, etc. This consolidation of single-party rule, however, did not involve a doctrinal repudiation of liberal democracy or of liberal values. Extraordinary measures were justified by temporary needs to protect the state and the regime against counterrevolutionaries.

Although the regime's authoritarian tendencies were somewhat intensified after the failure of the Free Republican Party experiment in 1930, most of these tendencies were checked or arrested by the more liberal or pluralistic countertendencies within the single party, the Republican People's Party (RPP). Organizationally the RPP never approached a totalitarian mobilizational party model. Ideologically, it did not provide a permanent justification for an authoritarian regime. Authoritarian practices and policies were defended not on doctrinal, but on purely pragmatic and temporary grounds. A liberal democratic state remained the officially sanctioned ideal. Institutionally attempts were made to partially open up the nomination and election processes starting from the 1931 elections, such as leaving some parliamentary seats open for independent candidates.[18]

As for its social bases, the RPP has often been described as a coalition between the central military-bureaucratic elite and local notables, the former clearly being the dominant element especially at the level of central government. This alliance was, at least partly, dictated by the circumstances of the War of Independence. These two groups were the only ones capable of mobilizing the peasant majority into a war of national liberation. After the consolidation of the republican regime this cooperation continued, since the Kemalists' emphasis on secularizing reforms did not pose a threat to the interests of local notables. Thus the RPP represented the old center, i.e., the world of officialdom, with some local allies in the periphery. But in contrast to mobilizational single parties, it did not attempt to broaden its social base or to mobilize the periphery.

The Kemalist regime was highly successful, on the other hand, in creating a set of new political institutions, among which the RPP itself and the Turkish Grand National Assembly (TGNA) stand out as the most important. Elections were also institutionalized and regularly held. The forms, if not the substance, of constitutional government were carefully maintained. All these political institutions survived with minimal changes in the multiparty era once such a transition was made in the late 1940s. Indeed, political institutionalization under the aegis of a single party provided a kind of "democratic infrastructure" that eventually facilitated the transition to democratic politics.[19] In this sense, the RPP regime can be described as a case of low political participation (mobilization) and high political institutionalization.

Other features of the Kemalist regime in Turkey might have also provided facilitating conditions for eventual democratization. First, the loss of all Arabic-speaking provinces at the end of World War I and the exchange of populations with Greece following the termination of the War of Independence made the new Turkish republic a much more homogeneous state. It thus facilitated the basing of its corporate identity on Turkish nationalism instead of Islamic religion or loyalty to the Ottoman dynasty. Indeed, a reason for the relative failure (compared, for example, with the Meiji restoration in Japan) of Ottoman modernization reforms in the nineteenth century might well have been that such reforms could not possibly have produced sufficient social integration and social mobilization in a multinational and overextended empire. The second facilitating condition was the complete secularization of the governmental, legal, and educational systems under the Kemalist rule. By strictly separating religion from politics the Kemalists created at least a precondition for liberal democracy, i.e., a rationalist-relativistic, rather than an absolutist, notion of politics. Thus it should be no accident that Turkey is the only predominantly Muslim country that is both democratic and secular. Obviously there is a link between Kemalist reforms and those of the nineteenth-century Ottoman modernizers, especially the Young Turks. But the speed, intensity, and scope of the secularizing reforms of the republic clearly surpass those of the earlier eras.

Regarding the relationship between the Kemalist reforms and the development of democracy in Turkey, a counterargument can be made to the effect that the traumatic experience of such a momentous culture change, and the deep cleavage between radical secularists and Islamic traditionalists[20] would make a stable democracy very unlikely. It should be stressed, however, that despite the radical nature of Kemalist secularism, it never intended to eradicate Islam in Turkey. It was anticlerical, to be sure, but not antireligious. It aimed at individualization or privatization of Islam, attempting to make it a matter of individual conscience rather than the fundamental organizing principle of the society. Consistent with this, freedom of religion at the individual level was always respected, while organized political manifestations of Islam were strictly forbidden.

Transition to Multiparty Politics and the Democrat Party Period

The transition from authoritarianism to competitive politics in Turkey is highly exceptional in that it took place without a *ruptura,* i.e., a break with the existing institutional arrangements. On the contrary, it is a rare example of *reforma,* where the transition process was led and controlled by the power holders of the previous authoritarian regime.[21] This transition started in 1945 when the RPP regime allowed the formation of an opposition party, the Democrat Party (DP), by some of the dissident members of its own parliamentary group. Despite some ups and downs on the road, the process proceeded relatively smoothly and ended in the electoral victory of the DP in the free parliamentary elections of 1950.

It is beyond the scope of the present study to give a full account of the transition or to assess its probable causes.[22] While such a momentous change cannot be explained by a single factor, it appears that the potentially democratic aspirations of the RPP regime and President Inönü's firm personal commitment to democratization provided the crucial impulse behind the move. In fact, whenever relations between the RPP old guard (the "bunker") and the DP opposition grew tense, Inönü intervened personally to soften the atmosphere and to reassure the opposition. The most significant of these interventions was his statement on July 12, 1947, after several rounds of talk with the hard-line Prime Minister Recep Peker and the opposition leader Celâl Bayar. The declaration included a promise by Inönü that the opposition party would enjoy the same privileges as the party in power and that Inönü himself would remain equally responsible to both parties as the head of the state.

Inönü's commitment to democratization, in turn, has to be explained by the structural and doctrinal characteristics of the RPP regime. The Kemalist regime evolved into a single-party model without, however, having a single-party ideology. No component of the RPP doctrine provided a permanent legitimation for the single-party system. On the contrary liberal democracy remained the ideal, and authoritarianism was justified only as a temporary measure arising out of the need to defend the Kemalist revolution against counterrevolutionaries. Kemalism as a doctrine was much closer to nineteenth-century liberalism than to the authoritarian and totalitarian philoso-phies of the twentieth century. Communism and fascism were never seen as models to be imitated. One reason for this might have been that the Kemalist regime was born in the immediate post–World War I period when democra-tic ideas and values were at the height of their appeal and legitimacy for the new nations.

The timing of the decision to democratize the Turkish system could have been influenced by favorable changes in the international environment. The victory of the democratic regimes in World War II, and Turkey's need for a rapprochement with the West in the face of the Soviet threat, no doubt provided an additional incentive for transition to democracy. Changes in the structure of Turkish society—notably the growth of commercial and indus-trial middle classes who favored a democratic regime in which their own party would have an excellent chance to win—on the other hand, do not seem to have played a decisive role in the transition. First, it is not clear why the commercial-industrial middle classes suddenly began to feel fettered under the RPP's statism, if statist policies really worked so much to their benefit. Second, assuming that this was indeed the case, there is no evidence that such internal pressures forced the RPP leadership into this decision. The experience of the Mexican PRI suggests that a pragmatic single party is capable of showing sufficient adaptability to accommodate newly emerging groups.

The DP came to power with a landslide electoral victory on May 14, 1950, also won the 1954 and 1957 national elections (Table 5.1), and remained in power for ten full years until it was ousted by the military coup of May 27, 1960. Socially the DP, led by a group of politicians who played fairly important roles in the single-party period, was a coalition of various types of oppositions to the RPP. It brought together urban liberals and reli-gious conservatives, commercial middle classes and the urban poor, and more modern (mobilized) sections of the rural population. The RPP, on the other hand, retained the support of government officials, some large landowners, and a substantial portion of the more backward peasantry still under the influence of its local patrons. The heterogeneous character of the DP coalition suggests that the dominant social cleavage of the era was cul-tural rather than socioeconomic in nature. The common denominator of the DP supporters was their opposition to state officials. In this sense, the rise of the DP was a victory of the periphery over the center.

The ideological distance between the RPP and the DP was not great. They differed significantly from each other, however, in their underlying attitudes toward the proper role of the state, bureaucracy, private enterprise, local initiative, and toward peasant participation in politics. While the RPP-oriented central elite had a more tutelary concept of development, the provincial elites around the DP emphasized local initiative and the "imme-diate satisfaction of local expectations."[23]

Table 5.1   Percentage of Votes (and Seats) in Turkish Parliamentary Elections
(1950–1977)

Party	Elections							
	1950	1954	1957	1961	1965	1969	1973	1977
DP/JP	53.3	56.6	47.7	34.8	52.9	46.5	29.8	36.9
	(83.8)	(93.0)	(69.5)	(35.1)	(53.3)	(56.9)	(33.1)	(42.0)
RPP	39.8	34.8	40.8	36.7	28.7	27.4	33.3	41.4
	(14.2)	(5.7)	(29.2)	(38.4)	(29.8)	(31.8)	(41.1)	(47.3)
NP	3.0	4.7	7.2	14.0	6.3	3.2	1.0	—
	(0.2)	(0.9)	(0.7)	(12.0)	(6.9)	(1.3)	(0.0)	—
FP	—	—	3.8	—	—	—	—	—
	—	—	(0.7)	—	—	—	—	—
NTP	—	—	—	13.7	3.7	2.2	—	—
	—	—	—	(14.4)	(4.2)	(1.3)	—	—
TLP	—	—	—	—	3.0	2.7	—	0.1
	—	—	—	—	(3.3)	(0.4)	—	(0.0)
NAP	—	—	—	—	2.2	3.0	3.4	6.4
	—	—	—	—	(2.4)	(0.2)	(0.7)	(3.6)
UP	—	—	—	—	—	2.8	1.1	0.4
	—	—	—	—	—	(1.8)	(0.2)	—
RRP	—	—	—	—	—	6.6	5.3	1.9
	—	—	—	—	—	(3.3)	(2.9)	(0.7)
Dem. P	—	—	—	—	—	—	11.9	1.9
	—	—	—	—	—	—	(10.0)	(0.2)
NSP	—	—	—	—	—	—	11.8	8.6
	—	—	—	—	—	—	(10.7)	(5.3)

Source: Official results of elections, State Institute of Statistics.

Note: The first row of figures for each party represents percentages of the popular vote, and the second row (in parentheses) presents the percentages of seats won.

Abbreviations: DP, Democrat Party; JP, Justice Party; RPP, Republican People's Party; NP, Nation Party; FP, Freedom Party; NTP, New Turkey Party; TLP, Turkish Labor Party; NAP, Nationalist Action Party; UP, Unity Party; RRP, Republican Reliance Party; Dem. P., Democratic Party; NSP, National Salvation Party.

Despite the non-ideological nature of the partisan conflict, relations between the two major parties quickly deteriorated. Especially after the 1957 elections the DP responded to its declining support by resorting to increasingly authoritarian measures against the opposition, which only made the opposition more uncompromising and vociferous. The last straw in this long chain of authoritarian measures was the establishment by the government party in April 1960 of a parliamentary committee of inquiry to investigate the "subversive" activities of the RPP and of a section of the press. With this, many opposition members were convinced that a point of no return had been reached and that the channels of democratic change had been clogged. The ensuing public unrest, student demonstrations in Istanbul and Ankara, and clashes between the students and the police led to the declaration of martial law. This put the armed forces in the unwanted position of suppressing the opposition on behalf of a government for whose policies they had little sympathy. Finally, the military intervened on May 27, 1960, with the welcome and support of the opposition. The National Unity Committee, formed by the revolutionary officers, dissolved the parliament, banned the DP, arrested and tried its leaders, and set out to prepare a new and more democratic constitution.

What is to be blamed for the failure of this first extended experiment of Turkey with democratic politics? One reason lay in the very nature of the DP, which was a coalition of diverse anti-RPP forces. This convinced the DP leadership that the party "could retain its unity only by keeping its ranks mobilized against the RPP. This was realized partly by accusing the RPP of subverting the government through its hold on the bureaucracy, and partly by raising the specter of a return of the RPP to power."[24] A second factor was that the DP leaders, having been socialized into politics under the RPP rule, had inherited many attitudes, norms, and orientations that were more in harmony with a single party than with a competitive party system. These included a belief that a popular mandate entitled the government party to the unrestricted use of political power. Coupled with the Ottoman-Turkish cultural legacy, which hardly distinguished between political opposition and treasonable activity, this attitude left little room for a legitimate opposition.

Perhaps an even more potent factor that eventually led to the breakdown of the democratic regime was the conflict between the DP and the public bureaucracy. The bureaucracy, which was the main pillar of the single-party regime, retained its RPP loyalties under multiparty politics, and resisted the DP's efforts to consolidate its political power. In the eyes of the DP leaders, this amounted to an unwarranted obstruction of the "national will." The bureaucrats, on the other hand, saw it as their duty to protect the "public interest" against efforts to use state funds for political patronage purposes. They were also deeply troubled by the DP government's careless attitude toward the "rule of law," as well as by its more permissive policies toward religious activities, which they considered a betrayal of the Kemalist legacy of secularism. These negative attitudes were shared by civilian officials and military officers alike.

Finally, all bureaucratic groups (again both civilian and military) not only experienced a loss of social status and political influence under the DP regime, but were also adversely affected in terms of their relative income. The DP's economic policies consisted of rapid import-substitution-based industrialization and the modernization of agriculture, largely through external borrowing and inflationary financing. Although a relatively high rate of economic growth was achieved in the 1950s, income distribution grew much more inequitable. Particularly badly hit because of the inflationary policies were the salaried groups. The 1960 coup found therefore an easy acceptance among military officers and civilian bureaucrats for economic as well as other reasons.

Turkey's Second Try at Democracy (1961–1980)

The 1960 coup was carried out by a group of middle-rank officers who, upon assuming power, organized themselves into a revolutionary council named the "National Unity Committee" (NUC), under the chairmanship of General Cemal Gürsel, the former commander of the army. The NUC declared from the beginning its intention of making a new democratic constitution and returning power to a freely elected civilian government. In spite of the efforts by some NUC members to prolong military rule, the committee kept its promise and relinquished power in 1961 following the parliamentary elections held under the new constitution and the Electoral Law.[25]

The Constitution of 1961 was prepared by the NUC and a co-opted Representative Assembly dominated by pro-RPP bureaucrats and intellectuals, reflecting the basic political values and interests of these groups. On the one hand, they created an effective system of checks and balances to limit the power of elected assemblies. Such checks included the introduction of judicial review of the constitutionality of laws; the strengthening of the Council of State, which functions as the highest administrative court with review powers over the acts of all executive agencies; effective independence for the judiciary; the creation of a second legislative chamber (Senate of the Republic); and the granting of substantial autonomy to certain public agencies such as the universities and the Radio and Television Corporation. On the other hand, the constitution expanded civil liberties and granted extensive social rights. Thus it was hoped that the power of the elected assemblies would be balanced by judicial and other agencies that represented the values of the bureaucratic elites, while the newly expanded civil liberties would ensure the development of a free and democratic society.

The 1961 elections, however, gave a majority to the heirs of the ousted Democrats (Table 5.1). The pro-DP vote was fragmented among the Justice Party (34.8 percent), the National Party (14.0 percent), and the New Turkey Party (13.7 percent), while the Republicans obtained only 36.7 percent of the vote. Following a period of unstable coalition governments, the Justice Party (JP) gradually established itself as the principal heir to the DP. In the 1965 elections, it gained about 53 percent of the popular vote and of the National Assembly seats. The JP repeated its success in 1969, when it won an absolute majority of the Assembly seats with a somewhat reduced popular vote (46.5 percent). Thus Turkey appeared to have achieved, once again, a popularly elected stable government.

Toward the end of the 1960s, however, the Turkish political system began to experience new problems. Partly as a result of the more liberal atmosphere provided by the 1961 Constitution, extreme left- and right-wing groups appeared on the political scene. This was followed by increasing acts of political violence, especially by extremist youth groups. The crisis was aggravated by the activities of various conspiratorial groups within the military. These radical officers, frustrated by the successive electoral victories of the conservative JP, aimed at establishing a longer-term military regime ostensibly to carry out radical social reforms. In fact the military memorandum of March 12, 1971, which forced the JP government to resign, was a last-minute move by the top military commanders to forestall a radical coup.

The so-called March 12 regime did not go as far as dissolving the Parliament and assuming power directly. Instead, it strongly encouraged the formation of an "above-party" or technocratic government under a veteran RPP politician, Professor Nihat Erim. The new government was expected to deal sternly with political violence with the help of martial law, to bring about certain constitutional amendments designed to strengthen the executive, and to carry out the social reforms (especially land reform) provided for by the 1961 Constitution. The interim government accomplished its first two objectives. Political violence was effectively stamped out. The constitution was extensively revised in 1971 and 1973, with a view to not only strengthening the executive authority, but also to limiting certain civil liberties that were seen as responsible for the emergence of political extremism and violence. The interim regime failed, however, in its third objective of carrying out social reforms, not only because of the conservative majority in the Parliament, but also because of the purge of the radical officers from the military in the months following the "March 12 memorandum."

The 1971 military intervention can be characterized as a "half coup," in which the military chose to govern from behind the scenes instead of taking over directly. If one reason for the intervention was the failure of Süleyman Demirel's JP government to cope with political terrorism, a more deep-seated cause was the distrust felt toward the JP by many military officers and civilian bureaucrats. Thus, in a sense, the 1971 intervention still reflected the old cleavage between the centralist bureaucratic elite and the forces of the periphery that commanded an electoral majority.

The interim period ended with the 1973 parliamentary elections, which produced a National Assembly with no governing majority. The RPP emerged, after many years of electoral impotence, as the largest party with a third of the popular vote and 41 percent of the Assembly seats (see Table 5.1). The RPP's rise was due on the one hand to the energetic leadership of Bülent Ecevit, who became the party leader replacing the octogenarian Inönü, and on the other to the new social democratic image of the party. As the 1973 voting patterns indicate, the new image of the RPP appealed to urban lower classes. This change signified a realignment in the Turkish party system, as the old center-periphery cleavage began to be replaced by a new functional cleavage. The RPP increased its vote particularly in the former strongholds of the DP and the JP, and among those strata that up to that time loyally supported the DP and the JP.[26]

The right, on the other hand, was badly split in the 1973 elections. The JP obtained only about 30 percent of the vote (Table 5.1). The Democratic Party, a splinter group of the JP, received just under 12 percent of the vote, as did the National Salvation Party (NSP). The NSP combined its defense of Islamic moral and cultural values with a defense of the interests of small merchants, artisans, and businessmen. Another new actor in Turkish politics in the 1970s was the Nationalist Action Party (NAP). Although it won only 3.4 percent of the vote in 1973, the NAP grew in the 1970s under the leadership of ex-revolutionary Alpaslan Türkes (one of the key figures in the 1960s coup) from an insignificant party into a highly dedicated, strictly disciplined, and hierarchically organized political force to be reckoned with. The NAP's ideology combined an ardent nationalism and anticommunism with strongly interventionist economic policies, and its tactics involved the use of militia-type youth organizations seemingly implicated in right-wing terror.

The composition of the 1973 National Assembly made coalition governments inevitable. First a coalition was formed, under the premiership of Bülent Ecevit, between the social-democratic RPP and the Islamic NSP. The coalition collapsed in the fall of 1974 and was eventually replaced by a "Nationalist Front" coalition under Süleyman Demirel, with the participation of the JP, NSP, NAP, and the RRP (Republican Reliance Party, a small moderate party led by Professor Turhan Feyzioglu, a former RPP member).

The 1977 elections did not significantly change this picture, although they did strengthen the two leading parties vis-à-vis most of the minor ones. The RPP, which increased its share of the popular vote by eight points, came close to an absolute parliamentary majority. The JP also improved its share of the vote and of the Assembly seats (Table 5.1). The NSP lost about one-quarter of its votes and half of its parliamentary contingent. The Democratic Party and the Republican Reliance Party were practically eliminated. The right-wing NAP grew considerably, however, almost doubling its popular vote while increasing its small contingent of Assembly seats fivefold.

Following the 1977 elections, a Nationalist Front government was formed again under Mr. Demirel, with the participation of the JP, NSP, and NAP. In a few months, however, the Front lost its parliamentary majority as a result of the defection of some JP deputies. Consequently, Mr. Ecevit was able to form a government with the help of these dissident JP members, who were rewarded with ministerial posts in the new government. The Ecevit government lasted about twenty-two months, resigning in November 1979, when the partial elections for one-third of the Senate and five vacant National Assembly seats revealed sharp gains by the JP, which won 47.8 percent of the vote while the RPP support declined dramatically (to 29.2 percent). Consequently, Mr. Demirel formed a minority JP government with the parliamentary support of its former partners, the NSP and the NAP. This government had been in office less than one year when it was ousted by the military coup of September 12, 1980.

How can we account for the failure of Turkey's second experiment with democracy? The immediate reason behind the military intervention was the growing political violence and terrorism that, between 1975 and 1980, left more than 5,000 people killed and three times as many wounded (the equivalent of Turkish losses in the War of Independence). Acts of violence, which became particularly acute between 1978 and 1980, also included armed assaults, sabotages, kidnappings, bank robberies, occupation and destruction of workplaces, and bombings. Some forty-nine radical leftist groups were involved in left-wing terror, while right-wing terror was concentrated in the "idealist" organizations with their unofficial links to the NAP. Thus, in a sense, the pattern that had led to the military intervention of 1971 was repeated, only this time on a much larger and more alarming scale. Just as in the early 1970s, the governments of the late 1970s were unable to cope with the problem even though martial law was in effect in much of the country. Martial law under the Turkish constitutional system entails the transfer of police functions to military authorities, the restriction or complete suspension of civil liberties, and the creation of military martial law courts to try offenses associated with the causes that led to the declaration of martial law. Thus it is a constitutional, albeit highly authoritarian and restrictive, procedure. In the crisis of the late 1970s, however, even martial law could not contain the violence. One reason for this was the infiltration of the police forces by right-wing and left-wing extremists. Another was the general erosion of the authority of the state as a result of growing political polarization in the country, as will be discussed below. It should be added here that a harmful side effect of martial law is the seemingly inevitable politicization of the armed forces, or the "militarization" of political conflict, which may pave the way for full-scale military intervention. Indeed, all three military interventions in recent Turkish history were preceded by martial law regimes instituted by civilian governments.

At a deeper level the incidence of political violence reflected a growing ideological polarization in the country. The polarizing forces were the NAP, and to a much lesser extent the NSP, on the right, and many small radical groups on the left. The NSP was not involved in violence, but its use of Islamic themes helped to undermine the regime's legitimacy among those committed to the Kemalist legacy of secularism, including the military. The parliamentary arithmetics and the inability and/or unwillingness of the two major parties (the RPP and the JP) to agree on a grand coalition or a minority government arrangement gave these two minor parties an enormous bargaining—more correctly blackmailing—power, which they effectively used to obtain important ministries and to colonize them with their own partisans. In fact this seems to be crucial for the crisis of the system. An accommodation between the two major parties would have been welcomed by most of the important political groups in Turkey, including the business community, the leading trade union confederation, the press, and the military, and would have been acceptable to a majority of the JP and the RPP deputies. A government based on their joint support would probably have been strong enough to deal effectively and evenhandedly with the political violence. However, the deep personal rivalry between Demirel and Ecevit, their tendency to see problems from a narrow partisan perspective, and perhaps their failure to appreciate the real gravity of the situation made such a democratic rescue operation impossible. As the experience of many countries has shown, antisystem parties can perhaps be tolerated in opposition, but their entry into government tends to put too heavy a load on the system to be handled by democratic means.

The radical left, unlike the radical right, was not represented in the Parliament, but extreme leftist ideologies found many supporters among students, teachers, and in some sectors of the industrial working class. Just as the JP was pulled to the right by its partnership with the NAP and the NSP, the RPP was pulled to the left by the radical groups to its left. Political polarization also affected and undermined the public bureaucracy. At no time in recent Turkish history had the public agencies been so divided and politicized as in the late 1970s. Changes of government were followed by extensive purges in all ministries, involving not only the top personnel, but also many middle- or lower-rank civil servants. Partisanship became a norm in the civil service, which had retained its essentially nonpolitical character until the mid-1970s.

A related phenomenon that contributed to a decline in the legitimacy of the political system was the *immobilisme* of the governments and parliaments in much of the 1970s. The very narrow majorities in the Parliament and the heterogeneous nature of the governing coalitions (be it the Nationalist Front governments or the Ecevit governments) meant that new policies could be initiated only with great difficulty. In the context of pressing economic troubles (such as high inflation, major deficits in the international trade balance, shortages of investment and consumer goods, unemployment, etc.), and international problems (such as the Cyprus crisis and the U.S. arms embargo), the inability of governments to take courageous policy decisions aggravated the legitimacy crisis. To put it differently this lack of efficacy and effectiveness served to delegitimate the regime. Perhaps the most telling example of such governmental failure of performance was the inability of the Turkish Grand National Assembly to elect a president of the republic in 1980. The six-month-old presidential deadlock ended only with the military coup of September 12. Other examples of lesser deadlocks abounded particularly in matters of economic and foreign policy.

The 1980 Coup and the 1982 Constitution

From the moment it took over the government on September 12, 1980, the National Security Council (composed of the five highest-ranking generals in the Turkish armed forces) made it clear that it intended to eventually return power to democratically elected civilian authorities. It made it equally clear, however, by words and deeds that it did not intend a return to the status quo ante. Rather, the council aimed at a major restructuring of Turkish democracy to prevent a recurrence of the political polarization, violence, and crisis that had afflicted the country in the late 1970s, and thus to make the military's continued involvement in politics unnecessary. The new constitution, Political Parties Law, and Electoral Law prepared by the council-appointed Consultative Assembly—and made final by the council itself—reflect these objectives and concerns of the military and indicate the extent to which Turkey's new attempt at democracy is intended to be different from its earlier democratic experiments.

The constitution was submitted to a popular referendum on 7 November 1982. The extremely high rate of participation (91.27 percent) was, no doubt, partly due to the provision that those who did not participate would forfeit their right to vote in the next parliamentary elections. The constitution was approved by 91.37 percent of those who voted. The counting was honest, but the debate preceding it was extremely limited. The council limited debate only to those views expressed with the purpose of "improving the draft constitution" and banned all efforts to influence the direction of the vote. The constitution was "officially" explained to the public by President Kenan Evren in a series of speeches, and any criticism of these speeches was also banned. Another unusual feature of the constitutional referendum was its combination with the presidential elections. A "yes" vote for the constitution meant a vote for General Evren for a seven-year term as president of the republic, and no other candidates were allowed. It is generally agreed that the personal popularity of General Evren helped increase affirmative votes for the constitution rather than the other way around.

The election of General Evren as president was one of the measures designed to ensure a smooth transition from the National Security Council regime to a democratic one. Another such transitional measure was the transformation of the National Security Council into a "Presidential Council"—with only advisory powers—for a period of six years, starting from the convening of the new Grand National Assembly. Also, during a six-year period, the president had the right to veto constitutional amendments, in which case the Grand National Assembly (GNA) could override the veto only by a three-fourths majority of its full membership. Finally, the constitution provided restrictions on political activities of former political leaders. The leaders, deputy leaders, secretaries-general, and the members of the central executive committees of former political parties were not allowed to establish or to become members in political parties, nor could they be nominated for the GNA or for local government bodies for a period of ten years. A less severe ban disqualified the parliamentarians of former political parties from establishing political parties or becoming members of their central executive bodies (but not from running for and being elected to the GNA) for a period of five years. These bans were repealed by the constitutional referendum of September 6, 1987.

In addition to such transitional measures, the constitution introduces highly restrictive provisions on political activities of trade unions, associations, and cooperatives. Thus there can be no political links between such organizations and political parties, nor can they receive financial support from each other. Political parties are also banned from organizing in foreign countries (obviously, among the Turkish residents of those countries), creating women's and youth organizations, and establishing foundations. Also the 1982 Constitution transformed the office of the presidency from a largely ceremonial one, as it was under the 1961 Constitution, into a much more powerful one with effective autonomous powers. Although the political responsibility of the Council of Ministers before the GNA is maintained, the president is given important appointive powers (particularly, in regard to certain high-ranking judges) that he can exercise independently of the Council of Ministers. Also he can submit constitutional amendments to popular referenda and bring about a suit of unconstitutionality against any law passed by the GNA. The constitution did not go as far as the "French" 1958 Constitution, however, in strengthening the presidency. The system of government remained essentially parliamentary rather than presidential.

The National Security Council regime also adopted a new electoral law which retained the "d'Hondt" version of proportional representation with some important modifications. The d'Hondt formula is also known as the highest-average system. Briefly, it ensures that in a constituency no reallocation of additional seats would take place to increase proportionality. The d'Hondt system, in its classical version, slightly favors larger parties, but the modifications introduced by the new law made such effect much stronger. The most consequential novelty of the new law is a national quotient (threshold) such that political parties obtaining less than 10 percent of the total valid votes cast nationally will not be assigned any seats in the GNA. This provision is designed to prevent the excessive proliferation of political parties which, in the opinion of the council, contributed significantly to the crisis in the 1970s. The ruling council indicated on various occasions that it preferred a party system with two or three parties, which would ensure stable parliamentary majorities. Another novelty of the Electoral Law is the "constituency threshold," according to which the total number of valid votes cast in each constituency is divided by the number of seats in that constituency (which varies between two and six), and those parties or independent candidates that fail to exceed the quotient are not assigned any seats in that constituency. The combined effects of national and constituency thresholds favor larger parties.

Return to Competitive Politics and the 1983 Elections

The provisional article 4 of the Law on Political Parties gave the National Security Council the right to veto the founding members of new political parties (all former political parties had earlier been dissolved by a decree of the council). The council made use of this power in such a way that only three parties were able to complete their formation formalities before the beginning of the electoral process and, consequently, to compete in the GNA elections. Notably, two new parties that looked like credible successors to the two former major parties (namely, the True Path Party as a possible successor to the JP and the Social Democratic Party to the RPP) were thus eliminated from electoral competition, although both parties were allowed to complete their formation after the nomination process was over. Earlier, another successor party, the Grand Turkey Party, established or joined by a large number of former high-ranking JP figures, had been banned outright by the council.

As a result of such qualifications, only three parties could contest the GNA elections held on November 6, 1983. These were the Motherland Party (MP), the Populist Party (PP), and the Nationalist Democratic Party (NDP). The MP was led by Turgut Özal, an engineer and economist who occupied high technocratic positions under Demirel, including the post of undersecretary in charge of the State Planning Organization. Özal became the deputy prime minister in charge of economic affairs in the Bülent Ulusu government during the National Security Council rule. The PP was led by Necdet Calp, a former governor and undersecretary in the prime minister's office. The NDP leader, Turgut Sunalp, was a former general who served, after his retirement, as the Turkish ambassador in Canada.

The November 1983 elections resulted in a clear victory for Mr. Özal and his party (Table 5.2). The MP won 45.2 percent of the total valid votes cast and 52.9 percent of the 400 assembly seats. Although a majority of the MP votes presumably came from former JP supporters, it appears that the MP also received votes from the supporters of the former NSP, NAP, and even the RPP. The PP came out as the second largest party with 30.5 percent of the vote and 29.3 percent of the seats, which was a better result than most observers expected. The PP appears to have gained the votes of a large majority of the former RPP voters. The main loser in the elections was the NDP. Despite the high expectations of its leadership, the NDP finished a poor third with 23.3 percent of the vote and only 17.8 percent of the seats. This seems to be related to the fact that most voters perceived the NDP as an extension of military rule, or as kind of a "state party," an image that the party leadership did not try to dispel. By contrast the MP was seen as the most spontaneous or the least artificial party of all three. In this sense, the election outcome can be interpreted as reflecting the desire of a majority of Turkish voters for a rapid normalization and civilianization.

The transition process proceeded smoothly following the elections. The legal existence of the National Security Council came to an end, the council members resigned their military posts and became members of the new Presidential Council. Mr. Özal was duly invited by President Evren to form the new government, and he received a comfortable vote of confidence from

Table 5.2   Percentage of Votes in Turkish Parliamentary and Local Elections
(1983–1994)

	Elections					
Parties	1983 (parliamentary)	1984 (local)	1987 (parliamentary)	1989 (local)	1991 (parliamentary)	1994 (local)
MP	45.2 (52.9)	41.5	36.3 (64.9)	21.8	24.0 (25.6)	21.0
PP	30.5 (29.3)	8.8	—	—	—	—
NDP	23.3 (17.8)	7.1	—	—	—	—
SDPP	—	23.4	24.7 (22.0)	28.7	20.8 (19.6)	13.6
TPP	—	13.3	19.1 (13.1)	25.1	27.0 (39.6)	21.4
WP	—	4.4	7.2 (0)	9.8	16.9[a] (13.8)	19.1
NAP	—	—	2.9 (0)	4.1	—	8.0
DLP	—	—	8.5 (0)	9.0	10.8 (1.6)	8.8
RPP	—	—	—	—	—	4.6

Source: Official results of elections, State Institute of Statistics.

Note: The figures in parentheses represent the percentages of parliamentary seats won by each party.

a. In alliance with the NAP and the Reformist Democracy Party.

Abbreviations: MP, Motherland Party; PP, Populist Party; NDP, Nationalist Democracy Party; SDPP, Social Democratic Populist Party; TPP, True Path Party; WP, Welfare Party; NAP, Nationalist Action Party; DLP, Democratic Left Party; RPP, Republican People's Party.

the GNA. Thus, with the 1983 elections, civilian government had been restored and a new phase in Turkish politics had started.

Post-1983 Developments

The period between 1983 and 1991 was one of great political stability as a result of comfortable parliamentary majorities enjoyed by the MP. The local elections of March 1984, in which all parties were allowed to compete, confirmed the MP's predominant position with about 41 percent of the vote. However, two parties that had been excluded from competition in the November 1983 parliamentary elections (the Social Democratic Party and the True Path Party) emerged as the second and third strongest parties, respectively, whereas the two parties permitted to contest the same elections and perceived by the electorate as the creations of the military regime (PP and NDP) performed badly. This anomaly led to a realignment in the party system. Thus, within a relatively short period, the PP merged with the Social

Democratic Party to form the Social Democratic Populist Party (SDPP), and the NDP decided to dissolve, with its deputies joining either the MP or the True Path Party (TPP).

The 1987 parliamentary elections kept the MP in power with a reduced electoral plurality (36.3 percent) but an increased parliamentary majority (64.9 percent of the seats) because of the changes made in the electoral law that favored the strongest party. The SDPP and the TPP emerged as the second and third largest parties, respectively. No other parties gained representation in parliament because of the 10 percent national threshold (Table 5.2).

The eight-year period in which the MP was in power as a one-party government not only provided political stability but also permitted fundamental reforms in the direction of a market economy. Thus, an outward-looking, export-led growth strategy replaced the import-substitution–based growth strategy of earlier decades. Market-oriented reforms also included the liberalization of the import regime, a realistic exchange rate policy, the introduction of the value-added tax, the convertibility of Turkish currency, and many others. The result was a dramatic increase in exports of goods and services and the opening up of more and larger sectors of the Turkish economy to international competition.

The same period also attested to gradual but important moves toward the demilitarization and civilianization of the regime and to certain modest but still significant steps toward democratization. The latter included the abolition of the "crimes of thought" (mainly communist, racist, and religious organization and propaganda), the repeal of the ban (introduced by the NSC regime) on the use of the Kurdish language, and Turkey's full integration with the human rights protection machinery of the Council of Europe (namely, the recognition of the right of individual application to the Commission of Human Rights and the acceptance of the binding jurisdiction of the Court of Human Rights).

Despite these accomplishments, the MP's popularity began to ebb in the late 1980s as a result of high rates of inflation and widespread rumors of political corruption. This decline first manifested itself in the 1989 local elections, when the MP vote dropped to 21.8 percent, and finally in the 1991 parliamentary elections, in which the MP ranked second after the TPP with 24 percent of the vote (Table 5.2). Following the elections a coalition government was formed between the TPP and the SDPP under the premiership of Süleyman Demirel, the former Justice Party prime minister in the late 1970s and now leader of the TPP. In summer 1993, Ms. Tansu Çiller became prime minister when Mr. Demirel was elected president of the republic upon the death of Mr. Özal.

The record of the TPP-SDPP coalition government in its first three years was mixed. Both parties had promised sweeping constitutional and democratizing reforms in their election campaigns. Yet, the only important piece of reform legislation in this period was the amendment of the criminal procedure law to provide certain rights and guarantees for detainees. Economically, Turkey entered a severe crisis in the early months of 1994, combining high inflation, recession, increased foreign and domestic debts, a soaring trade deficit, and a decline in its international creditworthiness. The most important political consequence of the disenchantment of many voters with the coalition government, as well as with the main opposition party, MP, has been a dramatic rise in the votes of the religious (Islamic) Welfare Party (WP). In the local elections of March 27, 1994, the WP's vote rose to an unprecedented 19.1 percent. The implications of this rise for the future of Turkish democracy are discussed later.

An Appraisal

On the basis of the above historical analysis, Turkey's overall degree of success with democratic government can be described as "mixed" or "unstable." Democracy has been the rule over the past four to five decades, but it has been interrupted three times since 1960. Democratic rule is now in place, however, and there appears to be no immediate threat to its existence. A more positive evaluation is also suggested by the fact that of the three interruptions one was only partial, and the other two were of relatively short duration. Furthermore, in both cases, the military rulers declared from the beginning their intention to restore democracy. That they faithfully kept their promises is even more significant. Thus the democratic process was interrupted not by fully developed authoritarian regimes, but by interim military governments that aimed to effect a "reequilibration of democracy." The overall trend then has been *not away from but toward* democratic government.

The transition in 1983 followed the pattern of *reforma* rather than *ruptura* or even *ruptura-pactada, reforma-pactada,* as did the transitions in the periods of 1946–1950 and 1960–1961. In fact it was even a purer case of *reforma* than the earlier ones. In the 1946–1950 transition the RPP government and the DP opposition at least agreed upon a new electoral law prior to the crucial elections of 1950. In 1960–1961 the military government actively collaborated with the two opposition parties in making the new constitution and the electoral law. In the most recent transition, on the other hand, the National Security Council excluded all organized political groups from any meaningful role in the transition. The 1982 Constitution was prepared by the National Security Council itself in collaboration with an all-appointed, no-party Consultative Assembly, and the November 1983 elections were held under conditions carefully controlled by the council.

This process of transition and the new constitution as its product have been questioned by important sectors of Turkish public opinion. The MP, which was the majority party between November 1983 and October 1991, did not seem to be in favor of major constitutional revisions. Mr. Özal often expressed the view that the new institutions created by the 1982 Constitution should be given a chance to function for a time before amendments could seriously be considered. Also underlying this position was his desire to avoid an open confrontation with President Evren, who declared himself the "guarantor" of the 1982 Constitution. The only significant amendment to the constitution during the years of the MP government was adopted by a law dated May 18, 1987. The amendment essentially consisted of the change in the amendment procedure itself, making constitutional change somewhat easier, and the repeal of the ban on the political activities of former politicians. The latter was submitted to a referendum that took place on September 6, 1987, and was approved by a very small majority (50.1 percent).

Regarding the two major opposition parties (SDPP and TPP) in the 1980s, they were both in favor of radical constitutional revisions, even writing an entirely new and more democratic constitution. However, since these two parties came to power in a coalition government in 1991, no constitutional amendment has yet been accomplished with the single exception of the repeal of the state monopoly over radio and television broadcasts (1993). A good measure of democratic consolidation in Turkey would be the ability of political parties to agree on certain important constitutional amendments through a genuine process of negotiation, bargaining, and compromise.

Theoretical Analysis

What are the historical, cultural, social, economic, and political factors that favored or impeded the development of democratic government in Turkey? Since Turkey is a case of mixed success, it stands to reason that the following list is also a mixed one.

Political Culture

Two important features characterized the Ottoman political culture. One was the predominance of status-based values rather than market-derived values.[27] This was the outcome of the "bureaucratic" nature of the Ottoman Empire, which was described above. Briefly stated, the fundamental relationship under Ottoman rule between economic power and political power was essentially the reverse of the European historical experience: instead of economic power (i.e., ownership of the means of production) leading to political power (i.e., high office in the state bureaucracy), political power provided access to material wealth. However, the wealth thus accumulated could not be converted into more permanent economic assets because it was liable to confiscation by the state. Despite the growth of a substantial commercial and industrial middle class under the republic and especially in the last forty years, such status-based values still persist. The impact of this historical-cultural legacy on the development of democratic government in Turkey has been, on the whole, negative, since the predominance of status-derived values contributes to the strengthening of an all-powerful centralized state and hinders the development of a "civil society."

Another feature of the Ottoman cultural legacy has been the dichotomy resulting from the cultural division in Ottoman society between the palace (great) culture and the local or provincial (little) cultures.[28] They represented two very distinct ways of life, with different operational codes, different symbols (state versus village and tribe), different languages (highly literary and stylistic Ottoman versus simple spoken Turkish), different occupations (statecraft versus farming and artisanship), different types of settlement (urban versus rural), different literary and artistic traditions (*divan* literature and court music versus folk literature and music), and sometimes different versions of Islam (highly legalistic orthodox Islam versus often heterodox folk Islam). The nineteenth-century reforms and the Westernization movement did not eliminate, but perhaps further exacerbated, this cultural dualism by making the elite culture even more alien and inaccessible to the masses. Linguistic differences even among the Muslim subjects of the empire further contributed to this cultural fragmentation. Finally, the *millet* system that gave the ecclesiastical authorities of non-Muslim communities substantial control over their communal affairs without, however, granting them participatory rights meant that these communities maintained and developed their own cultures quite autonomously from the central or great culture. All this led to a low level of social and cultural integration of the Ottoman society.

To be sure, the republic made important strides in bridging the gap between elite and mass cultures. In particular, the last five decades of multiparty politics helped to integrate the mass electorate into national political life. "The distributive and the redistributive functions of government received increasing emphasis, while the prevalence of the extractive function began to decline. Second, as an outcome of the first point, the citizens became more interested in national political life and came to identify themselves more closely with national political institutions of which political parties were the main example."[29] Still, the lingering elitist attitudes within sectors of the centralist bureaucratic elite have produced tensions in the political system and remain dysfunctional for the development of democratic government.[30]

There are other features of the Ottoman-Turkish political culture that are also incongruent with a democratic political system. It has been argued, for example, that "there is an element in Turkish political culture to which the notion of opposition is deeply repugnant." Turks have shown a predilection for organic theories of the state and society, and solidarist doctrines found easy acceptance among the Young Turk and Kemalist elites. The

Kemalist notion of "populism" meant a rejection of class conflict and a commitment to establish a "harmony of interests" through paternalistic government policies. This *"gemeinschaft* outlook," present in both elite and mass cultures, finds perhaps its most poignant political expression in the excessive "fear of a national split." Indeed, one of the most frequent accusations party leaders hurl at each other is "splitting the nation."[31] Thus it appears that the notion of a loyal and legitimate opposition has not been fully institutionalized at the cultural level. The line separating opposition from treason is still rather thin compared to older and more stable democracies. The tendency to see politics in absolutist terms also explains the low capacity of political leaders for compromise and accommodation. Whether such low tolerance for opposition is compatible in the long run with the institutionalization of liberal democracy is open to question.

A related tendency is the low tolerance shown for individual deviance and heterodoxy within groups. In other words Turkish political culture attributes primacy not to the individual but to the collectivity, be it the nation, the state, or one of its subunits.[32] Individuality and deviance tend to be punished, conformity and orthodoxy rewarded in bureaucratic agencies, political parties, and even voluntary associations. Finally, most social institutions (families, schools, trade unions, local communities) display authoritarian patterns in their authority relations. This tends to create incongruences with the democratic authority patterns in the governmental sphere and to undermine stable democracy.[33]

On the more positive side, however, there seems to be a widespread consensus that the legitimacy of government derives from a popular mandate obtained in free, competitive elections. A democratic system is seen as the natural culmination of a century-old process of modernization and especially of the Kemalist reforms, the purpose of which was to create a Western type of secular, republican, modern state. In addition to this long-standing elite commitment to democracy, the peasants and the urban lower classes have come to see competitive elections as a powerful means to increase socioeconomic equality and to promote their material interests. A survey among some Istanbul squatters demonstrated, for example, that a substantial majority of them believed in the importance of voting and found political parties useful especially as channels of communication with government.[34] This attitude reflects a realization that a noncompetitive system would be less responsive to their group demands. Although there was a great deal of public anxiety over increasing political polarization and violence in the late 1970s, a majority of Turkish voters do not seem to hold the democratic system responsible for the crisis. Furthermore, in spite of such polarization, a centrist political orientation has remained strong among Turkish voters.[35] While few people would like to go back to the circumstances that prevailed before the 1980 coup, there does not seem to be broad popular support for a prolonged authoritarian solution.

Historical Development

Certain historical factors favor the development of democratic government in Turkey. As the first part of this chapter demonstrates, the first movements toward representative and constitutional government started more than a century ago. Even if we discount the brief periods of democratic government under the Ottoman Empire and the early republic, the present competitive political system has been in existence for almost fifty years with relatively short interruptions. A generation born in the multiparty period and socialized into democratic values has already reached positions of authority in governmental as well as non-governmental spheres. Following Huntington we may argue that such longevity, or "chronological age," has helped to institutionalize democratic organizations and procedures.[36] That Turkey did not have a colonial past, unlike most of the Third World countries, is also a favorable historical factor for democratic development. Democratic institutions were not imposed from outside, but are seen as a natural outgrowth of internal political processes, which tends to increase their legitimacy in the eyes of the elites and the masses.

One may argue that some sequences of political development favor the emergence of democratic institutions more than the others. It has been posited, for example, that the optimum sequence is to establish national unity (identity) first, then central government authority, and then political equality and participation.[37] Turkish political development followed this optimum course. Simultaneously with the creation of the Turkish republic in place of the multinational Ottoman Empire, the question of identity was solved in favor of a Turkish national identity. The already highly developed central governmental institutions of the Ottoman state were further strengthened under the republic and penetrated more deeply into the society. The expansion of political participation took place a generation later in the mid-1940s, and proceeded within the already existing institutional framework of elections, legislatures, and parties.

Class Structure

The distribution of wealth and income appears to be highly unequal in Turkey. It is markedly so between the agricultural and nonagricultural sectors, within each of these sectors, between cities and rural settlements, and among geographic regions. A substantial proportion of the Turkish population has been, and remains, in a condition of low-end poverty. A study estimated that in 1973, 38 percent of all Turkish households were below the subsistence level. Ownership of land is also highly unequal. Another 1973 study found that 22 percent of rural households were landless. About 42 percent of all rural households own very little land or no land at all, and the land owned by this 42 percent makes up less than 3 percent of total privately owned land. Conversely, households with 1,000 or more acres of land, constituting only 0.12 percent of all rural households, own 5.27 percent of total privately owned land. Land distribution is particularly unequal in the eastern and southeastern regions, which display markedly feudal features.[38] With regard to overall income inequality, the general impression is that it further deteriorated in the late 1970s and the 1980s, especially as a result of high rates of inflation. Nevertheless, a 1987 survey carried out by the Turkish State Institute of Statistics showed that the share of the highest 20-percent income group in the total income declined in comparison to the studies done by the State Planning Organization in 1963 and 1973 (share of the highest quintile was 57 percent in 1963, 56.5 percent in 1973, and 49.94 percent in 1987). Consequently, an improvement is observed in the Gini coefficient (0.55 in 1963, 0.51 in 1973, and 0.43 in 1987). Since these studies used different methodologies, however, the results are not readily comparable.[39]

On the more positive side one may cite the existence of a rather substantial educated urban middle class of entrepreneurs, professionals, and bureaucrats, as well as a large group of middle-sized farmers. Under the liberal labor legislation that followed the 1961 Constitution, the number of unionized workers rose rapidly from less than 300,000 in 1963 to over 2.2 million in 1977. Thus the percentage of unionized workers reached 14.8 percent of the total economically active population and 39.8 percent of all wage earners.[40] Other alleviating factors ("dampening mechanisms") included the relatively high rate of economic growth (see below) and the availability of "exit" possibilities. Apart from more than a million Turkish workers (over 2 million together with their dependents) who have emigrated to Western Europe and to a much lesser extent to Middle Eastern countries, mass rural-to-urban migration helps to ease distributional problems in rural areas and reduces the propensity to resort to the "voice" option, that is, corrective political action.[41] Also contributing to the general lack of effective collective action aimed at income redistribution in rural areas are the strong in-group feelings and the absence of class-based politics among Turkish peasants who still compose roughly half the labor force. In some of the least developed regions (e.g., the east and the southeast), where land and income inequality is greatest and redistributive action is most needed, the low level of social mobilization and the strength of patron-client relationships tend to make peasant political participation more mobilized and deferential than autonomous and instrumental. In some areas (e.g., central Turkey), relative equality of landownership together with overall poverty also works against emergence of class cleavages among peasants by producing a "corporate village" pattern. This may explain why the social democratic RPP, which has based its appeal on the promise of a more egalitarian income distribution and has greatly increased its urban strength between 1969 and 1977, has not been able to achieve nearly the same degree of success in rural areas.[42]

National Structure (Ethnic and Religious Cleavages)

The breakup of the Ottoman Empire at the end of World War I made the present-day Turkey an ethnically, linguistically, and religiously much more homogeneous country than its predecessor. Over 99 percent of its population profess Islam; an estimated 15 percent belong to the Alevi (Shiite) sect; the rest are Sunnis. The Alevis are concentrated in the east central region and have tended to support the RPP. The Unity Party, formed in 1968 to represent the Alevis, has not fared well electorally. Its vote declined steadily from 2.8 percent in 1969, to 1.1 percent in 1973, and 0.4 percent in 1977. In the atmosphere of political polarization in the late 1970s, this sectarian cleavage led to violent clashes in several localities, the worst of which was the Kahramanmaras incident in which about 100 people lost their lives.

The only large linguistic minority is the Kurdish-speaking minority (again an estimated 10 percent to 15 percent). Although Kurds constitute a majority of the population in many eastern and southeastern provinces, a majority of Turkey's Kurdish-speaking population lives in western regions of the country, especially in the big cities, and is fairly well integrated into Turkish society. Since the late 1970s, a separatist guerrilla movement, Kurdistan Workers' Party (the Turkish acronym is PKK) has emerged in the southeastern region. Effectively suppressed during the NSC regime, the PKK became active again in the mid-1980s and intensified its terrorist attacks against the security forces as well as pro-government Kurds. With regard to Kurdish participation in political life, until fairly recently no ethnic-based political party specifically represented the interests of the Kurdish-speaking population. However, Kurds were active in all political parties and were well represented in Parliament. This pattern started to change in the late 1980s when for the first time an ethnic-based political party (Party of People's Labor or HEP in Turkish) was formed. However, the Turkish constitution and the Political Parties Law do not permit ethnic-based parties; consequently, the HEP was declared unconstitutional by the Constitutional Court. The HEP was immediately replaced by another Kurdish party, the DEP (Democracy Party), which was also declared unconstitutional in summer 1994.

In Turkey, sectarian and linguistic cleavages do not coincide and mutually reinforce each other, since most of the Alevis are Turkish speakers and a large majority of Kurdish speakers are Sunnis. Furthermore, neither group coincides with class cleavages, except that the eastern regions are generally much poorer than the rest of the country.

State Structure and Strength

One of the principal legacies of the Ottoman Empire is the strong and centralized state authority. The political center composed of the sultan and his military and civilian bureaucrats sought to eliminate all rival centers of power. The resulting situation has been referred to as the "absence of civil society," which means the weakness or absence of corporate, autonomous, intermediary social structures. The number of voluntary associations in Turkey rose tremendously in the multiparty era from a mere 802 in 1946 to 37,806 in 1968.[43] Yet organizational autonomy and the level of organizational participation in such associations are still much lower than in Western European and North American democracies. The relative ease with which interim military regimes abolished parties, restricted union rights, co-opted or neutralized professional associations, and curtailed the autonomy of universities testifies to the weakness of corporate structures.

The weakness of civil society is also evident in the weakness of local governments. The vast territories of the Ottoman Empire were ruled not by local bodies, but by centrally appointed governors. The first semielected, local administrative councils came into being, as we have already seen, only in the second half of the nineteenth century. As for the cities, the Ottoman state had no tradition of independent, autonomous municipalities. Nor did the republic attempt to change this centralized system. Although a law passed in 1930 enabled local communities to establish municipal governments, the whole system of local administration remained highly centralized. Local governments, especially municipalities, gained some vitality in the multiparty era. Nevertheless, their autonomous powers have been very limited, central control over their activities (called "administrative tutelage") exceedingly strict, and their financial resources totally inadequate. In this sense both provincial administrations and municipalities have had to depend very heavily on the central government.[44]

Historically the state has also played a dominant role in the economy. This Ottoman legacy was further reinforced under the republic when the Kemalist regime initiated a policy of economic interventionism (statism) in the 1930s. Statism meant the direct entry of the state into the fields of production and distribution. Public economic enterprises started to be created in those years and grew rapidly. Despite the greater emphasis on the private sector in recent decades, public enterprises still produce about one-third of the total output in the manufacturing industry. In 1990, 32.1 percent of the total value added in manufacturing was contributed by public economic enterprises and 67.9 percent by the private sector.[45] Under both the Ottoman state and the early republic, private accumulation of wealth depended, in large measure, on position in or access to the state.

This combination of factors, namely the absence of powerful, economically dominant interests able to capture the state and use it to serve their own purposes, and the weakness or absence of corporate intermediary structures, had important consequences for subsequent modernization. First, it led to what is known as the "autonomy of the state," meaning that the state apparatus is not the captive or the handmaiden of any particular social class, but possesses sufficient autonomy to make decisions that can change, eliminate, or create class relationships. This autonomous state, unhampered by established class interests and strong corporate structures, has a high capacity to accumulate and expand political power and to use it for the economic and social modernization of society. The implications for the development of democratic government are not, however, nearly as positive. As has been argued above, an autonomous, bureaucratic state is much less likely to develop democratic political institutions than a post-feudal society in which feudalism and the system of representation of estates left a legacy of autonomous groups with corporate identity and rights.

The nature and autonomy of the state in Turkey also means that the costs of being out of power are extremely high. Because of the high degree of governmental centralization and the large role of the Turkish state in the economy, "those in government have access, directly or indirectly, to an immense amount of resources in relation to the resource base of society, which they can distribute."[46] Conversely, a party that is out of power tends to get weakened since it does not have access to political patronage resources.

The Turkish state, strong and centralized as it is, has generally been effective in maintaining public order. When it was faced with widespread terrorism and violence as in the late 1970s, however, it had to turn to the army by declaring martial law. This may be related to the fact that police forces, being within the direct jurisdiction of the Ministry of Interior, are more susceptible to political influences and, sometimes, even to infiltration by extremist groups, as was the case in the late 1970s. Especially in a politically charged atmosphere, therefore, police action is not considered as impartial and as legitimate by the public as military action.

Indeed the Turkish armed forces are broadly representative of the society as a whole. They are not dominated or controlled by any particular social group or political force. They are strongly committed to the legacy of Atatürk and to a modern, national, secular, republican state. More so than in many Latin American countries, they also have been committed to democratic principles, as attested by their voluntary and relatively rapid relinquishment of power to freely elected civilian authorities after each intervention. They display, however, certain ambivalent attitudes toward democracy, characteristic of the military in other developing nations. In the elitist tradition described above, they tend to see themselves as the true guardians of the national interest, as opposed to "partial" interests represented by political parties. They also consider themselves the protectors of national unity that, in their opinion, is often endangered by the divisive actions of political parties. These attitudes, which signify a deep distrust of parties and politicians, are clearly reflected in those provisions of the 1982 Constitution aiming to limit the power of political parties. Similarly, the constitution's numerous restrictions on trade unions and voluntary associations suggest that the military's conception of democracy is more plebiscitary than participatory. In short the military, reflecting the larger society's somewhat ambivalent values toward democracy, seem to share both a belief in its general appropriateness and desirability for Turkey, and some of the antiliberal, antideviationist, intolerant attitudes embedded in the Turkish political culture.

Political Structure

Some aspects of the political structure in Turkey have been positive in their implications for democracy but others have been negative. On the positive side the major political parties have been moderate and non-ideological. Despite the polarization in the late 1970s, the ideological and social distance between the two major parties has not been great. Major political parties have not sponsored or condoned acts of political violence, nor have they called for military intervention.

Extremist parties, such as the NAP and NSP, have not had a significant electoral following. However, those parties played an important role in the 1970s because of the peculiar parliamentary arithmetic that resulted from the system of proportional representation. Although there were only four significant parties in the 1977 National Assembly, the system displayed the functional properties of extreme multipartism. Instead of the centripetal drive of moderate multipartism, the basic drive of the system seemed to be in a centrifugal direction. Standards of "fair competition" fell significantly and there was a corresponding increase in the "politics of outbidding."[47]

No major interest group is excluded from representation in the political system through a party or party faction. The constitution states, however, that the "constitutions and programs of political parties shall not be incompatible with the territorial and national integrity of the state, human rights, national sovereignty, and the principles of a democratic and secular Republic." To this is added a more specific provision banning parties that aim at establishing the sovereignty of a particular class or group, or a dictatorship of any sort. Thus the constitution excludes from political competition communist fascist, religious, and separatist parties. Political parties that violate these bans shall be closed by the Constitutional Court. Trade unions are also prohibited from establishing political linkages with political parties. They cannot engage in political activities, nor can they support or receive support from political parties.

A strong and independent judiciary has developed, including a Constitutional Court with full powers to declare an act of parliament unconstitutional. The 1961 Constitution took special care to safeguard the judiciary vis-à-vis the legislature and the executive. The 1982 Constitution broadly maintained the same principle with some, relatively minor, modifications. Security of tenure for judges and public prosecutors has been recognized by the 1982 Constitution in identical terms as those of its predecessor, according to which "judges and public prosecutors shall not be dismissed or retired before the age prescribed by the Constitution; nor shall they be deprived of their salaries, allowances, or other personal rights, even as a result of the abolition of a court or a post." Personnel matters for judges and public prosecutors, such as appointments, promotions, transfers, and disciplinary actions are within the exclusive jurisdiction of the Supreme Council of Judges and Public Prosecutors, itself composed primarily of judges nominated by the two high courts in the country and appointed by the president of the republic.

A vigorously free and independent press strongly committed to democratic principles has developed. The press has, in general, maintained its independent attitude and commitment to democracy even in times of interim military governments, although martial law entailed severe restrictions on the freedom of the press. With the transition to a civilian regime in November 1983 and the subsequent lifting of martial law, the press has strongly reasserted itself. It has shown willingness to publicize domestic and foreign criticism of human rights practices.

On the basis of the preceding observations we may conclude that, of our set of variables, that which pertains to political structures is probably the most favorable one to democratic government in Turkey.

Political Leadership

Turkish political leaders have, in general, been committed to the democratic process, and have denounced acts of violence and disloyalty against it. On the other hand, as our historical analysis has demonstrated, they have not, as a rule, shown a high capacity for accommodation and compromise in containing political conflict and managing political crises and strains. On the contrary their failure to do so seems directly responsible for both the 1960 and 1980 military interventions. In 1960, the deterioration of relations between the government and the opposition parties led to widespread public unrest that in turn triggered the coup. Similarly, prior to the 1980 intervention, a coalition government based on the two major parties, or at least some broad understanding between them, would probably have satisfied the military and held off their intervention. This unwillingness to compromise seems partly a function of the political cultural characteristics and partly of the high costs of being out of power in Turkey.

Development Performance

The rate of economic growth in Turkey has been comparatively high, if somewhat uneven. In the 1950s and the 1960s the average annual rate of real GNP growth was about 7 percent. Turkey was hard-hit, however, by the oil shock in 1974 and the subsequent "worldwide recession, concomitant with deteriorating terms of trade and continuation of trade policies geared more toward import substitution than export encouragement, including an exchange rate regime that discouraged inflows of capital and workers' remittances."[48] Thus the GDP growth rate fell to 2.4 percent in 1978, and declined further to 0.9 percent in 1979, and 0.8 percent in 1980. Moreover, the rate of inflation reached 70 percent in 1979 and above 100 percent in 1980. With the introduction of comprehensive reform measures in January 1980, whose chief architect was Turgut Özal (then the director of the State Planning Organization), economic growth has resumed at a modest rate of about 5 percent. These new policies aimed at greater reliance upon market forces and an easing of governmental interventions in the economy. They continued to be pursued by the military regime of 1980–1983, under which Özal was made the deputy prime minister in charge of economic affairs, and subsequently from November 1983 when he came to power as the head of his new Motherland Party.

The relatively high rate of economic growth since the transition to competitive politics has been one of the "dampening mechanisms" that discouraged the political participation of low-income strata. It seems, however, that the benefits of growth have been quite unevenly distributed across regions, economic sectors, and social classes. Nevertheless, it is not the case that the rich got richer and the poor got poorer; rather they both got richer, but the rich got richer at a faster rate.[49] The implications for the future of democracy of this economic development performance will be discussed in the next section.

International Factors

Turkey's close alliance with the West since the end of World War II has generally, but only indirectly, supported democratic developments in the country. Turkey has become a member of NATO and of the Council of Europe, and an associate member of the European Community. These relations have meant linkages between Turkish political parties, parliaments, trade unions, business and professional associations, armed forces, and their Western European and North American counterparts. Over two million Turks living in Western Europe (a very large majority in the Federal Republic of Germany) provide another, and vitally important, link between Turkey and the West.

While all these relations and linkages provide stimuli for democratic development, their effects have been far from decisive. Turks are proud and nationalistic people who do not like to be dictated to from abroad. A good example of this is that criticisms by the European Community, or the Council of Europe, or individual Western European governments of certain undemocratic practices during and after military rule usually create unfavorable reactions, even among those Turks who may be similarly critical of the same practices. The point is often made that Turkey will remain a democracy not to please its European allies, but because its people believe that this is the most appropriate form of government for their country. Nevertheless, the thought lingers no doubt in the minds of many Turkish leaders that an authoritarian Turkey, isolated and excluded from the club of European democracies, will probably experience greater difficulties in its international relations. The breakdown of authoritarian regimes in Greece, Portugal, and Spain in the 1970s and the democratization of Eastern Europe following the collapse of communist dictatorships make the position of a pro-Western but authoritarian European country extremely lonely and uneasy.

Future Prospects and Policy Implications

Policies Promoting the Growth of Civil Society

In view of the positive and negative factors discussed above, what kinds of policies and political/economic developments would be most likely to support, nurture, and sustain democratic government? If one of the most serious obstacles to democratic development in Turkey is the historical legacy of an exceedingly centralized, overpowering state and the concomitant weakness of civil society, then policies that aim at establishing a healthier balance between the state and the society will clearly be functional for democratic development. One obvious area where the state's role can, and probably should, be reduced is the economy. The market-oriented economic policies of Mr. Özal were important steps in that direction. Greater reliance on market mechanisms, greater emphasis on expanding exports instead of an inward-turned, import-substitution economic strategy, realistic exchange rates, and a sharp reduction in bureaucratic controls over private economic activities were the main ingredients of the new economic policy. Privatization as a corollary of these pro-market policies has received much attention and engendered extensive public debate in recent years. However, despite the fact that most political parties favor privatization in principle, relatively little has been achieved thus far.

Another set of policies promoting the growth of civil society would be the strengthening of local governments. One recent positive development in this regard has been the substantial increase in their revenues after 1980 through the allocation of a greater share of public funds. If local governments are seen with less suspicion by the central government and given greater powers and responsibilities, they will no doubt play an important role in socializing people into democratic values. Such a development will also mean a more effective power sharing between the central and local bodies and, consequently, an effective check on the power of the central government. Finally, it will lower the stakes of political competition, since an opposition party that controls important municipalities will be able to render some patronage services to its constituents and thus maintain a certain level of political influence.

A third group of policies with the same overall effect would be those that would promote the growth of voluntary associations. As I pointed out earlier, the 1982 Constitution introduced highly restrictive provisions on the political activities of voluntary associations as a reaction against the excessive politicization of many such associations and professional organizations in the 1970s. Despite such restrictions, however, voluntary associations continued to flourish following the retransition to democracy. Promoting civil society and its institutions became an important item in the political discourse of the 1980s and the 1990s.

These institutions of civil society include trade unions, associations, foundations, professional organizations, informal citizens' groups, discussion platforms, and the like. Although the constitution and the relevant laws prohibit political activity by such institutions, these restrictions are no longer strictly implemented, and many of these institutions are deeply engaged in political debate. The state monopoly on radio and television broadcasts was broken first on a de facto basis and then also legally by means of a constitutional amendment in 1993. Private radio and television networks have provided much diversity and vitality in political debates.

Policies Promoting Governmental Stability and Efficiency

It has been pointed out that the crisis of democracy in the late 1970s was due, at least in some measure, to the fragmentation of the party system and to the resulting fact that parliamentary balance was held by small antisystem parties. To this was added the incapacity of the political system to initiate new policies to meet new challenges, because of the narrow and heterogeneous governmental majorities in Parliament. Two sets of institutional measures taken by the military regime of 1980–1983 may prove to be helpful in preventing the recurrence of a similar situation. One is the change in the electoral system. The adoption of a 10-percent national threshold for representation in the Grand National Assembly, together with various other features of the electoral system that favor major parties, make it difficult for more than three significant parties to be represented in Parliament. One would have expected that such an electoral system would have forced political parties to coalesce around a few major ideological tendencies. Yet, paradoxically, the Turkish party system today is more fragmented than ever before. The center-right, which was represented by the JP in the 1960s and the 1970s, is now divided between the TPP and the MP. Similarly, the center-left, which used to be represented by the RPP, is now divided among three parties: the SDPP, the Democratic Left party of Bülent Ecevit, and the RPP (a reincarnation of the old RPP under the leadership of Deniz Baykal). The religious Welfare Party has also emerged as a significant electoral force.

The 1982 Constitution has also taken certain measures to increase governmental stability by strengthening the Council of Ministers vis-à-vis the Assembly. For example, while the vote of confidence taken following the formation of a new Council of Ministers does not require more than an ordinary majority, a vote of censure requires an absolute majority of the full membership of the Assembly. Furthermore, in a vote of confidence only negative (meaning no confidence) votes are counted (Articles 99 and 111).

A much more consequential novelty of the constitution designed to increase governmental stability concerns the scope of the power of dissolution. The 1961 Constitution permitted the executive branch to call new elections for the National Assembly only under very exceptional circumstances. This limited right of dissolution did not offer any help in cases of protracted government crisis when no majority coalition could be formed. The 1982 Constitution empowers the president to call new elections when a government cannot be formed within forty-five days either at the beginning of a new legislative assembly or after the resignation of a government. The constitution has also adopted a new procedure in the selection of the president of the republic to prevent the kind of deadlock witnessed in 1980.[50]

Finally, the broadening under the 1982 Constitution of the lawmaking powers of the executive is designed to increase the efficiency of government. This power was given to the Council of Ministers for the first time by the 1971 amendment of the constitution, under which the Council of Ministers could issue ordinances or decrees that could amend existing laws. The 1982 Constitution further expanded the power to issue such ordinances. It also empowers the executive to issue a special kind of law-amending ordinance during periods of martial law or state of emergency. They differ from ordinary ordinances in that they do not require a prior enabling act and, even more important, they are outside the scope of review by the Constitutional Court. Both ordinary and emergency ordinances are subject, however, to review by the assembly.

Policies Promoting Economic Growth and Equity

It has already been mentioned that the relatively high rate of economic growth in the 1950s and the 1960s has been one of the positive factors supporting democratic development. However, the dominant economic development strategy of the era presents a close resemblance to the one pursued by some relatively developed Latin American countries, notably Brazil and Argentina, during the populist semi-authoritarian regimes of Vargas and Peron, with the same negative implications for democracy. In both cases, economic development strategies were based more on import substitution (of essentially consumer goods) than on export encouragement. One reason given for the emergence of military-bureaucratic-technocratic regimes in these countries in the 1960s and the 1970s is the economic difficulties and bottlenecks associated with this kind of development strategy (industrial dependence on imported inputs and government protection; inability to export, leading to foreign exchange shortages, and then to unemployment and economic stagnation).

As the economic pie got smaller, political conflict became more virulent, the populist coalition broke down, and the middle classes came to see the demands of the popular sector as excessive. The resultant military-technocratic regimes tended to restrict political participation by suppressing or deactivating the urban popular sector, and to follow growth policies that increased socioeconomic inequality.[51]

Thus similarities between the Turkish case on the one hand, and the Argentine and the Brazilian ones on the other are unmistakable, with the exception that the military regime was of much shorter duration in Turkey. The most appropriate policy to avoid a repetition of this vicious circle seems to be an economic growth strategy encouraging exports and export-oriented, internationally competitive industries, combined with an effort to increase equity. While Mr. Özal's economic policies have been highly successful on the first front, they have not been marked by a strong concern for equity. Furthermore, during the 1980s and early 1990s foreign and domestic debts increased sharply, the public deficit grew, high rates of inflation became chronic, and very little was accomplished by way of privatization. These difficulties have become even more menacing under the TPP-SDPP coalition government, thus forcing Turkey once again to adopt severe stabilization programs in spring 1994.

Conclusion

Although still a developing country by most socioeconomic standards, Turkey has nevertheless been able to maintain a democratic political system since approximately the end of World War II. This is explained mainly by the strong elite commitment to democracy and the relatively favorable political structural factors such as the dominance of two major, well-organized, and essentially nonideological political parties. However, the fragmentation in the party system, already apparent in the 1970s, became even more acute in the late 1980s and the early 1990s. In the most recent local elections in March 1994, no party received more than 21 percent of the vote (Table 5.2). Such fragmentation does not augur well for government stability.

Even more disquieting than fragmentation is the growing ideological polarization (also apparent in the 1970s). In the local elections of March 1994, the combined vote of two center-right parties (the TPP and the MP) fell to 42 percent, whereas the combined vote for three center-left parties (the SDPP, the DLP, and the RPP) fell to 27 percent, an all-time low for the center-right and center-left tendencies. As a corollary, the two antisystem parties, the WP and the NAP, increased their combined vote to 27.1 percent. The WP represents an Islamic political philosophy, and it is doubtful whether its position can be reconciled with the secularist nature of Turkish democracy. The NAP, although considerably more moderate than was the case in the 1970s, still represents an ultra-nationalist position that is somewhat outside the mainstream of Turkish politics. Furthermore, the present economic crisis and the constant bickering among the moderate parties seem to work in favor of these two ideological parties.

Finally, the failure to resolve the Kurdish issue by peaceful, democratic means adds to the fragility of Turkish democracy. The military campaign against the PKK terrorists inevitably entails hardships for the local civilian population, as well as violations of human rights, which further polarizes the situation in southeastern Turkey. The constitutional ban on ethnic parties precludes the emergence of moderate, democratic Kurdish groups and parties. Human rights violations strain Turkey's relations with the West, including the European Union, the Council of Europe, and the United States. Western criticism of Turkey's behavior, in turn, creates an anti-Western backlash, which again adds to the popularity of the WP and the NAP. The increasing importance of religious and ethnic issues raises a number of difficult constitutional problems Turkish democracy has not previously confronted, such as Islam versus secularism, nation-state versus minority rights, and centralization versus decentralization. A full consolidation of Turkish democracy depends upon the peaceful resolution of these issues.

Notes

1. See Cyril E. Black and Carl Brown, eds., *Modernization in the Middle East: The Ottoman Empire and Its Afro-Asian Successors* (Princeton: Darwin Press, 1992).

2. For the differences between bureaucratic and feudal states, and the implications for their developments, see Samuel P. Huntington, *Political Order in Changing Societies* (New Haven and London: Yale University Press, 1968), ch. 3.

3. Halil Inalcik, "The Nature of Traditional Society: Turkey," in Robert E. Ward and Dankwart A. Rustow, eds., *Political Modernization in Japan and Turkey* (Princeton: Princeton University Press, 1964), p. 44. The following analysis borrows extensively from my (Özbudun) *Social Change and Political Participation in Turkey* (Princeton: Princeton University Press, 1976), pp. 25–29.

4. Niyazi Berkes, *Türkiye'de Cagdaslasma [The Development of Secularism in Turkey]* (Ankara: Bilgi Yayinevi, 1973), pp. 27–28.

5. H. A. R. Gibb and Harold Bowen, *Islamic Society and the West,* vol. 1, part 1 (London: Oxford University Press, 1950), p. 52.

6. Serif Mardin, "Power, Civil Society and Culture in the Ottoman Empire," *Comparative Studies in Society and History* 2 (June 1969): passim; Clement Henry Moore, "Authoritarian Politics in Unincorporated Society: The Case of Nasser's Egypt," *Comparative Politics* 6 (January 1974): pp. 204–208.

7. Serif Mardin, "Historical Determinants of Social Stratification: Social Class and

Class Consciousness in Turkey," A. Ü. *Siyasal Bilgiler Fakültesi Dergisi* 22 (Aralik 1967): p. 127.

8. Stanford J. Shaw, "The Central Legislative Councils in the Nineteenth Century Ottoman Reform Movement Before 1876," *International Journal of Middle East Studies* 1 (January 1970): pp. 57–62.

9. Roderic H. Davison, *Reform in the Ottoman Empire, 1856–1876* (Princeton: Princeton University Press, 1963), pp. 147–149, 167.

10. Robert Devereux, *The First Ottoman Constitutional Period: A Study of the Midhat Constitution and Parliament* (Baltimore: Johns Hopkins University Press, 1963), pp. 126, 148.

11. Engin Deniz Akarli, "The State as a Socio-Cultural Phenomenon and Political Participation in Turkey," in Akarli and Gabriel Ben-Dor, eds., *Political Participation in Turkey: Historical Background and Present Problems* (Istanbul: Bogaziçi University Publications, 1975), p. 139. See also, Serif Mardin, "Center-Periphery Relations: A Key to Turkish Politics?" *Daedalus* 102, no. 1 (Winter 1973): pp. 169–190; Metin Heper, "Center and Periphery in the Ottoman Empire, with Special Reference to the Nineteenth Century," *International Political Science Review* 1, no. 1 (1980): pp. 81–104.

12. Akarli, "The State as a Socio-Cultural Phenomenon," p. 143.

13. Kemal H. Karpat, "The Transformation of the Ottoman State, 1789–1908," *International Journal of Middle East Studies* 3 (July 1972): pp. 263, 268–270.

14. Feroz Ahmad, *The Young Turks: The Committee of Union and Progress in Turkish Politics, 1908–1914* (Oxford: Clarendon Press, 1969), pp. 143–144.

15. Ibid., pp. 161–162.

16. Özbudun, *Social Change and Political Participation,* pp. 38–41.

17. Frederick W. Frey, *The Turkish Political Elite* (Cambridge, Mass.: M.I.T. Press, 1965), p. 326.

18. For details, see my "Turkey," in Myron Weiner and Ergun Özbudun, eds., *Competitive Elections in Developing Countries* (Durham, N.C.: Duke University Press, 1987), pp. 328–368.

19. Ilter Turan, "Stages of Political Development in the Turkish Republic" in Ergun Özbudun, ed., *Perspectives on Democracy in Turkey* (Ankara: Turkish Political Science Assoc., 1988), pp. 64–68.

20. Nur Yalman argues, for example, that the dispute between rationalism and tradition "happens to be especially bitter in Turkey. It is rare to see such virulent opposition to a country's own traditions and history." "Islamic Reform and the Mystic Tradition in Eastern Turkey," *Archive européene de sociologie* 10 (1969): p. 45.

21. Juan J. Linz, "The Transition from Authoritarian Regimes to Democratic Political Systems and the Problems of Consolidation of Political Democracy" (Paper presented to the IPSA Round Table, Tokyo, March 29 to April 1, 1982), pp. 23–41.

22. For details, see my "Transition from Authoritarianism to Democracy in Turkey, 1945–1950" (Paper presented to the IPSA World Congress, Paris, July 15–20, 1985).

23. Frey, *The Turkish Political Elite,* pp. 196–197.

24. Turan, "Stages of Political Development," p. 73.

25. Ergun Özbudun, *The Role of the Military in Recent Turkish Politics* (Cambridge, Mass.: Harvard University Center for International Affairs, Occasional Paper in International Affairs, 1966), pp. 30–39.

26. Özbudun, *Social Change and Political Participation,* passim; Özbudun, "Voting Behaviour: Turkey," in Jacob M. Landau, Ergun Özbudun, and Frank Tachau, eds., *Electoral Politics in the Middle East: Issues, Voters, and Elites* (London: Croom Helm, 1980), pp. 107–143.

27. Mardin, "Power, Civil Society and Culture," pp. 258–281.

28. Ibid., pp. 270–281.

29. Turan, "Stages of Political Development," p. 82.

30. Ibid., pp. 100–103.

31. Serif Mardin, "Opposition and Control in Turkey," *Government and Opposition* 1 (May 1966): pp. 375–387.

32. Turan, "Stages of Political Development," pp. 96–97.

33. Harry H. Eckstein, *A Theory of Stable Democracy* (Princeton: Center of International Studies, Princeton University, Monograph no. 10, 1961).

34. Kemal H. Karpat, *The Gecekondu: Rural Migration and Urbanization* (Cambridge: Cambridge University Press, 1976), pp. 205–211.

35. Üstün Ergüder, "Changing Patterns of Electoral Behavior in Turkey" (Paper presented to the IPSA World Congress, Moscow, August 12–18, 1979), pp. 13–15.

36. Huntington, *Political Order*, p. 13.

37. Eric A. Nordlinger, "Political Development: Time Sequences and Rates of Change," *World Politics* 20 (1968): pp. 494, 520; Dankwart A. Rustow, *A World of Nations* (Washington, D.C.: Brookings Institution, 1967), pp. 120–132; Robert A. Dahl, *Polyarchy: Participation and Opposition* (New Haven and London: Yale University Press, 1971), ch. 3.

38. Ergun Özbudun and Aydin Ulusan, "Overview," in Özbudun and Ulusan, eds., *The Political Economy of Income Distribution in Turkey* (New York: Holmes and Meier, 1980), pp. 10–12.

39. *1987 Gelir Dagilimi: Hanehalki Gelir ve Tüketim Harcamalari Anketi Sonuçlari* [1987 Income Distribution: Household Income and Consumption Expenditures Survey Results] (Ankara: Devlet Istatistik Enstititüsü, 1990), p. 16.

40. Maksut Mumcuoglu, "Political Activities of Trade Unions and Income Distribution," in Özbudun and Ulusan, eds., *The Political Economy*, pp. 384, 404–405.

41. Albert Hirschman, *Exit, Voice, and Loyalty: Responses to Decline in Firms, Organizations, and States* (Cambridge, Mass.: Harvard University Press, 1970).

42. Özbudun and Ulusan, "Overview," pp. 17–18.

43. Ahmet N. Yücekok, *Turkiye'de Örgütlenmis Dinin Sosyo-Ekonomlk Tabani* [*The Socioeconomic Basis of Organized Religion in Turkey*] (Ankara: A. U. Siyasal Bilgiler Fakultcsi, 1971), p. 119.

44. Michael N. Danielson and Rusen Keles, "Allocating Public Resources in Urban Turkey," in Özbudun and Ulusan, *The Political Economy*, p. 313 and passim.

45. *Türkiye Istatistik Yilligi, 1993* [Statistical Yearbook of Turkey, 1993] (Ankara: Devlet Istatistik Enstitüsü, 1993), p. 393.

46. Turan, "Stages of Political Development," p. 104.

47. Giovanni Sartori, *Parties and Party Systems: A Framework for Analysis* (Cambridge: Cambridge University Press, 1976), pp. 139–140; Ergun Özbudun, "The Turkish Party System: Institutionalization, Polarization, and Fragmentation," *Middle Eastern Studies* 17, no. 2 (April 1981): p. 233.

48. *Turkey: The Problems of Transition* (Bath: a Euromoney Special Study, 1982), pp. 49–50; Zvi Yehuda Hershlag, "Economic Policies," in Klaus-Detlev Grothusen, ed., *Türkei* (Göttingen: Vandenhoeck and Ruprecht, 1985), pp. 346–369.

49. Özbudun and Ulusan, *The Political Economy*, passim.

50. As under the 1961 Constitution, if no presidential candidate obtains a two-thirds majority of the full membership of the Grand National Assembly on the first two ballots, an absolute majority of the full membership will suffice on the third ballot. Under the new procedure, a fourth ballot, if necessary, will be held only between the two leading candidates; if the fourth ballot does not produce an absolute majority, the Assembly will dissolve automatically and new general elections will be held immediately (Article 102).

51. Especially Guillermo O'Donnell, *Modernization and Bureaucratic Authoritarianism: Studies in South American Politics* (Berkeley: Institute of International Studies, University of California, 1973); Samuel P. Huntington and Joan M. Nelson, *No Easy Choice: Political Participation in Developing Countries* (Cambridge, Mass.: Harvard University Press, 1976), pp. 23–24.

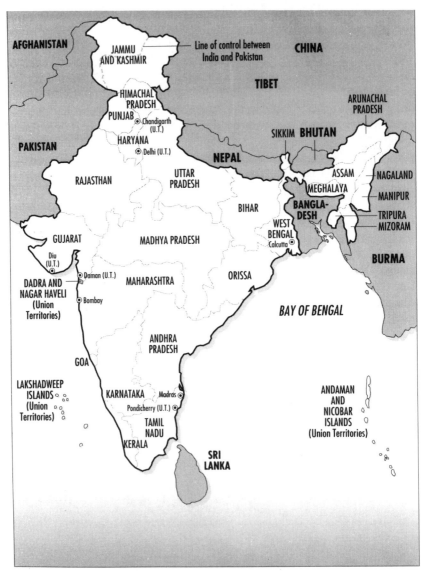

Reprinted from Robert L. Hardgrave and Stanley Kochanek, *India: Government and Politics in a Developing Nation*, Fifth Edition, Harcourt Brace & Company by permission of the publisher.

INDIA

6

India: Democratic Becoming and Developmental Transition

Jyotirindra Das Gupta

Developing countries are not supposed to offer conducive settings for democratic political systems. India's choice of democracy in a setting of poverty, ethnic diversity, and immense complexity of developmental problems must utterly puzzle any theorist of democratic politics. Anyone can imagine how precarious was the prospect of Indian democracy at the moment of its beginning. Nearly five decades of continuous development of constitutional democratic government in India may then call for two kinds of interpretation. Either democracy in India is a misnomer and the pessimistic expectation did not go wrong, or the theorists of democracy were wrong in writing off the possibility of democracy's compatibility with the most stringent tasks of both economic development and political integration in developing countries.

Before we settle for one or the other interpretation, it would be more appropriate to examine the nature of the past five decades' development of democratic politics in India. This will call for, in the first place, an understanding of some of the basic ideas permeating the nationalist movement. The unfolding of these ideas through organizational practice in pre-independence days covers a fairly long period. Indeed, the fact that the national ruling party is now more than a hundred years old may offer some solace to those theorists who worry about immature players taking chances with a sophisticated game like democratic politics in developing countries. For our purpose it is important to consider the inheritance of ideas and institutions that prepared the foundation of the new state. We will examine how a set of imported ideas was progressively indigenized to serve large-scale movements and enduring organizations that contributed to the subsequent development of democratic institutions. The second part of our discussion will examine the evolution of the major democratic institutions after independence. This will be followed by an examination of the performance of these institutions with respect to economic development, political participation, and national cohesion. Finally, an attempt will be made to analyze the significance of democratic development for India in terms of national and comparative implications.

Historical Review

The Colonial Period

Nationalist fascination with liberal ideas and organized associations began in India by the first quarter of the nineteenth century. The initial stirrings were mainly directed to internal investigation of the working systems of religion, social organization, and education.[1] Colonial domination of the coastal areas had already enforced a new exposure to the ways of the victors. This was, however, a selective exposure. The terms of selection were largely determined by the rules of consolidation of the colonizing power. The imposed constraints may explain why early nationalist liberation in India chose to stay close to moderate reformism.

Modern nationalism in India began with the notion that Indians should reexamine the very foundation of their existing organization of religion, society, and education. The architects of modern reforms believed that grave weaknesses in these organizations had to be overcome before Indians could seriously strive for active opposition to the colonial rulers. Since the problem of nationalism was perceived to be primarily internal, the immediate target of nationalist action was to be their own society and not the foreign rulers'. The emphasis on internal decay was rather unusual for a nationalist ideal and it turned the focus of the reforms to several unspectacular but patient organizational constructions.

Rationalism and Liberalism

Ram Mohun Roy (1772–1833), and the intelligentsia of his generation, felt that the most impressive aspect of the strength of the West lay not in its hardware and firepower, but in its development of rational thought. In fact, Roy welcomed British rule as a replacement of Moghul rule because it offered an opportunity for Indians to challenge and reconstruct their superstitious modes of social order in favor of a rational reordering. He had no doubt that such a society should be based on "civil and political liberty."[2] But he did not leave this transformation to the chance that the colonial rulers might extend their domestic spirit of liberty to liberate the colonized people. Rather, he worked on the assumption that the window on the West would make possible an organized political education, which would enable Indians to recall their original, rational libertarian philosophy. A combination of indigenous and received principles would thus aid the construction of a politically free and socially transformed order.

Ram Mohun Roy's faith in liberal political education was impressed in a number of modern voluntary associations set up by him and his urban followers in the fields of religious renovation, social reform, and educational modernization. Their constructive initiative was directed toward language reform, legal reform, establishing a vernacular press, defending the freedom of the press, and articulating the rights of women, particularly widows.[3] The associational activities spread to different parts of India during the 1860s and 1870s. By this time railroad and telegraph lines had facilitated national communication, and the regional isolation of political consciousness was giving way to an expanding network of public associations concerned with social reform and political protest across the country.

These efforts, however, lacked popular appeal. The liberal appeal to reason and scientific discourse could expand more smoothly only if the pace of introduction of modern education was made faster than what the alien rulers cared for. This pace was dictated by the colonial need for a supply of educated servants of the regime. A unique opportunity for educating the public was missed because the colonial rulers felt educational expansion would threaten their own security.[4] In fact, the abysmally slow growth rates of literacy and education made it easier for the conservative nationalists to gain support from the less educated public on the basis of traditional symbols of solidarity derived from religion, caste, locality, and speech community.

Nationalist politics in India took a new direction following the extensive armed rebellion of 1857. This revolt was effectively suppressed but it left some deep scars on both the rulers and the ruled. Henceforth, India came directly under Crown rule. Strategies of selective favors and suspicions were now used by the regime to deliberately fragment the national perception of British action along religious lines. While this put a premium on religious solidarity for both the favored and the unfavored alike, it seriously damaged the prospects of rational and liberal national mobilization.

Setbacks for Liberalism

The original appeal of liberal ideas in underdeveloped countries consisted of an admiration for the value of the individual and his reasoned preferences unhindered by traditional ties. It is interesting that the historical timing and fascination with liberal ideas in Japan and India were not very far apart. Paradoxically, it was the perceived threat from the liberal West that moved Japanese nationalism toward preemptive militarist modernism, while the colonial rulers in India positively weakened the growth of liberalism by an intensified racialist policy. This hastened the development of reactive communalism, whereby each religious community increasingly came to depend on exclusive mobilization to defend its members' interests.[5]

It is easy to argue that the structural features of Indian society could account for the use of traditional symbols for exclusive mobilization in

Indian politics of this time. This, however, would ignore the critical role of the political rewards, punishments, and prohibitions used by a newly centralizing effective power—Crown rule in India. For the strategists of Crown rule the need for Indian manpower offered an excellent opportunity to create a loyal base of support for the expanding colonial regime. Discriminatory preference seemed to offer a special dividend for the new rulers in a country where modern education and political consciousness was historically developing in an uneven spatial and ethnic distribution.

The strategy of selective preference deliberately encouraged the formation of particularistic organizations in Indian politics. The military component of this strategy was aided by a racial theory of graded competence—competence judged by loyalty and not by skill or achievement—whereby Sikhs, Rajputs, and Dogras were placed at the top of the scale of preference for recruitment and trust. The economic component of this preference meant a replacement of pre-colonial notables in the agrarian property structure by intermediaries drawn from groups promising loyalty to the regime. New revenue settlements (from the days of Permanent Settlement in eastern India to other types instituted in the rest of the country) created a rentier class innocent of productive needs but eager to strengthen the order and finance of the regime. The political component demonstrated, for example, a process of actively supporting the Aligarh movement for Muslim reformism against the anti-foreignism of the Muslim fundamentalists and for Muslim exclusivism against non-Muslims. Similarly, exclusive ethnic politics was actively encouraged. Dravidian sentiments were promoted to drive a wedge between northern and southern Hindus and, at the same time, the less advantaged Hindus in all regions were encouraged to press their claims against their superiors in rank.

By the end of the nineteenth century, it seemed clear that the strategy of colonial security and the scramble for new economic opportunities would leave no chance for the growth of secular liberal nationalism. However, two elements came to the aid of the latter. One was the *ideological affirmation* that modernization necessarily calls for a larger political and economic coalition in order to attain both national advancement and individual enhancement. The other was the *pragmatic assessment* of the benefits of a nationally extended market for enterprise, commodities, and employment. What is more important to recognize is the linkage between the two. The promise of extended profitability may not melt all segmental coins but it can soften many for a strategic transition. Nationalist ideological affirmation was expected to facilitate such a transition.

Learning by Organizing

Mutual need more than abstract altruism provided the first major springboard for the construction of a national political platform. Thus when the

Indian National Congress was created in 1885, it began as a platform of convenience. With various degrees of attachment to liberal principles, political associations that had grown up in the regional isolation of Bengal, Bombay, Madras, and other areas sought to build a coalition. Since the effective political authority in the country was centralized, it was natural to assume that a national bargaining instrument was necessary to augment the power of the constituents. Thus during the last quarter of the nineteenth century, the Indian Association of Calcutta, the Poona Sarvajanik Sabha, the Madras Mahajana Sabha, the Bombay Presidency Association, and a host of other active associations and individuals helped to form a national political organization that gradually evolved from pleas, petitions, and protest actions to one of the largest and most enduring mass organizations in human history.

During its formative decades, the Indian National Congress performed a number of important functions for democratic political development. It laid the foundation of a national political discourse that facilitated the formulation of political goals and demands in the public arena. It served as a forum for processing conflicting ideas regarding national goals and priorities. Democratic rules of procedure, tolerance of adversaries, and reconciliation of conflicting claims became part of the political education of the participants. From the very inception of the organization the founding leaders were eager to demonstrate their adherence to these democratic norms. Referring to the first phase of the Congress organization, one perceptive historian writes that "even though the Congress's democratic procedures were more symbolic than substantive, they indicated a commitment both to representative institutions and to an accommodation of India's pluralism in a future Indian constitution. This commitment was enunciated clearly at the first session of the Congress in 1885, and it remained central in Congress thinking through the drafting of India's constitution after independence in 1947,"[6] The founding leaders were highly successful professionals in their fields who did not have to live off politics. They were also aware of their distance from the Indian masses. In their attempt to speak for the people they recognized that their role was one of preparing the ground for popular self-expression and not one of formulating a corporate national will.

Their basic objective was to create a coherent national forum for representing what they perceived as nationalist interests. They were acutely aware of the social, regional, and religious diversities of the country, and the new organization was visualized as a medium for communication and coordination. That they demonstrated an eager commitment to representative institutions can perhaps be explained by a number of factors. Most of them were trained lawyers who were fascinated by the new legal culture and its linkages with liberal notions. Even those who were not in the new legal profession, including business professionals like Dadabhai Naoroji, appeared to be serious about preparing intellectually defensible cases for Indian representation based on empirical evidence. Thus the careful studies of the nature of Indian underdevelopment by scholars such as Naoroji, Ranade, Gokhale, and R. C. Dutt, using the modes of rational investigation normally employed by recognized intellectuals of the colonial home, set a rigorous standard of liberal discourse.[7] Few nationalist movements have yielded such a rich diversity of perspectives on the nature of underdevelopment and the sources of national misery. If Naoroji's work anticipated a dependence notion of underdevelopment, the others heavily emphasized the internal roots of mass poverty. No easy explanation was allowed to lend support to facile anti-foreignism.

One positive result of these patient empirical investigations was the gradual evolution of a consensual strategy of democratic development during the early phase of Indian nationalism. Ever since Ranade's essay on Indian political economy insisted on separating political liberalism from orthodox notions of laissez faire, the nationalist leaders generally agreed about the crucial need for active intervention by a democratic state for coordinated development of agriculture, industry, and education.[8] It is not surprising that the continuity of this consensus has served as a basis for democratic economic planning since independence.

Repression and Radicalization

The turn of the century brought some major changes in the course of nationalism. Although the Congress leaders had succeeded in establishing a viable organ of national representation, the increasing repression and racial arrogance of the colonial regime had made it clear that it was in no mood to listen to voices of dissent or demand. The ruling lords felt secure enough by 1900 that the bureaucratic personnel and the armed forces could be relied upon to deliver the required goods—more revenue squeezed from an already famished country and the use of India as a springboard for mounting expansion of the empire.

If the immediate interests of the colonizer were realized, the long-term prospects of liberal nationalism in India and elsewhere suffered a severe setback. The year 1905 marks a turning point in Asian history. By this time more radical nationalists were ascendant and the old liberal leadership was losing ground in the Congress and the nation. The arrogance and repression of the colonial regime offered a prime incentive to militant nationalism. In the ensuing struggle between brutal imperialism and militant nationalism, whichever gained, liberalism was the loser.

Japan's victory over Russia in 1905 created a new wave of self-confidence all over Asia. This coincided with intensified repression in India and enforced mobilization of Indian resources for British expansionism in Asia. Together these factors strengthened a radical response. Desperation drove the new course of struggle to employ emotional appeals based on highly evocative symbols of solidarity derived from literature, religion, and selective recall of history. Often the intensity of emotional activism erased the distinction between the methods of peaceful resistance and violent adventure. As more people joined the nationalist movement, with the attendant deepening of its social base, the process also paid a high price of creeping cleavage in the nascent nation.

Incentives for Diversion

Radical success using Hindu symbols and recalling the glory of the Hindu heroes mobilized larger numbers but also increased the distance between Hindus and Muslims. Muslim loyalists used this opportunity to carve out a separate road for exclusive religious nationalism. Democratization of the national movement by social deepening through popular mobilization, paradoxically, opened a wide opportunity for attack on both secular mobilization and the principles of democratic politics. The idea of a composite secular nationalism represented by the Congress was challenged from 1906 onward by the exclusive claims to representation based on religious community by the Muslim League and Hindu revivalists. This diversion from the major secular movement for national representation, of course, came in handy for the colonial rulers. Henceforth the political system also actively encouraged a divided system of representation, which reinforced incentives for segmental mobilization on ethnic lines. Beginning in 1909 and in a more elaborate form in 1935, a system of communal representation was introduced by colonial legislation to institutionalize separate electorates for specified ethnic groups.

Besides weakening the national challenge to colonial rule, official encouragement to ethnic solidarity also devalued the case for democratic politics. If the Congress language of democratic politics was embarrassing for some liberals in the administration, the open rejection of democratic politics by the founders of Muslim nationalism must have been a great relief for the regime as a whole. Sir Syed Ahmad Khan had struck the right note equally for the regime and minority religious separatism when he said that a democratic future for India would merely bring Hindu hegemony and oppression.[9]

Exclusive claims to represent a religious community were of course based on the idea that religious communities were homogeneous. The lines of division separating all religious communities in India among caste, language, socioeconomic class, and regional groupings could not, however, be easily erased by the leaders' rhetoric. But religious nationalists were not entirely wrong in pointing out the appeal of religion in India. The timing was also appropriate for building separate constituencies in each religious community by intensifying their rivalry for economic opportunities within the colonial regime. The emphasis, however, was entirely on dividing whatever pie the colonial strategists were prepared to concede and not on strengthening the movement for expanding the size of the total pie.

Social Deepening and the Gandhian Phase

Secular nationalists were not unfamiliar with national heterogeneity. Their case for a secular movement seeking to represent people across ethnic boundaries was based on the notion that an individual is not exhaustively identified by his ethnic markers. They were also sensitive to the crosscutting nature of ethnic identities characterizing the Indians: major religious communities are split into many language communities, which in turn are stratified into caste and class formations. Thus Hindi speakers constituted only about a third of the Hindus, while among the Muslims, Bengali and Punjabi speakers outnumbered the Urdu speakers. Given plural identities, the politically interesting affiliations are rarely derivable from social affinities. In fact, an eagerness to utilize one affinity by a political leadership that seeks an easy constituency of popular support may encourage other leaders to exploit the other affinities of the same individual. Thus, for example, the easier course of exclusive Hindu mobilization, by seizing upon the Hindi language loyalty in northern India, created negative political reactions among Hindus who spoke other languages. Similarly, Muslim nationalists' mobilization using the symbols of Urdu language community often left the much larger number of Muslims cold and uncomfortable. Again, religion, language, caste, and other affinities have to compete with the economic affinities developing among people locked into similar stations of both disadvantage and advantage.[10]

It was the common cause of the greatest number that the secular nationalist leaders wanted to use as the foundation of national struggle. However, neither the moderate politics of protest nor sporadic radical movements in regions (as conducted until the end of World War I) had been able to generate mass participation in a common struggle on a nationally significant scale. To be sure, both the moderate and radical styles had helped build an organized arena for nationalist struggles. But it remained for the Gandhian leadership to generate and coordinate mass-based political movements into an effective threat to the colonial adversary.

Probably, the best-known contribution of the Gandhian leadership was to socially deepen the base of the national movement by active incorporation of support from peasantry, labor, and other occupational groups in rural and urban areas. Mass mobilization helped nationalist leaders build a political coalition of social groups to challenge alien rule by peaceful struggle. In doing so, these leaders recognized their mutual differences regarding the future issues of centrality of the state, domain of bureaucracy, role of industrialization, agrarian reorganization, control of production, and pattern of distribution. Gandhi's idealization of peasant production, for example, sharply contrasted with Nehru's idealization of centrally planned industrialism.[11] Moreover, significant support existed for more straightforward concepts of capitalist and socialist industrialization. In fact, during the three fateful decades of the ascendance of Gandhi's leadership, what kept the prominent leaders and groups together was a prudent sense of tolerance of fundamental disagreements rather than any significant agreement on specifics of ideology.

This pragmatic process of inclusion meant that from the second decade of this century the Congress organization increasingly drew sustenance from organized labor, peasantry, trading communities, nationalist business (big and small), students, women's groups, and professionals. The initial impulse of unionizing labor or organizing peasants and other occupational groups did not always begin under the Congress leadership. However, Congress leaders in different regions gradually either joined the wave or brought the autonomous organizers into a close relationship with the Congress organization. Thus began an inclusionary process of linking mass participation in economic and political action into an institutionalized national organization.

Progressive success in incorporating interest groups called for a delicate task of balancing contradictory interests that was hardly easy for a political organization far from formal power. What made the task more difficult was the frequent need for complex conciliation of the conflicting interests of Indian owners and workers. When both the owners and the workers were aligned with the Congress, the latter could use its influence to mediate in cases of dispute. The joint pursuit of encouraging demands and containing demands by conciliation, in the larger interest of the national movement, helped train a leadership over decades in the art of managing conflicting interests in both the industrial and the agricultural sectors of the economy.[12]

Authority Formation and Coherence Creation

This transition from an elite-induced forum of protest to an institutionalized organization incorporating a broad spectrum of interests gradually endowed the Gandhian leadership with national authority long before it acquired state power. The readiness of this leadership to accommodate contending ideologies and interests, so long as their advocates were prepared to strengthen the common cause of national struggle and development, was a product of the conviction that consensus regarding national priorities is more important than either exclusive ideology or interest. For Gandhi this was much more than simply a matter of reiterating the primacy of the national collectivity over its smaller constituents. The way of accommodation was a part of his basic philosophy of *satyagraha* ("truth force"), or nonviolent resistance. In other words, this was not merely an issue of strategic prudence. Gandhi's strict philosophy of nonviolent resolution of disputes—where forsaking violence is never allowed to serve as a rationalization for acquiescence or submission to oppression—presupposed a theory of truth. According to this theory all that an advocate can claim for his case is incomplete knowledge. Arenas of contest enable rival advocates of incomplete knowledge to test their positions and to arrive at a new composition based on a creative resolution of dispute.[13]

While Gandhi's fellow Congress leaders were often uncomfortable with his strict adherence to nonviolence, they lost no time in recognizing the pragmatic value of consensus formation. The leaders close to Gandhi could use this consensus for strengthening their control of the growing organization, whereas others could at least hope to thrive on the assurance that dissenters would not be thrown out. Thus Gandhi's emphasis on nonviolence and peaceful resolution of conflict simultaneously served the purpose of generating organizational coherence and offering a novel technique of anticolonial resistance. His choice of targets and his capacity to channel isolated points of popular struggle toward a nationally converging course demonstrated an order of skill far superior to that of his colleagues. In addition, his detachment from office within the Congress not merely helped allocate a relatively smooth distribution of prized positions among his colleagues, but also impressed the importance of separation between power and authority.

Another aspect of the authority formation process actively pursued by Gandhi and his colleagues was the preemptive co-optation of outlying mass movements. This served both as a process of political education and a source of support. When Mohandas Gandhi began his political career in India in 1915, he had already earned a reputation for his political skill and moral saintliness during his two decades in South Africa. He used this reputation to gradually influence the Congress leadership, as well as to seek an entry into mass movements that were growing outside the Congress initiative. In fact, his successful conversion of local peasants' grievances against landlords in Champaran, Bihar, rural revenue agitation in Kaira, Gujarat, and a major industrial dispute in Ahmedabad into nationally significant resistance movements provided him with unique political capital from 1917 on.[14] These were followed by a succession of moves to enter, redirect, and nationally focus a diverse field of mass action that otherwise might have remained isolated efforts of limited import. Thus he succeeded in linking the national movement and religious demands of Muslim groups in the Khilafat movement, Sikh temple reforms, and Hindu lower-caste temple entry movements.[15] This process extended horizontally to areas that had never tasted an involvement in national movement and vertically to peasants, lower castes, and poor urban workers.

Although most successful in the practice of preemptive co-optation, Gandhi was not alone in its pursuit. Leaders like Jawaharlal Nehru, although lacking Gandhi's rural insight, supplemented his moves by inducing the support of more urban-based groups that were fascinated by the Western idioms of socialism and industrial development. These contrasting styles and idioms held together the growing support groups with contradictory future interests and perspectives through a conciliatory system maintained by the Congress through the fateful three decades before independence. This is where the Gandhian transformation of earlier liberalism into a strategy of inclusionary participation, progressively channeled within a frame of rules of peaceful conflict and organized collaboration in and with the Congress, helped build an important historical foundation for future democratic development.

This mass incorporation, however, brought the challenge of providing national incentives sufficient to preserve new elements in an enduring structure of solidarity. While Gandhi appealed to the moral imperative, he also recognized that it calls for unusual dedication and patience. Most of his colleagues had more use for mundane power and interest. Organizational expansion also required attention to the issue of sustenance of different levels of leaders and workers. Increasing access to local governing institutions and legislatures, although strictly limited by colonial needs, opened new doors to Indian aspirants.

From 1919 on politics had to make room for these new temptations. The constitutional reforms of 1909 had conceded limited Indian representation, but the extension of the franchise and the responsibility of the elected members were severely circumscribed. The reforms of 1919 provided for a relatively large measure of responsibility at the local and provincial levels in subjects such as education, health, and public works that were not "reserved" or deemed crucial for colonial control.[16] However, even these limited concessions were immediately followed by utterly repressive laws known as the Rowlatt Acts of 1919. Growing nationalist resentment against such dubious packaging of reforms eventually led to another round of reforms encoded in the Government of India Act of 1935. While this package conceded an extended electorate based on property qualification to cover about one-sixth of the adult population, it offered no effective concessions for self-government at the center. But it did provide for responsible government in the provinces subject to the discretionary powers of the appointed governors.[17]

Although these hedged reforms evoked strong negative reactions from the nationalist leaders, the latter were at the same time reluctant to miss the opportunities offered by the new institutions and their promise of public and private power. Despite initial resistance by the Gandhian leaders to the temptations of limited power, pressures both within and outside the Congress made them participate in the limited elections. In 1937 the Congress swept the provincial elections for general seats and formed ministries in seven (eight in 1938) of the eleven provinces.[18] Such electoral success during the preindependence decades helped the Congress organization accumulate valuable experience in constitutional, competitive politics and offered access to office and patronage.

Electoral reforms based on limited franchise were not, however, designed to offer instruction in democratic participation. The communal system of representation fashioned by these reforms put a premium on exclusive ethnic mobilization and collaboration with colonial rulers. The use of religious symbols in opposition to civic culture was now made doubly remunerative by the prospect of prizes for legislative access and colonial collaboration. The latter was made easier because of the bridge between the legislative and the executive arms of government in the British parliamentary system. The corrosive intent and effect of this colonial chemistry was not unanticipated by the Gandhian leadership, which tried to minimize these effects by several means. They scored impressive victories in Hindu as well as Muslim majority provinces and, at the same time, kept up the pace of mass movements in the form of active resistance and civil disobedience campaigns. Besides mass movements, they also extensively built up a network of constructive enterprises in the form of cooperative, small-scale industries and educational institutions and actively encouraged Indian initiative in large-scale industry and commerce. These constructive efforts provided sources of financial support both at individual and organizational levels and of productive engagement for organizational personnel during downswings of political agitation. But the taste of even limited parliamentary and executive access intensified an impatience for formal power. If Gandhi and a few other leaders could afford patience, most leaders found the decolonizing impulse following World War II to offer an opportune moment to settle for the prize of immediate power—even at the cost of a disastrous partition of the subcontinent.

Evolution of the Democratic System

Political reconstruction in India since 1947 has been remarkable for its consistent and continuous use of constitutional methods for generating national coherence, political stability, and the development of economic resources and political freedom.

The special properties of democracy in developing countries call for an understanding of a complex process of combined political, social, and economic development. Unlike the historically established democracies, which benefited from a sequence of social mobilization and economic development preceding political democratization, democratic systems in developing countries have the unenviable task of simultaneously and rapidly developing the polity, economy, and society. The task gets all the more difficult because public assessment at home and abroad tends to concentrate on a partial development at any point in time without considering the set as a whole. Thus, for example, cursory examination of a slow pace of economic development in isolation may easily mislead one to a negative judgment when, in fact, this might be due to a transitional diversion of resources from efficient performers to underprivileged beginners in order to spread the process of social and political development in a more even manner.

Political Inheritance and Renovation

The initial moments of a new regime can be critical. Ironically, the timing of Indian independence earned largely by nonviolent popular movement coincided with an unusually violent moment in the country's history. The architects of the new state soon realized the complex legacy left in 1947 by the departed rulers. The nation was in disarray. Partition of the subcontinent brought mutual insecurity and suspicion between India and Pakistan. A large part of new India was under princely rule. The most important problems on the agenda of reconstruction were political order and territorial integration. One can imagine the severity of the test these imposed at the moment of Indian independence. It is no wonder that few observers writing in those early years could summon enough faith in democratic development to foresee that the Indian system would survive the test. Fortunately the Indian leadership was aided by three important factors. The peaceful transfer of power made for a continuity of leadership and institutional structures. A professional bureaucratic system, already manned mostly by Indians, was available for immediate use and required expansion. Above all, the development of the Congress organization into a nationwide political institution, reaching remote corners and incorporating major political segments of the population representing diverse occupational groups, made for a unified exercise of power. Fortunately as well, this power was already endowed with a sense of authority earned in the course of the nationalist movement. Evidently, the partition of the country and the formation of Pakistan appeared to strengthen the legitimation of power in new India by eliminating a major challenge to nationalism and helped establish a new linkage between the Congress Party and the Muslim population. But the new leaders did not take their nationalist legitimation for granted. They sought to create a constitutional system that would institutionalize an authoritative democratic system of representation, competition, and exercise of power.

A comfortable Congress majority in the elected Constituent Assembly made for a largely consensual reiteration of some of the basic democratic principles enunciated in the earlier decades. The Constitution of India, operative since 1950, offered a complex coverage of elaborate legal and moral provisions, in the longest document of its kind, to a largely nonliterate people.[19] The basic principles enshrined in the justiciable part of the document provide for a parliamentary democratic system of government, fundamental rights, federalism tempered by a preeminent center, and secularism. The nonjusticiable part encodes a series of mild democratic socialist guidelines for the state. While codifying the rules of democratic government, the constitution carefully avoided the Gandhian principles of direct democracy, decentralized authority, and debureaucratization. The Gandhian leaders now needed Gandhi's mantle only for ceremonial legitimation.

In many ways the constitutional text could also be read as a developmental document, for it registered the basic aspirations of the members of a consensual intelligentsia to mold the country according to their tastes and preferences. An idealized blending of Western notions of liberal justice and indigenous notions of self-realization and social welfare had already become a part of nationalist culture that was widely shared by the educated classes. Constitutional encoding of these ideas satisfied their collective pride and reminded them of the social task ahead. Public responsibility was assumed to be mainly one of choosing the right legislators. The rest of the responsibility was now supposed to devolve on the state.

Accordingly, constitutional democracy in independent India cleared the way for an active state appropriate to the realization of simultaneous development on many fronts. A well-knit party, securing majorities in the national Parliament and in a majority of state legislatures, on the basis of elections held every five years, can pursue extensive intervention in the social, economic, and political spheres to generate and direct resources for national development. The power of the government is subject to several limitations. The federal provisions of the constitution, the fundamental rights, judicial review, various statutory commissions and, of course, the political opposition may serve as sources of curbs, limits, and warnings. However, these provisions are subject to considerable muting in cases of overriding "public purpose," which can be invoked with fair ease if the government can obtain the required majority support, simple or complex as specified by the constitution.

Besides providing for cabinet-style authority armed with legislative support, the constitution also offers some directions and perspectives for national development. Part four of the constitution spells out the duties of the state, but these articles are not binding on the state. It says that the fundamental principle of governance shall include the duty of the Indian state to promote the welfare of the people by securing "as effectively as it may" a social order in which justice—social, economic, and political—shall inform all the national institutions. A following specification reads like a catalogue of objectives that would be congruent with an ideology of a socialistic welfare state that carefully steers clear of revolutionary socialism.[20]

What is left out, however, is any sense of priority or urgency among the preferred objectives. The basic law of the country, then, has authorized the state to adopt a course of moderate reforms, but at the same time its amendment procedures ensure that a confident popular mandate can enable a responsible executive to go ahead with more radical reforms. The crucial issue was not what the legal language expressed but rather what the nature of democratic development in an inexperienced country would make of it.

Democratic Practice and Political Development

Democratic development in India has been served exceptionally well by a massive system of elections conducted at the national, state, and local levels. Ten general elections at the national level, nearly three hundred state-level elections, and innumerable local elections, organized on the basis of universal adult franchise since 1952, have generated a vigorous tradition of democratic representation and its regular renewal. By the end of the 1980s, the size of the electorate exceeded 500 million voters, and the voter turnout rate remained close to the 60-percent range at the national level and surpassed the 75-percent mark in several major states.[21] Nearly five decades of electoral participation to express citizens' choices at levels ranging from local to national, with respect to issues varying from rural to global, have demonstrated a quality of political development that was widely underestimated in the country and elsewhere. Political maturity of even the nonliterate voters has proven to be a positive resource for democratic functioning.

At the national level, the Congress Party has often enjoyed substantial electoral pluralities, which (because of the single-member-district electoral system) have been translated into large, and occasionally overwhelming, parliamentary majorities (see Table 6.1). If this process indeed helped the continuation of Congress dominance during the initial two decades in the national Parliament, many voters were also ready to withdraw support from that party at the level of state legislative elections as early as 1967. The message of defeat, although limited, was clear. The voters were not to be taken for granted by the Congress Party or the opposition parties. When the Congress Party regained its support in 1971–1972 and began to bend the constitutional system toward an authoritarian direction in the mid-1970s, it was served with a crushing defeat at both the national and state levels in 1977–1978. Rule by the Janata Party did not last long, however. The Congress Party was returned to national power in 1980 and 1984, then lost it in 1989, only to scramble back to power with the help of some allies in 1991. Some of the opposition members who had helped the Congress Party survive a major no-confidence motion in Parliament in 1993 subsequently joined the party, thus giving it a clear majority and its leader a more assured sense of mandate.[22] Dissent within the Congress Party occassionally alarmed the leadership but even the scary moments of threatened split and factional challenges in May 1995 failed to effectively endanger its position.

The continuity and regularity of nearly five decades of electoral participation have earned cumulative support from all of the major contestants in politics for the evolving institutionalized system of political competition. Increasingly, the object of durable support has turned out to be more the

Table 6.1.   Summary Electoral Data: National Parliament Results from Ten Indian
Elections, 1952–1991 (Lok Sabha)

	1952	1957	1962	1967	1971	1977	1980	1984	1989	1991
Electorate (in millions)	171.7	193.7	216.4	249.0	274.1	320.9	355.6	375.8	498.6	550.0
Voter turnout (in percent)	46	47	55	61	55	60	57	64	62	57
Congress Party percentage share of popular vote	45	48	45	41	44	34	43	49	39	38
Congress Party percentage share of legislative seats	74	75	73	55	68	28	67	77	37	44[a]

Sources: Government of India, Press Information Bureau, *Lok Sabha Poll 1991, 1991;*
Lloyd I. Rudolph and Suzanne H. Rudolph, *In Pursuit of Lakshmi* (University of Chicago Press,
1987), pp. 130–131; Robert L. Hardgrave Jr. and Stanley A. Kochanek, *India: Government and
Politics in a Developing Nation* (New York: Harcourt, Brace, Jovanovich, 1994); Government
of India, *India 1993* (New Delhi: Publications Division, Government of India, 1994).

a. This was the position in the original tabulation, but the Congress Party improved its
share, in delayed and by-elections held later, to about 47 percent by 1993; subsequent increases of share leading to slender majority was the result of party switching.

general institution for processing reasonable political rivalry[23] rather than
any particular great leader or dominant organization. The system has survived the death of Prime Minister Nehru in 1964, the assassination of Prime
Minister Indira Gandhi (Nehru's daughter) in 1984, the collapse of Congress
domination at the state level in 1967, as well as its failure to win a national
parliamentary majority in three general elections, and on more than one
occasion the inefficacy of the Janata Party alternatives at the national level.
At the same time, the story of the longevity of the constitutional system of
competition and representation may also reveal how the institution was able
to stick to its roots over time and across regions. Perhaps the biggest thing
in its favor was the basic contribution representation and competition could
offer by allowing various social, cultural, territorial, and ideological cleavages to have legitimate political voices.

The plural social environment and its sheer vastness offered incentives
for challenges to organized centers of power that sought to speak for the
entire nation. The early decades of Congress dominance following independence were marked by growing challenges from outside the party. Given the
federal structure of the polity, it was easier to organize the challenging
forces at regional levels. This was more a result of the practicality of scale
than of any necessary attachment to regional exclusiveness. Congress dominance was rudely shaken in the 1967 elections when about half of the states
chose the opposition parties for state-level governance, although Congress

rule continued at the federal level.[24] The nationalist mantle was no longer sufficient to hold together one national organization to reflect a consensual reconciliation of dominant interests.[25] When the Congress Party split into two organizations in 1969, the major group, led by Indira Gandhi, increasingly became more an electoral instrument serving the ruling leadership than a vehicle for accommodation. The moment of the split also reminded the rival organizations that henceforth the national scale of power would often call for a willingness and skill on the part of lower social formations to negotiate new structures of support and for new modes of cooperation with regional organizations. The split forced Indira Gandhi's Congress Party to seek the support of the Communist Party of India and a regional party of Tamil ethnic base, Dravida Munnetra Kazhagam (DMK), in order to continue in power. Radical socialism and regionalism now gained a new respect and acceptance at the center of national politics.

The dependence on other parties was soon overcome when bold populist moves to cultivate new support from disadvantaged groups turned out to be highly rewarding for Indira Gandhi and her Congress Party in the 1971 elections. The party won a commanding majority in the national Parliament, and the next year it won impressive victories in state legislative elections.[26] Meanwhile, in 1971 Gandhi also won widespread admiration for her role in the war that led to the independence of Bangladesh. It seemed as though her party was on the verge of restoring the old pattern of dominance. But unlike the earlier history, this time there was little organizational incentive for the regional and local Congress leaders to build sustained social bases of support in their constituencies. Loyalty to the party leadership at the top, access to the patronage system of the state and the party, and an ability to cultivate demonstrative spectacles of support for the top echelon were now regarded as the basic virtues of the successively lower layers of leaders and organization.[27] The old idea of a party-based state was transformed into a state-dependent party.

Formerly, the chief ministers of states were regarded as the builders of regional political bases and authority—a system that was congruent with the federal promise of the multiethnic polity. The new organizational system reduced this large reserve core of leadership—potential replacements for national leaders on demand—to a band of prime ministers' people who lacked regional political capital. The replacement of the polycentric organizational arrangement with a monocentric pattern also spelled a new danger. Regional problems and local conflicts were now transferred to the only authority that mattered—the prime minister's directorate. The concentration of power made it easy for dispersed conflicts to be transferred from local sites to the center. Ironically, the new strategy of strengthening a monocentric authority made the new leadership unnecessarily vulnerable by appearing to direct all of the dissents and disaffections of a plural society to one target.

Unfortunately for the new leaders, the problems of the early 1970s were too acute in terms of their depth, magnitude, and simultaneous demand on authority to make the new structure work. The refugee trail of the Bangladesh War, severe drought, energy crisis, and economic failures occurring together offered the most trying test for a newly reorganized authority. As resources were precariously depleted, mounting factional war within the ruling party and public protest against the government rocked the country. The opposition parties were aided by dissident factions within the ruling party and a convergence of nonparty political formations expressing popular disaffection. As the regionally initiated movements of unrest widened, the new ruling authority repressed them as an attack on the nation. This repression further polarized politics into a battle between an increasingly nervous ruling apparatus and an expanding coalition of opposition groups and parties.

Opposition Mobilization and the Emergency

History now presented an opportunity to the opposition that it had never tasted before. As we have seen, the single-member plurality system of electoral representation had discounted the electoral prospects of fragmented opposition parties. Extra-electoral politics of agitation now offered an incentive for these parties to mobilize popular discontent, form a coalition among them, and widen the scope of the coalition by inducting into it popular action groups from many regions, most notably Bihar and Gujarat.[28] The latter regions, in particular, could make use of the national prestige of leaders like Morarji Desai and especially Jayaprakash Narayan, whose Gandhian socialist credentials and continued ability to stay away from the small-time clash of economic and ethnic interests had won wide admiration. These ideologically diverse leadership resources helped forge a national unity of discontent although, inevitably, the nature of the coalition left a potential for rift. The goal of this national movement, as expressed in particular by Narayan, was to organize a popular initiative to replace a ruling leadership that was widely perceived as socially oppressive and politically authoritarian.[29]

While the pressure of the popular movements kept growing, the legal standing and the political stature of Prime Minister Indira Gandhi suffered a severe setback because of a conjunction of two critical events. Her own election of 1971 was invalidated in June 1975 by a high court decision on a case of electoral malpractice lodged by her socialist opponent.[30] Besides removing her from office, this conviction also entailed her debarment from elected office for six years. The Supreme Court, however, awarded a conditional stay of the judgment that temporarily allowed her to retain office, without the right to vote or participate in the proceedings of Parliament, pending consideration of a full-scale appeal. Meanwhile, a coalition of opposition parties in Gujarat scored a decisive victory in the state elections in the same month. Her spirited campaign in the state was of no help to the sagging Congress Party in the face of the widespread popular movement against her rule.

Indira Gandhi had a comfortable majority in Parliament. Her cabinet included several leaders of national stature and a fairly impressive political and administrative record. She could wait for the conclusion of the legal proceedings and, meanwhile, let another leader of her party exercise formal power without much reasonable fear of losing long-term grounds. Ever since the Congress split, her faction-ridden colleagues had owed their political stature considerably to her populist appeal. However, she did not have confidence in a patiently drawn institutional strategy to utilize her populist appeal in a manner that would strengthen both her party and her democratic authority. Instead, she opted for a system of extraordinary powers by invoking the internal emergency provisions of the constitution.

The Indian constitutional system was designed to serve the country in normal and crisis situations. It was assumed during the making of the constitution that internal and external stresses faced by a newly developing country would require certain temporary deviations from normal procedures to tide the system over a crisis. Thus a complex set of emergency provisions permit comprehensive or partial use of special executive powers, depending on the specific situation.[31] External aggression or grave internal political disturbance permit comprehensive use, while political crises confined to state levels or financial crisis on a national level may warrant limited use of these abnormal provisions. Many of these provisions have been used frequently before and after Indira Gandhi's emergency phase. In fact, the possibilities of a constitutional dictatorship utilizing these provisions were discussed in the constitutional literature on India from the very beginning.[32] But until June 1975, the actual pattern of use of the enabling powers did not entail systematic subversion of constitutional, democratic government on a national scale. This is the crucial point that should help us distinguish between the use of specific emergency powers and an emergency regime that deliberately seeks a transformation of the basic democratic structure into an authoritarian form of government.[33]

Indira Gandhi's choice of the emergency option was based on her claim that there was a deep conspiracy to destroy civil order and economic development in India.[34] The equation between her own political crisis and national crisis was hardly convincing. In order to register her point she set out to dismantle the democratic system of persuasion and replace it with an authoritarian mode of creating and enforcing public assent. Thus the emergency episode was marked by mass arrests, suppression of civil rights and all opposition voices, elaborate censorship of the media, and a carefully orchestrated campaign to celebrate the virtues of collective discipline promoted by the national leader, her increasingly powerful son Sanjay, and their nominees. A meek majority in Parliament endorsed the executive orders issued by the prime minister's inner court and the judicial system was emasculated by amending the constitution. These amendments also ensured the supremacy of the prime minister's role, thus formalizing a system that, as we have discussed, had been taking shape since 1971.[35]

Much was made of the logic of disciplined economic development, which presumably called for a strong state to guide the economy to serve the nation and especially the poor masses. With all the fanfare surrounding the new regime's twenty-point program—later collapsed into five points—this strong state failed to deliver a rate of progress strikingly different from previous or subsequent regimes.[36] Some of the early gains in grain production were due more to climatic favor than organizational changes. Extensive labor repression and the favor shown to terms of discipline dictated by employers helped register some gains in industrial production, but the overall process of economic development served the rich better than the poor. In any event the populist appeal increasingly wore off as the regime stepped into its second year. By early 1977 Indira Gandhi was confident that her party could get a fresh mandate by appealing once again to the people through parliamentary elections.

Emergency measures were relaxed before the elections. The opposition parties accomplished a rare measure of unity in the form of the Janata Party, based on the alliance brought about in the course of the Bihar and Gujarat movements. The March 1977 elections turned out to be a landmark event in the history of India's democratic becoming.[37] The Janata Party and its allies won an overwhelming victory over Indira Gandhi's Congress Party. That the Janata government did not endure beyond two years does not diminish the fact that the party system in India revealed a valuable reserve capacity to mobilize the political resources to replace the dominant system by a more competitive one in a time of democratic crisis.[38] This interesting case of institutional latency may reflect a deeper civic disposition to support a democratic system than what the manifest level of party competition would suggest.

Party Alternation and Governance Variation

The Janata government quickly dismantled the authoritarian emergency structure and reassured the citizens that future attempts to undermine the democratic system would be much more difficult. The leaders were aware that they represented more a coalition to restore democracy than a well-knit party with a disciplined program for the future. Many of the leaders, including Prime Minister Morarji Desai, were experienced practitioners of the craft of governance. Some were seasoned leaders of labor and agrarian popular movements. They began well in 1977 in their attempts to restore popular rights and to press the planning system to cater more to the rural lower-class groups. But factional conflict within the young party led to the fall of the Janata government in 1979. Meanwhile, Indira Gandhi's Congress Party split again, and her faction began using the name Congress (I) in 1978. The latter returned to power in 1980, and a new phase of Congress rule began.

Indira Gandhi's overwhelming victory, yielding a two-thirds majority in Parliament, restored her confidence in the populist craft of leadership. For a while, the opposition parties remained in disarray. The political space was increasingly converted into a field for family rule and arbitrary action. Having broken the back of the opposition, the new Congress leaders—some with criminal records—used manipulation within and outside the party to a point that undermined the democratic politics of reasonable rivalry and fair competition. Reckless disregard of rules and norms of fairness by the ruling party generated deep discontent. In 1983, Congress (I) was defeated in several state legislative elections.[39] That same year, extensive ethnic violence in Assam and Punjab conveyed ominous signals. Indira Gandhi was assassinated in 1984, consumed by the fire of violence in Punjab that for many years claimed a heavy human toll. These and other ethnic issues (analyzed later) continued to haunt her successors across parties. She was succeeded by her son Rajiv Gandhi, who won the 1984 national elections with a record vote.

Rajiv Gandhi's stewardship of the party and the country was the story of an inexperienced leadership that deeply distrusted the existing popular organizations. The new prime minister was more eager to bring a touch of novelty by projecting his youthful admiration for professional management in party and governance.[40] He held an assured majority in Parliament and an unmatched status in the party. His success in reaching accords with leaders in strife-torn Punjab, Assam, and Mizoram initially offered constructive possibilities for reducing the incidence of confrontational violence. His promise of economic liberalization, political decentralization, and a crusade against corruption remained largely unrealized, however. In fact, his impatience with organizational rules and processes, in both the party and the government, and his inability to dispel popular suspicion regarding his complicity or that of his aides in some of the largest-scale corruption cases in the country cost him dearly. The Congress Party was decisively defeated in the 1989 national parliamentary elections.[41]

The opposition campaign against the Congress rule had directed its major attack on Congress corruption. Although the campaign was impressive enough to bring the National Front—a cluster of parties led by the Janata Dal—and its clean-image leader V. P. Singh to power, the Front was haunted by a precarious dependence on the support of other non-Congress parties. The latter group mainly consisted of the Bharatiya Janata Party (BJP) and the Communist Party of India (Marxist) (CPM), parties of religious and Marxian persuasion, respectively, that rarely agreed with each other. Both, however, had stronger bases and greater internal cohesion than either the National Front or its components. The BJP was riding high. It had dramatically improved its position in the Lok Sabha—Parliament's more important lower house—from two seats in 1984 to eighty-five seats in 1989.[42] Its heady card of Hindu mobilization kept it at a distance from the parties of the left and center. Internal and interparty conflicts among these non-Congress parties led to the fall of Singh's government after barely a year. The government of his successor, Chandra Sekhar, lasted only about four months. Minority government, or its abuse, left a bad taste, and the 1991 elections promised another round of party alternation.

The Indian voters failed to return a clear majority in the 1991 parliamentary elections. However, the Congress Party's plurality placed it substantially ahead of the others. Yet even with the support of its allies, it fell marginally short of a majority when it was asked to form a government.[43] The new Congress government with P. V. Narasimha Rao as prime minister, despite its minority status for the first two years, succeeded in introducing many political and economic reforms that had positive implications for democracy and development. Rajiv Gandhi's assassination during the middle of the 1991 elections had called for a new leadership. When Rao was made the leader of the Congress Party and the prime minister, he was seventy years old. He was one of the most experienced persons in the party and the governing system, having served the party since the later decades of the freedom movement and the legislative institutions since the 1950s. He rose from the level of state politics in Andhra Pradesh, where he developed his unassuming style of rulership as chief minister in 1971. Later, he served in the central cabinet for many years as a senior minister in charge of defense and external affairs.

As prime minister, Rao brought back a consensual style, a respect for institutional structures, and an ability to work with colleagues who could outshine him in public. The new leadership restored the elective system within the Congress Party; after two decades, elections for party offices were held in 1992. A negotiating skill informed by an accommodating attitude was especially appropriate for the changing course of party politics and governance that had been occurring since the late 1980s. The ability of a minority government to succeed called for leaders who could command respect beyond party lines. Moreover, in a strong federal system such as India's, effective governance requires that national leaders work cooperatively with state-level leaders across parties. The need to cultivate collaboration among a number of parties did not, however, mean making them ruling partners. It was more often a question of building areas of agreement or points of consensus regarding rules, procedures, crucial national policies, or strategies in or outside of Parliament.

Strategic skills in making such agreements soon became evident in many moves by Rao to evoke cooperation from most of the national opposition and the regional ruling parties. The Congress leader was less often successful—although not on crucial systemic issues—in dealing with the BJP, which had once again improved its Lok Sabha strength from 85 seats in 1989 to 119 in 1991. The BJP had also gained impressive majorities in four state legislatures during the 1990–1991 elections. Yet just when its overconfidence and religious chauvinism were about to endanger the basic rules of the system, it lost control of three of those same four states in 1993.[44] This sobering democratic lesson took both the party and the scholars by surprise. However, in 1995 it made striking gains in the western states. It won power in Gujarat and became a partner of the ruling coalition in Maharashtra.[44] The electoral reverses of the Congress Party in the state elections in 1994 and 1995, as noted below, weakened the Rao leadership at the national level. But the dissidents led by Arjun Singh could not generate enough support to effectively change the leadership. Rao's ability to survive challenges remained impressive.

The increasing prominence of multiple parties is also an important product of politics at the state level, which is closer to the daily existence of most people in the country. Some of these states are huge: Uttar Pradesh alone has a population of more than 140 million.[45] Experiments in party alternation date back to the 1950s, when Kerala had its first period (to be followed by several more) of Communist Party government. Congress dominance of states was first broken in 1967; it was restored later, but then was broken again. Gradually, state politics offered various types of party rule—ranging, for example, from uninterrupted Communist Party (Marxist) dominance in West Bengal since 1977, well-entrenched regional party rule in Tamil Nadu since the 1960s, the dramatic rise and fall of a regional party in Andhra Pradesh in the 1980s, to the rise of a socialist party coalition that in 1993 defeated a strong bid by the Hindu-oriented BJP in Uttar Pradesh.[46]

Since the late 1980s, the non-Congress parties have generally controlled nearly half of all the state legislatures. However, Congress control did not remain regionally constant. Traditionally identified with the north as its political heartland, Congress Party support later shifted increasingly to reliance on the south and the west. This shift, too, was temporary. As of 1992 it held twelve of twenty-five states. In 1993 it won three, and in 1994 it lost three including two southern states. In 1995 it lost two key western states and won two eastern states. Most of the larger states are (as of early 1995) outside of Congress control, mainly as a result of a recent anti-incumbent mood of the voters in the state-level elections. As of April 1995 the non-Congress states were distributed among nine political parties.[47]

Although the plurality of party control and the fluidity of party support challenge the myth of single-party dominance in India, they should not be read as a sign of disarray or declining coherence in governance. Party variation in the states has not prevented policy coordination with the federal government, regardless of which party controls the latter. At the same time, policy practice at the state level has varied from radical agrarian reform under communist governments or populist welfare measures under southern regional parties to aggressive agrarian capitalism under Congress, Akali, or other parties.[48] These and other variations have often reflected innovative policy processes that stood in sharp contrast to a more rigid legacy of state-centric planning at the national level. That legacy, again, has been boldly revised by the Rao government, demonstrating that the efficacy of a minority government in a multiparty parliament can reasonably match its competition. This is discussed in a later section.

Mobilization, Moderation, and Institutional Development

Political parties and electoral participation reflect only one part of the Indian citizen's public engagement and involvement. Over nearly five decades of democratic practice the public space has grown in range and depth to reflect and often direct the processes of social deepening of national development. A wide variety of organized groups and associations have served as durable institutions for expressing popular claims, interests, and demands. As discussed before, many of these associational formations have a long history, dating back to the 1930s if not earlier. Organizations representing industrial labor, peasants, students, youth, and women have traditionally remained close to political parties.[49] Some of the more recent organizations, however, tend to disavow or disfavor party connections. Most organizations' linkages with parties, formal or informal, also bring them closer to other interest groups in the larger organizations that are concerned with more general objectives. A mutual dependence strengthens labor groups' bargaining position, for example, just as major national parties have found them to be important sources of organized support. This mutuality and intergroup linkage also induces a sense of moderation in the definition of particular interests and a respect for the institutional rules. Business associations—more prominent in large-scale industry—have generally used informal ties with parties to make the pursuit of their pressures more effective.[50] Associations to promote social causes, such as civil rights or environmental issues, have either tended to rely on bases of support from a variety of parties and pressure groups or mobilized new support bases to compensate for the failures of the established organizations.[51]

Despite a long history that predates independence, the growth of rural organizations involving peasants, agricultural workers, and farmers has been rather slow and regionally uneven. Persistent poverty in rural areas has not led to the expected nationwide coalescence or to collective action of extended duration. The expectation of many observers that the so-called green revolution would make the countryside's politics turn red did not materialize. Instead, patterns of rural coalescence and action have defied easy formulas that link economic conditions with political outcomes.

Although the incidence of poverty is highest among agricultural labor and marginal income groups, including tenants and smallholder peasants, their mobilization into organized associations has been hampered by wide variations in agrarian property systems, ecological contexts, social authority patterns (mainly exemplified in caste systems), technological diffusions, and policy approaches.[52] Thus radical mobilization, although initially successful in the 1960s in a few southern districts in Tamilnadu and Kerala under the auspices of two Communist parties, gradually veered toward a wider, multiclass agrarian coalition, which lent an important base of support for the parliamentary radicalism of the dominant Communist party, the Communist Party (Marxist), or CPM. The frequent induction of the Communist parties into power at the state level in Kerala, Tripura, and, more durably, in West Bengal can be understood in terms of their ability to forge a still wider coalition between urban and rural groups with varied class interests.[53] The gains of democratic incorporation, not surprisingly, have also been the loss of rural and urban radical espousal of exclusive causes of the most deprived classes.[54] Access to democratic power, as it were, has served to highlight the compulsion for inclusive combination rather than exclusive mobilization of particular classes. Moreover, this same broad combination has often encouraged shifting reformist coalitions between middle- and lower-caste formations in north Indian states, whereby status-based mobilization has gained precedence over class-based mobilization.

Region, Religion, and Ethnic Affirmation

India's complex ethnic divisions require a brief discussion before we analyze their political implications. The religious composition reveals a preponderance of Hindus (83%), with Muslims the largest minority (11.1%), followed by Christians (2.4%) and Sikhs (2%). At the state level, however, Hindus lack majority status in several states (Jammu and Kashmir has a Muslim majority, Punjab a Sikh majority, and Meghalaya, Mizoram, and Nagaland Christian majorities). However, language and regional loyalty significantly cut across religious communities. Hindus, Muslims, and Christians are dispersed all over the country, and they speak a variety of regional languages. According to a broad definition, nearly 43 percent of Indians (by a stricter definition, 31 percent) speak Hindi, the official language of the country, and the use of Hindi is limited mainly to six northern and central states of the twenty-five in India.[55] Some of these states are quite large—for example, Uttar Pradesh (140 million people in 1991), Bihar (86 million), Madhya Pradesh (66 million), and Rajasthan (44 million). These states have literacy rates that fall below the national average. Their rank in real per capita state income (average of 1991–1993) remains close to the lowest in the nation. Of these six predominantly Hindi-speaking states, only Haryana rises considerably higher in income and literacy.

Among the non-Hindi languages, the national proportions are Bengali

(8.3%, mainly in the state of West Bengal), Telugu (8.2%, in Andhra Pradesh), Marathi (8%, Maharashtra), Tamil (6.6%, Tamil Nadu), Gujarati (5.4%, Gujarat), Malayalam (4.2%, Kerala), Kannada (4.2%, Karnataka), Oriya (3.7%, Orissa), Punjabi (3.2%, Punjab and partly Haryana), Assamese (approximately 2%, Assam), and Kashmiri (0.5%, Jammu and Kashmir). Tamil, Telugu, Kannada, and Malayalam are southern languages that belong to the Dravidian family. The other languages included here belong to the Indro-Aryan family. Urdu, closely related to Hindi, is spoken by 5.7 percent of the nation's population, in Bihar, Uttar Pradesh, Andhra Pradesh, Karnataka, and Maharashtra.

Some of these non-Hindi-language communities and their associated states stand out with respect to a few key indicators. Kerala has the highest literacy and newspaper readership rates but poor per capita state income. Punjab, Maharashtra, and Goa have (along with Haryana) the highest per capita state incomes—considerably above the national average in 1991–1992. All of these regional and language communities are divided into a number of social classes and thousands of castes and subcastes (mainly among Hindus but also among non-Hindu communities). In many cases, regional loyalties are also undermined by strong subregional affinities. Thus, the issue of ethnic domination is less threatening because relative advantages (size, income, accomplishment) are often countervailing rather than mutually reinforcing. The distribution of ethnic plurality in this case militates against the domination of one homogeneous group; the cross-cutting cleavages tend to reduce the intensity of affinities.

Theories of democratic participation usually call attention to the *individual* citizen's political engagement or alienation. Developing democracies in multiethnic settings additionally require consideration of *collective* expressions that claim to be recognized as the voices and terms of communal solidarities. These collective entities are not just so many ascriptive fixtures that reflect some profound primordial divisions characteristic of premodern social formations. Social divisions that reflect regional, religious, cultural, caste, and language loyalties do not indicate *why, how,* or *when* they will be translated by political mobilization to produce *what* consequences for the polity. It is also important to note how these divisions are situated in the ethnic map of the country and what kind of institutional treatment has been available. Above all, we must pay careful attention to the dynamic character of ethnic boundaries and their political mobilization over the recent decades of economic development and institutional evolution. In other words, the political construction of exclusive communities should be distinguished from the idea of objective social solidarity with authentic interests. The definition of community interests is likely to vary depending upon how some articulate spokespersons want to use specific definitions to bargain for benefits. The fact that these communal spokespersons gradually generate their own competition because of either factional or subgroup rivalry has particularly interesting possibilities for generating cross-cutting collaboration and, therefore, moderating the intensity of political conflict.

Regional affinities in postindependence Indian history have been found to be compatible with a variety of political expressions. They have ranged from mostly *peaceful* identification with regional issues of autonomy, based on language, culture, and community within the federation, to *violent* movements for secession. The first category refers to two groups of states: the six Hindi states, with nearly 42 percent of the population, and about fifteen states with other language speakers, containing nearly another 54 percent. The second category of secessionist violence can also be divided into two groups: recent cases of violence in Punjab and in Jammu and Kashmir, and the earlier cases (during the 1950s and 1960s) of violence in small states like Nagaland and Mizoram. Together, all of these cases of violent mobilization account for less than 4 percent of India's population—in fact, much less when one considers the large minorities (or even majorities) of opinion in these regions that are opposed to violence and secession.

The population of Jammu and Kashmir (Kashmir, in short) in 1991 was 7.7 million (less than 1 percent of that of the country). It is the only state in India with a Muslim majority (64 percent), although Kashmir Muslims constitute only 5 percent of India's Muslim population. Any easy equation between Muslim religion and separatism is problematic for the rest of the Indian Muslims—nearly a hundred million by 1994—who are engaged in every aspect of national life throughout the country. For more than three decades, Kashmir has been ruled by Muslim leaders organized in contending parties.[56] The larger parties were the National Conference and the Congress Party—both of them secular.[57] This is the only state in the federation that has its own regional constitution and a special autonomy provision reserved for it in the national constitution. But the legacy of three international wars (the first in 1947) kept alive tension, intrigue, and foreign intervention. The situation was made worse by the leading political parties, which in recent years rightly accused each other of gross corruption, and by the Congress Party's manipulation of state politics from the center. Central rule replaced an unstable elected government in 1990.

By the late 1980s an increasingly powerful Islamic coalition in Kashmir began to threaten the established Muslim leaders. Although the Islamic groups had a dismal record in earlier elections, the declining integrity of the established parties and the irresponsible games played by the Rajiv Gandhi administration offered a new opportunity. In addition, during the 1980s the fallout from the Afghanistan war and the global wave of resurgent Islam produced a critical conjuncture.[58] Internal decline of authority and democratic institutions made it easy for the generous supply of sophisticated foreign arms and insurgents to press Kashmiri politics toward militancy and violence, which generated a high toll of repression from the central state. In the battle between terror and counterterror during the early 1990s, no matter who won the people always lost their opportunity for unintimidated choice. The rivalry for religious authenticity among the Muslim leaders equally overshadowed the basic security issues of the non-Muslims, who constituted nearly 36 percent of the state's population.

The explosive chemistry of region and religion produced by rival leaders who claimed the authentic right to speak for the community and rejected basic norms of democratic competition was exemplified during the 1980s in Punjab, which was 61 percent Sikh and 37 percent Hindu as of 1981. Punjab accounts for only 2.4 percent of India's population, and Sikhs nationally constitute only 2 percent, but they figured prominently in the political turmoil India experienced in the 1980s. Extensive violence connected with a militant separatist movement for a Sikh homeland claimed more than twenty thousand lives between 1981 and 1992. Nearly half of the killings were reported to be the work of the militants. Most of the victims of the violence during this period were Sikhs, who were targeted at a steadily increasing rate after 1987, probably because the community's response failed the militants' dream.[59] External armed involvement has been less conspicuous in Punjab than in Kashmir. External assistance from nonresident Sikhs (mainly living abroad) has been substantial. However, resident Sikhs have gradually opted for normalcy, and the electoral institutions registered increased effectiveness through several elections at the state and local levels from 1992 to 1994.

The trauma of the partition of Punjab in 1947 hit the Sikhs hard in many ways. The larger part of Punjab became the core territory of Pakistan, and the Sikhs had to leave for India. Worse still, the illusion of an identification between the territory of Punjab and holy Sikh land was broken. On the eve of partition, the Sikhs constituted only 13 percent of undivided Punjab (Muslims were 57%, Hindus 28%). The smaller Indian Punjab after 1947 also found them in a minority (Hindus 64%, Sikhs 33%). But the new situation offered a democratic system, and a popular movement was launched for a Punjabi-speakers' state. In 1966, the newly reorganized state of Punjab came into existence. But the Akali Dal (the exclusively Sikh political party), which led the movement to create that state, was still unhappy. Since 1921, the Akali Dal has claimed to speak for the Sikh religious community. The unique organization for managing Sikh temples, the SGPC—which serves as an institutionalized legislature for the Sikhs, with statutory recognition since 1920—has traditionally been controlled by the Akali Dal.[60] The SGPC lent a religious legitimation to Akali politics and gave the party access to its vast resources. Yet the nature of democratic competition in Punjab's politics never ensured a clear victory for the party in five state assembly elections (1967, 1969, 1972, 1977, and 1980) until 1985, when violence radically altered the politics of citizens' choice.[61]

In other words, when peace prevailed, the politics of fair competition revealed a willingness of the Sikh community to openly express its internal differences. These differences were caused by divisions based on class, caste, sect, location (rural-urban), ideology, and other sources. The Congress Party won the highest percentage of votes in all of the five state assembly elections before 1985, when it also stayed close to the highest. Each time it won substantial support from lower-caste and lower-class Sikhs, while the Akali Dal was closely identified with the more affluent Jat Sikh caste. This caste, even including its poorer members, constituted 65 percent of the Sikhs but only 39 percent of the state's population.[62] Not surprisingly, even the Akali Dal's quest for political power led it to seek collaboration with parties of different persuasions—until 1966 with the Congress Party and, subsequently, with the Hindu party, Jana Sangh (the predecessor of the BJP) and the Janata Party.

Nearly four decades of party competition provided Punjab with a system of governance that promoted agricultural development and economic prosperity at a rapid pace. Ironically, prosperity encouraged discontent and divisive pressures. The older Akali leaders, who by the early 1980s were riven by factional feuds, were increasingly challenged by younger Jat Sikh aspirants who were more confessionally purist, socially exclusionary, politically militant, and increasingly well armed. The competition to capture the centers of religious control put a premium on armed conflict and the use of Sikh temples as armed sanctuaries. Region and religion were tied together in an emotional equation symbolized by the notion of Khalistan as the Sikh homeland. The separatist case offered a spectrum of ambiguity such that the new militants and their nonresident remote supporters went for secession and terror, whereas several factions of the Akali leaders veered toward federalized autonomy. Most resident Sikhs had a hard time with this dissonance among political leaders. However, the Sikhs residing in other states of India—22 percent of all Sikhs living in the country—had the most difficult time.

Punjab was under president's rule in 1984 when the Indian military took the drastic action of forcing the militants to leave the Golden Temple complex they had occupied in Amritsar and to cease the use of the holy center for political and armed insurgency purposes.[63] This event led to a chain of intensified violence, including the assassination of Indira Gandhi; its aftermath of riots involving the killing of about 3,000 Sikhs, mostly in Delhi; and militant as well as counter-militant violence for many years that claimed more than 11,000 civilian lives.[64] As noted before, most of the victims of the militants' rage were Sikhs. Most of the damage and destruction affected the poor residents of Punjab. Gradually, the militants' political appeal declined, their internal feuds proliferated, and the self-confidence of the nonarmed citizens improved. The Congress Party, led by a Sikh chief minister, was returned to power in 1992 in an election that had a low turnout in a climate of stalking fear.[65] During the local elections in 1993 and 1994, the higher turnout rates matched those of the nation. The state of competitive democratic politics improved considerably as a result of the confident participation of the Congress Party, the two communist parties (CPM and the Communist Party of India), and several Akali factions functioning as competing Akali Dals. Secular democratic incentives for unmixing region and religion appear to have offered both elements a new constructive opportunity.

The long history of secessionism in India has probably made it less scary and more institutionally treatable. Northeastern politics has witnessed several moves for secession, beginning in 1950 when the case for separation of the Naga ethnic group from Assam and India was openly advocated.[66] Following continued violence, in 1962 the new state of Nagaland was created in the federation as a symbol and institution of Naga autonomy. The subsequent election in 1964 (with 77 percent voter participation) showed clear signs of increased moderation. Forces of moderation did not have an easy time, but the politics of negotiated settlement and party alternation made the federal coordination processes work through a succession of democratic governments. Secessionism was advocated for the Mizo people in 1966. The Mizo already had the status of an Autonomous Hill District in Assam—a substate system of statutory autonomy granted by the Indian constitution. But a deep resentment of Assam leaders drove some of the Mizo to insurgency. Subsequently, Mizoram's autonomy status was upgraded to a Union Territory in 1972 and to a state in 1986 following a series of compromises and negotiations. The state of Assam itself has seen violent movements initiated by members of its own dominant language community and directed against a variety of targets. Massive violence erupted in 1983. However, negotiated settlements between Assam and the federal government have been effective since 1985. Elections helped the movement leaders to gain power and, later, to lose it to their arch rival, the Congress Party.

The stories of violent ethnic demands and secessionism make exciting press copy, but the repeated success of democratic institutions in peacefully containing, preventing, preempting, or transforming such demands through negotiation tends to escape public attention. The inheritors of the Dravidian movement (in southern India), which in the 1950s advocated burning the constitution of India, became constructive partners with the nation in the 1960s. The movements for state reorganization during the 1950s and 1960s—violent at times—produced regional units based on language communities that have proved to be some of the most productive states; for example, Maharashtra, Gujarat, Punjab, Haryana, and Andhra Pradesh.[67] A series of federalizing institutions has allowed the flexible incorporation of new autonomy claimants, as exemplified in the settlement processes involving the Jharkhand and Uttarakhand movements in east and north India, respectively, in late 1994. These movements are also reminders that language-based, regional, and religious communities are political constructions that can be successfully challenged by the newly mobilized leaders who represent divisions within the communities.[68]

A notable feature of the role of religion in Indian politics until the late 1980s was the prominence of minority religions—Muslims in Kashmir and other states, Sikhs in Punjab, and Christians in Nagaland, Mizoram, and Kerala. Is it a coincidence that the focus on Hindu politics suddenly gained prominence also in the late 1980s? Is it surprising that even this prominence directed attention to a group of organizations that have performed well only in a limited set of regions? The major organizations seeking to speak for the Hindu community are the BJP, the Rashtriya Swayamsevak Sangh (RSS; national voluntary organization), the Vishwa Hindu Parishad (VHP; World Hindu Organization), and the Bharatiya Mazdoor Sangh (BMS; Indian Workers Organization).[69] These and several others are supposed to work as a disciplined family to promote an authentic form of Hindu nationalism. If these organizations are projected as the more conventional bearers of the banner of the community engaged in the legitimate public space, there are others on the side with ominous names, such as the Bajarang Dal and the Shiv Sena, that are better known for their confrontational propensities and militant manner. The boundaries of the Hindu community, however, are not so easily self-evident. The census figures indicate a massive Hindu majority (83 percent), but this is more a residual category than a measure of religious unity.[70] Distinctions of caste, language, faith, region, ideology, and class and the lack of a formal book, church, and congregations make Hinduism poor material for confessional mobilization. The long lineage of secular nationalism shared by most Hindus working in parties, pressure groups, and other organizations of the center, left, or revolutionary persuasions makes the case for Hindu confessional politics difficult. Opportunities may unfold, however, if Hindus can be made to see themselves as an unorganized majority victimized by organized minorities aided by unprincipled secularists. The BJP made such a case, but it did not prevail to the extent it desired.

Protracted violence in Kashmir and Punjab, the Congress Party's courting of the Muslim community's affection even when it entailed the reversal of a Supreme Court decision (in the Shah Bano case, 1986), the rise of Islamic fundamentalism in neighboring South Asian states, and the transnational Islamic resource conduits in India—these were some of the elements that contributed to the creation of a reactive Hindu nationalism. From 1984 to 1992, a series of campaigns to build a temple in Ayodhya, at a site where centuries ago a mosque had replaced a Hindu temple, offered mobilizing triggers to expand support nationally.[71] The payoff for the BJP was solid in the 1989 elections (as indicated previously), strikingly better in 1991, but instructively disappointing in 1993. Lower-caste and lower-class Hindu political leaders of secular radical persuasion succeeded in dislodging the BJP from power in its favorite state, Uttar Pradesh, where Ayodhya is located. The temple card also failed in two other states in 1993. All of these states were in the Hindi heartland; few areas outside of this bloc shared the spell cast by the Hindu nationalists. Before the spell took hold in the larger Hindu space, seeds of disenchantment appeared to have been planted by competing political mobilization reaching for the lower social strata among the Hindus and across religious communities. The success of Hindu organizations in the western states in 1995, as mentioned above, was actually associated with strong anti-incumbent and anticorruption campaigns. The temple card was considerably muted. A wider band of electoral support was cultivated by the BJP and the Shiv Sena. Once again, the institutions of political competition in India served to correct exclusive claims of community representation.

Democracy, Planning, and Liberalization

Strategy and Organization

Political democratization, in order to endure, needs more than institutional processing of pressures. It requires rapid development of economic and social resources so that expanding public demands can be effectively satisfied. But can a democracy in a developing country succeed in generating the required rate of development in a sustainable fashion? This question should be distinguished from one that concerns ideal or spectacular rates of development, and the distinction stems from a difference in basic values. A concern to maximize the rate of development can ignore how it is brought about and with what cost to freedom, stability, and national autonomy. Those who cannot afford to ignore these issues may, however, opt for an optimum rate consistent with other valued goals. But it is not necessary to assume that such an optimum cannot approximate or even surpass the maximum attained elsewhere. The linkage problem simply reminds us that the crucial issues to consider with respect to comparative economic development are not, after all, simply economic.

The idea of democratically planned development was pursued by the nationalist leaders long before independence. Gandhian strictures on centralization, large-scale industrialization, and bureaucratic management of development did not prevent the emergence of a wide area of agreement among other leaders regarding the importance of centrally coordinated planning for rapid industrialization. In 1938 Subhas Chandra Bose, the only major leader in Congress history who openly admired fascist discipline, became the president of the Congress and Nehru became the chairman of the party's national planning committee. Immediately after independence the Congress, as the ruling party, appointed an advisory planning board. As the first prime minister, Nehru initiated the Planning Commission and became its first chairman; he encouraged a process of thinking that assumed that economic development was a matter of scientific problem solving.[72] Nehru's admiration for scientism and its statist implications were not shared by his party men.

How has development fared? The country has experienced eight five-year and three one-year plans. During this period the economy registered a fairly steady, although unspectacular, rate of growth, experienced a partial renovation of agricultural production leading to self-sufficiency in food, developed a structure of industrialization that produces most of what the country basically needs, expanded the supply of educated and technical personnel able to execute most levels of sophisticated tasks, consistently held down the level of inflation to one of the lowest in the world, and in the process ensured a level of self-reliance and payment ability that kept it away from major debt crisis. At the same time disturbing poverty persists, inequality hurts, corruption prevails, the second economy thrives, and a number of shadows haunt the economic scene. Can the new course of liberalization do better?

The notion of people's capabilities, when applied to India, necessarily directs one to the rural situation. This is where the weight of decades of agricultural stagnation and technological obsolescence had dragged the largest segment of the nation's population to poverty and human incapacity. The most urgent task was to ensure a priority for rural development over everything else. Such a priority would have called for extensive intervention in the agrarian property structure through land reform followed by investment in productive support, technological change, and improvement in human resources. And yet this is where the record of development has been discouraging. Land reform, initiated immediately after independence, still remains largely unrealized, except in Kerala, West Bengal, and Kashmir. Drastic intervention in the rural property structure was, in fact, consciously avoided by leaving the reforms to the discretion of state-level legislation. The slow pace of land reform demonstrated a preference for a strategy of promoting production by offering financial and technical support to the relatively better-off segments of the rural population. The proportion of plan investment—implying mostly public investment—directed toward agriculture declined from the first through the second and third plans, the end period of which was accompanied by a severe crisis resulting from extensive drought.[73]

During this period public investment through planning was based on a preferred strategy of industrialization that encouraged considerably higher investment for developing organized industries, mining, power, and communications. A socialistic rhetoric was employed mainly to equate social progress with capital goods production under state control.[74] Scarce national resources were increasingly diverted to pursue import substitution under the leadership of the state. Foreign aid increased from a modest 10 percent of the first plan outlay to 28 percent in the third plan. At the same time the increasing self-empowerment of the national-level state through its expanding control of capital, strategic industries, power generation, communication networks, and employment created an impression that the ascendance of state capitalism was irresistible. Command over national, as well as external, resources and the apparatus of planned control of investment and enterprise by now had endowed the state with a degree of power that could be used to induce collaboration from larger private owners of resources in industry and agriculture. Indeed the prospect of such a collaboration could minimize the dependence of the ruling party on the poorer rural groups. Actually, as the ruling party's pursuit of industrialization strategy progressively intensified, its pursuit of the art of cultivation of mass support and its conciliatory coordination declined. A tired generation of Congress leaders appeared now to rely more on the formal instrument of the state, its tightly organized bureaucracy, its patronage powers, and its capacity to subsidize inefficient enterprise in order to consolidate and enjoy its power.

This was largely what one may call the Nehru phase of planned development. During his lifetime Nehru's influence welded the Congress Party to a level of coherence sufficient to maintain a semblance of united pursuit of planned development. Nehru's death in 1964 was followed by Prime Minister Lal Bahadur Shastri's conciliatory style of coordinating major factions and regions. If his capacity for consensus generation ensured a stable transition in politics, the new phase simply succeeded in maintaining the earlier developmental policy frame. No major departures were expected either. The consensus style, however, increasingly emboldened the chief ministers of the states to assert their role in national policy implementation. The process of regionalization of authority already developing during Nehru's rule grew stronger during Shastri's brief tenure. The strength of the state chief ministers within the party was dramatically revealed when, following Shastri's death in 1966, they helped elect Indira Gandhi as the third prime minister over the candidate of Congress organization leaders at the national level.

Indira Gandhi's style was inconsistent with a federalized system of authority within the party, but in 1966 consolidation was more important for her than anything else. The years 1966–1967 brought a severe crisis to the economy and the polity. Disastrous drought, legacies of wars with neighbors, economic debacle, and a close call in the 1967 elections appeared to offer the Congress Party an impetus for rethinking. However, although five-year planning was temporarily dropped, no radical reorganization of the premises of planning came about. The only major innovation was intensive modernization of agriculture with stepped-up investment for selected crops and regions aimed at national self-sufficiency in foodgrain production.[75] Again, the major goal was immediate production promotion and not the wider objectives of raising the long-term capability of the rural poor who composed the majority of the country. Neither the subsequent consolidation of Indira Gandhi's power from 1971, including the phase of emergency, nor her recovery of the popular mandate in 1980 were used as occasions to question the earlier priorities. The Janata Party rule, meanwhile, did raise some questions about priorities in the mid-1970s, but its tenure in office was too brief to effect significant change.

Human Base and Food Security

Indian planning began in a social context where nearly 85 percent of the population was rural, the national literacy rate was 12 percent, the majority of school-age children did not attend school, and for most people life was ruled by poverty, oppression, and morbidity. The state of the economy was equally dismal. Orderly management of the colonial economy during the five decades preceding 1950 had registered less than half-a-percent growth rate of per capita real output. Perhaps the only points of relief for the people were that life expectancy was short and the mortality rate was exceedingly high.[76] Clearly, something more than modest economic development was called for to make even a small step to alter such a nonhuman level of existence.

How does the record of democratic development stand as a response to that challenge? From the moment of independence in 1947 through the subsequent five decades, the people have lent an unexpectedly mature degree of support to the democratic process of economic development. What has this process yielded in terms of altering their level of living? How does it compare with the record of other developing countries following similar or different roads to development? Some basic indicators, despite their imperfection, can be revealing. Expectation of life at birth around 1940 was 32.1 years for Indian males and 31.4 years for females, and on the eve of planned development, around 1949, remained at 32.4 and 31.7 respectively.[77] During the years of development, these figures rose to 41.9 and 40.6 in 1960, 46.4 and 44.7 in 1970, and 50.9 and 50.0 in 1980. A recent report puts the combined figure for 1992 at 61, with women enjoying a slightly better share. By historical standards this rapid progress can be counted as encouraging. But by comparative contemporary standards, India's performance leaves room for considerable improvement. Sri Lanka, largely following a democratic path, succeeded in reaching a figure of 72 by 1992, and China, following a different path, scored 69. However, hidden under the Indian average are the figures for the state of Kerala, which are better than China's figures— China's for male and female, were 67 and 71, respectively, and Kerala's were 71 and 74, respectively.[78]

Food security, in the sense of general availability and the assurance of access to the stock of foodgrains, has been the most important issue facing the people. Indian planning began with the inherited base of production yielding barely fifty million tons. Production of foodgrains steadily rose until the crisis years of 1966–1967, when lower growth necessitated a sharp increase in imports, which in 1966 constituted 14.4 percent of total quantity available.[79] The drop in production and drag of foreign dependence pushed the state to begin a renewed effort to modernize agriculture, resulting in a big change on the food front. Production of foodgrains crossed the 100 million ton mark from 1971 and imports steadily declined. Dependence on imported food ended in 1978. In the subsequent three years, no food imports were needed. From 1980 to 1984 a small amount was imported mainly to augment the buffer stock. Production of foodgrains reached 182 million tons in 1993–1994. Net import of food from 1985 to 1994 was negligible or negative, and the size of the state reserve stock remained comfortable as of 1994.[80] The ability of the economy to cope with drought was demonstrated in 1987, when, unlike the previous drought years of 1965 and 1979, the growth rate of the national product was positive.

Success in generating self-sufficiency in foodgrains was accompanied by extensive state action to ensure that demands from the deficit states of the federation were met by transferring the surplus stock of other states in a coordinated manner. The role of the federal government in procurement and public distribution of foodgrains can be crucial for ensuring food security. In the absence of it, there would be little assurance that nationally available food would actually reach the neediest regions and groups. The magnitude of state involvement in procurement and distribution is indicated by the fact that from the mid-1960s, an average of close to 12 percent of foodgrains has been annually procured and distributed.[81]

The elimination of famines in India since independence contrasts not merely with their catastrophic recurrence during the colonial years but also with revolutionary China, where severe famine conditions claimed 15 million lives during 1959–1961.[82] The experience of democratic planning has demonstrated that democratic instruments can be made to deliver impressive results by a mutual reinforcement of popular voice and prudent policy. But that experience also shows that the reactive type of prudence, as distinguished from anticipatory prudence, can extract a heavy price from the country and especially from the poorer population before a crisis shakes the policy planners.

Thus, innovations on the food front should also be judged in light of the fact that the per capita availability of food has registered steady progress, although the actual access of the poorer people may still remain lower than in some advanced developing countries. India's daily calorie supply per capita as a percentage of requirement stood at 105, in 1991 (up sharply from 86 a decade previously), while the weighted average of all developing countries in 1991 was 109. The corresponding figure for China was 112, and for Sri Lanka 137. If the national average figures are disaggregated by income groups, lower-income groups in India will show worse scores than their counterparts in those two countries.[83]

Nutritional deprivation in India does not stand alone. Progress in providing mass education has been discouraging despite tremendous strides at the higher and technical education levels. The adult literacy rate in India in

1992 was 50 percent. In contrast, the developing countries of East Asia have exceeded 80 percent. The average rate for sub-Saharan Africa in 1970 was lower than that of India in the same period. Now India's rate lags behind that average. Primary school enrollment figures tell us an unexciting story.[84] If the premise of industrial priority explains the uneven emphasis on higher education and gross neglect of rural education at lower levels, it is difficult to imagine how comprehensive industrialization can be compatible with poor quality of labor. Fortunately, this disparity in educational investment was reduced by the end of the 1970s, indicating a better sense of balance among levels of schooling.

Induced Industrialization

The dominant intellectual climate in the 1950s could leave no doubt in the minds of any forward-looking leader of a developing country about the virtues of state-induced industrialization.[85] Industrialization, modernity, and efficient use of resources were universally equated, just as agriculture, traditionalism, and inefficiency were believed to go together. To imagine a situation of inefficient industry wasting resources and modernized agriculture offering a better return on investment and a sounder preparation for the future would have been a heresy unpardonable in the liberal, as well as revolutionary, West and, therefore, among educated people in India. If the heresy had reversed in many sophisticated circles by the 1980s, we should not forget the charm of the original equation.

Indian planning for industrialization was based on the assumption that a rapid rate and a comprehensive pattern of industrial growth can be obtained by assigning priority to the production of capital goods. If this called for going slow on agriculture and consumption goods, it was justified by the promise of future benefits for the nation as a whole. Expanded capacity in the capital goods subsector was supposed to lay the ideal foundation for subsequent production of consumption goods and absorption of labor. Such an expansion was beyond the capability of the private sector. Thus the logic of industrialization also provided a logic of centralization, extensive regulation, and a strategic role for the state in entering production, controlling supplies of inputs needed by private enterprise, directing crucial financial resources, administering key prices, and becoming the largest employer in the country. This logic satisfied the educated middle classes' sense of national mission for a number of reasons. It held a promise of national power and prosperity at the same time that an expanded public control offered a moral gratification. For here was an opportunity to use a socialistic language to control resources in the name of long-run public interest. After about forty years, it is time to ask, where has industrialization arrived?

Judging in the 1990s, it is apparent that India has acquired a comprehensive structure of industrial production (see Table 6.2). It has pursued a planned policy of import substitution that may be distinguished from the non-planned variants followed by many other developing countries.[86] Unlike Brazil, to take one example, the planned variant in India made it possible to develop heavy and light industries simultaneously despite a higher emphasis on the former. During the same period, Latin American countries gradually exhausted import substitution in light industries and then desperately scrambled for heavy industries, which led to political and economic crisis. In fact, India's policy of early emphasis on heavy industries may have allowed it to taste early and then to gradually cope with exchange crisis. Planned import substitution has also facilitated a pattern of industrialization endowed with a degree of self-reliance rare among noncommunist developing countries that achieved broad industrialization during the same period. The structure of capital goods industries in India is comparable to that of China, but unlike China, a diversified base of consumption goods industries was allowed to develop. Yet a strict regulation of the latter left room for few luxury goods, so that the flood of durable consumption goods characterizing so many industrializing countries was not reproduced in India.

These gains in industrial development were balanced by some disappointments, however. India's average annual percentage growth rate of industrial production during the period of 1960–1970 was 5.4 followed by 4.3 in 1970–1982 and 6.4 in 1980–1992. China's rates were 11.2, 8.3, and 11.1, Mexico's 9.4, 7.2, and 1.6, and South Korea's 17.2, 15.2, and 11.6, respectively.[87] Neither self-reliance nor comprehensiveness can serve as factors inhibiting high rates. India's planners have to admit that, with all their devotion to industrialism as the key to rapid development, India's performance on many important counts has moved slower than desired.[88]

The growth rate of industrial product may, however, be less important than the diversification of output indicating the creation of sophisticated capacity that makes an economy poised to move on its own. Between 1951 and 1960, sophisticated machinery and metal industries grew at a compound rate of 14.2 percent against the aggregate industrial rate of 6.4 percent, but during 1960–1970 the lead considerably narrowed, while between 1970 and 1983 the two converged around a low rate of 4.5 percent. However, the data for 1985–1991 dispelled fears of continued decline. Once again, the engineering and capital goods industries gained a comfortable lead.[89]

For Liberalization

But the sense of disappointment had already taken root. India's record of capital formation was encouraging; the rate of gross domestic savings rose consistently from about 10 percent in the 1950s to 25 percent in the 1980s (see Table 6.2). However, the inefficient use of capital, mainly by the large and abysmally wasteful public sector, deprived the country of its

Table 6.2   India Selected Growth Indicators, 1950–1951 to 1990–1991

Item	Unit	1950–1951	1960–1961	1970–1971	1980–1981	1990–1991	1950–1991 Annual Income (%)[a]
Population	million	359	434	541	679	846	2.1 (for 1980 to 1992)
Literacy	% total population	16.7	24.0	29.5	36.2	52.0	NA
Gross Domestic Capital formation	% of GDP	10.0	16.9	17.8	24.5	26.3	NA
Foodgrain Output	million tons	55.0	82.3	108.4	129.6	176.4	2.9
Industrial Production	1980–1981 = 100	NA	39.3	67.9	100.0	212.0	5.9
Consumer Price Index Industrial workers	Base 1982 = 100	NA	20	38	81	193	7.8
Government Expenditure (Center and state and union territories)	% of GNP	10.0	16.0	19.7	27.1	33.3	NA
Foreign Exchange Reserves (Excluding gold and special drawing rights)	10 million rupees ($1 = 31 rupees)	755	186	438	4,822 (1993–1994	4,388 = 4,728)	NA
Real National Income Growth Aggregate Per capita	decade %	(1951–1961) 3.8 1.8	(1961–1971) 3.4 1.2	(1971–1981) 3.0 0.7	(1981–1991) 5.2 3.0	(1991–1993) 2.3 0.4	

Source: Center for Monitoring Indian Economy, *Basic Statistics Relating to the Indian Economy,* August 1994; also August 1986 (Bombay; 1994 and 1986); Government of India, *Economic Survey,* 1993–1994 (New Delhi: 1994), various tables.

a. Rates of increase are tentative calculations; the data for different periods are not always strictly comparable because of source differences.

dividends.[90] It was easy for political leaders to expand the public-sector and public-control systems to reap political capital at the cost of the health and prospects of the economy. The socialist solace, if useful for a while for both the government and the opposition, this time merely served as a deceptive cover. Since the economy was mainly inward-oriented, the sore points of decay were not readily apparent abroad. Government attempted to cover some of the weaknesses through external and internal borrowing. The signs of industrial recovery were often false signals that concealed increasing payment burdens resulting from misguided industrial reforms in the 1980s. A narrow band of end users was being served by the fastest-growing industries—consumer durables that were affordable mostly to the wealthy segments of this poor country.[91] These were also the industries with higher import content. Already strained by severe fiscal and foreign exchange problems, the economy was pushed further to the brink of crisis.

The Rajiv Gandhi government showed little sign of readiness or capability to cope with the deeper problems. The National Front government offered some measures to reduce the fiscal deficit and import demand. But government instability during 1989, 1990, and early 1991 did not help. The drastic changes in the communist world at this time further hurt the Indian economy, abruptly shifting established patterns of trade and aid. The Gulf crisis of 1990 worsened the situation by suddenly reducing remittances while requiring an expensive evacuation of Indian workers from the war zone. By 1991, India was forced to seek International Monetary Fund (IMF) loans for financial rescue.[92] Thus, internal and external factors combined to create a conjuncture that, ironically, made it easier politically to opt for a major revision of the course of industrialization and economic development.

Narasimha Rao's minority government, in power after the 1991 elections, turned the moment of crisis into a season of opportunity. Prime Minister Rao utilized the common fears of a wide range of the Indian public to build broad consensual support for drastic action. He was ably assisted by his finance minister, Manmohan Singh, whose academic standing and economic connections facilitated the national and international negotiations to cope with the crisis. Rao and Singh gathered enough support within and across parties to break decisively with the past and embrace a bold strategic course of extensive economic liberalization. The package of policy reforms introduced in 1991 included stabilization policies to reduce the fiscal deficit and curb inflation, and structural reforms to increase the efficiency and capacity of Indian industries to compete abroad.[93] Liberalization called for a series of measures to deregulate the economy; the measures included industrial, trade, and financial-sector reforms of unprecedented scope. The system of planning was not abandoned—rather, it was revised to serve as an intersectoral federal coordinating mechanism. When the eighth five-year plan was released in 1992, it stated frankly that henceforth, planning would be largely indicative of the directions in which the economy and development process should be moving.[94]

The industrial reforms were designed to remove barriers to the entry of new firms and to projects for industrial expansion and diversification regardless of size. A few exceptions remained, but in general this delicensing policy was well received. Another delicensing policy removed bureaucratic scrutiny of investment proposals of large firms, which had been restricted to prevent monopoly practices. Regulations relating to foreign investment and technological collaboration were significantly liberalized. Although this policy signaled a major change, it still falls short of the freedom accorded to direct foreign investors in many other parts of Asia.[95] The public sector's operating space was substantially reduced; except for oil refining, all manufacturing industries were opened to private enterprise. The discretionary restrictions that had formerly benefited the small-scale industries were not significantly altered. Trade reforms and rupee convertibility processes were modest and cautiously paced. Financial-sector reforms consisted of liberalization of interest rates and measures to promote greater efficiency in the securities market.

The new directions of liberalization were reaffirmed and strengthened in all the successive budgets. Since the largest sector of employment—agriculture—was not directly the subject of these reforms, coordination between the center and the states became less problematic. In most states different ruling parties raised few disturbing issues. Yesterday's most vocal critic of liberalization and globalization—the CPM—gradually accepted some basic aspects of liberalization. Although dissent often blared from the public platforms of parties to the left and right of the Congress Party, the relative effectiveness of these policies rendered the criticism fairly harmless.

In late 1994, Rao claimed he wanted his Congress Party to rule for at least another decade to complete economic reforms that had received only three years' trial. Although this proclamation was obviously directed to the forthcoming elections in four states, it also indicated that the reformers knew it was too soon to expect any dramatic result.[96] Most observers agree that the liberalization measures have succeeded in reducing macroeconomic imbalances and in generating a positive climate for national and international investment. Progress in competitiveness through industrial deregulation and trade liberalization is also recognizable even within this short period. What are the developmental consequences of these liberalizing policies?

Beginning from a very depressing year, 1991, when the real GDP growth rate fell below 2 percent, the average annual rates for 1992–1994 exceeded 4 percent. Although this was worse than the 5.2 percent annual rate attained during the preceding decade, it was much better than the crisis base year. Agricultural production, which registered a negative growth rate in 1991, improved to an average of 3 percent growth during 1992–1994. In 1991 the industrial production growth rate had hit a low point of less than 1 percent. For the three succeeding years the rate improved, and by 1993–1994 the average approximated 4 percent. The consumer price index for the same two years recorded a 7.5 percent rise against the 1991 figure of 13.5 percent. Exports had hit a negative growth rate in 1991; by 1994 the average rate of growth approached 18 percent, and the import rise was moderate. Foreign exchange reserves tripled from a meager $5 billion to more than $15 billion. Foreign capital and direct foreign investment inflows continued to register exceptionally strong levels during 1993 and 1994. The debt component of the capital inflow kept declining, and the proportion of that debt in concessional loans was expected to rise in 1994–1995 from 39 percent in 1993 to 69 percent.[97] Concern about IMF leverage declined substantially. In April 1994, $1.13 billion of stand-by facility funds were repaid to the IMF ahead of schedule.[98] Thus, the bold moves of the Rao government seemed to reap a positive payoff for the economy and for the consensual strategy of national and international negotiation conducted by the leadership.

The initial accomplishments of liberalization do not warrant complacency, but neither should they be underestimated. Economic stabilization and structural reforms involve heavy transitional costs that impose a tremendous burden on the poorer people, especially on the most disadvantaged castes, classes, regions, and gender and age groups—for example, children. What world organizations celebrate as the virtues of stabilization may not always take into account the transitional destabilizing costs for the poor and for the political system and its effectiveness. For a developing country of India's size, complexity, and especially democratic politics, the feasibility of strategic choices is certainly more important than abstract economic prescriptions for crossing the critical threshold that would make liberalization irreversible.

Competing Claims for Justice and Responsive Transition

Economic liberalization is a part of the much wider process of developmental transition. These two aspects must be considered together in order to understand how the reforms are likely to work and for whom. Most of the emphasis in the liberalizing policies has concerned national-level decisions, which are more focused on the industrial sector and do not always directly affect policy at the state level. The most important issues affecting the daily lives of India's poor—food, agriculture, education, health, and human well-being—are closer to the state level. These issues are more directly concerned with improving the productive functioning of the people and their sense of efficacy as citizens, not merely as producers or consumers. The unconventional matching of liberal politics with liberal economic transition will increasingly call attention to the way these citizens will evaluate the developmental outcomes on their own terms and how they will act, individually or in concert. The proximate authority relevant for these citizens will usually be the local or state government. How will the reforms affect these citizens? Also, how will the citizens' reactions affect the capability of the political institutions?

It is important to consider the system of expectations the developmental processes have generated during the preceding decades.[99] Expectations for social responsiveness on the part of the political institutions were rooted in the planning system. The promise of poverty reduction through public allocation, investment, and management was an important part of India's early democratic functioning. The requirements of production had to be reconciled with the claims for employment and equity. The needs to reduce interregional and intraregional disparities were always an important part of the discourse on planned development. It was important to establish such major objectives as nationally shared values in order to generate a structure of collaboration among contending groups, parties, and publics. Over the historical course of India's planned development, these legitimating mechanisms have worked, both at the center and in center-state linkages. Fortunately, the limited scope of the liberalizing reforms and their cautious pattern of implementation make it likely that the departure from the old system will not be disruptive.

In fact, the pace of industrial restructuring, marketization, privatization, banking reforms, subsidy reduction, and fiscal deficit reduction has been so slow as to invite criticism that party politics was very much in charge. Reform of the public sector has implied selling some shares to private investors but not privatizing. Unionized labor has not yet been seriously disturbed. Major constituencies of support are offered compensatory benefits when old conduits are taken away. When the public-sector outlay for agriculture, including irrigation and flood control, was slated for reduction in the draft version of the eighth plan, the rural development outlay was increased. Meanwhile, the indirect effects of macroeconomic adjustments have also benefited agriculture by offering better incentives in terms of prices and investments. But the removal of biases against agriculture needs to be supplemented with public measures to supply subsidized food to the needy.[100] At the central level, a shift from subsidies to public aid for directly productive investments in agriculture can be gradually ensured if the transitional compensatory and supplemental measures are designed effectively. At the state level, however, there is less compulsion to shift from the path of subsidies, which will make the economic reforms in the countryside more amenable to a gradual transition while remaining responsive to the concerns of rural citizens.

The federalized political system in India has generally allowed for a variety of policy paths to serve the cause of the disadvantaged population within the national planning framework. Public investment to promote production in agriculture has been effective in reducing poverty and ensuring prosperity in Punjab and Haryana. In this group of cases, spectacular productive growth, although promoting capitalist agriculture, has been compatible with poverty reduction.[101] Radical land reform, on the other hand, in combination with extensive public support for promoting the well-being of the lower classes, has yielded social gains in Kerala exceeded by few governments in the developing world. By 1991, Kerala's life expectancy (for both men and women) exceeded that of China[102]; its fertility rate was lower than that of China, the United States, and Sweden; and its female literacy also surpassed China's. Democratic processes were strong enough to facilitate these accomplishments. During the period 1982–1992, West Bengal, which combined land reform with extensive public investment to raise agricultural productivity, surpassed the rate of growth of foodgrain production of Punjab and Haryana. West Bengal's record on this count was surpassed only by Mizoram and Nagaland—two states that are usually discussed more for their record of insurgent secessionism than for any other aspect of politics.[103] These selected cases are not models of responsiveness or of ideal development, but they do show what results democratic development can provide in some regions of the country even as other areas may lag far behind.

These cases also show how very different perceptions of priority may occupy different regions or segments of the population and how the pursuit of one objective may grossly neglect other competing objectives. Punjab's success in attaining prosperity was accompanied by an increasing concentration of property ownership in land. The lowest-caste or lowest-class Sikhs had less to rejoice about than their privileged partners. Yet their sense of disadvantage paled in comparison with the sense of violent persecution felt by some of the smaller sects within the Sikh community when they were the targets of attack by the group that dominated the community. Kerala's social accomplishments need to be read against its dismal record of production. The state that is famous for feeding its poorest members has by far the worst record of food production in the nation and also has the worst unemployment and the highest crime rate.[104] Kerala's social treatment of women is much more impressive than that of India's most prosperous states. At the same time, its rate of crime against women has also been the highest in the country during the past decade.[105] West Bengal's radical promise associated with the communist government is no consolation for the most disadvantaged castes and tribes.

Each of these disadvantages demands responsiveness and justice. Some of these claims for justice must be treated simultaneously, but they often compete with each other in a frustrating way. Disadvantages such as poverty, unemployment, gender oppression, and children's deprivations may call for coordinated treatment, but demands for ethnic affirmation, religious group rights, or regional autonomy may claim competing attention. The Indian experience of planned development—of which liberalization is a recent phase—is a story of competing and complementary claims of justice, complicating the problem of public responsiveness in a setting where democracy is supposed to be a productive force capable of energizing the economic system.[106]

Theoretical Review

Liberal democratic theories, as conventionally stated, are more preoccupied with political mechanisms for contestation and articulation than with what these mechanisms can accomplish for society. Such an emphasis on contest may be appropriate to societies where reasonable levels of living have been already accomplished or where crucial functions of development need not call for sustained collective endeavor. By excluding productive development from its charge, the state can simply be assigned some regulative and protective functions. But is this limited preoccupation justified by even the history of Western democracies? Perhaps the limited focus on *being* a democracy diverts our attention from the more complex historical issue of *becoming democratic*.[107] When the issue of active becoming is analyzed, it may show that there are more things in common between democratic evolution in the advanced and developing countries than is commonly assumed in the conventional literature.

Democracy in developing countries can hardly be appreciated merely in terms of degrees of contestation and expression, as many studies have sought to do.[108] A better way would be to focus on the gradual cultivation of ideas and institutions in civil society contributing to the formation and strengthening of a democratic *system,* through simultaneous development of social, economic, and political resources. This would imply an emphasis on the transformative role of the state and other political institutions. The basic concerns here, during a critical transition, would be less with the formal mechanisms of checks and balances, rights and obligations, and more with the authority of political institutions, the strength of operative (if not ideological) consensus, the weight and distribution of actual and latent opposition, and the ability of the system to evoke legitimating sentiments generally but not necessarily on the basis of performance. For in a fragile moment of beginning, rules can be easily violated by a state that comes to control most resources in the name of the public. But the same state will more often respect the rules where the absence of such rules may deplete, if not defeat, the economic and social power of the ruling leaders.

The rules of democratic legitimation and incorporation have served the ruling groups rather well in India during their five decades of operation. Unlike in neighboring Pakistan, which emerged from exactly the same colonial experience, India's leaders benefited from an early process of converting nationalist support into electoral support. Continued electoral support allowed them to dominate the developing civil society through state control over economy, education, communication, coercion, and extensive systems of patronage and subsidy. The dominant economic classes in industry and agriculture generally found the system profitable and conducive to a stable set of expectations in a national market of vast potential. If occasionally, as in the staggered sequence of modest reforms of land tenure or economic liberalization, some threats were posed to the upper, propertied classes, compensatory avenues of gains were offered to them through formal or informal channels.

Moreover, new entrants to privileged formations were encouraged through the use of public sector financing, licensing, and tax policies in industries, and by promoting relatively affluent peasant entrepreneurs. At the same time, the promise of expansion of privilege offered a mobility incentive to a wider number in rural and urban areas who developed a sense of stake in the system more on the basis of aspiration than accomplishment. The successful incorporation of regional aspirations in a federalized polity created another important constituency of support for this legitimated democratic system. If all this was not enough to impel the leaders to maintain the rules of the regime, the negative reactions of wide segments of the public threatening the brief interlude of rule violation during the emergency could make them fall in line. Besides, the gains of abiding by the rules were also appreciated by the opposition leaders when they realized—as in Kerala, West Bengal, Tamil Nadu, and other states—that access to power, and its prolonged use in cooperation with other parties ruling in the center, would not be denied. When leaders of capitalist, communist, and other persuasions develop and sustain a democratic system of rules with equal eagerness there must be something more to it than a mere veneer on class rule or a chance gift of colonial history.

All these leadership sets have worked through fairly structured organizational systems with relatively durable organizations and modes of mutual interaction. This organizational system has worked best when it has encouraged incorporation of multiple interests from civil society, including ethnic expressions. Such voluntary associations have also served as latent sectors of potential political leadership in moments of crisis as, for example, discussed earlier in the context of plebiscitarian adventures of central leadership. It is true that there have been occasions when the organizational system in the country witnessed disturbing challenges. However, these threats have, in most cases, been limited in time and territorial extension. Thus, communist insurrectionary challenge in the early 1950s and late 1960s remained confined to a few districts, separatism of the DMK or the hill peoples' secessionism failed to expand or converge, and religion-using Sikh separatism and Hindu communalism had to contend with rivals in their own communities. All these widely dispersed threats were also widely staggered over time, and in most cases yesterday's adversaries were turned into the next day's partners.[109]

This resilience or absorptive capacity has been considerably aided by an ideological consensus (evolving since the nationalist period) regarding liberal means of resolving conflict, the basic premises of self-reliant planned development, and the directive as well as responsive functions of the state in society. Thus no matter which political party has ruled at the center or at the state level, its functioning pattern has shared a degree of similarity that would have been hard to anticipate from its rhetoric before capturing power. This ideological collaboration reinforces the consensual readiness of political actors to play by mutually accepted rules.

How deep is the foundation of support for the system? Studies of advanced democracies show that basic agreements among articulate groups seem to be more decisive than their wider penetration among the masses.[110] Empirical studies of Indian political perception indicate a degree of penetration that clearly goes beyond this minimal requirement. As early as 1967 70 percent of Indian adults identified with a party, compared to 60 percent in the United States in 1972. The attitudes of non-literates and those with minimal education demonstrated strong commitment to parties, in fact considerably stronger than comparable U.S. cases. A high correspondence was demonstrated between party identification and party issue preference.[111] Another empirical study has found that partisanship is "not only associated with more [system] supportive attitudes, the attitudes themselves are richer and more basic to the viability of competitive institutions in India."[112] These studies also reveal that the perception of party differences among Indian partisans is informed by a remarkable tolerance of the ideologies of other partisans, who are rarely regarded as radical threats to the system.[113] Democratic political development has apparently not been constrained by the slow development of the so-called social and economic requisites of democratic being.[114]

Indian democracy can be understood as a deliberate act of political defiance of the social and economic constraints of underdevelopment. In fact it has been an adventure in creating a political system that would actively generate the social and economic development it lacked at its moment of foundation. This creative exercise in the autonomy of political initiative and inducement to reverse the expected sequence of democratic development called for simultaneous treatment of multiple issues like national cohesion, economic development, social justice, citizen efficacy, and human development. The requirement of combination also presupposed that exclusive attention to one objective could be self-defeating. Rather, divided attention implied that the system could benefit from a plurality of expectations from various publics. For example, success in managing challenges to national cohesion and promoting agricultural development may reduce the intensity of adverse reaction to the slow implementation of land reform. Thus it is not surprising that aggregate public confidence in the democratic system has not depended on the performance of particular governments in exclusive issue areas. When the "sons of the soil" or the backward castes are enthused to support a regime that offers them special mobility through a protected job market or job reservations, the system obviously gains allegiance at the transitional cost of economic efficiency.[115] But the consequent gains in the political efficacy of the system may allow it to promote efficiency in other areas of economic action.

Admittedly such balancing acts are favored by the configuration of social divisions, structural diversities, and the ecological differences in a complex country like India. It is also clear that these acts have been performed well enough to sustain the regime so far. But the limits should not be ignored. Success in balancing requires an imaginative leadership, which no system ensures in advance. Worse still, as one author had put it in a related context, it may be "a good net to catch allies, but one highly vulnerable to anyone with sharp teeth."[116] The art of balancing, even if forthcoming, may become vulnerable to resolute adversaries having independent access to crucial resources, particularly at a point when the resources of the state are dangerously depleted. Moments of economic crisis, international disturbance, tides of internal populism, or desperate actions by dominant classes to break a perceived stalemate may effectively challenge the hard-earned resilience of five decades.

Rapid development of the democratic system's resources of production, organization, distribution, communication, and legitimation can best preempt such danger. Unfortunately this art of balancing practiced in recent decades, by Congress as well as non-Congress leaders at federal and state levels, has thrived more on distributive skills—largely displayed in patronage, subsidy, and welfare promotions—than on rapid creation of resources.[117] It is tempting to believe that this is inherent in the process of democratic becoming in an inhospitable society. It is equally tempting to ask if the same society, with its compulsion for combined development, can be served better by alternatives to democracy, particularly at this point of development when the maturing experience of democratic becoming would scarcely make the people settle for anything less. However, neither logic nor the historical lessons discussed here would warrant a conclusion that democratic development in a context like India's must necessarily be more self-destructive than self-regenerating.

Future Prospects

Barely a decade after the launching of independent India's constitutional democracy, a major Western work on Indian politics confidently warned that "the odds are almost wholly against the survival of freedom and that . . . the issue is, in fact, whether any Indian state can survive at all."[118] Now that both the structure of freedom and the state have survived such dire predictions for nearly five decades, the issue can be turned around. The analysis in this chapter indicates that the successful maintenance of democracy in India has ensured the stability of the new state and reasonably steady development, achieved with a degree of self-reliance and relative freedom from world economic oscillation that is rare in contemporary history. The processes of democratic becoming have already crossed a threshold of reasonable success in a world that has witnessed, especially in recent decades, a resurgence of interest in democratic development. The appeal of the "glamorous" alternatives to democratic development has given way to more realistic assessments of the role of democracy in combined development.[119]

The initial decades of Indian democracy now deserve to be considered as a constructive enterprise of consolidating a political system while socially deepening its political structures. As competing groups canvass the lower depths of this maddeningly heterogeneous society to enlarge their political support, the new political recruits are unlikely to be already well schooled in cherished norms of civility. When inducted into the political process, their initial impulse may move them to seek social mobility or at least to affirm their political rights. These expressions may not necessarily be peaceful or graceful. A part of the first act of engagement in a legitimate public space may be the compression of the accumulated distress of centuries into moments of rage or excess. As one observer put it, in India this is the way freedom has "worked its way down."[120] Generally and mercifully, these moments have been brief, dispersed, noncumulative, and compatible with the basic rules of reasonable competition.

In India, wherever democratic institutions have become meaningful at the lowest level—that is, villages, districts, and intermediate units—popular participation has been systematically incorporated. The regularly elected *panchayats* in West Bengal, for example, have shown levels of citizen and institutional efficacy that are little different from those of the more visible legislatures in big cities.[121] Even outside of such structured representation, in most cases rural mobilization connected with upper- and lower-class issues has been expressed in organized forms. Whether it is a case of organized rich farmers or of a spontaneous march of the most disadvantaged subaltern formations, a disciplined harnessing of collective action can be noticed and negotiated with if the sensitivity exists to see it.[122] Too often we forget the logic of institutional becoming by indigenous trial and error, which allows these institutions to be shaped by their particular environment and, therefore, imparts to them a character that may depart from the standardized models obtained in Western literature.[123] Whatever the form, class expressions in the countryside have, through the use of democratic processes, become more attached to and influenced by the evolving institutions.

Job reservation as an expression of caste politics and as an instrument of social mobility on the part of backward castes has increasingly turned into a tool of the relatively upper castes. What is called "Mandalized politics" has built-in limits, in the sense that there are too few state jobs to be handed out to too many caste groups.[124] In July 1994, two of the most advanced castes in the state of Karnataka were included in the list of backward castes, and the span of reservation was extended to 73 percent of the population. The absurdity of this policy will limit its political profitability. But the most interesting secular contribution of this Hindu caste politics was the ability of lower-caste Hindu politicians to strike a crushing blow to Hindu communal politics by dislodging the BJP from power in its favorite state. Also, in early

1992 the lower-caste Hindu leaders in power in Bihar were highly successful in preventing communal riots when most other states' leaders appeared
either helpless or indifferent.

The expanding range and depth of popular politics have brought out
unfamiliar people, patterns, and idioms of political action that have often
made many observers at home and abroad uncomfortable. The lower-caste
chief ministers of Uttar Pradesh and Bihar are far apart from the anglicized
politicians of the Nehru family, who came down from their mansions to
serve the people below—people resembling today's chief ministers. A colonial hangover makes it difficult for many to accept the form democracy has
attained by making those people speak for and rule themselves. The changing nature of the national parties—which increasingly have tended to
become catchall federal coalitions, often with shifting support bases from
one part of the country to another—and a tendency toward plebiscitarian
cultivation of newly mobilized caste, class, and ethnic groups in regions
gave rise to the issue of the deinstitutionalization of authority.[125] Popular
demands not processed by familiar institutions of the older vintage helped
raise the issues of disorder and ungovernability.[126] If these labels were truly
descriptive of the system, how could it manage such a vast country? Some
economists have charged that the basic weakness of India's policy leadership lay in the fact that it was too exposed to, and too hampered by, contending interests to make hard choices.[127] These charges were made when
India was drifting from one plan to another in a manner that might have suggested a consistent capitulation to dominant classes. However, when the
economy was boldly made to change its course in 1991, this indicated that a
weak government could indeed make hard choices and thereby strengthen
itself and the system at the same time: The charges of ungovernability did
not seem accurate at that historical moment. The way an unspectacular
leader such as Rao dared to reintroduce internal elections within the
Congress Party following a lapse of two decades suggested that processes of
reinstitutionalization, organizational renewal, and restoration deserve as
much recognition as their ominous counterparts.[128]

The capacity of the democratic system to renew itself has not been
acquired without dissent or difficulties. The vitality of the system has
depended only partially on the state, or rather on the cluster of states that
work within the federal framework. The complex process of authority creation by gradually generating a sense of trust has, of course, been fairly
demanding and at times confusing. The nature of international connections
that developed following the end of the Cold War has also involved a rather
new course of learning.

But it is the civil society, with its expanding array of concerns and associations, that has offered the best course of learning for the democratic system. Democratization has encouraged and empowered a large number of
new organizations and movements seeking to express concerns and advocate causes that were not well articulated by conventional social and politi-

cal organizations. These civil-society formations have given a new sense of importance—if not receptivity—to issues that concern human rights, gender, children, health, security of groups threatened by communal or caste violence, autonomy of tribal groups, prevention of environmental degradation, and the rights of people victimized by either showcase public projects or ecological disasters. A new emphasis on the accountability of the political and social authority systems has been communicated by these civil-society formations. The lineage of voluntary associative action during the preindependence decades has helped, but the reach of the new formations is wider and deeper. They often derive strength from a variety of ideological positions or party affiliations. They are also, in many cases, multifunctional.

Thus, the People's Union for Civil Liberties and the People's Union for Democratic Rights work for civil liberties and also act as legal aid or, at times, as public interest groups.[129] By trying to expose and discipline the state and oppressive social authorities, these groups have, in fact, revitalized the democratic system. A number of national and regional women's organizations actively advocate rights and build self-help structures for women.[130] Other associations and movements advocate the rights of the rural poor and fight for the most oppressed castes.[131] Social action groups connected with the movements to protect the rights of those who are affected by the construction of dams on the Narmada River have gained national and international attention.[132] Their style of protest was popularized by ecological conservation campaigns such as the Chipko and Appiko movements.[133] All of these movements also highlight the need for special ecological sensitivity to the interests of the often neglected tribal peoples of India. In addition, tribal associations directly advocate cultural autonomy (in connection with regional demands and community issues, discussed earlier).

Space does not permit a full consideration of the wide range of organizations variously called social action groups, nongovernmental organizations, movement groups, and the like. One estimate claims that the number of these organizations in India may approach 100,000.[134] Fortunately, there is a new trend toward the formation of national federations such as the Jan Vikas Andolan (the Movement for People's Development), which brings together nearly 200 groups.[135]

These civil society formations have immensely enriched the institutional expression of India's developing liberal public culture. While expressing rights, they assist the democratic system in serving citizens on their terms and build networks and coalitions to serve wider publics and broader causes. In addition, they demonstrate the readiness of the system to be responsive to citizen needs and, thus, increase citizen efficacy and belief in the system's legitimacy. The formations call attention to the crucial connections between the institutions of governance and civil society. We will better appreciate the prospects of democracy in India if we focus attention on this growing reciprocity between the state and society, as reflected in the democratic developmental system.

Notes

1. For an early history of associations in India see, for example, B. B. Majumdar, *Indian Political Associations and Reform of Legislature (1818–1917)* (Calcutta: Firma K. L. Mukhopadhyay, 1965), ch. 2–5. See also S. Natarajan, *A Century of Social Reform in India* (Bombay: Asia Publishing House, 1962).

2. See Stephen Hay, "Western and Indigenous Elements in Modern Indian Thought: The Case of Ram Mohun Roy," in Marius B. Jansen, ed., *Changing Japanese Attitudes Toward Modernization* (Princeton: Princeton University Press, 1965), p. 318.

3. For details see J. Das Gupta, *Language Conflict and National Development* (Berkeley: University of California Press, 1970), pp. 78ff.

4. When the nationalists sought to persuade the ruling authority to introduce compulsory primary education, their move was turned down. As late as 1911 only 1 percent of Indians would be considered as literate in English and 6 percent in vernacular languages. According to high-ranking British administrators Indian "power to stir up discontent would be immensely increased if every cultivator could read." See Sumit Sarkar, *Modern India, 1885–1947* (Delhi: Macmillan, 1983), pp. 66-67.

5. For a discussion of preemptive militarism in Japan see Akira Iriya, "Imperialism in Asia," in James B. Crowley, ed., *Modern East Asia: Essays in Interpretation* (New York: Harcourt, Brace and World, 1970), pp. 122ff. Increasing racialism in colonial rule was typified in a comment like "we could only govern by maintaining the fact that we are the dominant race . . . ," quoted in Sumit Sarkar, *Modern India*, p. 23.

6. John R. McLane, *Indian Nationalism and the Early Congress* (Princeton: Princeton University Press, 1977), pp. 94–95. See also Bipan Chandra et al., *India's Struggle for Independence* (New Delhi: Penguin, 1989), pp. 74–76.

7. Dadabhai Naoroji, *Poverty and Un-British Rule in India* (Delhi: Publications Division, Government of India, 1969 [originally published in 1901]), p. 116. For a collection of others' writings see A. Appadorai, ed., *Documents on Political Thought in Modern India,* vol. 1 (Bombay: Oxford University Press, 1973).

8. See W. T. deBary, ed., *Sources of Indian Tradition,* vol. 2 (New York: Columbia University Press, 1963), p. 140; and Appadorai, *Documents on Political Thought,* vol. 1, p. 163.

9. See deBary, ed., *Sources of Indian Tradition,* vol. 2, pp. 194–195.

10. For a detailed discussion see Das Gupta, *Language Conflict and National Development.*

11. Gandhi's ideas are discussed in R. Iyer, *The Moral and Political Thought of Mahatma Gandhi* (New York: Oxford University Press, 1973). For Nehru's ideas see M. Brecher, *Nehru: A Political Biography* (New York: Oxford University Press, 1959). See also Ronald J. Terchek, "Gandhi and Democratic Theory," in T. Pantham and K. L. Deutsch, eds., *Political Thought in Modern India* (New Delhi: Sage, 1986), pp. 307–324; and B. Parekh, "Gandhi and the Logic of Reformist Discourse," in B. Parekh and T. Pantham, eds., *Political Discourse* (New Delhi: Sage, 1987), pp. 277–291.

12. The complexity of the job involved in keeping multiple interests together, and yet not exclusively serving a dominant interest due to populist compulsions of the movement, is discussed in C. Markovits, *Indian Business and Nationalist Politics, 1931–1939* (Cambridge: Cambridge University Press, 1985), pp. 180–181.

13. These ideas are analyzed in detail in Joan Bondurant, *Conquest of Violence* (Berkeley: University of California Press, 1965), esp. pp. 190ff.

14. See, for example, Judith M. Brown, *Gandhi's Rise to Power* (Cambridge: Cambridge University Press, 1972). For a detailed analysis of these movements, see especially pp. 52–122.

15. Ibid., especially pp. 190–249.

16. For a background of the 1919 reforms see S. R. Mehrotra, "The Politics Behind the Montagu Declaration of 1917," in C. H. Philips, ed., *Politics and Society in India* (New York: Praeger, 1962), pp. 71–96.

17. The Act of 1935 and its working is analyzed in A. Chatterji, *The Constitutional Development of India: 1937–1947* (Calcutta: Firma K. L. Mukhopadhyay, 1958), pp. 3–25.

18. The general seats were those that were not specifically designated for Muslims, Europeans, Anglo-Indians, Indian Christians, or Sikhs. For most purposes these would imply constituencies for Hindu candidates.

19. The official version of the constitution was in English. In late 1987 a Hindi translation of the document was approved by a constitutional amendment. Thus, the fifty-sixth amendment relatively enlarged access in a country where most people cannot read English. Hindi reading ability extends to about one-third of the country's population.

20. See *The Constitution of India* (as on September 1, 1991) (New Delhi: Ministry of Law and Justice, Government of India, 1991), pp. 13–15.

21. For example, during the ninth (1989) and the tenth (1991) parliamentary elections, the turnout rates in Kerala were 79 and 74 percent, respectively. The corresponding rates in West Bengal were 80 and 77 percent, respectively. These and other figures used in this section are from All India Radio, *Lok Sabha Poll* (New Delhi: Government of India, 1991); and David Butler, Ashok Lahiri, and Prannoy Roy, *India Decides, Elections 1952–1991* (New Delhi: Living Media, 1991), various sections.

22. The Congress government, led by Prime Minister P. V. Narasimha Rao, survived the no-confidence motion on July 28, 1993, by a margin of fourteen votes. A faction of the Janata Dal and some other small groups came to Rao's rescue. For details see the *Telegraph* (Calcutta), July 29, 1993, p. 1. For subsequent trials of strength within the party and parliament see V. Ramakrishnan, "Cracks in the Congress," *Frontline*, February 24, 1995, p. 18 and A. Phadnis, "Another Round to Rao," *Sunday*, May 14–20, 1995, pp. 34–39. A convention of rebel Congressmen threatened to split the party on May 19, 1995. The rebels had poor support in Parliament. On May 23, Rao comfortably won the parliamentary vote for the 1995/96 budget. See *India-West*, May 26, 1995, various newsreports, esp. pp. A-1, A-8, A-9, and A-13.

23. For an elaboration of the notion of reasonable action and its role in democratization see John Rawls, *Political Liberalism* (New York: Columbia University Press, 1993), pp. 48–54. To be reasonable is to respect "fair terms of cooperation and to abide by them willingly, given the assurance that others will likewise do so"; p. 49.

24. See Richard Sisson, "Party Transformation in India: Development and Change in the Indian National Congress," in N. S. Bose, ed., *India in the Eighties* (Calcutta: Firma K. L. Mukhopadhyay, 1982), pp. 1–23; and Stanley A. Kochanek, *The Congress Party of India* (Princeton: Princeton University Press, 1968), especially pp. 407–447.

25. The idea of the Congress Party as a national reconciler of interests has been extensively treated in many works, of which at least two may be noted: Myron Weiner, *Party Building in a New Nation: The Indian National Congress* (Chicago: University of Chicago Press, 1967); and Rajni Kothari, *Politics in India* (Boston: Little, Brown, 1970).

26. For details of the politics of the 1970s and its later impact see Robert L. Hardgrave Jr., and Stanley A. Kochanek, *India: Government and Politics in a Developing Nation*, 4th ed. (New York: Harcourt Brace Jovanovich, 1994), pp. 237ff.

27. See Myron Weiner, "Political Evolution—Party Bureaucracy and Institutions," in John D. Mellor, ed., *India: A Rising Middle Power* (Boulder: Westview Press, 1979), especially pp. 32ff.

28. For the Bihar and Gujarat agitations see Ghanshyam Shah, *Protest Movements in Two Indian States: A Study of Gujarat and Bihar Movements* (Delhi: Ajanta, 1977). See also Geoffrey Ostergaard, "The Ambiguous Strategy of J. P.'s Last Phase," in David Selbourne, ed., *In Theory and Practice: Essays on the Politics of Jayaprakash Narayan* (Delhi: Oxford University Press, 1985), pp. 155–180.

29. Jayaprakash Narayan explained his position in these words: "I am aiming at a people's movement embracing the entire nation. A movement cannot have a clear-cut program. The main purpose of a movement is to articulate people's wishes." See his collected writings published under the title *Total Revolution* (Bombay: Popular Prakashan, 1978), vol. 4, p. 141. Positive programs favored by him and the core groups of this movement in Bihar are stated in pp. 165ff. These include political accountability of the elected legislators to their constituencies, devolution of decisionmaking authority, and implementation of agrarian reforms through peoples' committees. See ibid., pp. 168–170.

30. The opponent was Raj Narain, who defeated Indira Gandhi in the election of 1977. The court case and the events following it are described in K. Nayar, *The Judgment: Inside Story of Emergency in India* (New Delhi: Vikas. 1977).

31. These provisions and their use in 1975 are discussed in Zubair Alam, *Emergency Powers and Indian Democracy* (New Delhi: S. K. Publishers, 1987), pp. 94–103. The fifty-ninth amendment of the constitution passed by Parliament in March 1988 empowers the federal government to impose emergency in Punjab.

32. See, for example, A. Gledhill, *The Republic of India: The Development of Its Laws and Constitution* (London: Stevens, 1951), pp. 107–109.

33. This distinction is discussed in detail in J. Das Gupta, "A Season of Ceasars: Emergency Regimes and Development Politics in Asia," *Asian Survey* 18, no. 4 (April 1978): pp. 315–349.

34. Why she ended up choosing this option has been subject to extensive speculation. A good analysis of possible reasons and explanations is in P. B. Mayer, "Congress (I). Emergency (I): Interpreting Indira Gandhi's India," *Journal of Commonwealth and Comparative Policies* 22, no. 2 (1984): pp. 128–150. How the emergency leaders defended this case is exemplified in D. V. Gandhi, ed., *Era of Discipline: Documents on Contemporary Reality* (New Delhi: Samachar Bharati, 1976), p. 2 and passim.

35. The constitutional changes, as intended and executed, are discussed in detail in Lloyd I. Rudolph and Suzanne H. Rudolph, "To the Brink and Back: Representation and the State in India," *Asian Survey* 18, no. 4 (1978): especially pp. 392–399.

36. The developmental implications of emergency are analyzed in Das Gupta, "A Season of Caesars," pp. 332ff.

37. See Myron Weiner, *India at the Polls: The Parliamentary Elections of 1977* (Washington, D.C.: American Enterprise Institute for Public Policy Research, 1978).

38. The political implication and the economic record of the Janata rule are analyzed in J. Das Gupta, "The Janata Phase: Reorganization and Redirection in Indian Politics," *Asian Survey* 19, no. 4 (1979): pp. 390–403.

39. The states were Andhra Pradesh, Karnataka, and Tripura.

40. Atul Kohli, "India's Democracy Under Rajiv Gandhi: 1985–1989," in Atul Kohli, ed., *India's Democracy* (Princeton: Princeton University Press, 1990 edition), pp. 319–333.

41. Harold A. Gould, "Patterns of Political Mobilization in the Parliamentary and Assembly Elections of 1989 and 1990," in Harold A. Gould and Sumit Ganguly, eds., *India Votes* (Boulder: Westview Press, 1993), pp. 14–49.

42. A good account of the rise is in Y. K. Malik and V. B. Singh, "Bharatiya Janata Party," *Asian Survey* 32, no. 4 (1992): pp. 318–336.

43. The deficit was later overcome. The context and the result of the 1991 elections are discussed in Walter Anderson, "Lowering the Level of Tension," in Leonard A. Gordon and Philip Oldenburg, eds., *India Briefing, 1992* (Boulder: Westview Press, 1992), pp. 13–45.

44. See Ramashray Roy, "India in 1993," in *Asian Survey* 34, no. 2 (1994): pp. 200–208; Y. Ghimire, et al., "The Saffron Resurgence," in *India Today,* North American Edition, March 31, 1995, pp. 35–49.

45. The 1991 census reported 139 million. Six other states have population sizes ranging from 86 million to 56 million. On the other hand, there are three states with less than 1 million people.

46. The literature on state politics is vast. Most of the major states' political development is discussed in Francine R. Frankel and M. S. A. Rao, eds., *Dominance and State Power in Modern India,* vols. 1 and 2 (Delhi: Oxford University Press, 1989 and 1990). Recent party positions in states are discussed in various chapters in Gould and Ganguly, eds., *India Votes,* passim.

47. As of May 1995, major non-Congress parties in power in states included Janata Dal (Bihar and Karnataka); AIADMK (Tamil Nadu); CPM (West Bengal, Tripura); BJP (Rajasthan, Gujaret, and the capital territory of Delhi); Telugu Desam (Andhra Pradesh); and Samajwadi Party and Bahujan Samaj Party (jointly in Uttar Pradesh). Maharashtra is ruled by a Shiv Sena and BJP coalition. Sikkim is ruled by the Sikkim Democratic Front. Jammu and Kashmir was under president's rule.

48. For a state-by-state analysis of policy processes and products, see Frankel and Rao, eds., *Dominance and State Power in Modern India,* vols. 1 and 2.

49. The literature on labor unions in India is extensive. For surveys of the role of trade unions in Indian politics, see S. Jawaid, *Trade Union Movement in India* (Delhi: Sundeep, 1982); and R. Chatterji, *Unions, Politics and the State* (New Delhi: South Asian Publishers, 1980), esp. pp. 27–86. For a survey of agrarian associations see A. N. Seth, *Peasant Organizations in India* (Delhi: B. R. Publishing, 1984); K. C. Alexander, *Peasant Organizations in South India* (New Delhi: Indian Social Institute, 1981); and M. V. Nadkarui, *Farmers' Movements in India* (New Delhi: Allied Publishers, 1987). Also, Leslie J. Calman,

Toward Empowerment, Women and Movement Politics in India (Boulder: Westview Press, 1992).

50. See Stanley A. Kochanek, *Business and Politics in India* (Berkeley: University of California Press. 1974), especially part 3.

51. See Harsh Sethi, "Survival and Democracy: Ecological Struggles in India," in P. Wignaraja, ed., *New Social Movements in the South* (London: Zed Books, 1993), pp. 122–148 and Barnett R. Rubin, "The Civil Liberties Movement in India," in *Asian Survey* 27, no. 3 (1987): pp. 371–392.

52. These are discussed in detail in an excellent analysis of the pertinent literature by Lloyd I. Rudolph and Susan H. Rudolph, "Determinants and Varieties of Agrarian Mobilization," in M. Desai et al., eds., *Agrarian Power and Agricultural Productivity in South Asia* (Berkeley: University of California Press, 1984), pp. 281–344; also Paul R. Brass, *The Politics of India Since Independence* (New York: Cambridge University Press, 1990), pp. 294ff.

53. The support bases in Kerala are discussed in T. J. Nossiter, *Communism in Kerala* (Berkeley: University of California Press, 1982); those in West Bengal are discussed in Atul Kohli, *The State and Poverty in India* (Cambridge: Cambridge University Press, 1986), ch. 3; and also his *Democracy and Discontent* (Cambridge: Cambridge University Press, 1990), chs. 6 and 10.

54. As one study of Kerala points out, "It seems that the agricultural labor movement . . . has now been integrated into the existing system. The reduction in militant struggles, the increasing institutionalization of collective bargaining and parliamentary politics are all indicative of this." See Joseph Tharamangalam, *Agrarian Class Conflict: The Political Mobilization of Agricultural Laborers in Kuttanad, South India* (Vancouver: University of British Columbia Press, 1981), p. 98. Another, more empirical survey conducted in Tamil Nadu reaches a similar conclusion. See Marshall M. Bouton, *Agrarian Radicalism in South India* (Princeton: Princeton University Press, 1985), p. 310.

55. Data pertaining to language and religion refer to the 1981 census. The population data refer to the 1991 census. These and other data used in this section are taken from *India 1992* (New Delhi: Government of India, 1993); and *Basic Statistics Relating to States of India* (Bombay: Center for Monitoring Indian Economy, September 1994), various tables.

56. For an excellent series of chapters covering different aspects of Kashmir politics see R. G. C. Thomas, ed., *Perspectives on Kashmir* (Boulder: Westview Press, 1992), esp. chs. 10 and 11 by A. Varshney and Leo Rose.

57. For a discussion of the National Conference see Vidya Bhushan, "The All Jammu and Kashmir National Conference," in S. Bhatnagar and P. Kumar, eds., *Regional Political Parties in India* (New Delhi: Ess Ess Publications, 1988), pp. 167–184.

58. The role of transnational Islam is discussed in M. K. Pasha, "Beyond the Two-Nation Divide: Kashmir and Resurgent Islam," in Thomas, ed., *Perspectives on Kashmir,* pp. 369–387.

59. The data cited here are from Paul Wallace, "Political Violence and Terrorism in India," in Martha Crenshaw, ed., *Terrorism in Context* (College Park: Pennsylvania State University Press, 1995), table 6.

60. SGPC stands for the Shiromani Gurdwara Prabandhak Committee. For the evolution of Punjab politics see Paul R. Brass, "The Punjab Crisis and the Unity of India," in Kohli, ed., *India's Democracy,* pp. 169-213.

61. For the elections and Akali power based on coalition with other parties see Paul Wallace, "Religious and Ethnic Politics: Political Mobilization in Punjab," in Frankel and Rao, *Dominance and State Power in Modern India,* vol. 2, pp. 446-449.

62. See Paul R. Brass, "Socio-Economic Aspects of the Punjab Crisis," *Punjab Journal of Politics* 13, nos. 1–2 (1989): pp. 1–16.

63. The president of India at that time was Zail Singh, a Sikh of lower-caste background. Most of the highest-ranking officers involved in the military action were Sikhs.

64. Wallace, "Political Violence and Terrorism in India," in Crenshaw, *Terrorism in Context.*

65. See Gurharpal Singh, "The Punjab Elections 1992," *Asian Survey* 32, no. 11 (November 1992): pp. 988–999.

66. For a discussion of Naga and Mizo secessionism see Bhagwan D. Dua, "Problems of Federal Leadership," in Subroto Roy and William E. James, eds., *Foundations of India's Political Economy* (New Delhi: Sage, 1992), pp. 98–104, 106–111; and S. Hazarika, *Strangers of the Mist* (New Delhi: Viking, 1994), pp. 86–119.

67. These movements are elaborated in my "Ethnicity, Democracy, and Development."

68. For a historical treatment of such constructions see Gyan Pandey, *The Construction of Communalism in Colonial North India* (Delhi: Oxford University Press, 1990). See also Partha Chatterjee, *The Nation and Its Fragments* (Princeton, N.J.: Princeton University Press, 1994), pp. 220–227.

69. For details see Malik and Singh, "Bharatiya Janata Party." See also Y. K. Malik and V. B. Singh, *Hindu Nationalists in India* (Boulder: Westview Press, 1994), pp. 139–177.

70. The 83-percent figure has been called "an artifact of categorization." Lloyd I. Rudolph and Susanne H. Rudolph, *In Pursuit of Lakshmi* (Chicago: University of Chicago Press, 1987), p. 37. For the census figures see the sources cited in note 55 above.

71. See S. Srivastava, *The Disputed Mosque* (New Delhi: Vistaar, 1991); and Manju Parikh, "The Debacle at Ayodhya," *Asian Survey* 33, no. 7 (July 1993): pp. 673–684. For the BJP view see L. K. Advani, *Ramjanma Bhoomi* (New Delhi: BJP Central Office, 1989), which contains speeches and official resolutions. Advani is one of the top leaders of the party.

72. For a discussion of his ideas on planning see Bruce F. Johnston and William C. Clark, *Redesigning Rural Development* (Baltimore: Johns Hopkins University Press, 1982), p. 24.

73. The proportion of plan outlay devoted to agriculture was 14.8 percent in the first plan (1952–1956), 11.7 percent in the second plan (1955–1961), and 12.7 percent in the third plan (1961–1965). The corresponding figures for organized industry and mining were 2.8 percent, 20.1 percent, and 20.1 percent. See the *Statistical Outline of India,* 1984 (Bombay: Tata Services, 1984).

74. For a critique of Indian plan strategies see John W. Mellor, *The New Economics of Growth: A Strategy for India and the Developing World* (Ithaca: Cornell University Press, 1976), especially pp. 274ff. For a sophisticated analysis defending the plan strategies see S. Chakravarty, *Development Planning* (Oxford: Clarendon Press, 1987), pp. 7–38.

75. This refers to the agricultural policies that have acquired the popular label "green revolution."

76. For an account of this colonial legacy see Dharma Kumar, ed., *The Cambridge Economic History of India,* vol. 2 (Cambridge: Cambridge University Press, 1983), pp. 947ff.

77. See the *World Development Report, 1987* (New York: Oxford University Press, 1987), p. 258; *World Development Report, 1994* (New York: Oxford University Press, 1994), p. 162; and *Human Development Report, 1994* (New York: Oxford University Press, 1994), pp. 136, 144. It was a total figure for 1992 at 59.7 and for women 59.9.

78. Ibid. See A. Sen, "Population: Delusion and Reality," *New York Review of Books,* Sept. 22, 1994, p. 70.

79. John Wall, "Foodgrain Management: Pricing, Procurement, Distribution, Import, and Storage Policy," in *India: Occasional Papers,* World Bank Staff Working Paper no. 279, May 1978 (Washington, D.C.: World Bank, 1978), pp. 8R89.

80. See Government of India, *Economic Survey, 1986–87* (New Delhi, 1987), pp. 8 and S-7 through S-15; and *Economic Survey, 1993–94* (New Delhi, 1994), pp. 2 and S-24 and passim. Also *Economic Survey, 1994–95* (New Delhi, 1995), pp. 2 and 5–25.

81. In 1992 the procurement rate was 12.2 percent of new foodgrain production. Even in the worst drought year of 1987, this rate exceeded 12 percent. *Economic Survey, 1993–94* (New Delhi, 1994), p. S-25.

82. See Amartya Sen, *Resources, Values and Development* (Cambridge: Harvard University Press, 1984), pp. 501ff, for an interesting comparison of the scale of famines in colonial India and socialist China.

83. *Human Development Report, 1994,* pp. 154–155.

84. Primary school enrollment as percent of age group for sub-Saharan Africa in the early 1980s was 77.6 percent, for East Asia 113.0, and for India 90.0, which in 1991 improved to 98.0. It was still lower then the low-income countries' average at 101.0—excluding China and India this average stands at 79.0. Compiled from the World Bank, *World Tables,* vol. 2 (Baltimore: Johns Hopkins University Press, 1984 edition), pp. 158–159; *World Development Report 1984* (New York: Oxford University Press, 1984), p. 226; *World Development Report, 1987,* p. 262; and *World Development Report, 1994,* p. 216.

85. For an idea of how the leading economists of the 1950s thought about desirable strategies of development and how in the 1980s they assessed their earlier thoughts, see Gerald M. Meier and Dudley Seers, eds., *Pioneers in Development* (New York: Oxford University Press, 1984).

86. Jagdish Bhagwati's distinction of several variants of import substitution would help one to place the Indian policy in a clearer perspective. See his "Comment" on Prebisch in ibid., pp. 201–202.

87. I have used total industrial growth rates because of easier availability, but growth rates in manufacturing are not very dissimilar. See the World Bank, *World Development Report 1984*, p. 220; *World Development Report, 1994*, pp. 164–165.

88. Thus, one estimate suggests that the annual percentage rate of growth of industrial product in India was 4.1 compared to 6.3 for nonsocialist developing countries and 4.3 for the nonsocialist world. See S. J. Patel, "India's Regression in the World Economy," in *Economic and Political Weekly,* September 28, 1985, p. 1652. How seriously such estimates need to be taken is an issue that may be controversial. See, for instance, K. N. Raj, "Economic Growth in India, 1952–55 to 1982–83," in *Economic and Political Weekly,* October 13, 1984, p. 1804.

89. From *Basic Statistics Relating to Indian Economy* (Bombay: Center for Monitoring Indian Economy, August 1984), Table 14.9-2, and August 1986, Table 14.11-2. The 1994 edition of this work reports, for 1985–1991, annual percent growth rates for aggregate industry as 8.2, for engineering goods, 12.0, and for capital goods, 16.0.

90. The record of the public sector is discussed in Baldev Raj Nayar, "The Public Sector," in Gordon and Oldenburg, eds., *India Briefing, 1992,* pp.71–101.

91. This point is developed in Vijay L. Kelkar and Rajiv Kumar, "Industrial Growth in the Eighties," *Economic and Political Weekly,* 27 January 1990, pp. 209-222. For the tastes of the growing affluent classes and their consumer durable preferences as witnessed in the 1980s see Suman Dubey, "The Middle Class," in Gordon and Oldenburg, eds., *India Briefing, 1992,* pp. 137–164.

92. The context of the crisis is described in Jagdish Bhagwati, *India in Transition: Freeing the Economy* (Oxford: Clarendon Press, 1993), pp. 39–69. See also Bimal Jalan, *India's Economic Crisis* (Delhi: Oxford University Press, 1991).

93. A good source for an elaboration of these reforms is Government of India Planning Commission, *Eighth Five Year Plan, 1992–1997* (New Delhi: Government of India, 1992), vol. 1, especially pp. 84–96.

94. Ibid., pp. 1-2.

95. See Asian Development Bank, *Asian Development Outlook, 1992* (New York: Oxford University Press, 1992), p.172.

96. The finance minister was quoted as saying it would take twenty years of GDP growth of between 6 and 7 percent for reforms to reach the poor masses. "Rao Wants Ten Years to Complete Reforms," *India Post,* November 18, 1994, p. B-15.

97. The data presented in this section is based on Center for Monitoring Indian Economy, *Economic Outlook* (Bombay: September 1994), various sections; and the same organization's *Economic Indicators* (August 1994). The 1994/95 estimate for foreign exchange reserves exceeds $19 billion. See *Economic Survey 1994–95* (New Delhi: Government of India, 1995), p. 2.

98. The Economist Intelligence Unit, Country Report, *India, Nepal* (4th quarter 1994), p. 15.

99. For an account of the evolving discourse see Ajit Mozoomdar, "The Rise and Decline of Development Planning in India," in Terence J. Byres, ed., *The State and Development Planning in India* (Delhi: Oxford University Press, 1994), pp. 73–108.

100. Robert Cassen, Vijay Joshi, and Michael Lipton, "Stabilization and Structural Reform in India," *Contemporary South Asia* 2, no. 2 (1993): p. 188.

101. For the Punjab case see Holly Sims, *Political Regimes, Public Policy and Economic Development* (New Delhi: Sage, 1988).

102. Life expectancy figures are China, male: 67, female: 71; Kerala, male: 71, female: 74 (1991). Fertility rates are China: 2.0; Kerala: 1.8; United States: 2.1; Sweden: 2.1 (1991). Female literacy rate, China: 68 percent; Kerala: 86 percent. See Sen, "Population: Delusion and Reality," p. 70.

103. The compound annual percentage rate of growth of foodgrain production (1982–1992) were West Bengal (6.5), Mizoram (9.3), Nagaland (6.7), Haryana (4.3), Punjab (4.0). The all-India figure was 2.7. See A. Saha and M. Swaminathan, "Agricultural Growth in West Bengal in the 1980s," *Economic and Political Weekly,* March 26, 1994, p. A-2. The investment aspect is discussed by John Harriss in "What Is Happening in Rural West Bengal?" *Economic and Political Weekly,* June 12, 1993, pp. 1237–1247.

104. Kerala's compound annual rate of growth of foodgrain production for the 1982–1992 period was -2.1, the lowest in India. See Saha and Swaminathan, "Agricultural Growth in West Bengal."

105. R. Krishnan, "A Fall from Grace," *India Today* (North American edition), November 15, 1994, pp. 116–117.

106. The productive notion is discussed in Claus Offe and Ulrich K. Preuss, "Democratic Institutions and Moral Resources," in David Held, ed., *Political Theory Today* (Stanford: Stanford University Press, 1991), pp. 144–145.

107. Tocqueville's idea that Americans have come to democracy without having endured democratic revolution and that they are born equal, instead of becoming so, may have implications for impressing such bias. Some of these implications are discussed in another context in Albert O. Hirschman, "Rival Interpretations of Market Society: Civilizing, Destructive or Feeble?" *Journal of Economic Literature* 20 (December 1982): pp. 350ff.

108. See G. Bingham Powell Jr., *Contemporary Democracies* (Cambridge: Harvard University Press, n.d.), for some samples, pp. 3ff.

109. The taming of the leading communist parties; the DMK, the Telugu Desam, and the Assam Movement are some examples.

110. See M. Mann, "The Social Cohesion of Liberal Democracy," in A. Giddens and D. Held, eds., *Classes, Power and Conflict* (Berkeley: University of California Press), pp. 388ff.

111. This congruence was revealed for all major parties and not just the Congress Party. Samuel J. Eldersveld and Bashiruddin Ahmed, *Citizens and Politics: Mass Political Behavior in India* (Chicago: University of Chicago Press, 1978), especially pp. 80, 90, 104.

112. John Osgood Field, *Consolidating Democracy: Politicization and Partisanship in India* (New Delhi: Manohar, 1980), p. 288. This work is based on data collected in 1966 as part of a cross-national project.

113. Ibid., p. 292.

114. See, for example, Seymour Martin Lipset, "Some Social Requisites of Democracy: Economic Development and Political Legitimacy," *American Political Science Review* 53, no. 2 (1959): pp. 69–105.

115. Backward caste demands usually benefit middle castes more than others. See Francine Frankel, "Middle Castes and Classes in Indian Politics: Prospects for Political Accommodation," in Kohli, ed., *India's Democracy;* and Weiner, *Sons of the Soil.*

116. Adam Przeworski, "Some Problems in the Study of the Transition to Democracy," in Guillermo O'Donnell, Philippe C. Schmitter, and Laurence Whitehead, eds., *Transitions from Authoritarian Rule: Comparative Perspectives* (Baltimore: Johns Hopkins University Press, 1986), p. 63.

117. I have excluded the issue of corruption. It is a long story, and allegedly, national and regional leaders, including prime ministers and chief ministers, have been involved. The issue of the Bofors arms deal in 1987 and N. T. Rama Rao's case in 1988, the securities scam in 1991–1992, and the sugar scandal in 1994 are just a few instances. The corruption issue needs to be seen in the light of the fact that democracy has encouraged and, at the same time, exposed corruption. But exposure does not necessarily eliminate corrupt leaders from politics. Popular toleration of corruption is as much a problem as that of multinational kickback incentives at the highest levels. See K. S. Padhy, *Corruption in Politics* (Delhi: B. R. Publishing, 1986), especially pp. 212–213, or press coverages such as a report on Harshad Mehta in *India Today,* July 15, 1993, pp. 22–33.

118. Selig S. Harrison, *India: The Most Dangerous Decades* (Madras: Oxford University Press, 1960), p. 338.

119. Barrington Moore Jr., who has inspired many scholars to defend "glamorous" options through his landmark work, *Social Origins of Dictatorship and Democracy* (Boston: Beacon Press, 1966), later conceded that "political glamour can be a disaster that produces enormous amounts of suffering. . . . If humanity is to work its way out of its current plight . . . there will have to be leaders . . . who can turn their backs on political glamour and work hard for [barely] feasible goals rather than glamorous ones." *Authority and Inequality Under Capitalism and Socialism* (Oxford: Clarendon Press, 1987), p. 125. Not surprisingly, compared to his earlier work, *Social Origins,* Indian democracy comes out in a positive light in this later work (p. 123).

I have used the notion of *combined development* in the sense of the political compulsion to pursue simultaneous or at least multiple objectives in a multiethnic developing country interested in comprehensive national development. This use should not be confused with other uses of the term in the literature (notably, Leon Trotsky's use to convey the advantage of historic backwardness). For an elaboration of the latter use see J. Elster, "The Theory of Combined and Uneven Development: A Critique," in J. Roemer, ed., *Analytical Marxism* (Cambridge: Cambridge University Press, 1986), pp. 54–63.

120. V. S. Naipaul, *India, A Million Mutinies Now* (New York: Viking, 1991), p. 517. Despite its title, this book is a highly perceptive study of the developing democratic processes.

121. See G. K. Lieten, *Continuity and Change in Rural West Bengal* (New Delhi: Sage, 1992), pp. 88–118.

122. For the rich farmers see the citations in note 52, especially the work by the Rudolphs. For the internal and external codes of discipline and harnessing relevant for understanding subaltern movements see Ranajit Guha, "Discipline and Mobilize," in Partha Chatterjee and Gyanendra Pandey, eds., *Subaltern Studies VII* (Delhi: Oxford University Press, 1993), pp. 69–120.

123. See the account of Indian "demand groups" and their departure from standard models in Rudolph and Rudolph, *In Pursuit of Lakshmi,* pp. 255–258.

124. Mandal refers to the Mandal Commission report and recommendation regarding job reservations for the scheduled castes, scheduled tribes, and other backward castes. The federal government had fixed a limit of 50 percent. Recently, Karnataka raised the limit to 73 percent. The document is *Report of the Backward Classes Commission, Parts 1 and 2, 1980* (New Delhi: Government of India, 1981).

125. See Rudolph and Rudolph, *In Pursuit of Lakshmi,* pp. 132ff., for a general discussion of the deinstitutionalization of the Congress Party and the state structure. For the changes in the support base of the parties see P. K. Chibber and J. R. Petrocik, "Social Cleavages, Elections and the Indian Party System," in R. Sisson and R. Roy, eds., *Diversity and Dominance in Indian Politics,* vol. 1 (New Delhi: Sage, 1990), pp. 105–122.

126. These issues are discussed in Atul Kohli, *Democracy and Discontent* (Cambridge: Cambridge University Press, 1990), especially pp. 387–397.

127. Pranab Bardhan, *The Political Economy of Development in India* (Oxford: Basil Blackwell, 1984), pp. 73–74.

128. See the discussion of political regeneration by James Manor, "The State of Governance," in Roy and James, *Foundations of India's Political Economy,* pp. 44–47.

129. See Rubin, "The Civil Liberties Movements in India," p. 376. The broader focus has included attention to the implementation issues of land reform from the vantage point of the poor peasants, protecting the rights of agricultural workers, the issues of caste discrimination, women's rights, and other issue areas; pp. 377–392.

130. The National Federation of Indian Women and the All India Democratic Women's Association are some national examples of the former, and the Self-Employed Women's Association (Ahmedabad) and the Working Women's Forum (Madras) are some regional examples of the latter. For a detailed account see Calman, *Toward Empowerment,* pp. 75ff and 96ff.

131. For a survey of these and most other organizations discussed in this section see S. Kothari, "Social Movements and the Redefinition of Democracy," in P. Oldenburg, ed., *India Briefing 1993* (Boulder: Westview Press, 1993), pp. 131–162.

132. The Narmada Bachao Andolan (Save the Narmada Movement) represents a coalition of groups. It has become more active since the late 1980s and the early 1990s. See J. R. Wood, "India's Narmada River Dams: Sardar Sarovar Under Siege," *Asian Survey* 33, no. 10 (October 1993): pp. 968–984.

133. These movements in northern and southern India are discussed in Sethi, "Survival and Democracy: Ecological Struggles in India," in Wignaraja, ed., *New Social Movements in the South,* pp. 128ff.

134. Kothari, "Social Movements," in Oldenburg, ed., *India Briefing 1993,* p. 142.

135. Ibid., p. 148.

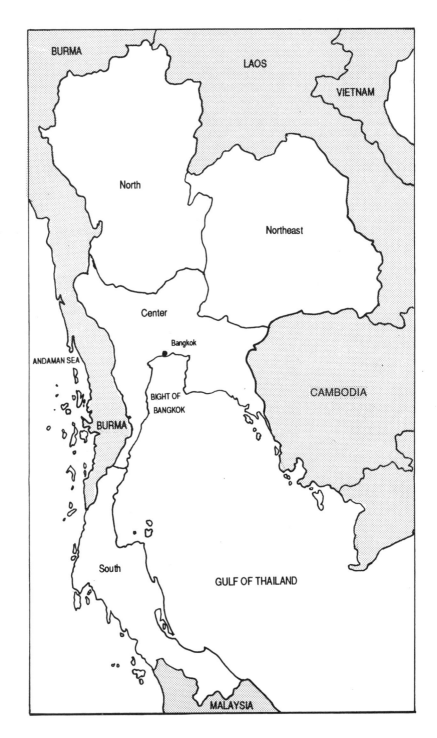

THAILAND

7

Thailand:
A Stable Semidemocracy

Chai-Anan Samudavanija

Historical Review

A lone in Southeast Asia, Thailand was never colonized, maintaining its
independence through the height of the Western imperial presence in
the region. Traditionally the Thai political system has relied on the monarchy as the basis for its legitimacy. The monarchy reigned and ruled and was
the focus for the loyalty, love, respect, and religious faith of the Buddhist
populace. The king and the dynasty were central to both the ideology and
reality of political rule. This was a classic centralized hierarchy, in which the
entire focus of legitimacy and status emanated downward from the king
through the royal elite to the ordinary citizen, and outward from the palace
in Bangkok through the provincial towns to the villages.

Independence in Thailand means that it never experienced the imposition and transfer of institutions from the West that took place in many developing countries. The absence of colonialism also means that traditional
structures, particularly the monarchy, the Buddhist Sangha (monastic order),
and the military and civil bureaucracy were not disrupted. Although
Thailand did not benefit from the process of democratization through the
transfer of colonial institutions, neither did it suffer the kind of destruction
of the social fabric that many European colonies in the Third World experienced. Because King Chulalongkorn (1868–1910) and his advisors were
able to respond effectively to the colonial threat the country also escaped the
necessity of overthrowing its colonial yoke. Since no independence movement was necessary the institutions and ideology concomitant with independence movements around the world—especially political parties and
mobilized mass movements—never emerged. The Buddhist Sangha, which
is the social and religious institution closest to the masses, was therefore not
politicized like its counterparts in Burma, Sri Lanka, and Vietnam. Its traditional linkage with the monarchy was not disrupted, but instead has been
fostered so that the two institutions have remained complementary to each

other.[1] In this sense Thailand faced only a limited political challenge. This allowed the country to defer its true political development to the present.[2]

Democracy as a system of government was introduced to Thailand in June 1932 when a group of junior army, navy, and civilian officers calling themselves the People's Party seized political power, overthrew the absolute monarchy, and established a constitutional regime. Prior to this, constitutionalism and democracy had been discussed among the Thai intelligentsia for a long time. In 1887, a group of princes and officials submitted a lengthy petition to King Chulalongkorn outlining the immediate problems facing Siam and suggested that a constitutional monarchy be instituted.[3] In the late 1880s Tienwan, a commoner and Buddhist scholar, argued in his magazine, *Tulawipak Pojanakit,* that the most effective way to promote justice was to institute a parliamentary form of government.[4] In the 1910s a group of lesser army officials attempted unsuccessfully to stage a coup to replace the absolute monarchy with a republican government. In 1917 Prince Chakrabongse submitted a memorandum to the king suggesting that it was time to grant some kind of constitution to the people. From the latter 1920s to May 1932—a month before the end of the absolute monarchy—the question of whether a democratic form of government was suitable for Siam was one of the major concerns of the regime. Starting from the reign of King Vajiravudh (1910-1925) the monarchy, as an institution, began to be questioned and criticized openly. With the increasing suffering from the Great Depression in the late 1920s, the desire for change was more pressing and resulted in growing awareness of the anachronism of the absolute monarchy.

The reactions of the kings to political reforms were quite similar.[5] Not all of them rejected constitutionalism and democracy as an ideal or a concept of governance, but the appropriateness of the model and practices were questioned. It had always been maintained by the old regime that while constitutional government might be desirable and even inevitable, it was still premature to establish such a system in Siam. The main reasons against the establishment of a constitutional government expressed by foreign advisors, the king, and senior princes were:[6]

1. There was no middle class in Siam. The Siamese peasants took little or no interest in public affairs. Most of the electorate were uneducated; hence to set up a parliament with real power without an educated electorate to control it would only invite trouble and corruption.
2. Parliamentary government was not suitable for the Siamese people, and it was even possible that there must also be certain racial qualities that the Anglo-Saxons possessed and the Siamese did not have to make democracy a successful form of government.
3. Not only was a real democracy very unlikely to succeed in Siam, it might even be harmful to the interests of the people. The parliament would be entirely dominated by the Chinese.[7]

4. The great bulk of the people of Siam were as yet not trained in political or economic thought.[8] As for the students who returned from Britain, Europe, and the United States, their idea of democracy was half-baked, and their Western ideas were often superficial and misunderstood.

It is clear that the arguments against the adoption of a constitutional government were not so much concerned with democracy as a concept but rather as a form of government, especially its political implications.

Yet it was admitted that Siam would ultimately be forced by circumstances to adopt a democratic form of government, and hence the regime should be well prepared to direct this change gradually. King Prachatipok, however, cautioned that the main danger and the obstacle to this gradual experiment lay in impatience.[9]

Those who were impatient were the Western-educated military and civilian bureaucrats. In the absence of a sizable middle class, a large and strong bureaucracy became the locus of power in the new institutional arrangements. Thai politics after 1932 have therefore been dominated by the bureaucrats, as best described by David Wilson:

> Some 30 years ago the bureaucracy much strengthened by the reorganization and development of the previous 40 years and by the new techniques of communications and control imported from the West—was cut free of the restraints of absolutism. As much as the leadership of the Thai revolution might have wished things to be otherwise, it was not able to muster much popular interest outside the bureaucracy upon which to base itself. As a result, politics has become a matter of competition between bureaucratic cliques for the benefits of government. In this competition the army—the best organized, most concentrated, and most powerful of the branches of the bureaucracy—has come out on top.[10]

It is ironic that soon after the success of the Westernized elites in their seizure of power from the monarchy, constitutional idealism gradually eroded into formalistic constitutionalism.[11] Since 1932 the bureaucratic elites have been the prime movers in shaping and operating political institutional arrangements under different constitutions. Because of periodic changes in the rules of the game, the scope of political competition, the level of political participation, and the extent to which civil and political liberties are guaranteed have varied according to the nature of the regime.

It should be noted that from 1932 to 1945 the only formal political institution in Thailand was a unicameral legislature composed of two categories of members—half elected and half appointed. The People's Party did not find it necessary to transform itself into a political party since its leading members and supporters were already appointed members of the National Assembly. Political parties in Thailand, therefore, emerged as late as 1946 and were only recognized as legal entities nine years later in 1955. What was institutionalized instead was the political role of the bureaucratic elites. The new leadership relied upon the bureaucracy to play a leading role in educating and mobilizing the masses to participate in elections, as well as to learn about democracy through the symbol of the constitution.

Since half of the assembly members were mainly military and civilian officers, the legislative process became an extended arm of, and provided an additional function for, the bureaucracy. Although the new military-bureaucratic elites formed the only organized political group in society, they were not united. On the contrary, soon after June 1932 the young military faction within the People's Party emerged and was, by 1938, able to eliminate the senior members. And since the civilian faction of the People's Party did not develop itself into a broad-based political party because of the resistance of the more powerful military faction, its power and influence gradually declined while that of the military faction rapidly increased, especially after its leader Luang Pibul became defense minister in late 1934 and prime minister in 1938.

From the beginning of constitutional rule, the role of the elected members of Parliament was oriented toward internal legislative activities rather than to act as a major political institution for participation and competition for major positions of government power. Hence the electoral process in Thailand, which began as early as 1933, did not lead to the recruitment of political leadership at the top. It was only a tool to legitimate the political system and process in which competition for power was not linked with the electorate but with the factions in the military.

It seems that the objective of the constitution was to establish and strengthen the power position of the new regime rather than to develop a truly democratic political system. The constitution and constitutional symbols were utilized to distinguish between the *ancien* and the *new* regime. In 1933 the National Assembly passed a bill on the protection of the constitution. In the same year it passed another bill establishing a special court to deal with 238 persons who were involved in the Baworadej rebellion. The special court had no provision for appeals or petitions.

The passage of the Protection of the Constitution Act and the special court legislation reflected the ability of the People's Party to control the National Assembly, as well as to utilize it in legitimating their power. Although there was an effort to educate the masses in democratic rule, such an effort was highly formalistic and symbolic rather than substantive, and in general public education was extremely limited.

The 1932 Constitution, therefore, provided considerable stability for the regime, as evidenced by the fact that factional rivalry and competition for power among the military did not result in the abolishment of either the constitution or the Parliament. Although there were eight cabinets in a period of six years (1932–1938), there were only two prime ministers, compared with the much more turbulent period three decades later (1969–1979) when there were ten cabinets with six prime ministers under four constitutions.

Political parties were not allowed to function in the first fifteen years of constitutional rule, and the voting method in the first election was indirect. (Each village elected its representatives; the village representatives chose those of the districts, who in turn chose the representatives of the province.) Political participation was a mobilized action in which officials of the Interior Ministry at the village and district levels played a significant role, a pattern not dissimilar to that existing in contemporary Thai politics. Hence early universal suffrage in Thailand did not lead to meaningful political participation or the emergence of political organizations, as happened in other societies. It should be pointed out also that universal suffrage was given to the people when they were not familiar with the principles and the workings of the new system. It is not surprising therefore that constitutional rule was finally replaced by an authoritarian military rule—first by Field Marshal Pibul, and later by Field Marshal Sarit and Field Marshal Thanom, respectively.

Pibul's cabinets from 1938 to 1944 marked the high point of rule by the army. During this period, there were seven cabinets with a yearly average of 51 percent military men in the cabinets. Also in this same period, the yearly average of the percentage of military expenditure to total national spending increased to 33 percent, compared with 26 percent during the 1933–1937 period. With the rise to power of Pibul, heroism and ultranationalism, with emphasis on leadership, began to develop. Such developments finally led to militarization, especially before the outbreak of World War II. In 1942 the government amended the constitution to extend the tenure of the Parliament for two years, and in 1944 the tenure was extended for another two years.

Although Pibul's rise to power did not in any way affect the constitution, his leadership style and ultra-nationalistic policies greatly affected civil liberties. His *ratthaniyom* marked the first and most systematic intervention of the state into the lives of the Thai citizenry. The Thai people were told what to do and what not to do by their "great leader." The state assumed its role in remolding the values and behavior of the citizens by imposing several orders, rules, and regulations. The nationalist drive also resulted in a number of discriminatory policies against the Chinese minority. Strangely enough, there was no challenge to the government's policies as being unconstitutional, either by the Parliament or by the press. This reflected the weakness of democratic values and the inherently autocratic traits in Thai society, which were utilized to a great extent by Pibul and his principal political adviser.

Before the outbreak of World War II the Pibul government was mainly controlled by members of the 1932 junior clique, including Pridi—a prominent civilian leader who was the chief ideologist of the 1932 coup group. World War II brought about a major conflict between Pibul and Pridi. The former chose to ally with the Japanese and the Axis Powers while the latter identified himself with the Allied Powers. When Thailand declared war against the Allies Pridi formed an underground movement against the Japanese and the Axis powers. As the tide of World War II turned against the Japanese and the Axis powers, Pibul's government resigned on July 24, 1994, when the Assembly failed to pass a bill proposing the establishment of a new capital at Petchuboon province in northern Thailand.

Postwar Politics

Postwar politics was largely a matter of struggle among three groups for dominance. One was the military group that supported Pibul and was based mainly in the army. The second group, at first centering on Pridi, was rooted in Parliament and the civil service. The third group, considerably smaller, was traditionalist and royalist in character. This group was led by Khuang Aphaiwong and Seni Pramoj.[12]

After Pibul's resignation, the National Assembly began to play a dominant role in the political system for the first time. Political parties were formed in late 1945 and early 1946. A new constitution was drafted and promulgated to replace the 1932 Constitution in May 1946. The new constitution was an attempt by the temporary civilian coalition of Pridi and Khuang to establish new institutional arrangements to minimize the power of the military. It provided for a bicameral legislature: the House of Representatives, to be elected directly, and the Senate to be elected indirectly by the House. At the first election of the Senate, most of the candidates were the appointed members of the former National Assembly who were Pridi's supporters.

Politics during this civilian interregnum was highly unstable. From August 1945 to November 1947 there were eight cabinets and five different prime ministers. Competition among civilian politicians, together with charges of corruption, economic hardship as the result of the war, and the mysterious death of King Ananda, led to a military coup in November 1947. The coup group abolished the 1946 Constitution and replaced it with an interim constitution, resulting in the January 1948 elections in which the Democrat Party won a majority. However, after less than two months of his premiership the leader of the Democrat Party, Khuang, was forced to resign by the army, and Field Marshal Pibul was installed as the new premier in April 1948.

In March 1949 a new constitution was promulgated. This constitution provided for a bicameral legislature like that of the 1946 version, but with an appointed Senate instead of an elected one. The new constitution barred officials from being members of the National Assembly, thus separating the once-powerful military and civilian bureaucrats from active involvement in politics. Such arrangements antagonized the military and finally led to the "silent coup" in November 1951 by the same officers who organized the 1947 coup.

The coup group reinstated the 1932 Constitution, which provided for a unicameral legislature with two categories of members—half elected and half appointed. Ninety-one (or 74 percent) of the total 123 appointed in the 1951 Parliament were military members, of whom sixty-two were army officers, fourteen were navy, and fifteen were air force officers. It is also noteworthy that thirty-four of them were the younger generation of middle-ranking officers (major to colonel). As David Wilson pointed out, with the reestablishment of the 1932 Constitution the principle of tutelage was again imposed on an assembly that had been free of it for six years. The government was therefore able to control the legislature through its appointed members and no longer faced serious difficulty in organizing a majority group to support it.[13] In February 1952 an Emergency Law providing the government with wide powers of arrest and press censorship was passed. In November of the same year an Anticommunist Law was approved by Parliament by an almost unanimous vote.[14]

Following their consolidation of power in the 1951 "silent coup," the 1947 coup group became deeply involved in politics and commercial activities. They built up their economic base of power by setting up their own business firms, got control over state enterprises and semigovernment companies, and gained free shares from private firms mainly owned by Chinese merchants. This active involvement in business ventures resulted in the division of the group into two competing cliques—popularly known as the "Rajakru," under the leadership of Police General Phao Sriyanond, and Sisao Deves clique, under the leadership of Field Marshal Sarit Thanarat. Each controlled more than thirty companies in banking and finance, industry, and commerce.[15] This split between Phao, the police chief, and Sarit, the army chief, was seen as an attempt by Pibul to maintain his power by manipulating and balancing off these two factions. However, the events of 1955 to 1957 culminated in the coup of September 1957 in which Sarit ousted both Pibul and Phao. This coup mainly concerned a succession conflict; "When a situation of considerable tension had developed in the Bangkok political scene, the Sarit clique moved with the army to take over the government and 'clean up the mess.'"[16]

After the September 1957 coup the constitution was temporarily suspended, resulting in the dissolution of the Parliament. The coup group appointed Pote Sarasin, the former Thai ambassador to the United States, as the premier of a caretaker government. A general election was held in December 1957 in which no party won a majority in the Parliament. Lieutenant General Thanom Kittikachorn, a leading member of the coup group, was chosen as the prime minister in January 1958. However, as a result of the inability of the government to control the internal strife within its supported party as well as deteriorating economic conditions, Sarit staged another coup in October 1958. This time he abrogated the constitution, dissolved the Parliament, banned political parties, arrested several politicians, journalists, writers, and labor leaders, declared martial law, and imposed censorship on newspapers. In 1959, an Interim Constitution was promulgated establishing an all-appointed constituent assembly whose main function was to draft a new "permanent constitution." The interim constitution also gave tremendous power to the prime minister. From 1958 to 1963 Sarit used the power given by Article 17 of that constitution to execute without trial eleven persons—five for arson, one for producing heroin, and four on charges of communism.[17]

Sarit's rule (1958–1963) has been characterized as a dictatorship, as a benevolent despotism, and as military rule. However, as a noted scholar of this period observed, Sarit's 1958 coup marked the beginning of a new political system that endured until at least the early 1970s. What Sarit did in effect was to overthrow a whole political system inherited from 1932, and to create one that could be termed more "Thai" in character.[18] Apart from his strongly anti-communist policy and his initiation of a National Development Plan that opened the way for the tremendous developmental activities of the following decades, the most significant change Sarit brought to the Thai political system was the activation of the role of the monarchy. As Thak rightly pointed out Sarit made it possible, without perhaps so intending, for the monarchy to grow strong enough to play an independent role after his death. The relative political weakness of Sarit's successors brought the throne even more clearly to the center of the political stage.[19]

After Sarit's death in 1963 Thanom became prime minister and commander of the army. In 1968 a new constitution was promulgated after ten years of drafting. The familiar vicious circle of Thai politics, evident in earlier periods, recurred. A semi-parliamentary system was established with a two-house legislature. Two years after that conflicts developed within the government-supported party, leading to a military coup in November 1971. Another interim constitution was promulgated, providing for a single constituent assembly composed entirely of appointed members, most of whom were military and civil bureaucrats.

The Breakdown of Military Rule

After the 1971 coup a new and ambitious strongman emerged: Colonel Narong Kittikachorn, the prime minister's son and Deputy Prime Minister Praphat's son-in-law. Narong was appointed assistant secretary-general of the National Executive Council, the supreme body of government administration after the 1971 coup. Apart from being the commander of the powerful Bangkok-based Eleventh Infantry Regiment, he acted as head of a new Committee to Suppress Elements Detrimental to Society, and was also made deputy secretary-general of a new anti-corruption agency. Narong was seen as the heir apparent to the prime ministership. This kind of dynastic succession, never before seen in the Thai military, generated tremendous discontent and criticism from the general public.

Leaders of the student movement were well aware that the growing popular animosity to Narong and the military offered a potentially unique
opportunity to put pressure on the military for political reforms, a new constitution, and an elected parliament. On October 6, 1973, student leaders and
political activists were arrested while they were distributing leaflets
demanding immediate promulgation of a new constitution. The government
announced that the police had uncovered a communist plot to overthrow the
administration.

From October 6 through October 13 hundreds of thousands of students
and others gathered to support the cause of the jailed students. Although the
government agreed to release the students and promised to quicken the
drafting of the new constitution, riot police on the morning of October 14
clashed with a group of demonstrators in front of the royal palace, thereby
sparking violence in other parts of the city. In the meantime a deep split was
developing within the military's own leadership. General Krit Sivara, army
commander-in-chief, began to adopt a position independent from the
Thanom-Praphat group. General Krit's intervention rendered further military suppression untenable, leaving Thanon, Praphat, and Narong no alternative but to flee the country, after being personally ordered by the king to
do so. The king appointed Professor Sanya Thammasak, former chief justice
of the Supreme Court and rector of Thammasat University, as the prime minister.

The Failure of Democracy, 1974–1976[20]

The student-led uprising of October 14, 1973, brought back once again the
period of open politics and democratic experimentation. The 1974
Constitution was patterned after the 1949 Constitution. It limited the number of senators to only 100, with much less power than the elected House of
Representatives. Government officials elected to the House or appointed to
the Senate had to resign their bureaucratic posts; votes of no confidence
remained the sole prerogative of the House; and the prime minister had to be
a member of the House of Representatives. These provisions set the stage
for a more open political system based on party and pressure group politics.

From 1974 to 1976 the political climate in Thailand became highly
volatile. Pressure group politics, mobilization, polarization, and confrontation replaced the usual political acquiescence and the achievement of
consensus through bargaining between established patron-client factions.
The students, labor unions, and farmer groups were most active in expressing grievances and making demands, which led them into conflict with government officials, business interests, and landowners.

Primarily because the previous governing elite (especially the army)
was discredited, and because the abrupt departure of Thanom, Praphat, and
Narong had damaged existing patron-client linkages, no single government
political party emerged. Several factional groups formed, each composed of

members of earlier government parties. Progressive elements also were unable to coalesce into a coherent political party, instead splintering into numerous competing groups. Fragmentation and political polarization of both left and right characterized Thai politics during this period. The Democrat Party, the nation's oldest, was divided into three competing factions; each formed its own political party to contest in the 1975 elections. The members of the defunct government party were also split into several competing groups, which subsequently led to the formation of four identifiable parties, namely, the Thai Nation Party, the Social Nationalist Party, the Social Justice Party, and the Social Agrarian Party. These parties were linked with the business community and the military-bureaucratic factions. Apart from these parties, there were two new parties in the center-left spectrum, the Social Action Party and the New Force Party, and two leftist parties, the United Socialist Front and the Socialist Party of Thailand. Although forty-two parties contested the January 1975 election, only twenty-two gained seats in the House. The Democrat Party, which had the largest number of seats in the House (72 out of 269), formed a ninety-one-seat minority government in February 1975, but the House on March 6 voted no confidence in the newly formed government. The Social Action Party under the leadership of Kukrit Pramoj, with only eighteen seats in the House, together with three other major parties and ten minor parties, formed a new coalition government. However, this government had a built-in instability because of the lack of trust among leaders of the various parties. Each party, aware of the possible dissolution of the House at almost any moment, focused on building its own small empire. As 1975 progressed, the pace of political maneuvering accelerated. On January 12, 1976—two days before the Democrat Party's scheduled vote of a no-confidence motion—Kukrit dissolved the Parliament. In the April 1976 election four major parties—the Democrat, Thai Nation, Social Justice, and Social Action—emerged as the dominant powers, compared with the multiplicity of small parties in the House elected fifteen months earlier.

The election results, shown in Table 7.1, demonstrated several continuing features of Thai politics. The national average voter turnout was slightly reduced, 46 percent compared with 47 percent in 1975. Only 29 percent voted in Bangkok, compared with the 33 percent that had voted fifteen months earlier. Leftist parties suffered a humiliating defeat as the electorate displayed a strong conservative tendency in its overall orientation, a preference for political safety over political development. The two socialist parties dropped from twenty-five to three seats, or in percentage terms from 10 to 1 percent of the House as a whole; the progressive New Force Party declined from twelve to three seats. Thus the perceived radical alternative so touted in the months after October 1973 was obliterated by the results of a free election. The Socialists won even fewer seats in April 1976 than in the House elected under military rule in February 1969.

Table 7.1   Comparative Election Results, January 1975 and April 1976, for the Largest Parties in Thailand

	January 1975		April 1976	
	Percent of Popular Vote	Percent of Seats	Percent of Popular Vote	Percent of Seats
Democrat	18.0	26.8	25.4	40.9
Social Justice	14.8	16.7	10.7	10.0
Thai Nation	12.2	10.5	18.1	20.1
Social Action	11.4	6.7	17.8	16.1
Social Agrarian	7.7	7.1	4.3	3.2
Social Nationalist	7.1	6.0	3.3	2.9
New Force	5.9	4.5	7.0	1.1
Socialist	4.7	5.6	1.9	0.7
Socialist Front	3.8	3.7	1.0	0.4
Peace-Loving People	3.5	2.9	—	—
Thai Reformist	2.0	1.1	—	—
Thai	1.7	1.5	—	—
People's Justice	1.7	2.2	—	—
Democracy	1.7	0.8	0.3	0.4
Labor	0.9	0.4	0.8	0.4
Agriculturist	0.7	0.4	—	—
Sovereign	0.6	0.7	—	—
Thai Land	0.5	0.7	—	—
Free People	0.5	0.4	—	—
People's Force	0.4	0.7	4.0	1.1
Economist	0.3	0.4	—	—
Provincial Development	0.2	0.4	0.5	0.7
Dharmacracy	—	—	1.4	0.4
Protecting Thailand	—	—	1.2	0.4
Democratic Front	—	—	1.0	0.4
Thai Society	—	—	0.7	0.4
New Siam	—	—	0.4	0.4
Progressive Society	—	—	0.1	0.4
Total	100.3	100.2	99.9	100.4

Sources: Chai-Anan Samudavanija and Sethaporn Cusripituck, *An Analysis of the 1975 Election Results (Kan wikrorh phon kan luak tang samachik sapha phu tan ratsadorn B. E. 2518)* (Bangkok: National Research Council, February 1977); Rapin Tavornpun, "Popular Votes in 1976 Elections," *The Nation Weekly,* 15 July 1976).

Note: Popular votes totaled 17,983,892 in 1975 and 18,981,135 in 1976. Seats totaled 269 in 1975 and 279 in 1976.

These election results confirmed certain basic trends. One fact was clear: while conflict between the political forces committed to change and those committed to maintenance of the status quo was continuing to escalate, most citizens long for the stability and security of an earlier, easier era. As they reflected on the extremes of violence that had become commonplace over the preceding months, many Thais were seriously asking familiar questions: "Can representative political institutions really survive in Thailand under these pressures?" And, of course, "When will the army finally intervene?"

The Democrat Party's leader, Seni Pramoj (brother of Kukrit), took over as prime minister on April 20, at the head of a grand coalition comprising the Democrat, Thai Nation, Social Justice, and Social Nationalist parties. Together these four parties controlled 206 of the 279 seats in the new House of Representatives. However, due in large measure to the weak and vacillating leadership of its aging head, the Democrat Party had by 1976 become divided into two sharply opposing factions, one progressive and the other conservative. The conservative faction, in alliance with other rightist parties, ultra-rightist groups, and the military, attacked the progressive faction as being leftist and communist. The factionalism and the weakness of civilian leadership coincided with the growth of leftist ideology and political polarization. Amid these situations came the fall of South Vietnam, Laos, and Cambodia to the Communists. Hence, when a crisis occurred in October 1976 following Field Marshal Thanom's return to Bangkok, the weak and faction-ridden civilian government was unable to control the violent and chaotic situation. On October 6, 1976, the military once again intervened.

The Resumption of Military Rule

The 1976 coup resulted in a familiar autocratic political pattern with even more extremist overtones. The 1974 constitution, parliament, and all political parties were abolished; martial law was proclaimed. The coup group appointed Thanin Kraivichien, a staunchly anti-communist judge, as the new prime minister. Over the months that followed, Thailand was immersed in intense reactionary rule. Several thousand students were arrested while others fled to join the Communist Party of Thailand in the hills.

The ultra-rightist policies of the Thanin government—especially its stipulated twelve-year plan for political development, its obsession with communism, and unnecessary aggressiveness toward communist regimes in neighboring countries—resulted in increasing polarization of the Thai society.[21]

Thanin's anti-communist zeal brought about rigorous indoctrination of civil servants, repressive educational control, pressure on labor unions, severe press censorship, and a rigid foreign policy. The military leaders, especially the emerging "Young Turks" in the army, became convinced that Thanin was leading the country to disaster, that his extremist policies were having a most divisive effect and were indirectly strengthening the Communist Party of Thailand (CPT). On October 20, 1977, the Thanin government was overthrown by the same group that had staged the coup that brought Thanin to power one year earlier.

The coup group eased social conflicts and political tension by abolishing the 1977 Constitution and replacing it with a more liberal one. A bicameral legislature with an elected lower House was again introduced and a general election was held in April 1979. However, the new military regime, like its predecessors, maintained its control over the legislature through the appointed Senate to ensure political stability.

The new government adopted a liberal policy toward the problem of communism by granting amnesty to the students and others who were arrested in the October 6 incident as well as to those who had fled to join the CPT. This move, together with other subsequent political measures and reduced support of the CPT by China, led to a diminution of the insurgency in the mid-1980s.

A significant political development from 1977 to 1980 was the rise to political influence of the Young Turks within the military establishment. The emergence of these young colonels as a pressure group coincided with the fragmentation of power among army generals. Their political importance stemmed essentially from their strategically important positions within the army organization, which provided a power base for the coup group and the government formed after the coup. Since parliamentary politics after the 1979 election was still unstable because of the proliferation of political parties and interplay conflict in the coalition government, and the military was still deeply split at the higher echelons, the Young Turks were able to exert pressure for changes in leadership. In 1980 they withdrew support for General Kriengsak's government, forcing the prime minister to resign, and installed General Prem Tinsulanond in his place. However, the Young Turks became frustrated a year later with the prime minister's choice of certain ministers (in a cabinet reshuffle occasioned by inter-party conflict in the coalition government). On April 1, 1981, the Young Turks tried and failed to capture state power, despite their overwhelming military forces. The failure of their coup attempt was due largely to their inability to get the tacit approval and support of the king, who openly supported Prem. The Young Turks' power and influence thus ended abruptly.

As a result of the failed coup thirty-eight officers were discharged, leaving a power vacuum in the army. At the same time Major General Arthit Kamlang-ek—who was responsible for the suppression of the April 1, 1981, coup attempt—rose rapidly to the rank of full general and became commander of the army in October 1982. Although he attempted to prove himself as a new strongman and as a successor to Prem, General Arthit found it difficult to advance his political career in that direction. The military's failure to amend the constitution in 1983 to allow permanent officials to hold cabinet positions made it impossible for General Arthit to enjoy the status his predecessors had as commanders of the army. As the army suffered a big split after the April 1, 1981, coup attempt, and the dismissed officers still maintained considerable influence among their troops, there was deep concern and widespread fear of a possible counter-coup if a coup was carried out.

In September 1985, while the prime minister was in Indonesia and General Arthit was in Europe, Colonel Manoon Roopkajorn, the leader of the Young Turks, and a group of officers in the Armored Cavalry Regiment still loyal to him, staged an unsuccessful coup. Two former commanders-in-chief of the armed forces (General Kriangsak Chommanan and General Serm Na Nakorn), two former deputy commanders-in-chief, and a serving deputy commander-in-chief of the armed forces (Air Chief Marshal Arun Promthep), were put on trial together with thirty low-ranking officers, while Colonel Manoon was allowed to leave the country. The September 1985 coup created a wider rift between the prime minister and General Arthit since the premier's advisers suspected that the latter was behind the unsuccessful bid for power.

Subsequently relations between General Prem and General Arthit became increasingly strained. On May 1, 1986, the government decree on diesel-fueled vehicle registration was voted down in the House, leading the prime minister to dissolve the Parliament.

The dissolution of the Parliament led to the formation of new political parties that openly declared their hostility toward General Prem. The scheduled election on July 27, 1986, was four days before the retirement date of General Arthit, and it was speculated by the premier's aides that General Arthit could make use of his positions as commander-in-chief of the armed forces and commander-in-chief of the army to influence the outcomes of the election. On May 27, 1986, the premier removed General Arthit as army commander-in-chief and appointed his former aide, General Chaovalit Yongchaiyuth, to the post.

The July 27, 1986, general election did not drastically change the political situation prior to it. Although the Democrat Party won the largest number of seats in the Parliament (100 out of 374), there were another fourteen parties elected with representation ranging from one to sixty-three seats (Table 7.2). It was therefore inevitable that a coalition government be formed, and it is interesting to note that this has been the pattern of government since 1975. The only difference is that coalition governments after 1983 have been more stable than their counterparts during 1975–1976 and 1979–1982.

The outcome of the 1986 election did not affect the pattern of leadership succession. General Prem, who did not run in the election and did not belong to any party, was invited by seven political parties (Democrat, Thai Nation, Social Action, People's Community Action, Thai Citizen, and United Thai) to head the government. It is clear that the support from the military was the key factor in the decisions of political parties to nominate him as the premier.

During the 1980s, bureaucratic and nonbureaucratic groups found a workable partnership in a stable semidemocracy. Party and electoral politics functioned once again under a constitutional system, although one much

Table 7.2   Results of the Thailand General Elections 1983, 1986

	1983		1986	
	Number of Seats Won	Percent of Seats	Number of Seats Won	Percent of Seats
Democrat	56	7.3	100	28.8
Chart Thai (Thai Nation)	73	22.5	63	18.2
Social Action	92	28.4	51	14.7
Prachakorn Thai (Thai Citizen)	36	11.1	24	6.9
United Democratic[a]	—	—	38	10.9
Rassadorn (People's Party)[a]	—	—	18	5.2
Community Action[a]	—	—	15	4.3
Ruam Thai (United Thai)[a]	—	—	19	5.4
Progressive	3	1.0	9	2.6
National Democratic	15	4.6	3	0.9
Muan Chon (Mass Party)[a]	—	—	3	0.9
Liberal[a]	—	—	1	0.3
New Force	—	—	1	0.3
Puang Chon Chao Thai (Thai People)	—	—	1	0.3
Democratic Labor	—	—	1	0.3
Independents[b]	49	15.1	—	—
Total	324	100.0	347	100.0

a. Parties formed after 1983.

b. In the 1986 election candidates had to belong to political parties in order to be qualified to contest.

more constrained than that during the 1974–1976 period. As prime minister, Prem did not directly involve himself in party and parliamentary politics because he did not consider himself a politician; in addition, the leadership of the military had no formal links with political parties. This altered the traditional pattern of Thai politics, in which conflicts between military factions had been carried over into the arena of parliamentary politics, and political parties and politicians were drawn into the vortex of military power plays, leading eventually to military coups. The period of Prem's rule (1980–1988) thus brought a new balance under semidemocratic institutional arrangements, satisfying the interests of the bureaucracy, the army (or certain factions of it), political parties, and the monarchy while holding at bay increasingly vocal and assertive interest groups.

Following the dissolution of Parliament by Prime Minister Prem in April 1988 and inconclusive elections in July (Table 7.3), Prem refused reappointment as prime minister, and on August 9 Chatichai Choonhavan— a party politician (leader of the Chart Thai Party, which had won the largest number of seats in Parliament) and a long-retired army officer—was named to head a six-party coalition government. The Chatichai administration

Table 7.3   General Election Results, 1988–1992

	July 1988		March 1992		September 1992	
Party	Number of Seats Won	Percent of Seats	Number of Seats Won	Percent of Seats	Number of Seats Won	Percent of Seats
Chart Thai	87	24.4	74	29.6	77	21.4
Social Action[a]	54	15.1	31	8.6	22	6.1
Democrat[a]	48	13.4	44	12.2	79	21.9
United Thai	35	9.8	—	—	—	—
Thai People	31	8.7	7	1.9	3	0.8
Rassadorn	21	5.9	4	1.1	1	0.3
Prachachon	19	5.3	—	—	—	—
Puangchon Chao Thai	17	4.8	1	—	—	—
Palang Dharma[a]	14	3.9	41	11.4	47	13.1
Kit Prachakom	9	2.5	—	—	—	—
Progressive	8	2.2	—	—	—	—
Saha Prachatipatai	5	1.4	—	—	—	—
Mualchon	5	1.4	1	0.3	4	1.1
Liberal	3	0.8	—	—	—	—
Palang Sangkom Prachatipatai	1	0.3	—	—	—	—
New Aspiration[a]	—	—	72	20.0	51	14.2
Solidarity[a,b]	—	—	6	1.7	8	2.2
Samakkitham	—	—	79	21.9	—	—
Chart Pattana	—	—	—	—	60	16.7
Seritham	—	—	—	—	8	2.2
Total	357	100	360	100	360	100

a. Formed the coalition government led by Prime Minister Chuan Leekpai of the Democrat Party, which took office in September 1992.

b. Formed in April 1989 from the United Thai Party, with supporters also drawn from the Prachachon, Progressive, and Kit Prachakom Parties, which disbanded at that time.

coincided with greater pluralism and openness in Thai politics, but his coalition government also suffered from allegations of increased political corruption, which eroded the legitimacy of party politics. More seriously, although Prime Minister Chatichai tried not to interfere in the corporate interests of the armed forces, the dominant military clique feared he would shift his support to a rival military faction. After two and a half years in office, his government was brought down in another military coup on February 23, 1991.

The military did not assume political power directly but appointed a highly respected businessman and former ambassador, Anand Punyarachun, as prime minister. The military did, however, control the drafting of a new constitution, which soon created heightened conflict because it did not require that the prime minister be an elected member of Parliament. In November 1991, while the draft constitution was being considered by the entirely appointed National Assembly, a huge demonstration demanding a more democratic constitution occurred in Bangkok. The king intervened by calling for passage of the draft constitution and appealing to the people to wait until after the upcoming election in late March 1992 to amend any articles they found objectionable. To counter the claims of the draft constitution's opponents that the new charter would enable members of the military coup group to perpetuate their power under civilian guise, General Suchinda Kraprayoon, who had masterminded the February 1991 coup and was the supreme commander as well as commander-in-chief of the army, announced publicly that he would not seek the premiership.

After the elections on March 22, 1992, no single party gained a majority of parliamentary seats, so a coalition of the five largest (and mainly military-backed) parties formed a government and invited General Suchinda to become prime minister. At this point it was fairly clear to the people that they had been betrayed by both the military and the military-backed political parties. Immediately after General Suchinda became prime minister, opposition parties and student organizations appealed to the people to oppose him. In early May 1992 huge demonstrations lasted for a week and started again on May 15. Suchinda's reactions were typical of the Cold War: He accused demonstrators of being lured by the Communists, who wanted to overthrow the monarchy. From May 17 to 20, troops under the command of his brother-in-law, General Issarapongse, fired on the people, killing hundreds and injuring thousands. On May 20, the king intervened by calling upon Suchinda and retired Major-General Chamlong, leader of the Palang Dharma (Righteous Force) Party and also of the demonstrations, to resolve the conflict. The bloodshed ended following the king's intervention, and Suchinda resigned on May 24. Even after Suchinda's resignation, the military-backed political parties were still trying to form a new government. On June 10, the king intervened again by appointing former prime minister Anand Punyarachun to head an interim government for the second time.

In new elections held in September 1992, the Democrat Party won the largest number of seats in the Parliament and formed a coalition with three other parties that had, along with the Democrats, been termed "angelic" parties by the media because of their opposition to the junta's draft constitution. However, the four "angelic" parties enjoyed only a slim five-seat majority in Parliament. To enhance the stability of the new government, the coalition was broadened to include the "devilish" Social Action Party (with twenty-two seats), which had formed part of the disgraced Suchinda government earlier in the year (Table 7.3). Democrat Party leader Chuan Leekpai became the first person without a military background (other than Anand in his brief interim administrations) to serve as prime minister since the mid-1970s.

Throughout 1993, the coalition government suffered form internal conflict and rivalry, making it unable to respond to rising expectations and demands from both the rich (the private sector) and the poor (the small farmers). The survival of Chuan's coalition government owed less to its political skill than to the absence of any particularly strong alternative to challenge it in Parliament. Its legitimacy was derived primarily from its constitutional status rather than its performance.

The present Thai political system can be called neither a democracy nor an authoritarian system. It falls between the two political modes but has been shifting incrementally away from semi-democracy toward democracy. The semidemocratic model, which was a political compromise between bureaucratic and non-bureaucratic forces, has been under pressure both externally and internally. Globalization and the demand for popular participation at both the national and local levels are major factors contributing to the shift toward democracy.

Historical Analysis

Constitutional Structure and Change

During the six decades from 1932 to 1994, Thailand has had fifteen constitutions, nineteen general elections, sixteen coups (nine of which were successful), and fifty cabinets. There have been twenty prime ministers, of whom eight were military officers and twelve civilians. During this period military prime ministers have been in power altogether for forty-seven years, while their civilian counterparts were in office for a total of only fifteen years. Moreover, some civilian prime ministers were simply fronts for the military.

Successful military interventions usually resulted in the abrogation of constitutions, abolishment of parliaments, and suspension of participant political activity. Each time, however, the military reestablished parliamentary institutions of some kind. This reflects the concern for legitimacy of every military group that came to power after 1932. But because of the weakness of extra-bureaucratic forces and the lack of broad-based support for political parties, what has occurred in Thailand since 1932 is referred to as factional constitutionalism.[22] This explains why there have been as many as thirteen constitutions and seven constitutional amendments in a period of fifty-five years. It also explains why democracy in Thailand has many versions and is still being interpreted differently by various groups.

In Thailand a constitution does not normally provide for the general and neutral rules of the game to regulate participation and competition between political groups. On the contrary, it has been used as a major tool in maintaining the power of the group that created it. What Thailand has experienced is not constitutionalism and constitutional government, but rather different kinds of regimes that adjusted and readjusted institutional relationships between the executive and the legislative branches according to their power position vis-à-vis their opponents.

Constitutional arrangements have basically presented three main patterns. One is the democratic pattern, which takes as its model the British parliamentary system, in which the elected legislature and political parties have dominant and active roles in the political process. Under such a system the prime minister must come from a major political party and is an elected MP. An upper house may be maintained but the number of its members is relatively small and its power minimal. In this model military leaders have no opportunity to become prime ministers and bureaucrats are not allowed to take political positions. The second, a semi-democratic pattern, favors a strong executive vis-à-vis the legislative branch. The prime minister does not have to be an elected member of the Parliament; the upper house is composed mostly of military and civilian bureaucrats with more or less equal powers to the lower house; and the total number of senators is almost equal to the number of elected representatives.

The third, the undemocratic pattern, has no elected Parliament. A legislature is maintained but its members are all appointed, and it acts as a mere rubber stamp on executive decisions that require enactment into laws. Under this system political parties are not allowed to function; hence no elections are held.

Table 7.4 shows the types of constitutions and the periods in which they were in effect.

The most important aspect of a Thai constitution is not the provision and protection of civil and political liberties, but the extent to which it allows the elected House of Representatives to participate in the political process. While, theoretically, the constitution is the highest law of the land, the constitution limits its own power by stating that citizens have political and civil rights and liberties "except where laws otherwise so stipulate." Thus laws, executive decrees, and so forth have precedence over constitutional rights and liberties. Such laws limiting rights and freedoms are framed in terms of national security, public order, and public morality. Seldom, if ever, is a law challenged on the basis of unconstitutionality. Even if a constitutional issue were to be raised, it would not be decided by an independent judiciary but by a Constitutional Tribunal composed of three ex officio officers (president of Parliament, chief justice of the Supreme Court, and director-general of the Department of Prosecutions) and four jurists appointed by Parliament. Thus, while the form and structure of constitutional government is visible, in reality the game is fixed; the political deck is stacked in favor of the executive.[23]

In other words constitutionalism was not designed so much to constrain the rulers as to facilitate their rule. The constitutions therefore did not prescribe the effective norms of political behavior, but were used to cast a cloak of legitimacy over the operations of succeeding rulers and to set the stage for a play to be enacted by the extra-bureaucratic performers—parliaments, political parties, electors.[24]

Table 7.4   Constitutions in Thailand: June 1932–January 1, 1995

	Types of constitution					
Constitution	Democratic	Time in effect*	Semi-democratic	Time in effect*	Un-democratic	Time in effect*
1932[a] (provisional)			√	5 months		
1932[b]			√	13 years 5 months		
1946[c]	√	1 year 6 months				
1947[d]			√	1 year 4 months		
1949[e]	√	2 years 8 months				
1932[f] (amended 1952)			√	6 years 7 months		
1959[g]					√	9 years 5 months
1968[h]			√	3 years 5 months		
1972[i]					√	1 year 10 months
1974[j]	√	2 years				
1976[k]					√	1 year
1977[l]					√	1 year 1 month
1978[m]			√	12 years 2 months		
1991 (March)[n]				8 months		
1991 (December)[o]**				3 years 1 month		
Total[p]	3	6 years 2 months	8 8	41 years 1 months	4	13 years 4 months

*Rounded off to months.
**Still in effect as of 1 January 1995.
Notes: a. 27 June 1932–10 December 1932 (provisional constitution); b. 10 December 1932–9 May 1946; c. 10 May 1946–8 November 1947; d. 9 November 1947–22 March 1949; e. March 1949 29 November 1951; f. 8 March 1952–20 October 1958; g. 28 January 1959–20 June 1968 h. 21 June 1968–17 November 1971; i. 15 December 1972–6 October 1974; j. 7 October 1974–6 October 1976; k. 22 October 1976–20 October 1977; l. 19 November 1977–21 December 1978; m. 21 December 1978–23 February 1991; n. 1 March–9 December, 1991; o. 9 December 1991–; p. Excludes a total of 1 year, 9 months when no constitution was in effect.

Having an elected House of Representatives means that a mechanism must be devised and agreement reached between elected politicians and non-elected bureaucratic politicians (military included) on the sharing of power in the cabinet. Whenever this relationship is strained the tendency has always been to abolish the constitution so that the elected House of Representatives will be automatically terminated. Similarly, having an entirely appointed assembly means that such mechanism and agreement have to be arranged among the bureaucratic elites, especially among the military.

Of Thailand's 15 constitutions since 1932, only 3 can be classified as "democratic" while 8 have been "semidemocratic" and 4 have been "nondemocratic" (Table 7.4). From June 1932 to January 1995, "democratic" constitutions were in effect for only 6 years and 2 months while the "semidemocratic" and "undemocratic" have been in effect for slightly more than 4 years and 13 years, respectively. In other words, during these 62 years there were only 6 years when political institutions could operate within the democratic rules of the game. Moreover, these 6 years were thinly spread out among three different short periods.

Political Institutionalization

The weakness of the democratic pattern of rule can be attributed to the low level of political institutionalization in Thailand, which is the consequence of three important factors: the frequency of coups d'état, the discontinuity of elected parliaments, and the weaknesses of political parties.

Military coups in Thailand are a means by which political leaders alternate in power. Therefore it is not necessary that political, social, and economic crises be preconditions for a military intervention, although they could facilitate the intervention, particularly when the civilian government's supporters are very strong and active. From 1932 through 1987 there have been altogether sixteen military interventions, nine of which were successful.

As military interventions have become more frequent the commitment of the military to democratic institutions has declined. This is indicated by the fact that in all the five coups during the 1932–1958 period the coup groups changed only the governments in power but did not abolish the constitution. Elections were held and political parties were allowed to function, although their roles in Parliament were limited by the presence of the appointed members of the assembly. After 1958, however, military interventions usually resulted in the abolishment of the constitutions and the "freezing" of participant political activities. In the following period of twenty years (1958–1978) there were altogether seven constitutions, only one of which can be classified as "democratic" (1974 Constitution); the rest gave vast powers to an executive branch that was dominated by bureaucratic elites. The high frequency of military interventions in Thailand has had diverse negative effects upon democratic political institutions and has bred more instability within the political system as a whole.

While democratic political institutions suffered setbacks and discontinuity, the military has greatly strengthened its organizations and expanded its roles in several areas. During the 1976-1982 period the defense budget averaged about 20 percent of the total government expenditure. The military has also been granted each year a considerable secret fund, which could be used for intelligence operations but has also been widely used for internal security and political purposes. Several civic action programs, political education projects, and rightist movements have been financed from this fund.

Most of the mass communication media, particularly radio and television stations, are under the control of the military—which has undoubtedly reinforced its political potency. Out of 269 radio stations—all of which are government-owned—the military stations account for some 57 percent, while 33 percent are operated by the Public Relations Department and the rest by other ministries and educational institutions. The army also runs two television stations.[25] The military can utilize radio and television programs for psychological warfare and/or mobilizing mass movements in times of political crisis. For instance, the Armored School Radio played a very active role during 1975 and 1976 in mobilizing the rightist movement against the student demonstrators, which eventually led to the coup on October 6, 1976.

In recent years the military has adopted a standpoint that serves to strengthen its legitimate role in politics. It has been emphasized that the military as an institution (or "national armed forces") is the principle machine of the state; therefore when a government composed of political parties fails to solve national problems, the military is entitled to use its own policies to solve those problems.[26]

In a country where participant political institutions are weak, the military can effectively rally public support by pointing to the instability of government and ineffective administration of state affairs by party politics. In their thinking, politics and government administration are inseparable; hence government officials could hold political positions, such as cabinet offices, concurrently with their administrative positions in order to ensure national security.

Historically, therefore, the military and civilian bureaucratic elites represent the most dynamic political forces in Thai society. They were prime movers in most of the events and changes. They are the most powerful political machine in the country, and have been able to control the political game fairly well. The circulation of the military and the bureaucratic elites is also worth noting. The control and command of military positions, especially those at the top of the pyramid and also at the politically important posts, can be utilized for multipurpose activities ranging from getting themselves appointed to the National Assembly to the chairmanship or membership of the public enterprise boards.

Unlike Malaysia and Singapore, where tenures of parliaments last without interruption, only four parliaments in Thailand completed their tenures; the rest were disrupted by coups d'état. While discontinuity of elected parliaments is a fact of political life, the appointed assemblies have been continued without disruptions. It is therefore not surprising that some military officials, such as General Prem, have been members of the appointed assemblies since 1958, while the majority of members of elected Parliament in 1980 served in the House of Representatives for the first time.

When parliaments could not complete their tenures, several bills proposed by the members had to be resubmitted, thus delaying the process of socioeconomic reform in response to the rapidly changing condition of society during these interim periods. Legislative supporting organizations such as legislative reference and research units were only established in 1974 and could not function effectively because of the lack of support from the government. Members on parliamentary standing committees keep changing from one parliament to another, preventing MPs from developing expertise in their chosen fields.

These consequences of parliamentary discontinuity have weakened the power of the legislative branch vis-à-vis that of the executive and prevented the legislature from becoming a potent force in the Thai political system.

Discontinuity of elected parliaments has had adverse effects on political parties in several aspects. Party organizations could not be developed and political mobilization could only be at best ad hoc. From 1946 to 1981, 143 parties were formed but only a few survived throughout these years. All of the parties are urban based with weak rural organization, and party branches are not very well organized.

When political parties were allowed to function they suffered from lack of discipline among their members, who pursued factional and individual interests rather than abiding by party policies. Usually political parties in Thailand are primarily groupings of individuals or networks of patrons and clients who are forced to be together by a political party law requiring candidates to contest elections under party banners. After elections almost all of the parties have no significant programs that would link them with the masses.

Unlike Singapore and Malaysia, which are one-party-dominant states, in Thailand no single party has ever dominated the political scene. When government parties won a majority in Parliament, factionalism within them usually led to political crises, culminating in military interventions. From 1975 to 1976, parliamentary seats were shared by from eight to twenty-two parties, resulting in highly unstable coalition governments.

Apart from the above-mentioned factors inhibiting the strength of political parties in Thailand, the development of a party system is affected by the hostile attitude of bureaucratic elites toward the role of political parties. As Kramol Tongdhamachart observes, "the bureaucratic elites often perceived political parties as the cause of national disunity and political instability and also as the political entity that could threaten their power positions."[27] When political parties were allowed to function, the bureaucratic elites usually imposed obstacles on their formation and performance, making it difficult for the parties to mature at a natural rate of growth. The 1981 Political Party Law requires the potential party organizers to fulfill several requirements before their parties can be registered and legally perform their functions. For example, they must recruit a minimum of 5,000 members with residence in five provinces in each of the four regions of the country. In addition, each province must be represented in the potential party with a minimum of fifty persons.[28]

To encourage a strong party system, the present constitution requires that, in the general election, parties must field candidates numbering not less than one-third of the total number of members of the House of Representatives. With thirty-six MPs (one-tenth of the total), Bangkok has the greatest share (but still slightly less than its roughly 13 percent of the population). Constituencies consist of up to three MPs, and voters can vote for as many individual candidates (of the same or different parties) as there are seats in the constituency. In such a system, major political parties have a tremendous need to mobilize funds for their campaigns, in the millions of dollars.[29]

The need for campaign funds has led to a closer relationship between political parties and business interests. Some prominent businessmen have thus become either deputy leaders or executive members of political parties, whereas in the past these people maintained relatively distant relationships with leaders of political parties. At the provincial level local businessmen are also more actively involved in politics both as candidates and as financial supporters of political parties. At the national level most of the businessmen who are party financiers prefer not to run in the election. However, because of their financial contributions, they are given cabinet portfolios in the coalition governments. Conflicts, therefore, usually arise between the elected politicians and the party financiers who are executive members of the parties and are given cabinet posts. The elected politicians call these party financiers "political businessmen," distinguishing them from the "grassroots politicians." Hence, although there has been more involvement from the private sector in the Thai political system, this development has created especially destabilizing effects. This is because, apart from cabinet positions, political secretaries to ministers, and a limited number of executive positions in public enterprises, there are no other significant official positions to which party financiers could be appointed. The competition for limited positions between these two groups of people in various political parties has markedly contributed to the overall instability of the system.

It is fair to say that most of the businessmen still prefer not to be formally identified with any political party. This is because party politics are not yet institutionalized, while bureaucratic politics provides more certainty. However, if there is continuity in the parliamentary system it is natural that compromises would be made between "grassroots politicians," who claim to represent a broader spectrum of national interests, and the "political businessmen," whose interests are more parochial. At present only the privileged groups have access to the formal political institutions through their alliances with political parties and lobbying. The underprivileged groups, i.e., the workers and farmers, have no formal links with political parties and take political actions independently. In other words, while all groups articulate their interests, only the interests of privileged groups are effectively aggregated by political parties.

Major political parties in Thailand have basically similar economic and social policies. In fact, these policies have been photocopies of the various National Social and Economic Development Plans. In other words, political parties and the technocrats are similar in their economic and social development strategies which are based essentially on a state-led model of centralized economic development under a free-market economy. Hence, political parties in Thailand have been merely electoral machines rather than full-fledged democratizing forces linking various sectors and allow for more active popular participation at the grassroots level.

However, in the past two decades electoral process in Thailand has become institutionalized in the sense that political parties and elections have been accepted as "necessary evils" by the state power elites. When electoral competition becomes stabilized, there is a need for political parties to search for a new platform to gain mass support. In the past, "democratic" parties campaigned on their anti-military and anti-dictatorship stance, but after May 1992—when the military suddenly lost political power—the parties were left with no effective political platform to distinguish one from another. This is the reason that since May 1992, political parties in Thailand have been categorized not along ideological, ethnic, or economic and social policy lines but by a strange criterion of being good or "angelic" parties and bad or "devilish" parties. (As noted earlier, "angelic" parties are those that opposed the military junta, whereas "devilish" parties cooperated with the military government.)

Without the threat from the Communist Party of Thailand and with the waning influence of the military, for the first time in Thai political history political parties have been able to capture the vacuum in the political space and have become the central decisionmaking entity. There is, therefore, an urgent need to develop a *political* platform in a democratic environment. This political platform is the policy of decentralization and more popular participation in economic and social development. Decentralization, especially a proposal for gubernatorial elections, has become a real dividing line between political parties that have otherwise similar economic and social policies. This political platform strikes at the core of the deep-rooted state-centric development of the modern nation-state, and Thai politics in the coming decade will be contested essentially on this major issue.

For the first time in modern Thai political history, "democracy" has been defined concretely as a political system that does not only allow for periodic elections, but also for more popular participation especially at the grassroots level on matters that directly affect communities. Once democracy is linked with participation, decentralization and the strengthening of local self-government become the major overriding issues. In the post–Cold War era, the Communist threat and the security imperative cannot be effectively exploited to deny popular participation. Thus, democratization in Thailand will be centered upon the ability of political parties to resolve the conflict between the popular demand for more participation (especially on communal rights to participate in local natural-resource utilization) on the one hand and the bureaucratic elite's resistance to surrendering its entrenched centralized administrative power on the other.

Like other problems concerning the weakness of political institutions, the impotence of Parliament and political parties in Thailand is inextricably linked with the perennial issue of the conflict between bureaucratic power and that of participant political institutions. Problems facing political parties must therefore be analyzed in a broader perspective and not restricted to internal characteristics of party organizations. It is impossible for any political party to develop its organization and to effectively perform its functions in a political system where coups d'état have become more or less institutionalized.

In historical perspective, democratic development in Thailand suffered setbacks because of certain unique circumstances. In the pre-1973 period, when extra-bureaucratic forces were weak and political competition was limited to a few personalities and their cliques, the commitment to democratic values among the political elite gradually declined. This is understandable because those who were committed to democratic principles had no effective base of support, and had to engage in the same game of power play. Hence in the 1930s, the leaders of the People's Party sought support from the armed forces in their competition for power. After being drawn into politics new generations of army officers quickly realized their indispensable role. The army officers who staged the coup in 1947 and remained in power until 1973 were not only uncommitted to democratic ideals, they also had strongly anti-political attitudes. Hence, when extra-bureaucratic forces became strong and began to play active roles in politics, they were regarded as destabilizing factors in national development. The military perceived legitimate politics in a very limited sense, involving activities centered in the Parliament and not outside. As General Lek Naeomalee (former interior minister) commented: "When people in our country want to have freedom or liberty, they are going to create confusion and disorder—in our democracy we have members of Parliament, but what do we get from having a Parliament? Can members of parliament help make our country stable?"[30]

It is evident that "democracy" perceived by military men is quite different from the liberal democratic tradition. Its scope begins with a general election and ends at the legislature that is not necessarily an entirely elected body. It is democracy without pressure groups and is conflict-free. In other words there is another set of values higher than liberal democratic values. These values are national security, stability, and order. The attachment to these values is still strong among military officers, and the increased activism of newly emergent groups has further convinced them that full-fledged democratic rule would be detrimental to national security.

Another factor that impeded political development is that rapid socioeconomic changes coincided with the growth of the Communist Party of Thailand. This contributed to the weakening of the overall political system, since any democratic movement that aimed at mobilizing and gaining support from the masses was usually suspected of being communist-inspired. It is therefore unfortunate that significant socioeconomic changes did not lead to a stable pluralist democracy. Ideological polarization during the 1973–1976 period was too extreme and intense. Moreover, political parties were unable to establish linkages to politically active groups such as student, labor, and farmer groups. As a result political participation under the full-fledged democratic rule in the mid-1970s was close to anarchy. The military was therefore able to exploit the situation, suppressing radical elements and co-opting the moderate and conservative sections of these pressure groups.

Economic Development and Social Change

Thailand's economy has grown rapidly over the past two decades, with an average per capita income growth of almost 5 percent per year between 1960 and 1980. (In 1961 per capita income was 2,137 baht compared with 12,365 baht in 1980. U.S. $1 = 22 baht in 1980.) Over the same period there was a rapid transformation in the structure of production, with the share of agriculture in total value added declining from 40 percent in 1960 to 25 percent in 1980. However, it was estimated that 76 percent of the Thai population still remained in rural areas, a decline of only about 10 percent since 1960. This labor force and population distribution reflects the unusually extensive pattern of Thai agricultural growth and the pervasive rural nature of the Thai economy and society. After two decades of development Bangkok still remains the primary city. While about 9.7 percent of the Thai population lived in Bangkok in 1980, 32.7 percent of total GDP in Thailand originated in Bangkok. Although the overall incidence of poverty was reduced from 57 percent in the early 1960s to about 31 percent in the mid-1970s, poverty remains largely a rural phenomenon.[31] It is estimated that in 1980 11 million people in the rural areas were living in poverty. The benefit of growth was not evenly dispersed but has widened the gap between the rich and the poor, and between the rural and the urban sectors.

The manufacturing sector expanded rapidly as a result of the policy of import substitution. Its share in the GDP rose from 10.5 percent in 1960 to

18 percent in 1980. The number of factories increased fivefold between 1960 and 1980. Figures in 1980 show that there were 3.6 million workers in industrial and service sectors. Apart from workers in privately owned factories, there was also a rapid increase in the number of workers in state enterprises, which rose from 137,437 in 1973 to 433,649 in 1983. Labor unions in state enterprises have been more politically active than labor unions in the private sector. In 1983, there were 323 labor unions in the private sector while there were 91 state enterprise labor unions. However, the former had altogether only 81,465 members compared with 136,335 members in the latter. Public enterprise workers in the Electricity Authority, the railways, and the Water Supply Authority are the most organized; their political significance is due to their control of public utility services in metropolitan areas, which gives them considerable bargaining power. Hence socioeconomic changes in Thailand are marked by the highly urban character of the society, with major potent political forces concentrated in the capital city.

By far the most important change in the Thai economy since the 1960s has been the rapid expansion of the "big business enterprises" (those with assets of more than 500 million baht). According to a 1983 study the value of capital owned by the big business enterprises amounted to nearly 74 percent of the GNP that year.[32] This growth of monopolistic capital was made possible by government development policies during the authoritarian regimes in the late 1950s and throughout the 1960s that favored the development of industrial capital outside agriculture. Such policies were aimed at creating a production base capable of transforming agricultural surplus into manufacturing commodities. As a result, policies of import substitution and trade protection were implemented. During the same period government after government pursued the policy of price controls in favor of urban communities at the expense of the agricultural work force. Prices of rice paddy have been kept low for the sake of city dwellers and consumers while farmers have to purchase chemical fertilizers at extra high prices as a result of additional transportation costs.[33]

Throughout the 1980s and early 1990s, the Thai economy maintained steady economic growth, averaging 6.0 percent annually in per capita GNP (and 8.2 percent in GDP) between 1980 and 1992 (one of the highest sustained growth rates in the world during this period).[34] Rapid expansion of the export sector, which grew at an average annual rate of 12 percent from 1991 to 1994, figured prominently in this boom. In the 1990s it is estimated that gross domestic product will continue to grow at an average of 8 percent per year, which would raise the per capita income level to about $3,000 by the turn of the century.

Economic development in the past three decades has resulted in the concentration of economic power in the capital city and has created a large urban working class. At the same time this development witnessed the growth of the bureaucracy, which, while remaining highly centralized, penetrated more into the rural areas. By 1980 the number of government employees (excluding military forces) reached 1.4 million, making the ratio between population (46 million) and government employees 33 to 1. In the same year, government expenditure on personnel services accounted for 35 percent of total government expenditures.[35] Bureaucratic expansion also resulted in a rapid increase in the number of students during the late 1960s and throughout the 1970s. This expansion, unprecedented in Thai political history, resulted from the heavy stress placed on education by the first three national development plans (1961–1976) and provided more than 30 percent of the total government funds each year to education at all levels. Most significant politically was the rapid expansion in the number of university students, which rose from 15,000 in 1961 to 50,000 in 1972, and has since increased greatly.[36]

In the 1980s and 1990s, Thailand's rapid growth was accompanied by a growing internationalization of its economy. The changing structure and increasing globalization of the Thai economy have created a large urban middle class not only in Bangkok but also in urban areas of the seventy-six provinces throughout the country. The rapid expansion of urban centers has brought about new social and economic problems such as traffic congestion, urban poverty, and environmental degradation. These problems, especially traffic congestion and lack of an alternative mass-transit system, are major concerns of the private corporate sector which seeks to increase its competitiveness in international and regional markets.

Unlike the 1970s, when latent demands for participation were escalating exponentially, mainly among strident and intellectual groups, socio-economic changes in the 1980s and 1990s led to increasing demands from the private sector to deregulate and supply basic services for new investments in emerging industries. It is clear that economics and politics are now inextricably linked with each other. In the 1970s the government was faced with an outlawed Communist Party, nonbureaucratic groups that were anomic entities, and the better-organized students and workers. The government succeeded in its attempts to control the workers, and rapid socioeconomic changes since the mid-1980s, as well as the dramatic convulsions in the socialist world, made the younger generation less ideological and more concerned with new opportunities in the business sector.

The main challenge of the government in the 1990s is the growing activism of the middle class, which had been small and politically inactive in the past. The May 1992 mass uprising reflected a trend of increasing activism of the commercial middle class, which is now larger than the professional official class.

The Consolidation of a Bureaucratic Polity

It is indisputable that socioeconomic changes led to the emergence of new groups in society, but whether the existence of these groups would lead to a pluralist democracy is another matter. In the case of Thailand socioeconomic changes occurred under situations of semi-imposed development. In this pattern of development, political and administrative structures such as the military and the bureaucracy have been able to grow alongside the growth of the private sector. In fact, they have been able to create new institutional structures of their own or to adjust existing structures and functions (or even the "style") to cope with pressures coming from extra-bureaucratic groups. The military and bureaucratic groups may "lose" the first battle, especially when intra-elite conflicts are high. However, as they had more and more experience with new environments and situations, their advantage in controlling political resources, especially the use of legitimate violence, made it possible for them to gradually gain control over extra-bureaucratic forces.

Rapid socioeconomic changes often create uncertainties and sometimes instability and disorder. In fact, democratic values and norms brought about by these changes are the antithesis of, and pose great challenges to, traditional values of the military elites, who welcome modernization and development as long as stability and order can be simultaneously maintained.

In the past five decades military intervention in the political process has taken only one form—a coup d'état. But during the 1980s, the military became more sophisticated in developing a national strategy that has helped to expand its legitimate role in the political system. It adjusted its strategies and tactics in dealing with emergent social forces. Cooperation and co-optation replaced intimidation and suppression. The experience the military gained during the 1970s and 1980s was not from its participation in conventional politics, but from its encounter with the Communist Party of Thailand in rural areas. The new generation of military leadership in the 1980s was politicized in a manner totally different from that of its predecessors. Their experience in organizing the masses in rural areas to counter political activities of the CPT convinced them that the most effective way to deal with pressure groups is not to suppress them but to find ways and means to control them. This approach is evident in the prime minister's orders No. 66/2523 and No. 65/2525. The former was known as the policy to defeat the Communist Party of Thailand, which stated that to destroy the CPT it was necessary to establish a truly democratic regime. Individual rights and liberty should be guaranteed and democratic groups encouraged to actively participate in politics. The army's role in implementing this order was therefore not only to suppress the CPT, but also to act as an instrument to solve political and socioeconomic problems. In a 1983 lecture on "The Changed Situation of the CPT and the Strategy to Defeat the Communists in 1983" Lieutenant General Chaovalit Yongchaiyuth,[37] deputy chief of army staff and the brain behind Order No. 66/2523, stated:

> Nowadays, Thailand has two policies to solve national problems. There is the political party policy, proposed to the Parliament by the government, and the policy of the National Army, the policy to defeat the Communists.

These two policies, however, have conflicting contents since one policy is formulated by the political parties but the other by the National Army. But facts, reasons and theory prove that the National Army can solve national problems, namely to win over the CPT, while the political party policy has not succeeded in solving any problems.[38]

From this statement it is clear that the military took another step in redefining and reinforcing its role in society. The open criticism of political parties reflected the attitudes of army leaders on the roles of participatory political institutions. In fact the military leaders were raising some very important questions, for example, the legitimate role of political parties, whether they really represent the people, and the extent to which parties could successfully cope with national problems.

In mid-January 1983 Major General Pichit Kullavanijaya, First Division commander, warned on a television program that the new electoral system would only result in bringing the "capitalists" into Parliament, and, if there were no change in the constitution, the military might well have to "exercise" (to step in) to protect the security of the nation and the interest of the people.[39] He also pointed out that the military has been an important force in society for 700 years and has to be given a proper role in politics.

Order No. 65/2525 reflects a tendency toward a limited pluralist system, especially points 2.3 and 2.4 of the order, which state:

2.3 Popular participation in political activities must be promoted to enable the people to have more practical experience which can serve to strengthen their attachment to and understanding of the principles of sovereignty. This must be done by involving the *tambon* councils, village committees and cooperatives, . . . encouraging the use of political parties as a means of promoting their own interests at the national or local level in accordance with the principles of democracy. . . .

2.4 Activities of pressure groups and interests groups must be regulated. Pressure and interest groups can act either to reinforce or to obstruct the development of democracy. Therefore, to ensure that their role be a constructive one and to deter any such group from hindering this development, their activities must be regulated. . . .[40]

Order No. 65/2525 (1982) identified six major groups that ought to be regulated: economic groups, the masses, students, progressive groups, the mass media, and the armed forces. While the first five groups were treated at length, the last—the armed forces—was given a very short guideline: "They should have a correct understanding of democracy and preserve this system."

The same order stated that the personnel who will be the main instrument for achieving democratic development are to be "*government* officials" in every agency, as well as ordinary people with idealism who are prepared to cooperate to bring about a model democracy (italics added). Hence the Thai military in the 1980s went one step further; that is, in the past it only criticized civilian regimes, but now it set the framework for the development of democracy.

Both the military and the bureaucracy compete with political institutions in organizing and mobilizing the masses in several ways. Although there are several private and voluntary associations, and interest groups, they are mainly Bangkok-based while the great bulk of people in rural areas are organized into groups by the military and the bureaucracy. At the village level the Ministry of Interior is in control of the village councils through the offices of village headmen and district officers. The army, through its Civilian Affairs Department, has not only organized and mobilized masses into groups such as Village Defense Volunteers, but has also infiltrated and taken over certain initially legitimate pressure/interest groups—e.g., student groups, labor, farmers, the media—and created polarization within these movements, weakening them as effective political forces. It was pointed out earlier that political parties had weak links with pressure groups and the masses. With the military's stand and approach to the groups mentioned above, it has been very difficult for political parties to establish a closer and more viable relationship with these groups. Political parties are thus reduced to ad hoc electoral organizations, rather than being a meaningful institution for political participation.

However, in 1993–1994 the northeastern nongovernmental organizations (NGOs) and the small farmers were able to unite in a grand coalition under the banner of the Northeastern Small-Farmer Convention (NSFC). Subsequently, the SNFC organized four long marches of small farmers to press their demands on the government. In early February 1995, the NSFC succeeded in persuading the government to set up a joint committee to take immediate action to solve small farmers' grievances, ranging from the postponement of farmers' debt with the Bank for Agriculture and Cooperatives to recognition of disputed forest-reserve land. It seems the elected government has found it necessary to respond to organized agricultural coalitions.

The present political system is therefore a unique one, in which the leadership of the military has not formed or openly supported any political party as it did in the past. The military and the bureaucrats, however, have their "informal political party," which is the appointed Senate.

The Senate is dominated by military officers and civil servants, with a few businessmen and intellectuals. Military officers are appointed to the Senate according to their seniority and positions (for example, all commanders-in-chief of the army, navy, and air force, chiefs of staff, divisional commanders) as well as for their loyalty to the prime minister. As for civil servants, the undersecretary of every ministry and those of equivalent stature are members of the Senate. These senators have a military whip, the army chief of staff, and a civilian whip, the undersecretary of the prime minister's office. Through their coordinating Committee on Legislative Affairs senators get slips recommending how to vote on various issues both in the Senate and in the joint sessions with the House of Representatives, the elected Parliament.

The role of the House of Representatives has been constrained by several provisions and procedures of the 1978 Constitution and parliamentary rules. For example, until recently, members of Parliament could not freely propose legislative bills unless the Committee on Legislative Bills endorsed the bills. This committee was composed of seventeen members—three appointed by the cabinet, six by the Senate, and eight by the House of Representatives. This provision of the 1978 Constitution was lifted in 1983. Until 1992, Senate control over the House was exercised through the requirement in the constitution that the following matters be considered by a joint session: consideration and passage of the Budget Bill, motion of the no-confidence vote, and consideration and passage of legislative bills concerning national security and economic aspects.

Ironically, whereas the elected Parliament has had to struggle for continuity and survival, the appointed Senate has always been entrenched and institutionalized. In April 1994 the coalition government proposed a series of constitutional amendments to the joint session of the House of Representatives and the Senate—one of which was an amendment to reduce the number of senators from two-thirds to one-third the number of members of the elected Parliament. All proposed amendments were voted down by senators, who formed an alliance with the opposition members of Parliament. The minister of defense, the secretary-general of the National Security Council, and almost all of the high-ranking civil and military officers who were senators voted against the government-backed constitutional amendments. Moreover, the opposition parties proposed a new constitution based on the 1978 semidemocratic version and gained total support from the Senate. The Senate is, therefore, an instrument for control of the political process—the legislative arm of the bureaucracy. It seems the military and civilian bureaucrats have adjusted their role and strategy from direct intervention in the political process by way of staging coups d'état to a more active legislative role, using the powers vested in a semidemocratic constitution to protect their waning political influence.

The semidemocratic pattern of rule described above is the outgrowth of the interplay of social, economic, and political forces in Thai society. It evolved from the nation's unique conditions that have existed for centuries. This semidemocratic pattern is a compromise between two sets of forces that have coexisted since 1932. One set of forces emanates from military and bureaucratic institutions, and values and norms associated with them. The other originates from more recent non-bureaucratic political institutions. These two forces operate within and adjust themselves to changes in the socioeconomic environment. In the Thai situation, changes resulting from social and economic modernization have not automatically strengthened voluntary associations and political groups because the military-bureaucratic structures, rather than the party system, have been able to incorporate and co-opt these new social groups, which then have their interests represented through bureaucratically created and controlled mechanisms.

During the 1980s, economic development brought increased criticism of the bureaucratic polity and of military domination of politics.[41] Ansil Ramsay observed that political participation in decision making in Thailand extended to "bourgeois middle-class groups," especially the business elite, who began to play a major role in Thai cabinets and in economic decision making. Other groups from middle-class backgrounds, such as leading academics and technocrats, also have increased their access to decision making.[42]

However, the growth of the middle class in Thailand that began in the 1970s did not lead immediately to democratization. Socioeconomic changes have enabled the middle class—largely composed of bankers, businesspeople, and other professionals (such as lawyers and doctors)—to participate more in bureaucratic politics rather than to fundamentally change the nature of the Thai political system from a "bureaucratic polity" to a "bourgeois polity." The business class—the owners of capital, especially those whose business ventures involve concessions from the state—has not been an independent class but has always sought a close alliance with the military and the technocrats. There was no strong reaction following the February 1991 coup; in fact, the middle class supported the overthrow of Chatichai's civilian government (at least partly in reaction to its high levels of corruption).

A number of recent studies about the role of business associations in Thailand and of the relationships between certain industrial sectors and the state have concluded that although Thai politics is highly unstable, the relationship between the state and the private sectors has been very stable and institutionalized. Both Anek Laothamatas and Richard Doner show in their analyses that the private corporate sector has been gaining acceptance from the state.[43] Such cooperation has led to a different political model—a kind of semiauthoritarian pluralism instead of democratic pluralism.

Clearly, state–private sector cooperation and semiauthoritarian pluralism are complementary. They formed an alliance in their drive toward industrialization, which is beginning to conflict with the impoverished agrarian sector. In January 1994 there were sixty-six mass protests across the country, most of which were caused by conflicts between officials and small farmers involving land rights, utilization of natural resources, and construction of dams affecting local communities.

Despite the fact that there have been more businessmen serving in the cabinets than in the past, they make little impact in policy matters. Their participation in the executive branch is usually counterbalanced by the use of advisers and technocrats. Such limitations on the role of the private sector and its leadership are due to the distrust of businessmen's direct involvement in politics on the part of the military and bureaucratic elites. The military, as pointed out earlier, has expressed its concern about the danger of "capitalist interests." Businessmen who have served as cabinet ministers often complained that they could not implement their policies because the bureaucrats did not give enough support.

Nevertheless, the democratic activism of the early 1990s does signal a possible long-term change in the political role of the middle class, or at least its professional and small-business components. The people's uprising in May 1992 has been termed the "revolt of the middle class" and the demonstrators the "mobile-phone mob." The professional class was the principal force driving the protests led by opposition parties, the Student Federation of Thailand, and the Campaign for Popular Democracy. The behavior of the middle class was best analyzed by the editor in chief of the *Manager* (*Poo Chad Karn* in Thai):

> The pro-democracy protests in May were a fascinating phenomenon that reflect a conflict of conscience in Thailand's capitalist culture, which apparently has not yet matured enough to create stability or an acceptable pattern of change. The neo-bourgeoisie turned out in droves to anti-government rallies—thus posting a threat to their own short-term interests in an attempt to secure a future economic system more conducive to their world view (*The Manager,* July 1991).

The reappointment of Anand Punyarachun can be seen as the triumph of the middle class, for he is their ideal leader. Anand initiated unprecedented reforms in major economic areas with emphasis on economic liberalization, competition, deregulation, transparency, and decentralization. Although his second term was brief (three months), he was able to convince the military to return to the barracks. A firm believer in pluralist democracy, Anand has had a fundamental problem in the past: how to minimize the entrenchment of the military in politics when the age of the middle class was dawning and the armed forces were losing legitimacy and prestige. During his two brief interim administrations, Anand laid a solid foundation for positive democratic development.

By 1994, the middle class and other democratic forces such as students and intellectuals had become disillusioned with the government. Failures of the democratically elected government to solve urban and rural problems diminished faith in representative government and reduced general calls for a Rousseauian type of communitarian democracy. However, the politically active public and the media have made it clear to the military that despite their increasing disappointment with political parties and the Parliament, they nevertheless still wholeheartedly oppose any move by the military into the political arena.

Theoretical Analysis

Politics has taken the shape of a vicious circle in Thailand. A constitution is promulgated and elections are held for legislative seats. A crisis is precipitated, and this triggers a military coup; the military then promises a constitution. Thus the process of democratization in Thailand has been cyclical; authoritarian regimes alternate with democratic or semidemocratic ones. In this situation neither authoritarian nor democratic structures are institutionalized.

Why, despite the social and economic changes that have occurred, is democracy in Thailand still unstable and why has there been the institutionalization of only semidemocratic rule? This is because a differentiated socioeconomic structure does not necessarily lead to the control of the state by societal groups. In Thailand socioeconomic change has occurred under conditions of semi-imposed, forced development, rather than being led by an autonomous bourgeoisie. An activist bureaucratic state competes with participant or nonbureaucratic actors, and this leads to greater bureaucratization, rather than democratization, as the state expands its development role.

The ability of the state to expand and adapt its role to changing situations and environments explains why emergent autonomous forces have failed to challenge the power of the military and the bureaucracy. Although there exists a sizable middle class in Thailand, it is mainly composed of salaried officials and other nonbureaucratic professionals whose interests are not institutionally linked with any of the participant political institutions. The capitalist and commercial class, which is predominantly Sino-Thai, is just beginning to take an active but cautious role in party politics. Neither the farmers nor the laborers, who together compose the majority of the lower class, have yet developed into a class for itself. Although there were some peasant and worker groups that developed consciousness of class antagonisms, they were easily suppressed by the authorities. This underprivileged class is not effectively represented by any strong political party, and is therefore a rather impotent political force in society. Moreover, the military and the bureaucracy have provided an important ladder for social mobility in the past century for many middle-class and lower-class children. This explains why there has been little class antagonism in Thai society despite distinct class divisions. The bureaucracy has therefore been able to function not only as the state mechanism, but also as a social organization.

It should be pointed out that Thai authoritarianism is not very repressive. Authoritarian regimes that attempted to be too repressive usually met with strong opposition from various sections of society. Once an authoritarian regime extended its controls and suppression to the general populace, it was usually opposed by the press, which has been one of the freest in Asia. An independent and long-standing judiciary is another institution that has always been safeguarding the encroachment of civil liberties. It is an autonomous body not subject to the control of the military and the bureaucracy, but with its own independent recruitment and appointment procedures. The independence and integrity of the judiciary branch is reflected in the appointment of a senior judge to head a government in times of crisis.

The existence of countervailing forces such as an independent judiciary, a free press, and some favorable social conditions such as relatively little class antagonism or ethnic and religious cleavage, are necessary but not sufficient conditions for a viable democracy in Thailand. These conditions do serve as important factors in preventing an authoritarian regime from becoming extreme in its rule. In other words they soften authoritarian rule and, to a large extent, contribute to the maintenance of semidemocratic rule.

The most legitimate institution, which has greatly contributed to social and political stability in Thailand, is the monarchy. It took the monarchy only three decades to slowly but firmly reestablish its prestige, charisma, power, and influence in the Thai political system. By 1985, after almost four decades of his reign, King Bhumibol Adulyadej had become the most powerful and respected symbol of the nation. He remains so a decade later. This is not surprising. He has survived nine constitutions, twelve general elections, and over thirty cabinets with fourteen different prime ministers. While politicians, military leaders, and civilian prime ministers have come and gone, the king has remained the head of state, the focus of his people's loyalty and cohesion, the fount of legitimacy. Because of the continuity of this institution in contrast to others in Thailand—especially elected legislatures and political parties—the king has gained political experience and developed mature insights into the country's problems.

It has been overwhelmingly accepted, especially since 1973, that the king remains the final arbiter of a national crisis. In 1984 and 1986, in the midst of the conflict between General Prem, the prime minister, and General Arthit, the commander-in-chief of the army, the monarchy played a decisive role in restraining many an ill-advised move by the military.[44] In the May 1992 upheaval, it was the king who intervened and prevented the escalation of conflict into civil war.

In this sense, the monarchy performs a highly important substituting function for other political institutions in bringing together national consensus, especially when there is a crisis of legitimacy. It has increasingly played the role of legitimater of political power, supporter/legitimater of broad regime policies, promoter and sanctioner of intra-elite solidarity, and symbolic focus of national unity.[45] The social stability of Thailand, despite its periodic coups d'état, can be explained by the existence and positive role of the monarchy. As long as the bureaucratic-military leadership is supported by the monarchy the problem of legitimacy is, to a large extent, solved. Hence it has been observed:

> If any significance emerged from the eventful and volatile political developments of 1984, it was perhaps that the highest institution in the land, the monarchy, revered as a symbol of justice and authority, is likely to be the single most important force capable of holding the country together during times of chaos and crisis and of assuring the viability of a democratic process in Thailand. With a clear commitment of the monarchy to a constitutional government, democracy Thai-style ultimately may have a chance to take root.[46]

This view merits further analysis. What kind of democracy is it that "may have a chance to take root" in Thai society? Democracy Thai-style has been identified in this chapter as a semidemocratic one. Is there any chance for a pluralist democracy or a polyarchy to take root in Thailand?

One of the most important conditions for the development of a pluralist democracy is the more or less neutral "umpire" role of the state. In the case of Thailand, however, the state and its machineries have always played an active and dominant role in society. It should also be noted that the state's principal machinery, the bureaucracy, has been able to adapt its role to changing conditions, most notably by utilizing the ideology of development to expand and legitimate its presence in society.

Although new forces have emerged as a result of socioeconomic changes in the past two decades, they have been under close surveillance by the bureaucratic elites. The privileged organized groups, such as the Bankers' Association, the Association of Industries, and the Chamber of Commerce, have been given access to the decisionmaking process in economic spheres, but their participation is of a consultative nature rather than as an equal partner. Likewise, labor unions have also been given a limited consultative role in labor relations, while the bureaucracy still firmly maintains its control over farmers' groups through the Ministries of Interior and Agriculture.

Although there have been frequent elections, popular participation remains relatively low. Where turnouts were high the successes were due to active mobilization by officials of the Interior Ministry rather than to voters' interest in political issues.

The Thai military and bureaucratic elites are by no means united but, despite factional strife and rivalry, they share a common negative attitude toward elected politicians. They are willing to tolerate the elected politicians only to the extent that the latter do not pose a threat to their interests.

The Thai case is different from the U.S. situation where elites are committed to democratic values. In the United States democratic values have survived because the elites, not masses, govern; and it is the elites, not the common people, who are the chief guardians of democratic values.[47] Past studies on Thai political culture have shown antidemocratic tendencies to be associated with a high level of education.[48] It was also reported that people who have high socioeconomic status, high educational levels, and good access to political information tend to have a higher degree of political alienation than other groups of people.[49] Furthermore, there is no difference in attitudes toward elections among voters with lower socioeconomic status. Electoral participation by the masses is ritualistic or mobilized participation rather than voluntary political action.[50] However, the new generation that reached maturity in the period following the October 1973 student-led movement for democracy is prodemocratic and has become an active section of the educated, urban middle class of the 1990s. Thus, the correlation between high levels of education and antidemocratic attitudes has no doubt weakened in recent years.

It is fair to conclude that a dynamic balance is currently maintained among various forces, each of which cannot possibly afford to dominate the political process on its own strength alone. The semidemocratic model seems to work quite well because, on the one hand, it permits formal and ritualistic political participation through a general election that produces an elected Parliament, but, on the other, the real center of power is in the executive branch, which is controlled by the military-bureaucratic elites who, in recent years, have begun to carefully select some business elites to join their regime on a limited basis.

A pluralist democracy is unlikely to develop from an entrenched bureaucratic polity, especially where that bureaucratic polity is not a static entity, but can utilize the ideology of development to redefine its role, and where it exploits traditionally powerful social institutions to further legitimate its dominance by evoking fears of communism and instability emanating from external threats (such as Vietnam and the Soviet Union). While socioeconomic changes have led to the growth of newly emergent forces, they could at best restrain the bureaucratic power rather than capture it and replace it with a group-based bargaining and mutual adjustment system. As for the masses, the persistence of the bureaucracy and lack of continuity in the functioning of political parties have greatly affected their socialization in the sense that they have been bureaucratically socialized rather than politically socialized. This is particularly true in the case of the rural population since they have to rely on the delivery of services from the bureaucracy, and therefore have to learn to survive or to get the most out of what is available from the bureaucracy and not from the parties. The politics of who gets what, when, and how in Thailand is in essence a bureaucratic allocation of values rather than a politically authoritative distribution of benefits.

The failures of the April 1981 and September 1985 coups did not discourage the military. They continue to view the coup as an acceptable technique to transfer political power. However, since the February 1991 coup and the subsequent popular uprising in May 1992, the military has suffered a great setback. Its leadership as well as the rank and file have been severely demoralized. The attitudes of the military leadership have not changed, although they are now under strong social pressure both domestically and internationally to avoid active intervention in politics.

Yet, however circumscribed the power of the military may be, and however expansive may be the growth of nonbureaucratic forces, the result cannot be interpreted as signifying a steady development of parliamentary democracy. The major constituencies of government remain outside the arena of its citizenry at large. The balance of power has not shifted to the democratic party system, but to the monarchy, whose charisma and grace enables it to control political power allocation and balance and referee often conflicting political power interests.

Future Prospects

In the past, democratic development primarily involved changes in the constitution to make it more democratic by giving more powers to the legislative branch. Such efforts usually led to the instability of the constitutions and the governments because formal political arrangements did not reflect the real power relationships in society. The problem of politics in Thailand is not how to develop a democratic system, but how to maintain the semidemocratic system so that a more participatory system of government can evolve in the long run. In other words, under the semidemocratic system in which an elected Parliament is allowed to function, political parties and Parliament could utilize the continuity of the political system (which is very rare in Thai political history) to strengthen their organizations. One of the least controversial and most practical aspects of democratic development is the development of the research and information capabilities of political parties and the parliamentarians. The strengthening of the supporting staff of parliamentary committees, as well as research capabilities of political parties, would greatly enhance the role of the Parliament in the long run. A well-informed Parliament can act more effectively in exercising its countervailing force vis-à-vis that of the bureaucracy.

The continuity of participant political institutions will have great impact upon local politics in the sense that elections for local government bodies, such as the municipalities and the provincial and the village councils, could continue to be held and allowed to operate alongside national politics. In the long run, it would be possible for political parties to extend their infrastructure to rural areas and mobilize support not only in national elections, but also in local elections. As long as the elected politicians are willing to make a compromise by not demanding the abolishment of the Senate or insisting that all ministers must be members of the elected Parliament, there is not likely to be a major disruption in the overall political system. This means that to be able to survive, participatory political institutions have to share power with the military and bureaucratic elite.

It seems that the most significant change in Thai politics since 1981 has been the inability of the military to dominate the political arena and sustain its influence in the long run as it used to be able to do. Some observers regard this as a progressive movement toward a more democratic system because of the more pluralistic nature of society. This led one scholar to conclude that the present Thai polity's strength is its ability to accommodate the demands of a wider range of groups than could the bureaucratic polity.[51] However, the stability and the strength of the present polity might, on the other hand, be attributed to its ability to accommodate the demands of the military and technocratic elites. In this sense, a fundamental change in the institutional framework, upsetting the existing power relationships, could precipitate a coup.

This does not mean that the Thai polity will maintain its semidemocratic pattern of rule forever. On the contrary, in the long run, when participant political institutions have the chance to prove their usefulness to the people, their image and credibility will be gradually strengthened. In the meantime, elected politicians should concentrate their efforts on developing party organizations (such as party branches), and on improving the capabilities of the Parliamentary research unit and committee staff so that their already accepted roles could be institutionalized. The improvement of legislative research and reference sections of the Parliament and the strengthening of parliamentary committee staff aids are less controversial than the proposal to reduce the number of senators. But such "internal" political reforms will have great effect in the long run. Another recommendation is state financing of political parties in order to reduce the dependency of elected politicians on nonelected party financiers. The German method of reimbursing political parties for their campaign expenses provided that they get more than 5 percent of the votes cast in the election should be adopted in Thailand.

Under the present political situation where there are many active voluntary associations and interest groups that seek to influence government decisions and policies, the Parliament should create a new standing committee to act as a channel for the expression of interests and opinions of various pressure groups. In this way groups would operate within the framework of the legislative process, and would reduce their perceived activist role play, which is not acceptable to the military. Instead of putting pressure on the cabinet through strikes, demonstrations, and protests, which so far have not been very effective in redressing grievances, pressure-group politics could best be legitimated through the provision of an institutional mechanism for their interactions with the government and the legislators. In the long run viable relationships would develop between political parties and interest groups. The above-mentioned recommendations are likely to be acceptable to the military and the bureaucratic elites because they do not directly threaten the existing power relationships. The idea of bringing group actions into the legislative arena is also likely to be welcomed by the military, which has been staunchly opposed to political activism outside formal political institutions and processes.

It is unrealistic to propose any drastic change in the constitution since such a move could induce a military coup. The most important issue in Thai politics is how to avoid the repetitive pattern of political change that I have described as the "vicious cycle of Thai politics." The main reason explaining the persistence of the semidemocratic system, or "authoritarian constitutionalism," is the nature of authoritarian rule in Thailand, which has often been characterized by moderation, flexibility, and careful avoidance of confrontation. As Somsakdi Xuto aptly observes,

> The general public, in particular, has been relatively little affected by exercise of authoritarian power. In short, Thai authoritarianism has been somewhat softened by the personal characteristics of pragmatism and accommodation. Thus harshness or extreme measures typically associated with authoritarian rule in other countries have remained relatively absent, particularly as applied to the general public.[52]

The idea of keeping the elected Parliament viable within the semidemocratic system is, of course, a second-best alternative. During the late 1970s and early 1980s, it was impossible for any government to effectively implement its programs because of its preoccupation with surviving. The absence of a coup in the 1980s enabled the government and the elected Parliament to perform their functions without disruption, which is very important in meeting the increasing challenges and uncertainties coming from international political and economic communities. The 1991 coup group did not succeed in reverting the political order back to the pre-1973 model, and the May 1992 popular uprising made the process of democratization possible. Perhaps improvement of the Thai political process has to begin by accepting existing politics for what they are and not what they should be.[53] It may be worthwhile to accept the role of the military in Thai politics by recognizing its sphere of influence especially in internal and external security matters. It also means that their participation in the legislative process through the Senate has to be tolerated by the elected politicians. Improvements of internal mechanisms of participant political institutions as suggested above would gradually strengthen these institutions and prepare them well for the more important tasks in the future. A viable and responsible government that would emerge in Thailand may not be exactly like the British parliamentary model that has been followed in form since 1932. It may be a mixed system in which the military-bureaucratic elites and the elected politicians share powers and each side competes for support from the masses in their responsible spheres of influence. The peculiarity of the Thai polity is that, apart from the institution of the monarchy, no other political institution can claim legitimacy on its own account.

It seems that accommodation and compromise, to preserve political stability at whatever cost, has led to political stagnation rather than development. It has become a question of stability for stability's sake rather than a foundation on which to build progressive reform. This social stability has enabled Thailand to sustain its economic and social development despite periodic coups d'état. However, as Seymour Martin Lipset rightly pointed out, in the modern world the prolonged effectiveness that gives legitimacy to a political system means primarily constant economic development.[54]

In the case of Thailand rapid development has expanded the private sector, but historically, the strength and autonomy of the bourgeoisie have not grown correspondingly to the extent that it could counter the political weight of the military and bureaucracy. This is because the bourgeoisie is largely composed of Sino-Thais who have been under the control of the military and bureaucracy for several generations. However, the new generation of Sino-Thai business elites is becoming more politically active than their parents, and younger businesspeople in general have increasingly shown their desire to be more independent by joining political parties, funding campaigns, and contesting elections. In fact, today it is mainly rich businesspeople (rather than the military) who sponsor political parties.

Despite the rapid rates of development and urbanization, political participation in Thailand will not be entirely autonomous but will remain in part bureaucratically mobilized for some time to come. The military and bureaucracy continue to shape the participation of nonbureaucratic forces and to constrain the functioning of the constitutional system. Only in recent years, with fewer disruptions in the political process and growing societal sophistication, has the Thai Parliament begun to emerge as a truly independent center of power, struggling hard to institutionalize its legitimacy.

Gradually, the Thai political system is moving toward a more democratic parliamentary system. All major political and socioeconomic groups realize that "the system is here to stay" and are trying to adjust to this new shift. In the age of globalization, there is no going back to the old model of authoritarian domination. Like other countries, Thailand is moving toward the twenty-first century not as an isolated nation but as a society that is being rapidly integrated into the emerging global economy and information age. Perhaps, for the first time since 1974, the possibility of genuine democratization is not beyond the reach of the Thai citizenry.

The dramatic events of 1992 signaled that Thailand has chosen to tread the path of democracy. Both the development of democratic institutions and the country's rapid economic growth are spurring the expansion of civil society, which in turn strengthens democratic pressures and possibilities. If those possibilities are to be realized in the coming years, Thailand urgently needs a continuous series of political reforms that will eventually reduce authoritarian residues left by the age-old structures and values.

New generations of Thais are much more confident than their forebears that they are a potent force in society. More important, they are the generation that shares a common democratic ideal and is committed to building a civil society in which the rule of law reigns supreme.

Notes

1. On Buddhism and politics in Thailand see Somboon Suksamran, *Buddhism and Politics: A Study of Socio-Political Change and Political Activism of the Thai Sangha* (Singapore: Institute of Southeast Asian Studies, 1982); and S. J. Tambiah, *World Conqueror and World Renouncer: A Study of Buddhism* (Cambridge: Cambridge University Press, 1976).

2. For more details on Thai political development before 1932 see Chai-Anan Samudavanija, "Political History," in Somsakdi Xuto, ed., *Government and Politics of Thailand* (Singapore: Oxford University Press, 1987), pp. 1–40.

3. Chai-Anan Samudavanija, *Thailand's First Political Development Plan* (Bangkok: Aksornsumphan Press, 1969) (in Thai).

4. On Tienwan see details in Chai-Anan Samudavanija, *Selected Works on Tienwan* (Bangkok: Posamton Press, 1974) (in Thai).

5. See Chai-Anan Samudavanija, *Politics and Political Change in Thailand* (Bangkok: Bannakit Press, 1980).

6. Benjamin Batson, *Suam's Political Future: Document from the End of the Absolute Monarchy* (Ithaca: Cornell University Southeast Asia Program, Data Paper no. 96, July 1974).

7. Ibid., p. 45.

8. Ibid., p. 10.

9. Ibid., p. 49.

10. David Wilson, *Politics in Thailand* (Ithaca, N.Y.: Cornell University Press, 1962), p. 277.

11. Toru Yano, "Political Structure of a 'Rice-Growing State,'" in Yaneo Ishii, ed., *Thailand: A Rice-Growing Society* (Monographs of the Center for Southwest Asian Studies, Kyoto University, English-language Series no. 12, 1978), p. 127.

12. Wilson, *Politics in Thailand*, p. 22.

13. Ibid., p. 20.

14. Thak Chaleomtiarana, *Thailand: The Politics of Despotic Paternalism* (Bangkok: Social Science Association of Thailand, 1979), p. 102.

15. See details in Sungsidh Piriyarangsan, "Thai Bureaucratic Capitalism, 1932–1960" (Unpublished M.A. thesis, Faculty of Economics, Thammasat University, 1980).

16. Wilson, *Politics in Thailand*, p. 180.

17. Thak, *Thailand: The Politics of Despotic Paternalism*, p. 201.

18. Ibid., pp. 140–141.

19. Ibid., p. 334.

20. For more details on Thai politics in this period see David Morell and Chai-Anan Samudavanija, *Political Conflict in Thailand: Reform, Reaction, Revolution* (Cambridge, Mass.: Oelgeschlager, Gunn and Hain, Publishers, 1981).

21. J. L. S. Girling, *Thailand: Society and Politics* (Ithaca, N.Y.: Cornell University Press, 1981), pp. 215–219.

22. Wilson, *Politics in Thailand*, p. 262.

23. I am indebted to Dr. William Klausner for his observation on this point.

24. Fred W. Riggs, *Thailand: The Modernization of a Bureaucratic Policy* (Honolulu: East-West Center Press, 1966), pp. 152–153.

25. Sethaporn Cusripitak and others, "Communication Policies in Thailand" (A study report submitted to UNESCO, March 1985), p. 37.

26. See details in Lieutenant General Chaovalit Yongchaiyuth, *Lectures and Interviews by Lt. General Chaovalit Yongchaiyuth 1980–1985* (Bangkok: Sor. Sor. Press, 1985).

27. Kramol Tongdharmachart, "Toward a Political Theory in Thai Perspective" (Singapore: Institute of Southeast Asian Studies Occasional Paper no. 68, 1982), p. 37.

28. Ibid., pp. 37–38.

29. A candidate uses about 800,000 baht in an election campaign, although the election law permits a candidate to spend not more than 350,000 baht. In highly competitive constituencies a candidate spends as much as 5 to 10 million baht to win a seat.

30. Matichon, September 16, 1979.

31. See details in *Thailand: Managing Public Resources for Structural Adjustment* (A World Bank Country Study, Washington, D.C.: World Bank, 1984), pp. 1–13.

32. Krirkkiat Phipatseritham, "The World of Finance: The Push and Pull of Politics"

(Paper prepared for the seminar on National Development of Thailand: Economic Rationality and Political Feasibility, Thammasat University, September 6–7, 1983), p. 21.

33. Saneh Chamarik, "Problems of Development in Thai Political Setting" (Paper prepared for the seminar on National Development of Thailand: Economic Rationality and Political Feasibility, Thammasat University, September 6–7, 1983), p. 38.

34. World Bank, *World Development Report 1994* (New York: Oxford University Press, 1994), Tables 1 and 2, pp. 163, 165.

35. Chai-Anan Samudavanija, "Introduction," in *Report of the Ad Hoc Committee to Study Major Problems of the Thai Administrative System* (Bangkok: National Administrative Reform Committee, 1980), pp. 6–7.

36. Frank C. Darling, "Student Protest and Political Change in Thailand," *Pacific Affairs* 47, no. 1 (Spring 1974): pp. 6–7.

37. Lieutenant General Chaovalit was promoted to chief of army staff and became a full general in October 1985. In May 1986 he was appointed to the position of army commander in chief.

38. Lieutenant General Chaovalit Yongchaiyuth, "Guidelines on Planning to Win over the CPT in 1983," Royal Military Academy, June 21, 1983.

39. That is, the party slate system requiring the electorate to choose the entire slate of candidates proposed by each political party.

40. Translated by M. R. Sukhumbhand Paribatra in *ISIS Bulletin* 1, no. 2 (October 1982): pp. 14–18.

41. Ansil Ramsay, "Thai Domestic Politics and Foreign Policy" (Paper presented at the Third U.S.-ASEAN Conference, Chiangmai, Thailand, January 7–11, 1985), p. 4.

42. Ibid.

43. Anek Laothamatas, *Business Associations and the New Political Economy of Thailand: From Bureaucratic Polity to Liberal Corporatism* (Boulder: Westview Press, 1992); and Richard F. Doner, *Driving a Bargain: Japanese Firms and Automobile Industrialization in Southeast Asia* (Berkeley: University of California Press, 1991).

44. Suchit Bunbongkarn and Sukhumbhand Paribatra, "Thai Politics and Foreign Policy in the 1980s" (Paper presented at the Third U.S.-ASEAN Conference, Chiangmai, Thailand, January 7–11, 1985), p. 18.

45. Thak, *Thailand: The Politics of Despotic Paternalism,* p. 334.

46. Juree Vichit-Vadakan, "Thailand in 1984: Year of Administering Rumors," *Asian Survey* 26, no. 2 (February 1985): p. 240.

47. Thomas R. Dye and L. Harmon Zeigler, *The Irony of Democracy: An Uncommon Introduction to American Politics* (Belmont, Calif.: Duxbury Press, 1971) pp. 18–19.

48. See, for example, Suchit Bunbongkarn, "Higher Education and Political Development" (Unpublished Ph.D. diss., Fletcher School of Law and Diplomacy, 1968); and Surapas Tapaman R. T. N., "Political Attitudes of the Field Grade Officer of the Royal Thai Army, Navy and Air Force" (Thesis submitted for the Degree of Master of Political Science, Chulalongkorn University, 1976).

49. Pornsak Phongpaew, "Political Information of the Thai People" (Unpublished research report submitted to the National Research Council, Bangkok, 1980), p. 131.

50. Pornsak Phongpaew, *Voting Behavior: A Case Study of the General Election of B. E. 2526* (1983), Khon Kaen Region 3 (Bangkok: Chao Phya Press, December 1984), pp. 155–156.

51. Ramsay, "Thai Domestic Politics," p. 9.

52. Somsakdi Xuto, "Conclusion," in Somsakdi Xuto, ed., *Government and Politics of Thailand,* p. 202.

53. Ibid.

54. Seymour Martin Lipset, *Political Man* (London: Mercury Books, 1963), p. 82.

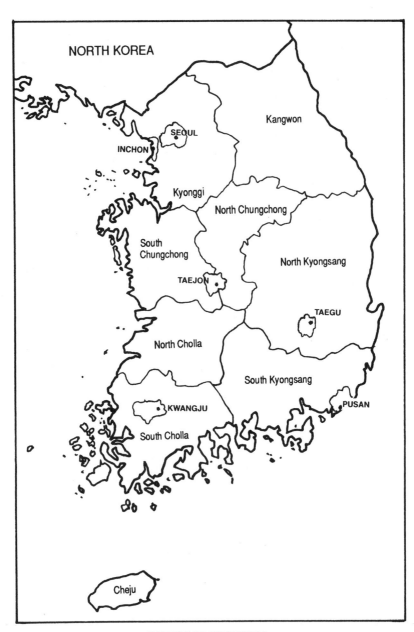

REPUBLIC OF KOREA

8

The Republic of Korea: Pluralizing Politics

David I. Steinberg

The Republic of Korea[1] has been a political and economic maverick. Known for its stellar economic successes that raised per capita gross national product (GNP) (in current dollars) more than 100 times—from about $67 to over $6,700 in just over three decades—today South Korea is also respected for the vigor of its internal political debate and the élan of its elections. It has a civilian regime that has evolved, in stages, peacefully from its military chrysalis. Its internal political culture is, however, more complex; traditional attitudes toward power, authority, and the role of the state are in contest with democratizing trends.

For most of its history, the Republic of Korea has been a highly bureau-cratic-authoritarian regime, although, ironically, it was held by the West (especially the United States) to be a bastion of the "free world" against North Korean, Chinese, and Soviet communism. Economically, it defied the usual donor prescriptions for development; instead of relying on internal market forces and promoting agriculture and then using those surpluses to develop industrially, it was a heavily dirigiste (state-directed) regime in keeping with its political history. Korea used state subsidies as an effective developmental weapon, investing first in industry and then, much later, using some of those surpluses to promote agriculture. South Korea's unique history, its experiences under colonial and foreign military occupation, as well as its social structure and economic growth have affected its politics.

South Korea is also an anomaly because of its unusual interplay between politics and economics. The dirigisme in economics had its origins in dirigiste politics. As in many states, the two have been very closely relat-ed. Although politics prompted many critical economic policies, Korea is unusual because in general its political leaders have pragmatically recog-nized the necessity to use professional economic advice effectively and to limit the intimacy and extent of political influence on such advice, barring exceptional circumstances. Politics may have led, but it did not completely control, economic policy formation. Ideology has not interfered with economics. Both state control and capitalism flourished in different sectors. Some of the most important political issues facing the state in the future, however, are related to how this past, interdependent interplay between politics and economics will evolve.

The political progress that has been so evident in South Korea has been a product of internal evolution, but it did not occur in isolation. Foreign influences—both positive and negative and including those of North Korea, Japan, and the United States—and even world opinion concerning Korea and the 1988 Olympics in Seoul have affected the parameters of Korea's internal political process, debate, and democratic governance. These influences are likely to remain influential, although not determining, factors. How far Korea has progressed along a democratic road and where that road will lead politics in Korea are the subjects of this chapter.

Historical Review and Analysis

The six republics[2] through which South Korea has traumatically traversed since independence in 1948 have run the gamut from authoritarianism to license, civilian to military rule, and back again, negotiating a civilianized military intermediary period. The diversity of these regimes masks a set of common core elements that have helped to shape, and will likely continue to influence, South Korea's future political directions. These include such factors as personal concepts of power, the institutional roles of the state, internal regional issues within a unified ethnic base, Korea's cultural heritage, concepts of hierarchy and class in Korean society, the effects of the urbanization process, and international influences on the political process.

Although both South and North Korea are ethnically and linguistically the most homogeneous states in Asia—a distinct developmental advantage that is not unrelated to the potential for both political and economic mobilization—this has not precluded the continued influence of regionalism, which since independence in 1948 has been a growing force in South Korea. This regionalism has had an increasingly important political influence in recent years.[3]

Since 1980 and the Kwangju Incident (see below), the two southwestern provinces of North and South Cholla (Chollanamdo and Chollabukdo, also called Honam, see map) have voted virtually as a block against the prevailing government party. In part a result of leadership issues, this has also been a product of economic and social discrimination by leaders whose origins and bases of support were from other regions. These two provinces—which had occupied the approximate area of the independent kingdom of Paek'che—were absorbed in A.D. 668 by the victorious Silla kingdom in the southeast (from which since 1961 the political establishment of Korea has come) upon unification, but regional, negative stereotypes of the southwest continued throughout Korean history, even though agriculturally that region was Korea's most productive. Contemporary prejudices against the southwest population are evident, although not virulent, and have even been reported in the press. However, the percentage of higher-level civil servants from that area was lower (in proportion to population) than from other areas, provincial incomes were below the average, business failures were higher, and infrastructure was less developed.

The Japanese colonial period (1910–1945) left important residues in most fields. The legal and administrative heritage from the Japanese era remains significant, but perhaps equally important was the solidification of a centralized administration that formalized the power of the central government in modern, bureaucratic terms. In theory, this centralized control was absolute during the Korean kingdom, but in fact it was vitiated by inefficiencies and the politics of the factionalized *yangban-* (gentry) dominated court. In a sense, the Japanese occupation gave the center, albeit foreign dominated, the actual power that the court had in theory. The U.S. military government (1945–1948) drew upon the Japanese tradition and added another centralized flavor, even though it recognized the need for more local authority and attempted (unsuccessfully) to decentralize certain fields, such as education.

The First Republic (1948–1960): Civilian Authoritarianism

Born on August 15, 1948, as a result of a UN-supervised election on May 10, 1948, for a Constituent Assembly, the Republic of Korea (South Korea) under its First Republic (1948–1960) may be characterized as a civilian regime, pseudodemocratic in character, that became increasingly authoritarian as its president, Syngman Rhee, aged.[4] Rhee had returned from a 40-year anti-Japanese exile in October 1945 in the wake of the U.S. takeover from the Japanese and the subsequent U.S. military occupation. Rhee's reign included the time of the traumatic, disastrous Korean War (1950–1953). Instigated by North Korea, the war devastated both North and South and ended near the 38th Parallel where it began. This division had been established in 1945 as the line north of Seoul that divided the peninsula into areas where the United States in the south and the Russians in the north would accept the surrender of Japanese troops. The issue was eloquently stated by Gregory Henderson:

> No division of a nation in the present world is so astonishing in its origin as the division of Korea; none is so unrelated to conditions or sentiment within the nation itself at the time the division was effected; none is to this day so unexplained; in none does blunder and planning oversight appear to have played so large a role. Finally, there is no division for which the U.S. government bears so heavy a share of the responsibility as it bears for the division of Korea.[5]

South Korea was strongly under U.S. influence, an influence that was tempered because the United States viewed South Korea as a critical area in which to block what was perceived to be Soviet and Chinese communist expansion. As an area also essential to the defense of Japan, which even then had become the linchpin of U.S. policy in the region, it had to be pre-served—whatever the excesses of the regime—but reformed if possible. The United States provided the vast percentage of all foreign aid, the bulk of all imports, and the core of the military forces and air cover protecting the South. The United States had a three-year military occupation of the South (1945–1948) and then saved and fed the Korean people during and after the war. South Korea could have been, and sometimes was, called a U.S. client state. This perception was only partly accurate. Reality tempered this con-clusion. The United States, in spite of its support, had very little influence over many of the critical political and even some economic policies the Rhee government promulgated. The United States needed South Korea as much as South Korea needed the United States.[6] Tensions between the two countries existed in both politics and economic policies. Contrary to public pronouncements of the democracy the South officially espoused and the United States endorsed, a steady deterioration in the political sphere and in U.S. relations was palpably evident.

Rhee was popular at first. He had a sterling, if autocratic, record as a freedom fighter against the Japanese colonial occupation, and he hated Japan—a quality that effectively delayed the normalization of relations with Japan until 1965, five years after his overthrow. He was a political conserv-ative, but the left had been eliminated as a political (and insurgent) force during the U.S. military occupation and in the 1948 Yosu-Sunch'on rebel-lion and the Cheju uprising.[7] Rhee's preoccupations seemed to have been with the retention of power, the reconquest of the North, and the extraction of the maximum U.S. economic and military assistance. Neither economic nor political development was a priority on either the Korean or the American agenda. Security issues prevailed.[8]

South Korea during this First Republic could hardly be designated even a "procedural democracy." Power was personalized and hoarded; the insti-tutions of democratic governance were in place, but they functioned inef-fectively. Although elections were held with regularity, they were manipu-lated and eventually blatantly fixed. There were opposition parties, generally conservative politically but more open in espousing somewhat more liberal political views. Most were simply antiregime movements, with-out constructive or coherent platforms, and were vehicles for individual leaders and effectively lacked power. Rhee did not even have a party at his first election. As one author noted, "Thus, political parties in Korea did not mean the existence of party policies or party politics. A political party was merely a grouping of men with common interests in power only to be dis-rupted as their interests conflict."[9] The National Assembly was a debating society whose power was constantly diminished, threatened, manipulated, and even coerced by the chief executive. An independent judiciary did not exist. The ostensible democratic process was continually corrupted by the leadership, which used the process for its own immediate ends. Rhee, for example, wanted to postpone the parliamentary elections scheduled for May 1950 because he perceived a loss of support in that body, but he was required to hold the elections by the United States. (The United States played a similar role in 1963 and a somewhat different but pivotal one in 1987.) Rhee then forced changes in the election procedures for the presidency in 1952; he was constitutionally elected indirectly by the assembly, but when relations with that body soured, he arranged to be elected directly by the populace because he recognized that he had more popular than legislative support or perhaps that he could more effectively manipulate the people. The issue of direct election of the president was a problem that resurfaced continually over the years under Presidents Park Chung Hee and Chun Doo Hwan, as well as under candidate Roh Tae Woo, and it was only resolved in 1987. In 1955, Rhee pushed through a constitutional change that revoked the two-term limitations on the presidency.

Political and mass-manipulated violence was evident. Key opposition figures died, some mysteriously. Civic organizations were mobilized for political purposes. Rent seeking by friends of Rhee's Liberal Party was endemic, replacing economic development efforts. In the 1956 elections, Chang Myon (John M. Chang), a prominent opposition Catholic liberal from the Democratic Party was surprisingly elected vice president (the president and vice president ran separately), much to Rhee's chagrin. For a period Chang had to take refuge on a U.S. ship. An assassination attempt against him failed. There were mobilization and only partly successful manipulation efforts to control the election processes in 1956 and again in the legislative elections of 1958. In the former, Chang Myon won the vice presidency; in the latter, Rhee's support dwindled, and the opposition gained more than one-third of the seats. The most blatant attempt to rig elections occurred in 1960, however; it caused such great discontent and anger that its aftermath brought an end to the First Republic.

In Masan, a student who had been tortured and killed by the police in connection with the election was found floating in the harbor. This sparked massive student demonstrations that began in Masan but soon spread nationwide. On April 18, 1960, Korea University students demonstrated in Seoul; on April 19, 1960, and shortly thereafter the movement that has since been known as the Student Revolution (or *sa-il-gu,* literally, four-one-nine, or April 19) reached a crescendo in Seoul, when professors joined the students in their march toward the Blue House (then known as "Kyungmudae" the presidential mansion). Around 200 students were killed by the police,[10] but the military refused to intervene. Syngman Rhee was forced to resign, an event that was prompted by the United States. He was spirited out of the country and later died in exile in Hawaii. His hated vice president, Lee Ki Bung, and his family died in a suicide pact.

The First Republic was a failure of governance, leadership, and economic progress. Even though there had been some modest growth in the economy (which had reached its nadir after the Korean War), there was less growth in politics. The disastrous Korean War cannot be considered the sole or even a primary explanation for the plight of the state. Although it was an international tragedy and exacerbated the poverty and economic straits of the country, the war and the consequent state of siege South Korea perceived it was under were used to perpetuate autocratic rule and major restrictions on civil liberties.[11] A national security law that gave wide, general powers to the state to arrest and detain antistate elements (however defined) was enacted in 1948, amended many times, and, in various permutations, was still in force and a matter for extensive debate in 1994. The law still limits any unofficially sanctioned contact with North Korea, antistate organizations, and views that support such organizations. More recently, it has been selectively enforced when the state has wanted to illustrate its power or exert control.[12]

In a sense, the failure of the First Republic was a failure of the donor as well, for the client state did not produce the reality or even the image of democracy or progress for which the United States had fought. Korea was called a "basket case," a state into which aid was poured but with few tangible results.

This bleak picture is not completely unredeemed. Although it did not produce democracy in its official mode, the twelve years of the First Republic did establish the internal need for the forms of democracy, if not its substance. This was reinforced by foreign influences, especially from the United States, which was so intimately associated with South Korea on the world scene that for its own propaganda purposes it needed at least the semblance of democracy in its ally. To achieve international respectability and legitimacy, South Korea also needed a positive image.

More important for the longer term were the educative process and exposure to the outside world, which created popular demands for effective participation in governance even if those demands could not be met at that time. In a sense, important elements of the urban population began to take seriously the state's public pronouncements about democracy, which it had cynically produced but had little inkling would be so important to the people and which would backfire against it and future authoritarian governments.

In part, the First Republic was also a failure because it had no believable positive ideals or ideology. It was a type of "soft authoritarianism," in part because of administrative limitations and in part due to U.S. pressures and influence, which subsequently diminished. It had difficulty rallying support for a negative cause—anticommunism—when it was obviously lacking the positive goal of democracy, which it had corrupted. This situation subverted the political legitimacy of those regimes that used anticommunism as their sole rationale. In addition, the First Republic used anticommunism to suppress rights, which was a continuing problem until 1987. Presidents Park and Chun attempted to substitute economic rewards for political progress in their search for legitimacy.

The Second Republic (1960–1961): Ineffectual Democracy

The Second Republic (1960–1961) was understandably an explosive, vibrant reaction to the repression of the Rhee era. It was the only period before 1987 in which South Korea had a semblance of democratic rule, and until 1987 the July 1960 presidential elections were the only free, unmanipulated elections Korea had experienced. Democracy gave way to license after a dozen years of repression, however, as the pent-up demands from labor, students, and many other elements of the population found their expression in the streets. During the short Second Republic, there were said to have been 500 major demonstrations by university students alone and an additional forty-five by the trade unions. Overall, there were around 2,000 demonstrations involving about 900,000 participants. The press was freed from control, and it expanded, with much of it becoming irresponsible and corrupt. The weak government could neither plan nor administer a state that was heady in its new freedoms and at the same time meet the strident demands from most segments of the populace.

With the revolution Hu Chung, an elder statesman, became head of the interim government. Then Chang Myon, the opposition vice president elected in 1956, was chosen prime minister and Yun Po Son became president. Although Chang was from North Korea (about 10 percent of the total South Korean population had northern origins, and this group has played a continuous and important role in high bureaucratic and military positions), his base of support in the Democratic Party[13] was located in the southwestern Cholla provinces, which (as noted above) have continued to be an area of opposition to the regimes in power.

Chang was known for his probity, but temperamentally and institutionally he was a weak leader who presided over an important but transitory democratic interregnum. Factional politics undercut his democratic goals, and the parliamentary system undermined democratic consolidation. He could not control the youth, some of whom wanted to march to North Korea in the spirit of reunification, the most longed-for goal of a people who had a single culture and who had long been united. Others wanted to reduce the armed forces by 100,000 troops. Both groups were viewed by the military as direct leftist threats to the existence of the state.

It is questionable whether any leader at that time could have simultaneously coped with the political and economic demands of the populace, satisfied the military and other conservative and powerful elements, encouraged both business and labor, and imposed enough order to make those processes work. Although the democratic experience clearly excited many in the urban population, the excesses associated with this period produced a backlash that resulted in the military coup.[14]

The Third and Fourth Republics (1961–1979): Military Hegemony

On May 16, 1961, a small segment of the South Korean military launched the first successful military coup in Korea since the founding of the Chosun (Yi) Dynasty in 1392. The coup was carefully constructed by a coterie of officers who were able to carry it out as a secret from the U.S. military advisers—who were present in each unit down to the battalion level—and from the top Korean military command itself. Troops were moved in contravention of UN military regulations. A Supreme Council for National Reconstruction, composed of thirty-six officers, was formed, and General Park Chung Hee soon became its chair, although Yun Po Son was kept on as titular president—without power—until March 1962.

The ostensible purpose of the coup was to save the state from destruction, both internally and externally, and to purify a corrupt regime—a rationale that has been a constant leitmotiv of the political vicissitudes in South Korea. There is evidence that the military had planned a coup against Rhee and the First Republic, but the Student Revolution had intervened.

The United States was strongly opposed to the coup for both practical and ideological reasons. Park was initially suspect as a communist sympathizer; he had been implicated in the 1948 leftist Yosu-Sunch'on uprisings, but was later pardoned. The coup was directed against a popularly elected government supported by the United States and was seen as destabilizing the security commitments on the peninsula. The coolness of U.S.-Korean relations accelerated as Park sought to solidify all political and economic power; he (1) created a pervasive intelligence network called the Korean Central Intelligence Agency (KCIA, renamed the National Security Planning Agency following Park's assassination in 1979), (2) eliminated all locally elected government and replaced it with appointed staff including many military officers, (3) distanced himself from the United States as much as possible while retaining the overall security umbrella, (4) engaged in an ill-considered currency reform and stopped joint economic planning, (5) reorganized the government, and (6) jailed many of those from previous administrations while confiscating illegally acquired wealth. Control was not limited to the public sector. The state reorganized and centralized professional and civic groups in attempts to control them more effectively and placed their trusted supporters in positions of authority (for example, in labor unions, teachers unions, and similar organizations).[15] No element of the society was left untouched.

If external approval for Park was not immediately forthcoming, internal support (except from elements of the military) was lacking as well. Park had no traditional leadership credentials: He was not from the *yangban* traditional ruling class and elite; he had no nationalistic pedigree, having been in the Japanese army; military officers did not yet have the cachet of state leadership; and he had no wealth. In addition, his relations with the state's chief protector, the United States, were strained at a time when that meant a great deal.

All of these factors produced two forces: the autonomous capacity to reform and the search for political legitimacy. Park owed no political debts to those associated with the Rhee or Chang regimes and their associates. He was able to meet his obligations to his and his military associates' classes at the Military Academy through extensive appointments in all sectors and at all levels of the government and state-controlled enterprises. He approached political legitimacy through economics. This search for such legitimacy through economic development was a major factor in the very successful export-promotion drive and the attempt to limit dependence on the United States that prompted him to diversify foreign support (from the World Bank, the Federal Republic of Germany, etc.) as early as 1962. In both efforts, he was successful on his own terms.

After ruling by decree, in December 1962 a referendum was held on a presidential system of administration. At the insistence of the United States and buttressed by the U.S. threat to suspend economic aid—and over Park's initial strong objections—an election was held in October 1963. At first Park was indecisive about running, but he had formed a political party, the Democratic Republican Party, which was funded in part through manipulation of various industries and the stock market. The mastermind of these activities was Colonel Kim Jong Pil, Park's nephew by marriage and the founder of the KCIA (he later also became prime minister, head of the New Democratic Republican Party, chair of the Democratic Liberal Party in the 1990s, and founder of a new party in the spring of 1995). Park, with his civilianized status, received 46.6 percent of the vote, and his opponent, Yun Po Sun, received 46.1 percent. It was widely believed that Park had fostered minor opposition candidates to run, splitting the opposition vote and enabling him to win.[16] He also mobilized the extensive military vote, a pattern that persisted for over a generation. The election process continued to be seen as a means to retain power rather than as a reflection of popular will.

The National Assembly, as in the Rhee period, was controlled—sometimes by strong-arm and illegal tactics, as in 1965, when legislation was forcibly passed concerning normalization of relations with Japan.[17] The legislature was thoroughly emasculated.

Park was able to defeat Yun Po Sun once again in the 1967 elections, with 51.5 percent of the vote, under a system in which his control directly and through the KCIA was pervasive. In 1969 he amended the constitution to allow a three-term (rather than a two-term) presidency (in 1955 Syngman Rhee had eliminated all term limitations).

The final election under the Third Republic took place in 1971, in which Park defeated a young legislator named Kim Dae Jung, who was from South Cholla Province. Kim's surprising showing of 45 percent of the vote created enmity that persisted and that resulted in Kim's abduction by the KCIA while he was in Japan and his attempted assassination in 1973.[18] Kim's party also won eighty-nine seats in the legislature, compared with 113 for the government. The election demonstrated that Park's support had eroded in rural areas, where government institutions and control over all institutional credit had previously ensured political compliance.

One scholar summed up the Korean experience from independence to 1972:

> Yet in the past twenty-five years South Korea has at no time really possessed democratic government, even though some of its borrowed institutions appeared to be functioning reasonably well. Except for the brief history of military rule from 1961 to 1963, elections for the presidency and the National Assembly were held on time, political parties were organized, and the press relatively outspoken. These developments, however, merely distorted the reality of Korean politics by directing the attention of outside observers to the superficialities rather than to the substance of political power.[19]

Park's internal and external political requirements prompted four critical economic decisions that profoundly shaped the structure of the state, its economy, and the political process. Park could take such actions because he owed no political, social, or economic debts to the entrenched elites—which he seemed determined to overturn—and because he effectively added a taut military command structure onto a strongly hierarchical bureaucratic and social system, thus developing a heightened capacity to implement policies at all levels and to a degree highly unusual in any society.

The first decision was to consolidate all economic power at the center, under Park's direct political control, through a deputy prime minister in charge of the Economic Planning Board, which combined both planning and budgeting functions. All banks and all institutional credit were nationalized. The Central Bank's autonomy was eliminated, and it was placed under the Ministry of Finance. The Agricultural Bank was placed under the governmental cooperative mechanism that controlled rural credit. This effectively gave the state political and economic power over the society as a whole— power it was not loathe to exercise.

The second decision involved the export drive, in which the state set the quotas for exports, rewarding and punishing businesses by providing or withholding institutional credit and providing other incentives (wastage allowances on production that gave export firms access to the lucrative, if small, local market, social prestige, and similar enticements), without which they could not compete either internally or internationally.[20] The dirigiste controls of the center were ubiquitous. Park, in contrast to many national leaders, took a personal, continuing interest in the economic programs of the state and met with business leaders and others. The rewards and consequences of conformity to state goals were considerable.

The third decision involved the development of heavy, chemical, and defense industries, which economists attribute to the need to deepen the economic structure of the state. Although doing so was necessary, the prime motivation may have been the Korean response to the 1969 Guam, or Nixon, Doctrine, in which the United States indicated it would no longer fight land wars on the Asian continent. South Korean suspicions concerning the reliability of the U.S. commitment to Korean defenses grew (the United States withdrew one of its two army divisions in Korea), and Park was determined to lessen his logistical dependency on the United States. Although the early push for these heavy industries resulted in underutilized capacity, inflation, and a heavily subsidized loan structure with which the state had problems for almost a generation, the result was the growth of Korean heavy-industrial capacity and exports, including automobiles; the changed structure of the Korean economy; and the increasing state dependence on the *chaebol,* the conglomerate industrial structure that in the 1990s began to vie with the government for political power.[21]

The fourth decision concerned the rural sector, with which Park had a special affinity because he had come from an impoverished rural background.[22] The erosion of rural support in the 1971 elections prompted the formation of the Saemaul Undong (the New Community Movement), a government-subsidized self-help, political mobilization, and corvée labor effort that, together with increasing subsidization of producer rice and barley prices, transformed the rural sector. The movement was later extended to urban areas and even to factories with more overt political ends.

Throughout all of this period and well into the mid-1980s, there was no traditional balance of power—not among the executive, legislative, and judicial branches of government nor between any element of the state and the private sector. The state was a monolith. Although the institutions may have been modern, the concepts behind their functioning were in many respects both traditional and a product of the colonial centralized administration reinforced by the military command structure. The National Assembly was to play only a modest role in the political process. It was at best a sounding board for the opposition. Its review of the government's budget, for example, was heavily circumscribed because it could not effectively deal with defense spending, which constituted a major portion of the budget. The Assembly was, and remains, heavily weighted in favor of the rural sector, which results in agricultural policy debate (including agricultural import issues of the early 1990s) playing a prominent role. The opposition was elected from major urban areas—especially, but not exclusively, from Seoul—where the population was sophisticated and not subject to the strictures of a controlled rural environment that is dependent on the state for credit and agricultural pricing policies. Until the mid-1980s few opposition legislators were elected from rural constituencies. The urbanization phenomenon, as I discuss later, was a critical element in the political transformation of the state.

During all of this period until 1987, the judicial system remained under executive-branch control. The very concept of an independent judiciary was undeveloped, a Confucian heritage reinforced by colonial rule and the U.S. military occupation. Until 1987, no law or decree was declared unconstitutional, even though that document guaranteed the usual democratic rights (subject, of course, to law). State control was administered through a highly competent but subservient bureaucracy, an appointed command structure that reached down into the villages, and the co-optation or suppression of civic organizations, which were seen in the former case as supportive of state policies and in the latter as opposed to the state. The KCIA influence was ubiquitous. It had effective executive and virtual extralegal judicial authority (arrest was often tantamount to conviction) far in excess of its putative role. This structure produced a rigid, monolithic political system to a degree perhaps unknown outside of communist societies, but one that overall was highly effective in pursuing its own shorter-term ends.

On December 6, 1971, Park declared a national emergency, supposedly because of the perceived North Korean threat. On July 4, 1972, Park revealed that secret talks had taken place with North Korea and that agreement had been reached that would relieve tensions: There would be peaceful reunification at some unspecified date, and a "great national unity" would be achieved. Ostensibly to mobilize the state to deal with North Korea, on October 17, 1972, Park declared martial law, and on October 20 he announced the repressive Yushin "reforms," which gave him absolute power and prevented any dissent.[23] This was the Korean equivalent of the Japanese Meiji Restoration. These reforms were ratified in the usual, formalistic national referendum in November 1972, and the Fourth Republic .(1972–1979) was ushered in.

Draconian laws were passed and emergency decrees promulgated. The first was the banning of all activities opposing or slandering the Yushin Constitution, including related press reports; the second was the establishment of special courts to try those who violated the first edict. Park established the Autonomous Council for Unification, a group whose function was to elect the president. One-third of that body was to be picked by the president, and the remainder would be chosen by the public. This arrangement assured the president of lifetime tenure. The local press was censored, and the foreign media that wrote on Korea was carefully screened, with offensive elements inked over before entry was allowed. The United States, in its operation of Armed Forces Radio and Television in Korea, went to great lengths to avoid reporting on anything the state might regard as controversial. For a period the government even restricted reporting on foreign events (some rebellions, demonstrations, and similar activities) it felt could incite the populace to take similar, antistate actions. The Fourth Republic was probably the most repressive regime in Korean history, not only because of its ideology and policies but also because of its efficiency, which exacerbated the degree of its control.

During this period, certain democratic-related institutions still existed. Opposition political parties were allowed, although they were ineffective. Elections were held, but they were manipulated, so that the regime attempted to appear externally as one that was essentially democratic in nature but that was forced to restrict freedoms because of the North Korean threat. The North Korean concerns were real, but they were also used by all regimes to suit their purposes and prolong their rule.

Social changes were also evident. In retrospect, it seems clear that the Park government inchoately attempted to change the Korean social structure, in which many traditional elements continued in spite of the Korean War and subsequent dislocation. The Japanese colonial period, the U.S. military occupation, and the Korean War did not eliminate the traditional Korean social structure (at least not to the outside observer—many Koreans felt the changes more acutely), which seemed socially, although not legally, intact. The descendants of the traditional *yangban* kept their status through two investments: urban real estate and higher education (including American Ph.D.s) for their children. Social mobility into the upper social classes was limited. During the 1960s and 1970s, however, social mobility occurred through the military channel, which was seen as an attractive career for males. This was virtually the only way very bright rural, impoverished males could afford to get a good, free education (through the Military Academy) and rise to positions of authority. It was only later in the 1980s that mobility through economic channels became widespread and military power was eclipsed; the military option then seemed less attractive.

The state also attempted to overturn the role of the literati, for whom Park seemed to have a distaste, although he eventually hired many from that background. One aim of the Saemaul Undong was to upset the traditional, elderly, *yangban* village leadership and replace it with modern, vigorous youth who shared the government's goals. The expansion of the number of students enrolled in higher education during the military period from about 100,000 to over 600,000 was intended not only to supply an educated workforce for Korea's new industrial strength but also to satisfy a pervasive hunger for education and to break up the virtual *yangban* monopoly on higher education.[24] A Ph.D. was the modern equivalent of passing the traditional imperial examinations. At a lower, blue-collar level, it was the military experience and training that provided the first waves of factory workers, mechanics, electricians, and drivers.

Although economic development continued and exports grew, despite the two global oil crises, student dissent continued even in the face of the repression. When events in Masan and Pusan seemed to be mushrooming as the political malaise was compounded, the government faced a decision on whether to increase repression or offer some conciliatory gesture to the students. On October 26, 1979, while they were at dinner, President Park and some of his closest associates were assassinated by the director of the KCIA, who, although he was the head of the most repressive instrument of state power, ironically had called for a softer line toward the demonstrators than others among Park's closest advisers.[25]

Interregnum and the Fifth Republic (1979–1987)

South Korea then experienced the second ebullient reaction to repression, similar to that following the overthrow of Syngman Rhee in 1960. This time, however, the joy was even shorter-lived. Choi Kyu Ha, a senior but ineffectual interim president, was effectively ousted by General Chun Doo Hwan on December 12, 1979, in a coup under which he gradually took over power even though Choi retained titular title for eight more months.[26] Chun was chair of the Council for National Emergency Security Planning and director of the National Security Planning Agency (KCIA). The United States did not publicly condemn the coup, which a few months later had tragic consequences for Korea and for Korean-U.S. relations.

The years 1979–1980 were difficult for Korea, both politically and economically. In March 1979 Park had recognized the need for major economic restructuring because of inflation. The heavy-industry program together with the expansion of subsidized credit to achieve state goals, and the construction boom in the Middle East—of which Korea was a prime beneficiary through construction contracts and labor supply (over 200,000 Koreans were working in that region)—pushed up wages, which the state had attempted to keep low, and increased inflation. The second oil shock had a more severe effect than the first in 1973 because Korea continued its heavy-industrial expansion, thereby overheating the economy. Structural adjustment was necessary. In 1980 the failure of the rice crop was a major disaster; it resulted in the only year since the Korean War in which the GNP dropped (by −4.3 percent).[27] The basic cause of the rice failure was the highly efficient implementation of a poor policy.

Economic concerns stimulated more basic political discontent, which was exacerbated by perceived regional inequalities. Park came from North Kyongsang Province (Chun was from South Kyongsang Province, but was reared and educated in North Kyongsang) in the southeast, an area that had received a major and disproportionate share of economic development projects and infrastructure. Higher levels of the bureaucracy were disproportionately staffed by people from that area. For example, the Kyongsang provinces contained 16 percent of the country's population, but from 1961 to 1987 they supplied 31 percent of the ministers, 35 percent of the vice ministers, and 39 percent of board directors. The Cholla provinces had been intentionally neglected.[28]

Kim Dae Jung, who had been kidnapped and saved by U.S. intervention but was under house arrest issued by the Park government, had been freed. His fiery defense of liberties and his opposition to the autocratic state resulted in his rearrest. Student demonstrations broke out in Kwangju, the capital of South Cholla Province. By May 18, 1980, the populace joined in, and a state of insurrection resulted as the center lost control over the town on May 21. The government sent in special forces, which tried brutally to put down the rebellion but were driven out. Officially, around 200 people were killed, although some estimates were as high as 2,000.[29] Martial law had been declared, and the Kwangju populace looked to the United States to broker a compromise. Finally, on May 27, after the U.S. commander had authorized the movement of regular troops (said to be less rapacious than the special forces that had committed atrocities), the city was retaken with little effort.

Many Koreans regard the Kwangju rebellion as the single most disastrous event to strike South Korea since the Korean War. The incident prevented the Chun regime from gaining the political legitimacy it sought. It soured U.S.-Korean popular relations and resulted in the rapid spread of anti-American sentiment. Many Koreans believed the United States intervened on behalf of the Chun government, allowing the movement of troops that participated in the massacre; the U.S. position is that this was not true and that the special forces that committed the outrages were not under the U.S.-headed Combined Forces Command. (About half of Korean forces were under this command in peacetime, about 90 percent during war.) Others had expected the United States to play a restraining role regarding the state. Subsequent high-level U.S. military statements, which seemed to justify Seoul's actions, exacerbated the issue. In 1994 questions concerning Kwangju remained unanswered or obscure, including such issues as Presidents Chun's and Roh's involvement in the actions.

General Chun retired from the military on August 21, 1980 (after promoting himself). On October 23, 91.6 percent of the electorate approved the new constitution of the Fifth Republic in the usual, controlled plebiscite. After martial law was lifted in January 1981, Chun was elected president for one seven-year term under the indirect system President Park had established to ensure his perpetual control over the process.

Saving Kim Dae Jung's life was the cost of the U.S. imprimatur on Chun's presidency. Kim was again sentenced to death for fomenting the Kwangju riots, which was untrue. At that point President Reagan invited

President Chun to the White House as his first official guest, but only after Kim's sentence had been changed. This was an effort—ill conceived, many would say—to improve relations with Korea, which had suffered under the Carter administration.[30] There had been two major points of tension. Carter had wanted to remove U.S. troops from Korea, both during his campaign and after he assumed the presidency, although the U.S. Joint Chiefs of Staff disapproved of the idea. Korea worried about the U.S. commitment to its defense in the wake of the Nixon Doctrine and the disastrous end to the Vietnam debacle. Carter had also stressed respect for human rights, which had been singularly lacking in South Korea. This closeness between the United States and Chun fueled anti-American feeling, especially among the youth. These sentiments were already running high in Kwangju.

The Chun government continued many of the repressive policies of the Park regime in addition to retaining its mode of electing the president. Labor unions were placed under even stricter control; the press was purged of dissenters. Around 5,000 officials were dismissed, as were several hundred journalists (from the private sector, indicating the degree of state control over the society as a whole); 172 "hateful" periodicals were closed down; 611 teachers and principals were fired; and 57,000 "hoodlums" were rounded up. All during this period, President Chun vowed to serve only the single term stipulated in the new constitution, but few believed him. In retrospect, his government was more thoroughly disliked than that of Park, because the economic accomplishments of the Park period were more striking and Park, although austere, was more respected than Chun.[31] Chun never overcame the Kwangju rebellion. Demonstrations continued, and in 1985 alone there were 3,877 on-campus student demonstrations.

The National Assembly elections on February 12, 1985, signaled the beginnings of a major change in the Korean political climate, if not the state's culture. Chun's Democratic Justice Party received only 35.3 percent of the multiparty vote, gaining eighty-seven seats, and the New Korea Democratic Party, led by Kim Dae Jung and Kim Young Sam and which had been formed only a month earlier, received 29.2 percent of the vote, with fifty seats. A proportional seating system, under which the party could allocate a certain number of seats at large depending on the seats it won in constituencies, finally gave 148 seats to the government and sixty-seven to the opposition. In April, the minor opposition parties collapsed into the main opposition group, giving them 103 seats, in what was called the *shin tang param*—the wind of the new party. The government lost in the five largest cities: Seoul, Pusan, Taegu, Kwangju, and Inchon. The legislature was becoming more important, elections were becoming more difficult to manage as the population urbanized and dependency on the government decreased, and state control over the society was unraveling. The government was still in control and had the elements of coercing and cajoling, but that control was becoming more tenuous.

These internal political events were influenced by Korea's preparations for the 1988 summer Olympics, for which Korea had lobbied hard, defeating Nagoya—an important psychological victory in view of colonial history. Chun had staked the reputation of his regime, and, indeed, of the nation, on the success of this event, a goal toward which the state had been mobilized. Continued repression would have irrefutably shattered the positive image Korea had assiduously cultivated, for as many said, it was hoped that the Seoul Olympics would give Korea the international respectability and attention the 1964 Tokyo Olympics had given Japan.

Dissent was growing and spreading from the students (who numbered over 1 million in higher education at the time, compared to 100,000 during the 1961 military coup) to the middle classes—which had vastly expanded—and to the urban population as a whole. The Cholla provinces, both urban and rural areas, were already thoroughly disaffected. To quell such dissent, in April 1986 Chun agreed to a dialogue with the opposition about which form of government was most suited to Korean needs: a presidential or a parliamentary system. The debate was not about the merits of each system alone. A parliamentary system with a titular but powerless president was thought to be more quickly responsive to popular feelings, but under such a system a strong prime minister would not be subject to single-term limitations and could perpetuate his rule. The opposition thought such a mode of government was a plot to continue the regime in power.

At the beginning of 1987, events were moving toward a climax that many felt would be bloody. A massive petition, denounced by the state, with over a million signatures, was circulated nationally, calling for the direct election of the president. In January the state admitted that a student detainee had been tortured and killed. The middle class became restive, demonstrations increased, and the local press began more open coverage of these incidents (such news could no longer be suppressed, as the events had been reported in the international press and on radio and television, which by then were available).

In a major departure from its quiet diplomacy, on February 6 U.S. Assistant Secretary of State for East Asia and the Pacific Gaston Sigur gave a major speech in New York City that effectively limited the parameters of the Korean government response to these internal events. He said the government had greater responsibility for solving these problems because it possessed the power and that the United States would not countenance military intervention through martial law or garrison command. This speech implied that the United States would approve of rebellion by the people if the military were brought in. Personal visits to Seoul by Sigur and other administration officials in June made the point palpable. The message, however unpleasant to those in authority, did not go unheeded. Although a major shift in the U.S. stance, this does not imply that the U.S. role was paramount. There were critical disagreements within the Korean military between rs and moderates, especially the National Military Security Command.

On April 13, President Chun cut off desultory negotiations that had continued with the opposition on the issues of the direct election of the president and of whether the state should have a presidential or a parliamentary system of governance. This move infuriated the public. On June 10, at the government's Democratic Justice Party convention, President Chun personally picked General Roh Tae Woo, his longtime colleague, as the party's presidential candidate and, thus, his successor. This was broadly interpreted as an act of such hubris that demonstrations increased in intensity and breadth. Some believed the move was a ploy by which Chun could once again assume the presidency following a single term by Roh. Civic organizations, professional associations, and even many of the wealthy—most of whom had remained quiescent during much of the troubles—joined in.[32]

Tensions mounted; demonstrations became more violent. The denouement came on June 29, 1987, when candidate Roh went on television and declared that he was in favor of the direct election of the president, the freeing of political prisoners, the restoration of Kim Dae Jung's civil rights, freedom of the press and labor, elected local government, and other reforms—in essence, he was giving in to opposition demands. The country, which had been on the edge of a bloody confrontation, suddenly breathed again. How and when Roh consulted with Chun on these issues is unclear, but the statement came as a major fresh breeze, dispersing the deepening political miasma.

This event, which became known officially as the Special Declaration in the Interests of Grand National Harmony, was an example of statesmanlike, expedient compromise in a society in which such compromise was especially difficult because the assumption of those in power is that the government is pure and, thus, that the opposition is unworthy of being taken seriously. The statement was, therefore, presented as a gracious gesture by the state rather than as a compromise. The popular relief was so great that some knowledgeable observers in Seoul believed that if an election had been held the next day, Roh would have won easily.

Korea was in a different, productive kind of political ferment in the second half of 1987. The constitution was revised to allow for the direct election of the president, and the rights of citizens were reinforced. Labor demanded increases in pay, and the number of strikes mushroomed. There were, for example, 276 labor disputes in 1986; but the number stood at 3,749 in 1987, 1,873 in 1988, and 1,616 in 1989.[33] Preparations began for the presidential campaign that was to culminate in the elections of December 16, 1987. In an example of the personalization of both the political party structure and the concepts of power, Kim Dae Jung and Kim Young Sam—each demanding leadership—formed their own political parties. Thus, despite three opposition candidates, Roh Tae Woo, the incumbent with the government's resources at his command, could defeat a profoundly divided opposition.

The results indicated that the opposition lost rather than that the government won. With 22 million people voting, Roh Tae Woo won 36 percent of the vote, Kim Young Sam 27 percent, Kim Dae Jung 26 percent, and Kim Jong Pil 8 percent (see Table 8.1). Although there were charges of government manipulation and fraud, it seems evident that democratic procedures were in place and basically worked.

Table 8.1   Official Election Results, 1987–1988

Party	1987 Presidential Election[a]	Thirteenth General Election, 1988[b]	
	% of Votes	% of Votes	Total Seats Won
Democratic Justice Party (Roh Tae Woo)	36.6	33.96	125
Unified Democratic Party (Kim Young Sam)	28.0	23.83	59
Party for Peace and Democracy (Kim Dae Jung)	27.0	19.26	70
New Democratic Republican Party (Kim Jong Pil)	8.1	15.59	35
Others	0.2	2.61	1
Independent		4.75	9

Source: Center for Korean Women and Politics.

Note: Translated by the Asia Foundation Korea Office. Translations of the names of political parties may not be official. Names of the party presidential candidates are in parentheses.

a. Voter turnout: 25,873,624 or 89.2% of registered voters.

b. Voter turnout: 19,642,040 or 75.9% of registered voters.

Analysis of the election results revealed important geographic splits within the electorate that had been masked by the state's mass mobilization techniques in previous elections. Most important was a regional split that may remain highly relevant in any future political prognosis in Korea. Kim Dae Jung, as a favorite son, carried his region of South Cholla Province by 90.3 percent and North Cholla by 83.6 percent; he also received the most votes in Seoul (which has a large population from that region), with 32.4 percent (see Table 8.2). Kim Young Sam won his home province of South Kyongsang with 51.6 percent and received 29 percent of the Seoul vote. Kim Jong Pil won his South Chungchong province with 44 percent. Roh swept his home province of North Kyongsang with 66.7 percent and Kangwon Province (where much of the military is stationed) with 60 percent; he received 30.6 percent of the Seoul votes and 41 percent of Kyonggi Province's (surrounding Seoul) vote. Regionalism, rather than class, status, or platform, had emerged as a primary force in Korean politics.

Table 8.2   Regional Voting Patterns: Direct Presidential Elections of 1971, 1987, and 1992 (in percentage)

Region	1971[a]		1987[b]				1992[c]		
	DPR	DNP	DJP	RDP	PPD	NDRP	DLP	DP	UNP
Kyongsang	71.8	28.2	49.9	42.5	5.1	2.5	68.8	10.0	12.0
N. Kyongsang	79.0	21.0	66.7	28.3	2.4	2.6	63.6	9.4	15.5
Taegu	67.4	32.6	70.9	24.4	2.6	2.1	58.8	7.8	19.2
S. Kyongsang	74.1	25.9	41.3	51.6	4.4	2.7	71.5	9.1	11.4
Pusan	56.1	43.9	33.2	54.7	9.5	2.7	72.6	12.4	6.3
Cholla	35.9	64.1	9.9	1.2	88.5	0.5	4.2	90.8	2.3
N. cholla	36.6	63.4	14.2	1.5	83.6	0.9	5.6	87.9	3.2
S. Cholla	37.2	62.8	8.2	1.2	90.3	0.3	4.1	91.1	2.1
Kwangju	23.0	77.0	4.8	0.5	94.5	0.2	2.1	95.8	1.2
Seoul	40.2	59.8	30.6	29.0	32.4	8.1	36.0	37.3	17.8
Other	54.0	45.2	42.3	26.5	13.5	17.7	36.7	28.6	23.8
Inchon	43.0	57.0	39.0	30.0	21.0	9.0	36.7	31.4	21.2
Kyonggi	51.0	49.0	41.0	28.0	22.0	9.0	35.8	31.5	22.8
Kangwon	61.0	39.0	60.0	26.0	9.0	5.0	40.7	15.2	33.5
N. Chungchong	58.0	42.0	47.0	28.0	11.0	14.0	37.6	25.5	23.5
S. Chungchong	55.0	45.0	27.0	16.0	13.0	44.0	36.2	28.0	24.7
Taejon	—	—	—				34.6	28.3	23.0
Cheju	58.0	42.0	50.0	27.0	19.0	5.0	39.2	32.5	15.8
Total	54.0	46.0	36.7	28.0	7.0	8.1	42.0	33.8	16.3

Source: Wonmo Dong, "Regional Cleavage and Political Change in South Korea." Paper presented at the Second Pacific Basin International Conference on Korean Studies, Tokyo, Japan, July 26–28, 1994.

A. Major political parties and presidential candidates in 1971: Democratic Republican Party (DRP), Park Chung Hee; New Democratic Party (NDP), Kim Dae Jung.

b. Major political parties and presidential candidates in 1987: Democratic Justice Party (DJP), Roh Tae Woo; Reunification Democratic Party (RDP), Kim Young Sam; Party for Peace and Democracy (PPD), Kim Dae Jung; New Democratic Republican Party (NDRP), Kim Jong Pil.

c. Major political parties and presidential candidates in 1992: Democratic Liberal party (DLP), Kim Young Sam; Democratic Party (DP), Kim Dae Jung; United Nation's Party (UNP), Chung Ju Young.

The Sixth Republic (1988–): The Pluralistic Society

The Sixth Republic (1988–) began on February 25, 1988, with the swearing in of President Roh, and was followed by preparations for the National Assembly elections, which were held on April 26. Roh's problem was to distance himself from the unpopular Chun Doo Hwan, establish his own control over the political party that Chun had dominated but that he, Roh, had inherited, and run a minority government. Roh on April 1 expressed regret for the Kwangju incident, stopping short of an apology for it, retained some members of the Chun cabinet, but was able to prevent Chun from having too great an influence over his appointees and the candidates for the National Assembly elections.

The government's Democratic Justice Party received only 33.9 percent of the popular vote in that April election, taking 125 assembly seats to 174 for the opposition parties. Kim Dae Jung's Party for Peace and Democracy received 19.2 percent of the vote, Kim Young Sam's Reunification Democratic Party 23.8 percent, Kim Jong Pil's New Democratic Republican Party 15.5 percent, and minor parties the remainder (see Table 8.1). Regionalism was again a critical element in the elective process, reaffirming the previous presidential voting pattern. The government had lost the legislative elections, an unprecedented event in Korean history and one that seemed to threaten the political power of the state. There was an evident need to reassert the government's political authority, which occurred in early 1990.

In January 1990, in an important move based explicitly on the Japanese model of political control (which has since proven ephemeral in Japan) and one designed to return legislative control to the government party, Kim Young Sam and Kim Jong Pil, with some of their party followers, joined the Democratic Justice Party (the government). The new party, called the Democratic Liberal Party, was formed with the overt purpose of changing leadership among factions of the same party and denying the opposition an opportunity to control the government. What was astonishing was not the attempt to retain control but, rather, the use of the Japanese example and even virtually the Japanese name (Liberal Democratic Party). The stated purpose of this move was to achieve national stability, but its aim was clearly to retain state power. This move, combined with some previous opposition defections, restored government control of the legislature, with 214 of the 299 seats.

In the aftermath of the election, Chun went into self-imposed internal exile in a Buddhist temple. Later, he was forced to testify about Kwangju in the National Assembly, but he shed little new light on that tragedy. Chun's younger brother was jailed for his corruption in the Saemaul Undong.

The presidency of Roh Tae Woo was significant in several aspects. In spite of his military background and close association with the Kyongsang and Taegu cliques, he was regarded as a leader who looked for consensus more than any previous president except Chang Myon. His economic policies were regarded as weak (in fact, the world economy had weakened and protectionism was rising); indeed, Korea suffered slower growth, which had previously been phenomenal, and higher inflation. Roh moved procedural democracy forward. As the cold war ebbed, Korea's relations with the former communist bloc improved, and he retired senior staff and effectively eliminated the military as a potential political force. He then retired in accordance with constitutional provisions.

Kim Young Sam claimed he won his party's nomination for the presidency by an open ballot for the first time (receiving 61 percent of the votes of the delegates) rather than by fiat. It seems evident, however, that Kim Young Sam had joined Roh Tae Woo's party in January 1990 with reasonable assurances that his candidacy would be backed by Roh. The possibility that Kim Dae Jung might win the presidency was anathema to the military and to many conservatives, and this was a means to prevent such a victory and retain control over the political process.

The Sixth Republic, which the Kim administration prefers be called the "civilian regime," has been the first in Korean history to provide continuity with a change in leadership. But a new political dynamic has been evolving in Korea. The state has been seriously challenged, and new forces are emerging to vie with the government for power. The most significant of these forces is the business community—more specifically the conglomerates, the *chaebol*. In 1992, this community began to emerge as a direct participant in the political process rather than simply a funder of political parties.

The *chaebol* were critical to Korea. They had been the unofficial chosen instruments in the export strategy and in the development of heavy industries.[34] Some were listed among the world's largest companies. In 1985, the top ten companies had aggregate sales equal to 80 percent of GNP. In 1993, the top thirty had assets of about 36 trillion won (about $45 billion) and controlled 616 subsidiary companies.[35] The state had gone into debt (over $40 billion) to expand industries, and the *chaebol* received much of the benefits—at least this was the public perception.[36] They had supported authoritarian regimes, which had kept down the costs of labor. Big-business interests in Korea, in contrast with the West, did not converge with popular values, so they were suspect. In addition, residual Confucian values suspect the profit motive. The *chaebol* were known as *mun'obal,* or octopus tentacles.[37]

The largest *chaebol* was Hyundai. Chung Ju Yung, former chair of that massive conglomerate, had been dissatisfied with the economic policies of the state and had formed his own political party, which won 11 percent of the seats in the assembly elections in March 1992. In fact, the government lost majority control of the legislature in that election, receiving only 149 of the 299 seats, but shortly thereafter it picked up some independent seats to gain a slim majority.

In the December 1992 presidential elections, Chung Ju Yung ran against Kim Young Sam, won a significant 16 percent of the votes, and then retired from politics when he lost. Kim Dae Jung also contested, as did some minor candidates. Kim Young Sam won the election with 42 percent of the vote (see Table 8.3), and Kim Dae Jung, in an important and graceful speech, retired from politics.

Kim Young Sam's election marked the civilianizing of the Korean political process, for he was the first president since 1961 who did not have a military background. He had been an advocate of democracy, had been placed under house arrest by Park Chung Hee, and had a long, distinguished record as a force for a more liberal political system. He was, by Korean

Table 8.3   Official Election Results, 1992

Party	1992 Presidential Election	Fourteenth General Election, 1992	
	% of Votes	% of Votes	Total Seats Won
Democratic Liberal Party (Kim Young Sam)	42.0	38.5	149
Democratic Party (Kim Dae Jung)	33.8	29.2	96
Unified National Party (Chung Ju Yung)	16.3	17.4	31
Shinjung Party (Park Chan Jong)	6.4	1.8	1
Others	—	1.6	—
Independent	1.4	11.5	21

Source: Center for Korean Women and Politics.

Note: Translated by the Asia Foundation Korea Office. Translations of the names of political parties may not be official. Names of the party presidential candidates are in parentheses.

Voter turnout: 24,095,170 or 81.9% of registered voters.

political standards, immensely popular in the early period of his presidency, with approval ratings at over 80 percent of the electorate at various periods. His was a smooth transition. This popularity, however, eroded over the first two years of his presidency.

President Kim undertook the establishment of his own base within his party and with the people in general. He was able to force high-level officials to reveal their financial assets, and he purged those who could not explain their wealth. Kim dismissed senior military officers on the grounds of corruption and of selling promotions, thus ensuring his control over what had been an independent power fiefdom within the state. He forced real-name bank accounts so the government could monitor tax compliance and limit *chaebol* speculation in real estate. (Previously, Koreans could legally register such accounts under any, even assumed, names.) In February 1995, he reformulated his party, effectively eliminating Kim Chong Pil, who then formed his own party.

There were also negative elements to Kim's performance, however. He used the threat and the actuality of tax audits to harass his opposition candidate, Chung Ju Yung. After promising during his presidential campaign that he would ban the importation of foreign rice, he reversed the decision and allowed rice imports. He softened the blow by agreeing in the first few years to a tariffication process of gradually lowering the tariffs over a period of years to ease the transition. Farmers and students demonstrated over this unpopular move and the apparent buckling to U.S. (and General Agreement on Tariffs and Trade [GATT]) pressures. The National Assembly is heavily skewed toward rural constituencies, which exacerbated the problem.

The heavy, if gloved, hand of the state was still felt. The government resisted eliminating the National Security Law, which gave the center immense potential power. There were, for example, 2,630 indictments under this law from 1980 through August 1991, of which about half took place after liberalization in 1987. In 1990 and 1991, 99.7 percent and 99.3 percent, respectively, of those indicted were found guilty.[38] Labor unions remained controlled, and some were still illegal or unrecognized—such as the National Council of Korean Trade Unions, which in 1990 had 190,000 members in 574 unions (or about 10 percent of all union members).[39] The government still prevented student-worker alliances and the presence of university-educated workers in factories, calling them "disguised workers" and "impure elements" through third-party intervention laws. Government guidelines for wage increases were announced annually for the spring labor negotiations. Demonstrations were broken up. Some political prisoners (including those in the labor field and some who had visited North Korea without state approval) remained in jail.

Progress was promised. After years of delay, there were plans to have the governors of provinces and the mayors of special cities (Seoul, Pusan, and others) elected directly by the people in 1995. Provincial councils had been initiated through such elections in March and June 1991 and were formally inaugurated in July of that year. These elections resulted in 4,304 office holders at the city, county, and urban ward levels and 866 for the metropolitan and regional councils. The results, which reinforced the regionalism that had been apparent in national elections, resulted in more than a two-thirds majority for the government party candidates and their supporters. Many undemocratic practices were charged, and election costs were said to be enormous.[40]

Appraisal of the Sixth Republic must await further events and the completion of the Kim Young Sam presidency. Early in his term Kim was probably the most popular president Korea ever had. The perennial issue of political legitimacy is no longer relevant in his case. There is virtual unanimity in the expectation that President Kim, in accordance with the constitution, will retire in 1997. The stability of democratic procedures and the forward motion toward more substantive democracy are unquestioned. Pluralism is well established and is unlikely to be relinquished by Korea's sophisticated population. Roadblocks along this path remain. They are formidable, if less concrete, than the accomplishments to date. These issues are discussed in the next section.

Theoretical Analysis

The Republic of Korea is now a pluralistic society in the process of continuous evolution. It is rent by a variety of contradictory forces, many of which are still generally unrecognized and inchoate, pushing the nation from the procedural democracy that has already been attained to more substantive and fundamental democratic concepts and performance. Other forces retard such growth. Ferment and modifications, progress and lapses are likely to describe this quiet but nonetheless profound political altercation, which over the longer term is likely to be fruitful and progressive.

Democracy is an evolving process, not an end in itself, through which such societal goals as social justice, equity, and liberty (however culturally defined) are sought. Societies do not reach democracy but alter and refine their political dynamics, institutions, and attitudes through processes and procedures generally known or perceived as democratic. Each state adapts procedures, processes, and political aspirations to its culture(s) and needs. As information expands worldwide, and as the UN Universal Declaration of Human Rights and other international criteria become more widely known, however, these procedures and at least the accepted and articulated political ends in many countries become similar; thus, the self-defined needs for and adoption of procedural democracy spread. International acceptability and legitimacy often seem to influence this articulated stance in many countries—thus, the continuing official adjectival modification of democracy with people's, guided, Asian, and similar expressions.

There is mutual interaction and influence between societal norms and democratic procedures, each affecting the other and producing (usually incremental) change. Law and the political process reflect to some major degree prevailing societal and intellectual norms, but either one can (and has) separately, in tandem, or sequentially prodded change in basic values— as is seen in the evolution in gender legislation and attitudes in the United States over the past generation.

The Republic of Korea has evolved politically in the past decade, for reasons noted earlier. This evolution continues. Korea today has all of the overt institutional elements of a democracy: There is intense political competition among a variety of political parties; a highly inclusive level of political participation; regular and now generally fair elections; an active and vigorous legislature; a judiciary freer than it has ever been in Korean history, and one that occasionally constitutionally questions executive-branch actions; much improved levels of civil and political liberties, including a vibrant press; a growing civil society; improved public accountability and transparency; and an increasingly stable political process. Why not, then, call it a democratic society?

The procedural forms and manifestations of democratic governance (those, in effect, that are enumerated in the previous paragraph) are in place and are unlikely to be strikingly altered for some time. They function, however, under considerable strain because their modern roles are subject to interpretation in the light of more traditional nondemocratic attitudes that still exist and that are widespread, thereby eviscerating some progress achieved and altering institutional and personal roles in this process. These more fundamental issues of attitude affect both the way these institutions function and the internal and external actors' expectations in the process of governance.

In an important article, one author postulates democracy as a spectrum along which its various forms exist.[41] In order to be stable, democracy requires consolidation, so that the democratic process is seen as legitimate and is unlikely to break down. In some societies, deepening is necessary to improve the quality, depth, and authenticity of democracy. Some societies may be described as semidemocracies, where the effective power of elected officials is limited, political parties are restricted, elections are compromised, and political liberties are circumscribed. South Korea seems to be beyond that stage.

Is Korea, then, a protodemocracy—one that is in its early stages of maturation but is not yet solidified? Or might Korea "drift indefinitely as a *democradura* in which constitutional rules provide no guarantee against a concentration of political power among the few, who then exercise their power in a personalistic fashion."[42]

Or does Korea represent a hegemonic party system under effective single-party control? Although not as extreme as the situation in Mexico, until recently the Kuomintang in China (and then in Taiwan) and the Liberal Democratic Party in Japan could be regarded as approaching this designation, although both have changed and political power has broadened in each state. Beginning in 1990 the Korean Democratic Liberal Party attempted to establish this type of one-party dominance (based on both the need for stability and the Japanese model), but it is too early to determine how successful in its own terms it will be. Since 1963, there has been an effort to establish a type of hegemonic political system, with election regulations that through a complex representational system give the party in power more seats than its proportion of the vote. Some scholars have called this a one-and-one-half party system.[43] If Korea is beyond semidemocratic status, where does it lie along the democratic spectrum?

The democratic forces affecting Korea have strengthened dramatically in the past decade. Yet as one specialist wrote:

> Power is highly concentrated in the executive organs of government with an enormous amount of coercive and allocative authority in the hands of state executives. Hardly anything socially consequential in South Korea is left untouched by the regulatory actions of the state, and few groups or organizations in society exist without some kind of state sanction. . . . Although it is true that all modern states intervene in their economies in one way or another, the South Korean state stands out in terms of the depth of such intervention, its dirigist [*sic*] policy implementation, and its ability to discipline the business sector while maintaining tight control over labor organizations.[44]

The Continuity of Korean Political Attitudes

These influences spring from a variety of sources, including the traditional Korean social structure, the Confucian cultural overlay of the role of government and the state, the colonial experience, the foreign military occupation and the domestic military regimes, the economic success of the highly dirigiste state, and the degree of anxiety concerning Korea's regional place in Northeast Asia and its tragic historical memory. Foreign powers have affected this process heterogeneously as well. We would be wrong to assume that economic and political developments must be synchronous—they often change at varying speeds and affect each other. This has been the case in Korea in the past, as economic growth outpaced political maturation.

Social tensions and inconsistencies were and are an inherent part of Korean, or any, society. The traditional, but only theoretical, Confucian moral and educational egalitarianism was, for example, in constant conflict with its own profoundly hierarchical reality and that of Korean society itself. The desire for mobility that pushed and pulled all to Seoul in order to rise in traditional Korean power terms was in contest with the social order.[45] In a sense, these issues still exist in a reduced, altered form.

Fundamental to the issue of democracy are concepts of power—its attributes, uses, and scope.[46] In many traditional societies, power is conceived as a limited good; since there is a fixed amount, sharing or delegating such power institutionally (from an executive branch to a legislative or judicial branch, for example), spatially (from a central government to provinces or to the periphery), or personally becomes problematic.[47] Power is then conceived as being personalized, and loyalties become directed to those who occupy positions of authority but not to the abstracted concepts nor the offices themselves. This situation gives rise to intense factionalism, which, indeed, has characterized Korean traditional court politics and the more modern political scene.[48]

The modern effect of these attitudes on politics and political parties has been profound. Political parties have been founded to provide the vehicles for individuals to perpetuate or achieve power. Few have had coherent platforms, although it should be noted that the far left of the political spectrum has been suppressed since the U.S. military occupation of 1945, and, indeed, the Communist Party was outlawed during the Japanese colonial period. A 1994 nationwide survey indicated that 69 percent of those interviewed believed political parties served the interests of their leaders, and 72 percent thought all of the parties were essentially the same.[49] Entourages and factions are formed around leaders, who are supported by, and in turn have obligations to protect and assist, their followers. This situation has encouraged the development of a bewildering array of political parties in modern Korea, parties whose names keep changing as alliances are formed and reformulated but whose policies and platforms remain obscure.[50]

The evidence for personalized concepts of power is pervasive. Recent examples include the 1987 election, when Kim Young Sam and Kim Dae Jung split the opposition vote because each wanted power, thus giving the victory to Roh Tae Woo. Roh Tae Woo had to put his personal stamp on the government party—inherited from Chun Doo Hwan—which he successfully accomplished. Kim Young Sam, after the Democratic Justice Party was transformed into the Democratic Liberal Party in 1990, has had to do the same thing. He did it again in February 1995. Political parties are critical to Korea and to the democratic process, but whereas in Western democracies the parties represent something beyond the individual leaders, continue after they leave, and breed successive leaders who rise from within them, in Korea the individual generally creates the party to suit his or her political needs or, in the more recent past, recreates it in the leader's own image.[51] Thus, simply strengthening political parties at this stage of Korean (or perhaps other countries') political culture might perhaps be seen as increasing personalism more than furthering democracy. Institutionalization of the political party culture seems critical to further progress. This institutionalization, however, needs internal reorganization. Autocratic control from party headquarters has vitiated the democratic process within the parties, as local leadership (until 1995, at any rate; there is discussion of change) is determined by Seoul. Simple institutionalization of parties is one of a number of needed reforms. It may be significant that President Kim Young Sam has been the first leader to keep the party name (although in February 1995 he did so after rejecting some two thousand alternatives, according to the press) thus perhaps indicating an early state of this process.

Hierarchies in themselves do not prevent democracy from evolving because societies may recognize equality in one sphere (e.g., voting) but not in another. But the pervasive nature of hierarchy in Korean society is an element that is retarding the full acceptance of democratic concepts, if not forms. The Korean social system was traditionally more hierarchical in the pre-Confucian period than was that in China. Rigid rank was hereditary, with the highest being "bone rank" in the Silla court. This continuity is reflected today in the Korean language, which requires discrete honorifics to establish the relative rank of all of those involved in conversations to a far greater degree than does Chinese, for example. When Korea adopted the Chinese civil service examination system, it effectively limited it to those from the *yangban* class, thus perpetuating an aristocracy, because status came from family and bureaucratic position—which in turn was generally determined by education in strict conformity to traditional canons of Confucian thought. A strong hierarchical tradition does not necessarily vitiate democracy, but it may slow its acceptance.

Hierarchical societies often fear change.

> The notion (or even the fear) that non-violent struggle, like violence, poses a radical or revolutionary threat to the system is understandable. This is particularly relevant to a hierarchically ordered society such as Korea, where any hint of change in the system portends the breakdown of the entire social order and is likely to be repressed at all costs.[52]

The Confucian system itself had a pervasive effect on Korean society—one that was known to be more Confucian in spirit than China itself.[53] Government was to be conducted by the example of the ruler and not by law, which was a "deteriorated form of norms applicable only to those uneducated [in proper conduct]."[54] Although constitutions have repeatedly established theoretical rights, these rights have been ignored in practice. In the fifteen years preceding 1987, no case came before the supreme organ of judicial review, the Constitutional Committee. Korea has correctly been called an "alegal" society.

The state, by virtue of its patriarchal role, had a right, even a moral obligation, to intervene in the lives and businesses of its citizenry to achieve desirable social goals.

> The King is father,
> And ministers are loving mothers.
> They only receive what love brings. . . .
> Peace and prosperity will prevail if each—
> King, minister, subject—lives as he should.[55]

These attitudes have not yet disappeared, although they may be more unconscious than articulated. The familial model ("father knows best"—the leader must be obeyed, and the individual sacrifices for the collective—family—good) is a critical, albeit residual but influential, analogy of political life. The state (father) correctly intervenes in virtually any activity to protect the family (society). This, for example, has justified the role of the intelligence agencies from traditional to modern times. The plot of the classic Korean novel *Ch'unhyang* is resolved through the return of the hero as the king's secret agent. Fears in the South of a German-style unification with North Korea may represent concerns not only about the economic costs, which would be massive, but also about the fact that a major influx of refugees and students going north could prevent the intelligence network—which is still pervasive, if less obvious and contentious today—from coping with such changes. Even with the freedoms now associated with contemporary South Korea, the ability of the state to establish limits on acceptable behavior is consequential, and popular acceptance of that ability is significant (as seen in July 1994, for example, when public mourning in the South over the death of Kim Il Sung in the North was forbidden). It is not without significance that in Korean the translated term for *agricultural extension* is *agricultural guidance.*

is paternal concept is related to the need for orthodoxy, and intervention has pervaded state attitudes toward the government's proper role in all fields. As one writer indicated, culture is an integral element of this approach, and culture is regarded as an arm of politics: "The Korean tradition strongly subscribes to the idea that culture should constitute the mainstay of the state."[56] The society traditionally did not allow autonomous centers of even local power to develop. In the modern period, therefore, the co-optation of civic groups that performed activities of which the state approved was common; equally common was the suppression of private organizations the leaders felt were inimical (or potentially inimical) to their immediate interests. "Private" universities, as only one example, are private only in the sense that they are not financed by the state; they are otherwise micromanaged by the Ministry of Education. Private businesses may be denied credit from private banks through state intervention, their management may be fired, and their tax returns may be audited—all powerful state tools. To the Confucian canon must be added the intentional spread by the political leadership of the past generation and a half of the concept of equating the state with the nation; thus, in all fields the state acts for the people as a whole. This is easier in an ethnically homogeneous society such as Korea. These attitudes remain, but the reality is far more hopeful, as I note later.

A strong element of regionalism has reemerged, retarding democracy; what has occurred might be reminiscent of the classic period of the contending states of the "Three Kingdoms" (until A.D. 668). One might consider North Korea as Koguryo; the regimes emanating from the Kyongsang area (Park, Chun, Roh, and to a lesser degree, Kim) are Silla governments, and the Kim Dae Jung opposition is Paek'che. These are real, not academic or arcane, issues and are often discussed among the intelligentsia. Kwangju residents often said the troops that went in to quell the disturbances were from Silla (the Kyongsang provinces). Kyongsang cultural influences have expanded, and many say the accents and food patterns of that region have replaced many of the more Seoul-oriented and gentry traditions that had previously been important. These changes are resented in many quarters. The elections at the presidential, National Assembly, and local levels have all demonstrated the importance of regional blocs. Whether the announced retirement of Kim Dae Jung from politics and government efforts to right the imbalances in infrastructure and industry in the Cholla region will affect this situation is unclear.

At various times some external forces have worked to retard or spur more democratic movements. The North Korean threat was and continues to be used to justify state control over South Korean society and to stifle the expression of unpopular political views. The tenacious hold all regimes have kept on the National Security Law is a reminder of that influence. To those in authority North Korea was a negative model, but South Korea was sometimes forced politically to follow a North Korean example, such as in land reform in the early 1950s. North Korea's nationalism has been appreciated in some South Korean circles, even if the regime and its leader have not been.

The United States has also been an important external influence. Over time, it had three objectives in Korea: security, democratization, and, more recently, economic—that is, market—openings. When security was paramount (during the Rhee, Park, and Chun periods), the United States opted, and was perceived by Korean intellectuals, to support security over democratization in spite of many public pronouncements to the contrary. As Korea allowed greater freedom of the press in the democratization process, there was more public debate over the security and economic issues the state had previously kept subdued—for example, atomic weapons in South Korea, market opening pressures from the United States, dumping issues, responsibility for the division of Korea, Kwangju, and similar issues. There was, thus, internal tension among the three elements of U.S. policy.

The impression of many Korean intellectuals has been that the United States supported authoritarian regimes more than democratic ones. Statistically, this is obvious, given the defense agreement between the two states. The agreement effectively mandated stability as the primary consideration. There were more authoritarian periods, and they lasted longer. Moreover, the U.S. foreign aid program ceased in 1975, before political liberalization. This assessment is not completely accurate, however, both because of its simplistic level and because there have been disagreements within the U.S. government in policy statements, as well as vigorous official but private protests in contradiction to muted public criticisms. The State Department has often been more concerned with democratic issues than has the Defense Department. Some ambassadors have privately protested human rights violations, both institutional as well as personal, while publicly remaining silent. U.S. interventions in 1960 to encourage Rhee to step down, in 1963 to force Park to hold an election, and in 1987 to limit Chun's potential use of the military are all examples of quiet interventions for democratic ends. Overall, foreign influences, including that of education, have been positive forces for pluralism.

The subservient role of women in society, who were exploited at wages less than half of comparable male earnings, probably began as an element that retarded democratic growth. This situation seems to have changed, with women becoming active in politics, articulate on social issues, and demanding of improvements in a variety of nongender conditions. Legislation has changed some of these inequities, but others remain. The number of women in public life is still small. About 1 percent of the winners in the 1992 local elections were women; they hold a limited number of supervisory civil service jobs. Their organizations and voting power, however, have been a positive force for democratic and pluralistic growth. They have been active in the nongovernmental organization (NGO) community in advocacy groups that strengthen democratic trends.

Law has represented punishment and obligations rather than the rights of the individual in relation to the state. The Western concept on which so much of democratic governance rests, the "Rule of Law," is capitalized here to reflect its Western importance; in Korea it is lower cased and is traditionally meaningless in societies in which modern law gave repressive power to a state or a colonial regime and allowed few, if any, rights for the individuals governed. Law, as Confucius indicated, was a tiger to be feared, not a protector of rights. Although the residual suspicion of law, courts, and lawyers remains (and both socially and institutionally private mediation and settlement are preferred to court action), the relative freedom of the judiciary to challenge legislation as unconstitutional and even legislative disputes over the nomination of judges have seen a partial revolution since 1987. It is not completely independent, but the judiciary is far more autonomous than it has been at any time in Korean history.

The bureaucracy and the scholar-literati class were essentially equal and enjoyed the highest status. The creation of the civil service examination system in China, which was transposed to Korea, is still profoundly felt, which accounts for the strong bureaucratic authority of those in key positions and for the effectiveness of this elite group (only about 2.5 percent of applicants pass the examinations). As a result, administrations are characterized by a top-down emphasis, which discourages criticisms or attempts at reform from below. This meritocratic pattern extends to many financial and corporate recruitment efforts as well. In a sense, the effective meritocracy of the bureaucracy encourages the pervasive role of the state and its interference in what Americans would regard as the rights of individuals to privacy. If emphasis on control and the status quo was an important consequence of the Confucian tradition, the positive aspects of that heritage also lie in its emphasis on education and in the concept of the role of a meritocracy, albeit within the prevailing cultural milieu, which sometimes vitiates these advantages.

The centralized Korean state was also a product of the Confucian tradition. It was easier to centralize in a relatively small state such as Korea. Further, although the authority of the king was theoretically absolute, it was in fact limited because he had to deal with his *yangban* court. Additionally, there could only be one Son of Heaven, and that was obviously the Chinese emperor, not the Korean king.

The concept of ideological conformity and loyalty came out of this tradition as it evolved. Thus, the very concept of a "loyal opposition" has essentially been an oxymoron in Korea—if one is in opposition, then clearly one is not loyal because one's loyalty is to the individual, who has personal power, and not to the concepts of governance. In modern Korea, the frequent use of words such as impure, ideological pollution, and related terms to describe any opposition individual or group (even within one's own party) conveys the necessity for orthodoxy and uniformity of opinion. It is significant that in premodern times the literati produced no tradition of satire of the establishment. (The only satire came from a few genre paintings by non-*yangban* and also through the peasant traditions of farmers' and mask dances. Satire was important, however, during the Japanese colonial period.) It was, until recently, illegal to criticize the head of state. Attitudes toward orthodoxy are in flux, however, and greater liberalization is evident.

It is significant that each regime has started off with the need for some ritual purification to solidify its own ranks, engender political legitimacy, and rid the establishment society of unwanted competition. These acts serve to reinforce orthodoxy as well, and they reestablish the paternalistic role of the state. The Chang Myon government, Park Chung Hee, Chun Doo Hwan, Roh Tae Woo, and Kim Young Sam have all done this in varying ways, although President Kim already possessed this legitimacy. The underlying message was clear: The state determines the rules of the distribution of power and is pervasive.

One part of the purification ritual has been the state's moral concern with intervening in the private lives of individuals. The sumptuary laws or edicts that relate to luxury or ostentation have been recurring elements of Korean life. Restrictions on the size of houses, use or purchase of foreign automobiles or luxury goods, expensive weddings, and the like—often applied ex post facto—are consistently, if ephemerally, enforced; these edicts demonstrate the state's control over society. These events create uncertainty in business (flower shops, for example, go out of business when weddings must be modest), and they have caused trade tensions with the United States, which accused Korea of intentionally excluding U.S. imports through an antiluxury campaign. In fact, the actions may have served dual purposes: demonstrating the traditional virtues of paternal government and modesty, as well as keeping away unwanted imports.

The military has receded as a force for authoritarian control, and it is a credit to the Roh and Kim governments that they have recognized the need for civilian control and, barring national tragedy such as a recurrence or imminent threat of a new Korean war, seem to have established the primacy of civilian rule. This situation is partly a result of the shift to economic over military domination of the state, partly because of the efforts of civilian politicians, and partly a result of splits within the military itself regarding its appropriate roles. The military, as I have demonstrated, was an important source of social mobility; although this is still true, its importance in that role has been overtaken by the business community. Although the class structure was far more rigid than was the case in many societies even during the past two generations, mobility is far more pronounced, and self-perceived middle-class status has resulted in little class solidarity among workers, farmers, and other strata of the society.

The Japanese colonial experience reinforced, perhaps solidified, this tendency toward centralization of authority and hierarchy. It was, in its own terms and for its own purposes, an effective mechanism that reached down to the village level. The U.S. military occupation did much to continue this tradition, even though certain policies (such as educational reform) were designed to break up centralization. These policies failed in the case of education, and educational control remained centralized.

In spite of the pluralism so evident in the society, during much of the Roh presidency there were many complaints that he was *mul* (watery, or wishy-washy). His policies were too weak, according to many who wanted more vigorous leadership and a determined economic policy when the economy did not expand as rapidly as it had in previous regimes. Thus, Koreans seem of two minds: They respect the need for democratic forms and yet need the reassurance of strong leadership for continued prosperity. In a sense, this tension represents the true debate in Korea over the future of democracy in that country. Democratic debate not only allows the expression of more liberal views, but also the strengthening of more conservative groups.

Political Changes

Perhaps the most important, overlooked force for democracy in Korea has been urbanization. Although some of the theoretical literature touches on this topic in matters concerning access to information and education—both of which are important—in Korea other forces were also operating.[57] In 1961, Korea was about 75 percent rural and 25 percent urban. By the late 1980s, the figures had been reversed. Voting patterns indicate that the government had the most trouble in, and often lost, the major urban areas. This occurred not only because these areas were more sophisticated and better educated (intellectuals in general tended to vote against the state). It was not because they had unique access to information; by that time, around 90 percent of Korean households had television, radios were ubiquitous, and newspapers were distributed in villages. It was also evident that the state elements of control were much less powerful in the anonymity of the cities, where the fiscal means of domination through rice and barley producer pricing, credit allocations, and rural mobilization and surveillance techniques were lacking. Thus, as urbanization expanded, the relative freedom of the population to express its voting preferences was far less restricted; as a result, the state lost control.

Urban autonomy gave rise to the autonomy of NGOs and public interest groups, which usually operated in urban areas. Many of these were advocacy groups, professional organizations, religious groups, and civic associations that had been under pressure from, or under the domination of, the state. Only about 16 percent of Koreans do not participate in civic groups, compared to 69 percent who do not participate in Spain.[58] It was evident in the events leading up to the June 29, 1987, liberalization announcement that NGOs had become far more active than at any previous time and that they publicly advocated positions opposed by the government. It is unlikely that at any foreseeable time these organizations will retreat from their pluralistic and important roles in furthering responsible and responsive governance. North Korea sometimes quotes NGO social criticism as indicative of the South's failures and, thus, reveals its concern about some NGO activity. It is likely, however, that NGO numbers and strength will expand. The NGO community is a critical force for pluralism and for democratic governance.

Pluralism has also come from and been evident in the growth of the business community, the rise in incomes of the population as a whole, and the growth of the middle class. Middle-class status has been variously defined; the World Bank believes about 55 percent of the population falls within that category, but the self-identification of those in that class, as reported by various polls, runs to 75 percent and higher. Middle-class status in Korea essentially conveys three messages: hope in a society in which the lives of the children will be better than those of the parents; a conservatism that has been evident in voting patterns, which indicates that this group wants to protect these gains; and a sense of participation in the political process. It is unlikely that this group will renounce the political gains Korea has achieved or the economic and social gains that have been garnered. The rise in per capita GNP from approximately $67 in 1961 to over $7,700 in 1994 has contributed immeasurably to the process of political maturity and increased political, social, and economic aspirations.

The desire for achievement and self-realization is perhaps a part of the reason Confucian societies have done so well. Together with the vortex theory, in which Koreans aspire and work toward the center and toward mobility,[59] this desire contributes to pluralism and eventually to more democratic substance.

The experience with political participation is also growing. The destruction of local, elected governments in 1961—partly because they were perceived as corrupt and partly because Park Chung Hee wanted his military command structure to be in place at all levels—eliminated popular participation in decisionmaking except in the rare national elections. The Ministry of Home Affairs, which controls the police and local government, has been the most powerful ministry except for the Economic Planning Board. Participation in the agricultural, livestock, or other cooperatives essentially constituted participation in state-controlled enterprises over which the members had no important say.

This situation has changed since 1987, and the cooperatives have voiced protectionist views on agricultural import policies that are inimical to state plans. These organizations are beginning to offer opportunities for a more intimate pluralistic experience than has been possible for many years.[60] As local elected government is reinstituted (with elections for governors and the mayors of special cities—those with over 1 million in population) in 1995, the rural sector may become more politically sophisticated as sources for instant information are in place. Literacy is virtually universal (over 95 percent). Electricity even in remote areas has given residents access to television and radio. Rural incomes are well below those of comparable urban families, but farmers are far less dependent on the state than they once were (about one-third of rural income comes from nonfarm sources), even if most of the institutional credit is still provided by the state through the cooperatives.

In the movement toward pluralism, the changing role of the private sector and the relationships between business and government have been in flux. Throughout the Park period, based on his leadership and on state regulation of and monopoly on credit, the government was able to control business and to force it into molds the center set. The expansion of the *chaebol,* however, and the dependence of the entire economy—and, thus, political legitimacy—on their performance mean the weight of power has shifted into an uneasy, liquid balance. Business needs the state, but the state cannot afford to see business slow or major firms collapse. The state has tried to control the *chaebol* because they are unpopular. It has publicly attempted to limit their growth, reduce the number of subsidiaries under their control (in 1993 Hyundai had ninety-five subsidiaries, Samsung had fifty-five, Lucky-Goldstar had fifty-four, and so on), force firms to focus on only three sectors, and limit their speculation in land. These regulations are only sporadically enforced, if at all. In a sense, the democratization process has inhibited the state from controlling its present competitor—the *chaebol*—even as it needs to do so to win popular support. The *chaebol* were largely a creation of the very state with which they now exist in an atmosphere of political tension.

We have seen the beginnings of the overt involvement of business in politics for the first time in Korean history. A review of the social backgrounds of the legislators since independence would indicate a remarkable paucity of those who have primarily identified themselves as businesspeople compared with most of the legislatures in other parts of Asia. Legislators have come from official, intellectual, journalistic, and military backgrounds; although many more have business interests, these interests have been subsidiary to other concerns. In part, this reflects the past irrelevance of the business community, which has now totally changed, and in part it reflects the public's suspicion of business as lacking in public responsibility.

Some specialists have raised the issue of future state-business relationships:

The more fundamental question is whether South Korean economic policy-making can break the government's reliance on an authoritarian style of rule. The return to open policies of exclusion now appears extremely difficult because of the increasing constraints posed by electoral politics. Yet South Korea still lacks the institutions, political alignments, and particularly stable party structure capable of supporting other alternatives.[61]

Thus, the accomplishments of the state have been remarkable in economic terms; those of the people in moving to pluralism and toward democracy have been historic. As in any society, important tensions still exist between the forces that are comfortable with traditional elements of control and those that wish to see these elements relinquished.

Conclusion: Korean Politics— From Procedures to Substance?

The record of progress in Korean political change is evident. The political experience since independence through the early 1950s augured poorly for the future of both Korean political and economic life, but there has been a startling improvement. If Korean economic growth has outpaced political change for the first two generations of South Korea's existence, Korea's political maturity over the past seven years—a product of subtle yet profound shifts in that process—has outpaced its recent economic accomplishments, which have been good but not spectacular. We can no longer characterize Korea as bureaucratic-authoritarian, a state-capitalist or mercantilist-authoritarian regime, or other such designations.

In the parlance of this volume, Korea in 1995 is a "mixed success" and a "partial democracy" or perhaps a "protodemocracy." It may more accurately be described as a procedural democracy rather than a substantive one.[62] But the political process is in a state of flux—stasis is not a prolonged condition of Korean political life. In which direction is politics moving in Korea, and what is the prognosis?

In considering the future of political life in Korea, in addition to examining positive factors, we must also look to the obstacles that will stand in the way of political maturity in order to determine the capacity of these elements to retard political growth. Some of these factors are internal; others are externally derived.

Of those external factors that might be involved in the potential collapse or implosion of political progress over the next decade, three stand out as possible, although all are unlikely. The first is the collapse of the world trading system through a universal recession, together with greater trade protectionism—including the Japanese refusal to supply Korea with the technology it now receives—which would cut Korean exports by a significant percentage. Korea is dependent on exports to a degree greater than most developing and developed states. In 1992, the ratio of exports to GNP was 26.1 percent, compared to 9.2 percent for Japan and 7.5 percent for the United States (Taiwan's ratio was 38.6 percent).[63] Korea's internal market is too small to absorb its present production, and a significant absolute decline in exports (although not in the rate of its increase) would have a profound effect on the society. Unemployment would rise, labor would be especially volatile, and the political system would probably be blamed for the crisis. There could be cries for a return to strong (authoritarian) leadership, as well as for controls over labor and other segments of the society.

The second scenario would involve unification with North Korea following what has come to be called the "German model"—that is, the precipitous amalgamation of North Korea into South Korea, the free flow of refugees from the North into the South, leftist students going north, and the collapse of the South Korean standard of living under such pressures. The *Economist* predicted a 25-percent immediate drop in South Korean living standards under such circumstances; others indicate that the costs of unification might run about $140 billion annually—about half of 1991 GNP—for ten years or around $1 trillion over a decade. Equally important, South Korea might try to impose an emergency government—even a resumption of military control—to meet this crisis because such economic and social disruption would likely force the collapse of the extensive South Korean intelligence network, which might cause great concern in military and ruling circles. The South Korean government has recognized that unification through immediate amalgamation is not in its interests (even if every regime stated that reunification was high on its agenda), however much the general concept of unification appeals to the people.

The third possibility is the launching of war by the North and the need to mobilize the South to meet that challenge. This situation would destroy much of the economic and political gains made by South Korea, although in the end that state would prevail even without U.S. support. It should be noted that each of these scenarios, which involve major actions that would impinge upon the Republic, is unlikely although not impossible. The July 1994 death of Kim Il Sung makes more obscure, but necessarily more unlikely, the prospects for immediate conciliation with North Korea simply because the North Korean government needs to consolidate its internal power.

The potential dangers to political progress are more internal, although the eventual triumph of a liberalized regime responsive to the wishes of its people in some Korean manner is likely over time. Such a system may be democratic in a sense that is readily intelligible as such to those from abroad, but equally it may be some unique amalgam of Korean practices that contains all of the elements I indicated earlier that make up democracy (an inclusive, representative, and contending system that guarantees a variety of rights), but does so in some uniquely Korean configuration. Japan has evidently evolved such a system suited to its own culture.

The first of these dangers is increased income inequality. Korea's Gini coefficient, by which income disparities are measured, has been about equal to those of Japan and Taiwan and far better than that of the Philippines. The reasons for this lie in the destruction of assets during the Korean War and in the land reform that equalized poverty in the predominant rural sector at that time. Income distribution has been deteriorating, a state economists often regard as natural under rapid growth conditions. Basically, everyone has become better off, as the incidence of absolute poverty has dropped from about 45 percent in the early 1960s to about 5 percent today (about half the percentage in the United States); those with wealth have gained disproportionally, however, and the disparities have become more obvious and, thus, more politically dangerous. Although income distribution is not too badly skewed, wealth distribution is because in Korea real estate prices have mushroomed, and much wealth resides in land—especially urban land.[64]

The National Assembly has rationalized the rural sector by enlarging the legal size of farms from 3 to 20 hectares. Although this plan may improve production and allow greater mechanization (there are shortages of farm labor, which is very expensive), it would force families off the farm into urban areas and increase the income disparities in the rural sector itself. If the *chaebol* are allowed to invest in agricultural land, they could increase their already massive control over the economy and have important political impacts.[65] A rise in anti-*chaebol* sentiment could be expected.

The issue of business overlaps with that of regionalism. In 1987, twenty-two to twenty-three of the fifty largest business conglomerates were owned by Kyongsang natives, whereas only three or four were in the hands of those from the Chollas. "The same study reports that more than two-thirds [66.7 percent] of the Cholla respondents said that they felt discriminated against in the process of obtaining employment and promotion due to their native [Cholla] origins."[66] For democracy to appear to be efficacious, economic gains and suffering need to be perceived as shared in some manner considered fair by the people, which in itself is a culturally determined concept.

There has been no extensive political polarization of labor in Korea to date, although labor may generally be expected to vote with one of the opposition parties. Class solidarity has not yet developed—political cleavages do not reflect social cleavages—but deprivation could mean the return to the streets for labor in a manner that might force a governmental crackdown on liberties, which are presently growing. The state has attempted to keep intellectuals out of labor unions; the leaders fear infiltration and more radical ideas. Labor remains one of the least democratically oriented fields in Korea.

Another issue is the role of the *chaebol* themselves. They were subject to criticism in the political campaigns of the 1980s and are vulnerable in part because they are so obvious and also because the economy of the state is dependent on their continuing success. Should they persist in growing at rates that outstrip the economy as a whole, and should they become perceived as abusive in their use of power, the state may begin to try to exert even stronger controls over both them and the society to deal with what might be regarded then as a political crisis. In a time of crisis the business community might demand political power to resolve a major depression.

Thus, more generally, a major issue for the future will be the relationship of business to the state. If the partnership is seen as too close—and a close and supportive relationship is in fact essential to the present growth in exports—then corruption may be charged, and small businesspeople might react negatively to the state and the political process on which it is based.[67] Since the state is so dependent upon exports, too distant a relationship could lead to economic decline. A fine line must be walked between the two extremes. The long dirigiste relationship between government and business is not likely to be broken, although the tether the state holds over business is likely to be significantly loosened.[68]

President Kim Young Sam has effectively set out on an anticorruption campaign that has been successful to date, but the issue is one that is not easily or continuously maintained or resolved. Official figures indicate that firms pay around 22 percent of their profits to voluntary donations—that is, to institutions the state deems appropriate, which may be the political parties or some leader's favorite charity or program. These donations are required both socially and politically. This is not the sultanistic corruption for individual gain of a Marcos or a Mobutu; it is institutional corruption that includes an element of institutional growth.

Personal corruption also exists and is important. The question is: When does such corruption revoke political legitimacy or undercut economic development? We could imagine a situation in Korea where this might become a major issue that would retard political progress because groups might feel the need to take actions to stop the cancer in the society. (This is, for example, a current issue in Cambodia.) Each regime, as we have seen, has attempted to purify the preceding regime. At this stage, a level of corruption that would threaten the stability of the state seems unlikely. As the political process expands to local levels, however, the financing of such campaigns has raised cries about the campaigns' excessive costs. Since electioneering is legally limited by time and type of activity, the costs incurred indicate the use of funds in what are evidently illegal manners. In 1994, a new election law was passed that limits campaign financing. This law will be tested in the 1995 local elections, the 1996 National Assembly elections, and the 1997 presidential elections.

Yet the forces for pluralism and democratic consolidation are more likely to prevail over time. The expansion of internationalized education, the changing concepts of power and responsibility, and the development of political institutions that encourage compromise and the sharing of power are all forces that are likely to grow. The historical demand and increased opportunities for social mobility are important causes for political hope and maturity.

The issue of unification remains a potent one—a longing now clouded by questions of costs and security. Looking beyond the process, however, the intense regionalism so evident in South Korea must raise the issue of whether unification might bring with it a more virulent regionalism under a unified peninsula. Koreans from the North have been accepted in the South, but they have been a self-selected, entrepreneurial group whose presence may have been justified to indigenes of the South as refugees.

A further element of opportunity exists for increased internationalization of the values associated with the political process and for a safety valve should economic decline set in. This is the Korean diaspora. There are over 1 million Koreans in the United States and a total of 5 to 6 million outside the peninsula (including perhaps 2 million in Manchuria). Most Korean extended families include members who live or have lived abroad, and many return for short or permanent residence. Many of those in Korea could find employment overseas should conditions warrant or require it. In this manner, foreign influences have begun to become internalized.

To enable the political process to work, Korea requires a concerted effort to encourage mobility in the society in order to meet the demands of both labor and management. As wages rise, this will mean a higher level of productivity, which in the Korean context necessitates new and continually improving levels of technology as Korea loses its competitiveness with the low-wage, labor-intensive states such as China, Vietnam, and Indonesia. The government recognizes this challenge, but it is a major concern that has to be addressed with all of the vigor with which Koreans have approached, for example, their export drive.

Institutional changes offer hope as well. The National Assembly has become a major, positive force with considerable power as an element in the pluralistic political process. It is unlikely to relinquish that role in the future. The judiciary has also matured and has reflected, in its increased autonomy, the new balances of power. It remains the least independent of the three branches of government because of residual negative attitudes toward law in the society, but never before in Korean history has it been so effective. The Korean intelligence agencies remain active but are lacking the pervasive powers of the past.

Might Korea have developed more quickly toward democratic goals under other systems of government? Some would argue that the parliamentary system introduced in 1987 would have been more efficacious than a presidential one in a democratic transition or that the partial proportional system of adding seats to parties getting certain percentages of votes in the legislature should have been eliminated at that time because the party in power had more seats than its percentage of the vote would indicate. These may be accurate observations, but political realities worked against such changes at the time because they raised other political fears.

The process of democratization is likely to be slower than some observers and Koreans might wish and may perhaps be too fast for some of the more traditionally minded. Some argue that it will be more than a generation until democratic attitudes are fully accepted.[69] Yet the prognosis is encouraging for those who believe the balance of rights and freedoms with responsibilities can best be achieved through that remarkably inefficient but equally remarkably enduring system we call democracy. What will occur in Korea will likely be a nationally grown system responsive to Korean social needs—a transplanted, hybrid democracy suited to the peninsula. Such a system that is responsive to local culture is, thus, not easily transferable to other societies. Neither in economics nor in politics can Korea indiscriminately be copied, however impressive its gains. Nor is the United States likely to serve as a model for whatever system evolves in Korea, however strong U.S. influence has been. The Republic of Korea thus remains an example to be studied and appreciated—a work in progress but one that is firmly rooted in its own traditions and culture.

Notes

The author is indebted to Sung-joo Han, the author of the original chapter in the first edition of this work, who at this writing was foreign minister of the Republic of Korea. He bears no responsibility for this chapter, however. The author also wishes to thank those who have read various drafts and offered suggestions. These include Larry Diamond of the Hoover Institution, John Merrill of the Department of State, Ahn Byong-man of Hankuk University of Foreign Studies, Moon Chung-in of Yousei University, and Kang Kyung-wha of Sejong University. The Sejong Institute staff discussed some of the theoretical issues as well. Sins of commission or omission remain, as always, those of the author.

1. The terms *Republic of Korea, South Korea,* and (in context) *Korea* are used interchangeably. When Korea refers to the entire peninsula, it is so stated. North Korea and the Democratic People's Republic of Korea are also used interchangeably.

2. A republic in Korea is a regime in which the constitution has been significantly changed. Thus, the election of Kim Young Sam as president in 1992 is not considered a new republic, as the earlier constitution from 1987 remains in force. The obverse is also true: Park Chung Hee was president under the Third Republic in 1963 (he came to power by coup in 1961) and under the Fourth Republic in 1972, when he introduced the Yushin Constitution ("revitalizing reforms"). The Kim Young Sam government prefers to be known as the civilian regime, rather than as a continuation of the Sixth Republic.

3. Some would claim that only since 1980 has this been an issue. Others contest that it was continually there, masked by other political factors, although it was true that Syngman Rhee and Chang Myon had no personal regional ties of significance.

4. Korean names as used here are normally presented in Korean order—the last name comes first; for example, *Park* Chung Hee, *Yun* Po Sun, *Chang* Myon, and the like. Syngman Rhee is an exception to this rule. Names have been romanized in accordance with the usage of those concerned. Similar last names do not imply relationships; 22 percent of Koreans are named Kim, 18 percent Lee (or Rhee, Yi, and so on). Diacritical marks have been eliminated from all names and places.

5. Gregory Henderson, Richard Ned Lebow, John G. Stoessinger, eds., *Divided Nations*

in a Divided World (New York: David McKay Company, 1974), p. 43. The Koreans still blame the United States for the division since they had no part in the decision, and this topic still incites anti-American attitudes.

6. A confidential (since declassified) Agency for International Development study concluded that U.S. leverage was limited since the Koreans knew the assistance had to be forthcoming because of American security interests and that it could only be delayed for relatively short periods. The real issue was not the assistance but any public U.S. display of dissatisfaction or displeasure with South Korean policies that could have had a destabilizing effect on the regime and that North Korea might exploit. There were many muted U.S. protestations about South Korean political, economic, and human rights policies. In the period from the Korean War to about 1970, North Korea appeared to be more of a threat because its economy was growing at a faster rate than that of South Korea.

7. See Bruce Cumings, *The Origins of the Korean War* (Princeton: Princeton University Press, 1990) (2 volumes).

8. This was also true of U.S. policy in Taiwan during the same period. See Neil H. Jacoby, *U.S. Aid to Taiwan: A Study of Foreign Aid, Self-Help, and Development* (New York: Praeger, 1966).

9. Kim Kyong-su, "Political Parties and Party Politics in Korea," in *Social Science Review,* Symposium on Korean Political Parties (Social Science Research Institute, Sungkyunkwan University, 1967). Kim Kyu-taik, in "A Statistical Analysis of the Elections in Korea" in the same volume, notes, "There were no parties which shared concrete policies and platforms from choice. Rather the personal background, consanguinial regional connections of individual candidates played a vital role in all campaigns."

10. Students have been a critical element in Korean politics. They have been the incipient literati, the heirs to power and prestige in a society that has traditionally been run by the gentry class. The first recorded student political demonstration occurred in the mid-fifteenth century when Confucian students at the state academy felt Buddhist influence was growing at the court. Students have been the conscience of the nation, but as the middle class has grown, higher education has expanded more than ten times since 1961, and the class structure of the student population has become diversified, popular support for student demonstrations has become more discerning and selective.

11. It is significant that until about 1970, North Korea was growing more rapidly than South Korea and had a higher standard of living. Stalinist regimes were effective in mobilizing resources for such reconstruction, but they failed in longer-term economic policies, perhaps because of centralized micro-management. Both North and South Korea were highly interventionist, but South Korea lacked ideological rigor and thus could be more pragmatic in its economic program. For a study of the Rhee period, see John Kie-Chang Oh, *Korea: Democracy on Trial* (Ithaca: Cornell University Press, 1968).

12. For a critical study of the National Security Law and other issues connected with human rights and law, see Laywers for a Democratic Society and the National Council of Churches, *Human Rights in South Korea: A Counter Report to the Human Rights Committee [of the United Nations] on the Initial Report Submitted Under Article 40 of the International Covenant on Civil and Political Rights* (Seoul: Seoul, May 1992). The book contains both the official report and the response and is, thus, especially useful.

13. Party names in South Korea mean little. They have had virtually no relationship to party platforms, which are inconsequential. Parties are generally designed to allow a leader to retain or achieve power, and the names are changed at a sometimes bewildering and rapid rate. Because such names are ephemeral, they are used sparingly in this chapter.

14. For a study of the Second Republic, see Han Sungjoo, *The Failure of Democracy in South Korea* (Berkeley: University of California Press, 1975).

15. The only groups Park did not centralize were student associations, which were considered too volatile and were intentionally splintered. Park also personally controlled top-level military promotions to prevent coup attempts by the officer corps.

16. These minor opposition candidates sponsored by the government were called *sakura,* the Japanese term for cherry blossom.

17. This event, which was extremely unpopular at the time, produced the largest demonstrations since the Student Revolution. As a result of normalization, Korea received $800 million in Japanese aid, investments, and credits over a ten-year period.

18. Kim Dae Jung was saved through the intervention of the American Embassy in Seoul. It was believed that the kidnapped Kim was to be thrown into the sea on a voyage from Japan to Korea. Japan reacted negatively and protested the violation of its sovereignty by the kidnapping on its soil.

19. James B. Palais, "Democracy in South Korea, 1948–1972," in Frank Baldwin, ed., *Without Parallel* (New York: Pantheon Books, 1973).

20. Without such government-approved credit, firms had to resort to the curb (informal) credit market, where interest rates were between two and three times the officially endorsed institutional rates. Firms deemed either politically or economically incorrect could not compete. In addition, firms were in far greater debt than is the case in most states—they owed between 300 and 450 percent of their assets. They expanded using borrowed funds, thus giving the state great leverage over private-sector policies, commodity choices, and personnel—power the state exercised.

21. On August 3, 1972, Park's presidential emergency decree (called the "8-3 decree") replaced high-interest loans with subsidized low-interest, long-term loans for the *chaebol*. See Carter J. Eckert, "The South Korean Bourgeoisie," in Hagen Koo, ed., *State and Society in Contemporary Korea* (Ithaca: Cornell University Press, 1993). This move gave a great fillip to their growth.

22. Park's principal adviser on rural policy said Park was likely to be the last president of Korea from a rural background (unless there was a coup by young officers, who often represented that sector of society) and that the amelioration of the plight of the peasantry was so important that the opportunity should not be lost.

23. It is significant, but often overlooked, that this declaration took place three weeks after President Marcos declared martial law in the Philippines. The Blue House in Seoul had a person monitoring the U.S. reaction to the Marcos self-coup; when there was no major protest, Park believed he could act with impunity without U.S. complaints.

24. Park was once quoted as having said that educated people who broke the laws, such as jaywalking, should be punished more severely than less well-educated people because they should have known better.

25. For a study of the first years of the military coup and its background, see Kim Se-Jin, *The Politics of Military Revolution in Korea* (Chapel Hill: University of North Carolina Press, 1971).

26. This coup, which also moved troops in contravention of UN Combined Forces Command regulations, was not publicly protested by the United States. Regulations called for prior notification of troop movements that might compromise security against North Korea, but the agreements did not stipulate any penalties if this were to happen. The Korean government notified the United Nations (United States, in effect) two days after the coup.

27. The rice crop failure was attributed to cold weather; this was accurate but misleading. The *tong'il* (unification) hybrid, high-yielding variety of rice was mandated by the state for political reasons even though scientists had warned of a likely failure. The superb implementation machinery of the state produced a major crisis. It is important to note that residual Confucian attitudes attribute the fertility of the state to the moral standing of its head; thus, crop failure had political overtones. See David I. Steinberg et al., *Korean Agricultural Research: The Integration of Research and Development* (Washington, D.C.: A.I.D., Impact Evaluation Report no. 27, 1981).

28. In fact, there was an outpouring of population from the Chollas over time because economic opportunities were limited, not only because of the pull of urban jobs and Seoul, which was a ubiquitous influence. From 1970, the two Kyongsang provinces contained about one-third of the total population; the Cholla provinces contained 20 percent in 1970 but had dropped to slightly over 12 percent by 1990. The relative lineup of ministers and vice ministers from these two areas was as follows:

	Kyongsang (%)	Cholla (%)
1963–1980	30.1	13.2
1981–1988	43.6	9.6
1988–1993	37.0	14.8
1993–1994	36.0	17.4

See Wonmo Dong, "Regional Cleavage and Political Change in South Korea" (Paper presented at the Second Pacific Basis International Conference on Korean Studies, Tokyo, July 26–28, 1994).

29. See Donald Clarke, ed., *The Kwangju Uprising: Shadows over the Regime in South Korea* (Boulder: Westview Press, 1988).

30. Some would argue it was not the fact of the visit that was a problem but rather the enthusiasm of the Republican administration in greeting the Korean president.

31. Professor Ahn Byong-man, in *Government and Politics in Korea* (pp. 221–231, in Korean), notes that of all of the presidents until 1992, Park was the most popular and Chun the least popular.

32. In the Philippines, the downfall of Marcos was virtually assured when the business and middle classes of Makati turned against him. In Korea, a similar movement could be discerned.

33. *Korea: Foreign Labor Trends, 1992–93* (Washington: U.S. Department of Labor, 1993).

34. There are many studies of the *chaebol*. For a summary of their role in economic development, see David I. Steinberg, "The Transformation of the Korean Economy," in Donald Clark, ed., *Korea Briefing 1993* (Boulder: Westview Press and The Asia Society, 1993).

35. *Newsreview* (Seoul), June 25, 1994.

36. There was also a widespread belief that the *chaebol* were in favor of inflation, which would reduce the size of their debt.

37. Eckert, "The South Korean Bourgeoisie."

38. Lawyers for a Democratic Society, *Human Rights in South Korea*, p. 51.

39. The U.S. Department of Labor (*Korea: Foreign Labor Trends*) estimates their membership at about 100,000.

40. Sae Wook Chung, "Local and Regional Council Elections in 1991: Features and Political Implications," *Korean Studies* 18 (1994). For a general study of local autonomy history and issues, see Cho Chang-Hyun, "The Politics of Local Self-Government in South Korea," in Kwang-Woong Kim and Yong-duck Jun, eds., *Korean Public Administration and Policy in Transition,* Vol 1 (Seoul: Jangwon Publishing Co., 1993).

41. Larry Diamond, "Democracy in Latin America: Degrees, Illusions, and Directions for Consolidation," in Tim Farer, ed., *Beyond Sovereignty: Collectively Defending Democracy* (Baltimore: Johns Hopkins University Press, 1994).

42. Doh C. Shin, "The Mass Public and Democratic Consolidation in Korea" (Paper presented at the American Political Science Association Annual Meeting, New York, September 1994).

43. See Ahn Byong-man, Kil Soong-hoom, and Kim Kwang-woong, *Elections in Korea.* Seoul: Seoul Computer Press, 1988.

44. Koo, *State and Society in Contemporary Korea*, p.2.

45. The classic discussion of this issue is found in Gregory Henderson, *Korea: Politics of the Vortex* (Cambridge: Harvard University Press, 1968). Korean history is filled with slave and peasant rebellions, in which social registers were frequently prime targets for destruction. The disappearance of a large slave population (said to be larger in percentage terms, although figures are lacking, than that in China) into the peasantry and the buying of official positions are evidence of this mobility.

46. Power is rarely discussed in developmental agencies concerned with democracy-related programs. Institutional reform and training are more often the foci. This may not be an oversight, as the capacity for donor organizations to affect power is marginal at best, whereas it is possible to help reform institutions.

47. For a study of power in Indonesia, see B. Anderson, "The Concept of Power in Javanese Culture," in Claire Holt, ed., *Culture and Politics in Indonesia* (Ithaca: Cornell University Press, 1972). The concept, however, applies to many traditional societies.

48. Many Koreans object to this characterization of their traditional political process because it was used by the Japanese as one excuse for their colonial occupation. It is difficult to see how the issue of factionalism as one prevailing element of the Korean political process can be denied. This is no justification whatsoever for Japanese rule.

49. Doh C. Shin, "Political Parties and Democratization in Korea: The Mass Public and the Democratic Consolidation of Political Parties" (Paper presented at the International Political Science Association XVL World Congress, Germany, August 1994).

50. In the early 1960s one Korean playwright wanted to write a satiric play on the potential for Korean export of political parties, which at that time seemed to be the only thing Korea could produce in quantity.

51. Personal responsibility is an attribute of personal power. If a problem occurs within the responsibility of a ministry, then the minister must resign as a symbol. Thus, the average tenure of ministers in Korea is very short—about a year or less.

To what degree does the individualized power structure and responsibility conflict with the Korean "corporate we"—the grouping of Koreans together for group responsibility in the family, business, or in language, where the use of "we" rather than "I" is the norm? There is a strong sense of Korean corporate identity in facing the external world. Put another way, how much is democracy dependent on individualism, and to what degree, if any? In any society, such inconsistencies can coexist. Thus, in Korea there is a tendency to consider the group—family, clan, entry or graduating class, school, region—before individual rights.

52. Roland Bleiker, Doug Bond, and Myung-Soo Lee, "The Role and Dynamics of Nongovernmental Actors in Contemporary Korea," *Korean Studies* 18 (1994): p. 108.

53. Some would disagree that Korea is a Confucian society, although its influence seems extensive. See, for example, Kim Yongkoo, "Ambiguity in 'The Clash of Civilizations?' A Korean View," *Korea Focus* (January–February 1994).

54. Seung Doo Yang, "Korean Perception of Law and Modernization," *Journal of Asiatic Studies* 31, no. 1 (January 1988).

55. Master Ch'ungdam (c. A. D. 742-765.). Translation by Peter H. Lee, quoted in David I. Steinberg, *The Republic of Korea: Economic Transformation and Social Change* (Boulder: Westview Press, 1989).

56. Uchang Kim, "The Agony of Cultural Construction: Politics and Culture in Modern Korea," in Koo, *State and Soceity in Contemporary Korea.*

57. Daniel Lerner, in *The Passing of Traditional Society* (New York: Free Press, 1958), discusses this issue. Auh Soo-young and Hahn Bae-ho, in "Urbanization and Political Participation in Korea," *Journal of Asiatic Studies* 31, no. 1 (January 1988), note that in Korea, the percentage of voting in rural areas is higher than that in cities and towns.

58. Shin, "Political Parties and Democratization in Korea." Some participation in the past has been mandated by the state, and it is unclear whether such local groups are included.

59. See Henderson, *Korea.*

60. See David I. Steinberg, "The Political Economy in Microcosm: The Korean National Livestock Cooperatives Federation," *Korean Studies* 18 (1994).

61. Stephan Haggard and Chung-in Moon, "The State, Politics, and Economic Development in Postwar South Korea," in Koo, *State and Society in Contemporary Korea.*

62. The distinction was made in a spring 1994 lecture at Georgetown University by Professor Ahn Byung-Jun of Yonsei University.

63. Korean Foreign Trade Association, *Major Statistics of the Korean Economy, 1993* (Seoul: 1994).

64. See D. Leipziger and D. Dollar et al., *The Distribution of Wealth and Income in Korea* (Washington, D.C.: World Bank, 1993).

65. Laws exist limiting businesses in land speculation, where the returns on urban land investments have been far greater than those in production.

66. Dong, "Regional Cleavage and Political Change."

67. The cream of the intellectual elite graduates (from Seoul National University and a few others) find employment in the *chaebol,* which pay higher salaries than smaller firms and the state, thus further limiting the capacities of both to compete with the conglomerates.

68. There is a perception in the United States that Korea has achieved its economic success through the magic of the marketplace. Although the private sector has been important, it has been lead by the center. See Robert Wade, *Managing the Market: Economic Theory and the Role of Government in East Asian Industrialization* (Princeton: Princeton University Press, 1990); World Bank, *The East Asia Miracle: Economic Growth and Public Policy* (Washington, D.C.: World Bank, 1993); and Woo Jung-en, *Race to the Swift: State and Finance in Korean Industrialization* (New York: Columbia University Press, 1990).

69. Doh C. Shin. His survey indicated that although the populace—by about 87 percent—does not want to see a return to military rule and wants a multiparty system, 56 percent does not want free competition among parties, and 79 percent feels more democratic forms are nec-

essary and that the age structure of respondents indicates that more than a generation may be required to change such attitudes. Although available too late for citation, the comprehensive volume by Sung Chul Yang, *The North and South Korean Political Systems: A Comparative Analysis* (Boulder: Westview and Seoul Press, 1994) has data on attitudes toward democracy and the political process.

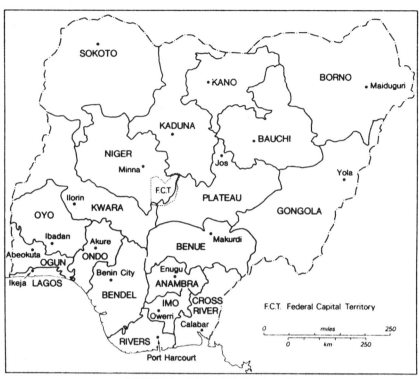

NIGERIA , 1976–1986 (19 States)

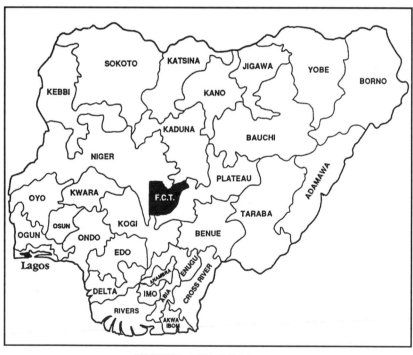

NIGERIA, 1991–? (30 States)

9

Nigeria: The Uncivic Society and the Descent into Praetorianism

Larry Diamond

From bountiful economic promise and vigorous democratic pluralism, Nigeria has descended over the past decade and a half into a developmental abyss. Once an epicenter of democratic energy, idealism, and innovation in Africa, with the freest press on the continent, it has now, by the mid-1990s, been governed continuously for more than a decade by repressive military regimes. Once one of the richest African countries (in national income per capita), it is now among the poorest. Once an assertive advocate for Africa and the Third World in global affairs, it is now financially and morally bankrupt, bereft of support or credibility from international creditors, and condemned in international human rights forums. Once admired for its grand cultural traditions, rapid educational expansion, and dynamic civil society, it is now infamous for its drug trafficking, smuggling, commercial fraud, and endemic corruption. Once a source of pride for African Americans, a rising economic and political giant in Africa, it is now a pariah state, to be sanctioned with the same moral outrage that ostracized South Africa's pariah state. Once a model of ethnic reconciliation and federalist accommodation, it is now again a seething cauldron of deep divisions and inflamed resentments. Once briskly on the road to development and democracy, it has collapsed into praetorianism—an institutional vacuum in which political rules are meaningless and raw power is the only object and arbiter of political affairs.

The progressive erosion of democratic and developmental promise is the overriding story of Nigeria since the early 1980s, but it is not the whole story. Military rule can no longer be termed, as it was routinely even by a succession of ruling generals, an "aberration." Yet Nigerians remain deeply committed to the goal of democracy, and after a decade of incessant venality and abuse, military rule has never been more thoroughly lacking in political legitimacy or societal respect. Indeed, the military has been able to survive in power for more than a decade only by continuously manipulating the promise and process of transition back to civilian, democratic rule.

417

Thus, the Nigerian experience with democracy remains paradoxical and conflicted. Thrice the country has undertaken to govern itself under liberal democratic constitutions, following carefully staged transitions. The first two republics were destroyed by antidemocratic behavior and then ended by popular military coups. The third was similarly undermined, before it was even fully born, by rank opportunism, fraud, and greed on the part of the politicians, but with the military actively orchestrating the destruction of its own democratic transition. And yet, Nigeria has never been content with authoritarian rule, and no military regime that has not committed itself to a democratic transition has been able to survive. Through three and a half tumultuous decades of independence—encompassing nine governments, six successful military coups, many other coup attempts, a civil war, and a dizzying economic boom followed by a crushing depression—Nigerians have maintained a passionate devotion to political freedom and participation.

Why has this commitment not produced a developing democracy? Why have political institutions repeatedly collapsed, and more recently, a promising program of economic reform along with them? Why the descent into praetorianism?

As this chapter shows, the explanation is cultural and social, but the real causal origins of Nigeria's developmental decay are political and institutional. At one level of explanation lies a culture of self-interest, fragmentation, exploitation, cynicism, dishonesty, and distrust—a striking absence of enduring shared commitments to the formal political community, most of all to the nation but also to lower levels of political authority (even ethnically homogeneous ones). This culture is reinforced by a fragmented and hierarchical social structure, in which horizontal networks of (more or less egalitarian) civic engagement and social exchange are largely absent or superficial, and social life is organized vertically into pyramids of patron-client relations, with material rewards flowing from the top down and support from the bottom up. Following upon the seminal work of Robert Putnam, I call this phenomenon "the uncivic society," denoting a political culture and social structure stunningly lacking the "horizontal relations of reciprocity and cooperation" (cutting across social cleavages) that breed the "honesty, trust, and law abidingness" that mark the "civic community."[1]

As Putnam and his colleagues have shown for the different regions of Italy, the presence of civic values and social structures is strongly correlated with democratic effectiveness and economic prosperity. In Italy, Putnam and his collaborators argue, these differing civic traditions can be traced far back in time. In Nigeria—a colonial construction from multiple peoples—where the challenge is to explain why the entire postcolonial system has become "uncivic," different causal dynamics appear. To be sure, many of Nigeria's ethnic communities had more or less "civic" traditions of horizontally bound "cooperatives and cultural associations and mutual aid societies" with strong ties of trust and reciprocity.[2] But as Peter Ekeh has argued in a highly influential analysis, these "primordial" norms and traditions of honesty and reciprocity did not carry over into the arena of the modern state, an alien institution toward which no primordial group felt any sense of ownership or identification.[3] Instead, the modern state was a resource, devoid of moral content or attachment, to be pursued, occupied, milked—and later plundered—for the individual politician and his support group. Unless the modern Nigerian state could become the subject of political identification across ethnic and communal lines, and unless it could impose strong institutional constraints against corrupt behavior in state office, these patterns were bound to intensify over time and to shape more and more profoundly patterns of political engagement at all levels.

The sudden boom in petroleum-based state revenue, and the failure of successive political regimes to impose effective legal and institutional constraints on the personal accumulation of state wealth, crystallized the emergent trends toward uncivicness in the formal political arena. As the struggle to capture ever larger amounts of state wealth became the overriding purpose of politics, parties and coalitions became more fleeting and opportunistic. Rules of any kind became increasingly fragile and untenable, and democracy increasingly hollow and superficial. Some civilian politicians came to recognize that, in the shrewd observation of President Shehu Shagari during the Second Republic (1979–1983), there were really only two parties in the country: the civilians and the military. What they did not comprehend—or could not organize themselves to overcome—was the primal principle that in a ruleless, Hobbesian struggle, the party with the guns always prevails.

Historical Review

Developments Before Independence

Nigeria has an enormous diversity of ethnic groups, as indicated by the presence of some 248 distinct languages.[4] Many of these linguistic groups are tiny and politically insignificant. But three comprise collectively two-thirds of the population: the Hausa-Fulani (two peoples who are typically grouped together because of their substantial cultural and political integration), the Yoruba, and the Igbo (see Table 9.l). In this respect, Nigeria has what Horowitz would term a relatively "centralized" ethnic structure, which presents a greater challenge to ethnic harmony.[5]

Although there were significant democratic traditions among the more decentralized and acephalous of Nigeria's ethnic groups (such as the Igbo and Tiv), and mechanisms for limiting power in the constitutional monarchies of the Yoruba, the history of democratic government in Nigeria must

Table 9.1   **Distributions of Nigerian Ethnic Groups, 1952–1953 and 1963**

Group	Percent of Population[a]		
	1952–1953		1963
Hausa	18.2 ⎫		
Fulani	9.9 ⎬ 28.1		29.5
Kanuri		4.2	4.1
Tiv		2.5	2.5
Nupe		1.1	1.2
Yoruba		16.6	20.3
Edo		1.5	1.7
Igbo		17.9	16.6
Ibibio-Efik		2.7	3.6
Ijaw		1.1	2.0
Total: Hausa-Fulani, Yoruba, and Igbo		62.6	66.4

Source: Etienne Van de Walle, "Who's Who and Where in Nigeria," *Africa Report* 15, no. 1 (1970).

a. The census has been a subject of continuing scholarly debate and political conflict in Nigeria for three decades, and hence no set of figures can be accepted as precise. Because the 1963 census was ensnarled in intense controversy, the 1952–1953 figures, compiled by the more neutral colonial administration in a less politically charged atmosphere, may represent more accurately the demographic balance of peoples.

begin with the history of the modern Nigerian state, the creation of British colonial rule. For half a century—from the time that separate protectorates were declared for Northern and Southern Nigeria in 1900 to the Constitutional Conference of 1950—Nigeria was ruled in essentially authoritarian fashion by the colonial power. But that fashion was not uniform across the country. Even after the formal amalgamation of the two protectorates in 1914, the British continued to rule Nigeria, in effect, as two countries. In the North, a native authority system was constructed to rule indirectly through the centralized and steeply hierarchical structures of traditional authority in the Muslim emirates. In the South, where power was more dispersed and there was more accountability of rulers to ruled, indirect rule worked poorly and even broke down in places. At the same time, Western (European) education and religion were permitted to spread rapidly in the South but heavily restricted in the Muslim North, creating enormous disparities in economic and technological development. In addition, political participation was permitted earlier in the South. From 1923 until 1947, only Southern Nigerians were allowed to elect members of the Legislative Council (advisory to the British governor).[6]

The separate character of development in Nigeria, and the political tensions to which it gave rise, were rooted in the regional structure created by the British. In 1939, Nigeria was divided into four administrative units: the colony of Lagos, and the Western, Eastern, and Northern Provinces. The power of these provinces grew, and in 1951 they were designated "regions," becoming constituent units in a quasi-federal system. The boundaries of these regions coincided with and reified the primary ethnic division in the country: the Igbo were the dominant group in the East, the Yoruba in the West, and the Hausa-Fulani in the North. But each region also contained significant minorities of other ethnic groups that feared and resented the domination of these "big tribes." Despite the intense lobbying for separate states by ethnic minority groups throughout the decade, and the profound concerns of Southerners about a system in which one region, the North, was more populous than all the others combined, the British were unalterably committed to this regional structure, and "after 1948 every effort was made to encourage 'regional thinking.'"[7]

The decisive first step toward self-rule and popular participation came in 1948, with several reforms in response to rising nationalist agitation. Africanization of the senior civil service was accelerated. The native authority system was democratized, and scrapped altogether in the East, in favor of a hierarchy of elected councils. Primary and secondary education were rapidly expanded and colonial efforts were extended to higher education.[8] Most important, a process of constitutional revision was launched that entailed extensive and unprecedented popular participation.

Out of this two-year process came the 1951 constitution, which launched the first period of full-scale electoral politics in Nigeria.[9] This provided for regional assemblies elected indirectly through a system of electoral colleges and a central legislature (half from the North) elected by the regional assemblies. No provision was yet made at either level for elected executives.[10]

The 1951 constitution made the regions the most important locus of political life. Through the end of colonial rule and the life of the First Republic, the growing regional emphasis was to tilt the national political balance decisively in favor of conservative forces, as the British had no doubt intended. Growing regional autonomy protected the position of the aristocratic Northern ruling class from the challenge and infiltration of better-educated and more cosmopolitan Southern elites and from any interference by the central government.[11] Moreover, the Northern Region's absolute population majority in the country made it likely that its dominant class would also be the dominant political force in Nigeria. But inherent in this strange federal structure was an explosive contradiction between the political power of the North and the socioeconomic power of the South, which generated deep insecurity and recurrent conflict.[12]

The regional system made control of regional government the sine qua non for both traditional and rising elements of the emergent political class.[13] This put an enormous premium on the 1951 regional elections. Given the coincidence of regional with ethnic group boundaries, it was virtually inevitable that these first elections would see the organization of political parties along ethnic and regional lines. Hence, although the leading nationalist organization, the National Council of Nigeria and the Cameroons (NCNC), had sought with some success to reach out beyond its Igbo core to construct a multiethnic, national base, it was able to win only the election in the Eastern Region. In the West and North, power was captured by openly regionalist political parties formed by ethnic elites for the express purpose of winning regional power against the challenge of the Igbo-led and better-organized NCNC.[14] In the West, the formation of the Yoruba-dominated Action Group (AG) followed years of intense competition between Yoruba and Igbo elites.[15] In the North, the transformation of the Northern Peoples' Congress (NPC) from a sagging cultural organization into a modern political party was in defense of both class and ethnic interests.[16]

The aggressive mobilization of Southern parties and groups stirred a "political awakening" among a new generation of Northern elites whose exposure to Western education had bred reformist inclinations and who had become alarmed to discover their region's massive and pervasive disadvantage in every aspect of modernization.[17] The social dominance of the traditional ruling class of the Northern emirates (the *sarakuna*) was threatened by political competition not only from militant and culturally alien Southerners, determined to dismantle the "feudalistic" structures of the emirates, but also from radical young Northern commoners (*talakawa*) similarly pledged to sweeping reform. Stunned by victories of the radical party, the Northern Elements Progressive Union (NEPU), in the early stages of the 1951 Northern elections, the "awakened" Northern elites revitalized the NPC just in time to win a sweeping victory in the final stage of voting.[18]

The 1951 victories of the NPC, the AG, and the NCNC in their home regions established a close identity between region, party, and ethnicity that was to heighten over the course of the 1950s. The constitution of 1954 not only created a genuinely federal system, but gave enormous autonomy and control over resources to each of the three regions. As the regions became the primary centers of power and wealth in Nigeria, the struggle between their ruling parties for socioeconomic resources came to dominate Nigerian politics. This struggle was manifested in repeated political conflicts over such issues as the timing of self-government, revenue allocation, and the NPC's effort to purge Southerners from the Northern bureaucracy and economy. But most of all, it was evinced in electoral competition.

Political competition during colonial rule peaked in the federal elections of 1959. By then, Nigeria had conducted three regional elections in the East, two each in the North and West, and one in the federation as a whole. The subsequent regional elections had tightened the grip of the ruling parties, but in the 1954 federal elections, the NCNC won not only in the East, but also (narrowly) in the West, joining the NPC in a coalition of expedience at the center. When the office of federal prime minister was created in 1957,

NPC President Ahmadu Bello chose (significantly) to remain the premier of the North, and the party's vice-president, Abubakar Tafawa Balewa, became prime minister. He then constructed a coalition cabinet embracing all three major parties. But this grand coalition would last only until the 1959 elections, which would produce the first fully elected national government and the one that would lead the country to independence the following year.

As with previous campaigns of the decade, the 1959 campaign was characterized by blatant appeals to ethnic prejudice and vituperative rhetoric, which completely drowned out the substance of party programs and proposals. Also, violence and repression marred the democratic character of the campaign. Repression was most prevalent in the North, where the NPC regularly used its control of traditional systems of justice and administration to obstruct, harass, and punish opposition candidates and their supporters. This repression reached new levels in 1959. Perhaps because electoral outcomes were not so much secured through institutional means of repression in the South, the campaigns were much more violent there. From the inception of electoral competition in 1951, parties fielded bands of thugs to disrupt, intimidate, and attack the opposition, and incidents resulting in injuries in the hundreds were not uncommon. In the high stakes of the 1959 election, such violence spread to the North as well, frequently victimizing Southern and NEPU campaigners.[19]

Despite the significant antidemocratic currents in the 1959 election, the "steel frame" of colonial administration maintained some semblance of political order and electoral integrity, and the keen anticipation of independence produced a postelection spirit of accommodation. Although battered by the extraordinary bitterness of the campaign, the tacit preelection alliance between the NPC and the NCNC matured into a coalition government led by the former, which was only a few seats short of an absolute majority in Parliament. The alliance was facilitated not only by the NCNC's desire to bridge the North-South divide on the eve of independence, but also by both parties' resentment of the AG's aggressive efforts to mobilize ethnic minority groups in their regions.

The First Republic

Nigeria thus achieved independence on October 1, 1960, with a functioning parliamentary system. Legislative power was vested in an elected Parliament, especially in the powerful lower chamber, the House of Representatives, which was responsible for the laws and finances of the federation. Executive power was vested in a cabinet, headed by a prime minister, who was to be appointed by the governor-general (and, after October 1, 1963, when Nigeria became a republic, by the president) upon demonstrating majority support in the House. Judicial power was vested in an independent court system, including a Federal Supreme Court with power to decide cases involving the constitutions and laws of the federation and the regions.[20]

Constitutionally, the system was democratic. Power was distributed among three branches of government. Regular parliamentary elections were required at least every five years. In the North, political rights were restricted to males. Otherwise, political and civil liberties were formally guaranteed in the constitution's detailed chapter on fundamental rights.

There were also other democratic features of the political landscape. A number of political parties competed for power. Their contestation was increasingly flawed, but still it existed. And although plagued by zealous partisanship, inexperience, irresponsibility, and economic and political pressure from the parties and governments that owned most of the newspapers,[21] the Nigerian press was a significant source of political pluralism and critical inquiry. In fact, some outside observers saw it as "the most potent institution supporting democratic freedom in Nigeria."[22]

In other dimensions, however, Nigeria fell much wider of the democratic mark. Loopholes in the constitution facilitated abuse. Each provision on human rights excepted laws that were "reasonably justifiable in a democratic society" in the interest of national defense, public order, etc. These exceptions could be widened much further during a state of emergency, which could be declared by a simple majority vote of each house of Parliament. In addition, the constitution enabled Parliament (by a two-thirds vote of each house) to take over the lawmaking functions of a regional government. In a system where parliamentary opposition was regionally based, this created enormous potential for intimidation.

More troubling was the actual performance of political actors. In all three regions, regional powers were used increasingly to harass and repress political opposition. In the North, "the freedoms normally regarded as essential if a two-party system is to work simply [did] not exist."[23] Genuine political competition was becoming constricted to the federal arena, as one-party states emerged in each region. In the regional elections of 1960 and 1961, each ruling party significantly consolidated its dominance, leaving the opposition shattered and demoralized.

Beyond escalating the insecurity in the federal system, the regional elections exposed again the shallow commitment of political elites to democratic norms of tolerance and fair play. These antidemocratic currents make it difficult to classify Nigeria at independence as a democracy. It was a semidemocracy struggling to establish fully democratic government.

The assault on the edifice of democracy continued relentlessly over the five and a quarter years of the First Republic. During these years, the political system was buffeted by a succession of five major crises that heightened ethnic and regional polarization, intensified political violence and intolerance, and heavily eroded the popular legitimacy of the regime.

The first crisis began as an internal conflict within the ruling party of the Western Region, pitting the AG national leader, Chief Obafemi Awolowo, who resigned as premier in 1959 to lead the party's federal campaign, against his successor as premier, Chief S. L. Akintola. The conflict was partially personal and factional, but also heavily ideological. Long committed to a moderate socialist program, Chief Awolowo moved, after the AG's sweeping 1959 defeat, to a much more radical stance, vowing to replace the regional system with a structure of multiple states and to forge a political alliance against the NPC. A transformation of the regional system threatened not only to unravel the social and political dominance of the Northern ruling class, but also to weaken the political classes of the Eastern and Western Regions, since smaller regions would mean smaller bases of patronage for the ruling parties and very likely different ruling parties in some of the new regions. Regionalism thus coincided with the conservatism of the Akintola faction, while Awolowo's antiregionalism was the logical spearhead of his radical challenge to the status quo.[24]

In a federal system with only three regions, no serious political conflict could long remain contained within a single region. When the Awolowo faction succeeded in deposing Chief Akintola as premier, the NPC/NCNC Federal Coalition took action. Seizing upon internal disorder in the Western Region House, it declared an emergency and prevented the Awolowo faction from taking power. After six months of heavily biased emergency rule, Chief Akintola was reinstated as premier at the helm of a new party. By the time the full effects of federal emergency rule had been felt, a fourth region (the Mid-Western) had been created out of the Western Region, Chief Awolowo and his close associates had been convicted of treason and sentenced to prison, and the AG had been destroyed as a national political force. The crisis not only alienated a large segment of Nigerian youth and intelligentsia who had been attracted to Awolowo's radical egalitarian appeals, but it also left the Yoruba feeling victimized as a people.[25]

The second crisis partially overlapped the first. By 1962, Nigerians were being mobilized intensively for the national census. With the distribution of power and resources between the regions hanging on its outcome, the census became the object of heated political competition. Controversy flared when the initial results revealed much larger population increases in the South—sufficient to end the North's population majority—and demographic tests showed some of the Eastern Region's figures to have been "grossly inflated." When the North then claimed to have discovered 8 million people more in a "verification check" (thus preserving its population majority), the ensuing crisis forced Prime Minister Tafawa Balewa to cancel the census and order a new one for later in 1963. But now that the census had been blatantly established as an instrument of ethnic and regional competition, mass political mobilization was even more intense and mutual suspicion even more profound. The result was a still greater fiasco—an "altogether incredible" national increase of 83 percent in ten years and a continued Northern population majority.[26] Despite bitter rejection by the Eastern Region's NCNC government, the NPC used its parliamentary power to win official acceptance of the figures.

The census crisis not only heightened the salience of ethnicity and region in politics, but it also marked the beginning of fiercely polarized competition between the NPC and the NCNC, who were both looking toward the critical federal election due before the end of 1964. With the decimation of the Action Group, the political system was realigning around a bipolar struggle: As progressive elements of the NCNC and AG began to unite, Chief Akintola's party moved closer to the NPC. But before these sectional tensions could cumulate in the electoral struggle, a third crisis erupted.

Late in 1963, wage laborers in Nigeria began to focus their indignation over declining real income and gross economic inequality into militant demands for government attention and higher pay. For the next year, the severely fractured trade union movement united in a concerted challenge to the country's political class. Following months of government arrogance and procrastination, the unions launched a devastating general strike in June 1964, which brought the economic life of the nation to a standstill for thirteen days. In addition to the overwhelming support of Nigerian workers, both organized and unorganized, the strike also drew widespread popular support, especially in the cities.[27] This came in response to the larger political issues in the strike: the enormous disparities in the official wage structure and the glaring corruption and extravagant consumption of the nation's political elite. The strike also drew some support from progressive AG and NCNC politicians, but it was really an expression of disgust with the entire political class. Although the government was finally compelled to make significant concessions, the effect of the strike was to further weaken the regime's legitimacy and to expose the weakness of its authority.[28]

By the time the strike was over, the two leading parties were busy organizing contending alliances for the 1964 federal election. The NCNC first formed an alliance with the Action Group, which was joined on September 1 by NEPU and the minority party of the Christian lower North in the United Progressive Grand Alliance (UPGA). Meanwhile, the NPC drew in Chief Akintola's party and various minor Southern parties to form the Nigerian National Alliance (NNA). These alliances—dominated by the Igbos of the East and the Hausa-Fulani of the North—reduced national politics to a bipolar struggle along the great cumulative divide of ethnicity, region, and party, reinforced by the ideological cleavage between progressive, antiregionalist forces (in UPGA) and conservative, regionalist forces (in the NNA).

With the entire distribution of national power and resources at stake, electoral conflict became more abrasively "tribalistic" and more violent than ever before. The class consciousness of the June general strike was drowned in an emotional resurgence of ethnic attachments,[29] and the democratic character of the 1964 election was obliterated by organized political thuggery and official obstruction and repression of opposition campaigns.[30] This led UPGA to boycott the election, provoking a tense showdown between the NPC prime minister and the NCNC president of Nigeria in which, for several days, the specter of secession and possible civil war loomed large. Wishing to avoid mass bloodshed, and unable to win military and police support, President Nnamdi Azikiwe finally yielded, and the NPC returned to the federal government more powerful than ever, with the NCNC obtaining a reduced role in a new and even more superficial coalition government. For the third consecutive time, the NPC had triumphed totally in a decisive confrontation with a Southern party.

This pattern prevailed through the final crisis of the First Republic, the October 1965 Western Region election, which pitted Chief Akintola's ruling party and the Action Group in a do-or-die struggle for control of the West. Hated for its corruption, extravagance, neglect, and collaboration with the "oppressor" of the Yoruba people, the Akintola regime was compelled to employ massive coercion as a substitute for legitimate authority. Still, it had to resort to wholesale electoral fraud to salvage a claim to reelection. With the announcement of this preposterous result, the Western Region erupted into popular rebellion. The wave of violence and destruction made the region effectively ungovernable. This only further accelerated the process of political decay, which had been advanced earlier in the year by a spate of scandals involving federal government corruption and by a growing consciousness of the degree to which official corruption, swollen salaries, waste, and recurrent political crises were squandering the nation's resources. These developments combined to rob the regime of what little legitimacy it still retained, especially among the educated "counter-elite" in the intelligentsia, the civil service, and the military.

Military Rule, 1966–1975

On January 15, 1966, a group of young army majors and captains overthrew the First Republic, assassinating the prime minister, the premiers of the Western and Northern Regions, and a number of high-ranking military officers. Although an ethnic motive has been deduced from their predominantly Igbo composition and the fact that leading Igbo politicians were spared, the coupmakers struck primarily "to end a corrupt and discredited despotism that could only be removed by violence."[31] Their disgust with the First Republic was shared by a broad cross-section of the population, which welcomed the coup in an effusive outpouring of joy and relief. However, the young coupmakers failed fully to execute their plans, and governmental power was wrested from them by one of their intended victims, Major General J. T. U. Aguiyi Ironsi, general officer commanding of the Nigerian army, who—like most of the plotters—was Igbo.

Initially, General Ironsi struck swiftly against corruption and graft, detaining a number of former political officeholders. He also promised an early return to civilian rule, appointing panels to draft a new constitution and to study problems of the judiciary and economy. But in administering the country, Ironsi tended to confirm mounting fears and suspicions (especially in the North) that the coup had been designed to impose Igbo hegemony on the country.

As concern grew over Igbo bias in his military promotions and choice of political advisers, Ironsi blundered disastrously on May 24, 1966. "Without waiting for the report of his constitutional study group or submitting their report to the promised constituent assembly," he announced a new constitution abolishing the federal system and unifying the regional and federal public services.[32] For Northerners, who had long feared that their educational disadvantage could open the way for Southern domination of their civil service (and the entire state system), this was anathema. Within days, hundreds of Igbos were killed in riots in Northern towns. Although Ironsi backed away somewhat from his original plan, Northern alarm and bitterness persisted, culminating in a bloody countercoup by Northern officers in July, which killed Ironsi and many other Igbo officers and soldiers. Out of the chaos and uncertainty, the army chief of staff, Lieutenant Colonel Yakubu Gowon, a Northern Christian from a minority ethnic group, emerged as a compromise choice for head of state.

At first, Gowon also spoke in terms of an early return to civilian rule. After reinstating the old regional system, he organized meetings of regional opinion leaders to prepare the groundwork for a constitutional conference. There support gathered for a stronger central government and the creation of more states. But Gowon could not bridge the years of enmity and suspicion, nor heal the wounds of two bloody coups. With the Eastern Region's governor and military commander, Colonel Chukwuemeka Ojukwu, refusing to recognize Gowon's authority, and with Eastern Region delegates insisting on extensive regional autonomy, the deliberations stalled and were abruptly ended in early October 1966 by a new wave of Igbo massacres in the North. Subsequently, more than a million Igbos poured back into the Eastern Region while Ojukwu ordered all non-Easterners to leave.

The soldiers proved even less adept than the politicians at managing the country's explosive divisions. Amid rising secessionist pressure in the East, efforts to negotiate some kind of compromise, confederal arrangement failed. With centrifugal pressures also growing in the West and Mid-West, the Northern emirs finally agreed to the creation of additional states as the only hope for preserving the federation. On May 27, 1967, Gowon announced the division of the country into twelve states (six in the North, and three each in the East and West). This at once broke the monolithic power of the North and granted the long-standing aspirations of ethnic minorities, who along with the Yoruba, found their commitment to the federation renewed. But the alienation of the Igbo was now irreparable. Three days later, Ojukwu announced the secession of the Eastern Region as the Republic of Biafra, and in early July the Nigerian civil war began.

Short of total defeat in war, there is probably no greater trauma for a nation than civil war. For the East in particular, which suffered immense destruction and hundreds of thousands of military and civilian fatalities, the thirty-month war was a horrific experience. Nevertheless, Nigeria emerged from the experience with a hopeful future, owing in part to General Gowon's magnanimous policy of reconciliation with the defeated East, and in part to the development of oil production, which by the end of the war in January 1970 was beginning to generate substantial revenue. With the specter of national disintegration now definitively laid to rest and a more effective federal system in place, attention turned to two overriding national problems: reconstruction of the economy and society, and renewal of civilian democratic government.

As part of the war effort, the public had accepted stern authoritarian measures, including strict controls on trade unions, a ban on strikes, and a crackdown on movements for new states.[33] But these were seen as temporary and democratic aspirations remained strong. Moreover, the presence in the wartime government of prominent civilians, led by the previously jailed Chief Obafemi Awolowo, had maintained some continuity with civilian rule.

With the end of the war, Nigerians eagerly awaited the military's program for transition to civilian rule. Not until ten months later, on October 1, 1970, was it announced. The military was to remain in power for another six years while it reorganized the armed forces, revived the economy eradicated corruption, conducted a new census, and managed the drafting of a new constitution and the resolution of such thorny questions of additional states and revenue allocation. Following this, genuinely national political parties would be organized and elections conducted. Although many Nigerians, not least the former politicians, were stunned and disappointed by the length of the transition, the setting of a definite date for return to civilian rule met with popular favor.

As oil production reached 2 million barrels a day in 1973 and oil prices quadrupled during 1973 and 1974, Nigeria entered a breathtaking economic boom. Ironically, this was when the popular consensus behind Gowon's rule began to unravel. Once more, the census generated a damaging political crisis, as it produced not only an incredible total count but bitterly disputed state results. With the North preserving its population majority by an even larger margin than in 1963, the census drowned in charges of fraud and ethnic domination, and the results were never formally adopted.

Alarmed by the resurgence of ethnic conflict, realizing that little progress had been made on most of the points of his transition program, and pressured by an increasingly venal circle of ruling military officers at the federal and state levels who sought to extend their control over the newly bountiful resources of power, Gowon shocked the nation on October 1, 1974, when he indefinitely postponed the return to civilian rule.[34]

At the time of his announcement, General Gowon committed himself to new reforms: a new constitution, new states, new military governors, and new federal commissioners. But no progress was forthcoming on any of these fronts in the subsequent ten months. Popular disillusionment sharply intensified as the twelve state governors, arrogant and brazen in their corruption, became ever more entrenched, while venality and mismanagement exacted a mounting toll on the national economy as well. The inept handling of the Udoji Commission's proposals for large wage increases for government workers brought a steep rise in inflation that reduced the purchasing power of urban workers. Strikes crippled banking and health services. Shortages of essential commodities occurred. The ports became hopelessly jammed with ships waiting to off-load fantastic amounts of cement inexplicably ordered by the government. And in yet another scandal, severe shortages of gasoline mysteriously developed, forcing dawn-to-dusk queues. General Gowon became increasingly remote not only from public opinion and protest, but from military officers outside his narrow ruling circle, who worried increasingly that the corruption and mismanagement of his regime were dragging the entire armed forces into disrepute.[35]

The Transition to the Second Republic

On July 29, 1975, General Gowon was overthrown in a bloodless coup by reform-minded senior officers determined to clear out the rot in the government and bureaucracy and return the country to civilian rule. The new head of state, Brigadier Murtala Muhammed, moved swiftly and boldly to achieve these goals. To great popular acclaim, he removed the twelve state governors within hours of taking power. Over the following weeks, more than 10,000 civil servants at every level of government were dismissed for abuse of office or unproductivity. Following this, the army itself was purged, and plans were drawn up to reduce its size from 250,000 to 100,000. Commissions were appointed to investigate several major scandals and the assets of public officers, to study and make recommendations on the creation of new states, and to explore the possibility of moving the federal capital from impossibly congested Lagos.

Most significant of all, Murtala Muhammed responded forthrightly to the mounting pressures for a transition to democracy. Through the previous decade of military rule, democratic aspirations had remained alive. These were sustained in part by the vigor of the Nigerian press, which, despite repressive decrees and continuous threats, harassment, and arrests, managed to preserve its freedom and integrity to a considerable degree.[36] "In the absence of a democratically elected Parliament, newspapers found themselves playing the role of a deliberative assembly, reflecting the feelings of the people [about] . . . government policies and actions."[37] Risking imprisonment, journalists and editors had taken the lead in exposing and denouncing corruption; in demanding the release of political detainees, the lifting of press restraints, and the restoration of other liberties; and in criticizing government policies and performance.[38] Through repeated strikes, boycotts, declarations, demonstrations, and other means of mass mobilization, university students also played a crucial role in demanding accountability, responsiveness, and basic freedoms from the Gowon government.[39]

On October 1, 1975, General Muhammed announced a precise deadline and detailed timetable for the restoration of civilian, democratic government. In five stages over a period of four years, a new constitutional and political foundation was to be carefully laid. First, the issue of new states would be resolved and a Constitutional Drafting Committee would be given twelve months to produce a draft constitution. Second, local government would be reorganized and new local governments elected, to be followed by the election of a Constituent Assembly to review and amend the draft constitution. Stage three would lift the ban on political parties by October 1978. Stage four would elect state legislatures and stage five a federal government, in time to transfer power to "a democratically elected government of the people" by October 1, 1979.[40]

Despite the tragic assassination of Murtala Muhammed in a failed coup attempt on February 13, 1976—when he was riding the crest of an unprecedented wave of national popularity—and despite a bitter debate within the Constituent Assembly over whether to establish an Islamic *shari'a* court of appeal at the federal level—which threatened explosive religious and regional polarization until it was resolved by compromise and skillful mediation[41]—General Muhammed's timetable was implemented faithfully and skillfully by his successor, General Olusegun Obasanjo.

Several aspects of the transition process appeared to augur well for the future of democracy in Nigeria. The volatile issue of new states, which had been the focus of intense ethnic and subethnic political mobilization, was tackled early and decisively with the creation of seven more states in April 1976. In addition to creating several new ethnic minority states, the major Yoruba state was broken into three states and the major Igbo state was split in two. The new nineteen-state system—containing four predominantly Hausa-Fulani states, four Yoruba, two Igbo, and nine ethnic minority states—seemed likely to weaken the ethnic and regional solidarities that had cursed the First Republic and to generate a more fluid and shifting pattern of alignments, with state interests representing an independent and, at least occasionally, crosscutting line of cleavage.[42]

The concern for generating crosscutting cleavages was also evident in the new constitution, which explicitly prohibited sectional parties and required broad ethnic representation in each party as a condition for recognition.[43] Including in the constitution provisions for an executive presidency, and requiring a presidential candidate to win at least a quarter of the vote in at least two-thirds of all the states in order to be directly elected, had a similar purpose. Together with the creation of a powerful Federal Electoral Commission (FEDECO) to certify parties and regulate campaigning, these innovations in "institutional architecture" seemed to produce a more durable political foundation.[44]

The new constitution was an elaborate and carefully crafted document. Closely modeled after the U.S. system, it provided for an elected president and vice-president (eligible for no more than two four-year terms); a bicameral National Assembly (with five senators from each state, elected by district, and 450 members of the House of Representatives, elected from federal constituencies of equivalent population); an independent judiciary, headed by a Supreme Court and State High Courts, with courts of appeal below them; and a detailed chapter on "fundamental human rights," guaranteeing not only life, liberty, and due process, but essential freedoms of expression, association, peaceful assembly, movement, and the press. The constitution's Fifth Schedule also contained an extensive new Code of Conduct for Public Officers, along with a bureau and tribunal for monitoring and enforcing compliance with its provisions.

Also auspicious was the widespread popular participation in the transition process. In the six months following the presentation of the draft constitution in December 1976, the country became consumed with a free and vigorous debate on its provisions, which continued in the deliberations of the elected Constituent Assembly.[45] The thoroughness and freedom of the public debate and the national consensus behind its result suggested that "Nigeria's Second Republic was established upon a genuinely popular foundation"[46] that gave legitimacy to its political institutions.[47]

The process of transition did not give the same careful attention to the development of political party institutions, however. Not until three of the four years had passed was the ban on political parties lifted. Aspiring political parties then had only three months to apply to FEDECO for registration. In this brief period, they had to establish a national network of local and state branches, elect party officials, and conduct national conventions. After thirteen years of prohibition of political parties, this severe compression of the period for political party development had precisely the consequences the military hoped to avoid: Most truly fresh political formations either fractured into more familiar forms or died stillborn. Only nineteen of some fifty emergent parties were able to file papers by the mid-December (1978) deadline, and of these only five were certified by FEDECO.[48]

These five new parties bore a strong resemblance to the parties of the First Republic, in part because of significant continuities in their leaderships and regional bases. Thus the Unity Party of Nigeria (UPN), strongest in the Yoruba states and led by Chief Obafemi Awolowo, struck many as the reincarnation of the Action Group. The National Party of Nigeria (NPN), based most powerfully in the far north and led in the presidential elections by former NPC Minister Alhaji Shehu Shagari, was widely seen as the successor to the NPC. The Nigerian Peoples Party (NPP), reduced primarily to an Igbo base after a damaging split cost it much of its northern support,[49] and then nominating Dr. Nnamdi Azikiwe as its presidential candidate, was seen to reproduce the NCNC. And the Peoples Redemption Party (PRP), also based in the emirate north and led by Mallam Aminu Kano, seemed to reincarnate the radical NEPU, which he had led in the First Republic. Only the Great Nigerian Peoples Party (GNPP), which split from the NPP when its leader, Waziri Ibrahim, refused to step aside for Dr. Azikiwe as presidential candidate, could not be obviously linked to a major party of the First Republic.

In fact, each of these parties was broader than its supposed antecedent in the First Republic. In particular, the NPN represented the broadest ethnic base ever assembled by a Nigerian party, perhaps the first truly "national" party in the nation's history. Although party power was based on the aristocratic and modern technocratic elites of the Muslim upper north, Yoruba, Igbo, and minority political and business elites played strategic roles in the party's formation, and the NPN showed signs of becoming the predominant party of an increasingly integrated and cohesive Nigerian bourgeoisie. Even after its traumatic split, the NPP continued to draw critical support from Christian areas of the Middle Belt (or lower north) that had never been associated with the NCNC, and the GNPP showed strength through much of the Muslim north and also in the minority areas of the southeast. While the UPN and PRP were more regionally based, they were the sharpest and least parochial in their substantive programs, seeking to build national constituencies around social democratic and socialist ideologies respectively.[50]

Nevertheless, in the brevity of the period for party development and under pressure of imminent elections, politicians tended to retreat into convenient and familiar ethnic alignments, and new political entrepreneurs were forced to look to established politicians for leadership. This not only snapped some significant crosscutting alignments—especially that represented by the original NPP—it also produced "a sad level of regional and tribal correlation in voting behaviour."[51] And it brought together politicians of such disparate ideological inclinations that their associations were bound to become sorely strained.

The Second Republic

The Second Republic was born in the elections for state and federal offices that took place in five rounds during July and August 1979.[52] Although largely successful, their legitimacy was tarnished by charges of administrative bias and, in particular, by a serious controversy over the presidential election. Pro-NPN bias was suggested by the pattern of disqualification of candidates by FEDECO, on the grounds of nonpayment of income tax.[53] The actual conduct of the voting was also disputed. Predictably, "the various parties complained of fraud, victimization, and all kinds of electoral malpractices in places where they had not won."[54] Numerous malpractices were in fact documented, and election tribunals did order some new elections, while courageously upholding the disputed election of the radical PRP candidate for governor of strategic Kaduna state. On balance, the 1979 elections were relatively free and fair in their conduct.[55] Parties were free to campaign and the results in most states seemed to reflect apparent political trends. Moreover, in contrast with previous elections, the 1979 contest was impressively peaceful, due in no small measure to the active efforts of the military government to check political thuggery.

However, a serious challenge to the legitimacy of the 1979 elections—and of the new republic—grew out of the ambiguous result of the last round of voting, for the presidency. Although the NPN candidate, Shagari, had won a plurality of the vote, the runner-up candidate, Chief Awolowo, and his UPN insisted Shagari had not satisfied the second condition for direct election because he had won 25 percent of the vote in only twelve, and hence not quite two-thirds, of the nineteen states. The ruling of the electoral commission that he was elected because he had won 25 percent in "twelve and two-thirds states" (i.e., a quarter of the vote in twelve states and two-thirds of a quarter in a thirteenth) was bitterly challenged by the UPN, but upheld by the Supreme Court. The controversy engendered lasting political enmity between the NPN and UPN that was to heavily color subsequent political developments.[56]

This tension congealed rather quickly into competing political alliances. Building upon patterns of electoral cooperation, the nine elected governors from the UPN, GNPP, and PRP began meeting late in 1979 as a kind of coordinating committee for the political opposition to the NPN. The self-styled "nine progressive governors" denounced what they alleged was repeated abuse of constitutional authority by the NPN federal government. Initially, this was countered by two alliances on the NPN side. One gave the NPP, by formal agreement, a share of executive and legislative offices in return for its legislative cooperation. The other, a de facto arrangement, drew into the NPN's expanding and patronage-rich political network a growing number of NPP, GNPP, and PRP federal legislators (mostly senators), who were constitutionally prohibited from crossing the carpet but who gave the president reliable and often pivotal legislative support.

The NPN-NPP accord never worked as intended. Disappointed with the lack of consultations and patronage, the NPP withheld legislative support on several critical issues. By mid-1981, the accord completely collapsed, and several (but not all) NPP ministers honored their party's call to withdraw from the government. Gradually, the NPP drew closer to the opposition alliance; later in 1981, the "nine progressive governors" became twelve when they were joined by the three NPP governors. These twelve states represented the full range of Nigeria's ethnic diversity: four predominantly Yoruba, two Igbo, two Hausa, and four ethnic minority states. Meanwhile, the informal alliance became more important for the NPN, and this also cut sharply across region and ethnicity: Many of the tacit collaborators with the NPN came from the two Igbo states and from elsewhere outside the party's far northern base. These developments raised the possibility of a historic realignment in which two new political parties, one more conservative and one more progressive, would contest for power on a national basis.

Despite the increasing polarization between the ruling NPN and the UPN-led opposition, there was some cause for hope in the fact that this cleavage was far less centered on ethnicity and region than was political conflict in the First Republic. As a result of not only expanding education and communication, but also the deep inequalities and contradictions engendered by the oil boom,[57] class and ideology were coming to play a more significant role in political conflict.[58] This was particularly so in the two states carried by the PRP in 1979—Kano and Kaduna, part of the core of the old emirate system. As these states became the focus of political conflict, cross-cutting cleavage became increasingly salient.

Three interrelated crises developed along this line in 1980 and 1981. The first was a deep split in the leadership of the PRP, not unlike that in the Action Group in 1962, save that the stance of moderation and national political accommodation was espoused by PRP President Aminu Kano and his aides, while it was the two elected governors of Kano and Kaduna who favored confrontation and a more radical, ideological approach. The latter faction was the larger of the two, containing most of the PRP's youth support, founding intellectuals, and legislative representatives. They supported the participation of the two governors in the meetings of the nine opposition governors, while the party establishment opposed it and ordered it to cease. Out of the mutual expulsions, two opposing party structures emerged, each claiming to be the genuine PRP. In a controversial decision early in 1981, FEDECO officially recognized the Aminu Kano faction, further eroding the legitimacy of that crucial regulatory body.

Aggravating this internal division was a deepening stalemate within Kaduna state between the radical PRP governor, Alhaji Abdulkadir Balarabe Musa, and the NPN-controlled legislature. This reflected the widening class cleavage in the far north, as a new generation of radical intellectuals and professionals sought to mobilize the peasantry in a struggle to dismantle the entire structure of traditional class privilege and power, based on land and the emirate system. Even though the legislature was controlled by his political and class opponents, Balarabe Musa plunged ahead with his radical program, abolishing exploitative local taxes, investigating land transactions, and inaugurating a mass literacy campaign. When he persisted in the face of intense legislative opposition, the NPN majority in the State Assembly, with the support of the establishment PRP, impeached him and removed him from office in June 1981. With opposition forces around the country bitterly condemning the nakedly partisan action as undemocratic and unconstitutional, the legitimacy of the Second Republic suffered. At the same time, speculation grew about a four-party alliance to wrest power from the NPN in 1983, which was further encouraged by the rupture of the NPN-NPP accord two weeks after the impeachment.

Just a few weeks later, on July 10, 1981, conflict in Kano state erupted into devastating violence, burning down much of the physical infrastructure of the Kano state government and killing the political adviser of the PRP governor, Mohammed Abubakar Rimi. The immediate precipitant of the riot was an offensive letter from Governor Rimi to the emir of Kano implying his possible removal for acts of disrespect to the state government. But the systematic character of the destruction, and considerable other evidence, indicate that the riot was organized to embarrass and intimidate the PRP administration and derail its agenda for change. Supporters of the governor and the radical PRP were convinced that the NPN and the PRP establishment faction were responsible—seeking to do by violence in Kano what could not be done by impeachment, given Governor Rimi's overwhelming support in the state legislature. The massive destruction had a traumatic and deeply polarizing effect on political conflict, heightening opposition fears that the NPN and its allies were not prepared to "play by the rules." In retaliation some months later, the radical PRP impeached the deputy governor of Kano, who had backed the PRP establishment faction.

The mere fact of conflict—even recurrent and intense conflict—between the ruling NPN and the congealing opposition forces was not in itself an ominous development for democracy. Nor did the occasional heavy-handedness of the NPN federal government represent a really grave threat to democracy: Despite the opposition charges of "creeping fascism," basic freedoms remained largely intact and a number of controversial government actions were reversed or enjoined in the courts.[59] What was dangerous was the aura of desperation and intolerance that infused these conflicts and the violence that often attended them. These danger signals were noted with increasing alarm by the nation's press, which repeatedly condemned "the politics of bickerings, mudslingings, . . . lies, deceit, vindictiveness, strife and intolerance that are again creeping back into the country's political scene."[60]

Of particular concern to independent observers and opinion makers was the growing trail of violence. Even in the first two years of the Second Republic (when the 1979 elections were history but well before the 1983 election campaign had begun), casualties mounted from the repeated clashes between thugs of rival politicians, parties, and party factions. In Borno state alone, the count had run to 39 dead, 99 injured, and 376 arrested by May 1981.[61] As the 1983 elections approached, violent clashes proliferated between supporters and hired bullies not only of rival parties, but also of rival candidates for party nominations, especially within the NPN and the UPN. In many states, escalating political violence brought temporary bans on public meetings and assemblies, and people became concerned for their physical safety. Reflecting the growing public cynicism, weariness, and disgust, the press repeatedly warned of the impending danger: "We are tired of celebrating politics as a rite of death. . . . If politics cannot inspire recognition and respect for fundamental human rights, the credibility of the captains of our ship of state is certainly at stake. . . . We can ask to be saved from politicians and their notoriously bloody style of politicking."[62]

But political violence and intolerance were not the only sources of public disillusionment. From the very beginning, concern was also manifest over the opportunistic and self-interested behavior of the politicians, as reflected in the prolonged debate over legislative salaries and perquisites that dominated the initial deliberations of the National Assembly. Cynicism was bred by the constant stream of suspensions, expulsions, and defections from the various political parties, which split not only the PRP, but later the GNPP and, to a lesser extent, the NPP as well. And within states controlled by each of the five parties, state assemblies became absorbed in bitter conflicts over leadership positions or threats to impeach the governor. The tremendous instability in party structures and identities suggested a general lack of democratic commitment among the politicians, who seemed obsessed with the quest for personal power and wealth.

Most of all, public disillusionment was bred by the unending succession of scandals and exposés concerning corruption in government. In 1983 alone, these included the mishandling of $2.5 billion in import licenses by the minister of commerce, the alleged acceptance by legislators of large bribes from a Swiss firm, the rumored apprehension in London of a Nigerian governor trying to smuggle millions of naira into Britain, and the revelation by a federal minister that the country was losing close to a billion dollars a year in payroll fraud. The issue was dramatized in January 1983 by a shocking fire that destroyed the thirty-seven-story headquarters of the Nigerian External Telecommunications in Lagos. The fire, condemned by a leading newspaper as "a calculated act, planned and executed to cover up corruption and embezzlement in the company,"[63] symbolized the rapaciousness of the ruling elite and visibly quickened the pace of political decay. Students took to the streets in several cities, carrying signs calling for the return of the military.[64]

Such incidents and revelations only reinforced the evidence in virtually every state and community of venality, insensitivity, failed promises, and callous waste: the skeletons of unfinished hospitals and schools, the treacherous craters in ungraded roads, the abandoned bulldozers, the rusting pumps beside the undrilled boreholes. These phenomena had spread malignantly since the oil boom but seemed to assume a wholly new and reckless momentum with the return of the politicians.

The devastating effects of corruption at all levels of government—which, by most estimates, drained billions of dollars from the Nigerian economy during the Second Republic—were compounded by the precipitous decline in oil revenue, from a peak of $24 billion in 1980 to $10 billion in 1983. As corruption and mismanagement prevented any kind of disciplined adjustment, the economy was plunged into depression and mounting international indebtedness. Imports of industrial raw materials and basic commodities were severely disrupted, forcing the retrenchment of tens of thousands of industrial workers and sending the prices of staple foods and household necessities skyrocketing. Shortages were further aggravated by hoarding and profiteering (especially of rice) by the powerful and well-connected. Sucked dry of revenue by the corruption, mismanagement, and recession, state governments became unable to pay teachers and civil servants or to purchase drugs for hospitals, and many services (including schools) were shut down by strikes. Everywhere one turned in 1983, the economy seemed on the edge of collapse. Still the politicians and contractors continued to bribe, steal, smuggle, and speculate, accumulating vast illicit fortunes and displaying them lavishly in stunning disregard for public sensitivities. By its third anniversary, disenchantment with the Second Republic was acute, overt, and remarkably broad-based.[65]

As the rot deepened, so did the popular aspiration for change. Beyond the chimera of popular rebellion (of which some leftist intellectuals dreamed and in fear of which the paramilitary wing of the police was rapidly expanded), only two possible avenues were open: to change the incumbents in power in the five weeks of national and state elections due in August and September 1983, or to displace the political system altogether and bring back the only alternative, the military. A large proportion of the Nigerian electorate had come, by 1983, to favor the latter option. My own preelection survey in Kano state, the largest and most volatile in the country, showed a majority of the state's electorate and two-thirds of the voters in Kano city favoring a military government. Probably an even larger proportion of the intelligentsia and the military had come to favor the systemic change, out of deep skepticism that reform from within was possible. Nevertheless, this group waited to see if change could come by constitutional means, viewing the elections as the last chance for the Second Republic to redeem itself.[66]

From the beginning of the process, the elections were gravely troubled. The two-week registration of voters during August 1982 ended amid widespread protests of incompetence, partisanship, and fraud. When the preliminary register of voters was displayed in March 1983, with millions of names missing, mangled, or misplaced, opposition fears heightened. These hardened into outrage and disbelief with the release (just ten days before the election) of the final register, which showed not only an absurd total of 65 million voters (possibly twice the legitimate total) but the largest increases in NPN states.[67]

Even more troubling was FEDECO's refusal to register a new and powerful opposition alliance that sought recognition as the Progressive People's Party (PPP). Bringing together the NPP and the largest factions of the PRP and the GNPP, the PPP seemed clearly to have satisfied the constitutional requirements. In fact, with control of seven state governments (as many as the NPN), the PPP was at least the second largest and broadest political formation in the country. But FEDECO even denied the NPP's request to change its name to PPP. Such rulings (hailed by NPN officials) badly tarnished the integrity of FEDECO and of the election.[68] Although the other party factions subsequently merged into the NPP, their northern campaign was to suffer from widespread identification of the NPP as an "Igbo" and "Christian" party—a major theme of the NPN campaign in the Muslim north. Anxiety further mounted as the election neared and FEDECO proved unable to cope with the staggering logistical preparations for five successive elections with tens of millions of voters in nineteen states.

Biased and incompetent administration was not the opposition's only concern, however. With full control of federal patronage and an extraordinarily well-financed national political machine, the NPN was a formidable national contender, even with its sorry performance in office. Probably the only hope for an opposition victory in the presidential election lay in uniting behind a common ticket. But months of negotiations between the UPN and the NPP (and their PRP and GNPP allies) under the rubric of their Progressive Parties Alliance (PPA) failed to produce agreement. Neither of the surviving political giants—Azikiwe of the NPP and Awolowo of the UPN—would step down for the other. As they divided the opposition vote, the Shagari campaign was able to brand them in the north as champions of alien ethnic and religious interests. Still, as they campaigned relentlessly against the corruption and mismanagement of the NPN administration, the two gathered new support around the country, including northern Muslim states they had previously failed to penetrate in their long careers.

Although it was apparent that the division of the opposition might enable President Shagari's reelection with a weak plurality, changes were widely expected at other levels. In particular, a number of massively corrupt and negligent governors figured to be booted out. Certainly no one was prepared for the scale of the NPN landslide, and even the most hardened skeptics were astonished by the degree of electoral fraud. Ballots were obtained in advance and thumbprinted en masse. Electoral officials at every level were bribed to falsify returns. Whole communities were disenfranchised. Although all the parties engaged in malpractices, those by the NPN were the most systematic and brazen. In many northern states, NPN agents collaborated with electoral officials and police to prevent opposition party agents from observing the polling and vote counting.[69] In the absence of this crucial check (guaranteed in the electoral law), unbelievable returns were reported and announced. Not only was President Shagari reelected decisively—and by incredible margins in some states—but the following week, the NPN increased its governorships from seven to thirteen, scoring shocking upsets in several opposition states while comfortably reelecting even its most venal incumbents. Subsequently, it was to increase its standing in the National Assembly from a small plurality to two-thirds, but by then the credibility of the elections had been shattered and most of the electorate was no longer bothering to vote.

Despite numerous appeals, few of the results were overturned in court. All but one of the most controversial gubernatorial outcomes were upheld. In that lone case, a defeated UPN governor was found to have been reelected by more than a million votes.

As they had in 1965, the people of the Yoruba states, where the rigging had been most outrageous, exploded in a frenzy of violent protest following the gubernatorial elections. More than 100 people were killed and $100 million in property destroyed.[70] Violent protest erupted in other states as well, claiming more than thirty lives. Both Awolowo and Azikiwe charged that the election was stolen and pronounced the country "on the brink of dictatorship." A pregnant calm returned by the inauguration on October 1, after which the reelected president took some steps to upgrade his cabinet and launch tough new austerity measures. But by then it was too little and too late.

The Renewal of Military Authoritarianism

Like the first coup eighteen years before, the coup that brought the military back to power on December 31, 1983, was widely welcomed and celebrated around the country.[71] The reasons for the coup were largely apparent in the declarations of the coupmakers: to redeem the country from "the grave economic predicament and uncertainty that an inept and corrupt leadership has imposed" on the country. The new head of state, Major General Muhammadu Buhari, added to the economic indictment the rigging of the 1983 elections. Observed a former army chief of staff, "Democracy had been in jeopardy for the past four years. It died with the elections. The army only buried it."[72] Any military hesitance to intervene was surely removed by the continued rapid deterioration of the economy (which saw food prices skyrocket between September and December) and the realization that militant junior officers, from whose ranks had come several unsuccessful coup attempts over the previous four years, could not indefinitely be kept at bay.

The government of General Buhari and his second-in-command, Major General Tunde Idiagbon, moved quickly to punish corruption and eliminate waste. More than 300 top officials in the civil service, police, and customs were dismissed or retired. Hundreds of former politicians were detained—including the president, vice-president, and prominent governors, ministers, and legislators. Huge sums of cash were seized from the homes of leading politicians, and the accounts of detained and fugitive politicians were frozen. Imports and travel allowances were slashed, black market currency operations raided, and government contracts placed under review.

These initial moves were highly popular, especially with the interest groups—students, trade unions, business owners, professionals—that had been most disgusted with the civilian regime. Newspapers and intellectuals also supported the professed intention of the new regime to restore account-ability to public life. But early on, it became apparent that the Buhari regime viewed accountability only in retrospective terms, and had no more inten-tion than the Gowon regime of allowing itself to be scrutinized and ques-tioned. With unprecedented harshness, arrogance, and impunity, the Buhari regime turned on the constituencies that had welcomed its arrival.

Political problems crystallized in March 1984 with the announcement of several controversial decrees. Decree Number 3 provided for military tri-bunals to try former public officials suspected of corruption and misconduct in office. The announcement of investigations and trials was popular, but protest arose over the severity of the penalties (a minimum of twenty-one years in prison) and in particular over the procedures, which placed the "onus of proving" innocence on the accused, prohibited appeal of the ver-dict, and closed the proceedings to the public. These provisions led the Nigerian Bar Association to boycott the trials.

In the subsequent year, Nigerians were gratified to see the conviction and sentencing of some of the country's most corrupt politicians, including former governors from a majority of the nineteen states. Acquittals of some other officeholders suggested that the tribunals were capable of fair and independent verdicts. But concern mounted over the continued detention without trial of politicians who had not been formally charged. Consternation also grew over the dearth of convictions of the most power-ful kingpins of the NPN, especially those from the party's northern power base. Given, as well, the heavily northern composition of the Supreme Military Council, the regime came increasingly to be derided as the "mili-tary wing of the NPN."

The disenchantment was fed not only by the narrow ethnic base of the regime, but also by its increasing repressiveness and arrogance, as mani-fested in its assault on the press. Decree Number 4 forbade the publication or broadcast of anything that was false in any particular or that might bring government officials into ridicule or disrepute. Under this and the internal security decree (Number 2) announced in January 1984, several prominent journalists and editors were arrested. Although journalists continued to test the regime's narrowing limits, the decrees and arrests had a chilling eff on news coverage and editorial commentary and alienated the inte'

Under Decree Number 2, which provided for the detenti' zen deemed a security risk, the Nigerian Security Organ' given a virtual blank check to arrest and intimidate

Some of Nigeria's most forceful and popular social commentators were imprisoned without trial. Others fell silent in a growing climate of fear.

Politics in the sense of articulation and representation of interests did not cease. As it had previously during military rule, mobilization continued by a panoply of assertive and clamorous interest groups. Repression became the reflexive response of the regime. Public declarations were discouraged and obstructed, meetings were forcibly dispersed, and group leaders were detained by the NSO. In addition, prominent interest groups, including the National Association of Nigerian Students and the Nigerian Medical Association, were banned. Toward the end, even public discussion of the country's political future was banned.

Public disaffection was intensified by the growing economic hardships, which followed from the severe austerity measures imposed by the Buhari government. Although these brought considerable progress toward balancing Nigeria's external payments, they came at the price of deepening recession. During 1984, an estimated 50,000 civil servants were retrenched, retired, or dismissed. Tens of thousands more industrial workers also lost their jobs as factories remained desperately short of imported raw materials and spare parts. Severe shortages pushed inflation to an annual rate of 40 percent. After three years of decline in GDP by an estimated 10 percent, the 1985 budget forecast only 1 percent growth, cutting imports again by more than half while assigning 44 percent of foreign exchange to debt service. At the same time, credible reports spread of renewed corruption in high places, including (incredibly, given its role in the demise of the Second Republic) the allocation of import licenses.

Escalating repression not only engendered deep resentment and bitterness among a people who cherished their personal freedom, it also dangerously cut the regime off from popular sentiments and relieved it of any need to be accountable for its conduct. In trying to impose a monolithic order on Nigeria's vigorously pluralistic society, the Buhari-Idiagbon dictatorship was risking a political convulsion. Rumors of failed coup attempts from the junior ranks circulated anew. Perhaps most fatally for the regime, its arrogance led it to ignore critical opinion and the imperative for consensus even within its senior military ranks.

Personal Rule and Protracted Transition

What was coming to be viewed around the country as an inevitable military coup finally happened on August 27, 1985. It was led by army chief of staff Major General Ibrahim Babangida (a pivotal figure in previous military coups and regimes), who became the first of Nigeria's six military rulers to ⁀ the title of president. From its initial statements and actions and the ⁀ᵗⁱc popular reception it received, the Babangida coup appeared to ⁀ rejection of the previous authoritarian trend. In his first address, General Babangida announced repeal of the odious Decree Number 4, vowing, "We do not intend to lead a country where individuals are under the fear of expressing themselves."[73] Shortly thereafter, all journalists in detention and dozens of politicians who had not been charged or tried were released, many to heroes' welcomes. The detention centers of the NSO were exposed to public view, and a thorough probe and restructuring of the dreaded organization was undertaken. Forceful and opinionated civilians were chosen to head crucial cabinet ministries, and the ruling military council was reorganized to disperse power. Babangida also promised to present a program of political transition, beginning with the revitalization of local government.

These and other initial moves earned Babangida wide popularity and a reputation for political skill and decisiveness. Here, it seemed, was a military politician with an ear for public opinion, a liberal and populist bent, the wisdom and self-confidence to draw in an extraordinary range of expert professional and intellectual counsel, and a determination to restore democracy, albeit with sufficient care and deliberation that it would survive this time— that his own coup would be, as he repeatedly promised and implored, the last in Nigerian history.

Over the course of his eight years of rule, these favorable images would crack and shatter. In their place a very different picture would take shape, of a brilliant and ruthless—but at times strangely indecisive—military politician, the first personal dictator in the country's history, obsessed with the aggrandizement of his own wealth, power, and glory, constantly manipulating the game of transition and the self-interests and divisions of the politicians to perpetuate himself in office. Admiration for a carefully drawn and intelligently staged transition plan gave way, with his repeated interventions in the process, to widespread cynicism and disgust for what one leading U.S. observer called "one of the most sustained exercises in political chicanery ever visited on a people."[74]

For most of Babangida's tenure, a transition to civilian democratic rule seemed likely, if not inevitable, and indeed civilian electoral politics resumed—under military control and scrutiny—fairly quickly. The transition process was initiated at the beginning of 1986 with Babangida's announcement of a return to civilian, democratic rule in 1990 and his appointment of a seventeen-member Political Bureau to initiate and lead what he termed the "collective search for a new political order." In the subsequent nine months, the "Politburo," as it came to be known, crisscrossed the country during a vigorous national debate that elicited a broad outpouring of popular and elite opinions on the design of a new democratic government.[75] While the military government's White Paper review panel accepted most of the approach and recommendations of the Politburo, it decided to extend completion of the transition program to October 1992, in order to permit, in President Babangida's words, "a broadly spaced transition in which democratic government can proceed with political learning, institutional adjustment and re-orientation of political culture, at sequential levels of politics and governance beginning with local government and ending at the federal level."[76] The efforts to reshape political culture and behavior would figure prominently in the high rhetoric and formal institutions of the Babangida transition, but already a more Machiavellian process of manipulation had begun. An overwhelming majority of the Political Bureau members favored adhering to the originally promised 1990 hand-over date, and they suspected that the minority recommendation (of two members) for 1992 had been induced or orchestrated by Babangida himself.[77]

This was only one of many surprises to be sprung upon the politicians—and the country—by General Babangida, whose stunning tactical maneuvers and, in the early years, brilliant manipulations of both political elites and public opinion earned him the nickname "Maradona" (after the Argentine soccer star). On taking power in August 1985, he announced his intention to complete an IMF agreement to stabilize and reform the horrendously imbalanced and indebted economy. But when the public debate he invited turned overwhelmingly against taking an IMF loan, he struck the ingenious stance of rejecting the IMF loan (and in theory its conditionality) while implementing on his own its harsh austerity and adjustment prescriptions. In the same speech announcing his new Structural Adjustment Program (SAP), on June 27, 1986, he banned all individuals who held party or government office in the Second Republic from future politics for ten years, but the next month he released the former president and vice-president from detention and cleared 100 former politicians of all charges. On September 23, 1987, twelve weeks after announcing the two-year extension of the transition, Babangida banned all the principal politicians and cabinet officers from all previous administrations (civilian and military, including his own) from seeking political or party office during the transition, thus supposedly clearing the decks for a "new breed" of politician. By then, however, any effort at legal accountability—such as his promise to try hundreds of Second Republic politicians for corruption—had quietly evaporated. Yet at the same time, he created (in response to a Politburo recommendation) an ambitious new state institution—the Directorate of Social Mobilisation (MAMSER)—to mobilize and educate the country for "a new political culture." Despite the serious and creative efforts of some of its practitioners to effect a new political awareness and responsibility at the mass level, MAMSER was doomed from the start by its inability to reform the elite political culture, which was powerfully shaped by political traditions, institutions, and leadership patterns well beyond its scope to redress.[78]

Much more potent was the impact on political values and expectations of Babangida's own cynical and corrupt style of governance, continually shuffling appointments (civilian and military) and doling out cash, contracts, and lucrative postings to solidify his grip on power. Every move was tactical and could be reversed with shifting political imperatives. Thus, two years later, after warning, threatening, and even arresting banned politicians for actively politicking (while monitoring their every move and dealing secretly with many of them), Babangida lifted the ban on the old politicians—too late in 1991 to enable any of them to contest for the December gubernatorial elections, but in plenty of time to unscramble the next year's race for the presidency. And thus, with his popularity badly slumping and the civilian political process gathering momentum, he created nine new states in August 1991, after promising to do so four years earlier—when his administration decided only to create the two new states of Akwa Ibom and Katsina—to bar any further consideration during his presidency of the multitudinous demands for new states.[79] New governments, state and local, became populist prizes to be awarded in exchange for support, and by late 1991, Babangida had increased the number of states from nineteen to thirty, and doubled the number of local government areas to 589. As more sober minds (including most of the Politburo) had warned, this proliferation only advanced the very trends of political fragmentation, fiscal inviability, and pervasive ethnic political mobilization Babangida had vowed to contain. With each new step in the proliferation of governments, "winning" communities celebrated and disaffected ones rioted. Sharp conflicts were spawned over the division of existing state assets, and state governments were left much weaker and more impoverished than ever before.

Warning signs of devious intent, apparent early on, formed a sharp contrast with the rigorous implementation of the transition program under the Muhammed-Obasanjo military regime.[80] The Constituent Assembly submitted its draft constitution to President Babangida in Abuja on April 5, 1989. This was somewhat late, and might have been much later had not the politicians in that body finally realized that the military was prepared to proceed, with or without their constitutional recommendations. The Armed Forces Ruling Council (AFRC) wasted little time in getting down to work on the draft constitution, "editing" the assembly's recommendations in a three-day, closed-door meeting that began on April 26, 1989. In his speech on May 3, lifting the ban on party politics, the president also announced the AFRC's final decisions on the constitution, altering some important draft provisions,[81] while trusting that the pent-up eagerness of the political class to get on with the business of politics would dampen the public outcry against the AFRC's rather brazen abridgments of the principle of popular sovereignty in constitution making.

In design, the six-year transition plan was not without promise. In fact, among recent transitions from authoritarian rule around the world, it was virtually unprecedented for its complexity and carefully crafted sequencing. It began with the establishment of regulatory commissions, such as the National Electoral Commission (NEC); the convening of the Constituent Assembly; and the holding of (nonpartisan) local government elections in

1987 and 1988. The subsequent four years entailed the return of party politics and the staging of five more elections at successively higher levels of power. In the second quarter of 1989, the ban on party politics would be lifted, and in the third quarter, two (and only two) political parties would be recognized to compete. In the fourth quarter of 1989, local governments would be elected anew on a partisan basis. In the first and second quarters of 1990, state legislatures and governors, respectively, would be elected, and in the third and fourth quarters they would begin governing. During the first three quarters of 1991, a new census would be conducted; in the fourth quarter, local government elections would be held again. In the first two quarters of 1992, the National Assembly was to be elected and convened; and finally in the last two quarters of 1992, a president would be elected and inaugurated. In theory, this would allow a new grassroots politics and (with the ban on the "old breed" politicians) a new set of political leaders to emerge democratically, organically, from the bottom up.

Despite the two-year extension, the public and the politicians (even the old breed) accepted the program and participated in its initial stages with enthusiasm. But this progressively gave way to mounting skepticism, anger, and alienation, as the military president altered the transition timetable four more times. In 1989, the denial of registration to all the political parties that applied necessitated a whole new process for forming parties that pushed back the early portions of the timetable. On August 27, 1991 (the sixth anniversary of his seizure of power), with a national census and state gubernatorial primary and general elections approaching, Babangida "threw the internal dynamics of the parties" and the fine calculations of countless politicians "into turmoil" with his surprise establishment of nine new states and forty-seven additional local government areas (with eighty-nine more added the following month).[82] Again the entire remaining timetable had to be pushed back, with the hand-over date postponed from October 1, 1992, to January 2, 1993. The third revision—which greatly eroded the credibility of the general's commitment to complete the transition—came in November 1992, when the regime seized upon the chaos and rampant fraud in the September presidential primary elections of both parties to disqualify all twenty-three presidential candidates (many of whom had only recently been "unbanned"!), dissolve the two party executives (appointing, once more, caretaker administrators), and reorganize the entire process again. Presidential elections were deferred from December 1992 to June 1993, and the hand-over of power was postponed a third time, from January 2 to August 1993.

Even with this third postponement, Babangida and his military cohorts were still expected to depart from power voluntarily, keenly aware of the political convulsion that would result if they failed to complete the transition to civilian rule. Rising public anxiety over General Babangida's ultimate intentions, his growing personalization of state power, and the deepening repression and corruption of his regime had helped to produce a trau-matic coup attempt on April 22, 1990 (the bloodiest in Nigeria's history), which leveled the presidential palace with tank fire, narrowly missed killing Babangida himself, and nearly plunged the country into civil war with its seizure of the national radio in Lagos and announcement that it was tem-porarily "excising" from the Federal Republic the five Muslim emirate states of the far north.[83] Still, Babangida did not cease his scheming to remain in power, provoking one last crisis over the June 1993 presidential elections that delayed the hand-over a final time, until his personal rule and then his "transition" came to an end.

Corruption, Alienation, Protest, and Repression

Political maneuver, cooptation, and corruption were General Babangida's favored instruments of consolidating and perpetuating what would prove to be, for Nigeria, an unprecedentedly personalized military rule. These instru-ments were serious enough in the damage they did to democracy, steeply eroding the already tattered integrity of the press, the judiciary, university officials, trade union officials, and many other elements of the state and civil society. But from early on, these alluring incentives proved inadequate for several reasons. Although the politicians generally played Babangida's game and sought and accepted his benificence, those key political leaders who were banned from the process (a group whose identities shifted over time) also had some incentive to destabilize it. More significantly, a vigor-ous and vigilant civil society had been developing, particularly among the independently owned newspapers and newly emerging newsweeklies, the professional associations, the trade unions, a growing number of human rights organizations, and the readily outraged and mobilizable university students. Many of these groups and individual practitioners were serious about democracy and social justice and quite prepared to question and chal-lenge Babangida's duplicity, illegality, and corruption, even at great risk to their positions and their lives. In addition, based mainly among the urban salaried middle class and wage earners, they were among the hardest hit by the regime's structural adjustment measures (such as reduction of consumer subsidies, retrenchment of public-sector workers, and the sharp devaluation of the currency that resulted from a much more market-oriented approach to the determination of the exchange rate). Thus, they generated the most stri-dent and vociferous criticism of SAP.[84] Further, the society was still deeply divided not only along ethnic but increasingly religious (Muslim-Christian) lines, and as Babangida leaned in one direction to consolidate his political base, he risked—and ultimately incited—eruptions of protest and intergroup conflict.

Coming from a more peripheral area of the Muslim north, and with his ethnic origins somewhat in question,[85] Babangida felt it imperative to solidify his support among the traditional power structure of the Muslim, Hausa-Fulani emirates. Increasingly, Christian Nigerians saw religious alignment and domination as the motive behind such controversial decisions as Nigeria's shift from observer to full membership status in the Organization of Islamic Conference in January 1986 and the removal of prominent, independent-minded Christian officers such as Ebitu Ukiwe (then the chief of general staff, the number two official in the regime) in October 1986 and Defense Minister Domkat Y. Bali at the end of 1989. Indeed, as resistance to his protracted rule and authoritarian manipulations increased, particularly among organizations centered in the predominantly Christian south, Babangida seemed to fall back increasingly on a northern Muslim political base. Reconstitution of the AFRC in February 1989 and of the federal cabinet at the end of the year were seen to be displacing Christians for Muslims, which some strident Christian leaders interpreted as a "carefully implemented design" to turn Nigeria into "an Islamic state."[86]

Perhaps most significantly, the country's deep ethnic and religious divisions, along with factional and personal ones, tore at the institutional coherence of the military itself, which was constantly seething with coup rumors, suspicions, and machinations, and which was gripped throughout Babangida's years by repeated shuffling and purging at the top and mysterious deaths of younger and middle-ranking officers. Babangida's obsession with his own security was apparently intensified only four months after his seizure of power by the discovery (or so alleged) of a coup plot against him by his high-ranking former ally, Major General Mamman Vatsa, who was executed three months later (March 1986) along with ten other senior officers allegedly involved in the plot.[87] The explosive coup attempt of April 22, 1990—avenged with the execution of sixty-nine military conspirators later in the year—followed closely the controversial departure of General Bali and the rise to fever pitch of Christian-Muslim political conflict. In the explanation broadcast by the coup leader, Major Gideon Orka, the desire to end the domination of the country by the "Northern aristocratic class" figured prominently, as did the ousters of Commodore Ukiwe, General Bali, and the southern Petroleum Minister Tam David-West (who was later sent to prison for alleged misconduct in office).[88]

To a degree previously unknown in Nigeria, religious conflict between Muslims and Christians led to repeated instances of mass-level violence during the Babangida years. In March 1987, a quarrel between Christian and Muslim students in southern Kaduna state led to riots that left nineteen dead and over 150 houses of worship (mainly Christian churches) destroyed. In April and May 1991, religious rioting broke out in Katsina state, leading to numerous arrests, and then in Bauchi state, where, after a reported 160 people were killed, the army was called in to suppress the rioting, and did so brutally (with death estimates running up to 1,000).[89] In October 1991, "at least 200 were probably killed" and thousands of Christians fled south during violent religious clashes.[90] In May 1992, a land dispute between Christian Katafs and Muslim Hausas in southern Kaduna escalated into wider religious violence in which up to 400 people may have died. These and other violent religious clashes all had important local causes or triggers, but they were stimulated by a political context in which religion was mobilized by various political forces and elite groups in their struggle for power, within a regime that was authoritarian but also transitional, and in which the authoritarian ruler himself sought to exploit religion to maintain his grip on power.[91]

For most Nigerians, however, the most alarming aspect of Babangida's rule was the steady drift toward dictatorship—personal, indefinite, and increasingly arbitrary and abusive rule by a general above any law or standard of accountability. As much as religious and sectional conflict, it was anxiety over the mounting concentration of authoritarian power in General Babangida's own hands, and his repeated willingness to use it bluntly, that motivated the April 1990 coup attempt and justified it to the nation. Orka's broadcast amounted to a sweeping indictment of Babangida's personal rule: his "cunning desire to install himself as Nigeria's first life president at all costs"; his "unabated corruption"; his responsibility for the "murders" of Major General Vatsa and other officers, who, Orka alleged, were falsely accused of plotting a coup; his use of the State Security Service (SSS) as a "tool of terror"; his creation of a national guard, independent of the armed forces, and, like the SSS, responsible to him alone; his appointment of himself as defense minister to replace General Bali; his unceasing harassment of organized opposition among students and university staff; his prodigious dispensations of cash to buy off the press and other potential critics; and, inter alia, his "deliberate manipulation of the transition programme."[92] The most stunning fact about this list was not merely its scope but the degree to which it reflected widespread popular fears, sentiments, and beliefs—and, to some considerable extent, reality.

Increasingly, Babangida was seen as the most massively corrupt ruler in Nigerian history. "Tales [had] been circulating for years of Babangida's large cash gifts to military officers, cabinet ministers, traditional rulers, and potentially contentious opponents; of Mercedes Benz cars given to major newspaper editors and directors of state broadcasting corporations; of the president's secret personal investments in banks and companies; of off-the-books oil being lifted offshore by private tankers."[93] Numerous recipients and one-time insiders confirmed the pattern of largesse, and one former top-ranking officer and longtime associate of Babangida's claimed he entered the presidency with a net worth in the tens of millions of dollars from previous corruption in weapons purchases and other transactions.[94] As in the Second Republic, foreign business leaders privately estimated the personal wealth of top officials in the hundreds of millions, and objective evidence pointed to annual leakages of revenue in the billions of dollars, approximating 10 percent of the country's total annual output of goods and services![95]

A confidential World Bank report "estimated that $2.1 billion in petroleum receipts were diverted in 1990 and 1991 to extra-budgetary accounts, much of which were disbursed to regime loyalists and strategic constituents."[96] And these did not include the diversions from one ministerial and parastatal account after another, the gigantic kickbacks on state contracts, the windfall gains from favoritism and nepotism in the privatization process, the continued rent-seeking through evasion of market practices in the state's foreign exchange auctions, and the other wanton abuses in the newly deregulated, heavily politicized, and rapidly mushrooming banking sector.[97] Nor did they include the bountiful cuts that might have come from the widely suspected complicity of military and state officials in oil smuggling, drug trafficking, and international commercial fraud schemes. Such ubiquitous, all-consuming corruption utterly ravaged Babangida's initially serious Structural Adjustment Program and drained his regime of moral authority.[98]

The widespread public awareness of boundless corruption—the fruits of which were readily displayed in the new luxury cars, expensive jewelry, and palatial homes of military, political, business, and other beneficiaries—was particularly enraging in the context of the catastrophic economic decline associated with the SAP (especially in the urban areas), and it added considerable fuel to the fire of protest. Indeed, a handbill falsely reporting that the U.S. magazine *Ebony* had named General Babangida one of Africa's richest rulers helped to trigger furious urban rioting against SAP in May 1989, during which more than fifty Nigerians were killed.[99] For the stability of the Babangida military regime, corruption was thus a two-edged sword. It oiled the wheels of a constantly whirring political machine, buying support, compliance, and alliances within and outside the military. But it also greatly intensified public alienation and revulsion toward the regime, the sense of acute injustice, the readiness to protest, and the need for repression to suppress that protest (as well as any concrete exposure of what was happening).

Lest the press take too seriously Babangida's initial promises of freedom, a chilling and potent message was sent in October 1986 when Dele Giwa, the founding editor of the crusading investigative newsweekly *Newswatch,* was assassinated by a parcel bomb. A decade later, Giwa's murder has still not been solved, but from the beginning, substantial circumstantial evidence fixed public suspicion on the state security apparatus and, in many minds, on the president himself.[100] These suspicions deepened with the government's unwillingness to launch an independent investigation and failure to record any progress of its own toward solving the crime. Six months later, the shadow this crime had cast over press freedom lengthened when the regime banned *Newswatch* for six months after it published an extensive account of the leaked Politburo report.[101] Between 1987 and 1992, "almost all the privately owned newspaper houses . . . suffered closure for a certain period of time," as the government cited sweeping and deliberately vague reasons of "national security and national interest." After the most powerful independent newspaper house, the Concord Group, was shut down for a time in April 1992, Babangida's attorney general declared, "Any malignant tumor requires a surgical operation."[102] Repeatedly as well, press facilities were stormed by security forces, "offending" publications were seized en masse, and vendors were arrested for selling them. As the controversy over the June 12, 1993, presidential election heightened in the subsequent weeks, the war on the press escalated, and on July 22, the military simultaneously shut down five media houses with a total of sixteen news publications.[103] Individual journalists suffered too (typically firing from government-owned papers and arrest and detention of those reporting for the independent press, but at times physical assaults as well) for covering issues of corruption, state incompetence, religious violence, or student protests, or for merely embarrassing the First Lady, the police, state governors (military and civilian), or other authorities.[104]

For organized groups in civil society and outspoken critics of the regime came similarly harsh repression from the general who had promised an end to fear and a transition to democracy. In response to peaceful student protests at Ahmadu Bello University in Zaria, police went on a rampage, killing several students (possibly more than twenty) and injuring many more. Sympathy demonstrations and further confrontation and violence followed.[105] Subsequently, the umbrella trade union federation, the Nigeria Labour Congress (NLC), was dissolved, taken over, and forcibly reorganized; the National Association of Nigerian Students (NANS) and the Academic Staff Union of Universities (ASUU) were both repeatedly banned by the regime; human rights organizations were monitored, harrassed, and intimidated with frequent raids and arrests; numerous politicians, interest group leaders, human rights activists, and government critics were arrested without warrant and detained without trial; court rulings ordering their release and other adherences to the rule of law were routinely ignored and flouted; and passports of democratic activists were seized to prevent their speaking out abroad. The decimation of the rule of law went well beyond national politics and the democratic struggle. In the absence of any legal accountability, the police (as well as the soldiers) became increasingly arbitrary and indiscriminate in their use of brutal and often lethal force; several police massacres occurred; and historically grim prison conditions became ever more abysmal, with detainees (especially the lesser known) increasingly subject to torture.[106]

All institutions suffered, perhaps none more than higher education. Over the years, probably thousands of students on individual campuses were punished, suspended, and expelled for demonstrating and participating in student union activities.[107] ASUU, too, found itself in constant battle with the regime and individual university administrations over political and economic issues. Partly as a result of the repression, and partly from corruption, underfunding, mismanagement, and the general economic depression, higher education (indeed instruction at all levels) essentially collapsed during military rule, with universities closing for prolonged periods, professors emigrating to safer and more remunerative positions abroad, and libraries, laboratories, and physical facilities stagnating or becoming unusable.[108] Virtually an entire generation of young Nigerians has been robbed of higher education, completely or in effect. When weighed with the massive dislocations and shortages of primary and secondary education as well, the implications are staggering and will diminish Nigeria's development prospects for decades to come.

The Abortive Third Republic

One of the most important features of the new political framework of the Third Republic was the *mandatory* two-party system, recommended by the Political Bureau (and accepted by the military) as a way of retaining democratic electoral competition while consolidating some of the past chaos of party politics and ensuring that political parties would crosscut and transcend the country's deep, complex, and volatile ethnic and regional cleavages. The period between May and July 1989 saw dozens of political associations canvassing support, but in the end only thirteen met the deadline and the substantial expense required to file a formal application with the NEC. Of these, the NEC rated six (and especially three or four) as having approached the standards for recognition more impressively than the others, but found all of them wanting.[109] In a stunning speech on October 7, President Babangida announced the AFRC's decision not to register any of the six political associations recommended by NEC for consideration, but rather to create by fiat two new political parties, the Social Democratic Party (SDP) and the National Republican Convention (NRC), one "a little to the left" and the other "a little to the right."[110] Subsequently, the military government proceeded to write the manifestos and constitutions of the two parties (synthesized from the documents of the preexisting associations).

Despite this jolt to the old politicians and wealthy newcomers who had asserted control over the aspiring parties, and despite the fact that the two new parties were initially administered by government-appointed civil servants, the politicians quickly sorted themselves out in largely predictable patterns and coalitions into the two new structures. During 1990, a succession of party meetings, from the ward through the local government to the state and finally the national level, elected party officers from the ranks and completed the transfer of party control from the government to the emergent (largely reemergent) political class. Interesting blends of old cleavages and coalitions and new faces, the two parties reproduced to some extent the emergent cleavage between southern-led "progressives" and northern-led "conservatives" that was taking shape toward the end of the Second Republic (and even the First). But the artificial nature of the parties' formation generated serious internal cleavages that remained to be worked out.

The most serious of these cleavages was within the SDP, which was torn from its beginning by a struggle between factions representing two of the six leading political associations that sought registration: the People's Solidarity Party (PSP), based among the old Yoruba, UPN stalwarts but reflecting a much more national progressive alliance, and the People's Front of Nigeria (PFN), led and financed by a leading dissident from the old NPN and the ruling coalition of the north, former General (and number two in the Obasanjo military regime) Shehu Musa Yar'Adua, who was determined to win the presidency and to control the SDP for that purpose.[111] This internal division within the SDP was never resolved and had much to do with the party's self-destruction in the controversy over the June 12, 1993, presidential election.

For all their "birth defects" and internal frictions, the two parties did generate a vigorous and not altogether predictable pattern of national political competition. Whereas the northern-based NPC and NPN had been the leading political force in the first two republics, the SDP—with its center of gravity in the south but important bases of support in parts of the north—appeared now to have the political edge. When the first partisan local government elections were finally held, in December 1990, the SDP won a majority of the local councils in fourteen of the twenty-one states and bested the NRC in total council seats (3,765 to 3,360) and council chairs (315 to 274), which were (in contrast to the previous republics) directly elected positions. It sustained its lead in the state elections a year later, capturing control of eighteen of the thirty state legislatures and 53.6 percent of the total seats. Yet, underscoring the competitiveness of the process and the significance of intraparty divisions (which cost the SDP likely gubernatorial victories in four states, including the strategic states of Lagos and Kaduna), the NRC won sixteen of the thirty governorships.[112]

In the July 1992 National Assembly elections, the SDP captured 53 of 91 Senate seats and 315 House of Representatives seats, to 275 for the NRC. In that election, as in the previous ones, party alignments showed significant crosscutting of ethnic and regional cleavages. To be sure, previous patterns of electoral alignment had clearly reasserted themselves. The SDP (widely seen as "the new party of the old 'progressive' front") established electoral dominance in the Yoruba west, the midwestern minority states of the southern delta (former Bendel state) that had also backed the UPN, the ethnic minority areas of the north (the Christian Middle Belt and the Muslim, mainly Kanuri, minorities of Borno), and the states of the Muslim north (particularly Kano and Kaduna) that had backed the radical PRP in the Second

Republic. The NRC inherited "the old 'conservative' front built around the Hausa/Fulani bloc, and including the Igbo East, [southern ethnic] minorities, and 'core' northern states."[113] Yet "the most remarkable thing about the National Assembly election results, and, indeed, the results of all elections contested by the two new parties, was the national spread of their victories."[114] In the north, the SDP won more Senate seats than the NRC and nearly as many House seats. In the south, the NRC was dominant in six of fourteen states. Only in four of the thirty states did one party sweep all the House seats (Table 9.2).

While the pattern of electoral outcomes showed some promise of generating the more national, crosscutting alignments that had gradually been taking shape in the first two republics, other, more destructive norms and practices also reasserted themselves with each new electoral step on the transition path. Although these local, state, and National Assembly elections were accepted by the NEC and the political parties as successful, and clear winners were less disputable than before, serious issues, particularly concerning the voting system, arose. The open as opposed to secret ballot system adopted at those elections reduced the real voter turnout to unprecedentedly low levels, as low as 10 to 15 percent in the December 1990 local government elections. Moreover, the system of open queuing behind candidates or their photographs in those elections (and in the party primaries that preceded them) did not eliminate fraud and abuse.[115] Fraud in the voters' register, bribery of electoral officials, vote-buying, intimidation, and even deadly violence were all widely evident once again and no doubt affected the outcome of some races (especially in the less carefully scrutinized primary elections).[116] This played neatly into the ambitions of the Machiavellian military president, who found little difficulty, for example, in finding reasons to cancel the September 1992 presidential primary contests of the two parties (after they had already been canceled once by the parties themselves, in August, amid nationwide protest over malpractices). In those contests, as in the past, votes and counts were brazenly bought and sold, and the procedures and results were bitterly disputed. "Delegates had been stuffing money into bread rolls to buy votes. One presiding officer was caught chewing ballot papers when the wrong candidate started to win."[117]

With Babangida having repeatedly jiggered the process without warning and skepticism mounting that he really meant to hand over power; with the politicians having richly justified the cynicism of the voters; with all of the major and long-running candidates for the presidency having been disqualified in Babangida's latest master stroke of October 1992; and with the party executive structures now in federal receivership, manned again by government appointees, the country approached the renewed presidential contest, rescheduled for June 12, 1993, with considerable wariness and exhaustion. Ironically, this skepticism may have helped to produce a much

Table 9.2 1992 National Assembly Elections: Sectional Patterns of Party Victories

		Senate Seats Won		HOR Seats Won	
		NRC	SDP	NRC	SDP
Northern States					
Bauchi		3	—	22	1
Jigawa		1	2	3	18
Kano	Hausa/Fulani	1	2	16	18
Katsina	dominated	1	2	20	6
Kebbi		3	—	16	—
Sokoto		3	—	29	—
Kaduna		2	1	7	11
Adamawa		3	—	14	2
Benue		—	3	1	17
Borno		1	2	3	17
Kogi		2	1	9	7
Kwara	Minorities	—	3	—	12
Niger		3	—	18	1
Plateau		—	3	3	20
Taraba		—	3	3	9
Yobe		—	3	1	11
FCT		—	1	3	1
Total		23	26	168	151
Southern States (East)					
Abia		2	1	12	5
Anambra	Igbo	—	3	4	12
Enugu		2	1	13	6
Imo		3	—	18	3
Akwa Ibom		3	—	18	5
Cross River	Minorities	2	1	10	4
Rivers		3	—	18	6
(West)					
Lagos		—	3	1	14
Ogun		—	3	—	15
Ondo	Yoruba	—	3	4	22
Osun		—	3	1	22
Oyo		—	3	3	22
Delta	Minorities	—	3	3	16
Edo		—	3	2	12
Total		15	27	107	164

Source: Eghosa Osaghae, "The National Assembly Elections of 1992," in Larry Diamond, Anthony Kirk-Greene, and Oyeleye Oyediran, eds., *Transition Without End: Nigerian Politics, Governance and Civil Society, 1986–1993* (forthcoming), Table 3.

fairer, if not entirely free and clean, election. The rescheduled primary election process (which selected national convention delegates through a more complex process of party caucuses and votes rising from the local to the state level) was again "characterized by vote-buying and sometimes sordid horse-trading. Yet the primaries were also remarkably orderly and free of the [previous] bickering and boycotts."[118]

With the cancellation of the 1992 presidential primaries, the major political titans in both parties now had to scramble behind surrogate candidates, as the field was left to a new crop of much less established, less resourceful, and less known aspirants. One striking exception, however, was the entry into the SDP contest of one of the country's wealthiest businessmen, Moshood K. O. Abiola. As the publisher of the Concord newspaper and magazine empire and one of the country's wealthiest, most generous and omnipresent philanthropists, Abiola was able to call on a far-flung network of friends, clients, contacts, and sources of information. As a leader of Yoruba opinion and holder of a prominent traditional title, but also an active and serious Muslim, Abiola was able to breach the country's regional and religious divides more effectively than any other candidate. In a close contest at the March 1993 SDP convention in Abuja, Abiola narrowly bested Shehu Yar'Adua's candidate, Atiku Abubakar, and the former SDP chairman (and former close Yar'Adua ally in the founding of the PFN), Babagana Kingibe. At the convention of the NRC, whose ranks of northern political leaders were more thoroughly depleted by the previous cancellation, a relative unknown, Bashir Tofa (a youngish Hausa banker from Kano who had been active in the NPN a decade earlier), emerged as the presidential nominee.

As he would repeatedly in the fateful coming months, Abiola hemmed and hawed in the face of a crucial decision: whom to choose as his vice-presidential running mate. Labor wanted trade union leader, Paschal Bafyau, who, as a northern Christian, seemed a perfect match for the Yoruba Muslim business tycoon. But the more powerful candidates were Abubakar and Kingibe. In the end, Abiola decided he needed Kingibe's superb organizational and rhetorical skills on the ticket to win the presidency, but this left Yar'Adua marginalized and the Hausa-Fulani establishment unrepresented (Kingibe, though a Muslim, was from the minority Kanuri group in the northeast). The choice appeared to earn him Yar'Adua's dedicated opposition, as the latter now looked beyond 1993.[119] In an effort to make amends with Yar'Adua that would later come to haunt him, Abiola allowed the embittered former general (the apparent winner of the canceled SDP presidential primaries the previous September) to place his own loyalists in the chairmanship and most other key executive offices of the SDP following the convention.[120] Meanwhile, seeking to repeat the magic of the Hausa-Igbo alliance dating back to the Shagari-Ekwueme presidential ticket of the NPN (and before that, to the NPC-NCNC governing alliance in the First

Republic), the NRC chose Sylvester Ugoh, an Igbo former minister in the Shagari cabinet, as its vice-presidential candidate.

Into the mix of calculation and ambition entered as well the Igbo counterpart to Yar'Adua in wealth, cunning, and ambition: former Second Republic Senator Arthur Nzeribe, who had joined Yar'Adua in launching the PFN and then contested against him for the SDP presidential nomination in 1992. A close Babangida confidant and business crony, Nzeribe abandoned his party altogether and launched a campaign lauding Babangida's indispensable leadership and demanding he remain in power four more years beyond the August 1993 hand-over date. Through the nebulous Association for a Better Nigeria (ABN) that incredibly claimed 25 million members, and with the support of other shadowy groups that appeared closely linked to the state security apparatus, Nzeribe sought through public relations and legal challenges to derail the June 12 elections.

The outlines of the most fateful and controversial election drama in Nigeria's history were thus in place. The ineffectual NRC standard bearer seemed ill-matched in stature and resources as Abiola and Kingibe barnstormed the country, mobilizing political support across ethnic and regional lines to an extent that seemed without precedent in the country. Meanwhile, as Yar'Adua withheld his active support (or even quietly tilted against the ticket in his home base of Katsina), Nzeribe went to court to try to stop the presidential election, citing alleged irregularities in the conduct of the 1993 SDP primaries. General Babangida played an ambiguous game. Nzeribe "was generally regarded as a proxy for senior military officers" who did not want to abandon the fruits of power,[121] but he was no doubt serving Babangida's own desire to extend his tenure indefinitely. Two days before the election, the Abuja High Court granted the ABN's suit with an injunction to halt the voting, but the regime overruled the court action the next day. In retrospect, the ruling generals, or Babangida himself, probably calculated that the election would once again discredit itself, through the usual fraud and disputes compounded by the judicially induced confusion in the voters' minds over whether the voting would even take place.

The military miscalculated. The confusion, apprehension, disgust, and apathy did produce a meager voter turnout for a presidential election (an estimated 30 to 35 percent). But to the pleasant and even proud surprise of a weary, cynical public, it also produced a historically peaceful and orderly poll—and a historically decisive outcome. Although the ABN won a new court ruling prohibiting the release of the elections results, returns from fourteen of the states released by the NEC on June 15 showed Abiola and Kingibe heading toward a sizable victory. Yet for ten days, the fate of Abiola, and of the transition to the Third Republic, hung in the balance as Babangida and his fellow ruling officers debated deep into the night how to handle the one outcome they had not anticipated—a decisive victory by the southern, Yoruba, SDP candidate in an election that both domestic monitors and international observers judged impressively free of the typical fraud, violence, and indiscipline.[122]

Reluctantly, NEC obeyed the regime's order this time to honor, not ignore, the court ruling, which now enjoined the release of the final results (despite other court rulings ordering precisely the opposite). But few doubted that Abiola had won, and when the final results did find their way to the Nigerian press, they gave the SDP ticket a landslide victory, with 58 percent of the vote and a majority in nineteen of the thirty states, including Tofa's home state of Kano. Particularly impressive were Abiola's inroads into the Igbo vote, winning 48 percent of the vote in the four Igbo states, even though his ticket lacked an Igbo or even a Christian candidate, while the NRC had an Igbo vice-presidential candidate. Abiola also won nine of the sixteen northern states, including several, such as Kano, Kaduna, and Borno, in the emirate upper north; the (mainly northern Muslim) Federal Capital Territory of Abuja; and a wide range of ethnic minority states in both the south and north (which were, like the Igbo states, overwhelmingly Christian), while failing only in two states to carry the minimum one-third of the vote required in two-thirds of the states for an outright presidential victory. Even allowing for the mandatory two-party system and the weakness of the opposition candidate, it was a victory of stunningly national breadth.[123]

Nevertheless, on June 23, the military announced its decision to suspend the NEC and annul the election results. In his televised address three days later, Babangida could only grasp at hollow straws of election malpractices, "widespread use of money" during the primary and general election campaigns, campaign overspending, low voter turnout, "conflict of interest between the government and the two presidential candidates," and a desire to save the nation from the "anarchy" of conflicting judicial rulings.[124] The length of time it took for the Armed Forces Ruling Council to announce its decision lends credence to widespread reports that the military was in fact deeply divided on the decision (with many southern officers opposed); that powerful northern interests lobbied intensely to block the southern business magnate from gaining control of the Nigerian state (and, by this logic, giving the Yoruba, already the most successful group economically, formidable control of the country's affairs); and that Babangida and his colleagues were truly surprised by the outcome. It could well be that they were prepared to hand over to Tofa, a weak and malleable figure who had previously called for a military president to rule Nigeria until the year 2000.[125] But despite his long record of business dealings and cordial ties with Babangida and numerous other military officers, Abiola was apparently judged too independent to be trusted to defer to the military in the future, to preserve the existing balance of power, and not to probe the massive abuses of a decade of military rule.[126]

The annulment of the country's clearest and fairest national election to date effectively scuttled the transition program and plunged the country into a political stalemate from which it had still not recovered two years later. Following an initial calm, rioting erupted in Lagos and other southwestern cities in early July, met with a brutal security response that left at least 100 protesters dead. For a time, ominous images of the past descent into civil war were replayed, "as southern ethnic groups, fearing a recurrence of the communal purges which had preceded the 1967 civil war, fled to their home regions."[127] The high pitch of regional and ethnic tension subsided somewhat. However, as when the Action Group was destroyed and Chief Awolowo was imprisoned during the First Republic, a deep sense of outrage and grievance festered among the Yoruba people and flared up intermittently on the streets of Lagos and other predominantly Yoruba cities.

True to the country's sad political history, at this peak moment of democratic crisis and challenge, the Nigerian political class fractured in pursuit of short-term interest. While human rights, professional, student, and trade union groups denounced the annulment and mounted scattered protests, most of the NRC and, critically, most of the top officers of the SDP—following the dictates of their patron, General Yar'Adua—abandoned Abiola and opted for Babangida's pledge of a continued transition with fresh elections.[128] But the overwhelming bulk of SDP elected officials—including the critical governors and senators—held fast to the legitimacy of June 12 and the demand for Abiola's inauguration. Moreover, public cynicism and disgust with Babangida personally (reinforcing mounting divisions within senior military ranks between his loyalists and opponents) were now too profound to permit him to extend his own tenure once more. Yielding reluctantly, and surprisingly meekly, to his own promised final deadline, Babangida left the presidency and the military both on August 26, handing over to a civilian-led Interim National Government headed officially by Yoruba businessman Ernest Shonekan, who had chaired the civilian Transitional Council Babangida had established in January 1993 to shore up his waning legitimacy. General Sani Abacha—the lone top military official to have survived with Babangida politically from the December 1983 coup—remained on as defense minister and, many assumed, the true power behind the civilian facade, guardian of the military's and probably Babangida's own interests. But neither Shonekan nor Abacha were doing Babangida's bidding any longer.

With the existing elected bodies continuing in place, and with Abiola now abroad campaigning for support for his claim to the presidency, Shonekan quickly set about to organize new presidential elections for February 1994 and to prepare a technocratic rescue of the collapsed economy. At the same time, "General Abacha broke from Babangida's shadow by purging the former President's loyalists from senior military and intelligence posts."[129] And the politicians continued to divide and bicker along ethnic, regional, and factional lines, symbolized by the removal from the

Senate presidency on November 2 of a staunch pro–June 12 loyalist, Senator Iyorchia Ayu, by a coalition of the NRC and SDP renegades. As the politicians maneuvered anew for the presidency, Abiola's prolonged absence eroded his active national support, which shrank back largely to his Yoruba base and a thinning coalition of "progressive" SDP politicians from around the country.

The above three trends—Shonekan's technocratic isolation from any political base, the politicians' fatal divisions, and General Abacha's rapid consolidation of personal control over the military—soon converged to produce the denouement for the putative Third Republic. A serious and respected international businessman, Shonekan tried to repair the devastated economy. As Babangida clung to power in his final years, all pretense of economic discipline had evaporated. Inflation had soared to over 90 percent, external debt ballooned to $30 billion, the naira had plummeted to a real worth of two U.S. cents (less than half the official exchange rate), and the annual budget deficit reached a whopping 15 percent of GDP.[130] With his regime crippled by "domestic protest and international censure," Shonekan sought "to break the stalemate with external lenders" by gambling "on the inflammatory issue of removing the petroleum subsidy," a reform long demanded by the IMF and international creditors. In early November he announced a 600 percent increase in the heavily subsidized domestic fuel prices. The gamble failed. A sullen, oppressed populace, struggling mainly now to survive from one day to the next, erupted in violent protest, and the Nigeria Labour Congress launched a paralyzing general strike. Three days later Abacha forced Shonekan's resignation and seized control of government in an audacious move that dissolved all the existing political structures and effectively ended the transition to the Third Republic.

The Descent into Praetorianism

With the Abacha coup, Nigeria's descent into praetorianism reached its nadir. Praetorianism, here, refers not merely to the predominance of the military in politics, or even the prominence of force as an instrument in the struggle for power, but rather, following Samuel Huntington, to "the absence of effective political institutions capable of mediating, refining and moderating group political action."[131] Politics in the praetorian polity is therefore pervasive and intense, as varied social forces become highly politicized and directly mobilized into politics, without the tempering restraints of an agreed-upon institutional order.

> In a praetorian system . . . no political institutions, no corps of professional political leaders are recognized or accepted as legitimate intermediaries to moderate group conflict. Equally important, no agreement exists among the groups as to the legitimate and authoritative methods for resolving con-

flicts. . . . Not only are the actors varied, but so also are the methods used
to decide upon office and policy. Each group employs means which reflect
its peculiar nature and capabilities. The wealthy bribe; students riot; workers strike; mobs demonstrate; and the military coup. Power is fragmented.
. . . Authority over the system as a whole is transitory, and the weakness of
political institutions means that authority and office are easily acquired and
easily lost.[132]

Thus, political allegiances are easily transferred or "sold out" in the quest
for power and benefits, and no allegiance is formed to the larger political
community.

These features of politics have been present in Nigeria since its birth as
a nation, and to some significant extent, independent Nigeria has always
been a praetorian polity (as Huntington recognized at the time he was writing in the mid-1960s). Certainly civil war is the ultimate manifestation of
the breakdown of institutional constraints and mediation of any kind. But
Nigerian history is more profitably viewed as an ongoing struggle between
institutionalism and praetorianism. The Obasanjo years were a time of serious and imaginative institution building. For a relatively brief time during
the Second Republic, those institutions offered promise of "mediating, refining, and moderating group political action" by parties, interest associations,
and ethnic and regional groups. Wanton abuse of the rules by the politicians
squandered that promise, and the country has been in political and economic depression ever since.

The early Babangida years offered renewed hope of institution building,
constitutionalism, a stable party system, a vital federalism, a reformed economy, improved governance, open policy debate, political legitimacy—and
hence a lasting reprieve from the repeated dynamic of civilian political failure and military coup. But this nascent institutionalism was again quickly
trampled under the stampede for personal enrichment by the ruling military,
the resurgent politicians, and most of all Babangida himself. Although the
politicians conspired readily in their own demise, Babangida's constant
shifting and manipulation of the rules did much to strip the party system, the
electoral administration, and the whole transition process of legitimacy and
effectiveness. In particular, the "recurrent banning and unbanning of candidates and party officials hampered the emergence of stable alliances or the
consolidation of popular constituencies."[133]

But even well beyond this, through his repression, cooptation, and
debasement of the mediating institutions of civil society; his ruination of his
own economic reform program through corruption, profligacy, and indiscipline; and his utter contempt for the judiciary and the rule of law, Babangida
degraded every institution he touched, and his fellow ruling officers followed his lead. Indeed, one of the most important legacies of Babangida's
rule—with his lavish dispensation of cash, cars, contracts, and kickbacks to

the officer corps, and his license to use political appointments for personal accumulation—was the degradation of the military's own professionalism and institutional integrity, so that increasingly it became a set of political actors, patrimonial ties, and factional alliances seeking after power, patronage, and wealth—another political party, but with an official monopoly of arms.[134]

With the predictable failure of the politicians to put their crumbling political house back together again after the earthquake of the June 12 election and its subsequent annulment, it was inevitable that the political wheel would turn back again to full military rule. But under General Abacha, it has reached a new level of depravity and ruthlessness, of deceit and contempt for constitutionalism. Perfecting the game he had learned as Babangida's real understudy, Abacha did promise, in his November 18 first address, a new transition to democracy, with a new constitutional conference to determine the country's political future. And, save for the remnant of the SDP that held fast to Abiola and June 12—now constituted in the National Democratic Coalition (NADECO)—most politicians jumped at the opportunity to rejoin the political process.

In a brilliant stroke worthy of Babangida at his Maradona best, Abacha filled his entire cabinet with a stellar cast of leading politicians from both parties of the Third Republic, and major political tendencies of the Second, while neatly balancing ethnicity and region as well.[135] Even more dramatically underscoring the fluidity of political attachments were the appointments of Iyorchia Ayu, the ousted SDP Senate president, as education minister; Olu Onagoruwa, an outspoken critic of military human rights abuses under Babangida, as justice minister; Alex Ibru, whose *Guardian* newspaper chain had suffered the sting of military repression, as internal affairs minister; and Abiola's own running mate, Babagana Kingibe, as foreign minister!

Kingibe was reported to have "played a key role in the planning and execution of the coup," and *Newswatch* speculated that the coup might well have occurred with the knowledge and support, or at least acquiescence of Abiola, his supporters, and even the independent human rights groups, which had coalesced in the Campaign for Democracy under the chairmanship of Beko Ransome-Kuti.[136] It is not implausible that both Abiola forces and prodemocracy advocates might have seen a military coup as the quickest and cleanest path to their goals, the implementation of the June 12 results and inauguration of Abiola as president, or, for some prodemocracy groups, the holding first of a sovereign national conference to rewrite what they regarded as the deeply flawed, military-bequeathed structure of the Third Republic. If so, however, their hopes were quickly dashed, as Abacha unveiled plans for a much more limited and controlled national conference, while steadfastly refusing to reopen the issue of June 12.

Any doubts about the Abacha government's intentions were dashed by the arrest of Abiola on June 23, 1994, after he had returned to Nigeria to form a "government of national unity" and then in a public speech on June 11 declared himself president; and by the harsh repression unleashed on the political and civic campaigns for democracy. In attempting to break an economically debilitating strike of oil workers that began on July 4, partly in support of calls for the restoration of democratic institutions and implementation of the June 12 election, "Abacha resorted to bribes, threats, arrests, and eventually, when these methods failed," forcible dissolution of both of the oil workers' unions.[137] In repressing popular mobilization and dissent, Abacha picked up where Babangida left off, once again dissolving the NLC executive; violently suppressing prodemocracy demonstrators (with numerous fatalities); breaking up opposition meetings; renewing the war on the press with a new wave of arrests, assaults, and closures; and arresting a wide range of prodemocracy leaders and activists, including the esteemed NADECO vice-chairman Anthony Enahoro, who in the era of nationalist politics, had moved the original parliamentary motion for Nigeria's independence.[138] Meanwhile, Abiola was charged with treason and imprisoned indefinitely while his health deteriorated and he was denied regular access to his physician.[139] Through it all, not one member of Abacha's stellar cabinet of politicians resigned in protest, and Kingibe, the former SDP chairman and Abiola running mate turned foreign minister, became the staunchest defender of the military regime on the international stage.

Appearing adept at the praetorian game, the Abacha regime came increasingly to resemble Babangida's in its later years of mounting abuse and personalization of power. Like Babangida, Abacha manipulated the politicians and what now passed, very thinly, for a transition process, adjourning the Constitutional Conference for three months in January 1995 when it passed a resolution demanding a return to civilian rule in January 1996; plying the delegates with "welfare packages" and more explicit inducements; and reportedly planning to create yet more state and local governments late in 1995 in order to "divert attention from pro-democracy agitations" and delay the transfer of power until 1998 (when presumably new reasons for delay would emerge).[140] Lending credence to this theory, he jettisoned the bulk of his civilian cabinet the following month (February 1995) in favor of largely military officers and began summoning "state military administrators, traditional rulers and community leaders" to his presidential palace in Abuja for meetings "reminiscent of the ones held by former President Babangida" as he sought their support to extend his rule in its dying days.[141] Having already retired numerous senior officers and shuffled top military commands to favor his northern Muslim (and even more narrowly, Kanuri Hausa) ethnic base,[142] Abacha launched a new purge in February 1995 in response to an alleged coup plot. The regime admitted to twenty-nine arrests of soldiers and civilians—including former generals

Obasanjo and Yar'Adua, who it claimed were linked to the plot—but press accounts put the number arrested at 300, and one reported the summary execution of sixty to eighty noncommissioned officers.[143]

As Abacha tightened his grip on power, democracy—or even the hope for its development under a civilian constitutional regime—seemed a more distant hope than ever in Nigeria, and prodemocracy groups became more despairing. To an impressive degree, democratic forces in the press, the associations, and the human rights community labored on courageously, preserving an important element of pluralism and source of truth in a new "dark age." But the very willingness of the Abacha regime to allow them to operate seemed now a sign of its confidence and contempt for their impotence, rather than any liberal instinct. Consumed with fear, factionalism, and greed, the military could hardly any longer be viewed as a potential source of rescue for democracy. Nor did the politicians seem likely to summon the courage to stand up to the Abacha regime's readiness for harsh repression, particularly when handsome rewards were still to be had from cooperation, even though the Constitutional Conference delegates (three-quarters of them elected, albeit indirectly) did feel the heat of popular anger sufficiently to call for a rapid transfer of power. Barring a societal explosion or a concerted campaign of international sanctions against the Abacha regime, its combined control of federal oil revenues and military might seemed to give it all the resources it needed to persist for some time to come. Nigeria's institutional vacuum had never seemed more immense, or its praetorianism more triumphant.

Analysis of the Historical Developments

Why the First Republic Failed

The proximate causes of the downfall of the First Republic were manifest in the statements of the coupmakers and have been widely acknowledged by students and observers of that experience. They included, first, the succession of intense political crises, the deepening polarization, the incessant political instability and strife; second, related to this, the style and tone of political behavior and conflict, the violence, repression, and failure to play by the rules of the game; and, finally, the "ten wasted years of planlessness, incompetence, inefficiency, gross abuse of office, corruption," and resulting lack of economic development.[144] These phenomena progressively destroyed the legitimacy of the republic.

It is tempting to attribute this decay and failure to an *undemocratic political culture,* lacking appreciation for "the conventions or rules on which the operation of western democratic forms depend."[145] To be sure, most Nigerian politicians manifested a weak commitment to democratic values and behavioral styles, as witnessed in the vituperation, intolerance, repression, violence, and fraud characteristic of electoral politics. But political values were far from uniformly undemocratic. Many Nigerian political leaders manifested a considerable pride in the democratic system and a sincere desire to make it work. A number of them had studied in Britain or the United States and had acquired a sophisticated intellectual and moral commitment to democracy. Moreover, the traditional political practices and values of many Nigerian peoples had significant democratic features. But values and beliefs do not wholly determine behavior. In Nigeria, democratic currents in the political culture were overrun by imperatives in the social structure. Political culture, in itself, cannot explain why political competition became a kind of warfare.

The most common conception is that the First Republic failed because of *ethnic conflict,* and, on the surface, this is indisputable. But this, again, can be a superficial and misleading explanation in itself. Certainly there were deep cultural divisions, and these were heightened by the centralized structure of ethnicity in Nigeria. But it was hardly inevitable that ethnic groups would contend in mortal political combat. This, too, must be viewed as an intervening variable, resulting from the interaction of ethnicity with social and political structures. Even the stimulus to ethnic conflict generated by the competitive pressures of modernization[146] provides only a very partial understanding of why ethnicity became so heavily politicized. Here we must make reference to three other factors: the establishment of political party competition in the absence of other crosscutting cleavages; the role of the federal structure in reifying the major, tripartite ethnic cleavage and heightening ethnic insecurity in general; and the role of the class structure in encouraging "tribalism"—the deliberate mobilization of ethnic suspicion, fear, jealousy, and hostility.

By any reckoning, the peculiar *federal structure* heavily contributed to the failure of the First Republic. Indeed, one may question the very use of the term *federal* for a system in which one region was larger and more populous—hence more powerful—than all the others combined. The additional fact that the Southern regions had huge advantages in their levels of technological and educational development made for an "acute contradiction" prone to "political upheaval."[147] Further destabilizing was the authoritarian social structure of the Northern emirates, which the federal structure was pivotal in preserving. The polarization and bitterness of national politics owed significantly to the Northern aristocracy's determination to control the federal government at all costs, not only to secure regional and ethnic interests, but also to preserve its class dominance against the mobilization of radical commoners and the winds of change whipping up from the South.[148]

Polarization was also advanced by the small number of constituent units in the federal system, enabling the tripolar structure to collapse into a bipolar struggle. That ethnic minorities lacked the security of their own regions added to the persistent tension. And with so few regions, each was compelled to exploit the internal conflicts of the others. There were simply too few regions to permit the federal system effectively to decentralize conflict and to insulate the politics of the periphery from the politics of the center.

Finally, the federal structure heavily contributed to one of the most powerful structural problems of the First Republic, the close *coincidence of major cleavages*: region, ethnicity, and party. Instead of complicating and crosscutting the centralized character of the ethnic structure, the federal structure heightened it by making the Yoruba, the Igbo, and the Hausa-Fulani, in effect, governmental as well as ethnic categories. This made the organization of political parties along this divide virtually inevitable. When every election and political conflict became a struggle for supremacy not just between parties but between ethnic groups and regions as well, everything was at stake and no one could afford to lose.

The polarizing effect of coinciding cleavages was compounded by the *cumulative pattern of conflict* it helped to produce. Until independence, some relief was provided by the shifting of alignments over time in a three-player game. But with the destruction of the Action Group in 1962–1963, conflict was reduced to a running struggle between the NPC and its Southern antagonists, with the Northern party prevailing decisively over the AG in 1962, over the NCNC in the census crisis, and over the combined forces of Southern progressives in the 1964 and 1965 elections. This pattern constituted the maximum formula for polarization: Each successive conflict involved the same cumulative line of cleavage, the same configuration of actors, and the same predictable outcome. Given that the triumphant party lacked any support in half the country, and was also feared and hated in parts of the other half, it is not surprising that it was ultimately toppled through a wholly different process.

The most basic cause of the failure of the First Republic had to do with the *structures of class and state*. Nigerian society in this era was a prime example of Richard Sklar's argument that, in the emergent states of Africa, "dominant class formation is a consequence of the exercise of power."[149] Colonial rule left in place a modern state that dwarfed all other organized elements of the economy and society. State control was firmly established over the greatest source of cash revenue in the country, cash crop agriculture, and the greatest source to be—mineral mining.[150] In addition, state monopolies were established in many other sectors, private indigenous enterprise was discouraged, and the parastatal sector was rapidly expanded.[151] In the classic sense of a class of autonomous capitalist producers, there really was no native bourgeoisie. By 1964, 54 percent of all wage earners were employed by some level of government, and most of the rest (38 percent) were employed by foreign capital.[152] Moreover, with the spread of Western education, media, and consumer goods, colonial rule fostered the rapid growth of materialist values.

In the South, material wealth became the mark of what Sklar termed the "new and rising class." Government power became the primary means for individuals to accumulate wealth and enter the rising class, and for the ruling parties to weld diverse professional, business, and traditional elites into a new dominant class.[153] In the Northern emirates, state power became the indispensable instrument for preserving class domination by reconstituting it on a modern foundation and broadening it through the incorporation of commercial and ethnic minority elites.[154]

The brutality and intolerance of political conflict followed from the sweeping nature of the stakes in controlling state power. Political and bureaucratic offices offered not only high social status and handsome salaries and perquisites,[155] but also vast opportunities for accumulation through bribery, embezzlement, favoritism, and other types of corruption.[156] Moreover, given the scarcity of private resources and opportunities, those who did not hold state office heavily depended on those who did. Political office could deliver or block the licenses, contracts, and public loan and investment funds that could make a new enterprise or a quick fortune, as well as the scholarships, government jobs, and military commissions that could quickly lift an individual from poverty into the middle class. By the same token, the loss of political office or access threatened an abrupt plunge in socioeconomic status. Few Nigerian politicians (or their clients) had alternative careers that could offer anything like the material and status rewards of state power. For communities, both rural and urban, state power was the source of schools, roads, clinics, pipe-borne water, electricity, factories, markets, and almost every other dimension of material progress. For cultural groups, it could be the primary threat to or guarantor of their cultural integrity.

Because of this enormous premium on political power, the competition for state control became a desperate, zero-sum struggle, a praetorian exercise in which rules mattered little if at all. To lose political power was to lose access to virtually everything that mattered. Hence, political actors—even those committed in principle to democracy—were willing to use any means necessary to get and keep state power. This breakdown of constitutional norms, in the context of the high premium on state control, in turn generated a high level of political anxiety—"the fear of the consequences of not being in control of the government, associated with a profound distrust of political opponents."[157] Elite accommodation and compromise could not bridge political polarization and bitterness so massively rooted in the relationship between state and society and the incentive structure it generated.

This relationship is also crucial to understanding the politicization of ethnic conflict. Although each ethnic group had a real cultural and psychological stake in its own communal identity and progress, "tribalism" was not a primordial force. Rather it was generated "by the new men of power in furtherance of their" class interests.[158] These rising and traditional class elements had to control the democratic state. To do this, they had to win elections, and in a largely illiterate, multiethnic society, with relatively scant crosscutting solidarities or national ties, no electoral strategy seemed more assured of success than the manipulation of ethnic pride, jealousy, and prejudice. As they appealed relentlessly to ethnic consciousness, the politicians inflamed group suspicion and fear to the point where these forces assumed an explosive momentum of their own.

"Tribalism" also functioned as a "mask for class privilege."[159] By focusing politics on ethnic competition for state resources and by distributing patronage to their ethnic communities, politicians diverted attention from their own class action and precluded effective class-based mobilization against it.

The extreme dependence of class formation on a swollen state is also crucial to understanding the escalating corruption that helped to delegitimate the First Republic. Significant personal wealth could only be accumulated through manipulation of state power and resources. Such wealth was not only desired in its own right but necessary to compete for power anew, by maintaining, extending, and enlarging the chains of clientage that substituted for effective political institutions.[160]

Why the Second Republic Failed

Of the two structural causes underlying the failure of the First Republic, one was understood and rectified in the subsequent period of military rule, while the other was not. By creating first twelve states in 1967 and then nineteen in 1975, the military governments dramatically reorganized the structural imperatives toward ethnic polarization. Innovations in the 1979 constitution further encouraged the development of crosscutting political cleavages. But the problem of statism and its corollary phenomena—corruption, clientelism, profligacy, and praetorianism—only grew worse during military rule. In this failure to alter the relationship between the state and society lies the primary reason for the failure of the Second Republic.

Despite the widespread disillusionment over that second democratic failure, it is important to appreciate the significant political progress that was achieved. Although ethnicity remained the single most important basis for political identification and alignment, the identity between party and ethnicity was perceptibly weaker in the Second Republic, and was beginning to decompose in historic ways when the system unraveled in 1983.[161] In this sense, the revisions in the 1979 constitution forbidding ethnic political parties and requiring visible evidence of crosscutting support as a condition for party registration must be credited with some real success. In particular, the much more complicated federal system made a profound difference. Although the Yoruba and Igbo states tended to vote as a bloc in 1979, the NPN made visible inroads there in subsequent years. In the north, the

Hausa-Fulani heartland became a major political battleground, with the NPN and PRP splitting control of the four key states in 1979. As had been envisioned, the ethnic minority states became the swing factor in national politics (and a powerful pressure group within the NPN), and their political alignment was the most fluid and hotly contested. And, on some issues, such as revenue allocation—where the oil states lined up against the states without oil—the nineteen-state system did generate crosscutting cleavage.

The kind of ethnic and regional polarization that savaged the First Republic simply did not emerge in the Second Republic. There was ethnic mobilization. There were charges of "big tribe chauvinism." There was north-south tension. There were all the traditional ethnic rivalries and hostilities. In fact, ethnicity remained the most salient political cleavage. But it was much more fluid and decentralized. *National* political conflict did not polarize around ethnic divisions. Rather, the Second Republic demonstrated that deep ethnic divisions can be managed by democratic institutional designs that provide opportunities to crosscut and incentives to accommodate ethnic differences.

And yet, politics were not significantly less violent, vituperative, and chaotic in the Second Republic than they had been in the First Republic. This was because state-society relations had not changed. State power remained the primary locus of national wealth, the chief route of access to the resources and opportunities of class formation. If the articulation of the private sector since 1966 opened possibilities for upward mobility outside the state that had not existed in the First Republic, so the petroleum boom opened possibilities for accumulation of wealth in office that could not have been imagined then. In fact, these possibilities were so fantastic that they brought an important change in the character of economic life, what Sayre Schatz has described as a shift from "nurture capitalism" to "pirate capitalism."[162] Power replaced effort as the basis of social reward, and the state became a mere resource to be carved up into "prebends"—offices to be used and plundered for individual and (ethnic or factional) group gain.[163] Under such circumstances, "a desperate struggle to win control of state power ensues since this control means for all practical purposes being all powerful and owning everything. Politics becomes warfare, a matter of life and death."[164] From this continuing enormous premium on political power followed the familiar consequences of political chaos, intolerance, and instability: the impeachments, decampments, expulsions, thuggery, rioting, arson, and massive electoral fraud that drained the Second Republic of the considerable legitimacy with which it began.

Perhaps no less than the above, political corruption also served to delegitimate and destroy the Second Republic. The continuing expansion of the state and the paucity of private economic opportunities steered the entrepreneurial and acquisitive spirit into all kinds of political corruption. The heavily clientelistic character of party politics furthered the spread of corruption during civilian rule. But significant responsibility must also be attributed to the failure of the legal system to restrain corrupt conduct in office. Since independence, corruption in Nigeria has offered not only immense opportunities for reward, but virtually no risk of sanctions.

The makers of the 1979 constitution understood that the conduct of public officers must be carefully circumscribed, monitored, and, if necessary, punished in order to reduce corruption. That is why the constitution contained a strict Code of Conduct and an elaborate enforcement machinery. The code required all public officers to declare all their assets at regular intervals to the Code of Conduct Bureau, which was empowered to monitor compliance and refer charges to the Code of Conduct Tribunal. The latter, a quasi-judicial body, had the authority to impose serious penalties on offenders, including vacation of office, seizure of assets, and disqualification from public office for ten years. But neither of these bodies ever worked as intended, because the National Assembly, upon which the constitution made their activation and supervision dependent, buried the enabling legislation. Without this legislation, the bureau was unable to hire any permanent officers or to investigate suspicions and complaints. In fact, most public officials went several years without declaring their assets. The bureau never really functioned. The tribunal never sat.

This was indicative of a fundamental flaw in the 1979 constitution. Crucial regulatory functions, on which the legitimacy of the Second Republic heavily depended, were left open to manipulation, sabotage, and abuse by the politicians. As a result, other sensitive regulatory institutions—the Federal Electoral Commission, the police, and, to some extent, even the judiciary—behaved or were perceived to behave as partisan instruments of the ruling party. The problem is unlikely to be resolved by the traditional checks and balances among the three branches of government. The integrity of the legislature and executive is so suspect, and the pressures for abuse so powerful, that some wholly new type of institutional check is necessary (see the last section of this chapter).

Another significant source of instability was the chaotic party system. The military architects of the transition to civilian rule appear to have drawn precisely the wrong lesson from the failure of the First Republic. Suspicious and mistrustful of party politics, they delayed the lifting of the ban on political parties as long as possible, after the Constitutional Drafting Committee declined Murtala Muhammed's invitation to "feel free to recommend . . . some means by which Government can be formed without the involvement of Political Parties."[165] With so little time for new parties to develop coherent identities, broad-based constituencies, and fresh leaderships, it was highly likely that the old political divisions and leaders and anxieties would resurface in a dominant role.

The character of political leadership was also a problem. It would have been difficult even for the strongest and most heroic leaders to contain the political violence and corruption generated by the high structural premium on state power. But President Shagari never put that proposition to a test. A weak leader prone to governing by consensus, he was unable to control the venal tendencies of his party machinery and closest advisers. The meetings of his cabinet and party councils became grand bazaars where the resources of the state were put up for auction. Hence, although Shagari was not a polarizing leader, and was more inclined than most to seek some reconciliation of differences, he could not deliver effective and accountable government. Most of the elected political leaders were corrupt, and they organized or at least condoned the political violence. But it is misleading to attribute these fatal excesses of the Second Republic to the failings of its political leaders. In the same context of statism, prebendalism, and feeble institutional constraints, the new generation of political leaders behaved no differently in the emergent Third Republic.

Similarly, it would be simplistic to blame the failure of the Second Republic on the economic depression brought on by the collapse of the world oil market. Even in the best of circumstances, this would have sorely strained an emergent democratic system. But the economy could have adjusted to this reality—painfully, but without the degree of dislocation and consumer hardship that occurred—if governmental capacity and resources had not been so relentlessly drained by corruption. With honest and effective government that was otherwise considered legitimate, the Second Republic could probably have survived this difficult period of adjustment. On the other hand, even with continuing economic boom, it would probably have been brought down by the corruption, mismanagement, deepening inequality, and political instability.

Why the Third Republic Imploded and Authoritarianism Persists

In the first edition of this chapter, written some eight years ago, it was possible to explain why, despite two democratic failures, authoritarianism in Nigeria had not been able to persist. That explanation pointed to Nigerians' strong cultural commitment to political freedom and participation and the vigor of the press and associational life, all of which undermined Gowon's sit-tight military regime while challenging Buhari's and Babangida's. It also noted the potential value of Nigeria's religious and ethnic diversity, which was difficult to manage under authoritarian (especially authoritarian military) rule, in which a narrow group tends to gravitate to dominance. Those factors remain salient, but after more than eleven years of military rule, they no longer appear to have the potency and promise that they once did.

To be sure, both Generals Babangida and Abacha felt compelled to play the transition game, to launch a political process and hold out the prospect of transition at a relatively near date, even if the goalpost was continually moved. In this long run of military rule, only General Buhari failed to do that, and he did not last long. Thus, military rule has persisted in a condition of at least partial diarchy, in which power (albeit often mainly symbolic) and resources were shared with elected civilian politicians. Even with the deepening praetorian trends, there apparently remains enough democratic vigor in Nigerian society and culture so that the soldiers dare not write off the politicians altogether.

Yet if (military) authoritarianism cannot endure and legitimate itself in pure form, neither, apparently, can democracy. In many respects, the politics of the Third Republic were a sorry replay of the corrupt, fraudulent, abusive, "anything goes" style of the First and Second Republics. Institutions did not work to restrain behavior and all was fair in politics as war. Had the transition process been allowed to wind its path to a presidential election without constant military interference, a Third Republic would undoubtedly have been born, and an interesting pattern of political conflict and allegiance would have progressed, taking up from where the most promising evolution of the Second Republic left off. Yet because the style of political behavior also resumed with little change; because the corrupt, prebendal logic of politics persisted; and because a hungry military was waiting in the wings, it is reasonable to expect that the cycle of democratic transition and military intervention would have been repeated once more, on similar grounds of massive corruption, electoral fraud, thuggery, chaos, and so on.

What differed in the transitional Third Republic, however, were two key factors, mirror images of one another. On the one hand, the military had become so corrupted, perverted, and politicized as an institution that it was no longer willing to wait for the cycle to turn, but wanted to hang on to power indefinitely and thus be able to distribute to itself the bulk of the material benefits of rule—the billions of dollars in oil revenue, an estimated 10 percent of GDP, that simply vanish into thin air each year. On the other hand, the Nigerian public is now more disgusted and disillusioned with military rule than ever before, and as in Latin America, this much longer and more profound experience of military repression and misrule is likely to inoculate the society for some time to come against the illusion that the military holds the answer to a blatantly malfunctioning civilian regime. This, perversely, may hold the greatest hope for the future: that if military rule were somehow displaced, there would be a much broader, more powerful and enduring societal distaste for its return. Thus, in the later years of the Babangida regime, many democratic activists and intellectuals who were dissatisfied with the stultified and artificial structures of the Third Republic (particularly the mandatory two-party regime) spoke of a "civilian to civilian" transition as the hope for its reform, after the military had departed government for good. Unfortunately, Babangida and his cohorts never gave them the opportunity to pursue that novel path.

Theoretical Reflections and Policy Implications

Numerous observers and commentators have attributed Nigeria's political and developmental travails to a culture of corruption, or in Richard Joseph's more precise formulation, a culture and supporting sociopolitical structure of prebendalism. There is indeed a "prebendal" culture in Nigeria, in which the systematic abuse of state office and resources for individual and group gain is expected and rewarded in the interactions of clients and patrons, politicians and constituencies, even while it is condemned rhetorically in the aggregate and abstract.[166] This dual normative code illuminates much of the opportunistic and seemingly contradictory behavior of social and political elites, who as political outsiders condemn incumbents, civilian and military, for their greed and corruption, but then leap at the opportunities for corrupt enrichment (and respond to the expectations for dispensation of patronage) when they become political insiders. It also helps to explain the popular intolerance for prolonged military rule, in which power is intrinsically more concentrated and the fruits of corrupt accumulation much less widely dispersed. Most of all, it goes a long way toward explaining the instability of democratic politics in Nigeria. The possibility, indeed expectation, that state power will be used to appropriate to one's self and supporters enormous wealth puts an impossible premium and strain on the electoral game; too much is at stake to obey the rules.

At the same time, precisely because it follows an unwritten code in conflict with the law, prebendal politics contradicts institutionalism and lacks any check. The clientelist pressures from below notwithstanding, simple human greed takes over as political barons compete not only for the top prize—the presidency—but for the status and power that accompanies wealth. Even when state resources were by far the greatest—at the peak of the oil boom in the Second Republic—most Nigerians were excluded from any real benefits of the prebendal game, and thus were forced to rest content with its relatively puny droppings of naira and foodstuffs around election time. They were the permanent outsiders, and over time their alienation from the system brought its collapse.

Precisely because it lacks any real institutional mediation or restraint, a democratic politics of prebendalism cannot possibly be stable. And its instability rises sharply in a multiethnic, deeply divided society like Nigeria, where patron-client chains are largely ethnic in nature, communities jealously evaluate who gets what in the distribution of the fruits of power, and the mammoth stakes in the prebendal game intensify ethnic political consciousness.

But underlying prebendalism is a more basic cultural phenomenon, with its own powerful correlates in social structure and politics. This, I termed at the start of this chapter the *uncivic society,* marked by the absence of the reciprocal, cooperative, crosscutting ties that breed that most crucial foundation of democracy—trust, and with it commitment to the larger political community. Because Nigerians have a strong rhetorical commitment to democracy, a penchant for political participation, and a relatively vibrant associational life, the deeply uncivic strains in the political culture and social structure have been neglected by many scholars. At the nonpolitical and micro level of the ethnic village or community, norms of reciprocity and bonds of trust and cooperation, nurtured through networks of horizontal collaboration, still survive in many places. But in the formal political arena, where state resources are distributed and developmental policies and priorities thrashed out, Nigeria has had since its birth as a nation an enormous deficit of civic engagement, in Putnam's sense of social networks "that cut across social cleavages" and thus "nourish wider cooperation."[167] Instead, the national political community has been stuck in a vicious circle of uncivicness, in which "defection, distrust, shirking, exploitation, isolation, disorder, and stagnation intensify [and reinforce] one another." Under such circumstances, the "strategy of 'never cooperate' becomes a stable equilibrium," and "we should expect," as indeed we have seen in Nigeria, "the Hobbesian, hierarchical solution to dilemmas of collective action—coercion, exploitation, and dependence—to predominate."[168]

As this chapter has shown, this culture of uncivicness has deep roots in colonial rule, which created a new and artificial state called Nigeria, and in the contradictions it spawned; but it has also been shaped by the country's ethnic divisions, by its poverty and underdevelopment (a major obstacle to the forging of crosscutting horizontal ties at the mass level, particularly in the least developed area, the far north), and by statism.

Sweeping state control over the economy provided an enormously powerful inducement to selfish, corrupt, uncivic behavior, because the stakes in holding power were so huge, and the costs of being out of power, in an economy that offered relatively few truly independent opportunities for wealth accumulation, were so steep. Once the oil boom filled state coffers with windfall income in the billions, statism greatly intensified the nascent structure of perverse incentives. While the boom made possible rapid expansion of the educational system and the middle class, it also generated numerous distortions and unrealizable expectations (fed by a dizzying economic growth rate averaging 7.5 percent in the 1970s). It undermined the country's only real base of productivity—in agriculture, displaced rural labor, deepened inequality, eroded moral values, increased inflation, discouraged entrepreneurship, distorted planning, and fostered corruption and waste.[169] On balance, both for democracy and development, oil has probably been more of a curse than a blessing for Nigeria, and for other developing countries as well.[170]

None of this, however, is meant to treat Nigeria's path of political development as "historically determined" from its inception as a nation or an oil exporter. Along the path to their own political development, other countries in the world have been caught in the grip of violent, protracted, "Hobbesian" conflict between warring groups and factions, hierarchically ordered and lacking any crosscutting ties. Those that broke free of that path did so through two crucial factors that have been missing in the Nigerian case. First, contending political elites broadly and consensually agreed to wage their conflicts through peaceful and democratic means. In most cases, and for most elites, this decision was motivated more by instrumental than by principled considerations. As a result of political experience and learning—from debilitating political stalemate and costly if not catastrophic violence—elites decided that the risks of continued praetorian competition were greater than the risks of democracy, or a constitutional order of some kind. Out of this decision emerged (from different theoretical perspectives) a system of "mutual security," a "decision phase" for democracy (to be followed by a later, consolidating and enculturating "habituation phase"), or an "elite settlement."[171]

What makes the shift to peaceful political competition possible and lasting is not a sudden conversion to democratic faith, or some miraculous appearance of trust on all sides. Rather, the existence of distrust, and a long history of coercion, domination, and conflict, require strong institutions in which contending elites can place their faith and trust. The deeper the history of conflict and enmity, and the stronger the pattern of generalized dishonesty, suspicion, cynicism, and abuse, the more powerful must institutions be to generate confidence in the political environment and ensure against individual defections from the rules.

The problem with Nigeria is that institutions to restrain uncivic behavior and induce cooperation, trust, honesty, and law-abidingness have been shallow and unstable. The fundamental challenge for the future is: How can they be made strong and enduring? Four factors are critical.

Part of the answer lies in the design of the institutions themselves. One of Nigeria's real political achievements since the civil war has been the innovation of institutional techniques for managing ethnic conflict: the multistate federal system, the devolution of resources and power (at least in statute, if not in reality) down to the local level; the requirement for nationally based, transethnic political parties; the generation in the presidency of a panethnic leader required to fashion broad national support to be elected; the mandate to "reflect the federal character" in national cabinet and other appointments; and the elaborate "zoning" provisions fashioned by political parties to ensure a fair ethnic distribution of key offices and nominations. There is room for further innovation—for example, to find means of electing the National Assembly (perhaps especially the Senate) that generate the kind of transethnic political appeals and constituencies that are fashioned in presidential elections.[172]

Most of all, the country must confront the profound ethnic grievance engendered by the virtually continuous hold of the north (and especially the Muslim north) on the leadership of the federal government since independence. With the annulment of the 1993 presidential election—which would have made Abiola the first southerner elected president—the issue has been raised to intense salience and continues to hang like a dark cloud over the future of the federation. While various proposals for confederation seem unrealistic—and the existing fragmentation of the federation into thirty states and almost 600 local governments equally unviable—one innovation discussed in the 1994/95 Constitutional Conference does hold promise. That would be to rotate or "zone" the presidency by constitutional mandate, so that over time both south and north (or by a more elaborate version, each of the six major sections of the country) would be able to have one of its own lead the nation.[173]

However, despite the increased salience of ethnicity, region, and religion in political conflict once again, these are more manifestations than sources of Nigeria's true dilemma, which is the struggle to overcome uncivicness in all its diffuse dimensions. The battle against corruption, exploitation, economic recklessness, and abuse of power, and the effort to develop civic norms and traditions, require what the economist Paul Collier has called strong "agencies of restraint." These are institutions that regulate the conduct of political officeholders, hold them accountable, and ensure a rule of law in political, economic, and social life.[174] Legal institutions are essential to controlling corruption, for until the structure of opportunities and incentives is radically altered—until corruption becomes risky and costly for its practitioners, through frequent exposure, punishment, and disgrace—it cannot be deterred or contained. The most important agency of restraint against abusive governance is therefore an independent judiciary; but even if it has true constitutional authority and political autonomy, it can be effective only if it is supported with adequate financial, technical, and staff resources, a competent legal profession (both for prosecution and defense), and an effective, apolitical police force. The central bank can be a crucial bulwark against fiscal irresponsibility, but only if it has true constitutional and political autonomy. A critical agency of restraint against corruption is an effective audit agency or auditor general's office, but this too needs independence and resources.

In Nigeria, the 1979 constitution added a potentially pivotal apparatus of restraint against corruption: the Code of Conduct Bureau and Tribunal. But as I have noted, neither of these bodies had the statutory autonomy and assured resources to function at all seriously during the Second Republic. The 1989 constitution strengthened the provisions of the Code of Conduct itself (governing how politicians conducted themselves—and their business affairs—in office) and retained the Bureau and Tribunal. But significantly, the Babangida administration rejected Political Bureau recommendations to make the apparatus a more effective agency of restraint and accountability, by publishing officeholders' declarations of assets "for general public assessment, claims, and counterclaims," and by giving the power to appoint these bodies to the Council of State. Moreover, although Babangida accepted the Political Bureau's recommendation to get the Code of Conduct bodies functioning before the transfer of power, it did not give them the authority, technical and staff resources, and administrative leadership to pursue their tasks effectively.[175]

In any case, the problem of oversight could not have been solved under the 1989 constitution (or its predecessor for the Second Republic) by giving the power of appointment of these bodies to the Council of State, since the Council was chaired by the president and included numerous serving politicians (such as all the state governors). Along with the Code of Conduct apparatus, Nigeria's constitutions have provided for several other crucial restraining, mediating, and regulatory bodies: the electoral commission (FEDECO, and then NEC), the federal and state Judicial Service Commissions, the National Population Commission (which conducts the politically sensitive census), and the Police Service Commission. One can imagine new agencies, such as a general accounting office (designed, like the GAO of the U.S. Congress to monitor government waste and fraud) and a network of federal and state ombudsmen. If they are to be effective, all of these institutions need exceptional insulation from partisan politics.

As Collier notes, colonial rule was sufficiently insulated and removed to ensure the autonomy of agencies of restraint. Since its departure, no effective substitute has been found. The search for such insulation now constitutes one of the greatest challenges of constitutional engineering in Nigeria, and in Africa. In an important intellectual contribution to that search, General Obasanjo proposed in 1989 that the incumbent president be the only politician on the Council of State (and not its chair), with all other members being required to relinquish any party memberships or affiliations.[176] Even that is probably one politician too many. Somehow, Nigeria must find a way to constitute the Council of State (or some such grand oversight agency) that provides maximum insulation from partisan, ethnic, and factional bias. It must then give that council power to appoint, supervise, and dismiss the members of these restraining agencies, even perhaps to set their funding. To restore judicial integrity, some Nigerians have also proposed shifting the power to appoint judges from the president and governors to the judicial service commissions or new independent bodies.

None of this can happen, however, without political leadership. That is the second crucial factor needed to shift Nigeria from praetorianism to institutionalism. And its absence cannot be viewed as a mere artifact of the historical and structural factors discussed above. Nigerians themselves rightly refuse to absolve their political leaders of historical and moral responsibility for the economic and political destruction they have wrought. In his trenchant and enduringly popular dissection of the situation, *The Trouble with Nigeria,* Chinua Achebe forthrightly indicts Nigeria's political leaders and predicts: "One shining act of bold, selfless leadership at the top, such as unambiguous refusal to be corrupt or tolerate corruption at the fountain of authority, will radiate powerful sensations of well-being and pride through every nerve and artery of national life."[177]

However romanticized that view may seem a decade later, it nevertheless reflects the real importance of political choice and example at the top. With each new turn in the cycle of regime change, a new leader had the chance for a fresh departure. Gowon and Shagari were both too weak and consensual in nature to confront the rapidly deepening patterns of corruption and prebendalism or to lead by example. Murtala Muhammed briefly began to do so, but lacked time and operated in ad hoc rather than institutionalizing fashion. For implementing unwaveringly the return to constitutionalism, General Obasanjo stands alone in Nigeria's postindependence history as a head of government who advanced rather than undermined civicness and institutionalization.

With his intelligence, charisma, and personal charm; his recruitment of outstanding intellectual and technocratic talent; his visionary twin programs of democratic transition and structural adjustment; the considerable international sympathy those programs initially garnered; and the national readiness for serious change after the debacle of the Second Republic, Ibrahim Babangida, more than any other Nigerian leader, had the potential to lead Nigeria onto a truly different, more civic and institutional historical path. Perhaps few leaders in the postcolonial history of the Third World have more thoroughly squandered such a critical historical opportunity and imperative.

A third factor that might help to move the country from prebendalism and praetorianism to institutionalism is civil society, the entire realm of associational life and mass media independent of the state and the purely political arena. Only from Nigeria's civil society has there emerged in recent years patriotic, disciplined, unselfish—*civic*—leadership, concerned more for the national political community than the private pursuit of wealth and power. The persistence against great odds of numerous Nigerian journalists, editors, and publishers (including a whole new creative generation who turned to ad hoc "guerrilla" publishing when their magazines and facilities were seized); of human rights organizations like the Civil Liberties Organisation (CLO), the Constitutional Rights Project, the Campaign for the Defense of Human Rights, and the National Association of Democratic Lawyers; of professional associations like NANS, the Bar and Medical Associations, the National Union of Journalists, and the National Women's Association; of trade unions like ASUU and the oil workers' unions

NUPENG and PENGASSAN; of writers, artists, and intellectuals like Wole Soyinka and Ken Saro-Wiwa, and their physical courage and resilience in the face of repeated arrests and constant harassment, have provided one of the few hopeful and inspiring currents in an otherwise grim story of democratic decay.

These and other civil society actors constitute a crucial foundation for the construction of a civic community from the bottom up. However, one of the most important social structural conditions for developing such civicness, crosscutting social ties, is still only partially developed. The human rights groups in particular remain largely southern and urban operations, and, as a result of developmental disparities as much as ethnic and regional frictions, the professional associations are also much more strongly based in the south than in the north. Moreover, civil society organizations have not been free of ethnic, regional, factional, and ideological rifts, divisions they can ill afford given their political and financial weakness relative to the authoritarian regime. To some extent, repression has worked to reduce the effectiveness of civil society groups and media as advocates for democracy, accountability, and human rights. And civil society groups have also been handicapped by their "mutual disaffection" with political parties and politicians, which has made it difficult for them to mobilize a large popular following and easy for the regime to marginalize them.[178]

Still, with all their weaknesses, warts, and divisions, these elements of civil society remain the last best hope for democracy in Nigeria. Their survival—even growth—through the "dark age" of authoritarianism has been encouraged and assisted to some degree by the international community—the fourth factor that will help to determine the future of democracy, and civicness, in Nigeria.

The international community has become more important to Nigeria's democratic future than ever before, for five reasons. First, it has been an important source of inspiration, moral support, and funding for leading elements of civil society, particularly the human rights groups, many of whose projects and reports are financed by grants from public and private foundations in the United States, Canada, Britain, Scandinavia, and continental Europe. Second, through the work of international human rights organizations like Human Rights Watch Africa and Amnesty International, and through attention in multilateral human rights forums, both private and diplomatic actors in the international community have exposed authoritarian abuses in Nigeria and focused moral outrage on the regime. Third, with the collapse of the Nigerian economy, its currency, and its standing among international creditors, Nigeria has become economically dependent on the international community to a degree unprecedented since the dawn of the oil boom. Without new lending and a rescheduling or buy-down of old debts, Nigeria is hard pressed to function in international commerce. This provides potential leverage that did not exist before 1983. Fourth, partly for reasons of self-image and pride, and partly because so much of their own personal wealth is deposited and invested abroad (particularly in Europe and the United States), Nigeria's military and political elites remain sensitive to international opinion and fearful of sanctions. Most of all they fear sanctions that would threaten their personal financial assets abroad, but they have also been stung by the ban on travel to the United States, affecting a number of officials and elites in the Abacha regime.

Finally, and most fundamentally, the international community is increasingly important because, in the context of uncivicness, praetorianism, and deepening national economic crisis and dependence, it is now the only potential agency of restraint on Nigeria's institutional horizon. Even with its sizable annual oil income, Nigeria needs the assistance and cooperation of international lending institutions, particularly the World Bank. That support should come at the price of stiff conditionality—not just economic but political. The World Bank, the IMF, and the established democracies as a group must come to grips with their own egregious miscalculations in betting on the Babangida regime and its economic reform program. They sought commitment to a specific economic policy reform agenda while paying little attention to broader patterns of governance. Yet those very patterns of uncivicness, abuse of power, and relentless venality fundamentally contradicted and inevitably undermined the economic reforms they were seeking.

For the international community, there are two lessons in this story. First, reform in Nigeria must cut to the heart of the problem, which is not merely statism and the scope it provides for rent-seeking, but the praetorian institutional deficit in politics and governance and the license it gives to corrupt accumulation by one means or another. Unless this problem is addressed, any economic reform program will ultimately be ravaged by the very leaders who initially author or concede to it. Thus, economic reform cannot succeed in Nigeria without the institutionalization of open and accountable governance, public dialogue and debate, shared sacrifices, consensus formation, and a rule of a law. A return to civilian, constitutional rule is necessary (though not in itself sufficient) for securing these conditions. A rapid transition to democratic and legitimate government is therefore the sine qua non for real developmental progress in Nigeria, and two years later, there remained no straighter path to that than the certification and implementation of the June 12, 1993, presidential election results.

The second lesson is that if the international community is to exercise effective leverage, it must hang together in imposing serious conditions and sanctions. General Abacha was able not only to survive but to consolidate his rule—while jailing the elected president and launching the greatest wave of political repression in the country's history—because the major democ-

ratic powers divided among themselves. And sadly, those divisions paral-
lelled the fractures within Nigeria's political class, over access to contracts,
commerce, and the source of virtually all Nigeria's wealth, oil.[179]

Absent powerful international pressures and restraints, Nigerians were
left waiting for some sudden unexpected eruption of fate or fortune. It
seemed unlikely that Abacha could prevail indefinitely against growing
grassroots pressure for complete military withdrawal. But then, who expected, when the military intervened at the dawn of 1984, that it would still be
ruling a decade later? Repeatedly, democratic actors and outside observers
have underestimated the capacity of the Nigerian military (even with its considerably reduced numbers) to hang on, backed by a loyal and ruthless state
security establishment and still numerous (if less distinguished) civilians
ready to serve for a price. The regime benefits, too, from the continuing deep
divisions within the political class and the general demoralization of a society heavily preoccupied with day-to-day survival.

But as institutions of all kinds continue to crumble and authoritarian
rule persists, political stability seems the least plausible scenario.
Frustration, outrage, and despair manifest themselves in the increasing erosion of state authority; the disengagement from its structures and rules, even
(through emigration) from the country altogether; the withdrawal into primordial and informal networks of production and exchange; the readiness to
turn to violence, organized and spontaneous; and the deepening descent into
crime and lawlessness—pure praetorianism.[180] These trends could converge
in an unexpected societal eruption—a new coup attempt, an urban riot that
cascades into a national uprising—or they could simply advance the progressive state disintegration that is now occurring.

Increasingly, one is tempted to conclude that the only thing standing
between Nigeria's current condition and that of collapsed states like Liberia,
Somalia, and Sierra Leone is oil. But oil remains abundant, and unless
domestic and international forces can rally their will for democracy,
Nigeria's praetorian descent figures to be long and ugly.

Notes

1. Robert D. Putnam, with Robert Leonardi and Raffaella Y. Nanetti, *Making Democracy Work: Civic Traditions in Modern Italy* (Princeton: Princeton University Press, 1993), pp. 88, 111.

2. Ibid., p. 162.

3. Peter Ekeh, "Colonialism and the Two Publics—A Theoretical Statement," *Comparative Studies in Society and History* 17 (January 1975): pp. 91–112.

4. James S. Coleman, *Nigeria: Background to Nationalism* (Berkeley: University of California Press, 1958), p. 15.

5. Donald L. Horowitz, *Ethnic Groups in Conflict* (Berkeley: University of California Press, 1985), p. 39.

6. Coleman, *Nigeria,* p. 50.

7. Ibid., p. 323.

8. Ibid., pp. 308–318.

9. In addition to James S. Coleman's classic work, the indispensable studies of this inaugural era of party politics in Nigeria are Richard L. Sklar, *Nigerian Political Parties: Power in an Emergent African Nation* (Princeton: Princeton University Press, 1963, and New York: NOK Publishers, 1983); and C. S. Whitaker, Jr., *The Politics of Tradition: Continuity and Change in Northern Nigeria, 1946–1966* (Princeton: Princeton University Press, 1970). Other important works on this period are B. J. Dudley, *Parties and Politics in Northern Nigeria* (London: Frank Cass, 1968); and K. W. J. Post, *The Nigerian Federal Election of 1959* (London: Oxford University Press, 1963). The following historical review of politics in the 1950s and the First Republic draws from Larry Diamond, "Class, Ethnicity and the Democratic State: Nigeria, 1950–66," *Comparative Studies in Society and History* 25, no. 3 (1983); and *Class, Ethnicity and Democracy in Nigeria: The Failure of the First Republic* (London: Macmillan, Syracuse: Syracuse University Press, 1988).

10. Michael Crowder, *The Story of Nigeria* (London: Faber and Faber, 1978), p. 231.

11. Whitaker, *The Politics of Tradition*.

12. Richard L. Sklar, "Contradictions in the Nigerian Political System," *Journal of Modern African Studies* 3, no. 2, p. 209.

13. Sklar, *Nigerian Political Parties*.

14. Ibid., pp. 88–112.

15. Coleman, *Nigeria*, pp. 332–352.

16. Whitaker, *The Politics of Tradition*.

17. Coleman, *Nigeria*, pp. 353–366.

18. Whitaker, The Politics of Tradition, pp. 361–362.

19. Post, *Nigerian Election of 1959*, pp. 276–292; and John P. Mackintosh, *Nigerian Government and Politics* (Evanston, Ill.: Northwestern University Press, 1966), p. 525.

20. Oluwole Idowu Odumosu, *The Nigerian Constitution: History and Development* (London: Sweet and Maxwell, 1963), pp. 193–197; and Frederick A. O. Schwarz, *Nigeria: The Tribes, the Nation or the Race—The Politics of Independence* (Cambridge, Mass.: MIT Press), pp. 196–211.

21. Ernest Adelumola Ogunade, "Freedom of the Press: Government-Press Relationships in Nigeria, 1900–1966" (Ph.D. diss., Southern Illinois University, 1981), pp. 165–218.

22. Frederick Schwarz, *Nigeria*, p. 162.

23. Mackintosh, *Nigerian Government and Politics*, p. 538.

24. Richard L. Sklar, "The Ordeal of Chief Awolowo," in Gwendolen Carter, ed., *Politics in Africa: Seven Cases* (New York: Harcourt, Brace and World, 1966), p. 156; and "Nigerian Politics in Perspective," in Robert Melson and Howard Wolpe, eds., *Nigeria: Modernization and the Politics of Communalism* (East Lansing, Mich.: Michigan State University Press, 1971), pp. 47–48.

25. K. W. J. Post and Michael Vickers, *Structure and Conflict in Nigeria* (London: Heinemann, 1973), pp. 88, 90.

26. Walter Schwarz, *Nigeria* (New York: Frederick A. Praeger, 1968), p. 158.

27. Robert Melson, "Nigerian Politics and the General Strike of 1964," in Robert I. Rotberg and Ali A. Mazrui, eds., *Protest and Power in Black Africa* (New York and London: Oxford University Press, 1970), pp. 771–774, 785.

28. A. H. M. Kirk-Greene, *Crisis and Conflict in Nigeria*, vol. 1 (London: Oxford University Press, 1971) p. 20; and Robin Cohen, *Labour and Politics in Nigeria 1945–71* (London: Heinemann, 1974), p. 168.

29. Robert Melson, "Ideology and Inconsistency: The 'Cross-pressured' Nigerian Worker," in Melson and Wolpe, *Modernization and the Politics of Communalism*, pp. 581–605.

30. Post and Vickers, *Structure and Conflict*, pp. 141–149; and Mackintosh, *Nigerian Government and Politics*, pp. 576–579.

31. N. J. Miners, *The Nigerian Army, 1956–66* (London: Methuen, 1971), p. 178.

32. Crowder, *The Story of Nigeria*, p. 269.

33. Kirk-Greene, *Crisis and Conflict in Nigeria*, p. 4.

34. Anthony Kirk-Greene, "The Making of the Second Republic," in Kirk-Greene and Douglas Rimmer, *Nigeria Since 1970: A Political and Economic Outline* (New York: Holmes

and Meier, London: Hodder and Stoughton, 1981), pp. 5–7; and Crowder, *The Story of Nigeria,* pp. 278–280.

35. Kirk-Greene, "The Making of the Second Republic," pp. 7–9; Crowder, *The Story of Nigeria,* pp. 280–281; and Billy J. Dudley, *An Introduction to Nigerian Government and Politics* (Bloomington: Indiana University Press, 1982), pp. 80–82.

36. Decree Number 53, for example, made it a criminal offense to publish or report "anything which could cause public alarm or industrial unrest"; granted the police and armed forces heads the right of arbitrary detention; and suspended the writ of habeas corpus. Victor A. Olorunsola, *Soldiers and Power: The Development Performance of the Nigerian Military Regime* (Stanford: Hoover Institution Press, 1977), p. 102.

37. *West Africa,* quoted in Olorunsola, *Soldiers and Power,* p. 88.

38. Olorunsola, *Soldiers and Power,* pp. 86–101; and Lateef Kayode Jakande, "The Press and Military Rule," in Oyeleye Oyediran, ed., *Nigerian Government and Politics Under Military Rule* (London: Macmillan, New York: St. Martin's, 1979), pp. 110–123.

39. Olorunsola, *Soldiers and Power,* pp. 60, 76.

40. Statement of General Murtala Muhammed, quoted in Kirk-Greene, "The Making of the Second Republic," pp. 13–14.

41. David D. Laitin, "The Sharia Debate and the Origins of Nigeria's Second Republic," *Journal of Modern African Studies* 20, no. 3 (1982): pp. 411–430.

42. Jean Herskovits, "Dateline Nigeria: A Black Power," *Foreign Policy,* no. 29 (Winter 1977/78): p. 179.

43. *Constitution of the Federal Republic of Nigeria 1979* (Reprinted by New Nigerian Newspapers, Ltd., Kaduna, 1981), p. 65, sections 202–203; and Richard Joseph, "The Ethnic Trap: Notes on the Nigerian Elections, 1978–79" *Issue* 11 (1981): p. 17.

44. C. S. Whitaker, Jr., "Second Beginnings: The New Political Framework," *Issue* 11 (1981): pp. 2–13; and Claude S. Phillips, "Nigeria's New Political Institutions, 1975–79," *Journal of Modern African Studies* 18, no. 1 (1980): pp. 1–22.

45. W. Ibekwe Ofonagoro, ed., *The Great Debate* (Lagos: Daily Times of Nigeria, 1981).

46. Richard L. Sklar, "Democracy for the Second Republic," *Issue* 11 (1981): p. 14.

47. Whitaker, "Second Beginnings," p. 7.

48. Phillips, "Nigeria's New Political Institutions," p. 15.

49. Richard A. Joseph, "Parties and Ideology in Nigeria," *Review of African Political Economy* 13 (May-August 1978): p. 82; and Joseph, "The Ethnic Trap," p. 18.

50. Larry Diamond, "Social Change and Political Conflict in Nigeria's Second Republic," in I. William Zartman, ed., *The Political Economy of Nigeria* (New York: Praeger, 1983), pp. 35–39. For a fuller review, see Joseph, "Parties and Ideology in Nigeria."

51. Martin Dent, *West Africa,* August 6, 1979, p. 1406; see also Joseph, "The Ethnic Trap," p. 20.

52. This section draws from several of my previously published works: "Cleavage, Conflict and Anxiety in the Second Nigerian Republic," *Journal of Modern African Studies* 20, no. 4 (1982): pp. 629–668; "Social Change and Political Conflict"; "A Tarnished Victory for the NPN?" *Africa Report* 28, no. 6 (1983): pp. 18–23; "Nigeria in Search of Democracy," *Foreign Affairs* 62, no. 4 (1984): pp. 905–927; and "Nigeria: The Coup and the Future," *Africa Report* 29, no. 2 (1984): pp. 9–15.

53. The most affluent party, the NPN, suffered by far the fewest disqualifications (6 percent), while its radical and much more humble northern challenger, the PRP, suffered the most numerous (49 percent). Moreover, the PRP and NPP presidential candidates were not finally certified to run until less than three weeks before the election, when the courts overruled FEDECO's provisional disqualification. Haroun Adamu and Alaba Ogunsanwo, *Nigeria: The Making of the Presidential System 1979 General Elections* (Kano: Triumph Publishing Company, 1983).

54. Ibid., p. 199.

55. Ibid., pp. 255–256; Walter I. Ofonagoro, *The Story of the Nigerian General Elections 1979* (Lagos: Federal Ministry of Information, 1979); and Larry Diamond, "Free and Fair? The Administration and Conduct of the 1983 Nigerian Elections" (paper presented to the 26th Annual Meeting of the African Studies Association, Boston, December 7–10, 1983), p. 25.

56. Richard A. Joseph, "Democratization Under Military Tutelage: Crisis and Consensus

in the Nigerian 1979 Elections," *Comparative Politics* 14, no. 1 (1981): pp. 80–88; and Whitaker, "Second Beginnings," p. 13.

57. Richard A. Joseph, "Affluence and Underdevelopment: The Nigerian Experience," *Journal of Modern African Studies* 16, no. 2 (1978): pp. 221–239; Henry Bienen and V. P. Diejomaoh, eds., *Inequality and Development in Nigeria* (New York and London: Holmes and Meier, 1981); and Michael Watts and Paul Lubeck, "The Popular Classes and the Oil Boom: A Political Economy of Rural and Urban Poverty," in Zartman, ed., *The Political Economy of Nigeria.*

58. Diamond, "Social Change and Political Conflict."

59. Prominent government actions overturned by the courts included the president's signing into law of the 1981 Revenue Allocation Bill after it was adopted only by a joint Senate-House committee; the jamming of Lagos State Television by the Nigerian Television Authority; and the deportation to Chad of a prominent GNPP leader in Borno state by the Ministry of Interior.

60. *Daily Star* (Enugu), July 22, 1981.

61. *National Concord* (Lagos), October 26, 1982.

62. *Punch* (Lagos), March 31, 1983.

63. *New Nigerian* (Kaduna), January 25, 1983.

64. Diamond, "Nigeria in Search of Democracy," pp. 906–908.

65. Newspaper interviews with a wide cross-section of Nigerians revealed a profound exhaustion and disgust with the greed, corruption, opportunism, thuggery, "witch-hunting and character assassination" that had "polluted" the political system. *New Nigerian,* October 3, 1982.

66. This interpretation was later confirmed by one of the key architects of the coup that overthrew the Second Republic, Major General Ibrahim Babangida. He revealed that the army had considered staging a coup as early as July 1982 but did not want to be fixed with the blame for preventing elections, and so decided to let them proceed. With the rigging of the elections they realized that the chance for self-correction had been lost. (*Nigeria Newsletter,* January 28, 1984, p. 12). In addition, a confidential source in the Shagari administration informed me that the president was warned in the spring of 1983 by a group of high-ranking military officers that a coup was inevitable if basic changes in the substance and style of government were not forthcoming.

67. For an extensive analysis, see Diamond, "Free and Fair?" pp. 43–52.

68. Another controversial FEDECO decision reversed the election sequence from 1979 so that the presidential election would be held first. This maximized the chances of an NPN bandwagon through the five rounds of voting.

69. See Diamond, "A Tarnished Victory for the NPN?" and "Free and Fair?"

70. Diamond, "A Tarnished Victory for the NPN?" p. 22.

71. This section draws on several of my previous articles: "Nigeria in Search of Democracy"; "High Stakes for Babangida," *Africa Report* 30, no. 6 (1985): pp. 54–57; "Nigeria Update," *Foreign Affairs* 64, no. 2 (Winter 1985/86): pp. 326–336; and "Nigeria Between Dictatorship and Democracy," *Current History* 86 (May 1987): pp. 201–204, 222–224.

72. Diamond, "Nigeria: The Coup and the Future," p. 13.

73. *West Africa,* September 2, 1985, pp. 1791–1793.

74. Richard A. Joseph, Testimony to the House Foreign Affairs Committee, August 1993, quoted in Rotimi T. Suberu, "The Democratic Recession in Nigeria," *Current History* (May 1994), p. 213.

75. The Politburo's mode of work, the extent of the national debate it heard and stimulated, and the breadth of popular involvement are officially recounted in the *Report of the Political Bureau* (Lagos: Federal Government Printer, 1987), pp. 7–12. For a candid inside account of the deliberations and recommendations of the Political Bureau by one of its members, see Oyeleye Oyediran, "The Political Bureau," in Larry Diamond, Anthony Kirk-Greene, and Oyeleye Oyediran, eds., *Transition Without End: Nigerian Politics, Governance, and Civil Society, 1986–1993* (forthcoming).

76. Address by Major General Ibrahim Badamasi Babangida to the Nation, "On Political Programme for the Country," July 1, 1987, p. 5.

77. Oyediran, "The Political Bureau."

78. Adigun Agbaje, "Mobilizing for a New Political Culture," in Diamond, Kirk-Greene, and Oyediran, *Transition Without End;* Larry Diamond, "Nigeria's Search for a New Political Order," *Journal of Democracy* 2, no. 2 (Spring 1991): pp. 64–65. The failure to achieve legal accountability for past corruption, and other early worrisome signs of potential breakdown, are trenchantly analyzed in P. Chudi Uwazurike, "Confronting Potential Breakdown: the Nigerian Redemocratisation Process in Critical Perspective," *Journal of Modern African Studies* 28 (1990): pp. 55–77.

79. Even the September 1987 decision to create the two states overrode a majority view of the Political Bureau, which declined to recommend for creation of new states out of concern (which proved quite prophetic) that it would open a Pandora's box to endless further mobilization for yet more states. Oyediran, "The Political Bureau."

80. For a comparative analysis of the two transitions, see Larry Diamond and Oyeleye Oyediran, "Military Authoritarianism and Democratic Transition in Nigeria," *National Political Science Review* 4 (1994): pp. 228–233.

81. For example, the Constituent Assembly's draft constitution provided for a single six-year presidential term, which the AFRC switched back to the 1979 formula of a maximum of two four-year terms (for governors as well). Provisions declaring Nigeria "a welfare state," making military coups a punishable crime, creating a post of head of the civil service, and establishing a separate account for the judiciary and an Armed Forces Service Commission were all expunged by the AFRC.

82. Suberu, "The Democratic Recession in Nigeria," p. 214.

83. For further discussion of the coup attempt, and its causes and implications, see Diamond, "Nigeria's Search for a New Political Order"; and Julius O. Ihonvbere, "A Critical Evaluation of the Failed 1990 Coup in Nigeria," *Journal of Modern African Studies* 29, no. 4 (1991): pp. 601–626. The five northern states to be expelled were Sokoto, Katsina, Kano, Bauchi, and Borno.

84. On the structure, mobilization, and victimization of civil society during the Babangida regime, see Bayo Olukoshi, "Associational Life," and Tunji Dare, "The Press," in Diamond, Kirk-Greene, and Oyediran, *Transition Without End.*

85. For example, Babangida, who hailed from an ethnic minority area of Niger state, was rumored to have a partially Yoruba lineage.

86. Quoted in Rotimi T. Suberu, "Religion and Politics: A View from the South," in Diamond, Kirk-Greene, and Oyediran, *Transition Without End,* p. 14, draft manuscript. As Suberu notes, Christian advocates were quick to point out that the February 1989 AFRC reorganization left all four army divisions under the command of northerners, and three of the four services headed by northern Muslims.

87. On the divisions in and deterioration of the military as an institution during the Babangida years, see Bayo Adekanye, "The Military in the Transition," in Diamond, Kirk-Greene, and Oyediran, *Transition Without End.*

88. The coup-plotters' bill of particulars is extensively quoted and analyzed in Ihonvbere, "A Critical Evaluation of the Failed 1990 Coup in Nigeria," pp. 615–622.

89. "Nigeria: Religion and Conflict," Research Directorate of the Documentation, Information and Research Branch, Immigration and Refugee Board of Canada (Ottawa, March 1993), pp. 9–13; Jibrin Ibrahim, "Religion and Political Turbulence in Nigeria," *Journal of Modern African Studies* 29, no. 1 (1991): pp. 65–67; Africa Watch, "Nigeria on the Eve of 'Change': Transition to What?" New York, October 1991.

90. Africa Watch, "Nigeria Contradicting Itself: An Undemocratic Transition Seeks to Bring Democracy Nearer," New York, April 21, 1992, p. 25.

91. Political interpretations of these conflicts can be found in Jibrin Ibrahim, "Religion and Political Turbulence"; Suberu, "Religion and Politics"; and Omar Farouk Ibrahim, "Religion and Politics: A View from the North," in Diamond, Kirk-Greene, and Oyediran, *Transition Without End.* It was widely believed at the time that Babangida's intervention in religious affairs went so far as to influence, even impose, the choice of a new sultan of Sokoto—the most important traditional ruler in the northern emirates, religiously and politically. In early November 1988, the late Sultan's eldest son, Alhaji Mohammed Maccido, was bypassed for the title (after Sokoto state radio announced he had already been nominated to succeed) in favor of the prominent banker and close Babangida associate Alhaji Ibrahim Dasuki. In response, wide-

spread rioting broke out in the ancient city of Sokoto, with crowds chanting in Hausa "We don't want," and ten people were reported killed in the violence. *West Africa,* November 14–20, 1988, p. 2161, and November 21–27, p. 2205.

92. Ihonvbere, "A Critical Evaluation of the Failed 1990 Coup in Nigeria," pp. 615, 618–619.

93. Larry Diamond, "Political Corruption: Nigeria's Perennial Struggle," *Journal of Democracy* 2, no. 4 (Fall 1991): p. 76.

94. This information is aggregated from a number of personal interviews I have conducted in and out of Nigeria since the late 1980s. The latter source is a former high-ranking Army officer and government official in the Babangida military regime.

95. The correspondent for the *Financial Times* of London was expelled from Nigeria after he reported (June 25 and 27, 1991) that at least $3 billion of the $5 billion oil windfall that Nigeria reaped during the shortages associated with the Gulf War was unaccounted for. In its August 21, 1993, survey of Nigeria, *The Economist* (London) reported: "The NNPC [Nigerian National Petroleum Corporation] has no published accounts. International economists calculate that, given known Nigerian oil production and world oil prices, the gap between what the NNPC should have earned and what the government says it earned was about $2.7 billion last year. This suggests a huge amount of money—nearly 10% of GDP [gross domestic product]— is disappearing each year out of government coffers" (p. 8).

96. Peter M. Lewis, "Endgame in Nigeria? The Politics of a Failed Democratic Transition," *African Affairs* 93 (1994): p. 330.

97. On the abuse of the banking sector and foreign exchange auctions, see Thomas Callaghy, "Political Passions and Economic Interests: Economic Reform and Political Structure in Africa," in Thomas Callaghy and John Ravenhill, eds., *Hemmed In: Responses to Africa's Economic Decline* (New York: Columbia University Press, 1994), pp. 492–493.

98. For the impact on economic reform, see ibid., pp. 489–496; Lewis, "Endgame in Nigeria?" pp. 336–339; and Peter M. Lewis, "Economic Statism, Private Capital, and the Dilemmas of Accumulation in Nigeria," *World Development* 22, no. 3: pp. 437–451.

99. Larry Diamond, "Nigeria's Third Quest for Democracy," *Current History* 90 (May 1991): p. 203.

100. Just before his death, Giwa had been questioned intensely by the deputy director of the SSS, who, preposterously, charged the liberal and nonviolent Giwa with plotting to import arms and foment a socialist revolution. *Newswatch* (Lagos), November 3, 1986, pp. 13–25; and November 10, 1986, pp. 15–22; *New African,* February 1987, pp. 13–15. The parcel bearing the booby-trapped bomb was marked "From the office of the C-in-C" [commander in chief] with instructions that it should be opened only by the addressee (Giwa), and on opening it Dele Giwa remarked to a colleague who survived the blast, "This must be from the President." Clement Nwankwo, Frank Aigbogun, Eluem Emeka Izeze, and Dulue Mbachu, *The Crisis of Press Freedom in Nigeria* (Lagos: Constitutional Rights Project, January 1993), p. 37. While journalists have privately pursued leads that appeared to substantiate official involvement in the assassination, they have been unable to get sources to go on the record and have been unwilling to pursue the story vigorously in print, for fear of similar retaliation. One exception was the Lagos newsmagazine *Newbreed,* whose editor in chief, Chris Okolie, and two associates were arrested by the SSS and detained for a month for a story linking Babangida's state security chief, Brigadier Halilu Akilu, to Giwa's murder. The case was dismissed when Akilu failed to make a complaint to the court. Babatunde Olugboji, Frank Aigbogun, and Clement Nwankwo, *The Press and Dictatorship in Nigeria* (Lagos: Constitutional Rights Project, October 1994), p. 16.

101. On the origins and struggle of *Newswatch,* see Ray Ekpu, "Nigeria's Embattled Fourth Estate," *Journal of Democracy* 1, no. 2 (Spring 1990): pp. 106–116 (reprinted in a more extended version in Larry Diamond, ed., *The Democratic Revolution: Struggles for Freedom and Pluralism in the Developing World* (New York: Freedom House, 1992), pp. 181–200).

102. *West Africa,* July 6–12, 1992, p. 1123. On the travails of the Nigerian press in this period, see also Dare, "The Press," and Nwankwo et al., *The Crisis of Press Freedom in Nigeria,* which surveys the history of press freedom and struggle in Nigeria and extensively documents abuses under the Buhari and Babangida military regimes.

103. Olugboji, Aigbogun, and Nwankwo, *The Press and Dictatorship in Nigeria,* pp. 10–12.

104. Africa Watch, "Nigeria Contradicting Itself," pp. 23–24; Olugboji, Aighogun, and Nwankwo, *The Press and Dictatorship in Nigeria*, pp. 10–22.

105. *West Africa,* June 2, 1986, pp. 1144–1146; June 9, 1986, pp. 1196–1197; and June 16, 1986, pp. 1247, 1250–1251.

106. These various human rights abuses are extensively documented in the reports of the Lagos-based Civil Liberties Organisation. See, for example, the 1992 and 1993 *Annual Reports on Human Rights in Nigeria* (Lagos, December 1993 and October 1994), and *Human Rights in Retreat: A Report on the Violations of the Military Regime of General Ibrahim Babangida* (Lagos 1993), which summarizes human rights abuses during the first seven years of the regime. See also the reports of Africa Watch and the annual reports of Human Rights Watch.

107. Africa Watch, "Nigeria Contradicting Itself," pp. 12–18. Decree 47 of 1989 authorized university officials to expel and suspend students for union activities and prescribed penalties of up to 50,000 naira (then about $5,000) and/or five years in jail for demonstrating or organizing a protest. Ibid., p. 16.

108. See, for example, the cover story, "Nation Without Future: The Collapse of Education in Nigeria," *Newswatch,* December 12, 1994, pp. 14–20.

109. NEC, "Report and Recommendations on Verification Exercise for the Registration of Two Political Parties," September 1989. For analysis of NEC's report and its reasoning, see Femi Badejo, "Party Formation and Competition," a paper prepared for the Conference on Democratic Transition and Structural Adjustment in Nigeria, Hoover Institution, August 27–29, 1990; and *Newswatch,* October 23, 1989, pp. 16–17.

110. General I. B. Babangida, "The Dawn of a New Socio-Political Order," address to the nation on Saturday, October 7, 1989; and *Newswatch,* October 23, 1989, pp. 13–26.

111. Oyeleye Oyediran and Adigun Agbaje, "Two-Partyism and Democratic Transition in Nigeria," *Journal of Modern African Studies* 29, no. 2 (1991): pp. 213–235.

112. Dan Agbese and Etim Anim, "The 1991 State Elections," in Diamond, Kirk-Greene, and Oyediran, *Transition Without End.*

113. Eghosa Osaghae, "The National Assembly Elections of 1992," in Diamond, Kirk-Greene, and Oyediran, *Transition Without End.* Both quotes are from p. 19 of the draft manuscript.

114. Ibid.

115. This "open ballot" system, adopted by NEC as a means to control voter fraud, and popular with some voters, was widely denounced as an abridgment of the basic democratic principle of ballot secrecy. It was ultimately abandoned for the presidential elections.

116. *Newswatch,* November 11, 1991, p. 16. Among the casualties of renewed electoral politics was the NRC (1992) presidential candidate Bamanga Tukur's campaign coordinator, who was murdered in Niger state, and the chairman of a local government in Edo state, who was shot dead by political rivals. Bola A. Akinterinwa, "The 1993 Presidential Election Imbroglio," in Diamond, Kirk-Greene, and Oyediran, *Transition Without End,* p. 8 of draft manuscript.

117. *The Economist,* August 21, 1993, "Survey of Nigeria," p. 6.

118. Suberu, "The Democratic Recession in Nigeria," p. 215. As Suberu noted, *West Africa,* in its edition of April 5, 1993, termed them "probably one of the most decent series of elections Nigerians are ever likely to have recorded in their electoral history."

119. Ajayi Ola Rotimi and Julius O. Ihonvbere, "Democratic Impasse: Remilitarisation in Nigeria," *Third World Quarterly* 15, no. 4 (1994): p. 679.

120. Confidential interview with a former campaign aide to Abiola, 1994.

121. Lewis, "Endgame in Nigeria?" p. 326.

122. Rotimi and Ihonvbere, "Democratic Impasse," p. 675.

123. The leaked election results were published in most major newspapers and periodicals, including *Newswatch,* June 28, 1993, p. 10. For an authoritative report and analysis of the election and its outcome, see Akinterinwa, "The 1993 Presidential Election Imbroglio."

124. Rotimi and Ihonvbere, "Democratic Impasse," pp. 674–675; Lewis, "Endgame in Nigeria?" pp. 326–327; Suberu, "The Democratic Recession in Nigeria," p. 215.

125. Akinterinwa, "The 1993 Election Imbroglio," p. 7. The remark was quoted in the *Daily Times* (Lagos), May 21, 1990.

126. Numerous Nigerian analysts and scholars have generally taken this view, including Suberu, "The Democratic Recession," p. 215, and Akinterinwa, "The 1993 Election

Imbroglio," pp. 23–24. The latter source cites a number of grounds for anti-Abiola sentiment in the military involving his independent views about development, contracts, and repeated arrogant behavior toward the military.

127. Lewis, "Endgame in Nigeria?" p. 327.

128. Initially, Babangida posed two options to the two parties: an immediate new presidential election process in July and August open to all the previous presidential aspirants save Abiola and Tofa, or the dissolution of all previously elected bodies and restarting of the transition under an interim government. The NRC favored the first, and the anti-Abiola wing of the SDP leaned initially toward the latter. A tripartite committee representing the Babangida regime, the NRC, and the Yar'Adua-controlled executive of the SDP settled on the compromise arrangement that was instituted: an interim government organizing new elections while existing democratic structures remained. Suberu, "The Democratic Recession," p. 216.

129. Lewis, "Endgame in Nigeria?" p. 328.

130. Suberu, "The Democratic Recession," p. 217.

131. Samuel P. Huntington, *Political Order in Changing Societies* (New Haven: Yale University Press, 1968), p. 196.

132. Ibid., pp. 196–197.

133. Lewis, "Endgame in Nigeria?" p. 331.

134. This view is widely shared by Nigerian scholars. See, for example, Suberu, "The Democratic Recession," pp. 215–216; Adekanye, "The Military"; and (from a much more sympathetic perspective on Babangida personally) J. Isawa Elaigwu, "Prospects for a Democratic Polity in Nigeria: The Ballot Box and the Barracks," in Diamond, Kirk-Greene, and Oyediran, *Transition Without End.*

135. Among the major political figures with roots in the Second Republic (as well as the Third) were two prominent claimants to Chief Awolowo's "progressive" leadership among the Yoruba, former Lagos governor Lateef Jakande and former UPN secretary-general and Awolowo confidant, Ebenezer Babatope; the radical PRP Kano governor Abubakar Rimi; the former Plateau and Rivers state governors, Solomon Lar and Melford Okilo; and two prominent northern cabinet officials in Shagari's NPN government who had also contested for the NRC presidential nomination in the Third Republic, Adamu Ciroma and Bamanga Tukur.

136. *Newswatch,* December 6, 1993, p. 12.

137. Human Rights Watch Africa, "Nigeria: The Dawn of a New Dark Age," October 1994, p. 5. The two unions were NUPENG (National Union of Petroleum and Gas Workers) and its white-collar sister, PENGASSAN (Petroleum and Natural Gas Senior Staff Association of Nigeria).

138. Ibid., pp. 6–12; and Olugboji, Aigbogun, and Nwankwo, "The Press and Dictatorship in Nigeria," pp. 24–39.

139. As this book went to press, in mid-1995, Abiola remained in detention, with Abacha refusing all public and private, domestic and international appeals for his release. Also still in detention and seriously ill was the prominent Nigerian novelist Ken Saro-Wiwa, detained since May 23, 1994, for his leadership of the Ogoni movement, which is protesting the environmental degradation of the sensitive Niger delta homeland of the Ogoni people from oil production, as well as the neglect of the region's developmental needs. In early 1995, Saro-Wiwa was put on trial for what were widely viewed to be trumped-up charges of murder. The first prosecution witness stated that the government bribed him and others to testify against Saro-Wiwa. On these two most important human rights cases, see *Human Rights Update: Bulletin of the Civil Liberties Organisation,* April 26, 1995, pp. 9–10.

140. *Newswatch,* January 23, 1995, p. 12.

141. *Newswatch,* February 20, 1995, p. 18.

142. Human Rights Watch Africa, "Nigeria: The Dawn of a New Dark Age," p. 16.

143. *Human Rights Update,* April 26, 1995, pp. 2–4; *Newswatch,* March 13, 1995, pp. 12–18. The report of mass summary executions was by *The Observer* of London, April 16, 1995. Nigerian human rights groups were deeply suspicious of the purge, and particularly the arrests of Obasanjo and Yar'Adua. Obasanjo had been one of the most forceful and internationally effective critics of continued military rule during both the Babangida and Abacha regimes; Yar'Adua, as a member of the Constitutional Conference, was a prime mover behind the resolution demanding a return to civilian rule in January 1996. In its *Update* (above), the

CLO noted that some of those detained are university-educated officers who had "consistently expressed opposition to military rule since General Abacha" seized power (p. 6).

144. Lieutent Colonel Ojukwu, quoted in Kirk-Greene, *Crisis and Conflict in Nigeria,* p. 146.

145. Mackintosh, *Nigerian Government and Politics,* pp. 617–618.

146. Robert Melson and Howard Wolpe, "Modernization and the Politics of Communalism," in Melson and Wolpe, *Nigeria: Modernization and the Politics of Communalism.*

147. Sklar, "Contradictions in the Nigerian Political System," and "Nigerian Politics in Perspective."

148. Whitaker, *The Politics of Tradition,* p. 402.

149. Richard L. Sklar, "The Nature of Class Domination in Africa," *Journal of Modern African Studies* 17, no. 4 (1979): p. 536.

150. Robert H. Bates, *Markets and States in Tropical Africa* (Berkeley: University of California Press, 1981), pp. 12–13; Claude Ake, Political Economy of Africa (London: Longman, 1981), pp. 63–65; Uyi-Ekpen Ogbeide, "The Expansion of the State and Ethnic Mobilization: The Nigerian Experience" (Ph.D. diss., Vanderbilt University, 1985), pp. 37–44.

151. E. O. Akeredolu-Ale, "Private Foreign Investment and the Underdevelopment of Indigenous Enterprise in Nigeria," in Gavin Williams, ed., *Nigeria: Economy and Society* (London: Rex Collings, 1976); Sayre P. Schatz, *Nigerian Capitalism* (Berkeley: University of California Press, 1977); and David Abernethy, "Bureaucratic Growth and Economic Decline in Sub-Saharan Africa" (paper presented to the 26th Annual Meeting of the African Studies Association, Boston, December 7–10, 1983), pp. 12–13.

152. Diamond, *Class, Ethnicity and Democracy in Nigeria,* pp. 178–179.

153. Sklar, *Nigerian Political Parties,* pp. 480–494.

154. Whitaker, *The Politics of Tradition,* pp. 313–354; Coleman, *Nigeria,* pp. 353–368; and Sklar, *Nigerian Political Parties,* pp. 134–152.

155. Richard Sklar and C. S. Whitaker, Jr., "The Federal Republic of Nigeria," in Gwendolen M. Carter, ed., *National Unity and Regionalism in Eight African States* (Ithaca, N.Y.: Cornell University Press, 1966), p. 122; and Abernethy, "Bureaucratic Growth."

156. Schatz, *Nigerian Capitalism,* pp. 190–195, 208–209, 231–232; and Larry Diamond, "The Social Foundations of Democracy: The Case of Nigeria" (Ph.D. diss., Stanford University, 1980), pp. 556–582.

157. Claude Ake, "Explaining Political Instability in New States," *Journal of Modern African Studies* 11, no. 3 (1973): p. 359.

158. Richard L. Sklar, "Political Science and National Integration—A Radical Approach," *Journal of Modern African Studies* 5, no. 1 (1967); p. 6.

159. Ibid.

160. Robert H. Jackson and Carl G. Rosberg, *Personal Rule in Black Africa: Prince, Autocrat, Prophet, Tyrant* (Berkeley: University of California Press, 1982); and Richard A. Joseph, "Class, State and Prebendal Politics in Nigeria," *Journal of Commonwealth and Comparative Politics* 21, no. 3 (1983): pp. 21–38.

161. See Diamond, "A Tarnished Victory for the NPN?"

162. Sayre P. Schatz, "Pirate Capitalism and the Inert Economy of Nigeria," *Journal of Modern African Studies* 22, no. 1 (1984): p. 55.

163. The term *prebend* was used by Max Weber to describe an office of a feudal state that could be obtained either through service to a lord or outright purchase, and then used to generate income for its holder. As applied by Richard Joseph, prebendalism is a system, as in Nigeria, where state offices are systematically "competed for and then utilized for the personal benefit of office holders as well as of their reference or support group." Richard A. Joseph, *Democracy and Prebendal Politics in Nigeria: The Rise and Fall of the Second Republic* (Cambridge: Cambridge University Press, 1987), p. 6; see also pp. 55–68 for conceptual elaboration of the phenomenon and its intimate, mutually reinforcing relationship to clientelism.

164. Claude Ake, presidential address to the 1981 Conference of the Nigerian Political Science Association, *West Africa,* May 25, 1981, pp. 1162–1163.

165. Murtala Muhammed, address to the Constitution Drafting Committee, App. II, *Constitution of the Federal Republic of Nigeria 1979,* p. 123.

166. For Joseph, the cultural or normative component, and its deep embeddedness in pervasive relations of clientage, constitutes a crucial distinguishing feature of prebendalism. A "prebendal system will be seen not only as one in which the offices of state are allocated and then exploited as benefices by the office-holders, but also as one where such a practice is legitimated by a set of political norms according to which the appropriation of such offices is not just an act of individual greed or ambition but concurrently the satisfaction of the short-term objectives of a subset of the general population." *Democracy and Prebendal Politics in Nigeria,* p. 67.

167. Putnam, *Making Democracy Work,* p. 175.

168. Ibid., p. 177. This culture of uncivicness is, in different words, brilliantly captured in Chinua Achebe's trenchant collection of essays, *The Trouble with Nigeria* (Enugu, Nigeria: Fourth Dimension Publishers, 1983). There he identified as a fundamental source of Nigeria's troubles "indiscipline" or "rampaging selfishness"—the "failure or refusal to submit one's desires and actions to the restraints of orderly social conduct in recognition of the rights and desires of others" (pp. 27, 30). This, he said, was closely related to lawlessness, and the key factor behind the extraordinary anarchy and carnage on the nation's roads and highways.

169. Richard A. Joseph, "Affluence and Underdevelopment: The Nigerian Experience," *Journal of Modern African Studies* 16, no. 2 (1978): pp. 221–239; Henry Bienen and V. P. Diejomaoh, eds., *Inequality and Development in Nigeria* (New York and London: Holmes and Meier, 1981); Michael Watts and Paul Lubeck, "The Popular Classes and the Oil Boom: A Political Economy of Rural and Urban Poverty," in Zartman, ed., *The Political Economy of Nigeria;* and Schatz, "Pirate Capitalism and the Inert Economy of Nigeria."

170. See Jahangir Amuzegar, "Oil Wealth: A Very Mixed Blessing," *Foreign Affairs* 60, no. 4 (1982): pp. 814–835; and Terry Lynn Karl, *The Paradox of Plenty: Oil Booms, Venezuela, and other Petro-states* (Berkeley: University of California Press, 1995).

171. See, respectively, Robert A. Dahl, *Polyarchy: Participation and Opposition* (New Haven: Yale University Press, 1971), pp. 33–37; Dankwart A. Rustow, "Transitions to Democracy: Toward a Dynamic Model," *Comparative Politics* 2 (April 1970): pp. 337–363; and Michael G. Burton and John Higley, "Elite Settlements," *American Sociological Review* 52 (June 1987): pp. 295–307.

172. Horowitz, *Ethnic Groups in Conflict,* pp. 635–638.

173. The six zones (similar to the scheme commonly used within the political parties) would be the predominantly Yoruba southwestern states; the southern minority states (now Edo, Delta, Rivers, Cross River, and Akwa Ibom); the Igbo states; the (predominantly Christian and minority) Middle Belt states; the northeastern states; and the northwestern states. Other versions of a possible zoning scheme have been floated and are plausible.

174. Paul Collier, "Africa's External Economic Relations, 1960–1990," in Douglas Rimmer, ed., *Africa Thirty Years On: The Record and Outlook after Thirty Years of Independence* (London: James Currey, 1991), pp. 155–168.

175. Diamond, "Political Corruption: Nigeria's Perennial Struggle," pp. 81–83.

176. Olusegun Obasanjo, *Constitution for National Integration* (Lagos: Friends Foundation Publishers, 1989), pp. 90–91. Other Nigerians have pondered whether it might be possible to have the council nominated from recognized and respected civil society organizations like the Nigerian Bar Association, the Nigerian Medical Association, the Nigeria Labour Congress, the National Association of Nigerian Students, and the National Council of Women's Societies.

177. Achebe, *The Trouble with Nigeria,* p. 17.

178. Lewis, "Endgame in Nigeria?" pp. 333–335; International Forum for Democratic Studies, "Nigeria's Political Crisis: Which Way Forward?" Summary Report of a conference in Washington, D.C. on December 7, 1994, pp. 12–14.

179. The United States imposed the most serious sanctions, including a ban on military aid and weapons transfers, as well as the visa ban. European Union member nations joined in rhetorical condemnation of human rights abuses and imposed similar punitive measures in principle, but these were not consistently enforced, as regime officials were able to make unofficial visits and weapons shipments continued. Human Rights Watch Africa, "Nigeria: The Dawn of a New Dark Age," pp. 18–19. U.S. reluctance to take more forceful measures derived partly from fear that if European nations, such as France, struck more accommodating postures, the Abacha regime might retaliate against the United States by expelling U.S. oil companies and assigning their lucrative production rights to European competitors.

180. The phenomenon of societal disengagement from the state in Africa is explored theoretically and comparatively in Victor Azarya and Naomi Chazan, "Disengagement from the State in Africa: The Experience of Ghana and Guinea," *Comparative Studies in Society and History* 29, no. 1 (1987): pp. 107–131; and in the contributions by those and other authors to Donald Rothchild and Naomi Chazan, eds., *The Precarious Balance: State and Society in Africa* (Boulder: Westview Press, 1988).

MAURITANIA

MALI

GUINEA

Senegal Oriental

Fleuve

THE GAMBIA

Casamance

Diourbel

Sine-Saloum

PORTUGUESE GUINEA

Thies

Cap Vert

ATLANTIC OCEAN

SENEGAL

── 10 ──

Senegal: The Development and Fragility of Semidemocracy

Christian Coulon

The Rough Road to Democracy

A survey of historical experience in Senegal shows that democracy has had mixed success in that country. To facilitate analysis, three periods, with their own specific characteristics, have been singled out. The first covers the period from the beginning of the century to independence (1960). It is characterized by the progressive extension of rights and liberties within the framework first of colonization and then of decolonization. The second period extends from independence to 1976 and is set off by a de facto one-party state. Since 1976, Senegal has embarked on an experiment in democracy that was daring when compared with the political systems of most black African countries until recently but that, as will see, is becoming increasingly problematic. A well-known student of Senegalese politics, Donal Cruise O'Brien, has described the Senegalese regime as a "democracy without alternation."[1]

It is important to emphasize, as will be pointed out later in more detail, that each of these periods is mixed in nature. Although the "democratic" periods are not lacking in restrictions concerning civil and political liberties, the era of the one-party state cannot be compared to a tyrannical regime, and even less so to a totalitarian one.

Conquering Liberties

Senegal became independent in 1960 at about the same time as most of the other countries in black Africa. Decolonization was brought about quasi-naturally, without violence or revolution, and with the agreement of the various interests. It was the culmination of a political process that began before World War II, tending to reduce political inequalities by encouraging the ever widening participation of Africans in public matters. On this point, it is necessary to emphasize the specific nature of Senegal's political experience.

In Senegal, as elsewhere in black Africa, political parties came into being after World War II. Unlike in other countries, however, "modern" political practices and elections were not unknown in Senegal before this date, at least for the (very small) percentage of the population that enjoyed French citizenship. Indeed, it is not possible to understand postindependent political development without taking into account this heritage, which has influenced the style of Senegalese political culture.

It is not our purpose here to undertake an analysis of French colonial politics in black Africa.[2] The ideology of and the experiments in assimilation, however, have left their mark on Senegal. Since the middle of the nineteenth century, a small number of Africans held French citizenship and, as such, participated in the election of a deputy to represent Senegal in the French National Assembly. A little later, when Saint Louis, Dakar, Gorée, and Rufisque became townships with full political rights *commune de plein exercice*, their inhabitants were called to the polls to elect members of the municipal councils. In 1879, the government set up a General Council in Senegal to be elected by the inhabitants of the four towns.

Democratic rights were limited to the famous four townships. To be a citizen and to participate in these different elections, one had to show proof of having been born in one of the four towns or of having resided there for at least five years. Such people were considered French, enjoyed the right to vote, and were subject to the French civil and penal codes. The other Africans in Senegal were French "subjects" with no political rights. They came under the jurisdiction of customary or Islamic law, as interpreted by the French, which did not prevent colonial administrators from inflicting sentences and fines on these "subjects" without any form of trial. In addition, these "natives" could be enrolled by force in public works projects. Up until the period just after World War II, the number of Africans who could claim citizenship was very small. In 1922, there were 18,000 *originaires* out of a total of 66,000 inhabitants in the four towns and 1,200,000 in the country.

However limited this experience was in terms of the numbers of people concerned, it clearly had an important impact on Senegalese political life. It fostered the habit of political competition, mobilized social forces (business establishments, religious organizations, ethnic-based groups, etc.) around political clans, and, above all, allowed a few Africans to be members of consultative bodies. In the nineteenth century the political class was made up mainly of Europeans and people of mixed blood. After World War I, however, and particularly after the election of Blaise Diagne, the first authentic African to reach the French National Assembly, African leadership became more pronounced and gradually conquered the different representative institutions.[3] In 1931–1932, Blaise Diagne became the first African to hold a cabinet position in a French government (as undersecretary of state for the colonies).

Thus, a class of African politicians developed in Senegal much earlier than in most colonies. They were true political entrepreneurs who controlled important support networks and appeared as real political bosses. If conflicts about factions and money issues often prevailed over questions of electoral platforms, these politicians, nonetheless, had to justify their positions before their African constituencies and defend their specific interests, which were sometimes opposed to the interests of the French colonial office. This democracy "of the few" set the tone for Senegalese political life and contributed to the creation of a class of professional politicians.

After World War II, the French Fourth Republic gave new impetus to the process of democracy in the colonial situation. In 1945, forced labor was abolished. The following year, the status of "native" was dropped and French citizenship granted to all former "subjects." The French Constitution of October 1946 that created the French Union called for participation of overseas territories in the central institutions. Henceforth, Senegal sent two deputies to the National Assembly and three senators to the Council of the Republic and to the Assembly of the French Union. Like other territories, Senegal was given a territorial Assembly and was included in the regional Council (the Grand Council of French West Africa)—with limited powers, however. Universal suffrage was adopted only progressively, and it was not until 1956 that all adult citizens, male and female, had the right to vote.

Important modifications to this political structure were made when the law of 1956 (called the *loi cadre*) was passed. The law called for a government council in each territory to be elected by the territorial Assembly and to be made up of a number of ministers, one of whom had the title of president of the government council. The road to autonomy was now open.

These constitutional modifications allowed for greater participation and more democratic management of public affairs by Africans. Rural inhabitants who had played no role in public life up to then could, henceforth, participate in public affairs. The sweeping social changes going on in the country—urbanization, upheavals in the rural areas as a result of the development of peanut farming, the emergence of a working class and of a middle class of civil servants—created new situations and new demands that engendered new organizations: associations of all sorts, trade unions, and political parties. Despite the diversity of their aims and ideologies, these movements had the common goal of promoting and defending the interests of Africans. At this time, the trade union movement began to develop, although the unions, and in particular the Senegalese branch of the French General Confederation of Labor (Confédération générale du travail, CGT), had already made themselves felt before the war in fierce strike actions like that of the railway workers in 1938. Regional and ethnic-based movements also started to bloom.

Above all, during these final years of colonial rule, political parties began to flower as well: the Rassemblement démocratique africain, which was the Senegalese section of the SFIO (the French International Socialist Labor Party), and the Mouvement nationaliste africain. At first, it was the SFIO of Lamine Guèye, Blaise Diagne's former lieutenant, that dominated political life. But very quickly, Léopold Sédar Senghor, a young politician who had been elected as deputy to the French National Assembly as a member of Guèye's party, set himself off from his former boss. Senghor accused Guèye and his party of being too tied to the interests of continental France and the French Socialist Party, of encouraging assimilation, and of favoring the old elite of the four townships. In 1948, he founded an independent movement, the Bloc démocratique sénégalais (BDS), which wanted more autonomy for overseas territories, sought to pave the way for an "African socialism," and defended the interests of peasants, whom the old politicians of urban areas had tended to treat as second-class citizens.

Senghor's BDS rapidly became the dominant party. It was more rooted than its rival in the rural areas, and although Senghor was a Catholic, it was much closer to the Muslim brotherhoods *(tariqa)* who held tight control over much of the peasantry. It was also much more open to currents of African thought, like negritude and African socialism, with which trade unionists and the new elite of young intellectuals and civil servants easily identified. In 1951, the BDS won the two seats in the French National Assembly. The following year, it carried forty of the fifty seats to be filled in the territorial assembly elections. The elections of 1956 confirmed this position.

The BDS gradually tried to gather rival political movements under its banner. A first attempt in 1956 brought several minor parties into the BDS, which now became the BPS (Bloc populaire sénégalais). The year 1958 witnessed the birth of a "unified party," the Union progressiste sénégalaise (UPS), which absorbed Lamine Guèye (who had become reconciled with Senghor) and his partisans.[4]

In was in this context, and after General de Gaulle came to power (1958), that the referendum of the project of the French Community took place. Under this project, African territories were to be granted extensive autonomy. The UPS suffered its first division over this issue. The majority of the party was in favor of de Gaulle's project, but the left wing broke off and founded the Parti du regroupement africain (PRA). The split did not affect the UPS unduly, however, and it won a massive victory in the referendum (92 percent of the votes), thanks to the support of rural leaders and marabouts (Muslim religious leaders). During the 1959 elections for the Senegalese National Assembly, the opposition was completely divided between the Marxist element, the Parti africain de l'indépendance, and the more conservative forces, the PRA and the Parti de la solidarité sénégalaise, and did not win a single seat. With 82.7 percent of the votes, the UPS's victory was absolute.

Thus, when Senegal became independent in 1960, first within the framework of the Federation of Mali and then as a sovereign entity, the UPS had a strong hold on the new country.

The long period we have just surveyed was essentially a time of formal questioning of the colonial order. To explain these political gains, one must focus mainly on the struggles of the elite and the different movements that sought to give Africans elementary democratic rights—to elect their representatives, to form associations, trade unions and parties, and to have adequate protection under the law. These struggles, of course, were led by a minority—those whose ambitions were frustrated by a colonial situation that only very reluctantly and incompletely encouraged the appointment of Africans to positions of responsibility. In contrast to what happened in Algeria, or to a lesser extent in Cameroon or in Madagascar, there was never any mobilization of the masses against the colonial regime, and even less so any attempt to take up arms against the colonizer.

One of the main explanations for this was that Senegalese peasants, particularly in the regions where peanuts—"the great wealth of the country"—were grown, were under the control of Muslim religious leaders, who exerted a sort of formal and indirect rule over the rural world in their role as middlemen between the "center" and the "periphery." The ties of these very popular religious leaders—and peanut producers—to the colonial system were strong enough to act as a kind of safety valve. The marabouts rendered services of all kinds to the peasants. They also had the charisma (*baraka*) that made them leaders whose protection was sought not only in the here and now, but also in the afterlife. In addition, because of their religion, the marabouts felt very little attraction for white culture and were, therefore, very reluctant, if not hostile, to accepting any form of assimilation. This religious power was a definite factor of political stability, and the success of Senghor and his party can be explained to a great extent by the relationship of trust he was able to cultivate among this class of religious leaders.

Léopold Senghor, who came from an ethnic group in the interior of the country and loudly proclaimed his African culture, appeared to be the natural spokesman of the marabouts and the peasants. Moreover, his status as an intellectual,[5] his active involvement in the African culture and literary movement of the time, as well as his pioneering efforts to defend "African socialism" attracted the sympathy of a great number of the young elite who could not identify with the older, urban-based leaders whose attitude they felt to be too "French."

Other explanations for the above political gains can be found in the age of political traditions in the country. Despite its status as a colony, Senegal was the only overseas territory to enter into modern political life at such an early date. As early as at the beginning of the century, a number of Africans had begun participating actively in electoral competition and acquired the habit of political debate. African politicians knew how to manage townships, how to make themselves heard in assemblies, and how to build a support network. At the outset, only a minority of the population was involved, and political struggles resembled private quarrels more than ideological debates. But, largely because these political activities took place in the urban arena, they had an impact that extended far beyond the few thousand people who were directly concerned. Hence, when political participation was widened, political "games" were not something new in Senegal. At the time of independence, a great number of leaders were immersed in the culture of political machinery, even if they endeavored to give it a new meaning. This was an inheritance that very few ex-colonies could claim. It made it very difficult to impose restrictions on a people who, for more than a century, had been used to political battles.

From a Dominant Party to a Single Party (1961–1976): Moderate Authoritarianism

In the period following independence, as a result of a series of crises, the regime sought to reinforce its control over society by strengthening the executive and the centralized power structure, and by developing a mass party. This authoritarian tendency was accompanied by restrictions on civil liberties, but, unlike many African countries, the regime never developed into a police state or promoted a situation of state-inspired political violence. Despite the UPS's monopoly over political life, despite many violations of civil liberties, and despite the personalization of power, freedom of speech in Senegal was never throttled. Social and political life in the country was constantly enlivened by debates on issues, by the voicing of opposition, and by the confrontation of clans and of ideas.

Senegal became a sovereign state in September 1960 after a short-lived attempt at union with the former French Sudan (April–August 1960) as the Federation of Mali. Ideological and personal antagonism, as well as differences in history and social structures between these two countries, explain the failure of this experiment.[6]

In August 1960, Senegal adopted a constitution that was inspired, both in spirit and largely in letter, by the French Constitution of 1958. The text granted political parties the freedom to compete for the people's vote, on the condition that they respect "the principles of a national sovereignty and democracy." It called for a bicephalous system of executive power, with a president of the republic to be elected for seven years by an electoral college made up of parliamentarians and representatives of municipal and regional councils. As guardian of the constitution and supreme arbitrator, the president insures the continuity of the republic and the regular working of institutions. The president of the Council, or prime minister, determines and carries out national policy and is responsible to the Assembly. Legislative power is invested in a single chamber, the National Assembly, whose members are elected for five years by direct, universal suffrage. The constitution recognized the independence of the judicial branch and set up a Supreme Court that, aside from being the highest administrative jurisdiction, ensures that the constitution is respected. In sum, then, the constitution called for a liberal, parliamentary democracy in which power is shared and civil liberties are guaranteed.[7]

Such a democratic foundation, however, hardly prevented the authoritarian evolution of a regime that was confronted, from the start, by major political crises. The most important was that of 1962, which brought into conflict the president of the republic and secretary-general of the UPS, Léopold Senghor and his prime minister, the party's assistant secretary-general, Mamadou Dia. This conflict provoked a profound split between the UPS and the National Assembly that fast turned into a struggle of clans and clienteles, as had always been the case in Senegalese political life. Above and beyond any question of personal or factional rivalry, however, fundamentally different ideological options explain the uneasy coexistence of these two men.

Mamadou Dia supported a strong socialist line and urged rapid, radical reforms in economic and social matters. He wanted to put a stop to the all-powerful French interests, which were backed by their African clients. His idea of democracy was based not on institutional pluralism, but on grass-roots action that gives initiative to the "powerless masses" through cooperatives and rural organizations. In order to bring about these changes, he thought it was necessary to build a party of the masses that would have pre-eminence over constitutional powers. Dia was not so attached as Senghor to the former "motherland," and encouraged the diversification of Senegal's foreign relations, particularly with Eastern bloc countries. His populist brand of socialism drew the favor of young civil servants and rural organizers—in short, of the "radical" wing of the UPS. Conversely, he met with the hostility, not to say hatred, of French businessmen and most Muslim religious leaders and traditional political authorities, who did not take kindly to the idea of radical changes that would reduce their own power. This power elite placed their faith much more in Senghor, whose humanistic form of socialism did not call for such rapid or profound changes. Senghor's lack of dogmatism, his concept of negritude that encourages cultural contact, and his less "authoritarian" view of the party not only reassured businessmen, but also the marabouts and the dignitaries with whom he had been dealing for so long.

After a series of complicated events, a motion of censure was voted against Mamadou Dia by forty-seven members of Parliament on December 17, 1962. He was accused of restricting parliamentary liberties and abusing power. Dia tried in vain to put down this parliamentary rebellion by force. The following day, he was arrested by the forces of order loyal to Senghor. In 1963, after a public trial, Dia was sentenced to life in prison, and several of his political friends also received prison sentences of varying lengths. In the period that followed, the regime hardened. Executive power was reinforced and the opposition tamed. The man who had given the image of moderate and democratic leadership, who had criticized his adversary's dictatorial tendencies, gradually turned more authoritarian in order to rectify the situation.

After Mamadou Dia was arrested, Senghor initiated a constitutional reform, changing the regime from a parliamentary to a more presidential type. Henceforth, the president of the republic was to be elected by universal suffrage. Presidential power was extended, and in "exceptional circumstances" and for a limited time, the president was enabled to govern without the Assembly. He also had recourse to referenda in order to have legislation approved.

The basis for election to the National Assembly was also modified. Senegal was transformed into a single constituency, and parties were authorized to present candidates at an election only if they offered a complete list of candidates. As G. Hesseling noted, "For the authorities, the ballot by list was supposed to encourage national unity. In reality, it meant that only one party could sit in the Assembly."[8] In 1967, another constitutional reform further increased the powers of the president by giving him the right to dissolve the Assembly.

Opposition groups were gradually eliminated, either by integration into the government party or by repression. The Marxist-oriented Parti africain de l'indépendance (PAI) had been outlawed in 1960. In 1963, Senghor began a major campaign to woo the Bloc des masses sénégalaises (BMS), a party that stood under the banner of African nationalism and was favored by some marabouts of the powerful Muslim brotherhood, the *mourides*. In exchange for two ministerial appointments and some seats in the Assembly, Senghor proposed a merger of the BMS and the UPS. A few members of the BMS accepted the offer, although others refused, including Senghor's great intellectual rival, the historian Cheikh Anta Diop. On October 14 the BMS was outlawed by decree. Its leaders refused to be intimidated and decided to found another political movement, the Front national sénégalais (FNS).

In January 1964, a new law went into force requiring political parties to request a "receipt" from the minister of the interior to be authorized to carry out their activities. A few months later, the FNS was dissolved, having been accused of encouraging violence and of being a cover for the activities of the partisans of Mamadou Dia.

Still, the Parti du regroupement africain (PRA), which had splintered off from the UPS at the time of the 1958 referendum (see above), continued to exist. The PRA was solidly anchored in a few places like Casamance, in the south of Senegal. Senghor attempted to buy out the PRA, and, in 1963, a minority group of the party swallowed the bait. Those who held back were taken to court. But, in 1966, the two parties reached an agreement: in exchange for three ministerial appointments and a few seats in the controlling organs of the UPS, the PRA merged with Senghor's party.

All the parties belonging to the legal opposition had now disappeared. From this point on the "unified party" was a de facto single party. In the legislative elections of 1968, the UPS was the only party to present candidates and it obtained 99.4 percent of the ballots cast.

The opposition now had a choice between two channels of expression: clandestine political activity or trade union organizations. But here also, the trend was to unification. In 1962, all Senegalese trade unions had been regrouped into the Union nationale des travailleurs sénégalais (UNTS), which was linked organically to the UPS. Despite having been bought out in this way, some union organizers did not hesitate to stir things up. Serious strikes took place in 1968 and 1969 as the result of pressure from the membership. Unable to control its rank and file, the UNTS was dissolved and replaced by a union more loyal to the government, the Confédération nationale des travailleurs du Sénégal (CNTS).

In 1973, by virtue of the 1965 law on seditious associations, the government abolished the Syndicat des enseignants du Sénégal (SES), the teachers' union and the second legal organization to openly attack the politics of the government.

The replacement, not to say monopolization, of political power by decisionmaking institutions had its effect on the management of the state and the society. As Sheldon Gellar writes, after Mamadou Dia's departure from power, "the technocratic perspective gained ground over the agrarian socialist perspective of the early 1960's."[9] The cooperatives and the rural organizations that were supposed to revolutionize social and economic relationships in the country were not done away with, but efforts were made to reduce whatever dysfunctional features they might have that would threaten the established order. On the other hand, centralized control of the marketing of peanuts was reinforced through the state marketing agency (set up at the time of independence)—for the simple reason that the sale of peanuts furnished most of the funds necessary for the functioning of the state and the salaries of its civil servants.

By the same logic, the state took steps to extend its control over the governing bodies on the local level. The Ministry of the Interior's power over townships was consolidated, and the latter's budgets were limited. The powers of regional governors were reinforced, and the regional assemblies were reduced to being organs to relay decisions and programs coming from the central state. In short, as Gellar concludes, "the subordination of local government to administration control coupled with the elimination of opposition political parties marked a sharp setback to democratization of Senegalese politics that was not reversed until the mid-1970's."[10]

Thus, throughout this period, one can observe in Senegal, as in most African countries, the setting into place of an authoritarian state and a one-party regime, aimed at concentrating all decisionmaking powers in the hands of the central authorities and at eliminating any group liable to oppose the established power structure. However, in Senegal this process never went so far as to set up an arbitrary or absolute dictatorship. If there were arrests, unlike in Guinea, there were never any concentration camps, nor were political opponents physically eliminated. Having lived in Senegal during this period, I can testify to the fact that people did not hesitate, even openly, to criticize the government. The political atmosphere was tense at times, but there were no reactions of fear, of silence, or of secrecy. Those who were arrested were regularly tried, even if the courts leaned to the side of the government. The attitude of the government toward the opposition was strict, for Senghor's policy was to "unify" all parties and movements; but such a policy implied the use of the carrot as well as the stick. After all, there were many more leaders of the opposition who chose to join the party in power than those who chose to go into hiding.

Furthermore, the government was (relatively) amenable to negotiation and power plays. In 1968, under pressure from the UNTS, the government agreed to talks on a tripartite basis (government, employers, unions) that resulted in an increase in wages and an attempt to lower the price of staple foods. The principle of authoritarianism never excluded the idea of maneuvers and tactics to come to terms with difficult situations. The strategy of defusing conflicts was not only used for parties and trade unions, but also for Muslim religious leaders who "held" (and who still hold today) much of the country. Rather than eliminate the "feudal enclaves" of the marabouts as Sékou Touré tried to do, the Senegalese government preferred to win them over by meeting some of their demands (particularly in agricultural matters) and by using them to govern the peasants, as the French had done. Such policies lessened, to some extent, the effects of centralization, which, on the other hand, the regime was attempting to reinforce. Strangely enough, the marabouts were an obstacle to the state's absorption of civil society.[11]

Finally, the progressive elimination of the opposition did not prevent power struggles within the government party. Much more than a mass party, the UPS was (and is still) composed of clientele networks that compete for control over the local, regional, and national organization of the party—and thus for control of the political resources attached to them. There is a long history of such struggles in Senegal, and they can be violent. This is the case, in particular, when choosing candidates for elections to the National Assembly. The UPS's timid attempts to centralize the mechanisms of the party and to introduce a code of morality were not strong enough to resist this fundamental characteristic of Senegalese political culture. The UPS has remained a political arena in which bosses compete with one another not out of any ideological motivation, but for the spoils they expect to pick up.

Thus, the existence of a single party did not stifle political life, and competition continued to prevail in the choice of party officials. It was very difficult in Senegal for the central party organ to impose a leader on a constituency if he had no local power base. Such practices had no ideological dimension and were but a fiction of real democratic proceedings, but they did serve to limit the all-powerful tendencies of the party and the state. They functioned both as safety valves for the regime, by preventing the crystallization of more radical tendencies, and as obstacles to the abuse of power.[12]

From independence to the middle of the 1970s, Senegal was characterized by a modified one-party state. The government had set up a regime that could be called authoritarian, but the process was never completed because the government either could not or did not want to do so. What factors explain this situation? We will first take into account elements that arose from the situation itself and examine later the structural features of the Senegalese political system.

At the outset, one has to stress the importance of the personality of President Léopold Senghor, the "father of the nation," who left such an indelible mark on the first years of independence. His regime reflected the leadership of a man who is both a great intellectual—one of Africa's most well-known writers and the pioneer of African socialism—and a first-class politician, skilled in political maneuvering and shrewd in his ability to adapt to situations or to predict them.

Senghor can in no way be defined as a dogmatic intellectual or politician. The father of negritude is also the man who promoted such ideas as *métissage culturel* (cultural crossbreeding) and *dialogue des cultures* (cross-cultural communication). He borrowed part of his socialist ideas from Marx, but he also endeavored to adapt such ideas to Africa, and even to go beyond them. His humanistic socialism is a far cry from the combative Marxism of someone like Sékou Touré. If he was in favor of the creation of a "unified party" and worked to bring it into being, he never conceived of the party as a monolithic institution, even if he always denounced the "fratricidal" struggle of factions within the UPS. While arguing that the absence of real social classes in Africa (a proposition one could debate) and the need to promote national unity justified the existence of a single large national party, he never rejected the idea of pluralistic democracy—when circumstances allowed it. And, as we will see, he became the promoter of pluralism in the middle 1970s.

Senghor's international status and his prestige as a writer were important factors in his moderation and liberalism. It was very difficult for the man who has long been thought of as a future Nobel prize winner in literature to behave as a tyrant and as a violator of civil liberties. He has always been very sensitive to the image that Senegal projected abroad, and he did not want to appear as the oppressor of the country's intelligentsia—remarkably large and lively for such a small nation. Whatever love-hate relationships he may have had with fellow artists like Sembène Ousmane, the filmmaker, or Cheikh Anta Diop, the historian—people who did not hesitate to voice their criticisms—Senghor endeavored to turn Senegal into a "black Greece." Such an ideal was incompatible with a hard-line regime suspicious of artistic creation and criticism.

Senghor also turned out to be a first-rate politician who could be firm when he felt it was necessary, but who was amenable to discussion and negotiation. His authority and his "untouchable position," to use a term coined by G. Hesseling, were as much the result of his political art as they were of his intellectual aura.[13] Two very good examples of this political know-how were the ways in which he was able to win the backing of Muslim brotherhoods, despite being a Catholic himself, and to "convince" many opposition leaders to rally to the cause of the government or the UPS.

If Senghor had so much authority and prestige, it was because a whole class of political and intellectual elites identified with him in a certain way, even if a few members of this group had uneasy relationships with him. Senghor was the "ideal portrait" of the Senegalese elite of the time. A brilliant craftsman of both the written and the spoken word, he was the best symbol of the all-important "master" figure in Senegalese culture. In the subtle and efficient way he played the politician's game, he was a real political boss, a most worthy heir of the great Senegalese politicians who preceded him.[14]

Under these conditions, it is easy to understand why the UPS never became a monolithic party. Local leaders in Senegal were too used to political competition (the "natural" mode of selecting leaders) and to the process of creating a clientele to agree to unite within a closed organization, where they would have to be at the leader's beck and call and where they would have to accept decisions from the top without complaining. Whatever authority Senghor had over his party, he was never able to turn the UPS into a mass party of ideology that toed the line behind him. The UPS remained a political machine, or rather, the sum of a number of political machines.

Nevertheless, Senegal's political and economic situation in the first years after independence gave rise to political and social tensions that pressed toward a hardening and a centralization of power. Although the country appeared to be much further along the road to "political modernization" than many other African countries (with its skilled political elite, electoral tradition, and experience in the management of public affairs, etc.), it was not saved from the structural problems that shook most of these new nations, even if it coped better than the others with these problems.

Between 1960 and 1970, Senegal was buffeted by three major political crises, which resulted in a redefinition of the structures of power and of the state along more authoritarian lines. The first was the short-lived Federation of Mali, whose demise not only put an end to the hope of achieving regional political union in West Africa, but also took its toll on Senegal's political climate. The impossible entente with Modibo Keita's Soudan (now Mali) created tensions within the UPS that led to sanctions against party officials and members who were suspected of encouraging Keita's plans. Emergency measures were taken to "set things in order": the Law of September 7, 1960, authorized the government to legislate in effect by decree in certain areas. The Decree of October 10, 1960, restricted the freedom of movement in the country for any person whose actions were judged to be a threat to public order and safety.

The second major crisis was the conflict between Senghor and Mamadou Dia, mentioned earlier. This rift, as well, was followed by purges in the party, a reinforcement of executive power, and the gradual elimination of the opposition. Senghor's aim was to get rid of the rival political clan that was guilty of questioning his supremacy. If the rules of the game of Senegalese political culture allow for struggles between factions, such conflicts must never reach the top of the political pyramid so as to threaten the position of the supreme leader, who is conceived as the ultimate arbitrator. In this sense, one would have to say that competition between political clans cannot lead to any true choice or even to any true alternative sharing of power.

In 1968 and 1969, it was not any struggle at the summit that shook Senegal, but rather a movement of revolt on the part of students and unions. Initially inspired by the French "revolution" of May 1968, the events provoked violent clashes involving a great number of intellectuals, civil servants, and workers who protested price increases and who felt their careers were stifled by the government's timid measures of Africanization in the public and private sectors. As we have seen, the government's response was to pull in the reins on the workers' movements. Essentially urban phenomena, these crises masked the profound malaise in rural areas resulting from the deterioration of the situation of peanut farmers. Peanut production had declined sharply after the agreements signed between African countries and the European Economic Community, putting an end to the preferential prices France granted Senegal. Moreover, the years of chronic drought in the Sahel had not helped matters any.

The peasants were losing their enthusiasm for growing a crop that paid them less and less and were increasingly devoting their efforts to the cultivation of staple foods. The state, however, was dependent on peanut farming to furnish an important share of its budget. Thus, the government cultivated the influence of local political and religious leaders to hold the rural world in line, but it did not hesitate to resort to force if necessary, carrying out veritable "dragon hunts," in the words of René Dumont, to collect taxes and to force peasants to pay their debts.[15] All these methods served to alienate the state from the rural population, who felt they were being taken back to the worst days of colonization. Thanks alone to the marabouts, who played the role of middleman and safety valve, this situation of structural conflict did not degenerate into a full-scale peasant revolt.

In the final analysis, the growing authoritarianism (in relative terms) of the regime corresponded to the elite's inability, or at least its difficulty, in holding the civil society and its movements in check. It was to correct these shortcomings that the regime changed its course.

Democratic Renewal and the Problems of Democracy

In 1974, Senegal began setting into action a series of institutional reforms that were to modify the nature of the regime profoundly by opening the political arena to multi-party competition, first on a somewhat timid basis and later in total freedom. Judged by outsiders to be exemplary in Africa, these initiatives did not solve the more structural problems of the country. They did, however, guarantee the stability of the political system, at least for some time. But closer analysis shows that this transition to democracy corresponded to an acute crisis between the state and the society that was masked by the often naive expectations generated both inside and outside Senegal by these reforms. Liberalizing the regime was an attempt—whose success must be qualified—to give new life to a state that was up against social, economic, and political constraints that it could hardly control.

This new chapter in the history of Senegal is marked, in the main, by the personality of Abdou Diouf, the chosen successor of President Senghor, who voluntarily resigned from office in 1981. Senghor's decision was motivated by his desire to be seen as a fighter for democracy. More a high-level civil servant than a politician, and more a technocrat than an intellectual, Abdou Diouf had carried out his career in the shadow of Senghor, first as first secretary to the president and then as prime minister. The date of his later appointment, 1971, coincided with a constitutional reform that reinstated the function of prime minister as a means of diluting executive power.

Abdou Diouf's role in the democratization of the country cannot be denied, but it was Senghor who initiated the reforms as early as 1974 by officially recognizing lawyer Abdoulaye Wade's Parti démocratique sénégalais (PDS), a party that proclaimed its allegiance to the tenets of social democracy. In 1978, a constitutional reform was adopted which put into place a system of "controlled democracy." The number of parties was limited to three, and they were required to belong to one of the following three systems of thought: (1) liberal and democratic; (2) socialist and democratic; (3) Marxist or communist. These restrictive measures were aimed at fostering political rigor and stability and discouraging opportunism and anarchy.

The UPS voted to become a socialist party at its 1978 convention and chose the second option. The PDS agreed, although reluctantly, to define itself as "liberal and democratic." As for the old African Marxist movement, the Parti africain de l'indépendance, it much more willingly accepted the communist label, although internal divisions within Senegal's extreme left wing had led to the proliferation of rival clandestine or semi-clandestine groups.

On the other hand, the Rassemblement national démocratique, the party of Senghor's old rival, Cheikh Anta Diop, was rejected from the official political scene. The party had been founded in January 1976 under an essentially nationalistic platform. In 1978, a fourth "conservative" option was recognized, thus allowing Boubacar Guèye's Mouvement républicain sénégalais (MRS) to participate openly in political life.

The legislative and presidential elections of 1978 were a great success for the Socialist party (which received 81.7 percent of the ballots cast and 82 of the 100 seats in the Assembly) and for President Senghor personally (who won 82.5 percent of the vote). But they also gave the country an official opposition, the PDS, which won eighteen seats in the Assembly, while Abdoulaye Wade received 17.4 percent of the presidential vote. It must be emphasized, however, that the elections were held in a tense climate and organized in a way that threatened the secrecy of the ballot. Furthermore, the rate of participation (63 percent of registered voters) showed a lack of enthusiasm on the part of the people for this experiment in democracy. This allowed the "illegal" opposition—particularly the RND, which had called for a boycott—to claim success in the elections.

With the arrival of Abdou Diouf as head of state in 1981, Senegal seemed to undergo an even greater renewal. While claiming to be Senghor's heir, Diouf set out to give new impetus to political life and to provide better management of state affairs. In his own words, they were to be "transparent" and more open to democratic debate.

Four months after coming to power, Diouf proposed a constitutional reform abrogating the Law of 1976, which had set limits to the number of parties and the number of possible ideological banners. This liberalization, to which Senghor declared his opposition, brought forth a multitude of political movements, including Cheikh Anta Diop's RND and the Mouvement démocratique populaire of ex-Prime Minister Mamadou Dia. Thus, today there are seventeen officially recognized political parties in Senegal, including a number of small leftist groups.

In the 1993 legislative elections, eight parties contested the 120 seats in the National Assembly. But it is worth noting that political movements based on religious, regional, or ethnic grounds are forbidden by the constitution.

This democratic renewal had its counterpart in the labor movement. Whereas the Confédération nationale des travailleurs sénégalais (CNTS), which is affiliated with the ruling party (PS), accounts for 75 percent of the unionized workers, other labor organizations have emerged. These include the Confédération des syndicats autonomes (CSA), the Union nationale des syndicats autonomes du Sénégal (UNAS), and the Union des travailleurs démocratiques du Sénégal (UTDS), all of which are more or less loosely linked to opposition parties.

Another result of democratization has been the proliferation of independent or opposition newspapers: *Wal Fadjri, Le Politicien, Le Cafard déchaîné, Sud-Hebdo and Sud-Quotidien, Sopi,* and many others. This new press has largely helped to develop democratic debates and to counterbalance the official voice represented by the progovernment daily newspaper, *Le Soleil,* and by the national radio and television authority.[16]

The legislative and presidential elections of 1983 were to be the most patent sign of democratic renewal in Senegal, as well as a popularity test for Senghor's successor and for his policy of change. Diouf won a large victory over the five rival candidates (receiving 83.5 percent of the ballots cast) and the Socialist Party kept absolute control of the Assembly with 80 percent of the votes and 111 seats. The opposition was left with only nine seats (eight for the PDS, one for the RND). But the participation of voters was even lower than in 1978 (58 percent of those registered), and many irregularities in balloting procedures were also officially noted, pointing to the limits and the difficulties of democratic renewal in Senegal[17] (Table 10.1).

Table 10.1   Senegalese Elections Results

	Legislative Elections					
	1983		1988		1993	
	% of Votes	Seats	% of Votes	Seats	% of Votes	Seats
Parti socialiste	79.9	111	71.5	103	56.6	84
Parti democratique senegalais	13.9	8	24.7	17	30.2	9
Others	6.2	1	3.8	0	13.2	9
	Presidential Elections					
Abdou Diouf (PS)	83.5%		73.2%		58.4%	
Abdoulaye Wade (PDS)	14.7%		25.8%		32%	
Others	1.8%		2%		9%	

The following two legislative and presidential elections confirmed the difficulties of creating a stable democratic order. The Parti socialiste and its leader, Abdou Diouf, succeeded in maintaining power, but this power existed in increasingly precarious conditions and in a climate of growing social and political tensions.

In the 1988 elections Diouf won 73.2 percent of the vote, but in the 1993 elections his share dropped to 58.4 percent. Similarly, the PS mobilized fewer and fewer voters, and its representation in the National Assembly decreased noticeably (71.5 percent of the vote and 103 seats in 1988, 56.6 percent of the vote and 84 seats in 1993). The major opposition party, the PDS, and its leader, A. Wade, were the main beneficiaries of that erosion of the socialist majority. Wade reached 25.8 percent of the vote in 1988 and 32 percent in 1993; the PDS, with 24.7 percent of the vote, won 17 seats in 1988, and in 1993, with 30.2 percent of the vote, obtained 27 seats. In the 1993 legislative elections minor parties (Parti de l'indépendance et du travail–PIT, Ligue démocratique, Jappo liggueyai Sénégal) mobilized 13.2 percent of the vote (9 seats) (Table 10.1). One should also note that Diouf and the PS have gradually lost the majority in Dakar, where the PDS and Wade won the vote by a head, but have kept their support in rural Senegal thanks to the influence of local bosses and religious leaders.

These last two elections took place in an atmosphere of rising discontent, disputes, and unrest. The opposition claimed the campaign and the vote were not free and fair. Numerous irregularities were reported by foreign observers.

In 1988 violent demonstrations arose in Dakar following the proclamation of electoral results, and several opposition leaders (including Wade) were arrested and detained in jail for a few weeks. After the 1993 legislative elections, the PDS calculated that it had taken sixty-three seats and therefore had an overall majority. Street protests were again organized by the opposition, and prominent PDS members were again arrested following the assassination of a Supreme Court judge.

Thus, political life in Senegal is marked by dramatic tensions between a ruling party that has dominated the state since independence and that cannot imagine losing power, and a boisterous opposition engaged in battles it seems bound to lose. In the last analysis, it appears the only way for the opposition to make itself heard is to negotiate some share of government power with the PS and its leader. Such a realistic strategy, which is a tradition in Senegalese politics, was arranged in 1991 when the PDS leader and three of his colleagues agreed to become ministers (Wade became minister of state) in the name of "national solidarity" following social and ethnic unrest in the country.

But at the end of 1992 the PDS cabinet members resigned their positions to concentrate on the electoral campaign. Since then, a kind of political guerrilla war has developed between the PDS and the government, although Diouf's policy of incorporating members of the opposition has officially continued with the cabinet appointments of three ministers and two assistant ministers belonging to minor opposition parties (LD-MPT, PIT, Rénovation).

One can conclude from these recent elections that political life in Senegal constitutes a balance between a culture of violent confrontation at the time of elections and a tradition of bargaining when politics becomes business. The problem with democratization in Senegal is that, as Leonardo A. Villalon puts it, "after more than three decades of rule by the same party, for many in Senegal real democratization can only mean change; democracy without alternation is not democracy." This is the reason the PDS slogan *sopi* (change, in Wolof) is so popular, especially among the urban youth. *Sopi* means not only a change of policy (the PDS program is not radically different from that of the PS) but above all a change of rulers and of methods of government.

It is not surprising in such a situation of blockage and powerlessness that the opposition is encouraged by a rising cynicism and that a growing portion of the electorate shows less and less interest in the constitutional democratic process (only 50 percent of the registered voters went to the polls in 1993). A well-known and sophisticated Senegalese social scientist, Mamadou Diouf, may therefore support the thesis that democracy in Senegal is a failure.[19] But as D. Cruise O'Brien and I wrote in 1989, one might perhaps be unwise to go too far in that direction, "for there are real freedoms in Senegal (of the press, of association, of speech) which it would be a pity to lose."[20] Further, as Robert Fatton has convincingly argued, one is better off with a flawed democracy and a chance at least to influence the government agenda than with the "specialists of coercion."[21]

Furthermore, we must recognize that the development of democracy in Senegal is not to be seen mainly as a political maneuver aimed at changing the facade of the political system without modifying the structure. The international image of Senegal was at stake: Senghor and Diouf wanted Senegal to be a model of liberty and democracy for Africa, and they counted on that prestige to attract Western aid and investments. But democratization also corresponded to a genuine attempt to regenerate a political system that was running out of breath and increasingly cut off from the realities of the country.

Senegal's enormous economic and social problems made it urgent to carry out reforms and to call for participation by the "living forces" of the country that had been marginalized for the benefit of traditional political bosses and bureaucrats, whose authority was based on clientelism and nepotism. The country had to find new forms of organization and control that were more pluralist in conception, more open to local initiatives, and less rigid.

In addition, the renewal of the democratic process and the reworking of state structures meant not only redefining lines of communications between the government and the civil service on the one hand and the citizens on the other but also boosting the economy by reinstating confidence among producers. This is the reason the democratization of the political system and the liberalization of the economy occurred with the support, and under the pressure and control, of the IMF and the World Bank.

Reform was also necessary to deal with the challenge of growing

Islamic mobilization. During the 1970s and the 1980s, Islam served as an ideology that structured social groups that could not find answers to their problems and expectations elsewhere. This was all the more true because the Muslim brotherhoods, which had traditionally been rooted in the rural milieu, had succeeded in adapting to the urban areas. Thus, the democratic renaissance has to be seen in a wider context than as a mere political manipulation or accommodation. Democratization and liberalization were aimed at strengthening the social foundations of the state so the legal country and the real country would coincide.

Paradoxically, from a sociological point of view the democratic process can be analyzed not only as a political promotion of the civil society but also as a more direct mode of incorporating society into the state, along with a redefinition of the role of the party and the ruling class in the political system.[22] This major transformation has failed. Problems have accumulated that democratization and liberalization have been unable to face. The country's very limited resources do not allow the state to improve its public image and to solve daily difficulties. The recent devaluation of the CFA Franc (January 1994) is intended to reduce imports and to stimulate exports, but for the ordinary Senegalese citizen it means increases in the prices of rice, sugar, cooking oil, electricity, water, public transport, and other needs.[23]

Democratization has helped neither to calm down the development of the regionalist movement in Casamance nor to weaken the rising of a militant Islam. The gap between the political system and the demands and aspirations of society remains very wide in spite of the progress of democracy. In such conditions it is easy to understand that democracy has not become a part of everyone's belief system. A large percentage of the people are not interested in the official political competition; many Senegalese do not see its benefits. They articulate their demands and grievances through other social institutions (religion, local and ethnic associations) or through violence.

The Search for Explanations

Having traced the different historical stages of Senegalese politics, we can now step back to consider the explanatory factors behind the regime's mixed success. We will be better equipped, as a result, to open the perspectives that seem to be the most plausible.

Political Culture

Just as the democratic performance of the regime has been a mixed success, so Senegalese political culture partakes of a mixed nature. It is a combination of rather authoritarian values and beliefs, compensated for by a propensity for debate, political game-playing, and a conception of power that depends more on the interdependence of actors (even if the relationships are unequal) than on organized violence. It must first be emphasized that the traditional political culture of Senegal's ancient local political systems was far from being locked up in a rigid authoritarianism, even if it was based on political and social hierarchies. Political competition between clans was indispensable for the exercise of power, and the Senegalese certainly did not wait for the birth of modern politics to discover the virtues (and the shortcomings) of political contests—they belong to their "natural" political universe. Moreover, among the Wolof (as among the Tukulor), political power holders were chiefs who were closely watched over by dignitaries, by the people, and, above all, by a whole political code that required them to work for the commonwealth. The Senegalese historian Cheikh Anta Diop has spoken in this regard of "constitutional monarchies."[24] The power of the "king" was limited, shared, and decentralized. It was governed by a political culture that defined a chief as a *samba linguer,* that is, as a man of honor who was supposed to protect those who were living under his authority and to be generous toward them. Dominant groups could not totally exploit or tyrannize their subjects without losing their favor. The "king" had duties toward his people, and if his power became too arbitrary, he could expect to be unseated and replaced. Power was thus held in check, if only because of its potential danger. As a Wolof proverb says, "A king is not a parent"; this means that the self-interested nature of power can lead its holder to sacrifice the interests of his family to his own interests.[25]

If traditional chiefdoms have disappeared today, this political culture has not disappeared with them. It survives, in particular, in the Muslim brotherhoods, whose leaders are viewed on the popular level as the holders of "good power," people whose "resources" profit those who are lacking in them.

The modern political elite has also been marked by these values. Of course, such values have become somewhat twisted in the system of patronage and clientelism that is the backbone of contemporary Senegalese political culture. One has to admit, however, that these kinds of behavior are ambivalent. It is true that they are responsible for the corruption, the prevarication, or at the very least, the manipulation of institutions for personal aims that are features of modern political life. On the other hand, they are also a way to control power. A "boss" who is unable to furnish the benefits expected will be disowned by his rank and file (his clients) in favor of a rival who appears to be more generous.

But the political elite of the present day have not only been nourished by these traditions and experiences. They have also been schooled in the ways of Western democracy. Senegalese leaders, more than others in Africa no doubt, are sons of France. They have learned from the former motherland the arts of politics on the most pragmatic level (political maneuvering), but also on the most noble. Hence, for Abdou Diouf, "knowledge of the other, the refusal to wear ideological blinkers, the search for the truth which leads one to listen to others, the expression of all opinions on acts of power, and the safeguard of the social and moral values of the country are all indispensable conditions for any pluralist democracy."[26]

Modern political culture in Senegal is thus a mixture of *liberalism,* which delights in discussions of philosophy and doctrine and which is hardly compatible with ideological dogmas, combined with a propensity for the *accumulation of power* (the more resources one has, the larger one's clientele, and the means to achieve such ends include compromise, as well as the crushing of rivals). A final element of this combination is the constant concern to convey an *acceptable image to the outside,* for Senegalese politicians have also conceived of their experiences as being models.

These values, however, appear more and more artificial or theoretical to segments of the population whose daily problems have not been solved by the intellectual debates, games of patronage, and pursuit of international prestige of the Senegalese political class. This explains the tendency for some to turn toward other systems of reference, such as militant Islamic organizations that purpose to solve the county's problems through ideals of rigor and nationalism. The lack of interest in elections and the growing development of different Muslim brotherhoods and associations attest to an evolution that could lead, in the long run, to radical transformations.

Historical Developments

The historical developments that have left their mark on the Senegalese political system have been noted and analyzed in the preceding pages. The essential features can be summarized here.

Traditional political systems in Senegal, although articulated around unequal power relationships (except in the south, in Casamance, where acephalous types of societies predominate), can be defined more as "constitutional monarchies" that allow for some political competition and control of power. We have shown what remnants of this remain in contemporary political life.

Second, if the colonial experience had sometimes been brutal (slavery; economic, social, and political destruction), it was nevertheless conditioned—one is tempted to say "softened"—by two elements: the existence, in the rural world, of a sort of system of indirect rule, based around Muslim brotherhoods that had taken on the role of the precolonial aristocracy; and, in the urban world, the existence of democratic institutions that mobilized the African elite and allowed it to gain access to certain positions of responsibility. This explains to a great extent why independence was acquired without revolutionary struggle. Structured as Senegal was by the marabouts, who had the confidence of the peasants, and by a class of experienced politicians, the conditions were not present for violent anticolonial sentiment to develop—contrary to what happened in the Portuguese colonies or in Zimbabwe, for example. Indeed, one could say that the absence of revolutionary and violent anticolonial struggle in Senegal helped to generate democracy by limiting violence as a method of political expression.

Class Structure

The structure of social classes in Senegal is extremely unequal. Nevertheless, certain social and political mechanisms have limited up to now the disruptive effects of this inequality.

It must be remembered that inequality was an inherent feature of traditional societies in Senegal. Such societies were divided into "orders" (free men, castes of craftsmen, slaves), which themselves were subdivided into several categories (noblemen or simple commoners in the first group, for example). An exception to this, as we have seen, was the south, where the idea of hierarchy in social structures was practically nonexistent, particularly among the Diola. These traditional social distinctions are far from having disappeared. Members of inferior social groups have, of course. been able to climb the social ladder to positions of leadership. But they remain the object of prejudices that depreciate them socially, and it is often difficult for them, in particular, to marry outside the social group from which they originate. In a 1977 interview, Léopold Senghor admitted it was a delicate issue that did come up when making appointments, although he always tried to play down the phenomenon.

Social inequality is, thus, not new in Senegal. However, whereas traditional social ranks were based on differences of social status and not necessarily on wealth, modern hierarchies are much more a matter of differences in income. These gaps are particularly acute between the urban and the rural worlds. The average income of wage earners in the public and private sectors is estimated to be ten times higher than that of farmers, and the income gap between town and country is widening despite the higher prices growers have been getting for peanuts in the last few years.

Since independence, the upper classes are dominated by the bureaucrats of the civil service, who make up the class of power wielders. "Senegal's proliferating state administration, accounting as it does for almost half of the national total of wage employees and for more than half of the national budget, may properly be called [in local terms] a ruling class."[27]

Under the influence of the International Monetary Fund (IMF), however, the public sector has been reduced. Since 1980, the Senegalese government has taken a number of measures to limit public spending, creating problems, in turn, for young university graduates who are finding it increasingly difficult to procure employment.

During the early years of independence, the state directed its efforts more to expanding the public or semipublic sectors than to developing domestic capitalism. It has had to change its position somewhat since the beginning of the 1970s in response to demands from Senegalese businessmen who felt their margin of maneuver between state-run companies and foreign interests was much too narrow. It is a growing category nonetheless—although very dependent on the state—not only for the supply of credit, but also for the marketing of goods.

Many of the most successful businessmen are merchants belonging to the *mouride* brotherhood. Religious networks have been put to use parallel to political networks. Thanks to these two factors, for example, the *mourides* have managed to gain control of the central market in Dakar, Sandaga.[28] Also among the *mourides* (and, to a lesser extent, the other Muslim brotherhoods) can be found a bourgeoisie of rural religious leaders. Marabouts in Senegal are the only big growers. They have at their disposal a free labor force to work their fields—that of their faithful (*taalibe*)—not to mention the Islamic tithe (*zakat*) that brings to them a share of the harvest from the private farms of other disciples. In exchange, the marabouts must take care of the moral, as well as the material, well-being of their followers: help them in time of need, supply them with fields to work, find them wives, and defend their interests before the state.

Up to now, these structures of patronage between unequal categories have contributed to the stability of the country, for they have allowed a certain redistribution of wealth. If these structures continue to govern the relationships between marabouts and *taalibe,* however, they work less and less well in the modern sector, even though it is customary in Senegal for a wage-earner to come to the aid of a great number of people. The urban explosion and the crisis in the rural world no longer enable these mechanisms to function on a large scale. Given the degree of peasant discontent, one cannot be sure that the marabouts will be able to continue to act as effective buffers. As "peasant leaders" of rural revolts, they may be tempted to make political use of discontent.

Ethnicity and Religion

For a long time, Senegal was free of any ethnic and religious tensions that might present a threat to nation building. However, the conflicts that have arisen in Casamance since 1980 have become a major political issue.

With the ethnic equilibrium that seemed to prevail for many years, Senegal had been relatively privileged compared to other African countries. The Wolof group, with 41 percent of the population, appeared to be the keystone of the edifice. Indeed, their language had gradually become the medium of communication in the whole country. There were several reasons for this: the great number of Wolof living in towns, their weight in the civil service, their dominant position among African traders, their geographic mobility, and their positions of leadership in Muslim organizations. Their domination was often viewed as intolerable by other ethnic groups, but at the same time, they appeared as models of social promotion for non-Wolof elites. Moreover, the Wolof domination did not prevent other groups from being present in representative institutions, including the head of the state. Senghor himself was a Serer (14 percent of the population).[29]

Also contributing to the reign of ethnic peace was the fact that the government never sought to impose Wolof as the only African language. Along with French, the official languages included six national languages: Wolof, Fulani, Serer, Malinké, Diola, and Soninké. But, on the question of introducing these languages into the educational system, the attitude of the government was much more reserved. The prestige of French was admittedly an inhibiting factor, but so was the Wolof question. Teaching African languages would naturally mean putting Wolof in a privileged position, not only because of the extent to which it is spoken in the country, but also because it has been studied more by linguists and could be immediately operational in school curricula.[30] And although non-Wolofs might well be able to function in that language, they would certainly object to any attempt to impose Wolof as a compulsory official language—for which certain Senegalese nationalist (Wolof) groups have been clamoring.

Another element that must be weighed is the overwhelming presence of Islam as the religion of 90 percent of the Senegalese people. Aside from the question of unifying customs—a point that is too often raised—there is no denying that the Muslim religion has, at the very least, inspired new feelings of belonging to a national and even an international community. The celebration of major Muslim feast days, for example, or the participation of the brotherhoods in the pilgrimage to Mecca, are ways of uniting people of different ethnic origins around common experiences and common symbols, even if, here again, Wolof leadership is an obvious element.

One could point out, of course, that Senegalese Muslims are divided into several brotherhoods (*murridiyya, tijaniyya, qadiriyya*), not to mention the groups of reformists or Islamists (the more activist being the Jamaatou Ibadou Rahman) who reject or criticize these traditional religious orders and advocate the unity of Islam. However, if such marginal beliefs have sometimes led to friction or even violent outbursts, particularly inside mosques, there is no seed here of any religious war. But in the last fifteen years, in Senegal as in many other Muslim countries all over the world, a new Islamic political culture is developing—especially among the urban youth and intellectuals—which advocates the creation of a Muslim state and the promotion of Islamic law (*Shari'a*). This Islamist ideology is the raison d'être of recently created movements like the Jamaatou Ibadou Rahman or Al-Falah, which are strongly influenced by the Iranian revolution and fundamentalist groups active in Arab countries. These movements, although they are very active, have mobilized only a small minority of the Senegalese Muslim community. More surprisingly, fundamentalism is increasingly present in some segments of Senegal's traditional Sufi brotherhoods, especially in the youth section of the *murridiyya* and the *tijaniyya*. In January 1994, a religious leader of the *tijaniyya* brotherhood, Moustapha Sy, head of an Islamic association called Moustachidina Wal Moustachidati (which claims 500,000 members) was sentenced to one year in prison for public orders offenses.

Christians (mainly Catholics—about 5 percent of the population), are found primarily among the Serer and the Diola. Islamic renewal movements in Senegal might raise problems for them one day, if those who advocate an Islamic republic were heeded or came to power. But for the time being, and despite strong pressure from Muslim groups, the government remains firmly attached to the notion of the separation of religion and state.

Religion is one aspect of the specific identity of the Diola people in Casamance. Very few Diola are Muslims, and where conversion has taken place, it is often only very superficial. Traditional religions and Catholicism (led by clergy who have a strong sense of ethnic membership) are ramparts against Islamization and militant Islamic movements. Other differences derive from the social and political organization of these societies, which are radically different from those of the northern pan of the country. Wolof and Tukulor societies are characterized by the tradition of a central state and by social systems based on a strict hierarchy. Diola society, on the other hand, like that of neighboring peoples, the Balante and Manjaque, is acephalous and egalitarian.

Other factors contribute to the strong sense of frustration in Casamance and the drive to actively proclaim local identity in the face of "internal colonialism." There is Casamance's geographic isolation. It is separated from the rest of Senegal by Gambia. The infrastructure, in matters of health and education particularly, is much less developed in Casamance. Finally, local commerce and civil service jobs are dominated by "northerners." All of this has created, as D. Darbon has written, "a general incapacity of communication between the Senegalese state and the people of Casamance."[31]

The specificity of Casamance was first expressed through the blossoming of prophetic movements, then by the development of opposition parties in the region (the PRA was, above all, a Casamance party, and more recently, the PDS has chalked up much higher scores in Casamance than its national average). Regional demands have become more and more radical and violent and have degenerated into a local guerrilla war between the Senegalese Army and sepatarist groups. On a number of occasions, Casamance was in a state of siege. A Casamance flag appeared along with a clandestine political movement, the Mouvement des forces démocratiques de Casamance (MFDC), led by a Catholic priest, Father Augustin D. Senghor. Recent negotiations with the MFDC have not stopped violence and general unrest in the region.[32]

In my opinion, there is a real regional movement in Casamance today.

It is an expression of the difficulties of communication and presents a real challenge to the Senegalese state. But, above and beyond Diola ethnic identity or Casamance regional identity, what is finally at stake is the kind of relationship that exists between a powerless central state and a "periphery" that has brought a number of mechanisms into play in its efforts to repel an intruding "center" whose actions are perceived as negative.

In sum, until recently Senegal's relative ethnic equilibrium and religious homogeneity have allowed the country to avoid conflicts that would have undermined the political stability necessary to democracy, but groups who are outside this "natural" national unity, like the Diola, might feel drawn to commit acts of violence to express themselves.

State and Society

The Senegalese state is heir to the French tradition of centralization. Senegal's administrative structures, as well as the national ideology that governs them, have been modeled on the French Jacobin state. Regions are void of power and autonomy, and any manifestation of ethnic difference is rejected, on principle, as being an obstacle to national unity. This tendency to centralization has also been reinforced by the colonial tradition. Finally, Senegal's leaders justify the state's domination as a condition for development. According to them, in order for development to be effective, efforts and initiatives must not be spread out too thinly.

All of these factors, in addition to the state's role as the main employer and the means by which the class of politicians and bureaucrats can accumulate wealth, have resulted in an administration that is omnipresent and that employs a great number of people. With independence, Senegal adopted a system of national planning and set up many state-owned companies, particularly after 1970 (between 1970 and 1975 approximately seventy-five state companies were created). A nationalized system for marketing farm produce was also erected. The central role played by the state in the organization of society, added to the "resource" it commands, has contributed to the forging of a political system based on clientelism and patronage.

The policy of centralization, however, has not been completely effective. First, the state does not have the material means to carry it out. Its budget is not big enough to allow effective presence in all sectors of the society. Its capacity to control and organize society is also limited by the vitality of so-called traditional societies and the presence of local leaders (like the marabouts), who either ignore or marginalize the role of the state or who refocus and deform the structures and initiatives of the "center" that might threaten their autonomy, in order to turn them to their own advantage.

When confronted with such "peripheral" forces, the state is often obliged to make concessions to local systems, for its political legitimacy depends to a very great extent on the support of these middlemen. This is what J. S.

Barker calls the "paradox of development": the government is torn between the need for political support that requires it to listen to the demands of the local community and the need to carry out a policy of development that drives it to transform the community.[33] Nevertheless, we have already noted the increasing tendency of the state to do without these middlemen and to communicate directly with the people. As we have seen in Casamance, the political risks of such an undertaking are enormous because of the danger of direct conflict breaking out between the state and the local community.

Recent reforms have attempted to lessen the weight of the administration, particularly in the realm of the economy. The signs of impotence were all too clear. Already heavily in debt, the public sector was also having to pay heavy costs for mismanagement, corruption, and absence of clear lines of responsibility. Since 1980, programs of structural adjustment have been implemented: the structure for marketing peanuts was redesigned, subsidies for state companies (almost all in the red) were curbed, and civil service hiring was brought to a halt.

If these measures liberalized the economy, they did not fundamentally change the nature of the Jacobin model. Although a failure from the political and economic point of view, it remained part of the political culture of the power elite. Unable to control society, the state has managed all through this period to maintain order. To be sure, discounting recent events in Casamance, it has never had to deal with any subversive or terrorist movements. But this absence of destabilizing forces is also due to the relative freedom of expression that political movements enjoyed in Senegal and the concern of Senegalese leaders to accept the principle of dialogue with members of the opposition. This is what President Diouf calls a "national consensus." If, in certain circumstances and at certain points in time, the government took a hard line and made decisions that were antidemocratic, the use of force was never looked upon as a *long-term* means of solving problems.

Another consequence of political stability is that the role of the army is much less noticeable than in the rest of Africa. The government has sometimes turned to the army for help (in Gambia and in Casamance), but in the last analysis, it does not owe its survival to military intervention. There is in Senegal today a tradition of nonintervention by the army in political life (members of the armed forces do not have the right to vote) that could only be brought into question in the event of grave difficulties.

Although this tradition is conducive to the consolidation of democracy, the centralizing ideology of the state is a major obstacle in this regard. The failing is one of communication. Paradoxically, the more the state becomes centralized, the further away it appears to be from society, and the greater is society's tendency to act autonomously. The Senegalese state is not an expression of the Senegalese society. It aims to control society without taking into consideration its specific features, its ethnic and cultural diversity, and the movements that society has engendered. From this point of view, one might agree with Mar Fall that the Senegalese state is, indeed, sick. It is suffering from the disease of isolation.[34] And the democratic renewal has done very little to modify the situation.

Political Institutions

As we have observed, presidential power has grown since independence. In Senegal, it is the executive that governs. For many years, the Assembly was a body where decisions were simply registered. The presence today of a number of opposition parliamentarians has made the Assembly a political forum, but its capacity for initiative to legislate or to control the government is extremely limited—in fact, if not by law. The judiciary would also seem to be subservient to the executive branch, even if it appears to have some margin of maneuver compared to other African states. Here again, there is no contrast between the two periods. Trials are conducted in a relatively unrestricted manner, but as Gellar notes, "the courts have rarely ruled against the government in important constitutional cases or political trials."[35]

In the party system, there have been some important changes with the evolution of a de facto one-party state to first a limited multi-party structure and then a totally unrestricted multi-party system. The government party, however, continues to play a dominant role in political life, and opposition parties have a limited influence and bargaining power. But distinctions must be made on this point. The PDS is the only movement with a wide social base (its clientele has about the same social profile as that of the Socialist Party, but the PDS is more popular among the urban youth than the PS) and a wide geographical base—although its position is stronger in regions with problems, like Dakar and Casamance. The political philosophy of the PDS is also rather moderate. It is, in fact, quite close to that of the Socialist Party on many issues, their principal criticism being the Socialist Party's incompetence or its unwillingness to carry out its program. The small parties of the extreme left, on the other hand, are much more ideologically oriented and divided by points of doctrine. Their social base is very narrow (teachers, students, and trade unionists), and their influence is practically nil outside of the towns. Yet, all of these groups have contributed in a big way to the development of a very active political press that enjoys great freedom compared to the systematic repression it experienced in the past.

Despite the apparent vitality of political life in Senegal, the party system still remains relatively impervious, as has already been noted, to movements in the rest of society. Politics is much more an arena for politicians than a channel for the expression and defense of new social interests and forces. The low voter participation in elections is one sign of this crisis, and the difficulty of Senegalese political movements in coping with Islamic mobilization is another.

Political Leadership

This last commentary underscores the limits of political innovation in Senegal, as well as the gap that exists between political leaders and the masses, who are looking outside official or institutionalized political channels for solutions to the problems they face. We can see taking hold and developing in Senegal today an informal political system that aims to compensate for the failure of the political system to adapt to social changes—but that also is an obstacle to the initiatives of political leaders. There is a sort of vicious cycle in the dichotomy between the "center" and the "periphery," between the state and what can be called *grassroots movements of political action.* Such movements are channeled through structures like Muslim brotherhoods or local development associations. Their strategy consists either in bypassing official institutions by creating their own organizational networks and schemes of action, or in recouping the benefits of initiatives from on high. Violence sometimes breaks out, as in Casamance, when problems of division and incomprehension fail to be overcome by passive resistance or manipulation.

It is not a question here of the democratic bent of Senegalese leaders. We have seen throughout this chapter that, even in the authoritarian period, the Senegalese government has been relatively open to dialogue and negotiation. For the most part, compromise and consensus have always been the rules of the game, at least in the long term. They are part of what can be called the political art of Senegal. The problem is much more that of a state whose centralizing ideology does not mesh well with grassroots dynamics.

Socioeconomic Development

The distance between the state and the society is a factor that has hampered development in the country. Since independence, the Senegalese government has endeavored to carry out what it calls "great development projects" (the building of dams and petrochemical plants, for example). It has given itself the tools that were supposed to free the country from dependence and underdevelopment through the creation of a whole series of state companies and strictly controlled peanut-marketing mechanisms—leaving the door open, however, for foreign investment. But these measures were undermined by bureaucratic structures that left no room for responsible participation on the part of producers or wage-earners. They also carried the threat of gigantic production structures that were not compatible with local traditions, particularly in rural areas. The outcome of these efforts was often financial disaster. In the final analysis, those who profited from these schemes were, above all, the experts hired as advisors and the technocrats.

Development has also been hampered by the decline in rainfall since the 1960s, bringing about drastic fluctuations in agricultural production and accelerating the country's food dependency.

It is true that other sectors have been relatively more successful: the phosphate mines, the petrochemical industry (with the refinery at M'Bao), and tourism. But this has not been enough to offset the effects of the slump in agricultural production, which remains the cornerstone of Senegal's economy.

A few statistics are sufficient to demonstrate the poor performance of the economy. Between 1980 and 1992, Senegal's annual growth rate per capita GNP was 0.1 percent; between 1980 and 1992 the GNP grew by 3 percent (2.7 percent in agriculture, 3.8 percent in industry). The balance-of-payments deficit went from $16 million in 1970 to $267 million in 1992. The external debt, which was $131 million in 1970, rose to $1,565 million in 1984 and to $3,607 million in 1992.[36]

Living standards remain very low for most Senegalese. Underemployment and unemployment pose a rising problem. According to an official survey (1991), 24.4 percent of the economically active population of the capital is unemployed, and the annual survey of the *Economic Intelligence Unit for 1992–1993* concludes: "The economic difficulties of the 1980s and the continuing structural adjustment programs designed to tackle them have so far made matters worse in this respect than better." Even in the medium term, Senegal's economy is unlikely to grow much faster than its population (2.9 percent per year).

On the whole, structural adjustment has been a failure in Senegal, as a report published in 1990 by Professor Eliott Berg recognizes.[37] "Senegalese society is in a situation of crisis without precedent; it is a victim of a growing and very disturbing phenomenon of pauperisation," writes Makhtar Diouf.[38]

The devaluation of the CFA Franc is supposed to have positive long-term effects on the Senegalese economy, but its immediate effect has been a substantial rise in prices (the average level of prices is likely to be 45 percent higher in 1994 than it was in 1993). Social and political unrest is inevitable in such a context.

It is nonetheless surprising to note that, in spite of this disastrous economic performance, Senegal has experienced continuous political stability. This is no doubt because of the function of mediation played by the Muslim brotherhoods and, on a wider level, the practice of clientelism, which has acted as a safety valve. But, as the gap between the state and society grows, one cannot be sure that these networks will continue to maintain a relative and fragile communication between the top and the bottom of the political and social system. One may well ask if the democratic process will be able to cope with these frustrations.

International Factors

International relations in Senegal are characterized by two tendencies that, at first sight, are contradictory. The first is the country's extreme dependence on the outside. Despite the efforts of its government to diversify agricultural production and equip itself with a dynamic industrial sector (development of the fishing industry, for example), Senegal's economic structure remains typically colonial. Seesawing agricultural output and the fluctuating world price of peanuts are grave threats to economic stability and an important contributing factor to Senegal's rising external debt. The situation was aggravated during the 1980s by the rise in the price of oil. In such conditions French aid, which had solved the problem for a long time, is no longer adequate. To improve matters, Senegal must appeal to the IMF—and agree to its conditions—as well as to other outside sources. France has remained the first supplier of technical assistance and Senegal's first trading partner (29% of total exports and 26.3% of total imports in 1991), and more and more financial aid and investment comes from other sources, including the European Development Fund and the IMF. The United States is also visibly present in Senegal through USAID and U.S. commercial banks. The aid of Arab countries, in the form of bilateral agreements or multinational business interests, was also very important in the 1980s but has slowed down since the Gulf War. The influence of France, however, remains preponderant on the political and cultural planes. France still has a military base in Dakar, and Senegal's intelligentsia is the most Parisian in all of black Africa. This dependence on the outside is matched by extremely active diplomatic involvement in Africa and the rest of the world. From this point of view, the Senegal of Abdou Diouf is as enterprising as that of his predecessor. Senegal has played a pioneering role in setting up regional economic bodies. The country has been a mediator in many inter-African conflicts (the Western Sahara, Liberia), and has made important contributions to the Organization of African Unity. Moreover, Senegal has been one of the initiators of the French "Commonwealth" (*francophonie*) and has always been an active participant in international institutions like the United Nations and UNESCO. In the eyes of the world, Senegal is one of the leaders of moderate Africa. The participation of Senegealese troops (500 soldiers) to the anti-Iraqi coalition during the Gulf conflict was the symbol of this international involvement.

Senegal's leading role in international relations implies the existence of a political regime that is stable and respectful of human liberties. We have already seen how important Senegal's international image was for Senghor in the past, and how important it still is for Diouf today—particularly as it concerns Western countries that are important sources of aid. This image has two complementary functions: it allows Senegal greater influence on the international scene than its demographic and economic weight would merit; and, by offering reassuring guarantees on the nature and stability of the regime, it helps attract international assistance: with aid receipts totaling $132 per capita, Senegal receives three times the average for sub-Saharan Africa.

With Abdou Diouf, however, another image has grown up around

Senegal, that of an Islamic country. Senghor developed close ties with certain Arab countries (Saudi Arabia, Kuwait, Iraq, and the Gulf States). But as a Muslim, his successor can go even further in this direction, and Diouf's participation in January 1981 at the Islamic Conference in Saudi Arabia, combined with his pilgrimage to Mecca, have had a considerable echo in Senegal. In 1992 Deker hosted the annual meeting of the Organization of Islamic Conference (OIC).

At the same time, Diouf knows very well that the Islamic card has to be played carefully if he wants to control the increase of Muslim expectations at the national level.

Senegal's relations with its neighbors have been more delicate. Relations with Mauritania have been very tense in recent years, reflecting the conflict between Arabic-speaking groups and black Africans within Mauritania. In 1989 violence in Mauritania against blacks led to violence against the numerous white Mauritanian petty traders in Senegal. Expulsions took place on both sides, and diplomatic relations on both sides were broken until 1992. The failure of the confederation with Gambia (which ended in 1989) and uneasy relations with Guinea-Bissau (linked to the guerrilla conflict in Casamance) have hampered Senegalese aspirations to regional leadership.

Summary

In the last analysis, Senegal still appears today to be a semidemocracy. The factors that have played in favor of democracy relate to Senegal's history and political culture, as well as to its relative ethnic equilibrium and religious homogeneity. In addition, one cannot overlook the international image that this little country has tried to project. On the other hand, the weight of the state, economic—and, to a certain extent, political—dependence, and the phenomenon of clientelism have functioned as limits to democracy.

Future Prospects

Formal democracy is a political tradition in Senegal, despite a period of about ten years during which some violations were committed. More than elsewhere in Africa, Senegal has used pluralism and negotiation (sometimes accompanied by threats, it is true) to overcome the difficulties it has encountered. There is no doubt that the majority of the political elite strongly favors democratic government. The problem is whether democracy can solve the fundamental issues facing the country.

The first of these concerns Senegal's economic survival. As has been pointed out, despite its efforts to take better advantage of its (scarce) resources, Senegal has been hit head-on by the world recession and the drought. It has also had to face the consequences of the neocolonial structure of its economy, as well as the shortcomings of its political and administrative apparatus—its unwieldiness and lack of flexibility and its clientelist practices. Up to now, public funds, international aid, and foreign investment have served to develop the ruling elite and the bureaucracy rather than the country's productive forces. In such conditions, democracy is fragile and artificial. It can benefit, at the very most, certain elites by giving them channels to express their opinions, but it has not changed the living conditions of the majority of the people. This explains their growing mistrust of institutions and political parties and their lack of interest in electoral, political, and public affairs. The success of ideologies and movements outside the formal political scene is thus not very surprising, and the renewal of Islam has to be seen in this light.

Here, then, is the second big issue facing Senegal. It is one of utmost importance, for it reveals the existence of another political culture that may not be fundamentally antidemocratic, as is often thought, but which brings into question the political heritage and traditions that have dominated the intelligentsia and the ruling elite up to now. For a long time, Islam, and especially the brotherhoods that structured it, served as institutions of social, political, and economic mediation. Today, however, Islam has become an ideology of mobilization and protest. The failure of modernization has contributed to the rise of a religion that appears as a weapon in the combat against the West and its values as expressed by the elite of the country. Henceforth, the marabouts are no longer simple clients of the ruling elite and of the state. Riding on the wave of popular opinion that sees Islam as a universal remedy to poverty and decadence, the marabouts have become more demanding partners of the state, setting themselves up as lesson givers, or even as a counterelite. In this sense, Islam is no longer simply an element of popular culture. It has become an ideology aiming to remodel society and the state. The young, and particularly young intellectuals, as well as members of the frustrated petty bourgeoisie, no longer identify with the values of the West, or with Marxism, but have thrown themselves into Islamic movements.

It is very difficult for the state and for democracy to cope with this dynamic social force. What we are witnessing is the transition from a relatively tolerant and open kind of Islam to an Islam that is setting itself up as an autonomous political force. Whereas the first type was compatible with democracy, the second is more of an obstacle, for it implies a totalitarian vision of society.

The problem of Casamance represents a third challenge for the regime. The revolts that have shaken the southern part of Senegal in the last years cannot be stopped by mere administrative reforms. I have tried, briefly, to give reasons for this. It must be emphasized that this is not just a rebellion of a particular ethnic group. What is being questioned, above all, is the kind of communication that exists between the "center" and the "periphery." It is the culture of the Jacobin state itself that is under fire, particularly by a people who do not live in the same social and cultural universe as those of the rest of the country and feel they have been ignored for too long.

In short, these three critical issues show the limits of a democracy that has been too much the exclusive concern of a relatively privileged minority and that remains cut off from the realities of the country. The inhabitants of Senegal will only be able to feel concerned about pluralism and liberalism if this minority is able to provide for their security and dignity. As of now, the above problems not only impose limits to the liberalization of the regime, but threaten the country's political stability.

It would be presumptuous of us to claim to have lessons to teach or to have miracle solutions to the crisis facing Senegal today. However, in light of the above analysis, it is possible to indicate a few directions that could allow Senegal to consolidate its democratic gains and to make these gains more meaningful for a greater number of its inhabitants.

The most fundamental point concerns the economic survival of the country, and, more specifically, that of its most underprivileged categories. On the whole, massive state intervention and huge agroindustrial complexes have been failures. Not only have such schemes prevented any grassroots initiative, but they have failed to improve the income of the social groups they were meant to benefit. Worse, the effects have often included a profound breaking down of the groups concerned—and erosion of the legitimacy of a regime that has been unable to meet people's expectations and fulfill promises made.

Unfortunately, structural adjustment policies have not been very successful, as we have seen. In the minds of many Senegalese they mean pauperization, and the devaluation of the CFA franc will make daily life more difficult in the immediate future.

Such steps cannot be carried out simply by limiting the role of the state. But another aspect of democratization must be worked out: Senegal has to invent a new means of communication between the "center" and the "periphery." And that means that the state has to be more open to local realities. I believe that only a policy of decentralization would be able to put such dynamics into motion and reestablish confidence between the summit and the base, for political pluralism will function in a vacuum if it is not anchored in local societies. Unfortunately, both the Jacobin tradition and the monocratic presidential system work against such transformations, justifying the monopolization of power in the name of "national interest." In his contribution to a debate on democracy in Senegal, Pathé Diagne observed that democracy loses much of its meaning when it is structured around a monocratic and centralizing power system that prohibits people "from achieving their full material and cultural potentials by refusing to allow them to set up their own assemblies and local administrations in their own specific context and geographic space."[39]

Decentralization is certainly not a panacea for all the problems in Senegal, and it might even be a threat to national unity, but it can bring institutions closer to the people and thus prevent disastrous clashes, such as might well occur one day in Casamance.

Finally, if decentralization really is to work, both the state and the forces behind it have to anchor themselves more deeply in Senegal's cultural environment. The elite's Westernized consumption patterns and concept of the state only serve to widen the gap between the ruling class and the majority of the people, who live in another universe and who have no means of gaining access to the "superior" culture. Muslim nationalism feeds on this gap. And refocusing the political culture around "indigenous" values, practices, and realities would help narrow and, finally, close this gap, which is detrimental to democracy.

What national or extranational forces might foster such changes?

I have emphasized already the rather large consensus that exists in Senegal around the concept of pluralism. Such orientations, however, could be brought into question by the rising forces of Islam, which are gaining support among certain elites seeking new forms of action and legitimacy. Among the social categories mobilized by the Islamic revival can be found the young intellectuals and, to a lesser extent, the business class, no doubt because they perceive the Muslim religion as a way of setting themselves off from the political and administrative elite that governs the country. As for the latter, it is undermined by a conflict of generations that pits the former political bosses and dignitaries against young technocrats. The older generation has strong local backing but it is incapable of coping with the mutations the country is undergoing, and the younger generation is more competent but less rooted in the "real country." What they do share, however, is their mutual support for the democratic form of government.

The values and institutions of democracy find much less favor, on the other hand, among the lower social classes, who do not perceive their utility, or rather their effects, on daily life. For these classes the state is often a foreign entity that is ineffective and oppressive. Competition among political parties is a game that does not concern them directly because it cannot solve their problems or fulfill their aspirations. In such conditions, democracy lacks pertinence and cannot throw down roots in the "real country."

The most important task on the international level, I believe, is not merely to consider Senegal as a politically strategic region but to try to overcome the difficulties that restrict the impact of democracy. From this point of view, any action that limits the state is a necessary, although insufficient, condition, for there is the ever-present risk that giving free rein to economic forces would create new forms of inequality and reinforce the neocolonial structure of the economy. International aid must not only help to develop an entrepreneurial class in the strictest sense of the word. It must allow local communities to have control of their own affairs and give them the means of innovation. Thus, heavy capital outlay or aid schemes for "massive development projects" should give way to an aid emphasis on smaller-scale and intermediate technology, featuring projects that are less ambitious but closer to the people. It bears repeating that any policy that tends to bring the "center" closer to the "periphery" promotes stability and democracy.

On a strictly political level, it is also vitally important that Senegalese political parties not be isolated, but be in constant contact with democratic movements in the world. To be shut off from the outside carries with it the threat not only of political sclerosis, but also of authoritarianism. Anything that facilitates the exchange of experiences and ideas encourages the development of democracy and renewal. Dialogue of this sort could not but help to widen the perspectives of Senegalese political parties.

Finally, the industrialized nations of the West must be reminded that they should not set themselves up as the supreme models of democracy. African history has shown us that the dynamics of African politics can also invent original forms of participation and pluralism. Nothing is more dangerous for the West than to appear to be the sole source of democracy. The West should content itself, on a much more modest level, with facilitating the changes that propose an alternative to authoritarianism and tyranny. From its contact with Africa, the West could also learn to respect differences, which is the very core of the concept of democracy.

Notes

1. Donal Cruise O'Brien, "Au Senegal, la democratie sans alternance," *Le Monde Diplomatique,* (April 1993).

2. On this subject, see Michael Crowder, *Senegal: A Study in French Assimilation Policy* (London: Oxford University Press, 1962).

3. See J. H. J. Legier, "Institutions municipales et politiques coloniales: Les communes du Sénégal," *Revue francaise d'histoire d'outre-mer,* no. 201, p. 445. On this period see also the fundamental work of G. Johnson Jr., *The Emergence of Black Politics in Senegal: The Struggle for Power in the Four Communes, 1900–1920* (Stanford: Stanford University Press, 1971).

4. On the political life in Senegal in this period, the following works can be consulted: R. S. Morgenthau, *Political Parties in French West Africa* (Oxford: Clarendon Press, 1964); K. Robinson, "Senegal: The Elections to the Territorial Assembly," in J. W. Mackenzie and T. Robinson, eds., *Five Elections in Africa* (New York: Oxford University Press, 1960); P. Mercier, "La vie politique dans les centre urbains du Sénégal: Etude d'une periode de transition," *Cahiers internationaux de Sociologie* 6, no. 17 (1959).

5. Senghor was the very first African to pass France's prestigious *agrégation* examination, which allows successful candidates to teach at the higher levels of the lycée and is often a stepping stone to a university career (translator's note).

6. See W. F. Foltz, *From French West Africa to the Mali Federation* (New Haven: Yale University Press, 1965).

7. Among the many studies of this constitution and its different reforms, one may consult the following works: J. C. Gautron and M. Rougevin-Baville, *Droit public du Sénégal*

(Paris: Pedone, 1977; 1st ed. 1970); D. G. Lavroff, *Le Sénégal* (Paris: Librairie générale de droit et de jurisprudence, 1966); G. Hesseling, *Histoire politique du Sénégal* (Paris: Karthala, 1985).

8. Hesseling, *Sénégal,* p. 247.

9. Sheldon Gellar, *Senegal: An African Nation Between Islam and the West* (Boulder, Colo.: Westview Press, 1982), p. 31.

10. Ibid., p. 41.

11. On this subject, see my work, *Le marabout et le prince: Islam et pouvoir au Sénégal* (Paris, Pedone, 1981).

12. On clan struggles, see, in particular, F. Zucarelli, *Un parti politique africain: L'union progressiste sénégalaise* (Paris: Librarine générale de droit et de jurisprudence, 1970); and C. Coulon, "Elections, factions et idéologies au Sénégal," in Centre d'étude d'Afrique noire et Centre d'études et de recherches internationales, *Aul urnes l'Afrique* (Paris: Pedone, 1978), pp. 149–186.

13. G. Hesseling, *Sénégal,* p. 137.

14. On Senghor, the following works will be found very useful: J. L. Hymans, *Leopold Sedar Senghor: An Intellectual Biography* (Edinburgh: Edinburgh University Press, 1971); I. L. Markovitz, *Leopold Sedar Senghor and the Politics of Negritude* (New York: Atheneum, 1964).

15. R. Dumont, *Paysanneries aux abois* (Paris: Editions du Seuil, 1972).

16. See M. Paye, "La presse et le pouvoir," in M. Coumba Diop, ed., *Sénégal: Trajectoire d'un Etat* (Paris and Dakar: CODESRIA and Karthala, 1992), pp. 331–377.

17. Donal Cruise O'Brien, "Les élections sénégalaises du 27 février 1983," *Politique africaine* 11 (1983): pp. 7–12.

18. Leonardo A. Villalon, "Democratizing a (Quasi) Democracy: The Senegalese Elections of 1993," *African Affairs* 93 (1994): p. 163.

19. Mamadou Diouf, "L'échec du modèle démocratique au Sénégal, 1981–1993," *Africa Spectrum* 1 (1994): pp. 47–64.

20. Donal Cruise O'Brien and Christian Coulon, "Senegal," in D. Cruise O'Brien J. Dunn, and R. Rathbone, eds., *Contemporary West African States* (Cambridge: Cambridge University Press, 1989), p. 150.

21. Robert Fatton, *The Making of a Liberal Democracy: Senegalese "Passive Revolution"* (Boulder: Lynne Rienner Publishers, 1985), p. 170.

22. O'Brien and Coulon, "Senegal," pp. 150–153.

23. The former French colonies in black Africa belong to the Franc zone. The CFA Franc was created in 1945. Originally the term CFA meant *colonies françaises d'Afrique* (French African colonies), but later, at independence, it was changed to *communauté financière africaine* (African financial community). Since 1958, one CFA Franc has been worth 0.02 French Franc. This fixed parity was not modified until the 1994 devaluation, which cut the value of the CFA Franc in half. This devaluation is often presented as a consequence of the poor performance of the CFA economies and as a means to stimulate African exports.

24. Cheikh Anta Diop, *L'Afrique noire précoloniale* (Paris: Présence Africaine, 1960).

25. In addition to Diop's work mentioned in note 24, see A. Sylla, *La philosophie morale des Wolof* (Dakar: Sankore, 1978).

26. Abdou Diouf in the Preface of J. M. Nzouandeu, *Les partis politiques sénégalais* (Dakar: Editions Clairafrique, 1984), p. 7.

27. Donal Cruise O'Brien, "Ruling Class and Peasantry in Senegal: 1960–1976", in Donal Cruise O'Brien, ed., *The Political Economy of Underdevelopment: Dependence in Senegal* (London: Sage, 1979), pp. 213–214.

28. V. Ebin, "A la recherche de nouveaux 'poissons': stratégies comerciales mourides par temps de crise," *Politique Africaine* 45 (1992): pp. 86–99.

29. W. J. Foltz, "Senegal," in J. S. Coleman and C. Rosberg Jr., eds., *Political Parties and National Integration in Tropical Africa* (Berkeley: University of California Press, 1964), pp. 16–64.

30. See Donal Cruise O'Brien, "Langue et nationalité au Sénégal," *Année africaine 1979* (Paris: Pedone, 1981), pp. 319–338.

31. D. Darbon, "Le culturalime des Casamançais," *Politique africaine* 14 (1984): p. 127. See also Darbon's *L'Administration et le paysan en Casamance: Essai d'anthropologie administrative* (Paris: Pedone, 1988).

32. See J. C. Marut, "Sénégal: Les évolutions politiques en Casamance," *L'Afrique politique 1994* (Paris and Bordeaux: Karthala and CEAN), pp. 59–99.

33. J. S. Barker, "The Paradox of Development: Reflections on a Study of Local-Central Relations in Senegal," in M. F. Lofchie, ed., *The State of the Nation: Constraints of Development in Independent Africa* (Berkeley: University of California Press, 1971), pp. 47–63. On the same theme see the work of J. L. Balans, C. Coulon, and J. M. Gastellu, *Autonomie locale et intégration nationale au Sénégal* (Paris: Pedone, 1975).

34. Mar Fall, *Sénégal: L'Etat est malade* (Paris: L'Harmattan, 1985).

35. Gellar, *Senegal.*

36. Banque mondiale, *Rapport sur le développement dans le monde 1994* (Washington).

37. Eliott Berg, *Adjustment Postponed: Economic Policy Reform in Senegal in the 1980s* (Washington, D.C.: USAID, 1990).

38. Makhtar Diouf, "La crise de l'ajustement," *Politique Africaine* 45 (1992): p. 81.

39. Pathé Diagne, *Quelle démocratie pour le Sénégal* (Dakar: Editions Sankore, 1984), p. 48.

11

South Africa: Divided in a Special Way

Steven Friedman

In late April 1994, South Africa joined the growing late–twentieth-century fold of new democracies. Although claims of South African uniqueness have become overworked, aspects of its history do make it an unusual case study of contemporary democratization.

As with Russia and in contrast to most Latin American countries, South Africa's 1994 elections were its first experience in choosing a government by universal franchise in competitive elections. But in contrast to virtually all new democracies,[1] the country had an unbroken experience of regular elections and pluralist politics—restricted to its white minority.

These features give a distinct character to South Africa's first experience with democracy; they combine with a complex political and social history to create circumstances at once hostile and unexpectedly propitious to democratization. In this chapter I examine the roots of South African democratization and its implications for the study of comparable societies; I also analyze possibilities for and obstacles to democratic consolidation.

Divided and Doomed?

South Africa has always fitted neatly into the group of societies labeled "deeply divided." Until 1994 the central feature of the country's politics was rule not by an unelected elite but by an ascriptive racial minority. The 5.2 million whites—about 13 percent of the population—participated in regular multiparty elections but denied that right to their 30.6 million black African compatriots, who make up about 76 percent of the population. Belatedly, in 1984, the government extended the franchise to the two black minorities— the 3.4 million "colored" (mixed race) people, who make up about 9 percent of the population, and the 1 million Asians (3 percent) (see Tables 11.1 and 11.2)—but on terms that preserved political segregation white government was forced to begin to adapt racial legislation), racial identity and

531

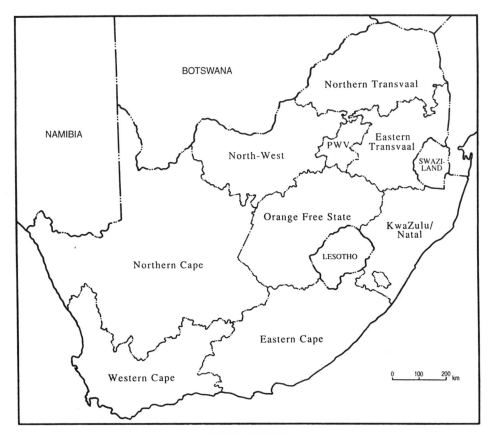

SOUTH AFRICA

Table 11.1   Estimated Population by Race, April 27, 1994

Race	Number	% of Total
Black African	30,645,157	76
White	5,171,419	13
Colored	3,435,114	9
Asian	1,032,943	3
Total	40,284,633	101[a]

Population by Race Under Eighteen Years of Age

Black African	14,405,685	82
White	1,410,261	8
Colored	1,378,670	8
Asian	380,865	2
Total	17,575,481	100

Source: Central Statistical Services, *Estimated Population and Number of Voters by Province and District as of 27 April 1994,* 1994.
a. Does not add up to 100 because figures are rounded.

Table 11.2   Percentage Population by Language, 1993

Race	Number	% of Total
Black African		
Zulu	8,340,000	29
Xhosa	6,959,000	24
Tswana	4,015,000	14
North Sotho	3,460,000	12
South Sotho	2,230,000	8
Shangaan	1,440,000	5
Other	2,274,000	7
Total	28,718,000	99[a]
White		
Afrikaans	2,920,000	60
English	1,960,000	40
Other	9,400	0
Total	4,889,400	100

Source: Race Relations Survey, SA Institute of Race Relations, Johannesburg, 1994; 1993–1994 author's calculation.

Note: This table seeks to quantify South Africans by ethnic origin. Since ethnicity is a highly sensitive issue, however, official censuses do not ask respondents for ethnic affiliation. Language is, therefore, used as the indicator.

The last language census was conducted when the four black "homelands" that were granted "independence" had not been enumerated. In an attempt to rectify this, I have included population figures for these territories and assumed that all of the black residents spoke the language of the ethnic group for which the homeland was created. This cannot be verified, and the figures should be regarded only as rough estimates. The figure for Tswana speakers is particularly open to question, since it assumes that all inhabitants of the former Bophutatswana homeland speak this language. This is not the case, but no figures exist that indicate the proportion of non-Tswana speakers. Any errors are the author's, not those of the *Race Relations Survey.*
a. Does not add up to 100 because figures are rounded.

ensured continued white dominance. Prior to the mid-1970s (when the also determined property rights and the consequent right to engage in economic activity, entry to' educational institutions, access to residential areas and to private and public facilities—and the right to live in the cities.

Inevitably, race was the society's primary social and political divide: The central issue in white politics was how to maintain control over the black majority, and this, equally inevitably, prompted black resistance. Statutory racial domination appeared to divide society into two camps[2] and largely to exclude the possibility of choice between them; birth, rather than social class, interest, or personal choice, determined political identities and loyalties.

Democratization in this context appeared to face very different constraints than those analyzed by O'Donnell and Schmitter.[3] The central divide was not that between the unelected elite and the citizenry but that between two social blocs, one of which ruled not only by force but also on the strength of a mandate conferred by over 2 million electors who entrusted it with defending their privilege. It seemed more appropriate to influential scholars[4] to analyze South Africa as a divided society—and a particularly intractable one at that. Politics seemed a zero-sum game, in which the minority would retain its dominance through force and manipulation or lose it by the same means: The victory of the majority would have to be bought at a price so high that prospects of building a democratic polity on the ruins would be negligible.

Thus far, the conflict has proved less intractable than it previously appeared. Although conflict gathered momentum from the 1970s, minority rule ended not with a convulsion but with a negotiated compromise that left much of the society's administrative and economic capacities intact. To some extent, minority democracy had been broadened by including the disenfranchised majority. If this did not guarantee a democracy, it at least made its prospects far more plausible than had seemed possible during much of South Africa's history.

These unexpected developments did not necessarily negate a "divided society" analysis—not all scholars who analyzed South Africa in these terms asserted that the conflict was intractable. But they did insist that it could be resolved only by negotiating institutional forms that recognized the society's divisions. The most popular option was a negotiated compromise, or "elite settlement,"[5] which acknowledged that the society was composed of blocs rather than of individuals. Since this was the way in which a political settlement was achieved—and the settlement did incorporate features that seemed to offer minorities a guaranteed share of power—the diagnosis seemed to be confirmed.

Although a divided society analysis clearly describes crucial aspects of South African reality, I argue that it fails to capture the complexity of the country's divisions and that a flawed diagnosis leads to equally faulty prescriptions for democratization. The argument begins with a brief examination of the society's political history and its implications for political culture.

The Roots of Exclusion

South Africa's divisions are rooted in an unusual colonial history that played a contradictory role in shaping contemporary politics. The country's southernmost region, the Cape, was colonized by the Dutch in 1652. Since the bulk of black settlement was located further inland, and the indigenous Khoi and San peoples were quickly conquered, the colonizers soon saw South Africa as an African New World and themselves as white pioneer settlers: They proclaimed themselves "Afrikaners" or Africans. Their relationship with the colonial governors dispatched by the Dutch East India Company was tense and sometimes conflictual. Something akin to a "white politics" soon took root.

Intra-white divisions developed a new character in 1806, when the British annexed the Cape. This action was followed eighteen years later by the arrival of the first group of British settlers, who, like their Dutch predecessors, saw the country as a permanent home. Conflict between white settlers and the British administration began early. Successive governors ruled autocratically, prompting settler resistance.

Afrikaner resentment was particularly strong, and its form was also significant for later political development. As the settlers penetrated into the interior, they faced their first serious military challenge from the Xhosa-speaking peoples, and a series of border wars ensued. The settlers complained that the British administration seemed unwilling to help. Their dissatisfaction was strengthened by the activities of the London Missionary Society's Reverend John Phillip, whose complaints about the settlers' treatment of the indigenous peoples were denounced as meddling negrophilia.[6] Resentment was enhanced by the fact that the "meddlers" were British.

In the 1830s, therefore, when the more independent Afrikaner settlers decided to leave the colony and journey inland to escape British rule, two of the central features of white politics were already evident. The common experience of frontier society—and of resistance to an often authoritarian colonial administration—had instilled in the Afrikaner *trekkers,* or pioneers, a strong spirit of independence and internal democracy. But this was accompanied by a far more overt brand of racism than that of the British administration.

British colonialism was never as racially inclusive as its Portuguese[7] and French equivalents; it never sought to define colonized territories as provinces of the "mainland" or their inhabitants as subordinate compatriots. Most instruments of South African racial domination were introduced by British administrations.[8] But the British were open to extending the rights of citizenship to colonized blacks who were able to acquire property and a

British education. When representative institutions were introduced in the Cape, the small stratum of blacks who could meet these standards were indeed granted the franchise. For the vast majority of black people, British colonialism was indistinguishable from rule by Afrikaner pioneers; for the tiny elite, it made a world of difference. The cultural influence of British colonialism was also shaped by the Anglican church, which wanted to recruit the indigenous colonized, not merely to administer them. This implied both a friendlier approach and an emphasis on education—the modernizing black elite was almost invariably educated in Anglican mission schools.

The Afrikaner settlers adopted a more consistent approach to the people they colonized. They were concerned with establishing an egalitarian democracy among themselves. This implied formal equality of all citizens; thus, they could retain control over their polities only by excluding non-Afrikaners (and blacks in particular) from citizenship. As the settlers established states in the interior through conquest, they rejected any possibility of black inclusion, proclaiming the principle of "no equality in church or state."[9]

Much of South Africa's subsequent white political history can be explained by these early divisions. The South African state was born following an 1899–1902 war in which Britain defeated the Afrikaner, or Boer, republics and incorporated them in a polity that became the Union of South Africa in 1910. Consistent with British policy toward colonies that had dominant white-settler populations, the Union was granted significant autonomy and representative institutions for whites (and those blacks who qualified for the Cape franchise).

For more than five decades, white electoral politics constituted a battle between Afrikaner nationalism, which mobilized the descendants of the citizens of the defeated Boer states, and the British tradition, represented by the 40 percent of the white population who were descendants of either British settlers or other non-Afrikaner European immigrants. Although neither side was inclined to include the black majority in the oligarchic democracy the Union created, Afrikaner nationalist governments were even less inclined to compromise on exclusion. The issue was settled with the triumph of Afrikaner Nationalism—and its vehicle, the National Party (NP)—at the polls in 1948. The NP implemented a strictly exclusionary race policy that, after several ideological twists, hardened into apartheid in the late 1950s. Since Afrikaners remained a majority of the white electorate, they remained in power until 1994.

White Politics and Black Resistance

This unusual form of colonization is highly significant because of its influence on the political culture of the colonized elite. Elsewhere, the fight against colonialism was almost invariably fought against a single group of colonizers whose political culture was rejected by the resisters. South African colonialism was noteworthy because it represented a struggle between two sets of colonizers, one of which—albeit in its cultural-religious dimension more than its legislative practice—was made to appear relatively accommodating by the rigid exclusivism of the other.

One manifestation was the stress the early black resistance placed on the conscience of the British colonizer. The African National Congress (ANC), the principal vehicle of majority nationalism, was formed in 1912 (when it was called the South African National Native Congress) by the small elite that owed its formal education to the missionaries. Its leaders dressed, talked, and acted like British gentlemen. In 1913, when they prepared to oppose the Union's first overt act of exclusion—Land Acts that deprived black Africans of the right to own property in all but a small part of the country's land surface—they turned to the Crown for help. They did so repeatedly, without success, for three decades.

By the 1940s, the ANC Youth League, led by a group of impatient professionals and intellectuals (which included Nelson Mandela, who half a century later became the country's first president to be elected by universal franchise, and Oliver Tambo, ANC president during its exile), insisted that appeals to the Crown were an implausible source of salvation. The league, whose leaders were initially suspicious of cooperating with whites,[10] impelled a change in resistance strategy from moral suasion to mass mobilization. Beginning in 1960, when the ANC and the Pan Africanist Congress—a more militant breakaway group formed in 1959 by black nationalist intellectual Robert Sobukwe—were banned, this tactic gave way by force to guerrilla war.

The 1950s, which were remembered for almost three decades as the "golden age" of legal black mobilization, were not as golden as the fond memories suggested. During this period the ANC had support but little organization—its membership peaked at around 100,000.[11] Some of its most celebrated campaigns were centered around issues that were more important to its elite than to those on whose behalf it sought to speak.[12] The period also held no serious prospect of accommodation; resistance met with continued police harassment, and the government ignored ANC appeals for dialogue.

The post-1960 period began a process that seemed inevitably to lead to irrevocable polarization. The ANC turned to revolutionary guerrilla war; exile extinguished the limited democracy within the movement and strengthened the influence of the Stalinist South African Communist Party (SACP). Internally, a state of emergency closed off all avenues of legal mobilization. The ensuing decade was quiescent, and resistance was restricted to isolated conspiratorial activity.

The first public sign of renewed resistance repeated the history of the 1940s. Young black intellectuals rejected the perceived passivity of their elders and demanded an assault on apartheid. In 1969, university students formed the South African Students Organisation (SASO). SASO's chief intellectual architect, Steven Biko, articulated the philosophy of Black Consciousness (BC), which stressed black assertiveness, unity, and self-reliance in the struggle to end white rule.[13] In the early 1970s, a set of BC organizations emerged. Although their influence on intellectuals was always far greater than on the grass roots, they helped to shape the climate of resistance that began to reemerge in the 1970s and played a major role in producing a generation of black leaders.

SASO's formation was followed four years later by the first sign of mass resistance—a wave of strikes in the industrial port city of Durban that were the catalyst for the reemergence of a black trade union movement. In 1976, protests by black pupils against Afrikaans as a medium of instruction triggered violent conflict in Soweto, outside Johannesburg (the country's largest black township) which spread to other parts of the country; conflict persisted in some parts for nearly two years.[14] The protests were quelled, and in late 1977 almost all BC organizations, which the government saw as instigators of revolt, were banned. Biko died in police detention in 1978. But both events reshaped apartheid. The strikes led to a series of adaptations that culminated in the legal recognition of black union rights in 1978; the Soweto turmoil began a series of adaptations that recognized black permanence in the cities.

Equally important, both events also rekindled internal resistance, which reemerged in 1980 and 1981 as a rash of student protests, which were quelled, and reemerged again in 1984. By this time, students and workers (the union movement continued to grow, and industrial conflict became a routine feature of the economic landscape from 1980) were not the only participants. The Soweto conflict gradually triggered the formation of a host of associations—residents' groups (or "civics"), youth organizations, women's groups, religious groups—that were committed to resistance. In 1983, these groups formed the United Democratic Front (UDF), which was located firmly within the ANC tradition and among whose features was a commitment to nonracialism as a strategy as well as a goal. (This ensured a rivalry between the UDF and the BC organizations, which reemerged in 1979 with the formation of the Azanian People's Organisation, AZAPO.) The UDF's initial focus was on resistance to the 1983 Constitution, which offered colored and Indian peoples a subordinate role in Parliament but excluded black Africans, who were expected to be content with ethnic "homelands" and autonomous local governments. In late 1984, these local councils, which had been elected by only a fraction of their constituents (the UDF had mobilized a boycott of the elections), raised service charges. This act led to a rejection of their legitimacy that, fused with economic hardship, produced two years of violent protest in which resistance was often imposed coercively. The government of state President P. W. Botha reacted by declaring two states of emergency, one each in 1985 and 1986; the latter lasted until the end of the decade.

In the townships, 1984 began a period of violent confrontation in which both militants and police appeared eager to outdo the other's brutality. Violence against opponents or against those who chose not to boycott was matched by mass arrests, "hit-squad" murders, and attempts to trigger violence between black political rivals. The ANC responded by moving from sabotage directed at government installations to a "people's war" that, although never sustained, was often expressed through urban terrorism. Both camps framed their strategies in apocalyptic terms, and a violent stalemate began that appeared irrevocably to polarize the society.

Even in these times the earlier cultural legacy did not disappear. Black Consciousness, which posited race polarization as an inevitable step on the road to an antiracist society, did not prove to be an enduring influence on mass resistance, despite its vital role as a catalyst. AZAPO barely developed a support base beyond a coterie of ideologues; on the elite level, many BC activists gravitated to the UDF and then the ANC:[15] In both movements BC "graduates" played a significant and growing role.[16] The union movement, whose largest vehicle is the Congress of South African Trade Unions (COSATU), supplemented its militancy with a pragmatic willingness to negotiate ever more elaborate compromises with employers. During part of the 1980s the township UDF affiliates, some of whose supporters brutalized or killed opponents, were sometimes either negotiating with local municipalities and business groups or putting out feelers with an intent to do so.

Although the host of civil society groups that emerged in the 1980s— primarily within the UDF fold—were often hastily convened instruments of political resistance, and although many lacked the organized base they claimed, a strategy that relied on open mobilization produced a culture of popular democracy. Although sometimes more rhetorical than real, this culture was an important antidote to the conspiratorial culture of exile and guerrilla war. Leaders of this internal mobilization, such as unionist Cyril Ramaphosa, and UDF activists such as Trevor Manuel, Dullah Omar, and Sydney Mafumadi played key roles in the ANC government after 1994. Activists schooled in the struggles of the 1980s were often (but not always) more committed to democratic principles such as accountability than were the former exiles. Although in the 1970s and 1980s polarization was undeniable, it was mixed with attitudes that suggested that the image of a society hurtling toward a violent showdown with an authoritiarian outcome was overly simplistic.

For a variety of reasons, this had always been the case. Until their closure by the government in the mid-1950s, the Anglican and Catholic mission schools had not only been the primary source of education for the black elite, they were also a key source of opposition to racial exclusion. An Anglican priest, Trevor Huddleston, was one of three people given a special award for service by the nationalist movement. Indeed, the Christian church has exerted a significant influence on both sides of the divide in a country that still ranks as one of the most strongly Christian in the world.[17] Within white politics the divide ensured the continued existence of a small but vocal liberal opposition, the Progressive Party. Its most prominent member in Parliament, Helen Suzman, personally met nearly every ANC leader imprisoned after 1960, as she devoted a considerable part of her parliamentary work to an attempt to ameliorate the conditions of political prisoners.

As resistance militancy grew beginning in the early 1950s, it became unfashionable for most African nationalist politicians or sympathetic analysts to acknowledge explicitly any difference between English and Afrikaner colonial politics—or between white liberalism and Afrikaner nationalism. But the earlier experience nevertheless continued to influence resistance politics.

In 1958, to the dismay of some of its sympathizers, the ANC urged white voters to reject the NP and, by implication, to support its slightly less segregationist opponent, the United Party. In 1961, the ANC called a general strike to protest the proclamation of a republic[18] (a presumably unique act by an anticolonial movement). Indeed, during the 1950s, when the ANC remained a legal movement that openly mobilized mass protest, its embrace of more militant strategies often masked the extent to which it continued to rely on moral suasion—and incrementalism—rather than attempted revolution.[19] Throughout its period in exile, appeals to the conscience of the Western democracies remained a linchpin of its strategy. Until the 1980s, even guerrilla war was designed more to draw international attention to apartheid than to overthrow the government.[20] Indeed, a cardinal principle of ANC military strategy during that period was that civilians were not to be attacked, a stipulation that owed something to moral commitment but that also owed much to a desire not to alienate potential Western support.

This is not to say that the fight for majority rule was conducted solely within the parameters of British liberalism or social democracy. The SACP was the ANC's firmest internal ally, the Soviet Union its most loyal international one. From the 1950s, left-wing thought—including a militant anticolonialism—exerted a strong influence on the ANC. But given the nature of white rule, this was hardly surprising. What was surprising was the persistence of a significant, albeit partial, reliance on intervention by liberal democracies and their internal allies to hasten the end of minority domination.

This was clearly a consequence of a history in which British colonialism, at least since 1910, had not been the most oppressive force with which the majority and its political leadership were forced to contend. In this context it was understandable that black nationalist leadership would adopt a less dismissive attitude toward liberal democratic institutions than those of resistance elites elsewhere, who experienced Europe's proclaimed values as an undiluted source of subjugation. The fact that the willingness to value these institutions was not restricted to political elites is perhaps best illustrated by an anecdote told by a political scientist. He interviewed an ANC guerrilla who, detained without trial, insisted that his main demand was the right to be tried in open court by a judge—an appointee of the regime he was seeking to overthrow.[21] This attitude was not atypical; similar demands were voiced repeatedly by ANC militants.

An obvious objection to this analysis is that South Africa is not the only country in which a minority racial democracy subordinated the majority against the stated wishes of Britain. Zimbabwe is a seemingly similar case,[22] but there this situation has not blurred or complicated racial divisions. But Zimbabwe white society was far more politically homogeneous than South Africa's; there was no white cultural cleavage and, therefore, little of a (albeit ambiguous) "liberal tradition" to oppose the dominant minority mores. Further, in Zimbabwe the tension between indigenous whites and the colonial power only began in the 1960s; in South Africa it dates back to the early nineteenth century.

A legacy that ensures an understood difference between liberal democratic institutions and the system that subjugated the majority may do more to explain aspects of the South African transition than many analyses suggest.

The Ambiguous Legacy of Oligarchic Democracy

The claim that South Africa's pre-1990 political experience might have in any way fostered enthusiasm for democracy is, at first glance, absurd. Oligarchic democracy would seem on the surface to have done little or nothing to impress the virtues of democratic politics upon those who were excluded from it. First, white democracy was not as democratic as its beneficiaries chose to believe. Power changed hands through the ballot only twice—in 1924 and 1948. On both occasions, the change installed a government more hostile to majority aspirations than its predecessor.

More important, for much of its forty-six-year reign beginning in 1948, the National Party—with no serious electoral challenge—acted primarily as an ethnic patronage network, using public resources for the economic advancement of Afrikaner nationalists. In addition to negating central principles of democratic government, such as the requirement that public benefits not be distributed in a partisan fashion, the NP packed the military and the bureaucracy with its supporters, increasingly blurring the divide between party and state. Beginning in 1950, when the SACP was banned, attempts to quell black resistance prompted the incremental erosion of civil liberties. Black movements were banned, and individuals considered a threat to the state were arbitrarily restricted or detained without trial. The press was nominally free but was subject to an estimated one hundred laws restricting reportage and comment. Although whites were also victims of executive action, the brunt of the negative consequences was borne by blacks, for whom the virtues of competitive white elections were not immediately apparent.

More important still was the fact that apartheid operated in a manner that discredited electoral politics. In 1958, when Hendrik Verwoerd was elected prime minister, the NP implemented an ideology and an accompanying strategy that purported to abandon white dominance. Apartheid, or "separate development," as Verwoerd preferred to call the ideology, was not, he insisted, a system of racial mastery; rather, it sought to recognize inherent cultural difference by creating separate polities for the country's "ethnic groups." This strategy rested on the reality that, as in the rest of Africa, the black population is multiethnic. The largest language group, the 8. 3 million Zulus, make up only 29 percent of the population; the second largest group consists of Xhosas (6.9 million), 24 percent, and Sotho speakers, 20 percent (5.7 million) (see Table 11.2). The remaining one-quarter of the population speaks a variety of languages and has varying ethnic affiliations. By seeking to accommodate each group in a separate "state," the NP could argue that it was not denying majority rule since there was no majority: The country was a patchwork of minorities. It could argue, too, that blacks were no longer disenfranchised; they could enjoy the vote in their ethnic "homelands," which would be led to full independence. Much later, after the urban conflicts in the mid-1970s had revealed the impossibility of complete territorial segregation, segregated local government institutions known as Black Local Authorities were created as a vehicle for black African representation. In the mid-1980s, the parliamentary franchise was extended to the two black minorities—"colored" (mixed race) and Indian peoples—in racially separate houses that in the event of deadlock could be overruled by the whites' house.

This strategy was a twentieth-century product of the political culture discussed earlier. Black subordination was rationalized by excluding the majority from the state (or, in 1984, the white house of Parliament) and offering it alternative, ethnic forms of representation. But it was a disingenuous policy, just as apartheid was a rather implausible attempt to clothe racial domination in democratic and anticolonial garb. It was also a relatively effective method of transferring some of the responsibility—and the opprobrium—for administering racial exclusion to blacks themselves.

None of the black representative institutions enjoyed the power needed to change national legislation, and so they were forced to operate within the constraints of apartheid law. "Homeland governments" were unable to undo the rules that ensured that they presided over territory populated almost entirely by those considered too unproductive to labor in the cities. Local black councils could not challenge residential and industrial segregation, which ensured that they represented the poorest parts of the city and were also denied access to a business tax base that might have provided some resources with which to render public services. Election to any of these institutions brought the right to administer apartheid in exchange for the perquisites of office and the power to dispense some patronage.

Black nationalist organizations responded to the creation of these subordinate imitations of representative government by attempting to frustrate their work. The election boycott became a key instrument of strategy, aimed both at demonstrating the unwillingness of most black people to accept the strictures imposed upon them and at ensuring that if the minority wished to rule over the majority, it would have to do so without the aid of black surrogates. Beginning in the mid-1970s, this strategy included periodic—and, in the 1980s, escalating—attempts to weaken elected institutions by exacting violent retribution on those who held office in them. It seemed inevitable that for some, if not all, resistance activists, rejecting the legitimacy of these elections would translate into denying the legitimacy of all ballots and of the representative institutions they created. That it did, in some cases, have that effect is demonstrable.[23]

To these factors must be added the more obvious apartheid legacies that seemed to lay infertile soil for democratic consolidation. These included vast income inequalities, severe educational disadvantage for the majority, racial polarization, and the exclusion of the majority from competitive politics. All of these factors appeared to offer a very bleak prognosis for postapartheid democratic culture and practice.

The constraints on democratic consolidation posed by these factors are very real. But the effect of oligarchic democracy on majority political culture was far more complex than conventional analyses suggested.

Although the apartheid era was marked by phases of severe repression and black rights were always severely circumscribed, even in the more benign periods of white rule, the system never abandoned all vestiges of democracy. As noted earlier, some opposition members of Parliament achieved small improvements in the conditions of black political prisoners; some judges, albeit rarely, acquitted black nationalists accused of political crimes; white opposition newspapers that denounced apartheid. During all but the two periods noted previously, limited opportunities existed for public mobilization. The expression of antiapartheid opinion, although sharply circumscribed, was never completely prohibited.

More important, the privileged were genuinely enfranchised. Despite some irregularities by party organizers, white elections were perceived as fair, and few restrictions were placed on the liberal opposition.[24] This may have strengthened the value placed on the franchise by those excluded from it. The contrast between the powerlessness that awaited those who won apartheid elections and the power conferred on those who won the white equivalents was recognized, which prompted an inevitable demand for the real thing. Indeed, enfranchisement came to be seen as the status that distinguished the privileged from the dispossessed; the franchise became the central goal of resistance. This helps to explain the behavior of the majority in April 1994, when the vote was achieved. The press was filled with accounts of black citizens who patiently endured severe inconvenience as they waited for hours to vote.[25] The most remarkable feature of the polling days was the sharp drop in violence (in a society in which 16,757 people had died in political conflict since 1990[26]) as rivalries took second place to enthusiasm for voting.

White democracy was never hermetically sealed from black society, particularly from its intelligentsia. White elections were always *about* blacks, and this forced any black politician or intellectual who wanted to understand the political environment to watch these events with more than passing interest. Although it became de rigueur to proclaim indifference to white elections, those who did so clearly knew a great deal about the events they dismissed as "irrelevant." This imparted a vicarious experience of democratic politics.

These ambiguous and, at times, contradictory features of the apartheid order posed some significant obstacles to democratization. But they also created some often ignored factors that were more propitious to democratization than they seemed.

The Consequences of Differential Inclusion

It should be clear that the apartheid system was more complex than it seemed. Characterizing the system as one of unambiguous racial domination is valid as a moral judgment but not as an analytical tool.

Indeed, one of the system's more important effects for our understanding of the environment that shapes the effort to build a postapartheid democracy was its attempt to offer some black people a stake in the system. As noted earlier, subordinate political entities were created that, although they wielded little power, offered opportunities for patronage to those willing to assume office. Most of the conservative black elites who joined the system used the opportunity primarily to enrich themselves and a small group of followers; they failed or did not try to build a popular support base. But there was one notable exception.

This exception was the Inkatha movement (in the 1990s the Inkatha Freedom Party [IFP]) led by Mangosuthu Buthelezi: it governed KwaZulu, the Zulu "homeland." Buthelezi was no ordinary homeland leader. He had been a member of the ANC; in the 1970s, Inkatha had enjoyed the ANC's blessing since the protection offered by homeland office appeared to give Inkatha an opportunity to mobilize lawful resistance to apartheid. Although he ended his tacit alliance with the ANC in 1979, Buthelezi continued to resist cooperation with key elements of apartheid strategy. He refused to accept "independence" for the homeland, which would have stripped Zulus

of their South African citizenship, and in the late 1980s he refused to negotiate with the NP until restrictions on his more militant opponents were lifted. Inkatha, therefore, enjoyed sufficient antiapartheid legitimacy to recruit
significant Zulu support. In the 1980s, when the rift with the ANC hardened,
Buthelezi and Inkatha proved adept at mobilizing ethnic sentiment among
more traditional Zulu speakers. Equally important, Inkatha forged an
alliance with sections of the Zulu chieftaincy who, although they were
salaried employees of the KwaZulu administration, wielded significant
patronage.

All of this ensured that Inkatha and its support base stood to lose significantly if the powers apartheid bestowed upon them disappeared with the
system. As the prospect of universal franchise neared, the movement did not
resist the system's demise but was determined to influence the shape of the
new order sufficiently to ensure that the elements of the old system that benefited it were preserved. The movement's interests diverged from those of
the NP; whereas the NP needed to retain a hand on the levers of national
power, the Inkatha movement needed strong powers for the Natal (later
KwaZulu Natal) province, where its support base was concentrated, as well
as protection for chiefly privilege. Unlike most other homeland leaderships,
whose lack of support ensured their quick demise once the settlement die
was cast or who attempted to ensure their political survival by joining the
ANC, Inkatha wielded sufficient power to threaten the stability of a transition that did not secure its interests. It therefore emerged as a third element
in the negotiation equation, complicating attempts to reach a settlement.

A further important consequence of the homeland system for the
postapartheid order was the fact that in territories largely deprived of an
industrial or a commercial base, the most attractive patronage vehicle was
the bureaucracy. This led to the creation of public services with almost half
a million personnel. These services rewarded scores of officials with promotions for which they were unqualified and, in some cases, with benefits
exceeding those paid to their senior equivalents in Pretoria.[27] The route by
which many homeland officials had acquired their status—and the reality
that this was often nearly the sole source of salaried work in homelands—
also ensured that they viewed the bureaucracy as a vehicle for personal
advancement rather than as a public service. Although homeland officials
voted overwhelmingly for the ANC in the 1994 election, they were a significant brake on democratic consolidation after the election, a point to which
I will return.

If apartheid created or reinforced black elites whose enthusiasm for
racial democracy was ambiguous, it also made it more difficult for resistance leaders to view their fight as purely racial. The fact that some blacks
were willing to serve apartheid (and that some whites were willing to oppose
it) had a noticeable effect on the thinking of black antiapartheid activists,
particularly in the 1970s, when this policy's effect became highly visible.

The emergence of Inkatha as a significant black minority bloc created a pluralism within "black" politics that could only be suppressed at great cost.

But this aspect of apartheid's differential treatment of black South Africans was perhaps less significant than the effect attempts to reform the system beginning in the mid-1970s had on the structure of black society. I have already noted that the first sign of a retreat from apartheid was the recognition of black permanence in the cities. But this was qualified: Perhaps because they realized the probable political consequences of urban permanence (particularly since, as noted earlier, Afrikaner nationalism was not ideologically equipped to cope with subordinate inclusion), apartheid's planners sought to limit the numbers of black people who qualified for inclusion.

Access to the cities had been selective for much of the century. When the number of those included was widened in the late 1970s, the new residents were granted trade union and limited property rights, as well as greater opportunities to perform skilled labor and to own businesses. But efforts to draw a line between them and the excluded were continued and refined. In some cases, the government sought to enlist black people who were allowed to stay in the cities in excluding those who were not. A clear case of this was the government strategy regarding "illegal" migration to the cities in the 1970s and early 1980s. After failed attempts to remove shack settlements, the government usually allowed those who had arrived first to stay if they excluded those who came later. As an attempt to limit black urban settlement, the policy was a failure; as an attempt to encourage interest divisions among shack dwellers, it was a significant success.

This could also be said of the reforms' general effect. Through market forces as much as the conscious designs of official planners, the reforms created significant interest differentiation within black society. Although this situation never create a black stratum that had enough of a stake in its relatively privileged status to cause it to defend apartheid, it allowed the emergence of the black class and interest differentiation that apartheid had suppressed. In time, a black business and managerial class emerged, as did a skilled and semiskilled working class.

By far the greatest division which this policy created was that between the urban "insiders" of whatever class—those who enjoyed access to formal housing and urban services—and the "outsiders" who lived in rural areas or on the fringes of the cities in shack settlements or migrant worker barracks.[28] Despite the rhetoric of political elites, which assumed an overarching black solidarity transcending such divisions, hostility between the insiders and outsiders was first manifested as early as 1976.[29] This hostility became particularly intense, often prompting violence, in the mid-1980s.

The impact on attempts to consolidate a democracy in a divided society proved contradictory. The effect within the urban areas was to create the conditions for accommodation of a sort, whose features are discussed later.

The organized insiders invariably provided the most effective support for the fight against apartheid, and some of the upwardly mobile interests "reform apartheid" allowed to emerge have been the most strident postelection advocates of legislation to weaken white economic power.[30] But the insiders became part of a common urban culture that is not free of conflict but whose shared assumptions and attributes may outweigh the division between black insiders and outsiders.

The opposing effect, however, has been the strengthening both of differential access to resources that exclude millions of outsiders from effective participation in the polity and of the common assumptions that may underpin urban accommodation. The obvious divisions to which scholars of divided societies draw attention, although clearly salient, may prove less significant than the divisions between those on the outside, who are almost invariably black, and those on the inside, who are black as well as white. These divisions persist in the postapartheid order.

The Historic Compromise

This background provides some insight into why a settlement seemed so unlikely and why it was negotiated. It has become a truism to point out that a settlement was reached because the antagonists acknowledged that continued conflict could destroy the country. But this does not explain why they preferred not to destroy it; if South Africa is as polarized as some theorists of divided societies would have us believe,[31] the parties would be unlikely to see saving the country as an important goal if the price of doing so was coexistence with the "enemy." The fact that they did view doing so as important suggests that polarization is not necessarily as complete as some theories suggest.

In hindsight, the roots of the transition lie in the NP's forced concession allowing black people to live and work in the cities permanently.[32] The trade union movement which emerged after union rights had been conceded quickly became the most organized black force.[33] When the 1976 conflict was seen—by government planners as well as apartheid's critics—as a reaction to a policy that had deliberately starved black urban areas of services and resources to encourage their residents to "return" to their segregated rural homelands, the recognition that black South Africans were a permanent part of the urban white heartland, and that some form of political representation was therefore necessary, heralded the beginning of apartheid's end.

That end did not come without something akin to a convulsion. In the 1980s, the administration of NP President Botha sought, against rising resistance, to take the 1984 local government reforms further by devising a subordinate form of black representation in central government, and by repressing mobilized resistance to Botha's reforms. Violent urban resistance increased. The ANC, in exile, abandoned the use of guerrilla war merely as a political instrument and, reacting to heightened resistance within the country, declared a "people's war" in which civilian casualties were unavoidable.[34]

Conventional wisdom at the time saw little prospect of a negotiated settlement less than a decade later; the South African tragedy appeared to have entered a new period of stalemate in which the government could rule only by force but the opposition was too weak to overthrow it. The 1986 emergency was not an attempt to resist a black role in national government; it was, rather, an attempt to dictate the terms on which such a role would be granted. The NP's strategy was to crush the "radicals" in the hope of negotiating a limited form of black participation in government with the "moderates," in particular Buthelezi. When it became clear that he would not negotiate on these terms—to do so would have invited being labeled a beneficiary of repression—and that no other "moderates" had appreciable support, the subsequent settlement became inevitable.

This settlement was greatly speeded by a variety of factors, including a change in NP leadership—Botha suffered a stroke and was replaced in 1989 by the pragmatic F. W. de Klerk—and an international climate that offered the NP real incentives for negotiating a compromise. Equally important, the government's often successful assault on internal insurrection in the late 1980s affected ANC thinking, confirming an already lingering fear that the overthrow of the state by force was not feasible. Again, international influence played its part. Change in the Soviet Union, the ANC's principal foreign backer, was crucial. But so too, ironically, was a victory the ANC had been seeking for decades: the commitment of the United States in particular to pressure Pretoria to negotiate a settlement.[35] As the ANC won respectability in American and European democracies, these countries began to cajole the ANC to the bargaining table. The sensitivity to opinion in the Western democracies that had marked the ANC's early years survived into the late 1980s.

De Klerk first tested the waters by releasing imprisoned veteran ANC leaders such as Walter Sisulu, Govan Mbeki, and Raymond Mhlaba (now premier of the Eastern Cape province). He lifted the bans on the ANC and other resistance movements on February 2, 1990, and nine days later released Mandela, by then the acknowledged leader of the ANC. Almost immediately, the ANC signaled a willingness to return from exile to begin talks. Key exiles such as Thabo Mbeki (son of resistance veteran Govan), who had played a key role in covert ANC-government contacts in the 1980s and who was elected deputy president in 1994, Communist Party leader Joe Slovo, and ANC intelligence chief Jacob Zuma returned to their birthplace to begin negotiating the transition.

By the time the adversaries met at the negotiating table, they had recognized the inevitability of living with the other. But this recognition was grudging; they still viewed each other as adversaries who were forced to continue their fight by other means. This sentiment shaped the four-year process that culminated in a settlement, as well as the nature of the polity it produced.

The Unfinished Bargain

The earlier negotiation period—up until September 1992—was marked by clear antagonism between the two major parties. The first attempt at negotiating a settlement, the Convention for a Democratic South Africa, which convened in December 1991 and collapsed in May 1992, failed because the ANC and NP still sought to defeat each other at the table rather than to reach a compromise.[36] The collapse of the talks was followed by a period of intense hostility as the two groups tested their respective strength. The foundation for renewed negotiations was laid only after each party had recognized its inability to defeat the adversary. The result was a pact between Mandela and de Klerk in September 1992, known as the Record of Understanding.

This agreement signaled a mutual commitment to negotiate a settlement. During the discussions that produced the Record of Understanding and the ensuing few months, both parties made significant concessions designed to demonstrate their good faith.[37] But the Record failed to recognize—or chose to ignore—the interests of Inkatha. The IFP feared any pact between the ANC and NP as a sign that the two groups were making common cause against it; further, the Record bound the parties to actions that affected IFP core interests but about which it was not consulted.[38] This set in motion a sequence of events that prompted the IFP to cement a tactical compact—later named the Freedom Alliance—with the white right and two of the homelands that had been granted an "independence" by Pretoria that their elites hoped to preserve.

From the signing of the Record until a week before the 1994 election, the negotiations were dominated by tensions between the Freedom Alliance and the two major negotiating parties, which prompted escalating violence. Particularly in the later stages of the negotiations and the ensuing run-up to the election, this situation created the impression that the ANC and the NP had combined to steer an agreed settlement to finality against opposition from the right and, to a lesser degree, the left. The right's constant complaint that it was being confronted by an ANC-NP alliance seemed to many commentators and citizens an accurate description of a profound political realignment.

This perception was strengthened by developments in the negotiation process in 1993. In midyear the IFP and its allies, alleging that the ANC and the NP were determined to conclude the negotiations without considering their demands for an extremely vigorous form of federalism, withdrew from the talks. By then, the ANC and the NP had agreed that an election on April

27, 1994, was a necessity. With more than a dozen smaller parties, they pressed on without the Freedom Alliance toward a settlement in November 1993.

The agreement produced an interim constitution—to be replaced by a "final" one within two years of the election—that had much more strongly liberal democratic features than either party's history had seemed likely to produce. But it also contained elements that had clearly been agreed upon in closed meetings between the two major parties. The constitution provides for a bicameral legislature, to which the executive—including the president—is responsible and which is elected by closed-list proportional representation. The executive is a government of national unity, in which parties nominate one cabinet minister for every 5 percent of the vote they win. The constitution introduces a bill of rights justiciable by a constitutional court, entrenches the independence of the judiciary, and includes thirty-four principles which will govern the writing of the final constitution by the first elected Parliament. It establishes elected provincial governments, with powers stipulated in the constitution, thereby ensuring a limited form of federalism.

These general provisions are, however, mixed with many others—such as the stipulation that any party winning 20 percent of the vote can nominate an executive deputy president (a clause designed to ensure de Klerk a deputy presidency) and job guarantees for public servants demanded by the NP—that suggested a big-party trade-off. Further, the clauses stipulating the circumstances under which the center may override provinces' powers are so vague they seemed to offer little guarantee of the federal system the IFP and its allies wanted. These and other features strengthened perceptions that the compromise reflected the emerging ANC-NP consensus.

The election campaign that followed did not explode that idea. To be sure, the NP and ANC campaigned vigorously against each other—so much so that in the Orange Free State the NP threatened to challenge the election's fairness, complaining that it was barred from campaigning in the province's black townships.[39] This phenomenon, the enforcement by parties of "no-go" areas in which rivals could not function, was a pervasive feature of the campaign,[40] but it was most prevalent in what many saw as the campaign's central feature—the IFP's attempt to mobilize a boycott.

In early March, the participating parties tried to woo the IFP and its allies by enacting changes to the constitution that incorporated some IFP demands.[41] The concessions persuaded a section of the white right to register. Former military chief Constand Viljoen, who had led the right-wing alliance, formed a Freedom Front, which contested the poll. But the IFP stayed out. Its attempt to mobilize a boycott in its KwaZulu home base and in the Pretoria-Witwatersrand-Vereeniging (PWV) area, where a group of IFP-supporting Zulu migrant workers was based—and the reaction to that attempt—triggered violent conflict. On March 29, 1994, seventy-six people were killed in downtown Johannesburg when an IFP protest march was met by sniper fire. The center of the country's largest city had never witnessed such an event. The violence heightened fears of a bloodbath as the election drew nearer—fears that were largely vindicated—and on polling days on which they were not.

About two weeks after the Johannesburg incident, international mediators, led by former U.S. Secretary of State Henry Kissinger, arrived at the invitation of the major parties to attempt a brokered settlement. The attempt was a failure, and the mediators returned home before their work began. Days later, the IFP agreed to join the campaign after signing an agreement with the NP and the ANC.[42] This ensured that, in one respect, the South African transition was unique: It was the only transition in which a major party entered a founding election a week before the poll. The IFP's reasons for joining so late were never fully explained. The most persuasive interpretation is that the Zulu king, Goodwill Zwelithini, who commands significant symbolic support among the more traditional Zulu speakers and who had implicitly backed the IFP boycott through early 1994, told Buthelezi that he would urge his subjects to vote.[43]

On the surface, the party was irrevocably handicapped, since it had only days to campaign. In reality, its boycott campaign had been mobilizing supporters for months: It had turned all of the KwaZulu part of the province[44] into a no-go area, just as the ANC had done with the areas it controlled. Nor were these the only parties to do so. Despite the fervor with which election rallies were held, competitive campaigning was limited by the no-go area phenomenon. Some parties tried to campaign in their rivals' strongholds, were driven out, and did not try again. In a sense, this reflected the spirit of the transition: Faced with unpleasant realities, parties simply resigned themselves to those realities. Indeed, one of the more competitive aspects of the campaign was the attempt by a host of voter education organizations, ranging from private companies to party-affiliated organizations thinly disguised as nongovernmental organizations (NGOs), to grab their share of the market. None of these groups made significant inroads; a survey conducted among black voters in the campaign's last weeks found that only 9 percent had been reached by direct voter education.[45]

Polling days, which began on April 26 with a day set aside for special voters, were marked by two phenomena. The first was the chaotic nature of the Independent Electoral Commission's[46] (IEC's) administration, which led to long delays for voters as necessary supplies failed to arrive—in some former black homelands, supplies did not arrive until April 28—and forced the parties to agree to an extra polling day in these areas on April 29. The second phenomenon was the remarkable patience and bonhomie of the electorate.

The parties, however, were less given to good cheer. The IEC's incompetence had also resulted in a host of electoral irregularities, which included significant breakdowns in ballot security. As the chaos extended into the vote-counting period,[47] the parties filed hundreds of complaints against each other, alleging that the result had been compromised. The prospect that the result would be overturned was very real, but this did not occur because the parties settled the election in the way they settled everything else—by negotiating a compromise. In a series of closed meetings, each agreed to drop its claims against the others; on May 6, the chair of the IEC, Johan Kriegler, announced the results and declared them "substantially free and fair." He was able to do so because the parties had extended their penchant for deal making to the election results themselves:[48] The negotiated transition had ended in a negotiated election.

The reason, perhaps, was twofold. First, with one exception, the results conformed with preelection opinion poll results. Second, the two major minority parties, the NP and the IFP, either achieved their minimum goals or, in the IFP's case (the one exception, since it did better than the polls had predicted), exceeded them. The ANC, as expected, won comfortably, winning nearly 63 percent of the vote and 252 seats. But the NP, which won just over 20 percent of the vote (82 seats), and the IFP (10.5 percent, 43 seats) prevented it gaining a two-thirds majority, which would have allowed it to control the writing of the final constitution. The NP gained the 20 percent required to ensure de Klerk a deputy presidency and control of the Western Cape province, where it won 53 percent of the vote. The IFP won the KwaZulu Natal province, which it had expected to lose, by a whisker—50.3 percent. (See Tables 11.3 and 11.4.) The result could have been written by consociational theorists.

Table 11.3 National Results, 1994 South African Elections

Party	Number of Seats	Number of Votes	Percentage Vote
African National Congress (ANC)	252	12,237,655	62.7
National Party (NP)	82	3,983,690	20.4
Inkatha Freedom Party (IFP)	43	2,058,294	10.5
Freedom Front (FF)	9	424,555	2.2
Democratic Party (DP)	7	338,426	1.7
Pan Africanist Congress (PAC)	5	243,478	1.2
African Christian Democratic Party (ACDP)	2	88,104	0.5
African Muslim Party	0	34,466	0.2
African Moderates Congress Party	0	27,690	0.1
Other (ten parties failed to win 20,000 votes)	0	97,140	0.5
Total	400	19,533,498	100.0

Source: Electoral Administration Division, Independent Electoral Commission, *Republic of South Africa 1994 General Election: National and Provincial Results by Province District,* May 26, 1994.

Note: Voter turnout was 86.87 percent.

Table 11.4   Provincial Election Results, 1994 South African Elections

	ANC		NP		IFP		
	% of Votes	Seats	% of Votes	Seats	% of Votes	Seats	Total Seats
PWV	57.6	50	23.9	21	3.7	3	86[a]
Western Cape	33.0	14	53.2	23	0.3	0	42[b]
KwaZulu/Natal	32.2	26	11.2	9	50.3	41	81[c]
Northern Transvaal	91.6	38	3.3	1	0.1	0	40[d]
Eastern Transvaal	80.7	25	9.0	3	1.5	0	30[e]
North West	83.3	26	8.8	3	0.4	0	30[d]
Orange Free State	76.6	24	12.6	4	0.5	0	30[e]
Northern Cape	49.7	15	40.5	12	0.4	0	30[f]
Eastern Cape	84.4	48	9.8	6	0.2	0	56[g]

Source: Electoral Administration Division, Independent Electoral Commission, *Republic of South Africa 1994 General Election: National and Provincial Results by Province District,* May 26, 1994.

a. Five seats each were won by the FF and DP; 1 seat each by the PAC and ACDP.
b. Three seats were won by the DP, 1 seat each by the FF and ACDP.
c. Two seats were won by the DP, 1 each by the FF, ACDP, and Minority Front.
d. One seat was won by the FF.
e. Two seats were won by the FF.
f. Two seats were won by the FF, 1 seat by the DP.
g. One seat was won by the PAC, 1 seat by the DP.

The manner in which the election ended—the parties' agreement not to contest the result, and a gracious concession speech by de Klerk—strengthened the impression that the cartel that had appeared to take shape during the negotiations had cemented. Some even believed the IFP might be available to join it.

The Illusory Cartel

This impression was at most half true. As with Codesa, the 1993 negotiation process that followed the Record of Understanding was dominated by the two major parties; the presence of a host of smaller parties was a thin veneer.[49] But the division between the negotiators and the Freedom Alliance obscured the differences between the NP and the ANC. Determined to drive the negotiations to a conclusion that would allow an election on April 27, the date that had been promised to both an ANC constituency impatient for change and the international community,[50] the major parties repeatedly "resolved" these differences by agreeing on creative short-term compromises that, in effect, left the contested issues unresolved.

The most significant point of disagreement was the nature of the government of national unity. Throughout the negotiations the ANC had insisted that the party that won the election should control the government—it was willing to include its stronger opponents in the executive and to consult them on decisions but not to allow them a veto. The NP held out for a share of power—a veto on at least the important decisions. The interim constitution ostensibly settled this issue in the ANC's favor; it declares that cabinet decisions should be made by majority vote. But the NP continued to assure its constituency that the ANC would be bound to govern with NP consent.

This was not the only issue that was unresolved. The arrangement for executive decisions was one of the clearer agreements on the issues that divided the two parties. On many others—the powers of provincial government, procedures for allocating cabinet posts, whether minority party ministers were bound by majority cabinet decisions—the preelection compromises ensured vague constitutional stipulations which were open to differing interpretations.

The fact that some important business remained unfinished was confirmed after the national unity government—composed of the ANC, the NP, and the IFP—had been installed. In its early months there were disputes over the allocation of cabinet portfolios and the chairs of parliamentary committees; repeated and often successful attempts by the ANC parliamentary caucus to veto cabinet decisions, which increased executive accountability to the legislature at the expense of weakening consensus within the government; and strident public attacks on the ANC by the NP and the IFP, which indicated that the two smaller governing parties had determined to act as much like a parliamentary opposition as like partners in a coalition government.

None of these events should have surprised those who had studied the negotiation period closely; they simply confirmed what had been evident then. The two major parties had merely agreed on the terms of transition; they had not become allies or partners, let alone a cartel.

Throughout the negotiation period, ANC and NP negotiators had proved adept at bargaining compromises that saved both the transition and the country from crises that threatened irreversible breakdown. They were far less adept at cooperating to prevent these crises. If a big-party cartel had indeed solidified during the negotiations, we would expect its members to work together on at least two key issues—public order and economic recovery. These were not only the two central issues facing the society but they constituted the most palpable threat to the transition to which both parties were committed.

There was little or no cooperation on either issue. In the area of public order, continuing violence remained largely a subject of political contest. Rather than seeking to bind their constituencies to the maintenance of order, each party largely restricted itself to blaming the other for bloodshed. In the area of economic recovery, there was a degree of multiparty cooperation in soliciting foreign investment. On issues of direct relevance to economic revival, however, from the refusal of black city dwellers to pay for urban services through socioeconomic policy issues such as housing, to industrial conflict, the dominant pattern was mutual finger pointing rather than cooperative remedial action. This may have represented more a continued distance between the two parties' constituencies than antagonism between their leaders; but neither was eager to risk alienating its constituency by cooperating with the other; negotiation was often portrayed as a continuation of war by other means rather than a process of reconciliation.

The South African pact was a remarkable exercise in conflict resolution, driven by a mutual acknowledgment that the society's only option was to negotiate its way out of stalemate—a realization that went beyond the two major parties. This explains the late decision by a large section of the white right and then the IFP to contest the poll. This acknowledgment survived severe tests, not the least of which was the election itself. But it did not create an elite cartel, nor did it ensure cooperation between the major protagonists. This situation has both theoretical and practical consequences for the consolidation of democracy.

The Unconsociational Pact

The fact that the settlement was a pact between the two major parties vindicated analyses that had insisted that only pacted democratization offered a route to a settlement that would leave enough of the economy and social fabric intact to allow even a tentative democratic experiment. This condition flowed from the balance of power between majority and minority. Since the mid-1970s, the majority had gradually acquired sufficient capacity for mobilization to frustrate the NP government's attempts to reform the society on its own terms. But the minority remained firmly in control of the instruments of coercion—hence the 1986 state of emergency, which bottled up resistance mobilization until de Klerk's opening in 1990. Although the resistance movements could frustrate the government's initiatives, they could not seize power. The result was a stalemate that could only be broken by an accommodation between the antagonists.

When the government of national unity was installed in May 1994, this accommodation was only partial. Since the dangers to public order and economic revival that had hastened the negotiations toward a settlement did not evaporate when the new order assumed office—and since the balance of power that had created the rationale for a compromise settlement remained following the election—it seemed reasonable to assume that the society's survival prospects depended on further attempts to consolidate cooperation between the ANC and the NP.

If, however, that assumption implied that the two parties would have to accept joint responsibility for governing the society, it was open to serious question. In theoretical terms, it implied that the society could be rescued from the consequences of its divisions only by consociational arrangements. But the claim of consociationalism's prime academic champion, Arend Lijphart, that the institutions created by the new constitution *are* consociational[51] is erroneous; nor are attempts to address the challenges that face the new democracy likely to move the political order in a consociational direction. More important, perhaps, this analysis argues that the future of the new South African order does not depend on its ability to create consociational arrangements.

The Consociational Mirage

Since the new order could only be created by negotiation between the two major parties, it seems logical to conclude that it can only be consolidated in the same way. The balance of power between majority and minority seems to demand this, and comparative evidence seems to confirm it. Terry Lynn Karl's study of the relationship between transitions and the polities they produce found that pacted transition is likely to produce "consociationalist or corporatist democracy" in which "party competition is regulated to varying degrees determined in part by the nature of foundational bargains."[52]

Karl's thesis seems confirmed by the fact that the new democracy does have one apparently consociational feature: the national unity government. But Lijphart's claim that the constitution meets his specifications is difficult to understand since this is the only one of his prescriptions (except for proportional representation, which is hardly an exclusive property of consociational systems) that was included in the interim constitution. Even this one fails to meet his criteria.

The multiparty cabinet is not a consociational arrangement if that term is understood to include, as Lijphart insists, consensual decisionmaking and minority vetoes, at least on key issues.[53] As we have seen, this stipulation was abandoned in the last hours of the negotiations.[54] Nor is power sharing strong enough to allow the minority parties a joint say in the distribution of cabinet portfolios or parliamentary committee chairs—minority parties that failed to secure enough support to gain a cabinet seat have been allocated more significant committee chairs than the NP. Perhaps more significant, no judge appointed to the constitutional court is sympathetic to the NP's perspective. The NP's regular resort to statements criticizing government policy initiatives suggests either that it was not party to formulating those initiatives or that it did have input but its view on vital issues was ignored.

The constitution that created the joint government formula is only an interim document. It is not certain that the proportional distribution of cabinet seats will be retained; indeed, the ANC will probably face severe constituency resistance if it seems willing to retain this distribution. Proportional representation also seems destined to be modified significantly in the final document.[55] Since the society's divisions remain, will the likely abandonment of even those constitutional features that resemble consociational arrangements not invite the resumption of the stalemate that prompted the settlement? The answer is that it will not. In the early months of the new order, the evidence began to suggest overwhelmingly that executive power sharing had been abandoned because there was no great need for it.

Gatekeeper Without a Gate

Executive power sharing as an antidote to deep social divisions has little value unless the parties bring the society's major interests to the arrangement. Consociationalism seeks to abridge the politics of competition by institutionalizing negotiation, and, in negotiation theory, the negotiators must be strong enough to bind to any bargains they reach the interests affected by these compromises. In a context in which the largest party in the government has established its right to rule by winning almost two-thirds of the popular vote, the rationale for minority party participation must surely rest on those parties' ability to bind to the bargain strong minority interests without whose compliance the majority will be unable to govern.

The fact that South Africa has strong minority interests whose compliance is essential to stable democratic government is unquestioned. Whether the NP is the conduit to those interests is highly questionable. There are three organized minority interests—formal business, the security establishment, and the top echelons of the bureaucracy—with which the majority party must reach an accommodation if it is to govern effectively. None of the three appears to see the NP as an essential—or even a necessary—interlocutor.

Established business remains largely in the hands of whites. But business—even its organized variety—is not politically monolithic; nor does it see the NP as a guardian of its interests. The four-year negotiation period was marked by informal negotiation between the ANC and business; in the immediate preelection period, many business leaders hastened to court the presumed new governing elite. In a parallel process to the political negotiations, organized business participated in an array of socioeconomic negotiation forums that sought to form agreement on policy either with the ANC directly or with key interests in its camp, such as the Congress of South African Trade Unions or the South African National Civic Organisation (SANCO).[56] In the postelection period, business leadership has sought to deal directly with the ANC; the NP has been at most a bit player. This tendency has been so pronounced that some left-wing analysts have lamented the "alliance" between the majority party and white business. They greatly overstate the reality—relations between the ANC and business are not completely harmonious and may be subject to severe stress. But whatever tensions lie ahead, neither side is likely to resort to the NP as an intermediary.

The apartheid order's security establishment—the military and police leadership—is the second crucial minority constituency. During the negotiation period, both security arms sought to cement their future by placing a distance between themselves and the NP, insisting that they would serve any elected government. Both the military and police portfolios in the new government are occupied by ANC ministers (the defense minister and the deputy minister are former ANC guerrilla commanders). In the military portfolio in particular, relations between elected politicians and those in uniform seem harmonious—too much so to please some members of the ANC. The NP's exclusion from all security portfolios, although deeply disturbing to the party, does not appear to have upset the generals. Again, the relationship may be far less harmonious than it appears, particularly in view of tensions between the military leadership and former ANC guerrillas, which triggered a mutiny by a sizable number of the latter in October 1994. But the NP has played little part in attempting to resolve the tensions and is unlikely to play a bigger role in the future.

The third crucial constituency is the bureaucracy or, at least, the section of it that is white. Here, the tensions between the old and the new have been palpable as ANC ministers seek ways of changing the racial and political complexion of the upper and middle levels in the face of severe nervousness and more than a little obstruction by the officials. Conflict has often been public and has impaired effective government. Whereas the NP clearly sees itself as the guarantor of civil servant interests—it fought uncompromisingly for the constitutional clause that protects their jobs—that perception is not shared by the officials themselves, who in the last two years of the old order increasingly resented the NP's perceived refusal to consult them on decisions that affected their interests or to grant them a role in negotiating their future. Despite the conflict between the new government and the old bureaucracy, the Public Servants' Association, which represents most of the white officials, insisted three months into the new order that only two government ministries were operating effectively—both headed by ANC ministers.[57] Again, the NP does not seem to hold the key to accommodation.

None of this necessarily means that the NP's role in government is devoid of purpose. There are two rationales for its continued presence. The first is the probability that whatever the positions of the strong, organized constituencies, the morale of the white citizenry would be damaged if it were no longer a part of the government. The damage might not be nearly as severe as some suppose—one of the features of white politics since the mid-1970s has been the tendency of voters to resist changes until they are made and then to adapt to them quickly when the consequences appear less baleful than whites had feared. It seems likely that adaptation to majority government would follow a similar course. The second rationale, articulated explicitly by Mandela himself, is blame sharing. The president told an interviewer in August 1994 that it was essential to include minority parties in government because the new administration faced a severe challenge to undo the social and economic legacy of apartheid in adverse circumstances; stability would be far better served, he argued, if all major parties took joint responsibility for failures.[58]

These reasons may indeed suggest that a continued NP presence in the executive would enhance both stability and the consolidation of democracy. But they offer no rationale for consociational power sharing. They also suggest that the NP role will be temporary. Five years may be ample to prepare whites for majority government, whereas blame sharing may last only as long as the majority party is insecure enough to believe there is blame to share. If there is great cause for blame, it is not clear why minority parties would want to share it; their criticism of government policy throughout much of 1994 suggests they are already unwilling to do so.

The third party in government, the IFP, is an even less likely consociational partner than the NP. The IFP was not party to the agreements that produced the unity government formula. Although in the early stages of negotiation it had advocated a multiparty government, the election results confirmed that it is a regional party whose support is concentrated overwhelmingly in KwaZulu Natal. Its interests seem to lie more in continuing its campaign for provincial autonomy than in a minority share of national office. This, combined with a stated perception by IFP strategists that the IFP can substantially enhance its electoral support when, as they confidently expect, the ANC-led government fails to meet voter expectations,[59] may explain why IFP leaders have criticized the unity government as an artificial, forced coalition and have repeatedly predicted its demise. If the joint government does endure, the IFP may withdraw from it long before the next election to begin campaigning more vigorously against the ANC.

Consociationalism is, therefore, not a South African option since there is little point in pinning hopes for stability on an "elite cartel"[60] in the government if the cartel does not represent many key elites. It is worth mentioning that the ANC's capacity to directly represent organized interests in its own camp is also not self-evident. Whereas the glue of liberation symbolism binds the ANC camp together effectively enough to ensure that none of its organized interests formally distance themselves from it, the months following the election were marked by tensions not only between ANC ministers and the ANC's parliamentary caucus and extra-parliamentary organization but also between the ANC and key ANC-aligned interests such as COSATU and organized black business. The link between political parties and the organized interests whose members vote for them is not sufficiently direct to suggest that consociational arrangements would bind the society and underpin democracy. Since the society remains divided, however, and the balance of power ensures a continued need for pacted compromises, how will stability and democracy be ensured in the absence of conditions favorable to consociationalism?

The Corporatist Connection—The Deal-Making Society

If the majority party is forced to reach accommodations with strong minority interests and cannot use the minority parties in government as intermediaries, the obvious implication is that it must deal with these interests directly. Corporatism, then, is the most feasible route to consolidating the new order. In the South African context, this may operate on two levels. The first is formal corporatism—structured negotiation between government and private interests.[61] The second is an informal variety in which accommodations are reached between the majority party and organized minority interests within the state. The feasibility of bargaining occurring between the ANC and the organizational expressions of minority society is strengthened by the fact that bargaining between the ANC and private interests—and between those interests themselves across racial and political divisions—has become a significant element of social and political life. Its foundations were laid well before the founding election.

Bargaining's visible vehicle was the forums that emerged during the last two years of the negotiation period.[62] By far the most important of these vehicles are two tripartite institutions made up of organized business, labor, and government—the National Economic Forum and the National Manpower Commission. Following the election these institutions were merged into a council that was granted legal recognition.

There is no guarantee that this formal corporatist arrangement will secure the compromises needed for economic recovery. But its prospects are enhanced by the fact that its origins predate political negotiation by a decade. Since the early 1980s, trade unions and employers have been developing stable negotiation relationships (albeit often conflictual ones) that have delivered increasingly complex compromises, even, as during the 1980s, in periods of increased polarization. Despite the high unemployment rates typical of developing countries, South Africa has a developed formal economy, and negotiated accommodations between business and labor are widely accepted as a precondition for economic recovery.

Accommodations between the majority party and old-order interests within the state also would not start from scratch. An important feature of the political negotiation period was a parallel process between the military and the police on the one side and the ANC on the other.[63] No similar negotiation occurred with organizations representing old-order public servants, but formal negotiation channels with public servants' unions now exist and are an obvious potential vehicle.

These are not the only routes for negotiating South African divisions. The deal-making culture that delivered the political settlement is not restricted to political elites nor to formal negotiating forums. It is pervasive in the major metropolitan areas. In the private realm, it has been more effective in delivering limited forms of cooperation than has the political process.

A propensity toward deal making across divisions does not imply that the divisions are illusory. Indeed, the ideological positions and rhetoric of the organized interests and activist groups within the ANC camp that participate in deal making are more militant than those of the movement's national political leadership. But in practice, the purpose of the rhetoric is to negotiate deals on more favorable terms, not to revolutionize society. The deal-making game is based on the unstated premise that the society is indeed divided into racial camps but that this does not preclude the willingness of those in the camps to negotiate instrumental compromises. On occasions they have done even more, agreeing on limited forms of cooperation. Black-led unions debate socialist strategy as they work with investment bankers to place worker provident fund contributions in socially responsible companies; civic associations breathe rhetorical fire as they enter into development partnerships with some financial institutions; and these are just two examples. At times, as occurred in debates on housing policy, militant populists in the ANC may find themselves in alliance with private construction companies against ANC pragmatists and financial institutions.

South African urban political culture contains at least elements of a phenomenon that, if the starker typologies of divided societies are accepted, should not exist—interest alliances that cut across the central racial divide. Further evidence of this was an ANC decision to allow ministers to employ personal aides at inflated salaries, which was denounced by the Public Servants Association (PSA). The PSA was immediately supported by COSATU, which months earlier had threatened to strike because the jobs of PSA members were guaranteed by the constitution. In Johannesburg, ANC-aligned civic associations joined with white-run city governments to denounce an ANC local government restructuring plan. We should not make too much of these examples. The crosscutting alliances are remarkable precisely because they are rarities. But they do caution against simplistic caricatures of South African divisions.

If private interests are able to deal with each other—with or without a state intermediary—across the divisions, the intensity of conflict within the state is reduced. It is further mitigated by a factor generally ignored by those who have repeatedly predicted a postelection white backlash: The vast majority of whites need the state far less, if it all, than they did during the heyday of white rule. The Afrikaner majority within a minority used the state to great effect to force its way into the market economy. But the strategy succeeded so well that except for a small white "underclass," whites have no further need for it. White desiderata from government may be little different from those of the affluent members of societies in which ascriptive identities play no part in politics—limited or no intervention in private economic activity rather than a share of the spoils of state power. This reinforces the prognosis that a minority share of state power is not essential to stability.

The Parameters of Division

The fact that deal making across the racial divide outside the state is possible suggests the need for a more nuanced approach to the dividedness of South African society. South Africa *is* divided, as shown by the election results, which largely confirmed Donald Horowitz's prognosis that elections in divided societies are "tantamount to a census."[64] One estimate suggested that around 2 percent of whites voted for the ANC and about 6 percent of black Africans voted for the NP.[65] I have cited other evidence that shows that South Africans do define themselves politically by ascriptive criteria.

But these divisions do not preclude a common commitment to the South African state—among elites and, if survey evidence can be believed, also among the citizenry. At the very least, this commitment may express a resignation to the reality that there is no alternative to a common state, a perception acknowledged by Buthelezi's remark, at a time when he was felt to harbor secessionist ambitions, that "history has condemned us all to be South Africans." The roots of this commitment lie in dynamics, many of whose elements require further study and analysis. But some pointers can be offered.

One element is economic interdependence. Apartheid's attempt to divide the country into racial enclaves failed. No single magisterial district in the country has a white majority and, therefore, a territorial basis for separation. Nor is KwaZulu Natal an IFP-dominated enclave; it won only half of the votes in the province, which is clearly not a basis for secession.

Since the early 1970s, economic growth has been impossible unless skilled black labor played a growing role in industry. But apartheid's reinforcement of disproportionate white access to skills and resources ensured that the economy and society will require white skills for some time. The result is a single economy in which for decades, blacks will need whites, just as whites will need blacks. In the cities, this is reinforced by both a common consumer culture[66] and increasing black penetration of upper-income brackets—albeit as income disparities within the society are growing.[67]

Another element has already been noted—the workings of both classical and reform apartheid, which, although they created divisions within black society, also narrowed the divisions between black and white city dwellers. The divisions within white society discussed earlier are, therefore, also pertinent. Although white liberalism and radicalism were always a minority position—and the number of whites who identified unambiguously with black political aspirations probably never exceeded 3 percent of the white population—the cleavages in white society have always been significant enough to ensure that it did not present itself to black South Africa as an undifferentiated, hostile whole. Even 3 percent of the white population constitutes a sufficient complement of "race defectors" to challenge the notion that racial divisions are immutable. I have already noted one other factor that significantly weakens white society's enthusiasm for protracted conflict—the success of a racial capture of the state, which worked to lessen the capturer's dependence on that state.

One further element is seemingly obvious, but it is rarely mentioned in current debates: demographics. Not only does black South Africa outnumber its white counterpart by around six to one, but the trend is growing; whites make up only 8 percent of the current population below age eighteen (see Table 11.1).

Given the racial voting patterns evident in the election, this element suggests that elections in this divided society are likely to produce permanent minorities and majorities.[68] But this does not mean that whites will stake everything on a share of the state. It is no accident that one of Lijphart's desiderata for consociationalism—curiously ignored by both Lijphart himself and his South African disciples—is relative numerical equivalence between the contending blocs.[69] A "big-bloc" cartel in which one partner purports to speak for nine of every ten citizens and the other for one in ten is likely to be so skewed that it cannot endure; elites on both sides of the divide may be aware of this. This situation may encourage moderation among majority leaders, if they realize that any attempt to forestall "undiluted" majority rule is doomed to be temporary, and also among the minority, since it highlights the futility of permanent control. The demand for guaranteed participation in government becomes, at best, a holding operation.

Whites are numerous enough to ensure that they will not disappear. Frederik Slabbert has noted that even if "white flight" reaches Algerian proportions, the most extreme case on the continent, there would still be at least five million whites in the country a decade into the next century.[70] The demographic balance, therefore, seems to indicate that whites are too small a group to harbor realistic aspirations to state power but that they are too numerous to be ignored or subjugated.

Whites appear aware that control of the state is passing into other hands, which creates abundant opportunities for the pursuit of interests outside the state. Is the prospect of pursuing private interest sufficient to assuage a once-ruling minority that faces a permanent life in opposition? If South African white politics is a guide, it may be. For at least the first two decades after 1948, "census-type" elections ensured a permanent Afrikaner Nationalist (NP) majority. This situation relegated English-speaking whites to cast protest votes for an opposition, the United Party, that having once ruled, disintegrated as its prospects of ever doing so again waned. This response did not enrich white democracy, but it posed no threat to stability, despite the fact that English speakers wielded immense economic power. They did not rebel or challenge their political relegation but instead opted out of politics; the material rewards of the market proved to be more than adequate compensation. In time, some reentered politics, this time on the side of the white majority.

One potential flaw in the analogy is that both minority groups had a common interest in resisting majority rule. But although it is premature to suggest that the minority will defect to the new governing majority, the early evidence suggests that the minority has already resigned itself to being ruled by the majority and in some cases is seeking to extract maximum benefit from ANC rule. White businesspeople besiege ANC ministers, but their concern is to sell "change-oriented" services rather than to safeguard their identity.

For the moment, white elites can afford to contemplate majority rule with equanimity because they possess the means to restrain it through control of the military and the economy, a situation that will endure for longer than many in the ANC camp believe. But when and if this situation changes, the key white decision will be whether to stay or to leave—not whether to acquiesce or to rebel. Why else would only 11 percent of whites *who support right-wing parties* (around 4 percent of all whites) express unqualified confidence in a white-ruled separatist state?[71]

This argument does not deny a need for minority safeguards. Whites may continue to feel that the balance of power needs to be translated into concrete legal provisions. But until 1994 the NP demand was for guaranteed minority *participation* in government, not merely for protection. The realities may force it—or another champion of minority interests—to concentrate on the latter and to abandon the former.

One element may be added: the sensitivity of the contending elites to international opinion. The roots of this phenomenon in resistance political culture have been described earlier in this chapter; its white counterpart may stem from cultural roots in Europe and from an economy dependent on and sensitive to world markets. The bombast of white rhetoric during the apartheid period that insisted that the country could ignore international isolation was always tinged with wishfulness. In 1989, when changes in international alignments gave the Botha administration an opportunity to regain a toehold in the world, it hastened to take that opportunity. The willingness of whites, in a crucial 1992 referendum, to endorse de Klerk's negotiated settlement strategy owed much to a perception that rejection would mean renewed isolation.[72]

It must be stressed that most of these observations apply only to the world of the insiders. Outside of that world the divisions may remain far more intractable. At present, this is no threat to stability, since the insider-outsider divide ensures that resources—including the capacity to organize—are so heavily concentrated in the larger cities that the insiders dictate the patterns of political life. This situation echoes the weakness of many new Latin American democracies[73] and obstructs a deepening of democracy. If the consequence of this division is that universal franchise allows organized urban interests to secure state policies that further strengthen the divide—

and, ironically, some of the policies advocated by the more radical urban populists promise to do just that[74]—the need for survival may impel outsiders to challenge the urban stranglehold in ways that will render the deal-making culture very fragile indeed. But the remedies for a division between city and countryside—between those, black and white, who can organize and reach accommodations and those who cannot—do not lie in the remedies proposed by theorists of divided societies.

For the present, the dominance of the insider political culture softens the edges of divisions and ensures that the society is more complex than some divided society theories suggest. It also ensures that the remedies for these divisions are likely to be more complex, too.

Democracy Deferred?

To insist that power sharing within the state is no key to stability is not to argue that stability will be achieved or democracy consolidated. It could be argued, contrary to the consociationalists, that South Africa has had a lucky escape. Larry Diamond has pointed out that elite pacts "inevitably become outdated with time, requiring revision or complete abandonment."[75] During the negotiation phase, it did appear that a power-sharing pact was the only route to reasonably stable change. But transitions, as many of their scholars remind us, are defined by their uncertainty, and subsequent events have undermined that assumption. If South Africa is indeed infertile ground for power sharing, the consequence may be not ruin but, rather, avoidance of a cartel that might have imperiled democracy and stability—particularly since neither of the two major parties is necessarily committed to democracy as a principle rather than as an expedient.[76]

Whereas the society may have averted the dangers of "a venal, self-interested 'partidocracia,'"[77] the realities described here suggest great obstacles to a consolidated democracy. If South Africa is indeed becoming a society in which the crucial pacts are made outside of the formal representative system, democracy may rest on shaky foundations. Power sharing in the formal political system may be unnecessary largely because the representative system is less important than political analysis assumes it to be. As Frances Hagopian[78] has shown, a political order bounded by pact making outside the formal representative system sharply narrows prospects for political choice and contestation. South Africa's new order may have little choice but to engage in this sort of pacting.

Such pact making may also severely threaten the new order's legitimacy and survival prospects. The relationship that emerges between the majority party and the security establishment will be crucial. On the one hand, aggressive political intervention in military and police affairs could pose severe threats to stability; on the other, a pact—explicit or implicit—on the security establishment's terms would have baleful consequences for democratization and, ultimately, for stability.

In itself, corporatism is not necessarily inimical to democracy. Pacts between governments and extra-parliamentary interests can be subjected to public scrutiny and, thus, to political contest. Formal corporatism can underpin democracy,[79] and in South Africa democracy might be unattainable without it.[80] But if Adam Przeworski[81] is right to insist that a defining feature of democracy is its contingency—the uncertainty of outcomes—and if Diamond, Linz, and Lipset's insistence[82] that it must be characterized by extensive competition between political parties is accepted, South Africa faces a far more formidable obstacle to democratization than pact making: the reality that, for all its elites' capacity to strike bargains, it remains a divided society.

South African elites are, arguably, *becoming* "consensually unified"[83] in the sense that they have regular access to each other and seek to bargain with or outmaneuver, rather than eliminate, each other. But they and the society still lack the "sense of community" Dankwart Rustow believed essential for democracy to be born out of protracted conflict.[84]

One often-stated reason for the necessity of a sense of community is that it ensures that some issues are beyond contest, such as the security and prosperity of the common state. It is easier for politics to become a debate over means rather than ends. In South Africa, this sense of community is still not firmly established since divisions are severe enough to ensure that security remains contested. The sense of community may stretch to include a common commitment not to destroy the society, but it may not go far enough to ensure sufficient cooperation to avert the crises that at times seem to make that destruction a possibility.

There is a second consequence of a lack of community—it ensures a politics in which voter choices are determined by membership in an ascriptive group, resulting in electoral outcomes predetermined by demography. Voting of this nature was deeply entrenched in the white electoral system for many years. The 1994 election results, survey evidence,[85] and observed political behavior confirm that most South Africans continue to define their political identity racially.

The development of a competitive party system would, therefore, depend upon a split in the ANC or upon a sharp improvement in the fortunes of one of its black-led rivals. Given the interest differences within the ANC, this possibility is regularly posited, but for now it seems unlikely. As long as whites are seen to control significant power and resources and racial socioeconomic inequality remains significant, there will be ample perceived reason to continue to rally around a unifying movement. In fact, many Afrikaans-speaking whites remained within the NP for years after they had lost confidence in its ideology and programs. As Larry Diamond[86] reminds us, however, there are theoretical, empirical, and normative reasons to insist that political culture is not static. Survey evidence and political behavior have shown that South African political culture is neither as polarized nor as inflexible as scholars of divided societies seem to imply. But its "plasticity" is unlikely to be sufficient to cause much uncertainty about electoral outcomes for some time. A dominant party system—either of the Indian variety (in which rule by a particular party is the norm but occasional voter rebellions install a weak alternative, primarily as a brief warning to the dominant party) or, more likely, similar to that in Botswana, where the same party has ruled since independence but regular elections are held—may, therefore, represent the limits of what is possible.

One important caveat should be added here. Dominant party systems are usually buttressed by the extensive use of patronage. Limits on state spending capacity, the constitutional guarantee for public servants[87] (which could limit the majority party's capacity to dispense public service jobs), and the private economy's potential to absorb ambitious and talented ANC voters could weaken the majority party's ability to dispense favors. But this should not be assumed: The state still commands substantial resources, and there are limits to business's absorptive capacity. Even if the ANC's patronage capacity remains limited, symbolic power may prove sufficient to ensure a majority for many years. A dominant party system, therefore, remains the likeliest possibility, even if it is not guaranteed.

Although this likelihood may not—justifiably—fit accepted notions of democracy, it creates potential space for relatively vigorous public debate and a fair measure of government accountability. Whether the space is used will depend on the citizenry's resolve to do so. Not long ago, that possibility seemed unlikely. Naomi Chazan's observation that "structures of democratic government were implanted in Africa with very little prior preparation"[88] applies in large measure to South Africa, too.

But again, political culture in South Africa has proved to be more plastic than many expected. Increasing majority participation in the market economy; four years of transition, which gave the society a taste of predemocracy; and an admittedly ambiguous legacy of domestic antiapartheid mobilization have, as the examples of fractiousness in the ANC constituency show, created a climate in which the majority party cannot expect a free ride from its constituency. It may be significant that 28 percent of black respondents to a 1991–1992 survey cited "accountability" as their primary requirement from a majority government,[89] a high figure given the conventional wisdom that democracy is likely to be judged in instrumental terms alone—as a deliverer of material goods denied by white rule—by black voters. The new South African government will be forced to recognize the durability and indispensability of constituencies it does not control.

Even if political actors choose the authoritarian route, the elite may lack enough coherence to agree on the targets for authoritarianism—beyond the right wing if it opts for violence. If the majority party falls into authoritarian hands, it may find its security forces an unwilling implementer of repression against the establishment. The costs of similar action against the left would be vast, given the nature of the ANC constituency. Equally important, authoritarianism could encounter resistance from a substantial section of the citizenry.

The result could, therefore, be as messy as the compromises that produced it. The new order may entrench a dominant party but allow for large doses of "syncretism"[90] in which ideological concessions and corporatist arrangements allow for a significant measure of participation by minority elites and organized private groups, subject to the continued political control of the ruling party. There are signs of syncretism in postelection ANC strategy, evidenced not only by the revealing inaugural slogan "One Nation, Many Cultures" but also by an early attempt to create out of the Reconstruction and Development Programme, the ANC Alliance's proposed project to redress socioeconomic inequalities, a hegemonic but accommodating unifying project in which all will participate but the ANC will retain some autonomy to define their contribution.

Although these points predict possible outcomes if the new order negotiates the challenges that face it, some seem to argue against its ability to do so. The factors described here may rule out minority rebellions and military coups; if they also exclude the possibility of action against violence or of governance sufficiently effective to provide the preconditions for economic growth, the postapartheid order may face a decay that could produce one of these outcomes in the future. The danger for the new order lies not in what it will do with the formal power it now commands but in whether it can translate office into sufficient power to govern.

Theoretical and Policy Considerations

South Africa, once considered the paradigmatic intractable divided society, turns out to be a case study of a very different sort.

The new democracy is fragile and will remain so for some time—if it consolidates at all. But if the first democratic attempt does fail, it is unlikely to be torn apart or be driven to authoritarianism by the tenacity of ascriptive divisions. These divisions do exist, and they are politically salient. They may prevent the prospect of party alternation in government, attenuating, or imperiling democracy. But they are unlikely to contain the seeds of irreconcilable racial conflict.

Influence Without Power?

This prognosis has potentially important theoretical implications. Once conventional wisdom assumed the society could be changed only through revolution; when the alternative of a negotiated transition began to appear more plausible, the prognosis was replaced by an analysis that assumed that only power sharing offered a prospect of stability and democratic consolidation.

My analysis has argued against that proposition. But if my interpretation of South African realities contradicts consociational analyses, it also raises questions about another influential diagnosis and remedy—that of Donald Horowitz, who insists that electoral system design can provide inducements for moderation that offer a surer prospect for creating a democratic center in countries riven by identity politics.[91] Whereas Lijphart fails to explain "how hostile and intolerant masses are going to produce . . . tolerant and open-minded leaders,"[92] Horowitz is forced to acknowledge that centripetal electoral systems in deeply divided societies are not immune to manipulation by competing ethnic elites.[93] Given South Africa's racial demography, "vote pooling," if it had any effect (which it might not in a polity in which the majority party is currently separated from its nearest rival by 42 percentage points), could encourage alliances between a relatively moderate ANC and its most militant black-led rivals.[94] To the extent that constitutional design may influence the development of the polity, a nascent federalism may offer minorities more than either power sharing at the center or modified electoral systems.

But this serves merely to introduce the central point—that both schools of analysis (which are not the most pessimistic offerings of the divided society theorists) assume that in divided societies, divisions can be accommodated only within the state. By contrast, this analysis contends that it is possible to envisage a divided society, particularly one in which the majority substantially outnumbers the minority, in which the minority is reduced to a permanent opposition but retains enough influence in civil society to offer it a continued stake in that society.

Divided society theorists are right to assume that in a society such as South Africa, minorities need access to decisionmaking. But they do not allow for the possibility that the minorities may acquire such access in ways other than guaranteed representation in the executive or the legislature—such as through corporatist bargaining or lobbying. This possibility depends on the strength of the private economy; in South Africa, this economy is still strong enough to offer minority interests a viable alternative to the state.

If, as an often-quoted pessimistic analysis of plural societies insists, the state in these societies is likely to distribute goods in a way that invariably "favours one community and hinders others,"[95] then power sharing is the only antidote to enduring conflict. But this thesis is weakened if the state is not the only vehicle for interaction between the contending blocs. Private deal making suggests that the South African marketplace provides an alternative site for transactions in which there is scope for positive-sum bargains.

Nor, perhaps, do these theories allow for the possibility that the divisions they describe may be more complex and more plastic than they would suggest. It is too early to assume that the deal-making culture described earlier will prove sufficiently tenacious to withstand significant shocks. But the fact that this deal-making culture exists at all is possible cause to question the assumption that social blocs divided enough to identify almost instinctively with rival political parties may not also be consensually unified enough to strike bargains.

In South Africa, this phenomenon may be partly a result of apartheid's relative success in creating and strengthening divisions *within* the ascriptive—and subordinate—majority. These divisions did not create new identities, but they may have created new interests that provide at least a partial counterweight to the politics of racial outbidding.

In sum, to conclude that a society is divided is insufficient to describe its prospects for stability or democracy—the way it is divided is equally, or even more, crucial. We likely do not yet fully understand how South Africa is divided, but an attempt to reach that understanding is vital if we are to measure more fully the prospects for its new democracy.

The Perils of the Closed List

Although constitutional engineering is not a necessary antidote to ascriptive divisions, institutional design—the rules and conventions of competition and representation—does have relevance. The nature of South African divisions demands an urgent reconsideration of the country's electoral system, but again the remedy may lie in further weakening one of the features of the new system of which consociationalists would approve.

Agreement on closed-list proportional representation had two rationales. First, the need to ensure minority representation in a divided society was seen to demand the rejection of a majoritarian or plurality "first past the post" system. Second, high illiteracy rates among the electorate were believed to militate against an electoral system that required voters to do anything more than simply indicate party preference.

When the new polity began operating, however, it soon became clear that closed-list proportional representation has high costs in a divided society with South Africa's demographic profile. First, the overwhelming ANC majority ensured that this party was represented in the legislature by over 250 members, only a handful of whom were able to occupy cabinet posts or senior positions on committees. The inevitable result, given that legislators were not responsible to a geographic constituency, was that a large number of MPs had nothing to do. Their boredom and frustration seemed unlikely to strengthen their enthusiasm for participation in representative democracy or, indeed, for racial or political reconciliation, particularly since many were drawn from the more militant sections of the movement. It is conceivable that the ANC caucus's insistence on overturning some agreements reached in the cabinet was partly a consequence of frustration by MPs excluded from the contact with opposition parties that occurs in the cabinet and whose only route to influence was through a rebellious caucus.

This point has not been lost on the legislators. A contrived "constituency system" has been developed that assigns to legislators a geographic area for which they are responsible; the establishment of relatively large committees (with a maximum of forty members) has also offered many more MPs a role in the parliamentary process. But the constituency system still does not ensure that MPs are accountable to a constituency; they have little incentive to serve that constituency because the party leadership determines their prospects of surviving the next election. The committee system is an incomplete reform since it is not yet clear whether committees will play a significant role in legislating or simply oversee the work of ministers and officials. There is also a limit to the extent to which large committees can keep all members usefully employed.

Second, the interim constitution stipulates that MPs who resign or are expelled from their parties cease to be members of Parliament, which is arguably a logical consequence of an arrangement in which voters choose parties rather than people. Thus far, predictions that this policy would ensure slavish adherence to party lines have not been vindicated—at least within the ANC. But no ANC MP has voted against the party line, which relegates votes in the legislature to a symbolic ritual.[96]

In South Africa, divisions operate to remove the presumed benefits of closed-list proportional representation and to sharply increase its costs. A rudimentary analysis of the 1994 election results[97] suggests that a "first past the post" constituency system would have indeed increased the ANC majority to over two-thirds. One could therefore argue that the system fulfilled its purpose in the first election. But a constituency system would not have significantly altered the NP and IFP share of seats and may be of little use to these two parties in future elections. More important, if demographics are indeed likely to ensure an ANC majority for many years, closed-list proportional representation may be a highly inappropriate system.

Given the strong possibility of an enduring ANC majority, the vibrancy of Parliament may depend on the extent to which differences within the majority party are able to find some expression in the political process. This would open the possibility of issue-based alliances between ANC legislators and those representing minority parties. An arrangement in which open differences are accommodated within a single movement is consistent with the internal ANC culture, but a closed-list proportional representation system prevents its expression.

This is not necessarily an argument against proportional representation. The rough analysis mentioned earlier found that none of the parties that failed to gain cabinet seats would have gained any parliamentary representation in a "first past the post" system. Since the right-wing Freedom Front, the black nationalist Pan Africanist Congress, and the liberal Democratic Party all represent perspectives that demand inclusion in the legislative process, this exclusion would have imperiled democratic stability. But it is an argument for one of the systems that combines proportional representation with voters' choice of individual legislators. The practicability of such a system is enhanced by evidence that the electorate is not as incompetent as had been assumed. Under 1 percent of the ballots in the 1994 election were spoiled, despite the weak penetration of voter education.

South Africa, then, may confirm the importance of institutional design in divided societies. In this case, however, its role lies not in diminishing racial antagonism but in opening democratic possibilities within the parameters imposed by a probable racial majority in future elections.

An Unruly Civil Society

Given the nature of South African divisions, the relative strength of civil society is remarkable, despite the fact that its vigor and its capacity to constrain authoritarian trends may be exaggerated. In principle, there is nothing odd about the existence of strong private interest groups and voluntary associations in a divided society. But deep divisions should produce interest groups that are firmly committed to the prevailing norms of their camp and that are loyal to the political parties that represent those camps.

As the section on deal making suggested, South Africa's civil society partly confirms this prognosis. But it is the deviations from the norm that are significant. On the side of the previous order's established, white-led interests, the existence of a minority tradition has, as noted earlier, ensured that business has never been a monolithic and enthusiastic supporter of apartheid. Further, there have always been white professionals willing to endorse antiapartheid principles and programs, which was important in assuring the transition. Business lobbied for and supported key reforms beginning at least in the late 1960s; during the prenegotiation and negotiation phase, it was at times an important source of institutional and financial support for activities designed to promote a settlement.[98] The partial deracialization of workplaces during the 1980s provided an important counter to polarization. White lawyers have played important roles by highlighting human rights abuses and in shaping the interim constitution; white town planners and architects have helped to frame postapartheid urban and housing policies.

On the other side of the divide, the civil society organizations that emerged in the 1980s were, as noted earlier, created specifically to pursue the antiapartheid "struggle." But although these groups may share similar values, interest diversity within and between them is palpable, which ensures vigorous contests concerning the postelection government's policy direction. COSATU's challenge of some government decisions is one example. The overwhelmingly black-member churches remain strong, and although the South African Council of Churches was labeled "the ANC at prayer," these churches have never been mere conveyor belts for ANC strategy or policy. In fact, Nobel Laureate Desmond Tutu, the Anglican archbishop of Cape Town, denounced the violence of antiapartheid protest during the 1980s, and his attacks on the new political elite's salaries played a major role in persuading the new government to announce voluntary cuts in its pay. There is also a less vocal but important set of private black associations, ranging from business groups to mutual savings clubs to welfare associations, that are not products of political mobilization and that, therefore, are both independent and lacking aspirations to state power.[99] An independent African church movement is more widely supported than the "mainstream" churches, and political independence is one of its cardinal principles.

All of this suggests that South African civil society is sufficiently vigorous to constrain a postsettlement government's authoritarian ambitions. In contrast to most other African countries, substantial expertise exists within civil society that could vastly enhance the society's capacity both to steer its way through the transition and to deal with the political and socioeconomic problems that will face the new state. The deal-making culture also injects an important element of civility into South Africa's private realm. The existence of strong private interests is not in itself a guarantee of a strong civil society; the role of those interests in encouraging and entrenching political civility (compromise and tolerance) is also vital.

Although civil society is an important potential constraint on authoritarianism, its role in underpinning democracy is not guaranteed. First, deal making across the cleavages is far more pervasive than the interest identifications and alliances which cut across them. Second, civil society is largely an insider phenomenon. Third, even within the insider world, the voice of authentically independent private associations is muted. Further, many of the most vocal and influential black-led associations are not nearly as representative as they claim to be. Perhaps more important, the extent to which they represent interests, rather than access to symbolic influence, is open to question: the civic associations which led the fight against apartheid in the urban black townships of the 1980s presume to speak for entire "communities" in which a diversity of interests and values cannot be captured by single organizations whose claims of influence rest more on their contribution to antiapartheid activity than on their ability to articulate the range of interests that have become salient now that the fight against white rule has ended.

Civil society may, therefore, prove strong enough to impose limits on state power but too weak to offer most citizens a channel for social and political participation. There is a strong possibility that institutional changes that are justified as means of according political influence to civil society will weaken that which they purport to strengthen by elevating private associations that have political influence to a spurious role as representatives of all of "civil society."

Postsettlement South Africa could provide an important test for some current theories of the role of civil society in democratization. The important role civil society has played in many contemporary democratic transitions[100] is no guarantee that this society will continue to strengthen democracy after the transition has produced a founding election. South Africa will test this proposition, albeit in a context which is in some ways unique.

The Perils and Possibilities of Federalism

The establishment of a nascent federal system provides an important source of pluralism since two provinces—Western Cape and KwaZulu Natal—are dominated by opposition parties.[101] A significant postelection trend has been the assertiveness of provincial governments. Ironically, since the ANC resisted federalism during the negotiations, those governments controlled by it are as inclined to demand enhanced powers as the two governments controlled by the NP and the IFP. This situation may strengthen democratic prospects by creating cross-party alliances. In fact, ANC provincial premiers have cooperated with their NP and IFP counterparts in the fight to secure greater powers from the center.

But the early evolution of the provincial government system created by negotiators may also weaken prospects for democratic government. First, failure to agree on an appropriate relationship between region and center has potentially destabilizing effects. Federalism is not confederalism; it implies a role for central government and a recognition of allegiance to a common polity. For some analysts, the assertiveness of provincial governments is evidence of a regional identity that crosses party divisions. For others (and for some ANC national leaders), it is evidence of ethnic identity or "tribalism" since in parts of the country there is a strong correlation between geography and ethnicity.[102] The accuracy of these diagnoses varies: There is some evidence of both regional and ethnic identities. But the demand for provincial powers is not restricted to those areas in which these identities are manifest. It is voiced, for example, with much enthusiasm in the populous PWV province, which is ethnically heterogeneous and in which there is little sign of a regional identity. Whereas citizens in parts of the country may identify with their region, there is little sign that they are demanding greater powers. The tussle between the center and ANC provinces seems to have much more to do with the desire of elites to maximize their power than with identities.

Continuing conflict over the appropriate division of powers could, in the absence of broad ground rules of agreement, severely weaken a coherent government. The conflict is exacerbated by a process in which the provinces have demanded—and in some cases acquired—greater powers without concomitant fiscal responsibilities. Decisionmaking is, therefore, not constrained by the need to account for spending to electorates. Since closed-list proportional representation has ensured a weak link between provincial governments and their electorate, there is a danger both that federalism will become a vehicle for unaccountable regional elites and that conflicts between provinces and the center will exceed the creative tensions in established federal systems, further complicating the challenges of governance. This is particularly a concern because the weakness of state administration is most clearly manifest in the provinces since it is their governments that are served by the former homeland bureaucracies. In parts of the country that were formerly homelands, public administration is in disarray, and even limited service provision has ceased.

The immediate effect of this bureaucratic incapacity is to further strengthen the insider-outsider division. It is much easier to administer the better-endowed metropolitan areas. Citizens in these areas are also much less dependent on government, at least on its national and provincial tiers. Basic services and infrastructure are the responsibility of relatively high-capacity local authorities, and the market economy and a higher level of associational life also cushion the effects of government incapacity. Poorer areas—particularly the former homelands—have no such advantages.

The longer-term consequence may be to imperil the legitimacy and effectiveness of the new order. If South Africa is to avoid a society in which the democratic polity is the preserve only of those who live in the established sections of the urban centers, the authority of government in those areas in which such authority has declined will need to be established and extended. Whether this will occur is not assured; whether authority will be established without destroying democracy is even less sure.

Conclusion: Strengthening the State

For much of the negotiation period, it was often assumed that postelection democratic consolidation would be imperiled by the prospect of too strong a state. Since the election, it has become clear that the real threat is too weak a state.

Enhanced stability in the months after the election often tended to mask the real challenges to the new order's authority—and to the coherence of the society. Two of these challenges merit specific mention. The first is the challenge to public order posed by a high—and perhaps rising—crime rate, as well as limited progress toward ensuring a state monopoly of the instruments of coercion, which, as Naomi Chazan points out, is a sine qua non for the consolidation of democratic transition.[103] The apartheid period spawned not only a host of armies—official and otherwise[104]—but also the rise of vigilante groups on left and right with ready access to arms. The agreed-upon process of integrating the various armies has been turbulent, and the potential threats to stability are clear.

The second challenge is the refusal of most urban residents to pay for municipal services. This is a legacy of the antiapartheid conflicts of the 1980s, one of whose vehicles was a service charge boycott designed to weaken urban administration. Appeals by ANC leadership to resume payment have been ignored, and payments by colored, Indian, and some white residents have also declined. The failure of the state to secure voluntary citizen compliance with its fiscal obligations obviously weakens the viability of the new order. Prospects of overcoming these and other challenges are severely weakened by turmoil within the bureaucracy, which was discussed in part in an earlier section.

In South Africa, as in any other society with a strong private realm, government effectiveness will depend in part on recognizing and accommodating civil society since it is here that much of the society's capacity resides. But this is not to suggest the abdication of government functions to the private realm; as Chazan reminds us, a strong state remains a precondition to a strong civil society.[105] The most obvious example is the maintenance of public order, which, as the experience of the National Peace Accord brokered in 1991 shows,[106] cannot be delegated to civil society alone.

This problem is not South Africa's alone. In this and many other developing societies, debate over the appropriate limits to state power may be meaningless without concerted study of the conditions required to ensure the development of states that are strong enough to govern at all. Democratic governance is, after all, impossible in societies in which governance itself is not assured.

Notes

1. The exception, as we will see later, is Zimbabwe. See Masipula Sithole, "Zimbabwe: In Search of a Stable Democracy," in Larry Diamond, Juan J. Linz, Seymour Martin Lipset, *Democracy in Developing Countries: Africa* (Boulder: Lynne Rienner, 1988).

2. Advocates of this view acknowledge that the political camps produced by apartheid are not entirely racial, although they are predominantly so. But legal status under apartheid was determined entirely by race. See Charles Simkins, *The Prisoners of Tradition and the Politics of Nation-Building* (Johannesburg: Institute of Race Relations, 1988).

3. Guillermo O'Donnell, and Phillipe Schmitter, *Transitions from Authoritarian Rule: Tentative Conclusions About Uncertain Democracies* (Baltimore: Johns Hopkins University Press, 1987).

4. The most influential works of the divided society theorists, at least in South Africa, have been those of Arend Lijphart, *Power-Sharing in South Africa* (Berkeley: University of California, Institute of Strategic Studies, 1985); Donald Horowitz, *A Democratic South Africa? Constitutional Engineering in a Divided Society* (Cape Town: Oxford University Press, 1991); Hermann Giliomee, "The Communal Nature of the South African Conflict," in Hermann Giliomee and Lawrence Schlemmer, (eds.), *Negotiating South Africa's Future* (Johannesburg: Southern, 1989).

5. Michael Burton and John Higley define "elite settlements" as pacts in which "national elite factions suddenly and deliberately reorganize their relations by negotiating compromises on their most basic disagreements." Michael G. Burton, and John Higley, "Elite Settlements," *American Sociological Review* 52 (1987): pp. 295–307.

6. T. R. H. Davenport, *South Africa: A Modern History, Second Edition* (Johannesburg:

MacMillan, 1981), pp. 33–35. Ironically, Phillip advocated race segregation but saw this as a means of protecting black tribal polities from white conquest.

7. This argument is developed in Douglas Pierce, *Post-Apartheid South Africa: Lessons from Brazil's "Nova Republica"* (Johannesburg: Centre for Policy Studies, 1992).

8. To name one of many examples, it was a British governor of Natal, Theophilus Shepstone, who introduced the system of segregation, or indirect rule, which compelled blacks to live "as far as possible" in separate areas under the rule of tribal chiefs. See C. W. de Kiewiet, *A History of South Africa: Social and Economic* (London: Oxford University Press, 1968).

9. See, for example, Leonard Thompson, *Politics in the Republic of South Africa,* (Boston: Little Brown, 1966), p. 27.

10. Although some "Youth Leaguers" retained this position, Mandela and Tambo in particular were reconciled both to nonracialism and to alliances with the white left as early as the 1950s.

11. Tom Lodge, *Black Politics Since 1945* (Johannesburg: Ravan, 1983), p. 75.

12. A case in point is the 1953–1954 campaign against the removal of black people from Sophiatown, a nonracial freehold area to Johannesburg's west. Many were happy to go because they believed they would no longer be victims of the rackrenting that was rife in the township. Ibid., p. 104.

13. The origins of Black Consciousness predate SASO by two or three years. Its first stirrings began in the University Christian Movement, which was strongly influenced by black theology. Domestic black theologians played a significant early role in the movement. Its intellectual origins lay in U.S. black separatist movements, the negritude theorists, and the work of Frantz Fanon. Biko and his allies, however, significantly adapted these theories to the South African context. See, for example, John Kane-Berman, *Soweto: Black Revolt, White Reaction* (Johannesburg: Ravan, 1978).

14. Ibid.

15. A key catalyst was the conviction of the BC movement's intellectual vanguard on political charges in the 1970s. They were imprisoned for five years on Robben Island, where Mandela and other ANC leaders were also held. The ANC leaders won the ensuing debate, and several of the BC prisoners emerge as confirmed nonracial democrats.

16. The list is long, but two examples illustrate the point. Patrick Lekota, who later became the ANC premier of the Orange Free State province, was one of those imprisoned in the BC trial. Cyril Ramaphosa, ANC secretary general and chief negotiator at the constitutional talks, played a minor role in BC activities before becoming a trade unionist.

17. A 1993 survey found that 56 percent of black youth, popularly regarded as the most alienated section of black society, attend church at least once a week. See D. Everatt and M. Orkin, *"Growing up Tough": A National Survey of South African Youth* (Johannesburg: Community Agency for Social Enquiry, 1993).

18. Edward Roux, *Time Longer Than Rope: A History of the Black Man's Struggle for Freedom in South Africa* (Madison: University of Wisconsin Press, 1964), p. 423.

19. During this period the movement appealed to NP prime ministers to negotiate, but received no response. See Roux, *Time Longer than Rope.* Mandela, at his 1964 trial for treason, insisted that he would have accepted a minority of racially reserved black seats in Parliament as a step toward full franchise.

20. This policy changed in the mid-1980s, when the ANC proclaimed a strategy of "people's war," which was largely an attempt to capitalize on internal resistance. See Tom Lodge, "Mayihlome!—Let Us Go to War! From Nkomati to Kabwe, the African National Congress, January 1984–June 1985" in G. Moss and I. Obery, (eds.), *South African Review 3* (Johannesburg: Ravan, 1986), pp. 226ff.

21. Tom Lodge, University of the Witwatersrand, comments at a private seminar.

22. Sithole, "Zimbabwe."

23. One manifestation has been a tendency among civic associations allied with the ANC to insist that representative democracy be subordinated to "people's forums" that are allegedly installed by popular or participatory democracy but whose representativeness would not be open to test. Steven Friedman, "Bonaparte at the Barricades: The Colonization of Civil Society," *Theoria,* no. 79 (May 1992): pp. 83–95.

24. There were some restrictions on white political competition. Communists were not permitted to contest elections; nor was anyone convicted of a political offense, which often

included individuals who were not communists. See, for example, Roux, *Time Longer than Rope,* pp. 378ff.

25. Benjamin Progrund, "South Africa Goes to the Polls," in Andrew Reynolds, (ed.), *Election '94 South Africa: The Campaigns, Results and Future Prospects* (Cape Town: David Phillip, 1994).

26. Figures supplied by Human Rights Commission.

27. Officials in the former Transkei homeland received, for example, double the housing subsidies of their counterparts elsewhere in the country. This benefit has since been reduced to ensure parity. *Daily Dispatch,* London, May 10, 1994.

28. This strategy was developed in the 1979 Riekert Report, which advocated concessions for black Africans who were in the cities legally and more efficient controls to keep out those who were not. See Doug Hindson and Marian Lacey, "Influx Control and Labour Allocation: Policy and Practice Since the Riekert Commission" in G. Moss, (ed.), *South African Review One* (Johannesburg: Ravan, 1983): pp. 97–113.

29. The 1976 incident occurred at the Mzimphlope hostel, Soweto, whose residents attacked neighboring suburbs during the township conflict. See Kane-Berman, *Soweto,* p. 113. Unpublished research indicates that clashes between hostel dwellers and permanent residents predate this incident.

30. Organized black business, which has lobbied vigorously for preferential treatment, is a case in point.

31. Giliomee, for example, although insisting that a negotiated settlement was possible, posited as an alternative a struggle "of survival, involving the basic issue of personal and communal identity and integrity." But if divisions had this much conflict potential, why was a settlement attempted? Giliomee, "The Communal Nature," p. 126.

32. For a description of this policy and its effects see Kane-Berman, *Soweto,* pp. 69–102. For the reforms and their effects see Hindson and Lacey, "Influx Control."

33. For an account and analysis of the growth of the trade union movement, see Steven Friedman, *Building Tomorrow Today: African Workers in Trade Unions, 1970–1984* (Johannesburg: Ravan, 1987).

34. Lodge, "Mayihlome!"

35. In the mid-1980s, the Comprehensive Anti-Apartheid Act imposed U.S. sanctions, thus meeting a long-standing ANC goal. But the act also mandated attempts by the administration to persuade the parties to seek a negotiated settlement. Chris Landsberg, "Directing from the Stalls: The International Community and the South African Negotiation Forum," in Steven Friedman and Doreen Atkinson, (eds.), *The Small Miracle: South Africa's Negotiated Settlement* (Johannesburg: Ravan, 1994), pp. 276ff.

36. Steven Friedman, (ed.), *The Long Journey: South Africa's Quest for a Negotiated Settlement* (Johannesburg: Ravan, 1993).

37. Ibid.

38. The agreement covered the bearing of "traditional weapons"—a penchant of IFP supporters—and security at migrant worker hostels, which were regarded as an Inkatha stronghold. See Friedman, *Long Journey,* pp. 160ff.

39. Analysis Department, Independent Electoral Commission, Weekly Report No. 4.

40. A history of political conflict in the 1980s—in which warring parties asserted control over territory by force—combined with white farmers' and right-wing municipalities' use of their power to exclude campaigners, resulted in 165 no-go areas in which rivals were denied varying forms of access. Sixty-two of these were hard no-go areas in which they were denied all access. See Steven Friedman and Louise Stack, "The Magic Moment: The 1994 Election," in Friedman and Atkinson, *The Small Miracle,* p. 310.

41. The changes slightly increased the powers of provinces, which were conceded a double ballot—one for the national legislature, the other for their provincial equivalents. This move, which had been resisted by the ANC and demanded by the IFP, changed Natal province's name to KwaZulu Natal and made a symbolic concession to the white right's demand for a separate state. Doreen Atkinson, "Brokering a Miracle? The Multi-Party Negotiating Forum," in Friedman and Atkinson, *The Small Miracle,* p. 37.

42. The agreement recognized the constitutional status of the king of the Zulus and provided for postelection international mediation of the IFP's demands. Ibid., p. 38.

43. Tension between Buthelezi and the monarch dated back to the 1970s. Their alliance

was built on the former's power, through the KwaZulu administration, to determine and pay the king's salary and those of the chiefs. Both the NP and the ANC tried to persuade the monarch that his future could best be secured by the new order, and they seem to have succeeded. Ibid., p. 39.

44. The province of KwaZulu Natal includes both the former homeland of KwaZulu and the formerly white areas. Under apartheid, the IFP controlled the KwaZulu section.

45. SABC/Markinor, *End of Campaign*, April 1994.

46. The choice of an electoral administrator was constrained by the ANC's refusal to accept the apartheid state as election manager and the NP's refusal to accept an international agency such as the United Nations. The parties agreed on an independent commission, chosen by an all-party committee, which would monitor and administer the poll. Friedman and Stack, "The Magic Moment," pp. 301ff.

47. The results were announced a full week after the polls closed as a consequence of inefficiencies and attempted fraud. Ibid., pp. 319ff.

48. It was frequently claimed after the election that the parties had negotiated the percentage of the vote each received. No conclusive evidence has been produced to support this claim.

49. Atkinson, "Brokering a Miracle."

50. Landsberg, "Directing from the Stalls," p. 290.

51. Arend Lijphart, "Prospects for Power Sharing in the New South Africa," in Reynolds, *Election '94*, pp. 221–231.

52. Terry Lynn Karl, "Dilemmas of Democratization in Latin America," *Comparative Politics* 23, no. 1 (1990): pp. 1–21.

53. Arend Lijphart, *Democracy in Plural Societies* (New Haven, Conn.: Yale University Press, 1977).

54. The constitution does contain a vague appeal to consensus seeking, but this is of no binding effect. See *Republic of South Africa Constitution Act,* clause 89(2).

55. Both NP Minister of Constitutional Development Roelf Meyer and his ANC deputy, Mohammed Valli Moosa, have declared their intention to press for an end to closed-list proportional representation.

56. SANCO is the national vehicle of civic associations, which emerged in the 1980s to mobilize township resistance to apartheid. See Khehla Shubane and Pumla Madiba, *The Struggle Continues? Civic Associations in the Transition* (Johannesburg: Centre for Policy Studies, 1992).

57. *Citizen,* Johannesburg, September 1, 1994.

58. *Sunday Times,* Johannesburg, August 14, 1994.

59. Interview, IFP member of Parliament.

60. Lijphart, *Democracy in Plural Societies,* uses this term approvingly to describe one of consociationalism's key features.

61. See Alan Cawson, *Corporatism and Political Theory* (London: Basil Blackwell, 1986); and Phillippe C. Schmitter, "Interest Intermediation and Regime Governability in Contemporary Western Europe and North America," in Suzanne Berger, (ed.), *Organizing Interests in Western Europe: Corporatism, Pluralism and the Transformation of Politics* (Cambridge: Cambridge University Press, 1981), pp. 285–327.

62. Khehla Shubane and Mark Shaw, *Tomorrow's Foundations? Forums as the Second Level of a Negotiated Transition* (Johannesburg: Centre for Policy Studies, 1993).

63. Mark Shaw, "Biting the Bullet: Negotiating Democracy's Defence," in Friedman and Atkinson, *The Small Miracle.*

64. Horowitz, *A Democratic South Africa?*

65. Calculations by Professor Lawrence Schlemmer, Human Sciences Research Council.

66. See, for example, Heribert Adam, and Kogila Moodley, *The Negotiated Revolution: Society and Politics in Post-Apartheid South Africa* (Johannesburg: Jonathan Ball, 1993).

67. These are the findings of a study by Michael McGrath of the University of Natal and Andrew Whiteford of the Human Sciences Research Council. *Financial Mail,* August 12, 1994.

68. Steven Friedman, "South Africa's Reluctant Transition," *Journal of Democracy* 4, no. 2 (1993): pp. 56–69.

69. Lijphart, *Democracy in Plural Societiest.*

70. Frederik van Zyl Slabbert, *The Quest for Democracy: South Africa in Transition*

(Johannesburg: Penguin, 1992), p. 15, calculates that at a "conservative estimate," there will be 5.8 million white South Africans by 2010—10 percent of the population.

71. Results of survey by Lawrence Schlemmer presented to Human Sciences Research Council Symposium, *The Transition: Four Years On,* Pretoria, February 2, 1994.

72. Television interviewers repeatedly encountered white voters who declared that they had decided to vote "with [our] heads rather than our hearts." The context suggested strongly that the "heads" argument was strongly influenced by likely international implications of a negative vote.

73. Larry Diamond, *Democracy in Latin America: Degrees, Illusions and Directions for Consolidation,* paper prepared for the Inter-American Dialogue Project on "Reconstructing Sovereignty in a Democratic Age," November 1993.

74. Policies advocated by urban insider groups such as SANCO would, for example, significantly improve the quality of urban housing but would also deny even rudimentary improvements to outsiders. See Steven Friedman, *The Elusive "Community": The Dynamics of Negotiated Urban Development* (Johannesburg: Centre for Policy Studies, 1993).

75. Larry Diamond, "Introduction: Political Culture and Democracy," in Larry Diamond, (ed.), *Political Culture and Democracy in Developing Countries* (Boulder: Lynne Rienner, 1993).

76. Friedman, "South Africa's Reluctant Transition."

77. Diamond, *Democracy in Latin America.*

78. Frances Hagopian, "Democracy by Undemocratic Means? Elites, Political Pacts and Regime Transitions in Brazil," *Comparative Political Studies* 23, no. 2 (1990): pp. 147–170.

79. Schmitter, "Interest Intermediation."

80. Steven Friedman, *Another Elephant? Prospects for a South African Social Contract* (Johannesburg: Centre for Policy Studies, 1990).

81. Adam Przeworski, "Democracy as a Contingent Outcome of Conflicts," in Jon Elster and Rune Slagstad, (eds.), *Constitutionalism and Democracy* (Cambridge: Cambridge University Press, 1988), pp. 59–80.

82. Larry Diamond, Juan J. Linz, and Seymour Martin Lipset, (eds.), *Democracy in Developing Countries: Latin America* (Boulder: Lynne Rienner, 1989).

83. John Higley and Michael G. Burton, "The Elite Variable in Democratic Transitions and Breakdowns," *American Sociological Review* 54 (1989): pp. 17–32.

84. Dankwart A. Rustow, "Transitions to Democracy: Towards a Dynamic Model," *Comparative Politics* (April 1970).

85. Lawrence Schlemmer and Ian Hirschfeld, "Voter Expectations and Orientations," in Schlemmer and Hirschfeld, (eds.), *Founding Democracy and the New South African Voter* (Pretoria: Human Sciences Research Council, 1994), pp. 45–67.

86. Diamond, *Political Culture and Democracy in Developing Countries.*

87. See article by Giliomee, *The Star,* October 19, 1994.

88. Naomi Chazan, "Between Liberalism and Statism: African Political Cultures and Democracy," in Diamond, *Political Culture and Democracy in Developing Countries.*

89. Schlemmer and Hirschfeld, "Voter Expectations."

90. See Theodor Hanf, "The Prospects of Accommodation in Communal Conflicts: A Comparative Study," in Giliomee and Schlemmer, *Negotiating South Africa's Future.*

91. Horowitz, *A Democratic South Africa?*

92. Hanf, "The Prospects of Accommodation," p. 100.

93. Although Horowitz is clearly confident that vote pooling will encourage ethnic accommodation, he acknowledges in a footnote that "there are no guarantees . . . that politicians will play by these rules." Horowitz, *A Democratic South Africa?* p. 183.

94. Vote-pooling electoral systems are those that provide strong incentives to candidates and parties to seek support from supporters of rival parties. They include systems that require winning candidates to obtain not only a majority but also a particular distribution of votes (e.g., 25 percent from each region in presidential elections) and preference systems in which voters are required to list candidates in order of preference; "inferior"—second, third, and subsequent choices—count toward the allocation of seats. Advocates of these systems argue that they provide strong disincentives to polarization by forcing or encouraging parties to appeal to rival party supporters and to reach vote-pooling agreements with those parties. See ibid., pp. 163–203.

95. Alvin Rabushka, "Prescriptions for the Plural Society: Theory and Practice in the South African Context," in Nic Rhoodie, (ed.), *Intergroup Accommodation in Plural Societies* (Pretoria: Institute of Plural Studies, 1978).

96. In the first session of the 1994 Parliament, there was only one vote on a bill.

97. Had each magisterial district been a constituency, the ANC would have won 72 percent of the seats, the NP 19 percent, and the IFP 9 percent. No other parties would have won seats. Own calculations from Independent Electoral Commission, Electoral Administration Directorate, *Republic of South Africa 1994 General Election: Results by Province/District* (Johannesburg: IEC, 1994).

98. There are many examples. A group of senior businesspeople made the first public contact with the ANC in the mid-1980s. They also include business's role in breaking key log-jams in the negotiations such as the impasse over federalism (Richard Humphries, Thabo Rapoo, and Steven Friedman, "The Shape of the Country: Negotiating Regional Government," in Friedman and Atkinson, *The Small Miracle,* pp. 166ff) and the IFP's refusal to contest the election (Landsberg, op. cit., p. 294) and its prominent role in the 1991 National Peace Accord, which sought to counter political violence by encouraging negotiated peace accords between warring local parties. A business-funded organization created specifically to encourage a negotiated settlement, the Consultative Business Movement, provided the secretariat for the first multiparty negotiating forum, the Convention for a Democratic South Africa. Friedman, *Long Journey.*

99. Naomi Chazan, "Governability and Compliance During the Transition," edited transcript of address in Riaan De Villiers, (ed.), *Governability During the Transition: Proceedings of a Conference Organised by the Centre for Policy Studies on Government in Post-Apartheid South Africa* (Johannesburg: Centre for Policy Studies, 1993), pp. 13–15.

100. O'Donnell, Schmitter, *Transitions from Authoritarian Rule.*

101. The government of national unity formula also applies to provincial executives. The ANC, thus, holds executive portfolios in opposition-controlled provinces just as smaller parties hold seats in ANC-dominated executives.

102. See comments by Deputy President Thabo Mbeki, *Business Day* October 20, 1994.

103. Chazan, "Governability."

104. In addition to the ANC and PAC guerrilla armies, those of the ethnic homelands are to be integrated into the national military. See Shaw, "Biting the Bullet."

105. Chazan, "Governability."

106. Mark Shaw, *Crying Peace Where There Is None: The Function and Future of the Local Peace Committees of the National Peace Accord* (Johannesburg: Centre for Policy Studies, 1993).

The Contributors

Kathleen Bruhn is assistant professor of political science at the University of California, Santa Barbara. She is currently completing a book on the emergence and consolidation of the Party of the Democratic Revolution in Mexico.

Christian Coulon is co-director of the Center of Black African Studies at the University of Bordeaux. He is author of numerous articles and several books on politics and development in Francophone Africa, among them *The Marabout and the Prince: Islam and Power in Senegal, Local Autonomy and National Integration in Senegal,* and *Muslims and Power in Black Africa.*

Jyotirindra Das Gupta is professor emeritus of political science at the University of California, Berkeley, where he has also served as chairman of the Program in Development Studies. His work has focused on politics, language planning ethnic mobilization, and socioeconomic development, both in India and in comparative perspective. His publications include *Language Conflict and National Development* and *Authority, Priority and Human Development.*

Larry Diamond is senior research fellow at the Hoover Institution, co-editor of the *Journal of Democracy,* and co-director of the National Endowment for Democracy's International Forum for Democratic Studies. He is author of *Class, Ethnicity and Democracy in Nigeria: The Failure of the First Republic* and *Developing Democracy: Toward Consolidation* (forthcoming). In addition to his continuing study of Nigeria, he is currently analyzing U.S. and international programs to promote democracy and comparative problems of democratic consolidation.

Steven Friedman is director of the Johannesburg-based Centre for Policy Studies, an independent research center that specializes in political analysis. He is author of *Building Tomorrow Today: African Workers in Trade Unions 1970–1984* and editor of two studies of the negotiation process that culminated in South Africa's first universal franchise elections: *The Long Journey* and *The Small Miracle.*

Bolívar Lamounier is co-founder and senior researcher of the Instituto de Estudos Econômicos, Sociais e Políticos de São Paulo (IDESP). Among the many works he has authored, edited, or co-edited in Portuguese are *Parties and Elections in Brazil* (with Fernando Henrique Cordoso) and *How Democracies Are Reborn* (with Alain Rouquie and Jorge Schwarzer). He has been a member of the Brazilian Presidential Commission for Constitutional Studies (1985–1986) and several other Brazilian high-level commissions.

Daniel Levy is professor of educational policy, Latin American studies, and political science at the State University of New York at Albany. He is author of *University and Government in Mexico: Autonomy in an Authoritarian System, Mexico:*

Paradoxes of Stability and Change (with Gabriel Szekely), and the forthcoming *The Third Sector: Latin America's Private Research Centers and Nonprofit Development.* His articles focus on the politics of Latin American universities, Mexican politics, and nonprofit organizations.

Juan J. Linz is Sterling Professor of Political and Social Science at Yale University. His English-language publications include *Crisis, Breakdown and Reequilibrium* — Volume One of the four-volume work, *The Breakdown of Democratic Regimes,* which he edited with Alfred Stepan. His *Problems of Democratic Transition and Consolidation,* co-authored with Alfred Stepan, is forthcoming. He is co-editor, with Arturo Valenzuela, of *The Failure of Presidential Democracy.*

Seymour Martin Lipset is the Hazel Professor of Public Policy at the Institute of Public Policy, George Mason University, and senior fellow at the Hoover Institution, Stanford University. A prolific author, he is the only person to have been president of both the American Sociological Association and the American Political Science Association. His most recent books are *Jews and the New American Scene* (with Earl Raab) and *American Exceptionalism: A Double-Edged Sword.*

Ergun Özbudun is professor of political science at Bilkent University in Ankara, Turkey. He is also president of the Turkish Political Science Association and vice-president of the Turkish Democracy Foundation. He has written widely on democratic politics both in Turkey and in comparative perspective. He is the author and editor of many books, including his *Social Change and Political Participation in Turkey* and *The Political Economy of Income Distribution in Turkey.*

Chai-Anan Samudavanija is professor of political science and a Royal Scholar at Chulalongkorn University in Bangkok, Thailand. He is also chairman of the Chaiyong Limthongkul Foundation and president of the Institute of Public Policy Studies in Bangkok. He has written 30 Thai-language books on Thai politics and numerous works in English, including *The Thai Young Turk* and *Political Conflict in Thailand* (with David Morell). He was a member of the 1974 Constitutional Drafting Committee and adviser to two prime ministers.

David I. Steinberg, representative of The Asia Foundation in Korea, was formerly Distinguished Professor of Korean Studies at Georgetown University. He was president of the Mansfield Center for Pacific Affairs and had a long career with the Agency for International Development, Department of State, serving in a variety of positions including director for Philippines, Thailand, and Burma affairs. He is author of some ten books and monographs, including *The Republic of Korea, Economic Transformation and Social Change,* and *The Future of Burma: Crisis and Choice in Myanmar.*

Arturo Valenzuela is Deputy Assistant Secretary for Inter-American Affairs in the U.S. Department of State. He is on leave as professor of government and director, Center for Latin American Studies, Georgetown University. Among his books are *Political Brokers in Chile: Local Government in a Centralized Polity; The Breakdown of Democratic Regimes: Chile; A Nation of Enemies: Chile under Pinochet* (with Pamela Constable); and *Military Rule in Chile* (edited with J. Samuel Valenzuela).

Index

585

About the Book

This second edition of the highly regarded *Politics in Developing Countries* again presents case studies of experiences with democracy in Asia, Africa, Latin America, and the Middle East, along with the editors' synthesis of the factors that facilitate and obstruct the development of democracy around the world. The new edition adds a chapter on South Africa and brings the other nine studies current through 1994.

The recent developments covered in the book include:

- The reemergence of democratic politics in Chile
- The impeachment of President Collor and the crisis of democracy in Brazil
- The growing pressure for substantive democratization in Mexico
- The 1994 elections in Chile, Brazil, and Mexico
- The leadership transition in Turkey following the death of President Ozal
- The growing ethnic and religious strife in India
- The overthrow and reemergence of democracy in Thailand and the country's economic boom
- The quest for democratic consolidation in South Korea under new President Kim Young Sam
- The political and economic crisis in Nigeria
- The difficulties facing the one-party dominant regime in Senegal following the 1993 elections
- The 1994 elections and democratic transition in South Africa

Larry Diamond is senior research fellow at the Hoover Institution. He is author of *Class, Ethnicity and Democracy in Nigeria: The Failure of the First Republic* and coeditor, with Juan J. Linz and Seymour Martin Lipset, of *Democracy in Developing Countries* (4 vols.).

Juan J. Linz is Sterling Professor of Political and Social Science at Yale University. He has written widely on authoritarianism and totalitarianism, fascism, and transitions to democracy and is coeditor of the four-volume work *The Breakdown of Democratic Regimes.*

Seymour Martin Lipset holds the Hazel Chair of Public Policy at George Mason University. Among his books are *Political Man, The First New Nation,* and *Consensus and Conflict.*